The Cannon Film Guide

Volume II (1985–1987)

Austin Trunick

BearManor
Media

Orlando, Florida

Published in the USA by
BearManor Media
1317 Edgewater Dr. #110
Orlando, FL 32804
www.BearManorMedia.com

Softcover Edition
ISBN-10: 000
ISBN-13: 978-1-62933-889-7

Printed in the United States of America

Dedication

For my uncle, Jon Gordon, whose affection for
b-movies clearly must have rubbed off on me.

Cannon surprised attendees of the 1986 Cannes Film Festival with a sixty-page spread in the trade papers promoting an over-ambitious slate of films, quite a few of which would never be made.

Table of Contents

Foreword by James Bruner

Menahem Golan continued to ignore Chuck Norris, his brother, Aaron, and me as he slowly thumbed through the script, pausing every so often to read a line or two. I had convinced Chuck and Aaron to take a chance on the storyline and the direction of our careers was at stake, but Menahem's poker face gave nothing away. In the creative universe at Cannon Films, there were no committees making decisions. Menahem's personal approval of a project was the alpha and omega.

After an eternity, Menahem took off his reading glasses. He held up the script - and grinned his infectious grin. "Of course, we cannot call it *American Ninja.*"

Chuck mentioned the other title we had in mind: *Invasion U.S.A.*

At the time, *Missing in Action* was in post-production and this was my first real experience in developing a film with Menahem. He had wanted Chuck to star in a movie titled *American Ninja* - and had even pre-sold the film on the concept alone, with no plot or story, which was the rule, rather than the exception for Cannon. Following the rule and his gut instinct, and understanding the worldwide marketplace, Menahem brought unrivaled success to Cannon Films.

I learned that while Menahem had extremely strong opinions, to put it mildly, he could also think on his feet and be persuaded to see another approach to a film. After *An Eye for an Eye* and *Lone Wolf McQuade*, Chuck was breaking out of the strict martial arts genre and didn't want to do a ninja movie, but he had a deal with Cannon and a ninja movie was going to be his next film. Unbeknownst to Menahem, I suggested a solution to Chuck: he would play a former government agent whose code name was 'American Ninja'.

In the end, everyone was happy: we got to make a big, fun, blockbuster action movie and Cannon got a successful *American Ninja* franchise with Sam Firstenberg and Michael Dudikoff.

At the time, Cannon Films was renting space in the old CNN Building on Sunset Boulevard and Ivar in Hollywood. Shabby would be too nice of a word to use to describe the space. My wife, Elizabeth Stevens, who was invited by Menahem to come along on the adventure, observed that Cannon was like a collection of starving international film students who had been thrown into a whirlwind to cobble together movies. There was a strong *David vrs. Goliath* vibe: Everyone was a rebel of some kind and there was a crazy, creative energy that permeated the place. Cannon was a place where people weren't just talking about making movies, they were actually making movies.

Flexibility, the ability to move fast and the concentration on popular genres and pop culture made Cannon successful and unique for its time. Traditional movie studios and production companies, then and now, generally move at a glacial pace. It can be years between the approval of a concept and the release of the final product.

When Menahem called to pitch me on writing a film, he talked about scheduling production in a matter of weeks, not years. More time for writing and pre-production would have most probably been helpful, but it was not part of the tried-and-true Cannon *modus operandi*.

The phone rang. Menahem was calling from New York. In typical fashion, he had a one line pitch: "Jimmy, Chuck Norris, Charles Bronson. *The*

Delta Force. You wanna write it?" Hell yes, I wanted to write it. As usual, there was no plot, just a strong title and two of the most popular action stars of the day.

I had pitched Menahem a Delta Force project right after *Missing in Action* came out. I had learned about Delta from a close friend, James P. Monaghan, an ex-Special Forces officer who had helped train the original Delta operators, but Menahem wasn't interested until he saw a small article about Delta in *Time* Magazine a couple of years later. Now Delta was *current* news and he was ready to green-light a film.

Maybe it was the increased financial pressure, but Menahem's free-wheeling, high-risk, indie film approach changed when Cannon built its new headquarters on San Vicente Boulevard in Beverly Hills and started to try to compete with the major studios, but that's another story.

It amazes me that quite a few Cannon films remain popular worldwide to this day, almost forty years after they first burst on the scene. Why is that the case? Well, with a few noticeable exceptions, the vast majority of Cannon films were intended as popular entertainment and to a great extent, popular entertainment tends to stand the test of time.

By chronicling and preserving the unique and inspiring story of Cannon Films—and of Menahem Golan and Yoram Globus, two outsiders, who set out like countless others to conquer Hollywood, and succeeded, at least for a time—Austin Trunick is doing a tremendous service to everyone who loves the movies.

James Bruner
Los Angeles, 2021

James Bruner is a screenwriter and producer for film and television. His Cannon credits include Missing in Action, Invasion U.S.A., *and* The Delta Force.

Preface

The Cannon Film Guide, Volume II: 1985–1987 operates under the assumption that most of its readers have already read *The Cannon Film Guide, Volume I: 1980–1984*. It's not absolutely necessary to read these books in order—Cannon themselves flipped the sequence on the first two *Missing in Action* movies and that was one of the best decisions they ever made—but it helps paint a more complete and linear portrait of the company. Cannon worked with many of the same players again and again over the years, and so to cut back on redundancy I've avoided going into extensive detail on the major figures' pre-Cannon biographies if I already did so in the first book.

As in the first volume, film franchises are written about in single chapters covering the entire series of movies. This is, again, to avoid redundancies, since cast and crew members often carried over from one production to the next. For example, that's why the full *American Ninja* series, which began in 1985, is included here. It's also why Cannon's entries in the *Death Wish* series, which spanned from 1982 to 1987, are covered in the first volume.

This period is also where exact release dates for Cannon's output can become very fuzzy. It was not all that uncommon for a finished (or half-finished) film to sit on Cannon's shelves for years before it was released, either in theaters or direct to video. These books are organized according to when the films were widely released in the United States, rather than when they were shot or first shown at festivals. (As most of the nine movies in the Cannon Movie Tales series were barely seen in the U.S. until video releases in the late '80s, the decision was made to include those in *Volume III*.)

There are a number of well-known "Cannon" movies from this middle period that aren't *actually* Cannon movies, per se. The company picked up many outside productions for theatrical or video distribution in the mid-1980s, and so for this reason and others their logo would appear on some releases of films in select regions or formats. As much as I love classics such as *Cobra* and *Highlander*, my focus was on the films that originated in-house or otherwise received that magical Golan and Globus touch. Please see this volume's "Intermission" chapter for a run-down on how many of those films came to be associated with Cannon.

Thank you for reading—I hope you enjoy learning about how and why these movies were made at least half as much as you enjoy watching them.

Austin Trunick
Connecticut, 2021

Introduction

On the last episode of *The Cannon Film Guide*...

Cousins Menahem Golan and Yoram Globus arrived from Israel to take Hollywood by storm. They were two of the most famous and successful names within their native film industry, but success in the American market had eluded them for the nearly two decades of their lives they had already dedicated to the movie business. If they were going to make it in America, they decided, the best way to go about it would be to acquire an established foothold in the country. In 1979, they bought out a collapsing movie company called Cannon, best known for importing softcore films from abroad and releasing a steady stream of grindhouse-caliber schlock. In a matter of months, Golan and Globus moved in and began churning out their own, distinct brand of grindhouse-caliber schlock.

One of the keys to understanding Cannon is to break down the way they did business, which explains how they were able to consistently turn a profit on movies that rarely made much money in theaters. Where Menahem Golan was the company's creative leader and vocal spokesperson, his younger cousin, Yoram, was the quiet, financial mastermind who kept the engine running through constant critical derision and countless box office flops. Cannon pre-sold their movies to foreign markets, video distributors, and cable companies, often with little more than a title, a piece of dummied-up artwork, and once in a while a star's name already attached. (That sometimes happened before the star signed onto the project, or even knew about it.) Once the pitch had been sold to enough exhibitors, Cannon sent the movie into production, usually at a budget that was lower than the amount they had already brought in. This way, they came out ahead even before the movie was made, and whether or not anyone went to see it once it was finished.

In a look few other studio moguls could pull off, Menahem Golan (left) and Yoram Globus (right) were photographed wearing *King Solomon's Mines*-style costumes for the company's 1985 catalog.

Cannon was also ahead of the curve when it came to recognizing the potential in alternative markets. Along with the video revolution and the growth of premium cable came a hunger for content, which was necessary to fill rental shelves and late-night television schedules. It was a void that

Cannon was happy to step in and fill with their low-budget, high entertainment fare. They were the kings when it came to making movies that people wouldn't necessarily buy tickets to see, but might watch from their couch over pizza and/or several beers.

This model worked, and worked well. They started small, with the raunchy comedy *The Happy Hooker Goes Hollywood* (1980) and a few cheap-but-effective horror films: *Schizoid* (1980), *New Year's Evil* (1980), and *Hospital Massacre* (1981). Along with those came history's only dystopian science fiction, Bible-themed, disco musical, *The Apple* (1980), an absolutely insane feature directed by Golan himself, which the company expected to be the next *Saturday Night Fever* (1977), but which flamed out immediately upon release. Cannon rebounded with *Enter the Ninja* (1981)—also directed by Golan—which was an influential hit, kicking off the ninja craze of the 1980s and inspiring dozens of low-budget ninja movies, many of those produced by Cannon itself.

The following year brought an even bigger hit with *Death Wish II* (1982), a violent sequel to the eight-year-old vigilante film that turned Charles Bronson into a box office star in the United States. The aging, mustachioed action hero became one of Cannon's unlikely leading men, starring in eight films for the company while in his sixties. This included two more *Death Wish* sequels, and numerous variations on Bronson as a cop who doesn't play by the rules.

As their number of releases grew rapidly each year, so did Cannon as a company. They opened a number of international divisions, the most notable of which was Cannon Italia, in Rome, where they employed many filmmakers and actors from the country's once-booming exploitation industry. It's here where they turned bodybuilder and TV star Lou Ferrigno into *Hercules* (1983), and based the productions for many low-budget adventure films, comedies, and thrillers in the years to come.

They had another ninja-themed hit that same year with *Revenge of the Ninja* (1983), directed by Sam Firstenberg, a young filmmaker who had already worked for the Golan-Globus machine in many, varying capacities for almost a decade. By placing its Japanese-American star front and center for the first time, the film cemented martial artist Sho Kosugi as cinema's foremost ninja, and laid the framework for many of Cannon's low-budget action hits to come.

The year 1984 would prove to be the company's most successful from a business standpoint. *Breakin'* (1984) was rushed into theaters so that it would be the first movie to highlight the growing breakdance scene; what could have been a shameless, cynical cash-grab proved to be an earnest, brightly colorful film starring several of the dance form's most talented practitioners. The movie was not only a box office hit, but a genuine pop culture phenomenon—one that Cannon followed up in record time by conceiving, shooting, and releasing a sequel into theaters just seven months later.

Cannon had another number one hit on their hands with *Missing in Action* (1984), one of two movies shot back-to-back and starring former karate champion Chuck Norris. When the initial film was rejected by their distribution partner, Warner Bros., Cannon had the uncanny idea to flip their order and release its more exciting sequel first, and stumbled almost backwards into a hit action franchise that turned Norris into a star.

While Cannon was making real headway into the box office rankings, they were also starting to be taken seriously by filmmakers, who saw them as a risk-taking alternative to the major studios. This led to projects with such celebrated names as Oscar-winner Faye Dunaway and maverick filmmaker John Cassavetes. Their reputation among Hollywood's creative renegades would only grow as they moved into the heart of the decade.

By the end of 1984, Cannon was reaching the pinnacle of their respectability, not only as a box office challenger but as an outlet for serious filmmakers. They had a stable of reliable directors who could turn around quality films on time and under budget: names like Firstenberg, J. Lee Thompson, Michael Winner, and Boaz Davidson. Soon, those ranks of trusted Cannon directors would grow to include Andrei Konchalovsky, Albert Pyun, and Tobe Hooper.

In front of the camera, the roster was equally formidable. In Charles Bronson and Chuck Norris, they had a pair of bankable stars under lengthy contracts. In short time they would welcome a new, home-grown action hero in Michael Dudikoff, who would headline many exciting films for the company throughout their remaining years.

Despite all of the momentum they rode into the year, 1985 also marked the beginning of the end for Cannon. With grander ambitions came a level of risk the company hadn't dared gamble with in their early years. The folly of several much larger-budgeted flops were compounded by bad investments. Cannon rolled into 1986 with a larger slate of films than any other studio in Hollywood; by the end of 1987, they would be struggling to find the money needed to simply put the movies they'd made into theaters.

Cannon's middle period was a time of unrivaled ambition and excitement, but also a self-inflicted disaster. The films they released during this time came from an uninhibited mix of genres; new ideas and old; from low-budget action films to high-budget failures, including numerous hidden gems and honest-to-goodness classics. Those three years at Cannon saw a whirlwind of productivity as wild and chaotic as any ever witnessed in cinema history.

Welcome to *The Cannon Film Guide, Volume II.*

The Cannon Film Guide
Volume II (1985–1987)

This VHS copy of *The Ambassador* was rented out by The Maltese Falcon video store of Seattle, Washington.

The Ambassador

Release Date: January 11, 1985
Directed by: J. Lee Thompson
Written by: Max Jack
Starring: Robert Mitchum, Ellen Burstyn, Rock Hudson, Donald Pleasence
Trailer voiceover: "There are those that want him silenced. There are those that want him dead … He's fighting for peace, *and* his life!"

Even if *The Ambassador* (1985) had turned out to be the worst movie Cannon ever made, it would still have been worth watching just to see its two aging legends, Robert Mitchum and Rock Hudson, sharing a screen. We should be thankful that Golan and Globus had the good sense to pair these two together before they were gone. Sure, it was in a cheap, sleazy, b-movie thriller, but one that's at least pretty entertaining.

The Ambassador was the second film British director J. Lee Thompson made for Cannon, after *10 to Midnight* (1983), and six more would follow. He was a natural pick for the project, having twice directed Robert Mitchum more than two decades earlier, and notably having coaxed from him one of the actor's best-ever performances in the classic thriller, *Cape*

3

Fear (1962). Mitchum had recently starred in Cannon's *That Championship Season* (1983), a prestigious affair that the actor infamously sabotaged by drunkenly knocking out a photographer's teeth with a basketball at the premiere party. With his out-of-court settlement with the assaulted photographer costing him far more than he'd made on the prior feature, Mitchum needed a quick paycheck—and Cannon was surprisingly eager to give him one. (That costly outburst apparently didn't curtail Mitchum's drinking at all, which reportedly led to numerous arguments with co-star Ellen Burstyn, who didn't approve of her scene partner showing up drunk on set.)

Rock Hudson, meanwhile, was brought on to co-star in *The Ambassador* as a last-minute replacement for former *Kojak* (1973–1978) hero Telly Savalas. You have to imagine it felt like a lucky coup for Cannon to the snag the ailing Hudson, who had in the 1950s and 1960s been one of the box office's leading stars but had not appeared on the big screen for several years following a heart attack and open-heart surgery, and had yet to make his return to TV and join the cast of *Dynasty* (1981–1989). Hudson would be diagnosed with HIV just months after filming wrapped on *The Ambassador* in the early weeks of 1984, and he'd pass away from AIDS-related complications the following year. Unbeknownst to the cast or filmmakers, *The Ambassador* would ultimately be Rock Hudson's final theatrical appearance.

Although Hudson was in poor health throughout filming—he fell ill several times during the shoot, holding up the production—he hardly let it show in his performance. From the looks of it, Hudson was having a blast playing the rough-and-tumble Frank Stevenson, an American security officer stationed in Israel and best friend of the U.S. Ambassador to Israel, Peter Hacker (Mitchum). While Hacker's our hero, Stevenson's the one who has his back, ready to jump into action at any moment. Hudson essentially gets to do the most fun stuff, from throwing punches to jamming a pistol in an extortionist's crotch, to making wisecracks while he waterboards a goon over the back of a speedboat.

EMBAJADOR EN ORIENTE MEDIO

Two aging icons, Robert Mitchum and Rock Hudson, huddle under a jeep in the Israeli desert while filming *The Ambassador*.

Mitchum plays the titular ambassador of *The Ambassador*, a highly respected figure within both political and intellectual circles. In Tel Aviv, his Peter Hacker is a beloved university lecturer, particularly among the young, liberal-minded students who long for peace between the Israelis and the Palestinian Liberation Organization. Back home in America, he's widely regarded as a prime candidate to receive a position in the Presidential cabinet. As the movie takes pleasure in heavy-handedly explaining, Peter Hacker is viewed as the world's best hope to bring peace to the Middle East.

Unfortunately for the world, Hacker's attempts to reconcile the warring factions—primarily through bringing together youths from both sides in an effort to form a united peace movement—are repeatedly thwarted, often with sudden violence on the part of those more adamant in their stances. Hacker's tireless campaign for Israeli-Palestinian harmony is further threatened by two newly-arisen complications which, in both cases, would likely bring a permanent end to his peace-making efforts. The first is the existence of a sex tape which shows Hacker's wife in bed with, of all people, a well-known leader of the Palestinian Liberation Organization. The second, even more dangerous

5

issue at hand is the appearance of a mysterious assassin who has his sights set on Hacker.

The twisting, turning story claims to have been adapted from Elmore Leonard's 1974 novel *52 Pick-up*, although the only major commonality the two stories share are their sex tape-based extortion plots; Leonard long disavowed himself from ever having had any involvement in *The Ambassador*. (Golan and Globus bought the rights to the book shortly after publication, but didn't make a proper film out of it until John Frankenheimer helmed their next version of *52 Pick-Up* in 1986, starring Roy Scheider and Ann-Margret.)

The Ambassador is packed with plenty of tense set-pieces—one memorably framed within the lens of a sniper's scope—and sudden, unexpected bursts of action. Its leads get to drop some fun one-liners, and the plot thankfully leaves no loose ends hanging. The politics on display are a bit slanted, sure, but this tight little thriller never feels overly preachy, either.

His career is in jeopardy
His marriage is in ruins
And his life is in danger
"The Ambassador"...He's through negotiating

Early promotional artwork for *The Ambassador*. In some catalogs, the movie was advertised under the title "Peacemaker."

Mitchum and Hudson were joined by a few very noteworthy co-stars. Best known for his roles in *Halloween* (1978) and *The Great Escape* (1963), and for playing the iconic Bond adversary Ernst Blofeld in *You Only Live Twice* (1967), Donald Pleasence was both one of cinema's all-time great bad guy actors and a staple of '80s horror movies. (He'd thrice return to Cannon's fold for *Hanna's War*, *Ten Little Indians*, and *River of Death*, in 1988 and 1989.) Pleasence plays Israel's no-nonsense Defense Minister, Hacker's frequently flustered, frustrated boss who doesn't approve of his free-wheeling methods. If Mitchum was playing a rogue cop rather than a bureaucratic negotiator, Pleasence would have been the hot-tempered chief of police trying to take away his badge and his gun.

The ever-reliable Ellen Burstyn—of *The Last Picture Show* (1971) and *The Exorcist* (1973)—plays Alex, Hacker's unhappy and heavy-drinking wife, and seems to relish the opportunity to sling bitter barbs at Mitchum with a boozy slur. Despite her infidelity, their relationship is endearing. Both readily admit their imperfections and are quick to forgive the other. In spite of their off-screen differences, Mitchum and Burstyn showed really great chemistry. From reading contemporary reviews, it seems critics at the time were surprised to see the prestigious actress—at this point in her fifties and already a five-time Oscar nominee—doing nude scenes, somehow forgetting that she'd starred in the X-rated *Tropic of Cancer* (1970) before garnering all of that acclaim.

The cast also boasts Italian actor Fabio Testi, star of cult giallo *What Have You Done To Solange?* (1972) as well as Menahem Golan's pre-Cannon thriller, *The Uranium Conspiracy* (1978), as Burstyn's Palestinian paramour. (He was cast in this role after being unceremoniously fired from playing Bo Derek's sexual conquest in Cannon's *Bolero* [1984], allegedly for having herpes.) Among several of Cannon's recurring Israeli actors popping up in small roles is Zachi Noy, star of the *Lemon Popsicle* franchise and recently seen wearing a hook for a hand in *Enter the Ninja* (1981), who provides some comic relief as a bumbling extortionist.

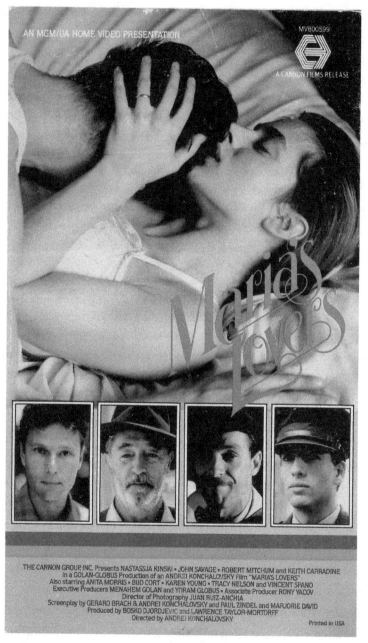

Maria's Lovers on VHS: "She's every man's dream girl, but the only man she wants can't have her!"

Maria's Lovers

Release Date: January 18, 1985
Directed by: Andrei Konchalovsky
Written by: Gerard Brach, Andrei Konchalovsky, Paul Zindel, Marjorie David
Starring: Nastassja Kinski, John Savage, Robert Mitchum, Keith Carradine
Trailer Voiceover: "America, a time of celebration... for her, it is a time of innocence, passion, and the discoveries of womanhood."

Maria's Lovers (1985) is one of those classic, age-old tale of boy loves girl, boy marries girl, boy can't bring himself to make love to girl so boy hops the rails, girl gets pregnant by a gypsy drifter, and boy's erectile dysfunction is miraculously cured. Tell me you haven't heard *that one* a thousand times before.

As far as erotic, World War II period dramas go, *Maria's Lovers*, well . . . it's a Cannon movie. Nastassja Kinski is as alluring as ever as a virginal waif who's the object of desire to every hot-blooded male in her small, American town, but even she's unable to overcome a plot which spends a lot of time meandering to nowhere in particular, and many unintentionally hilariously lines of dialogue that it somehow took a team of four writers to come up with. (One of them—Paul Zindel—was a Pulitzer-winning playwright!)

9

Maria's Lovers is noteworthy, however, for making Andrei Konchalovsky the first Soviet citizen to direct a Hollywood movie at a time when nearly every Hollywood film featured at least one Soviet bad guy.

Andrei Konchalovsky began his career in film as a writer, co-authoring several screenplays with the great director Andrei Tarkovsky, including his lengthy 1966 masterpiece, *Andrei Rublev*. (That's the most times you'll see the name "Andrei" typed in a single sentence in this book.) Konchalovsky's father, Sergey Mikhalkov, was an esteemed children's author who, on the request of Joseph Stalin, penned the lyrics to the national anthem for the Soviet Union. Not long after his collaborations with Tarkovsky, the young Konchalovsky went on to direct his own films. Even while clocking in at more than four hours long, his *Siberiade* (1979) was a hit at the Cannes Film Festival, and took home the prestigious Grand Prix award.

A painted pre-sales advertisement. The film was described to buyers as "a passionate tale of fiery obsession."

Konchalovsky eventually befriended actress Nastassja Kinski, who introduced him to Menahem Golan. His relationship with Cannon proved to be a fruitful one for both sides, as Konchalovsky helmed four films for the studio—*Maria's Lovers*, their highly acclaimed *Runaway Train* (1985), *Duet for One* (1986), and *Shy People* (1988)—and then parlayed that into further work in Hollywood, including the buddy cop classic *Tango & Cash* (1989).

Given their friendship, it's unsurprising that Konchalovsky chose to collaborate with Nastassja Kinski for his first Hollywood feature. Kinski was the estranged daughter of infamous German actor (and crazy person) Klaus Kinski, who'd previously starred in the Cannon feature *Schizoid* (1980). Her breakout role in Roman Polanski's *Tess* (1979) turned her into a film star, but by the early Eighties she'd achieved full-blown sex icon status thanks to her role in a racy remake of *Cat People* (1982), and a popular pin-up poster by Richard Avedon in which the actress was photographed wearing nothing but a dangerous-looking python.

After a brief introduction which uses repurposed, doctored footage from John Huston's war documentary *Let There Be Light* (1946), we're slowly eased into the movie. World War II has just ended, and lovelorn G.I. Ivan Bibic has returned home to his rural, picturesque Pennsylvania town suffering from a debilitating case of PTSD. He's played by John Savage, best known for his starring roles in *The Deer Hunter* (1978) and the film version of *Hair* (1979). He would return to Cannon a couple years later to play the titular Beast opposite Rebecca De Mornay in the Cannon Movie Tales version of *Beauty and the Beast*.

Naturally the first thing Ivan does on returning home is call upon his childhood sweetheart, Maria (Kinski), the memories of whom had kept him going through the many dark nights spent in a Japanese prison camp. Unfortunately, he wanders up to catch her necking with another handsome soldier, Captain Al Griselli (Vincent Spano), and flees home to mope to his father.

Ivan's old man is played by the one and only Robert Mitchum, an old Hollywood legend who'd quickly become something of a Cannon regular. As mentioned in the prior chapter on *The Ambassador* (1985), Mitchum had made a costly out-of-court settlement after he'd gotten blotto and used a basketball to wreck a photographer's face at the premiere for his first Cannon feature, *That Championship Season* (1983). Burt Lancaster was originally to play this role in *Maria's Lovers* but had to drop out to undergo bypass surgery, and Mitchum was available to take on the work.

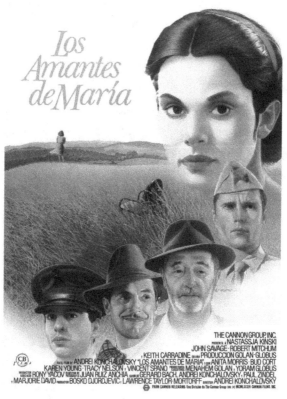

A Spanish poster featuring artwork by painter Keith Batcheller, who would go on to design the home video covers for many Disney films in the 1990s and 2000s.

Ivan and his dad have a pretty weird relationship. First off, Pops doesn't seem too thrilled to have his son home from the South Pacific. Second, he all but encourages his son to slip out and bump uglies with Ms. Wynic, a nutty, middle-aged lady who lives down the street and has known Ivan since he was just a kid. Judging from Mitchum's wink, it's clear that he's been hitting that, too.

Back at her place, Ms. Wynic wastes no time going "full Mrs. Robinson" on the younger Ivan by dropping a barrage of racist and unsubtle innuendos. ("They tell me the oriental women are different, you know what I mean?" she giggles. "Don't tell me. You'll make me blush!") At one point, the crazy lady becomes so aroused by Ivan's youthful masculinity that the buttons on her blouse fly off. Eventually they get it on, and afterward we are treated to what might be the most wack-ass, out-of-nowhere line of pillow talk ever written:

"Do you know the sound of a head being cut off?" Ivan blurts, the reek of sex still hanging in the air.

In case Ms. Wynic wasn't turned off enough by that romantic little non sequitur, Ivan goes on to describe that sound in graphic detail, and then tells a story about the time he saw a rat feast on the remains of one of his fellow prisoners in the Japanese camp. He somehow brings the story back around to Maria, and how he spent his nights imagining he was married to her to drown out the torture, killings, and all of the other horrors happening around him. (Ivan's a buzzkill.)

Later, a homecoming celebration is thrown for the returning war hero at one of the local watering holes. As her new boyfriend canoodles with a blonde tart who talks like a chorus girl in *Grease*, Ivan takes the opportunity to slip in and win back a receptive Maria. Despite the film taking place outside of Pittsburgh, almost every minor character in the film speaks with a thick Jersey—"Joy-zee"—accent. Kinski, on the other hand, retained a good amount of her German accent for Maria. The weirdness of this heavily-accented girl living in heartland America is explained away by giving her a backstory where she's a Yugoslavian immigrant.

It doesn't take long before Ivan and Maria sneak away on the back of his motorcycle to visit the scenic patch of pasture where they used to meet up before he went to war. There, the two rekindle their flame. ("You're different," Ivan remarks, showing his keen eye for observation. "Before you were the same, but now you're different.") After watching the sun rise, Ivan returns Maria to her home to find her understandably livid boyfriend, Al, waiting for them there. "Damn you, baby!" Al howls at them. "And damn you, too, clown!" However, he doesn't really put up any more of a fight to preserve his relationship with Maria.

At this point we're about a third of the way into the movie, and this is where it really takes a turn into bizarre-land. Ivan's father, who has no name, by the way—Mitchum is simply credited as "Ivan's father"—heads over to Maria's house to drop off a homemade dresser. He finds her there bent over, tantalizingly scrubbing the floors in a wet, see-through nightgown. In a brief, incredibly awkward conversation during which he fondles her thigh as she reveals her desire to marry his son, Ivan's father gets all freaky-deaky and tries to get in on that sweet Maria action by asking her for a kiss.

"Let me kiss you. I'm almost your father," he says, as if it weren't weird at all.

She counters with a somehow-even-creepier reply: "Fathers don't need to ask their daughters for a kiss."

Their kiss isn't a peck on the cheek, either: it's about as sexy a 66-year-old man lip-locking with his teenage daughter-in-law can get.

THE CANNON GROUP, INC.
presenta a

NASTASSJA KINSKI

JOHN SAVAGE

ROBERT MITCHUM

KEITH CARRADINE en

UN FILM DE
ANDREI KONCHALOVSKY

Los Amantes de María

Ivan is no good in bed, which makes Maria sad.

After that shiver-inducing father-daughter moment, Ivan and Maria get married, and he's soon carrying his new bride over the marital threshold. Despite Maria putting on such an enthusiastic, overblown display of arousal that it would make a coked-up cam girl blush ("Come, my love. Come into me. Come! Come! Come!" she squeals), Ivan discovers he can't get it up for Maria. It turns out he's so in love with his dreamed-up fantasy image of her that it's rendered him impotent. We know right away how big of a problem this is going to be, not only because Maria's spent half this scene begging Ivan to put a baby in her, but in the next scene we learn she works in a maternity ward and spends all of her days coddling the babies she'll never be able to have.

As you might guess from the film's title, Ivan and Maria aren't about to just go on living happily ever after in this unconsummated marriage of theirs. The first sign of trouble arises when the textbook definition of a handsome goofball rides into town. This chucklehead is played by Keith Carradine, son of John and brother to David and Robert, and the most musical member of the Carradine clan. Konchalovsky had originally hand-picked guitar legend Stevie Ray Vaughan for the part, but when the role was expanded it was decided that a seasoned actor would be a safer choice. It's not like Carradine was a slouch in that department, anyway—"I'm Easy," the track he wrote and performed in Robert Altman's masterpiece *Nashville* (1975), won an Academy Award for Best Original Song. It's nice to see his musical talents put to use here, even if his character is a bit ridiculous.

Carradine makes his entrance on a blue motorcycle, wearing one of those old-timey leather helmets that makes him look like the Red Baron, and with a grinning bulldog riding in his sidecar. He wears a pencil moustache, yellow suit, and a big ol' plaid bowtie, and goes around begging the local businesses for work as a barroom musician. (He's supposed to be some kind of gypsy, but his outfit screams "zany used car salesman.") As if this yuckster didn't seem goofy enough for you yet, he introduces himself as Clarence Butts. It wouldn't be any more obvious that his character is up to no good if he arrived in town pulling a wagon marked "Snake Oil" behind him. He soon encounters Maria at the local soda pop shop and romantically serenades her with a slimy rendition of "Makin' Whoopee." She rebuffs his advances. Mr. Butts later finds Ivan drinking away his sorrows at a local saloon and advises him to go out and get laid, inadvertently striking out with both halves of the unhappily married couple.

Having grown justifiably suspicious, Maria later follows and spies on Ivan through a window as he sticks it to the nutty old neighbor lady once again. When Ivan returns home and fails to get it up for his nubile young wife, she confronts him about his dalliances, and suggests he leave her as it's clear that other women are able to do something for him that she can't. ("I'd rather lose you than destroy you, Ivan," she pleads, perhaps displaying a little too much generosity.) Obviously, the thought of leaving the woman of his P.O.W. camp fever dreams doesn't sit well with Ivan, and so he flips the hell out, laughing like a crazy person, whipping out his package and jiggling it at Maria as she cries. ("Cut it off, that's what you want!" he screams. "Do it! Do it!") Oddly, the scene ends with Maria quietly going to bed while Ivan eats a watermelon in total darkness.

Tensions are obviously high the next morning as Ivan and Maria get dressed up and head out to attend an engagement party for her ex-boyfriend, Al, and his new fiancée. As a romantic big band tune spins on the Victrola, Maria dances from suitor to suitor—Al, Ivan's own dad—allowing them to get a little too close and handsy as her husband watches.

What happens next feels like a cliché moment ripped from a bad rom-com, but *Maria's Lovers* goes for it anyway. Just as the party's guests pose for a commemorative photo with the newly-engaged couple, Al drops a bombshell and announces that he can't marry his fiancée because he's still in love with Maria. *At that very moment* the photographer goes ahead and snaps the photo, so that the flashbulb goes off and captures this betrayal just as it registers on his new girlfriend's face.

As the stunned crowd of party-goers stand around with their mouths agape, Ivan and Al head into the kitchen, we assume, to duke it out mano-a-mano. Instead, Ivan makes an indecent proposal and practically *begs* Al to take Maria from him. ("Just do it," he commands, looking like a mad animal. "Go get her. Get her dresses. Get her stockings. Get her little doo-dads, her perfume, *and her goddamn little underwear!*") When Al suggests that Ivan doesn't love Maria, he decides he'll prove how much he loves her . . . by pressing *his motherflipping hand on a red-hot stove*, because everyone in this movie is out of their damn minds.

Ivan sulks for a while longer so that the movie can hammer home what a broken, shattered man he's become, in case that wasn't made clear enough a few minutes ago *when he purposefully burned his motherflipping hand on a red-hot stove* in an insane gesture of love. Eventually he returns home to find Maria basking in the afterglow of a rigorous masturbation session, and for some reason that's apparently the final straw for him. So, Ivan hits the rails, running away to a nearby town where he starts a new life and finds a job working in a meat processing plant with John Goodman and Bud Cort. (This was John Goodman pre-*Roseanne*, pre-Coen Brothers, and even pre-*C.H.U.D.* [1984]—he looks so young! His other pal, Cort, is best known as Harold from Hal Ashby's cult classic *Harold and Maude* [1971], though he's certainly more grown up here but no less distinctive. This was Goodman's only foray into a Cannon film, but Cort returned to play a peacenik NASA scientist in 1986's *Invaders from Mars*.)

The cover for the Spanish press book for *Maria's Lovers*.

A few months pass. Maria has reconnected with slimy Mr. Butts after bumping into him on a ferry full of gypsies straight out of an Eastern European fairy tale. (Actually, it's more like bumping *and grinding* into him—Butts is so brazen with his bad touching that he feels inclined to comment on the woody he's pressing into her backside. "Feel that? Not bad, huh?" Ugh.) Over a pair of creepy scenes he somehow melts her icy exterior with a few eccentric, slam poetry-style pick-up lines:

"You're like a flower stalk. You'll bend, but you won't break. Just bend, flow with me like water. Wind through the flowers."

. . . and a sappy song, and eventually they wind up in bed together at Maria's house. After deflowering the young housewife he's unable to shut up about her having been a virgin, and invites her to join him on the road. ("You're a class act, all the way. Squeaky clean. No mileage!") With lines like that, it's no wonder Maria declines his invitation.

And, holy hell, we take another jarring time jump to the next Fourth of July, and Maria looks like she's about ready to drop a kid. Everyone saw that coming, right? She somehow manages to track Ivan down in his newfound, equally poor rustbelt town to tell him the news, but he seems totally cold and unfazed by her condition. She goes so far as to even beg him to come back to her, but he tells her he doesn't love her anymore. She leaves him, crushed.

Not long afterwards, Ivan is out drinking with John Goodman, Bud Cort, and a trio of floozies when you'll never guess who shows up. Clarence Butts *himself* walks through the front door of the bar, peddling the same wares he was selling in Ivan's hometown. Ivan buys him a drink, but when Mr. Butts starts bragging about bedding a virgin housewife, Ivan puts two and two together and flattens him with a nasty uppercut.

Ivan spends a night tossing and turning and having nightmares about flesh-eating rats, but soon his dad shows up at his apartment to tell him that Maria had the baby, a son, and that she's alone—and also, he's dying. (Not that his imminent death plays into the remainder of the film—they just felt like slipping that in there, apparently.) The errant husband rushes home to see his wife and her bastard child, and immediately falls in love with the baby. Somehow, for some inexplicable reason, this baby manages to miraculously cure Ivan of his erectile dysfunction. With his deus ex boner, Ivan proceeds to excitedly mount his joyous wife despite her being just a day removed from childbirth.

"We're making love, Maria!" Ivan coos, once again demonstrating his keen skills for stating the obvious.

"We're making our own baby now!" Maria adds, in her thick German/Yugoslavian accent.

The End.

Maria's Lovers was released in theaters in the early weeks of 1985. Critics weren't entirely unkind to the film, and many were quick to point out how the movie had a distinctly foreign feel to it, which made sense since it was an American story starring a German actress by a Russian director produced by a duo of Israelis. If the movie was in another language and subtitled, perhaps we'd be able to chalk up the odd verbiage and heightened melodrama to something being lost in translation. As is, though, it's a beautifully picturesque film where every single character behaves in a totally bonkers, nonsensical fashion, which will probably leave most viewers smacking their foreheads in absolute bafflement.

Hot Resort on VHS, with cover art virtually indistinguishable from any other
sex comedy on video store shelves in the mid-1980s.

Hot Resort
Hot Chili

Release Dates: January 1985 (I), June 1985 (II)
Directed by: John Robins (I), William Sachs (II)
Written by: John Robins, Boaz Davidson, Norman Hudis (I), Menahem Golan (as Joseph Goldman) & William Sachs
Starring: Tom Parsekian, Michael Berz, Bronson Pinchot, Dan Schneider (I), Charlie Stratton, Allan Kayser, Joe Rubbo, Chuck Hemingway (II)
Taglines: *Hot Resort:* "Where anything you want is everything you get!"
Hot Chili: "Sometimes a little spice is *all* you need!"

Film number one: Four young men—a nerd, a player, his sidekick, and their chunky friend—get jobs at a Caribbean resort. Rather than take their duties seriously, the boys are more interested in trying to get laid. Fortunately for them, nearly every woman who checks into their hotel is either a bombshell bimbo or some kind of sex maniac. Standing in their way is their real buzzkill of a boss, a short-tempered (and deeply closeted) taskmaster hell-bent on running a tight ship. Hijinks ensue, bawdy jokes are made, and many, many, many women appear topless, but our hero finds true love in the end. This movie is called *Hot Resort*, and was released by Cannon in 1985.

Film number two: Four young men—a nerd, a player, his sidekick, and their chunky friend—get jobs at a Mexican resort. Rather than take their duties seriously, the boys are more interested in trying to get laid. Fortunately for them, nearly every woman who checks into their hotel is either a bomb-shell bimbo or some kind of sex maniac. Standing in their way is their real buzzkill of a boss, a short-tempered (and deeply closeted) taskmaster hell-bent on running a tight ship. Hijinks ensue, bawdy jokes are made, and many, many, many women appear topless, but our hero finds true love in the end. This movie is called *Hot Chili*, and was released by Cannon in 1985.

These two movies are totally unrelated, but you can probably understand why they're being lumped together here for the sake of discussion. Somehow, for some reason, The Cannon Group managed to make the same movie twice and release the two films within months of each other.

By 1985, we'd more or less reached the nadir of the teen sex comedy genre. The big time success of movies like *Animal House* (1978) and *Porky's* (1981) came just before the start of the home video boom, leading to hun-dreds of cheap knock-offs flooding the rental market. Because T&A was usu-ally their main draw, these were movies that didn't really need to be funny, well-made, or even feature real actors to be successful. They were cheap to make, and easy to sell: all you needed was an outlandish premise, and that didn't even have to be original. (*Animal House* inspired dozens of frat house comedies, 1979's *Meatballs* led many others to be set on campgrounds, and so on and so forth.) By the time the 1980s hit their midpoint, the theatri-cal viability of these raunchy comedies had begun to peter out in favor of more sentimental, character-driven teen fare, mostly thanks to John Hughes, *The Breakfast Club* (1985), and its ilk. However, that barely slowed the pro-liferation of R-rated teen sex comedies on video store shelves, where both of Cannon's 1985 entries, *Hot Resort* and *Hot Chili*, made their inauspicious debuts.

Both films owe as large a debt to Cannon's own *The Last American Virgin* (1982) as they do to the contemporary trends in the video market. *The Last American Virgin*—and even more so the Golan and Globus-produced Israeli film it remade, *Lemon Popsicle* (1978)—did pretty well for Cannon, so it made sense they'd try to repeat their past success. But where *Virgin* found some level of adolescent honesty amid its raunchy humor and gratuitous nudity, Cannon's *Hot* films mostly walked a path of crudeness for crudeness' sake, and nudity purely for the purpose of titillation. (Which is to say, they probably didn't disappoint the hot-blooded teen boys who stayed up to catch them on late-night cable broadcasts.)

Hot Resort was so much in the vein of Golan and Globus' *Lemon Popsicle* movies that early sales ads were illustrated with the likenesses of that series' stars: Zachi Noy, Jonathan Sagall, and Yftach Katzur.

In *Hot Resort*, four horny knuckleheads become quick pals on their first day on the job at the Royal St. Kitts Hotel in the lovely Caribbean. (The tiny island of Saint Kitts was just then starting to become a tourist destination, and this newly-opened resort was one of its first; meanwhile, Cannon had recently filmed 1984's *Missing in Action 2: The Beginning* nearby.)

Among the group are your token playboy with an inflated ego, Marty (Tom Parsekian), and his wise-ass compadre, Brad—played by Bronson Pinchot, soon to become Balki of TV's *Perfect Strangers* (1986–1993). There's also a nerdy virgin by the name of Kenny, played by Michael Berz in his only on-screen appearance. (He would, though, go on to write two Cannon Movie Tales—*Sleeping Beauty* and *Snow White*—the latter of which he also directed.) Rounding out the group is a loveable chunko named Chuck, played by Dan Schneider, whose movie debut came in Cannon's *Making the Grade* (1984) one year earlier.

The boys' main antagonist is their short-fused, drill sergeant-like manager (Samm-Art Williams) who barks orders at his staff like he's R. Lee Ermey in *Full Metal Jacket* (1987). There's also a flamboyant concierge who helps run the hotel, played by Stephen Stucker in more or less the same, over-the-top gay stereotype he played in the first two *Airplane!* movies.

Marty is clearly the group's alpha male, and thus receives the closest thing *Hot Resort* has to a storyline. Not long after arrival he meets and falls head over heels for a pretty, young hotel guest named Liza (Debra Kelly), who is vacationing in Saint Kitts with her ice queen best friend, Franny (Marcy Walker of TV's *All My Children*.) Liza becomes our hero's sole conquest, his love for her instilling in him valuable lessons about monogamy even amidst the endless parade of bikini-clad lady-flesh bouncing around the resort.

Meanwhile, his buddies get up to all sorts of mischief, mostly of a carnal variety. The Riddler himself, Frank Gorshin, briefly shows up to provide lewd tips on how to pick up women. Brad gets repeatedly called to deliver "room service" to one of the hotel's more buxom guests—you can guess the *type* of service—while another lad gets locked up with an overzealous, sex-craved hotel maid. Other sequences include an amorous couple getting stuck in a compromising position in the back seat of a car—requiring the aid of the fire department, the jaws of life, and a crane to rescue them—and a lengthy scene where our horny heroes are hired to drive around the hotel owner's geriatric father and help him, as he puts it, "pick up some broads."

Their antagonists show up in the form of an Ivy League rowing team made up of snotty rich kids who dress like Abercrombie and Fitch models, speak with absurdly WASP-y accents, and diminutively address the hotel staffers as "boy." The team is in town to film a soup commercial, but of course at the eleventh hour the clients decide they want a second team racing in the background, and the only young men around to pilot that other boat are . . . you guessed it, our favorite chuckleheads. Suddenly the hotel's managers are on the lads' side and heavily invested in their winning the race, for whatever reason. As pointless as it all seems, at least it's easy to root against the pomp-ous, Ivy League twits during the movie's big, boat race finale.

Although the movie was never given the opportunity to set the box office on fire—Cannon opted for a straight-to-video release—a couple real-life love connections were made on set. Co-stars Bronson Pinchot (Brad) and Marcy Walker (Franny), were briefly engaged after the shoot, but never married. The two romantic leads, however, Tom Parsekian (Marty) and Debra Kelly (Liza), *did* marry after filming wrapped.

Director John Robins, who took over the film from John Marshall, passed away just a few years after making *Hot Resort,* having spent most of his career directing television programs like *The Benny Hill Show* (1969–1974). Along with Frank Gorshin, another famous face—or, more accurately, famous voice—makes a cameo appearance in the film. Mae Questel, who plays one half of an old Jewish couple staying at the hotel, was the primary voice actor for not only Betty Boop, but Popeye's better half, Olive Oyl, dating all the way back to the 1930s. Also, keep an eye out for Cannon regu-lar Victoria Barrett, who would later star in *America 3000* (1986) and *Three Kinds of Heat* (1987).

You might recognize the theme song used throughout *Hot Resort,* since Dave Powell's "Body Shop" was already used by Cannon in both *Breakin'* and *Ninja III: The Domination* (both 1984), and will no doubt be stuck in your head by the time the movie's credits finally roll. Hopefully you're a fan of the song, because you'll be hearing it again soon . . .

. . . in our next movie, *Hot Chili.* Released to video just a few short months after *Hot Resort,* the totally-unrelated-but-similarly-titled sex comedy *Hot Chili* makes the loose plot of *Hot Resort* feel as complex and nuanced as an entire season's worth of *The Wire* (2002–2008).

Hot Chili on VHS: "South of the border, the food isn't the only thing that's hot!"

Hot Chili was something of a pet project for Cannon chairman Menahem Golan. He co-wrote the screenplay under the pseudonym "Joseph Goldman," a fake name he'd resurrect again and again as a writer (and occasionally, actor) in the 1990s. Golan would sit in his office and describe scenes that he wanted to appear in the movie to the film's director, William Sachs—who had recently salvaged *Exterminator 2* (1984) as a hired fixer, filming and adding new footage when Cannon deemed the original director's cut unfit to be released. When Golan eventually caught wind that Sachs was shooting scenes he hadn't written, Golan hopped on a plane to Mexico so that he could oversee the production himself.

Golan's heavy-handed interference resulted in a film that Sachs was so displeased with that he tried to have his name removed—that is, until he discovered that would prevent him from receiving his residuals. Although he's practically disowned it, *Hot Chili* does occasionally benefit from the director's surreal touch. Take, for instance, the opening shot: the camera slowly tilts downwards from a herd of mooing cows as an iguana enters the frame. As the lizard opens its jaws, we hear a loud, gross, and obviously human belch ring out. *Hot Chili* begins on a very weird—but very funny—foot.

In addition to his fixer work on *Exterminator 2*, Sachs was the filmmaker behind a string of off-the-wall, cult-ready flicks that included *The Incredible Melting Man* (1977), *Galaxina* (1980), and a satirical documentary about UFOs, Bigfoot, and Atlantis called *Secrets of the Gods* (1976). With his past work in mind, it makes sense that some of the movie's bizarre humor and weird eroticism feel more like something from a film by Buñuelor Fellini than a *Porky's* knock-off sprung from the mind of Menahem Golan.

This time around, our quartet of mischievous horndogs is comprised of good-natured New Yorker named Ricky, played by a "Charles Schillaci"—who'd soon change his professional name to Charlie Stratton and star in the *Gremlins* knock-off *Munchies* (1987)—and his lascivious pal, Jason, played by Allan Kayser, who would go on to fame as Bubba on *Mama's Family* (1983–1990) and appear in *Night of the Creeps* (1986). Joe Rubbo makes his return to Cannon as *Hot Chili's* Arney, playing essentially the same comic foil he did in *The Last American Virgin*. The token nerd in the crew is Stanley (Chuck Hemingway), whose obnoxious catch phrase—"I just wanna fuuuuuuuuuuuck!"—is delivered in a nasal, proto-Urkel whine.

Instead of a tropical island resort, *Hot Chili*'s degenerate teens head to the Tropicana Cabana, a top-of-the-line Mexican hotel where they've secured summer work as hired hands, and have plans to chase some sun-kissed tail. At first, the gig proves to be a mixed bag: while the resort is reasonably luxurious and, indeed, well-populated with bikini-clad hotties, the young men mostly find themselves spending their days scrubbing floors and nights sharing sleeping quarters with a horse.

The hotel stable, of course, is no place for seducing women.

Sales ads like the one above did not beat around the bush regarding what sort of film *Hot Chili* would be.

Their menial labor is personally overseen by the hotel's stickler of an owner, Señor Esteban Rodriguez Cortez the Third, who insists on only being addressed by his full name. His cartoonish accent leads him to pronounce his generational suffix as ". . . the turd," which is a running joke throughout the film. (No one ever said this was a cerebral comedy.) He's played by Cannon regular Jerry Lazarus, who had already appeared in *Treasure of the Four Crowns* (1983), *Over the Brooklyn Bridge*, and *Breakin' 2* (both 1984), and would later have roles in *The Delta Force, Murphy's Law* (both 1986), and *Surrender* (1987).

When their situation seems to be at its most insufferable, the boys glimpse a light at the end of the tunnel in the form of the hotel's buxom cook, Chi-Chi, who inexplicably introduces herself to the guys while wearing nothing but a teensy-tiny kitchen apron. She's played by Louisa Moritz, another returnee from *The Last American Virgin*, in which she was also paired up with Joe Rubbo. (She also appeared in 1980's *Schizoid* for Cannon.)

Between the burping iguana, Cortez "the Turd," and the mysteriously bare-assed kitchen wench, you get a pretty good indication of what kind of film *Hot Chili* strives to be within its first seven minutes. Then the guests start showing up and the boys' futures begin looking even brighter. Beyond the pair of honeymooning senior citizens and a stray German aristocrat, practically everyone who checks in to the Tropicana Cabana is an attractive woman who is just aching for sex with an inexperienced teenage boy. How lucky for our heroes!

The movie, for the most part, plays out in a series of close encounters with the resort's zany guests. Some scenes offer little more than your standard sex comedy T&A tropes, but others border on the surreal. One such recurring thread involves a guest billed only as the "music teacher," played by Bea Fielder, a German actress who had previously appeared in several of the *Lemon Popsicle* films. This striking blonde—who is rarely clothed—gets off on teaching young men how to play musical instruments. She lures her prey by ordering room service, and then surprising them with a nude instrumental serenade. The increasing absurdity of her appearance—first, seen calmly straddling a cello while stark naked, next playing the piccolo while floating topless in a pool, and then huffing and puffing into a tuba, and finally letting it all hang out while banging on a set of bongos—might have been considered a bold artistic statement were this a foreign language film. Here, in a raunchy Cannon sex comedy, it's utterly baffling.

If these nude music lessons instill *Hot Chili* viewers with a dash of Fellini, then the numerous scenes of the resort's bourgeois clientele being comically tortured is straight from the book of Luis Buñuel. Poor Stanley gets lost while hauling luggage, leading a stuck-up rich girl—once again, played by Victoria Barrett—on an endless goose chase around the resort in search of her room. Their winding path appears to go on for days, taking them through hotel hallways, lavish gardens, and a local bullfighting ring, with the footage occasionally sped up to create a madcap, *Benny Hill Show*-type effect. (This turns their bickering into high-pitched, Chipmunk gibberish, and cartoonish spring noises are added every time she kicks Stanley or wallops him with her purse.) This goes on, and on, and on, and on—well past the point of being funny, but then continues until the sheer ridiculousness of continuing to prolong the gag makes it laughable all over again.

Disappointingly, the rest of the film's humor is more pedestrian. You have the well-trod cliché of oversexed seniors in Mr. and Mrs. Houston, a pair of over-the-top old Texans on their honeymoon, played by a pair of prolific character actors in Ferdy Mayne and Connie Sawyer. (Combine their two resumes and you'll have nearly five hundred screen credits.)

You've also got Brigitte, a German dominatrix played by Taaffe O'Connell—of *Galaxy of Terror* (1981) and Cannon's own *New Year's Evil* (1980)—who indoctrinates our young heroes in her particular brand of lovemaking. Ripping another page from Cannon's own *The Last American Virgin* playbook, her lessons continue until just the moment her boyfriend returns by surprise and catches her in bed with poor Arney.

The boyfriend naturally speaks in one of those wacky German accents that are typically reserved for Nazis or mad scientists, where all of the S's are replaced with Z's, and W's with V's—think Dr. Strangelove, or Arte Johnson on *Laugh-In* (1968–1973):

"I vill kill your little room zervice salami, zen I come back and kill you!" he threatens her.

"Ohhh, yah, Brigitte luffs it ven you kill her!" she moans, on edge of orgasm and still fully decked out in her leather bondage gear.

Later on in the film, Ricky's parents and little sister show up at the Tropicana Cabana, forsaking their annual vacation to the Catskills to spend time with their son at his place of work. This puts a serious wrench in his plans to woo the pretty blonde Allison (Kathleen Kriss), who is vacationing with her ice cold, upper class mother. (She's played by Flo Gerrish, also of Cannon's *Schizoid* [1985], *The Naked Cage* [1986], and 1987's *Over the Top*). The movie culminates in one madcap evening of unchecked sexcapades, where almost every character—including Ricky's folks, and the boys' hot-headed boss "the Turd," who hooks up with the Germans guests' shirtless manservant—gets caught on video engaged in carnal hijinks with someone who isn't their spouse. The tape is played over dinner the next evening, and once all infidelities are revealed—and everyone finishes up slapping each other—the movie cuts to an obligatory bullfighting scene, where every character is in the audience and happily enjoying each other's company again.

On the whole, *Hot Chili* feels positively unhinged. It's incredibly juvenile and sexist, sure, but that's par for the course when it comes to this style of movie. Left to his own devices, you get the sense that director William Sachs might have made this into one of the weirder entries into the '80s sex comedy canon. Even if they weren't aware of Menahem Golan's personal interference, though, many viewers would probably come away with the feeling that this was a movie being pulled in several directions. The film feels as if it were tossed together and rushed onto video as an afterthought after things went sour between the director and producer. Moments of sloppy editing are present, too: characters' relationships to one another change, and in his letters home to his parents—which serve as narrative voiceovers for the first half of the movie—Ricky sometimes refers to events in the film that haven't happened yet.

Besides the previously mentioned "Body Shop," Cannon harvested much of this film's score from *Breakin'* and *Rappin'* (1985).

While not a very good movie by any means, the more bizarre elements of *Hot Chili* make it far more memorable than its (slightly) older Cannon sibling, *Hot Resort*. Still, it's unsurprising that neither of these films saw the light of day again on home video for thirty-five years after their straight-to-video premieres.

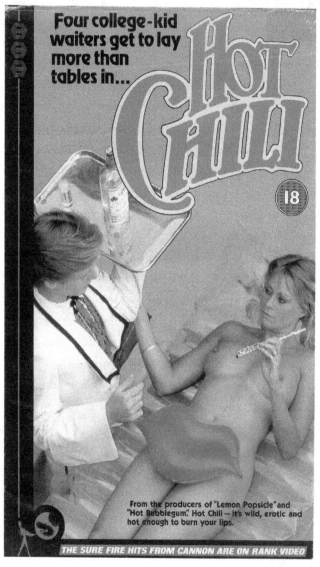

The U.K. videocassette edition of *Hot Chili* came courtesy of Rank Video, who handled many of Cannon's British VHS releases.

Interview: *Hot Chili* Director William Sachs

By the mid-Eighties, William Sachs was easily the longest-tenured film-maker at Cannon: having worked for the company in varying capacities since the late 1960s, Sachs' employment predates the arrival of Golan and Globus by more than a decade.

He started out as an assistant editor working on the studio's low-budget features and many European imports, but was promoted to director on *Joe* (1970) after John G. Avildsen was fired. Sachs retitled the film and pulled Peter Boyle's character to the forefront. *Joe* was met with critical praise, and became one of the top-grossing films for the year—and was the movie that put the original incarnation of Cannon on the map. Sachs turned down a co-director's credit, but made a name for himself anyway as one of Hollywood's best film doctors, and found himself hired more than twenty times over the following decades to fix movies that no one else could. Among these salvage jobs were video-era b-movie classic *Leprechaun* (1993), and of course Cannon's own *Exterminator 2* (1984), which Sachs was interviewed about in *The Cannon Film Guide, Vol. I.*

At the same time, Sachs built up his own filmography as a director. His widely-varied catalog of films includes *There Is No 13* (1974), *The Incredible Melting Man* (1977), *Van Nuys Blvd.* (1979), *Galaxina* (1980), and *Spooky House* (2002).

At many points Sachs ran into producers with whom he didn't see eye-to-eye, which resulted in films which were tampered with against his desires. One such film was the Cannon feature *Hot Chili* (1985), over which he butted heads with Menahem Golan the whole way.

I know *Hot Chili* isn't a film that you're very happy with. I know that Menahem came in and ran over what you were doing.

William Sachs: I don't even talk about that one! But, whatever. Actually, Menahem came and told me once, "You know, this is Burt Lancaster's favorite movie." I don't know why, but one day he came into the editing room and announced that. [Laughs] I don't know if that was actually true.

I wrote the script with Menahem at his house. I spent three years sitting in his office listening to him. And then in some interview, they asked him something about me and he said, "I don't know who he is." [Laughs]

Wowwwwww.

I could tell you the whole story, if you want.

I'm very interested. How was it even pitched to you? I figure it must have started out, at least, as more of your own project. Or, at least you thought it might be.

Menahem came to me. I was supposed to direct a film called *Number One with a Bullet* (1987). They had a great script. I forgot who wrote it, but it was really good. And then Menahem rewrote it and I *hated* it. So I got mad, and I didn't want to do it. So then Menahem says, "*Lemon Popsicle*! Do a *Lemon Popsicle*! Make a new one!" That was their Israeli hit. I think Boaz Davidson did it originally.

The sadly unused, original name for the film—"Ooh, What a Zexy Summer!"—was another masterpiece movie title by Menahem Golan, the man who came up with the phrase "Electric Boogaloo."

Yeah, they remade it as *The Last American Virgin* (1982).

Right. And so he said, "Make a new one." I told him, "I don't want to do that." Yes, yes, he kept pushing. I finally said, "Okay, *fine.*" So I wrote something, and he didn't like it. He goes, "I will write it with you!" He used another name, Joseph Goldman or something.

We wrote in his office, and I even went to his house on a Jewish holiday. His wife makes this really nice dinner and we sit down, and he gulps the whole thing in two bites! He goes, "Come back to work at the table!" I said, "No, I want to eat! When do you rest?" Menahem points to the ground and says, "When I'm there!" So now he's resting, anyway.

He says, "Come outside!" So I go outside, and we're standing by the pool, and he was mad at Boaz Davidson for something. And he lived in Cheviot Hills, which is in LA. He points to a roof—there's this house, a pool, a yard, a wall, another yard, trees, and then there's this distant roof. He says, "That's Boaz Davidson's house. Spit on him!" I said, "I can't really spit that far!" And he goes, "Just spit, then!" and he spits in the pool. So, I spit in his pool. [Laughs]

He was coming up with all this crazy stuff that I hated. He tells me to write it down. But while he's dictating, I wrote down what I wanted to write down. [*Laughs*] He was so out of control! So we go shoot the movie, and on the third day he calls me up and says, "I'm pulling the plug!" I ask why, and he says, "Because there's nothing in it that I wrote!" He says, "Stay there, I'm coming." We were in Mexico, at this resort. I had my wife and my son there, and we kind of had parties for three days. The food was great. The people were great. We had fun.

He had a "friend," who was one of the females in the movie. And she liked my version, so he comes down and she's telling him to do my version. But he said, "No, no, let's do my version!" So I had to shoot his scenes, which were the naked violinist, the cellist who is naked and all that stuff. He was standing there, laughing and laughing.

Anyway, so the movie's a mishmash. I like some of it. Like, the tango scene, I like—that's mine. But, it's a crazy movie! It's half his, half mine, and it doesn't go together. I liked the title music with the postcards.

I was wondering if there were moments in the film that you were still happy with.

I don't like watching my movies when I've finished them. I want to move on. When I watch movies, I just remember all the horrible things that happened. I don't love it. There are bits that I think are fun. There's some silly, crazy stuff that I like, but it's not my movie. It's his movie with my stuff in it.

Just a quick Menahem story. I'm working on that script, right, and I'm sitting in his big, giant office and they had a coffee table area where I was working on a yellow pad. He's on the phone and he's screaming at some agent, "I don't care who she is! She's an actress! An actress is an actress!" and he slams the phone down. He was talking about Katharine Hepburn! [*Laughs*] And she ended up working for him!

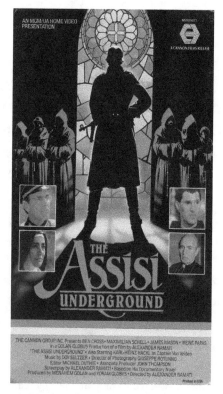

The Assisi Underground on VHS.

The Assisi Underground

Release Date: May 3, 1985
Directed by: Alexander Ramati
Written by: Alexander Ramati
Starring: Ben Cross, Maximilian Schell, James Mason, Irene Papas
Trailer Voiceover: "The incredible, true story of a battle for human dignity!"

The small town of Assisi in central Italy was the setting for one of the Second World War's many inspirational stories of resistance. In 1943, a Franciscan priest by the name of Father Rufino Niccacci oversaw a secret system that sheltered hundreds of Italian Jews from the Nazis. Hiding them in the town's monastery and convents, he helped them obtain falsified papers so that some could live as normal lives as was possible during wartime. He was able to help others escape Axis-occupied territory by disguising them as monks, and teaching them Catholic prayers and blessings to fool enemy soldiers. The heroism of Father Niccacci and all of his associates in Assisi saved hundreds of lives.

Such a tale is deserving of a fine movie adaptation. Perhaps someone other than Cannon will attempt to make that film one day.

The Assisi Underground, originally intended to be a TV miniseries, isn't a bad movie; it just isn't a particularly exciting one. While there are a few tense scenes where snooping Nazis almost catch our hero and his protected flock, a lot of the film focuses on the duller details of what went on. There are too many scenes of the Jewish refugees just hanging out in the monastery, dining, chatting, and playing games, and unnecessarily long shots of printers forging documents. A lot of the film is just our priest convincing locals to join his cause which, while true to the real story, doesn't make for the most exciting viewing experience. Originally released in a three-hour-long festival cut, the movie was trimmed down to just under two hours for its video release.

The film was directed by Polish writer Alexander Ramati, who had penned the 1978 novel that served as its source material. During World War II, Ramati had worked as a journalist and spent time in Assisi throughout 1944, where he first met Father Niccacci and learned of his story. His next (and last) film was 1988's *And the Violins Stopped Playing*, another adaptation of one of his own novels about World War II.

Father Niccacci is played by Ben Cross, who had just starred as Harold Abrahams in 1981's critically-acclaimed *Chariots of Fire*. (You started humming that film's theme song as soon as you read the title, didn't you? Admit it.) Cross, who passed away in 2020, remained prolific throughout his career, appearing in almost one hundred films and TV shows—from the criminally-underrated *Paperhouse* (1988) to the 2009 *Star Trek* reboot.

Irene Papas, of *Antigone* (1961) and *The Guns of Navarone* (1961) renown, played the nunnery's Mother Superior, while Maximilian Schell of *Judgment at Nuremberg* (1961) played a Nazi who was compelled to help Father Niccacci because of his devout Catholic upbringing. Other recognizable actors in smaller roles include Angelo Infanti (Michael Corleone's traitorous bodyguard in 1972's *The Godfather*), Delia Boccardo (the goddess Athena in Cannon's own *Hercules*, 1983), and Italian politician Allessandra Mussolini, who plays a nun, which feels a little like awkward casting in a Holocaust film. (Yes, she is the granddaughter of *that* Mussolini . . .)

The biggest name in *The Assisi Underground*'s credits, though, is James Mason, who plays Father Niccacci's boss, Bishop Nicolini. A three-time Oscar nominee—for *A Star is Born* (1955), *Georgy Girl* (1966), and *The Verdict* (1982)—who starred in nearly one hundred and fifty movies across a half-century-long career, Mason was also known for movies such as *North by Northwest* (1959) and Stanley Kubrick's *Lolita* (1962). This would be his final role, as he passed away of a heart attack just months after shooting wrapped.

While not a terrible film by any means, there are better war dramas out there—even within Cannon's own filmography.

IT'S THE STREET SENSATION
THAT'S SWEEPIN' THE NATION!

Rappin'

VIDEOPHONIC™
SOUND DIGITALLY
DUPLICATED

THE CANNON GROUP INC. PRESENTS MARIO VAN PEEBLES · TASIA VALENZA · CHARLES FLOHE · MELVIN PLOWDEN IN A GOLAN-GLOBUS PRODUCTION OF A JOEL SILBERG FILM RAPPIN' DIRECTOR OF PHOTOGRAPHY DAVID GURFINKEL MUSIC SUPERVISOR LARRY SMITH CHOREOGRAPHY BY EDMOND KRESLEY UNDERSCORE BY MICHAEL LINN WRITTEN BY ROBERT LITZ & ADAM FRIEDMAN PRODUCED BY MENAHEM GOLAN YORAM GLOBUS DIRECTED BY JOEL SILBERG ASSOCIATE PRODUCER JEFFREY SILVER

Printed in USA

The U.S. VHS release of *Rappin'*, "a fast-talking, fast-dancing film that does
for street talk what *Breakin'* did for breakdancing."

Rappin'

Release Date: May 10, 1985
Directed by: Joel Silberg
Written by: Adam Friedman, Robert Litz
Starring: Mario Van Peebles
Trailer Voiceover: "Party people in the place, listen to me / I'm gonna tell you a story about an MC / or a rapper, that's a person who rhymes to the beat / A musical rhythm on city streets . . . You must see *Rappin'!* / This movie *had* to happen!"

Somehow, in some way, Cannon always finds a way to surprise you. What if I told you *Breakin' 2: Electric Boogaloo* (1984) wasn't the studio's most insane exploitation of mid-'80s hip-hop culture? How could a movie get crazier than Boogaloo Shrimp *breakdancing on the ceiling*, right? Or, what about the power of breakdance bringing a man *back from the dead?* Well, our next movie has all of that wackiness and *then* some. *Rappin'* (1985) was the company's spiritual continuation of the *Breakin'* series, and man oh man, is it wild.

The film was directed by Joel Silberg, an Israeli filmmaker whose prior Cannon credits include *The Secret of Yolanda* (1983) and the first *Breakin'*

(1984), and who would go on to direct 1990's *Lambada*. Like both of the company's breakdance films, *Rappin'* was rushed through production at a breakneck speed, hitting theaters almost one year to the weekend after the first *Breakin'* took the box office by storm. To put the pace at which Cannon worked into better perspective, *Breakin' 2* was released for Christmas of 1984—and *Rappin'* had already begun shooting eight weeks later.

Cannon assumed, probably correctly, that they'd oversaturated their market for urban dance films after releasing two *Breakin'* movies in roughly a six month period, which is why they shifted from popping and locking to rap for the third film in this unofficial trilogy. The hopes, surely, were that it would be met by the same resounding success as the two earlier films thanks to the similar way it tapped into a growing trend then buzzing at the edge of popular culture, ready to explode into the mainstream. (Their inability to reach a deal with Adolfo "Shabba Doo" Quiñones to make a third *Breakin'* movie also factored into this pivot.)

To Cannon's credit, rap music was far from the pop music-dominating genre that it is today, but this wouldn't have been many Americans' first exposure to the form. *Rappin'* came out post-Grandmaster Flash, post-"Rapper's Delight," and years after Blondie's "Rapture." Heck, Run-D.M.C. had already released two hit albums by the time *Rappin'* landed. Sure, it beat Def Jam's *Krush Groove* (1985) to the theaters by a few months, but if you were to ask any hip-hop head which of the two has more cred, well, they sure as hell aren't going to point at Cannon's movie.

The original *Breakin'* felt like a loving (if cheesy) tribute to an under-exposed element of hip-hop culture. *Rappin'*, on the other hand, feels like it was cooked up by a bunch of unhip, old men in suits wanting to cash in on a hot, new music fad before it fades away. Nowadays, *Rappin'* isn't helped by the fact that hip-hop became *the most* culturally influential pop movement by the end of the millennium, but it's hard to imagine the film didn't feel exploitative even on the day it was released. Perhaps the biggest factor contributing to this is how few people involved in the making of *Rappin'* were even remotely associated with the actual hip-hop scene. Rather than turn to someone well-known within the community—as they did when they recruited street dance all-stars such as Shabba-Doo and Boogaloo Shrimp for *Breakin'*—Cannon instead turned to Mario Van Peebles for their lead.

To be fair, he's an incredibly appealing actor, and would go on to become a big name as an actor and director. The son of Blaxploitation godfather Melvin Van Peebles—writer, director, and star of *Sweet Sweetback's Baadasssss Song* (1971)—Mario made his big screen debut with a small role in his father's influential independent movie, but it was Cannon who gave him his first meaty adult role when they cast him as the villainous "X" in *Exterminator 2* (1984).

If you set out to make a film with the sole purpose of highlighting "the street sensation that's sweeping the nation," as the posters put it, you would probably want to cast at least a few people who were good rappers. Unfortunately, that was not the case when it came to *Rappin'*. Whether or not Van Peebles has any natural rhyme-spitting ability we may never know, as the moments where his character raps are so painfully and obviously dubbed that the lip-matching resembles, well, Franco Nero's in *Enter the Ninja* (1981).

As the story goes, Cannon screened an early cut of the film for Master Gee of the Sugarhill Gang, who was the older brother of actor Leo O'Brien, who plays Van Peebles' rapscallion kid brother in the film. The Sugarhill Gang was the group responsible for 1979's "Rapper's Delight," the first-ever rap single to hit the Billboard charts, and later performed on-screen by the Muppets' Swedish Chef, Adam Sandler's elderly neighbor, and Kangaroo Jack. (That was in *The Muppets* [2015–2016], *The Wedding Singer* [1998], and *Kangaroo Jack* [2003], respectively.) Master Gee, already by that point a member of hip-hop's old guard, found Van Peebles' attempts to rap so laughable that he volunteered to re-dub his musical segments in post without taking any on-screen credit.

Rappin' isn't set in Los Angeles or New York, but in that other hotbed of street culture known as . . . Pittsburgh, Pennsylvania? (We'll go with it.) Our hero, John Hood (Van Peebles), is a man with a cool name and an ill-defined criminal past. We first meet him as he's being released from an eighteen-month prison stint for assault. Our rapping narrator explains to the audience that Hood has a new lease on life:

"Yes, you went away an underachiever / Now you're coming back a true believer!"

Recognize that voice? Yes, that's everybody's favorite gangsta-rapper-turned-TV-actor, Ice-T, again, long before "Cop Killer" and very, very long before *Law & Order: Special Victims Unit* (1999). He returned to Cannon again after making appearances in both *Breakin'* movies, not only to play himself, but ghost-write some of the film's rhymes and perform its cheesy, rapped narration. (He also rap-narrates the movie's theatrical trailer, which loosely summarizes the movie's plot.)

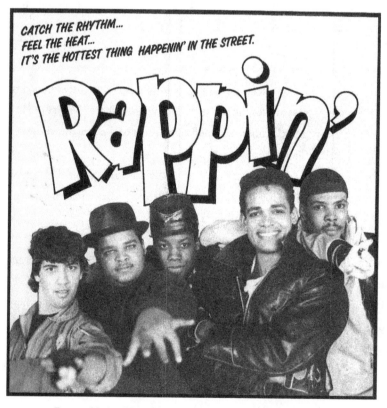

Rappin' John Hood (second from right) and his crew.

It turns out that John Hood—or "Rappin' John Hood," as he's known—was scared straight by his time in the slammer. He's washed his hands of his old, criminal lifestyle, and has dedicated himself to walking the path of the straight and narrow. Likely due to him being the leader of a violent gang just one and a half years earlier, Hood is notorious within his stunningly diverse neighborhood. As he makes his way down the street he's greeted with nervousness by the proprietors of an Asian fruit stand, a Greek hot dog cart, an Italian deli owner, an Irish food truck operator, and his elderly Jewish neighbor. (If the Irish restaurateur looks familiar, it's probably because you recognize the actor, Clayton Hill, as the escalator-riding sweater zombie in 1978's *Dawn of the Dead*.)

The members of Hood's old gang, the Wild Things, are happier to see him back in town—they include his best friend, Ice, played by Eriq La Salle, the future Dr. Peter Benton of *E.R.* (1994–2009) fame, in his debut role. Happiest of all, though, are his kid brother Allan (Leo O'Brien of 1985's *The Last Dragon*) and his sassy grandmother, played by Eyde Byrde. The Hood siblings immediately break into an uncomfortably awkward hip-hop number titled "Two of a Kind," where they casually rap-splain to grandma about how they sneak into porno movies together and their shared preference for "girls with big behinds." Grandma counters this weirdness by rap-scolding Allan into doing his homework. Good for Grandma.

Hood heads out to a welcome home party thrown by the Wild Things at the local club. One of his gang members, Richie, gets into an absurdly-choreographed breakdance battle—with pirouettes and coordinated kicks—that looks more like an audition for *Swan Lake* than anything you'd see on the street. (The actor, Richie Abanes, was a Broadway dancer, and is now a very prolific Evangelical author behind books such as *Harry Potter and the Bible: The Menace Behind the Magick* and *What Every Parent Needs To Know About Video Games*.)

It's not long before John Hood gets some bad news. It turns out his old flame, Dixie (Tasia Valenza), has been stolen away by a rival gang leader: an extremely clean-cut white guy named Duane. Now, Duane (soap opera hunk Charles Grant) used to be Hood's right-hand man, but he's taken over their old crime biz, stealing away some of Hood's old lackeys along with his girlfriend. It's pretty clear, though, that Dixie and Hood aren't one hundred percent over each other, which pisses off Duane, who becomes hell-bent on fighting his old partner in crime. (Beyond his many soap roles, Grant—here credited as Charles Flohe—appeared in two more films for Cannon: 1986's *The Delta Force*, where he was credited as Charles Floye, and the same year's *P.O.W. The Escape*, where he was credited as Charles R. Floyd. Make up your mind, man!)

Our hero has a bigger problem than a stolen girlfriend, however: Hood's hood is about to be demolished by a corrupt businessman named Thorndike, played by Harry Goz. If you recognize the actor's face, it's either from *Marathon Man* (1976) or *Mommie Dearest* (1981)—if, more likely, you recognize his voice, it's because he played Captain Hank Murphy on Adult Swim's *Sealab 2021* (2000–2005). Thorndike has hired a wimpy goon named Cedric (Rony Clanton) to clear out all the tenants who live on Hood's street by any means necessary, which mostly entails turning off their heat during the bitter cold of a Rust Belt winter.

So, to recap: Hood needs to win back Dixie's heart, and save his neighborhood from a greedy developer, all while trying to live a crime-free life in spite of the dastardly Duane's attempts to lure him and his crew into a rumble. These three story threads eventually converge, all thanks to the healing powers of rap music.

It turns out that Dixie works in A&R at a big-time music label, because Pittsburgh is also a major hub of the music industry within the *Rappin'* cinematic universe. With his new outlook on life, John Hood now considers himself a rapper, not a fighter, and would rather solve his problems with freestyle rhymes instead of his fists. Dixie is convinced Hood can become a big star and possibly even change the world with his raps, but Duane's obviously not happy about his new girlfriend spending all of her extra time with her hunky ex. For Hood, becoming a rap superstar would be a means of helping out his poverty-stricken neighborhood.

I won't bother continuing with a play-by-play. Instead, I'll highlight just a few of the movie's many "Did that really just happen?" moments. Not all of them, obviously, as that would take many more pages.

One of the movie's most memorable musical numbers is a little piece called "Snack Attack." John Hood's crew includes a guy who goes by the name "Fats," and you can probably guess what his defining physical trait might be. (He's played by Melvin Plowden, a local high school student who auditioned for the filmmakers when they came to town.) After making countless jokes about Fats always being hungry, the Wild Things visit their pal Richie where he works, at a grocery warehouse. Fats can't help but help himself to the merchandise, which triggers a group rap about all of the things he loves to eat.

A few choice rhymes:

"I like my prosciutto thin and lean / With hot linguini that's fresh and green ..."

"White asparagus and hollandaise / Scallops, shrimp and fresh béarnaise ..."

"A real green salad, fresh and nude / When it comes right down to it, the boy loves food!"

As they rap, they trash literally dozens of dollars' worth of groceries, which gets Richie fired from his job, so they steal several boxes of food on their way out. To throw off some suspicious cops, they pretend to be a charity service and start to distribute their contraband to their malnourished neighbors. This turns John Hood's reputation around and earns him the nickname "Rappin' Hood." (Get it? As in, Robin Hood? "Rappin' Hood?" GET IT?)

At another point, Cannon's favorite "rap talker," Ice-T, auditions for Dixie's boss with his early single, the anti-violence anthem "Killers." He's credited here under his birth name, Tracy Marrow, while his backing group is credited as "Ice-T," and includes his Rhyme Syndicate compatriots Hen-Gee and DJ Evil E. Dixie's boss isn't impressed by the future Grammy winner, and instead signs John Hood to a record deal after he sees him break up a slapstick bar fight between two drunks—by rapping about the dangers of alcohol. (His *Rappin'* co-star, Mario Van Peebles, may have felt a need to make that up to him, as he gave Ice-T his first major role by casting him as a police detective in his 1991 directorial effort, *New Jack City*.)

There's a scene where Hood's pals Richie and Moon—the latter played by Kadeem Hardison, or Dwayne Wayne of *Cosby Show* spin-off *A Different World* (1987–1993)—are comically launched from the hood of a moving car into the back of a garbage truck, and somehow aren't dead afterward.

At another point, Hood and his Merry Men hijack an oil tanker and use it to restore heat to their neighbors, who are being frozen out of their homes, and they do it in the most silly, convoluted way possible. They accomplish their charitable grand theft auto by recruiting a local prostitute to seduce the truck driver and take him into her apartment, and then have Fats pretend to be her husband returning home early from work. As the poor truck driver hides under the bed, the portly, lovable Fats bounces up and down on the mattress, squashing him. This whole segment takes the form of a musical montage. The best things about it are all of the lowbrow sound effects added to the action, such as a slide whistle when the trucker drops his pants, and an exaggerated springing noise from Fats bouncing on the mattress. It's like a Road Runner cartoon, but with a trucker trying to get it on with a prostitute!

Every single one of these scenes is a great time in its own right, but wow oh wow, *Rappin*'s credit sequence really takes the cake. Almost every major cast member is given a solo rap verse as the Wild Things dance and strut their stuff through the streets of Pittsburgh. Whoever came up with this idea was either a madman, brilliant, or possibly both, because these last few minutes are where it becomes painfully clear that most of *Rappin*'s cast should never, ever have been allowed anywhere near a microphone.

Sure, it's bad when Duane butchers his verse by showing off just how little flow a man can possibly possess, but it's even worse when the filmmakers inexplicably decide they need to put an extra spotlight on all of the movie's walking ethnic stereotypes one last time before the movie ends. John Hood's elderly Jewish lady neighbor raps "Oy vey!" over a bit of klezmer music; the Greek hot dog stand owner drops a lyric about Zeus; the Italian deli owner spits a rhyme referencing Ancient Rome, and the poor Asian grocer was asked to rap about a "Chinese proverb" in pidgin English. This big finale ends with the entire cast dancing together in the street, and I'm crying just thinking about it.

As fun as it may be to point out the many, many things wrong or just plain *weird* about the movie, it's hard to rag on *Rappin'* too much. It's a feel-good film with an easy-to-get-behind—if predictable—plot about a reformed gangster saving his neighborhood through the power of music. For what it's worth, the cast is also very likeable, even if only a handful of them can actually rap.

Plus, the soundtrack—that is, outside of the music sung by the main cast—is pretty damn good. *Rappin'* actually featured quite a few professional musicians who were mostly relegated to background dressing in the film itself. Just like Ice-T and Rhythm Nation, Staten Island's Force MDs—the R&B group behind the mid-80s hits "Tender Love" and "Love is a House"—audition a song for Dixie's boss, only to be passed over for Rappin' Hood's freestyle truth bombs. Claudja Barry, best known for her dance hit "Boogie Woogie Dancin' Shoes," rips out a lively rendition of her New Wave single "Born to Love" in a crowded club. Singer Eugene Wilde, who had #1 R&B hits with "Gotta Get You Home Tonight" and "Don't Say No Tonight," duets with Joanna Gardner on a late-night radio ballad called "First Love Never Dies."

The guest musicians who stand out most are likely the Jackson 5-ish kid rap group, Tuff, Inc., who perform their lone, adorable single "Golly Gee" for the rest of the neighborhood kids, who clap and dance along. A fellow prepubescent singer, Warren Mills, lays down "Flame in the Fire" in the recording studio. Meanwhile, Golden age rapper Lovebug Starski also provided two songs for the movie.

With this much *good* music in the film, it's unsurprising that Atlantic Records left all of John Hood's songs from the movie off their official soundtrack release.

Rappin' was a rush job, even by Cannon's ridiculously fast-paced standards. The movie shot in Pittsburgh through February and March of 1985, and hit theaters on May 10th—meaning, the entire film was shot, edited, marketed, and released in less than four months. It wound up making just under $3 million on its sub-$1 million budget, but was still considered a financial disappointment considering that its predecessor, *Breakin' 2*, brought home roughly five times that amount at the box office. The results were so underwhelming that Cannon put off making another dance or musical trend cash-in movie for *three* whole years. Then came *Salsa* (1988), followed by *Lambada* (1990).

Viewed today through the dual lenses of kitsch and camp, it's really a wonder *Rappin'* doesn't have a larger cult following. Imagine midnight screenings, where fans dress up in sleeveless sweatshirts and fly sneakers, bust out their best ballet moves during the breakdance battle, and shout all of the movie's wackiest lines along with the characters on screen, from "Hay is for horses" to "Bathroom, fool!" But, it's never too late for that to change.

John Hood (Van Peebles) and his kid brother rap to their grandma about their shared love of girls with "big behinds" in a press kit still from *Rappin'*.

Interview: Actor Mario Van Peebles

For the Van Peebles, filmmaking is a family business. At the age of two, young Mario was already making appearances in his father's short films. His dad, Melvin Peebles, displayed a talent and proficiency for filmmaking from the start, but when the young, Black director went to Hollywood in the 1950s looking for work behind a camera, doors were repeatedly slammed in his face. Frustrated but not beaten, Melvin moved his family to the Netherlands—where he added the "Van" to his surname—and then France, where he learned the language, and wrote the novel he'd eventually turn into his first feature, *The Story of a Three-Day Pass* (1967). With his third film, *Sweet Sweetback's Baadasssss Song* (1971), he made his biggest impact. Widely credited with launching the Blaxploitation genre, its unprecedented success proved to studios that there was an audience for Black cinema—and to other independent filmmakers, how much could be achieved outside the studio system.

Mario Van Peebles followed his father into the film industry after playing the son of his real-life father's character in *Sweetback*. First as an actor, the younger Van Peebles rose to prominence with roles in films such as *Exterminator 2* (1984) and *Heartbreak Ridge* (1986). After cutting his directorial teeth in television, Mario moved into feature-filmmaking with his stunning debut, *New Jack City* (1991), which—just like his father's best-known work—became the highest-grossing independent film of its year. It was followed in quick succession by memorable works like the Black Western *Posse* (1993) and *Panther* (1995). Ever since, he's remained highly active as an actor, director, writer, and producer; he wore all four of these hats in his 2003 film *Baadasssss!*, a compelling docudrama portraying the making of his father's famous feature. [Portions of the interview below originally ran in a feature published by *Under the Radar* magazine in 2021.]

You became directly involved with your father's filmmaking with *Sweet Sweetback's Baadasssss Song* (1971), and you later dramatized that part of your childhood in *Baadasssss!* (2003). You were a very young kid, though, when his first feature, *The Story of a Three-Day Pass* (1967), was made. What do you remember of those years and the making of this film, from a child's point of view?

Mario Van Peebles: My father was in the Air Force, and he'd broken the cardinal rule which was "Don't get too good at a job you don't want to have." He won the bombing competition. After Pearl Harbor, there was this thing where they thought we should always have this threat in the sky. He was the navigator on all of those big, globetrotter missions, and his team won. They'd say, "If we're going to drop a bomb, where does it go?" They would drop these dummy bombs, and his team kept winning. And so, the Air Force wanted to keep him around as their Black guy who, you know, represented the "New" Air Force. He didn't want to do that.

He had a girlfriend come visit him on the base. He was an officer, she was white, and you couldn't have women on base, so they pretended they were cousins. They asked for her ID, and her maiden name is Marx. She said, "Oh, that's my slave name." [*Laughs*] That was my mom.

They hung out on the base together. My mom is white, my dad is Black, and they pretended to be cousins, which was all fine until I started to come along. Then they decided, "We've got to get out of here." After his last mission was done, he couldn't get out. He didn't want to be brought back in, and he was concerned his name might appear on some re-up papers. So, they split and got across the border to Mexico. Hence, I have the name "Mario," because I was born in Mexico.

In a way, perhaps the movie *Three-Day Pass* was inspired in some way by the relationship between my mom and dad, and to some extent I would be a product of it. [*Laughs*] And according to them, they had a lot of fun making me, so that's good to know.

Later, my dad tried to get work as a filmmaker, and there's a long story behind that. Hollywood said, "We don't need any elevator operators," and he said, "No, I want to be a filmmaker." They said, "We don't need any elevator operators who want to be filmmakers." He and my mom always talked about going to Europe, so they went to Europe and he went on a long trek to learn French, start to write, and did that. He made shorts, some of which I'm discovering now, which are great. Those include the first one I was ever in, when I was two years old. Then he made his first feature, which was *Three-Day Pass*.

I remember seeing the film at the San Francisco Film Festival, when it won the festival as the French entry. That was bananas, because they thought Monsieur Melvin Van Peebles would be a French guy, maybe a French-Dutch guy? Definitely not a brother from Chicago. [*Laughs*] So when he shows up at the airport, the little lady with blue hair says, "Monsieur Van Peebles, delegacion français?" He rolls up and says, "Yeah, baby, that's me." It's like, "Whoever you are, I'm waiting for a *very* important auteur." And then he says, "Oui, c'est moi, Monsieur Van Peebles." And she's like, "Oh, shit!" [*Laughs*]

And so his film wins, and then Hollywood is embarrassed. That's how he got to make *Watermelon Man* (1970), and I became a P.A. on that. And then *Sweetback*, but you saw my take on that.

I think the French got a little bit of a kick out of the poor, Black American kid having to go to France to make it. I think there was a bit of a "stick it to the Yankees" energy going on there, and my father was happy to let them play with that.

You went on to become a very accomplished filmmaker in your own right. I'm sure you have many, many answers to this, but I'm wondering if you can share any of the lessons you took from your father that you bring with you each time you step onto a set as a director.

When I went to direct *New Jack City* (1991) and I talked to my dad about it, he said the best thing to do would be to commit Rudyard Kipling's "If –" to memory. It's a great poem: "If you can trust yourself when all men doubt you, but make allowance for their doubting too. If you can wait and not be tired by waiting . . ." There are portions of that poem I've had to reference all the way through my career.

The other thing was that no matter what business you're in, there are going to be some "isms." Lookism, racism, sexism, classism. You should be in a business that you love, and then make changes to those isms through and with it.

The other thing is that great allies come in all colors. They don't always look like you, or vote like you. Melvin has great friends of all races, all genders. He never let the isms make him bitter, otherwise it poisons your art.

I think that was a huge lesson to see. This is a guy who has friends and supporters of all colors and types. He draws from the whole smorgasbord of humanity. I think that happened with me. The first guy who gave me a break was a tall, Republican cat named Clint Eastwood, who doesn't look like me, doesn't vote like me. The two people who got me into the Academy were Poitier and Clint Eastwood. It's not always going to be people directly in your little tribe. You have to look beyond that, and I think it was really helpful to see that early on. It expands your universe.

You can see it in my casting, right? On *New Jack City*, I mixed it up. I thought, if we want kids to say 'no' to drugs, you better have role models to say 'yes' to. I had Russell Wong, who's Asian, and Judd Nelson, who's Jewish. I got Ice-T to play the cop, not the gangster, and I got a sister to play the prosecutor. Make inclusive films.

Van Peebles (center) starred as the villainous "X" in *Exterminator 2*. The young actor was allowed to design his own costumes for the film.

The Cannon Group gave you two of your first big roles as an adult. Can you tell me a little about what you remember of making *Exterminator 2* (1984) and *Rappin'* (1985)?

Of course! [*Laughs*] I learned so much during those early days working with The Cannon Group. Here's the thing: you'd be amazed by what you can accomplish when you're not worried about taking your credit. For example, on *Exterminator 2*—and there are so many stories I could tell about that film, man—I realized they were going to put me in some sort of weird, spandex outfit. I wasn't feeling it, so I went out and made my own wardrobe. As long as I wasn't charging them and the director was cool, which he was—he became a friend of mine, Mark Buntzman—they didn't give a shit. They said, "You'll do it for free?" I said, "Absolutely!" Boom. I got in there. I said, I want to make this guy look like the Road Warrior meets Grace Jones meets Billy Idol. That was the look I was looking for.

Man, I did more stuff on that movie. For a number of reasons, I got to run it down into the end zone. No one was paying attention! [*Laughs*] Because it wasn't costing them anything, it wasn't affecting the bottom line. It was wonderful. I got to carry on.

And then on *Rappin'* I learned a really valuable lesson, which was "Don't forget to entertain." [*Laughs*] It meant that I was trying to act in a movie that was about rapping. What a mistake! Just understand that you'll never be able to complete a punchline if you don't tell the joke. Right? So, I was thinking and reflecting, "*What does this mean?*" I'd been to Stella Adler, and was trying to figure out that stuff. I didn't realize, oh, they just want to know if the Fat Boys are going to be in the movie, or if Run DMC was going to be involved. I realized I'm misreading this. I was trying to elevate this thing, and make it into something else. People aren't watching *Rappin'* for acting, they're watching *Rappin'* for rapping. So, that was a valuable lesson, to understand what you're in.

The very next film I got, *Heartbreak Ridge* (1986), I did just that. I decided I'd make a character that would blend in, and where you'd believe his personal arc and evolution, so that he doesn't start out the same character that he winds up being. But, there would be a balance in humor and resilience that would draw you in. I used some stand-up stuff that I'd written, and Clint introduced me to the Warner Bros. folks, and let me write songs for the movie. I was ready to do everything that was needed so that I could get in where I fit in. At Cannon Films, there were a lot of places for that personality, where you could get in where you fit in, and learn what to do and what not to do. It was very helpful.

Grace Quigley on VHS. This copy belonged to a National Video franchise which, before Blockbuster, was the largest chain of rental stores in North America.

Grace Quigley

Release Date: May 17, 1985
Directed by: Anthony Harvey
Written by: A. Martin Zweiback
Starring: Katharine Hepburn, Nick Nolte, Kit Le Fever
Trailer Voiceover: "What happens when a hardened criminal teams up with a sweet old lady? ... *Grace Quigley*: A film that brings new meaning to the word 'life.'"

If anyone were to put together a list of the best actresses in the history of cinema, there's no conceivable measure by which the great Katharine Hepburn would *not* rank somewhere near the top. Hepburn is a leader in both popular opinion—*Bringing Up Baby* (1938), *The Philadelphia Story* (1940), and *The African Queen* (1951) are just three of the many bona fide classics in which she starred—and by the gold standard known as the Academy Award, of which she's won more statuettes—four, in total—than any other actor who has graced the business. Hepburn received the Best Actress award for *Morning Glory* (1934), *Guess Who's Coming to Dinner* (1968), *The Lion in Winter* (1969), and *On Golden Pond* (1982), and did not attend the ceremony to accept a single one of them. (She was nominated for Best Actress eight more times.)

With a screen career that stretched more than sixty years, the working legend had her pick of projects in her final decades. Shot when she was 73 years old, *Grace Quigley* (1985)—a comedy about a headstrong, old woman who partners with a professional hitman to start a business that euthanizes the more miserable members of New York's elderly community—is certainly one of the strangest movies she ever chose as a starring vehicle, and perhaps one of the most fascinating ones.

The story of how screenwriter A. Martin Zweiback's treatment for *The Ultimate Solution of Grace Quigley* found its way into Katharine Hepburn's hands is the sort of thing that usually only happens in movies. Seriously, you can't make this up: sometime in 1972, the wily writer snuck up to the front gate outside the home of director George Cukor. He wrapped his 25-page story treatment into a tight bundle, and then chucked it over the wall in hopes that the Hollywood legend might somehow stumble across it. It just so happened that Cukor was lunching with his old friend, Katharine Hepburn, whom he had directed in ten films (including *The Philadelphia Story*.) Hepburn spotted the airborne script as it came crash-landing onto the lawn. The actress read the pages, fell in love with them, immediately attached herself to star, and personally helped Zweiback shop the film around Hollywood for the better part of the next decade.

As you might expect, studios weren't exactly lining up to bankroll a black comedy about suicidal old people, even with a septuagenarian living legend eager to play the lead. For a while, Columbia seemed ready to finance the movie. Hepburn was insistent that the co-starring role go to her friend, *Bullitt* (1968) and *The Great Escape* (1963) actor Steve McQueen, but the movie continued to sit in development hell. After McQueen passed away from cancer in 1980, Nick Nolte eventually replaced him, but Columbia was no longer interested in making the film.

Although he was already in his forties, this was still relatively early in Nolte's career—he was best known at that point for the acclaimed, late

Seventies TV miniseries *Rich Man, Poor Man*. (His breakout film, *48 Hrs.* [1982],had not yet opened by the time Cannon picked up *Grace Quigley*.) A bit of a late bloomer, Nolte would later become famous for his appearances in *The Prince of Tides* (1991), *Affliction* (1998), and unflattering mugshots. (Nolte was briefly attached to 1983's *That Championship Season*, but *Grace Quigley* wound up being his first and only Golan-Globus appearance.)

The Cannon Group eventually stepped in to take over the project, but not before Hepburn could shuffle up the talent again, this time swapping out directors. Zweiback, who had long been geared up to direct his screenplay himself, was replaced by Anthony Harvey, the English filmmaker who had directed Hepburn's Oscar-winning *The Lion in Winter* (1968)performance, and her acclaimed 1973 TV version of *The Glass Menagerie*.

Director Anthony Harvey, Katharine Hepburn, and Nick Nolte in a press photo for *Grace Quigley*. All three agreed to work well under their normal rates to keep the film's budget under $5 million.

Before we get into the plot summary, it must be pointed out that multiple versions of *Grace Quigley* were released, and that there are stark differences between them. The version described here in detail is the one that received the widest release, and made it onto home video. (It's the only version that doesn't require an Indiana Jones-like dive into a hidden, trap-filled temple to locate.) Afterwards, we'll go over many of the ways that this best-known cut of the movie differed from the ones that came before and after it.

The movie opens on an elegant, elderly dynamo, the titular Grace Quigley (Hepburn), wandering alone through the snowy streets of New York City. The movie wastes no time pounding home just how lonely an existence Grace leads. She lives by herself in a rent-controlled apartment with a parakeet as her only companion, having tragically outlived the rest of her family. Her new, nasty landlord threatens to evict her because she's late on her rent, and has disregarded the strict, no pet policy. Grace finds herself at the end of her rope. That is, until she inadvertently witnesses a hitman taking out her landlord with a point-blank bullet to the brain.

Horrified as you would expect, Grace flees the scene and hides herself in the backseat of a nearby parked car—which, it turns out, belongs to the hitman, who hops into the driver's seat and speeds away with the scared, old lady unknowingly in tow. She manages to escape the ordeal undiscovered, as well as learn the name (and home address) of the mysterious murderer-for-hire.

A morbid idea crosses Grace's mind.

Meanwhile, we get to better know our ruggedly handsome assassin, Seymour Flint (Nolte). We learn that he's a conflicted man whose morally dubious job causes him headaches, nosebleeds, and other crippling side effects, which he pays a therapist $75 an hour to help rid him of. (The therapist is played by Chip Zien, the voice of *Howard the Duck* [1986].) Suffice to say, it's not a gig he takes a great deal of pleasure from. That's why he's repulsed when the elegant, well-composed Grace shows up at his apartment door and tries to hire him to end her life. And yet, through a one-two punch of extortion and persistence, Grace gets the dumbfounded Seymour to hear her out: she delivers a heartbreaking story of how she failed twice before to kill herself, and tries to convince him that the dignity to choose when she leaves this world would be the greatest gift he could possibly give her.

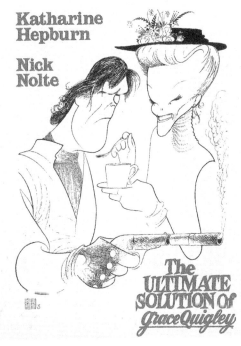

An early ad for the film featured an illustration by Al Hirschfeld, history's most recognized caricaturist.

For the time being, Seymour seriously considers Grace's bizarre proposal, but the situation quickly grows out of hand. Grace comes to the realization that she's far from the only New Yorker of advanced age who would welcome a friendly nudge off their mortal coil. To help finance her own assisted suicide, Grace works as an agent of sorts, finding prospective customers for Seymour while collecting a percentage of their fee for herself. This gradually gives Grace an unexpected, newfound lease on life, where her continued existence helps others make their welcome way into an early grave.

As for poor Seymour, he's still at odds with his chosen occupation and it's harder for him to get on board, even if their old folk liquidation business is booming. When he sends his hooker girlfriend, Muriel (the wonderfully innocent Kit Le Fever), to cheer up one of Grace's lonely pensioners, the old man dies from a heart attack—with a smile on his face. Eventually, Grace wins Seymour over, and he rubs out a whole group of her unhappy, elderly friends in one go.

Our formerly suicidal heroine becomes a mother figure to the emotionally damaged killer-for-hire, taking care of him and even convincing him to make an honest woman out of his call girl sweetheart. Once in business together, it's not long before Grace and Seymour have a long line of old folks cued up around the block, practically begging for their help into the afterlife.

The good times don't last long, though. Grace has a run-in with a particularly crabby cab driver, and basically blackmails Seymour into murdering the man out of petty vengeance. For poor Seymour, who had only signed on to kill people who actually *wanted* to die, this brings back his nosebleeds and headaches. He decides the only way out of his situation is to knock off Grace once and for all, as she attends her friends' funeral, which leads to a wacky hearse chase across New York City. They reconcile when one of their jilted customers attempts to kill them both. Grace, though, feels so guilty about forcing Seymour to murder a man against his will that she throws herself off the roof of her own building. He gets there just in time to save her *and* reveal that he never actually killed the cab driver after all—he'd fibbed about doing the deed—and they both live happily ever after.

A cartoonish sales catalog entry for *Grace Quigley*, which Cannon marketed as "a hilarious, off-beat comedy."

If that last paragraph feels abrupt, well, that's more or less how the last act of the film plays out. It moves fast, doesn't feel entirely logical, and the happy ending comes from so far out of nowhere that it seems pasted on to the movie. Stating that the tone of *Grace Quigley* feels off-kilter would be an understatement: the film never seems sure whether it wants to mimic one of the old, screwball comedies that Kate would have headlined forty years earlier, or a depressing message movie about a person's right to die.

The Ultimate Solution of Grace Quigley debuted at the '84 Cannes Film Festival in a cut that ran a half hour longer than the version we can see today. This cut—assembled by director Anthony Harvey—wasn't well-received by the international critics, mostly because of the grim subject matter being made far worse by a much darker original ending. In this earlier version, overcome with guilt from making Seymour carry out a murder he felt wasn't justified, Grace kills herself by wandering into the surf at Coney Island and being pulled out to sea. Seymour tries to save her, but winds up drowning as well. To recap: a grim comedy about euthanizing old people, which ends with both of its heroes dying—is it really a wonder how critics *didn't* walk out of the theater with smiles on their faces?

Menahem Golan decided that this ending needed to go, and hacked it away along with another thirty minutes of additional footage.

And so, *Grace Quigley* premiered in New York the following spring with not only a shorter runtime, but a shorter title. Even with a thrown-together happy ending, the premise still didn't sit well with critics and the film was widely panned. Cannon, embarrassed, dialed back their release plan, and *Grace Quigley* quietly slipped out of theaters before most movie-goers realized it had ever been there.

Meanwhile, the film's writer, A. Martin Zweiback, pleaded with Cannon to let him take a crack at editing the movie. While he had been granted an executive producer credit when he was pushed out of the director's chair, it was largely ceremonial. Despite spending more than a decade fighting alongside Hepburn to get the film made, Zweiback reportedly wasn't welcome on set. (It's telling that when the press was invited to visit the New York film set

63

to write puff pieces on the production, Zweiback conducted his interviews by phone from his home in California.) Cannon eventually acquiesced to Zweiback's request, allowing him some time in their editing room to put together his "Writer's Cut" of *Grace Quigley*.

In Germany, the film's title translated to "Grace Quigley's Last Chance." Other international titles include "A Game of Life and Death" (Brazil), "Homicide Agency" (Italy), "Eliminate Me!" (French Canada), and "Mom's Little Killer" (Denmark).

Although it's rarely been seen, Zweiback's cut is said to be more dark and surreal. This version opened with a nightmare sequence, where Grace dreams about her family members walking off into the ocean and drowning, one-by-one, creating a bleak bookend for Grace's suicide at the end of the movie, and more firmly establishing that she'd outlived her entire family. It also scrapped much of the movie's original score, replacing the music with rock music by The Pretenders. This "Writer's Cut" version was shown only a few times in Los Angeles. Zweiback himself phoned up critics and begged them to attend the screenings, hoping that it would lead to Oscar buzz for Hepburn or, at least, encourage Cannon to put out what he viewed to be a proper cut of the movie.

Before their relationship went sour, Zweiback was briefly signed on at Cannon as a screenwriter for *A Great Wind Cometh*—which was filmed and released years later as *Hanna's War* (1988)—and something else called *The Mummy of Beverly Hills*, which was never made. Of course, both deals fell through in the kerfuffle over *Quigley*.

By every published indication, it seems like Zweiback's feelings about the film were correct: his version of *Grace Quigley* received a far warmer response from critics than the ones that played at Cannes or in New York. However, Cannon—and director Anthony Harvey—publicly disregarded his version of the film. When *Grace Quigley* ultimately arrived on home video, it was in Cannon's critically-panned second cut, with the slapped-on happy ending.

Perhaps someday an enterprising home video label will procure one of the movie's alternate cuts and we'll be able to judge for ourselves whether there was a good movie at the heart of *Grace Quigley* or not. Until then, the undeniably messy *Grace Quigley* is the only one we have to go on.

Still, *Grace Quigley*—the version we got—is better than its reputation would lead you to believe. Gene Siskel summed things up succinctly in his 1987 review of the film, calling the movie "better than awful, but still disappointing."

First off, you have a gung-ho performance from the long-dependable Katharine Hepburn. Months before filming began, Hepburn drove her car into a utility pole and almost lost her foot in the accident; she was hospitalized for three weeks, but the production went on as scheduled. Although she was hobbled at the time of shooting and the tremor she developed late in life is on full display here, the actress clearly loved the role, and put a lot of energy into her part. (It's fun to see her climbing onto the back of a motorcycle at seventy-three years old.) Nick Nolte, in his role, seems to be having a good time as well. The supporting cast is also very strong, including Kit Le Fever as the hooker with a heart of gold, and several familiar New York character actors in Walter Abel, Elizabeth Wilson, and William Duell, playing some of Grace's eager-to-die old friends.

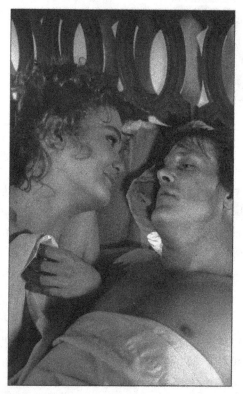

Muriel (Kit Let Fever) cozies up with Seymour (Nick Nolte) in a Spanish lobby card for *Grace Quigley*.

Likely far more famous than the film itself is the (possibly apocryphal) exchange of witty barbs between its two co-stars, which supposedly occurred during filming and only boosted both actors' respective mythologies. As it is told, one morning Nolte showed up late on set after one of his then-famous alcoholic benders. Hepburn loudly scolded him:

"I hear you've been drunk in every gutter in town!"

Nolte's response?

"I've still got a few left to go."

Interview: Actress Kit Le Fever

Their first major role can turn a lot of young actors into nervous wrecks: there's an added level of intimidation knowing that the eyes of your cast-mates and the film's crew are all trained on you. Now, imagine having to do your first big, on-screen performance opposite a true, living legend, Katharine Hepburn, and one of Hollywood's top leading men, Nick Nolte.

Kit Le Fever rose to exactly that challenge in *Grace Quigley* (1985), her first screen credit, playing Muriel, a prostitute who wins the heart of Nolte's unhappy hit man.

I'd love to know more about your background. What were you doing before *Grace Quigley*? I know it was your first feature film.

Kit Le Fever: I started acting in high school. The drama teacher came into a tenth grade play that each class was doing. During the rehearsal, he stopped me and said, "You know, you're very good. Would you like to join the acting class?" So, that's really how it started. After high school I went to the American Academy of Dramatic Arts, which was a good school at the time. Then, I worked small jobs—that's what you do, you waitress, and you work temp jobs, and at every job you tell people that you're an actor, so you can be available to go on auditions. It was kind of a difficult way to make a living but at the time rents were very cheap. I lived in a New York studio apartment for $165 a month. [Laughs] I didn't have too much trouble making the rent. You just keep the dream alive, and you keep trying.

One day my agent called me and told me that he had this role of the hooker in this movie. Many famous actresses started out by playing a hooker with a heart of gold. It's like a standard part, you know? So, here was this opportunity to play a hooker and he said to me, "Well, it's a long shot . . ."

I wanted to call him back and scream, "I do really well on a long shot! Long shots are good luck for me!" [Laughs] You do the best you can, you hope for a showcase. The *Grace Quigley* audition came out of the blue, but I don't believe in "out of the blue." I think things are meant to be. There were two auditions and then three callbacks.

Oh, wow. That's a long process.

They probably saw two hundred people for this role before I went in, because I was a c-list actress. I wasn't anybody. I never made a film before. I went to the audition, and then I got a call back. The final callback was on Friday. My belief is that my agent knew that they had chosen me for the role, but he wasn't going to tell me because the agent that I worked with directly wasn't in the office that day. So, they made me wait until Monday. So, that weekend was really interesting, personally, because it was down to me and one other girl. I thought to myself, there's one other person in this world who knows how I feel. One of us is going to get our heart broken.

You always hold in your heart this feeling, like someday, something's going to happen to me that's going to change my life. I never imagined in a million years that I would make a movie with Katharine Hepburn. She wasn't my favorite person, but she was so high up in the clouds that you would never think it could happen. You know, Bette Davis was who I was hoping for! [Laughs] When it happened, it was stunning.

Do you recall who you auditioned for?

Anthony Harvey was there at one of the callbacks. He said, "You can play this part in your sleep." I was having a little trouble with the nerves, so he said that. I'll never forget that, actually, because he was really good to me.

I was really scared, because when I read the script, I thought, "Oh, what a shame. This woman has to do a striptease on a table. There's no way I can do that. No way!" So then I thought, wait a minute. Hold on. Maybe she does it for him, for Seymour. Looking at it from that perspective, I could do that!

Of course, Hepburn didn't come to any auditions. The day I met her was really funny. One day they do this testing of makeup and costumes, changing and trying things to get it right. I was sitting in the makeup chair with the makeup artist just talking away. Hepburn kept coming through the room to go to the camera and then back to her dressing room. I didn't say anything. I was just talking to the makeup artist because I was so scared. At one point she'd had enough, and she stopped by my makeup chair and put her face right in my face. Like, right up to my face, and said [mimicking Hepburn's voice], "Hello . . ." Later in the day, Anthony Harvey is there with us and asks, "Have you met yet?" And she says, "Yes, I presented myself to her." [Laughs] She was just so good to me.

Katharine Hepburn, Nick Nolte, and Kit Le Fever stroll the boardwalk in *Grace Quigley*. Scenes were filmed in all five boroughs of New York City.

I imagine your striptease scene must have been pretty intimidating to do, this being your first film.

When I did the striptease, I kept thinking, "Oh, my God. The thing that kept me going was I said to myself, "Look, it doesn't matter what you say. It doesn't matter if you're nervous. When the director says, 'action!', you have to do this." I told myself that constantly for four or five weeks before we shot that.

Tony Harvey said, "Don't worry about it, it's going to be a closed set." To me, that meant that there wasn't going to be anybody on the set. But that's not what it meant. [Laughs] It meant that it was a three-quarters set: the set had a back and two sides. There must have been a hundred people crammed into every available space when we did that striptease.

We did the first shot as a long shot. After we finished that first round, everybody was coming over to me, from costumes, makeup, Tony was there choreographing me. Everybody was surrounding me. Hepburn came up to where we were, reached across the table and slapped me on the arm really hard and said, "You did good!" [Laughs] She was the only one who said that!People on the crew were surprised that I had never done a film before, because I handled myself so well. I mean, no way was I going to mess up with Hepburn around.

One day, I froze. I just got cold. I got stiff—everything felt like it was stuck. I looked around and I thought, "What am I doing here, standing on the street with Katharine Hepburn? What the heck is going on?" And she looked at me and it was like she knew exactly what I was saying, even though I didn't say any of that out loud. She looked at me and said, "Isn't this a terrible business? Don't you just feel wooden?" [Laughs] She knew exactly what I was thinking.

What was the general vibe like on set?

Well, Anthony Harvey was a terrific director. So he set the tone, he made everyone feel good. There was a very positive energy. At the same time, because Hepburn was there, everyone was doing their best. She set a very high bar, and everybody followed that. She didn't take any guff, and she wasn't going to put up with antics, of which there were a few. Of course you had Nick and his entourage doing their thing. There were a few clashes but all in all, I think it was pretty good. He'd come to work with a hangover, which was a no-no. [Laughs]

Hepburn recommended me for another film. A friend of hers had written a script about William Randolph Hearst and Marion Davies [*The Hearst and Davies Affair*, 1985]. She thought that I should audition for them, so she called a producer and she told him "If you don't see this girl, I'm going to make a lot of trouble for you." [Laughs] So, they saw me, but they didn't audition me. Later she called me. She said, "Kit, it's Kate. How'd it go?" I said, "Well, they gave me a script, but they wouldn't audition me. They said I didn't look sixteen." She says "Sixteen? I can't imagine. Eighteen, maybe . . ." I think Virginia Madsen was the one who got that role.

I went to visit her at her house after the movie. I also wrote to her, and for years she wrote back to me. She'd send me back these little notes. She was just so great to me.

Different cuts of the film were shown in different places. The screenings at Cannes and in New York were not so well reviewed, but then you have the LA version that the writer cut together, which didn't get a wider release, but those reviews are all very positive.

That was a heartache, for sure. My agent said to me in January, "Haven't you done anything else? Nobody cares about this movie anymore." [Laughs] Oh, wow. The dream of my lifetime comes through, and she says it doesn't matter anymore. I was learning the business.

It was funny, because they released it in the movie theater around the corner from my apartment. I lived on Horatio Street in the Village. A bunch of my friends, we all got together and went. One of my friends threw confetti up in the air and then the manager of the theater came out and got really mad, and my friend quickly said "She's in the movie!" So he goes, "Oh, okay!"

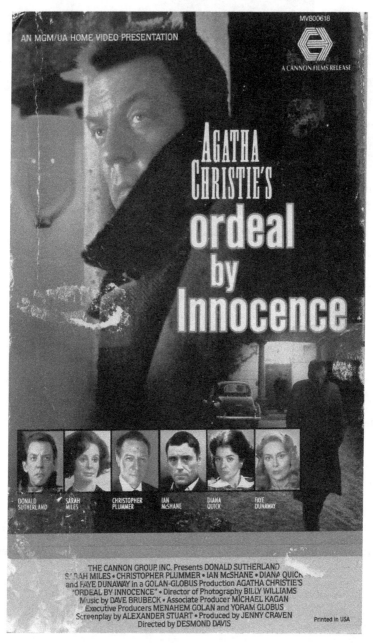

Ordeal by Innocence on videocassette. This rental copy belonged to Fox Video in Shavertown, Pennsylvania.

Ordeal by Innocence

Release Date: September 13, 1985
Directed by: Desmond Davis
Written by: Alexander Stuart
Starring: Donald Sutherland, Faye Dunaway, Christopher Plummer, Sarah Miles, Ian McShane
Tagline: "Once the murder was solved, the real mystery began . . ."

Considering that she is second-best-selling writer of all time behind only William Shakespeare, it's no surprise that Agatha Christie's works are frequently the subject of media adaptations. The British mystery author achieved her record-holding status not only through overwhelming popularity—her most successful book, *And Then There Were None*, has sold numbers similar to *The Hobbit, Alice in Wonderland*, and the first Harry Potter novel—but also through being incredibly prolific: Christie penned more than eighty books across a career that spanned a half-century. Over time, those works have been turned into more than 150 feature films and television shows. Cannon themselves dipped into the Christie pool three times in total: the first being 1985's

Ordeal by Innocence, adapted from the 1958 novel of the same name, followed by *Appointment with Death* (1988) and *Ten Little Indians* (1989).

Ordeal by Innocence stars esteemed Canadian thespian Donald Sutherland as Dr. Arthur Calgary, an American paleontologist returning home from a years-long Antarctic expedition, but making a pit stop first in jolly old England to do a good deed for a stranger. Early in his acting career, Sutherland was known for his roles in acclaimed films like *The Dirty Dozen* (1967), Robert Altman's *M*A*S*H* (1970), *Klute* (1971), Nicolas Roeg's *Don't Look Now* (1973), and Robert Redford's *Ordinary People* (1980). (These days, more people likely recognize him from his role in the blockbuster *Hunger Games* franchise.)

Dr. Calgary drops by the stately home of Leo Argyle, the patriarch of a large, upper-crust family. He hopes to return a lost address book to Argyle's son, Jacko, to whom he had given a ride the last time he was in town, and then found the booklet left behind in his car. Calgary is perturbed to learn that ol' Jacko is dead: hanged, in fact, for murdering his stepmother. Worse yet is that Jacko's ride with Calgary was his only alibi for the crime, and had Calgary been available to vouch for him, an innocent man would not have gone to the gallows. Calgary quite understandably feels guilty for this, which drives him to become an amateur gumshoe, following up on various leads found in the misplaced address book in hopes that his detective work can clear the dead man's name. To his surprise, however, he finds that Jacko wasn't an entirely innocent character, and that his family members weren't necessarily upset to see him hanged . . .

Cannon's adaptation of *Ordeal by Innocence* is set in the 1950s and was shot in, and around, the same picturesque, historic English town of Dartmouth where Christie's original story took place. Sutherland spends a lot of time knocking on doors, ducking about among the town's 17th-Century buildings, and riding back and forth across the fog-covered Dart River on a commuter ferry. It's a rather good-looking film as photographed by cinematographer Billy Williams, who'd just won an Oscar for *Gandhi* (1982) two years earlier.

This moody sales catalog ad invokes a Film Noir-style vibe that doesn't quite match the movie, but looks cool nonetheless.

Ultimately, this little whodunit gets a big boost from its marquee ensemble, on whom Cannon likely dropped most of the film's budget. The murdered mother is played by Cannon regular Faye Dunaway, fresh off *The Wicked Lady* (1983). Dunaway insisted on being lit and made up to appear as young as possible, despite being the same age as the actors playing her children. Although she appears only in a few brief flashbacks, Dunaway received second billing under Sutherland. Meanwhile, the priggish patriarch of the Argyle family is played by the great Christopher Plummer, already midway into a career that would span more than half a century. Playing the eldest Argyle daughter is Sarah Miles of *Blow-up* (1966) and *Ryan's Daughter* (1970). Her bitter, wheelchair-bound husband is none other than Ian McShane. At the time, McShane was living with erotic film actress Sylvia Kristel, star of Cannon's *Lady Chatterley's Lover* (1981) and *Mata Hari* (1985). In the United Kingdom, he's best known for playing the title character on the BBC series *Lovejoy* (1986–1994); elsewhere, he's known for playing the spectacularly foul-mouthed whorehouse operator, Al Swearengen, on HBO's acclaimed Western series, *Deadwood* (2004–2006).

A brigade of BBC notables rounded out the rest of the cast, chief among them Diana Quick and Phoebe Nicholls of *Brideshead Revisited* (1981), Annette Crosbie, Anita Carey, and Michael Elphick. These big names were touted with a lineup of colorful headshots on the movie's poster and VHS cover.

Cannon spent so much on their cast, however, that they were left with insufficient funding to actually shoot the movie. Entire scenes were cut out of the script for budgetary reasons, including several that would have established a bit of crucial backstory for the movie's accused murderer. When shooting wrapped, Cannon found that their film was too short. (Surprise, surprise.) They needed additional footage to hit the 90-minute theatrical mark, but were unable to bring back either Billy Williams, the cinematographer, or the director, Desmond Davis—whose primary claim to fame was the mythological fantasy film, *Clash of the Titans* (1981). And so, filmmaker Alan Birkinshaw was recruited to shoot pick-up scenes with Sutherland and Plummer not in England, but in New Jersey. (Birkinshaw would later return to Cannon to helm their third and final Christie adaptation, 1989's *Ten Little Indians*.)

This wasn't the only post-production shakeup. Italian composer Pino Donaggio—a Cannon regular, having already provided the soundtracks for *Hercules* (1983) and *Over the Brooklyn Bridge* (1984)—had supplied a lush, orchestral score for the film. Unfortunately, once the film was re-cut, it also needed to be re-scored, and Donaggio had already moved on to his next project. And so Cannon scrapped Donaggio's music and turned to famed jazz artist Dave Brubeck, who initially balked at their request that he score an entire movie in under two weeks. They negotiated, and Cannon caved to an agreement that they'd instead recycle several of Brubeck's older compositions in newly-recorded versions. Although we'll never see a version with Donaggio's original score, it's hard to imagine that it wouldn't have been a better fit: Brubeck's piano- and sax-centric, light jazz music sounds like the cross between something you'd hear in a '90s pay cable erotic thriller, and something from a lesser-known Peanuts holiday special. It's quite good on its own, but it doesn't match the tone of this buttoned-down, British murder mystery one bit.

In spite of all its star power and a few decent reviews, *Ordeal by Innocence* wasn't supported by Cannon with much of a theatrical release. Its biggest splash came at a royal premiere in London in February 1985, which was held for charity purposes and attended by Queen Elizabeth II, Prince Philip, and cast members from the film. The Queen spent the screening seated next to Menahem Golan, who recounted later how she was impressed by the number of murders that occurred in the film. (Oh, to have been able to overhear *that* conversation . . .)

AN MGM/UA HOME VIDEO PRESENTATION

924

DRAMA

THE CANNON GROUP, INC. presents JACLYN SMITH • SHELLEY WINTERS • CLAIRE BLOOM • NIGEL TERRY
in a GOLAN-GLOBUS Production of an ANTHONY RICHMOND Film "DEJA VU"
Associate Producer MICHAEL KAGAN • Photography DAVID HOLMES • Music by PINO DONAGGIO
From the Novel "Always" by TREVOR MELDAL-JOHNSEN • Adaptation by JOANE A. GIL
Screenplay by EZRA D. RAPPAPORT & ANTHONY RICHMOND and ARNOLD SCHMIDT
Produced by MENAHEM GOLAN and YORAM GLOBUS • Directed by ANTHONY RICHMOND

Printed in USA

Jaclyn Smith plays dual roles in "a tale of a love that wouldn't die!"

Déjà Vu

Release Date: October 25, 1985
Directed by: Tony Richmond
Written by: Tony Richmond, Ezra D. Rappaport, and Arnold Schmidt
Starring: Jaclyn Smith, Nigel Terry, Shelley Winters, Claire Bloom
Trailer voiceover: "A film of consuming passion that crosses the boundaries of time."

This supernatural, romantic thriller was intended to showcase former Charlie's Angel and future fashion mogul Jaclyn Smith in multiple roles. It was directed by first-timer Tony Richmond—at the time, Ms. Smith's husband—and based on a 1979 novel by Trevor Meldal-Johnsen.

In it, Nigel Terry plays Gregory Thomas, a successful author living in London, whose bride-to-be—Maggie, a rising film actress, played by Smith—drags him out to see an old, black-and-white ballet movie at the local repertory theater. He is immediately struck by how the film's lead actress, a prima ballerina named Brooke Ashley, looks *exactly* like his wife. (Exactly, as in, she's also played by Jaclyn Smith.) Upon learning that she died in a mysterious fire fifty years prior, Gregory decides to write a screenplay about her life, and becomes obsessed with researching the details of her untimely passing.

As he bangs out a first draft at his typewriter, he imagines a romance between Brooke and her Royal Ballet choreographer, Michael Richardson. (In these flashbacks, Nigel Terry also pulls double duty, playing the ballerina's paramour.) An old article about Ashley's death reveals that Michael Richardson was not a fictional character born of Gregory's imagination, but a *real* person who was actually engaged to the dancer, and died along with her in the apartment fire. (*Spooky!*) It also leads him to an old, Russian fortune-teller, who was Brooke's bestie at the time of her death.

Enter Shelley Winters as Olga Nabokova, a thick-accented, vodka-swilling gypsy-type who puts two-and-two together and figures out that Gregory must be the dead ballerina's lover reincarnated. She uses hypnosis to help Gregory tap into his past life, where we get to watch his courtship of Brooke Ashley and learn about her maniacally overprotective mother, Eleanor Harvey—played by Claire Bloom, of *Clash of the Titans* (1981) and *Crimes and Misdemeanors* (1989). Eleanor *hates* Michael, and will stop at nothing to tear apart their relationship and keep her daughter from dropping her dance career to start a family with him. As time goes on, Gregory and Olga's mystical tomfoolery with hypnosis seems to wake Eleanor's restless spirit, who does what any other sensible ghost would do, and takes possession of Gregory's dismissive fiancée.

Déjà Vu takes forever to confirm that the ballerina's crazy, old mother is the one who set the deadly blaze, despite never bothering to suggest another suspect for the crime or otherwise trying to throw viewers off her trail. Instead, the movie slowly cuts back and forth between flashbacks to Michael and Brooke's romance, to Gregory's current-day problems, like receiving anonymous death threats and trying to mend his damaged relationship with Maggie. (She's quite justifiably concerned that he's been ignoring her while he obsesses over this long-dead ingénue.) Along the way, somebody impales his poor cat on a fence post, and Gregory receives nightly visits from a genuinely creepy vision of the grim reaper.

From right to left: Nigel Terry, Jaclyn Smith, and Jaclyn Smith in a catalog ad for *Déjà Vu*.

In the end, Eleanor's homicidal spirit manages to take full control over Maggie's body. One night Gregory wakes up to her trying to stab him with a knife. He knocks her out with a mean, right hook and carries her off to Olga's house, where they're able to exorcise the evil spirit . . . or, so they think. Later, Maggie/Eleanor wakes up and tries to set Gregory on fire again, but only succeeds in burning herself alive while he escapes.

The movie ends, not with Gregory under even the slightest level of police suspicion for the grisly death of his famous, actress wife, but instead with the writer moping around Paris in a sad sack montage. Eventually, he attends a ballet where he meets a French woman who—based on the expression on his face in the film's freeze-frame, closing shot—we have to assume is being played by Jaclyn Smith yet again, making a vague statement about how true love transcends death, or time being a flat circle, or something like that.

Déjà Vu is a bit of a dud, even by Cannon's standards, and the studio seemed to sense that, giving the film a minimal theatrical release and choosing not to screen it in advance for critics. It's not that it's poorly-made, or even that poorly-acted. (Well, Winters' hammy Russian accent *is* hilariously bad, and it's hard not to giggle through Terry's over-the-top thrashing and moaning during his frequent nightmares.) A couple of issues are how sluggishly the movie is paced, feeling long even when it runs just over 90 minutes, and that the murder mystery itself never really feels all that mysterious, since the film lacks any red herrings—or, even a second suspect—that would typically make it so that the audience didn't have the whole thing figured out by early in the movie's runtime.

The biggest problem, though, is Terry and Smith's total lack of chemistry: for a love so strong that we're supposed to believe it transcends the course of multiple lifetimes, it's hard to tell if the two actors even like each other. By the way that Maggie invites George in for a drink after they catch a movie at the beginning of the film, you'd think they were newly dating; it's not until a good ways into the film that it's even mentioned that they're engaged to be married in just a few weeks. The movie's passionless, almost fully-clothed love scenes don't help this matter, either.

It's not the cast's best work. Despite being the obvious main character in the film, poor Nigel Terry somehow only received fourth billing in its opening credits. (Although, it's nice to see him not in armor or a crown for once; the British actor was frequently typecast in medieval-themed productions, from 1968's *The Lion in Winter* through John Boorman's *Excalibur* in 1981.) Winters, of course, was a Cannon regular, her relationship with Menahem

Golan dating all the way back to the 1975 film *Diamonds*. (Her appearance in *Déjà Vu* came sandwiched between 1984's *Over the Brooklyn Bridge* and 1986's *The Delta Force*, both directed by Golan.)

As for the director, this would be the first and the last film that he would ever helm. Tony Richmond had built his career as a talented cinematographer, notably working as director of photography on Nicolas Roeg's *Don't Look Now* (1973), *The Man Who Fell to Earth* (1976), and *Bad Timing* (1980), all three quite handsomely-shot movies. He'd also worked on the crime thriller *Nightkill* (1980), starring Robert Mitchum and Jaclyn Smith, after which he married the lead actress the following year. After *Déjà Vu* fizzled out—Richmond did *not* work as DP on this one—he went back to camera operation, and continued to find steady work on a wide range of Hollywood pics, from *Tales from the Hood* (1995), to *The Sandlot* (1993), to *Legally Blonde* (2001).

It's hard to imagine Jaclyn Smith spent much time looking at *Déjà Vu* in her rearview mirror, either. After five seasons playing Kelly Garrett on *Charlie's Angels* (1976–1981), the former shampoo model continued her acting career, regularly taking on TV movie roles. The same year *Déjà Vu* failed to make a splash in theaters, Smith launched a signature clothing line for the Kmart chain of department stores. As a designer, her brand grew into a mini fashion empire that is still going strong more than thirty years later, and now includes wigs, fragrances, and home goods in addition to clothing.

As no doubt confused several of their employees at the time, this was actually the second project called *Déjà Vu* in development at Cannon in the early '80s. The first was a contemporary noir film set to star Robert Mitchum (yet again) and Yves Montand, written by *Death Wish II* (1982), *America 3000* (1986), and *Over the Top* scribe David Engelbach. While that was in the works, this film was to be called "Always." When the Mitchum movie fell through, its title was forfeited and given to this movie so that it wouldn't be confused with Henry Jaglom's *Always* (1985) which came out that same year and also featured Shelley Winters, before her role wound up on the cutting room floor. (If your head isn't spinning yet, consider that Jaglom also directed his own movie titled *Déjà Vu*, which came out in 1997.)

An early, pre-sales advertisement for the film featured artwork by famed
movie poster painter Keith Batcheller.

Interview: Screenwriter Arnold Schmidt

Arnold Schmidt, Ph.D. is a Professor of English at California State University,
and has taught courses in the fields of literature, film, creative writing, and
humanities. He's published research articles that have been translated into
multiple languages, a book on Byron's impact on Italian nationalism, and an
anthology of British nautical melodramas.

Prior to his career in academics Schmidt worked in the film industry,
acting as an assistant producer on the Academy Award-nominated short film
The Silence (1982), and penning the story to an Emmy-nominated episode of
Alice (1976–1985). He crossed paths with Cannon in the early 1980s, having
been recruited to rewrite 1985's *Déjà Vu.*

Can you tell me how you came to be involved with *Déjà Vu?*

Arnold Schmidt: I came onto the project after the first script, and
there was another writer after my version. I was Publicity Director at Coast
Productions, where I met Tony Richmond, who was doing TV commercials. I had earlier worked on a screenplay with another director, Ray Rivas,
who recommended me to Tony when he needed the existing script revised.

**What do you view as your biggest contributions to the script? Were
there places you were asked to focus? What were the primary challenges
you faced?**

84

My instructions were to start fresh and develop my own adaptation, not rely on the earlier work. I stayed pretty close to the book, which isn't particularly long and certainly lends itself to adaptation. (The book doesn't present a lot of interior character action, or the personality of a strong narrative voice, both of which can be tricky in adaptation.) I selected and blocked out the key scenes, working to present them as visually and dramatically as possible.

This alternate artwork was used for ads and foreign video releases, and better invokes the movie's supernatural elements.

What can you tell me about any of the people you collaborated with on the movie?

I met Jaclyn Smith, and I know that she mentioned the script to me in passing, but not in the way of a lengthy discussion. That's my recollection, anyway. The person I primarily met with was Tony. We worked in his office at Coast, and at his and Jaclyn's house in Bel Air. The process was pretty straightforward. I read the book and outlined my ideas for presenting the story. I then started drafting the script, passing it along in stages to Tony for notes, until finished, then revised.

Did the final movie meet your expectations, based on the script?

One of the reviewers of the film described it as not scary enough for horror fans and not romantic enough for the romance audience. I'd agree with that.

You've since taught courses and given talks related to screenwriting. Is there anything you learned during your experience on this film that you've passed on to your students?

I've certainly used it as an example of adaptation and collaboration with a director, working to think visually in terms of scene construction.

This may not be useful to you, but I have used one incredibly minor detail in class: early in the film, after they see the footage of Brooke in the ballet, they return home and have a drink. She asks him what he'd like, and he answers her.

I tell my students to get to know everything about their characters, so they understand them well enough to know how they might act in any given situation. One way to do that, in addition to thinking about characters' psychologies and writing their biographies, etc., is to consider everyday details that rarely show up on the page/screen. I say they should know details like whether their characters drink tea or coffee and how: straight, milk, sugar, whatever.

It seems to me that in this scene, each lover might know the other's preferred drink. Tiny details, and, of course, people drink different things at different times. So I don't use the scene to indicate something wrong about the script for *Déjà Vu*, but rather as a way for students to think about how minor details can telegraph to the audience information about the types and levels of intimacy of relationships.

What would it tell the audience if she just brought the drink she knew he'd want? (He always drinks the same thing; he's so consistent in character and habit; he's predictable.) What if she brought one drink when in fact he wanted another? (Has she misread him? Doesn't know him as well as she thought she did? Or does the fact that he's in the mood for something different say something about his state of mind?) In screenwriting, details accumulate and have importance because we have so little time to create character. The point for students is not what precisely do the details mean in this particular scene in *Deja Vu*, but how they can use details to communicate meanings in their own writings.

In addition to your questions, the only thing I'd like to add was a bit about my meeting at Cannon itself. Tony and I went to their offices for a meeting with Menahem Golan. We walked into the broad expanse of an enormous office, mostly empty of furniture except for a formidable desk at the far end. In my recollection, it's a wide shot. It seemed so far away as we walked toward him. We approached the desk, itself mostly empty except for a notepad and a telephone, and sat down. I don't remember the conversation, which wasn't particularly long, maybe fifteen minutes. Then, things concluded, and Mr. Golan stood up, slammed his hand on the desk very dramatically and said, "Let's make a movie!" It was a great moment, right out of Fitzgerald's *Last Tycoon*. It's one that's always stuck with me.

The first American VHS edition of *Lifeforce*, released by the beloved cult
label Vestron Video.

Lifeforce

Release Date: June 21, 1985
Directed by: Tobe Hooper
Written by: Dan O'Bannon & Don Jakoby
Starring: Steve Railsback, Peter Firth & Mathilda May
Trailer Voiceover: "The terror has just begun!"

Vampires from space! Zombies loose in the streets of London! A psychic villainess who doesn't wear any clothes! Patrick Stewart locking lips with a highly-decorated American Air Force Colonel! Esteemed British stage actors somehow keeping a straight face through all of this! *Lifeforce* has it all, indeed.

It wouldn't be a long reach to assume that *Lifeforce* was just the sort of movie Menahem Golan and Yoram Globus had dreamed of making when they bought out the failing Cannon Films and set about turning it into their version of a major Hollywood studio. The duo had been linked to the film adaptation of Colin Wilson's sci-fi novel as far back as 1979, when it was announced—under its working title, *Space Vampires*—as one of the first twenty features to be produced by Cannon under its new ownership. They went so far as advertising it with a two-page ad in *Variety* in early 1980, a whole five years before the movie would finally arrive in theaters.

Although they'd briefly offered the job to Michael Winner, who had already directed *Death Wish 2* (1982) and *The Wicked Lady* (1983), Cannon found an ultimately better-suited filmmaker to head up *Lifeforce*. By the early to mid-1980s, there were few rising directors with more cachet than Tobe Hooper. The native Texan had a breakout hit with *The Texas Chain Saw Massacre* in 1974, a tense and gory horror movie that set box office records for an independent release. He spun that success into a string of films which ultimately culminated in the Steven Spielberg-produced *Poltergeist* (1982). Now considered a classic of the genre, *Poltergeist* was the highest-grossing horror film of the year and went on to earn a trio of Academy Award nominations, including Best Visual Effects, Best Sound Editing, and Best Original Score. While there was controversy surrounding whether it was Hooper or Spielberg who actually directed that film, it didn't stop Menahem Golan from playing suitor to Hooper post-*Poltergeist*. Golan was ultimately able to woo Hooper over to Cannon under a three-picture deal, which was to include *Invaders from Mars* and a live-action Spider-Man movie. Hooper was also on the hook to produce, rather than direct, a sequel to his classic *Texas Chain Saw Massacre*. After he was forced to direct the film himself, 1986's *Texas Chainsaw Massacre 2* replaced Cannon's never-produced Spider-Man film—which seemingly every director at Cannon was linked to at one point or another—as the third movie in Hooper's three-picture contract.

By his own accounts, Hooper was downright giddy to be given his crack at *Lifeforce*. He was instantly taken with the source material, the 1976 novel *The Space Vampires* by Colin Wilson, a copy of which had been handed to him by Menahem Golan at their first meeting. (Wilson was a highly prolific English author, best known for his non-fiction work on true crime and occult subjects, and for his 1956 study on social alienation, *The Outsider*; he also dabbled in science fiction, obviously.) *Lifeforce* would be known under the more evocative title *Space Vampires* until deep into post-production, when the powers that be at Cannon became nervous that the name was too hokey and forced the change, afraid that audiences would confuse it for one of the cheap exploitation movies they'd made in the past. *Lifeforce* was certainly *not* cheap. With a budget of around $24 million, it was, at that point, the most expensive movie Cannon had ever made—more than double what they'd spent on any movie prior.

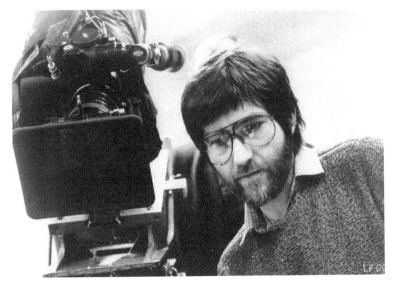

A publicity shot of Tobe Hooper from the set of *Lifeforce*.

Much of that cash went into assembling the sci-fi movie dream team behind *Lifeforce*. Among those joining Hooper was special effects trailblazer John Dykstra, the Academy Award-winner who'd designed most of the visual FX for *Star Wars* (1977) and *Star Trek: The Motion Picture* (1979). Handling the makeup and animatronics would be Nick Maley, another *Star Wars* alum best known for his design work on Yoda and the eclectic group of aliens that made up that movie's cantina band. The adaptation would be co-written by Don Jakoby and Dan O'Bannon, the latter of whom had also written the screenplay for the 1979 classic *Alien*. (Jakoby also penned *Death Wish 3* for Cannon, but opted there to be credited under a pseudonym.) The art direction and production design were by Robert Cartwright and John Graysmark, both veterans of Stanley Kubrick's 1968 masterpiece, *2001: A Space Odyssey*. The film's other major off-camera contributor was composer Henry Mancini, the four-time Oscar-winning legend remembered for his iconic *Pink Panther* and *Peter Gunn* themes; somewhat surprisingly, *Lifeforce* was his first science fiction score.

Let's review: *Lifeforce* had the director of *Poltergeist*, the effects and makeup artists from *Star Wars*, the screenwriter of *Alien*, the art and production designers from *2001*, and the guy who wrote the *Pink Panther* theme song. That's a *lot* of star power (behind the camera, at least.)

Lifeforce opens with the crew of the international space shuttle *Churchill* nearing the objective of its mission, to converge with and study Halley's Comet as it makes its closest orbit to Earth in 75 years. (The actual comet last passed by Earth in 1986, less than eight months after the movie's release.) Hidden within its tail the crew locates an awe-inspiring object: a needle-shaped vessel measuring more than 150 miles in length. With their radio blocked by the comet's radiation, they make a snap judgment to move in and investigate the alien ship. Inside they find countless, bat-like monsters—desiccated, and clearly dead—as well as three nude humans, two male and one female, preserved in suspended animation. (One of the males is played by Mick's younger brother, Chris Jagger; the part had originally been offered to Billy Idol.) The astronauts bring the three humanoids back to their shuttle in their coffin-like chambers, stowing them in the cargo hold.

Thirty days pass. At mission control, the team has not heard from the *Churchill* since it intercepted the comet, though the shuttle has remained on course for its return. When the ship becomes stuck in orbit, an American rescue team is sent to investigate. They find the *Churchill*'s interior incinerated, the remains of the crew burnt beyond recognition—and the three mysterious humanoid lifeforms, perfectly safeguarded within their crystal coffins.

Back on Earth, the alien girl is deemed deceased and prepared for an autopsy. The girl (Mathilda May) sits up on the operating table and pulls the shocked guard into a sexual embrace. They kiss, and (literal) sparks fly, electricity whipping around the room and forming an indoor thunderstorm.

Lightning leaps from the guard's mouth and into the girl. In an impressive display of special effects, the guard's life force is drained from him, and we watch as his body withers away into a near-skeletal form. She then escapes the compound to wreak nude, psychic mayhem through London.

Mathilda May, credited in the film as "Space Girl," is confined to her see-through coffin in one of the film's Italian posters.

It's in these scenes that *Lifeforce* showcases what most have come to consider its two main selling points: John Dysktra's stunning special effects work, and Mathilda May's persistently naked body. *Lifeforce's* special effects were done pre-CGI, and still hold up to this day. The film's early scenes set in outer space are particularly impressive. That's no green screen when the astronauts are floating through the alien spacecraft: the ship's massive interior was actually built on a soundstage at London's Elstree Studios—the same stage used to shoot parts of *Star Wars*—and the actors were suspended by cranes to create the illusion of zero gravity. Because the movie's effects were often so complicated to set up, it led to sometimes needing several days for the crew to get shots which might last only seconds. This was possible because of the prolonged, 117-day schedule afforded to the production: roughly *six months* of shooting, another Cannon record.

It wouldn't be a surprise if many viewers—especially those of an adolescent, male variety—barely noticed the special effects with *Lifeforce's* main villain being a young, attractive, and totally unclothed woman. From her first appearance in a glass coffin until almost the end of the film, the female space vampire rarely dons any clothing and when she does, promptly loses it. As she hypnotizes doctors, feeds on their life essence, incapacitates security guards, and escapes the government compound, actress Mathilda May— who turned nineteen years old on the set of the movie—bares everything in a performance that must rank somewhere near the highest percentage of full frontal nudity in a non-erotic film. (Certainly the most seen in a big-budget summer blockbuster, for sure!) Mathilda May spent so much time on set disrobed that Hooper would come to describe her nudity as "her costume." This included an outdoor night shoot where the female vampire is seen walking away from the compound and into the darkness, when temperatures dropped below freezing. (A production assistant hid behind the tree she walked past, holding a blanket to toss around the poor, naked girl as soon as Hooper called "cut.")

The casting team saw somewhere between fifty and seventy actresses while searching for their female vampire. Unsurprisingly, many of them expressed an unwillingness to go through with the tremendous amount of nudity called for in the script. Mathilda May was a relatively new, French actress with only a couple small credits to her name. Speaking very little English at the time she took on the role, she memorized her lines phonetically. Prior to acting, May had been a premiere ballerina. This makes sense when watching her on screen in *Lifeforce*: the way she moves and carries herself has an intentionally alien quality. It's as if she approached her performance as a space vampire as a dancer as much as an actor.

Another Italian poster, which doesn't beat around the bush in regards to the film's content.

Where Cannon had, by most reports, left Hooper to his own devices while developing the movie, its non-stop full frontal nudity was the only thing they supposedly insisted upon. To their credit, it makes total sense within the film: what use would an invasive, alien species have for modesty, anyway?

It is weird, however, considering how the movie was marketed to audiences as the next, big sci-fi blockbuster. Imagine *Star Wars*, but in place of Darth Vader there's a bare naked lady. Or, try swapping out the Xenomorphs of the *Alien* franchise with nipples and brief flashes of pubic hair. It's no wonder many audience members walked out of theaters so confused.

With the astronauts largely out of the way, the movie introduces us to a new set of characters. Dr. Fallada is the chief researcher overseeing the autopsies of the aliens; his rather macabre area of expertise is death and what comes afterward. (He's played with cool, Shakespearean posture by Frank Finlay, a prolific British character actor.) There's also a prominent doctor, Bukovsky, played by Michael Gothard, best remembered as the Bond antagonist, Emile Locque, from *For Your Eyes Only* (1981). They're soon joined by Special Air Service Colonel Colin Caine, portrayed by Peter Firth, who'd earned an Academy Award nomination for his starring role in *Equus* (1977) and would have a small but pivotal role in *The Hunt for Red October* (1990). Making his return to the plot at this point is American Air Force Colonel Tom Carlsen (Steve Railsback), the only survivor of the ill-fated *Churchill* mission, who crash-lands on Earth in his shuttle's missing escape pod. Those who recognized Railsback would most likely have seen him opposite Peter O'Toole in the classic *The Stuntman* (1980), or playing Charles Manson in the 1976 television adaptation of *Helter Skelter*.

With the female vampire loose in London, our heroes soon have their hands full with an even more immediate problem. Two hours after he was killed by the vampire, the dehydrated corpse of the first guard wakes up on the autopsy table, moaning and reaching for the closest doctor. Just like the female vampire—but far less sexy, obviously—the dried, withered husk drains the doctor's life force, regaining his original appearance while leaving his victim shriveled and lifeless. (This impressive corpse puppet, which played a big role in the movie's marketing materials, required more than twenty puppeteers to operate.) Acting fast, the doctors capture the creature for observation and eventually figure out that the vampires' condition is contagious: exactly two hours after being drained, victims will awake with the need to feed. The new vampires who don't manage to find victims of their own will ultimately self-destruct in a cloud of dust. The doctors come to the grim realization that they'll essentially have a zombie pandemic on their hands if they don't catch their escaped vampire.

An early sales catalog entry for *Lifeforce*. Cannon used variations on this artwork to advertise the film in trade papers as early as 1979.

They eventually figure out that the sexy dreams that astronaut Carlsen keeps having about our buxom, buck naked bad guy are actually the residuals of a psychic link with her. Tapping into that connection, they learn that she's able to mentally possess humans when it meets her needs, and they trace down her latest body to a mental institution in the English countryside. Colonels Carlsen and Caine make haste to intercept her along with a government liaison, Sir Percy Heseltine. Sir Percy is played by yet another esteemed British thespian, Aubrey Morris, who had appeared in such cult favorites as *A Clockwork Orange* (1971) and *The Wicker Man* (1973).

Our heroes are greeted at the institution by the movie's far and away most famous actor, Patrick Stewart, who sports much more hair than viewers are used to seeing him with. Though nowadays he receives top billing on many re-releases of *Lifeforce*, he was little-known to filmgoers when the movie was made, with his most significant appearances being in *Excalibur* (1981) and David Lynch's *Dune* (1984). It would be two more years before he became a science fiction icon as Captain Jean-Luc Picard on *Star Trek: The Next Generation* (1987–1994), and fifteen years before he stepped into the role of Professor Charles Xavier in the *X-Men* franchise.

Not long after welcoming them into his institution, it becomes evident to our heroes that Dr. Armstrong (Stewart) is the latest human to become possessed by the vampire. They dope him up and tie him down, trapping her spirit inside the future Captain Picard. The female vampire fights back, attempting to seduce Carlsen through their mental link—and Patrick Stewart shares his first-ever on-screen kiss with Steve Railsback, of all people. They manage to sedate him (her) again, but not before they learn they were duped and that the alien had been purposefully trying to lead them out of London so that they would be distracted while the vampiric plague spread through the urban populace.

The female vampire's spirit escapes during the chopper ride home. It's an unforgettable special effect: as blood pours out of the mouths of Patrick Stewart and Aubrey Morris dummies, filmed upside-down and in slow motion, the blood reassembles itself mid-air into a bloody, syrup-covered Mathilda May before bursting into a gory mess.

Returning home, they find that their city has been overrun by the shriveled monsters while they were gone, as thousands of Londoners are consumed in a bacchanalia of vampire sex and feeding. The vampires' endgame is finally revealed, as well, when the alien ship arrives in Earth's orbit and starts sucking up the glowing life forces released in the vampire attacks across the city. The British capital has been placed under NATO quarantine, but our intrepid heroes fight their way into the city to stop the vampires once and for all.

The whole finale of *Lifeforce* is a glorious spectacle, packed with hundreds of zombie-like extras tearing their way through a burning backlot dressed convincingly like London. The buildings destroyed in the background of many shots were actually built (and then demolished) within a model of London at a nearby amusement park, with footage of the fleeing extras laid in front of them. You also have a pair of stuntmen executing full-body burns, spectral blue beams cutting paths through the chaos, and a pillar of glowing light rising up into the orbiting spaceship. You can't argue that what Cannon achieved in the movie's final sequences doesn't look and feel like the big-budget, Hollywood blockbuster they had longed to make.

Another striking Italian poster for *Lifeforce*.

Lifeforce leaves its ending wide open on the off-chance that a sequel might have been in order. Sadly, it wasn't. The movie opened in fourth place at the box office, behind in-genre competitors *Cocoon* and *The Goonies*. Over the following weeks, audiences would be spoiled with sci-fi, fantasy, and horror choices as other 1985 titles such as *Back to the Future*, *Mad Max Beyond Thunderdome*, *Explorers*, *Red Sonja*, *Day of the Dead*, and even a re-release of *E.T.* made their way into theaters. In a less-stuffed release window, *Lifeforce* might have been able to draw in more of those genre fans, but in the summer of 1985 it only managed a meager $11.6 million at the U.S. box office, less than half the movie's production budget.

Hooper, who had already moved on to filming his next Cannon picture, *Invaders from Mars*, blamed the movie's chilly reception on the title change from "Space Vampires" to *Lifeforce*, believing it made critics expect a more serious film than what was delivered. (In Hooper's mind he was making a throwback, Hammer-style movie, along the lines of 1955's *The Quatermass Xperiment*.) The American reviews largely ranged from tepid to outright shredding the film, with *The New York Times*' Janet Maslin condemning it as "hysterical vampire porn."

The movie fared better in Europe, where it was released under its original "Space Vampires" title and ran fifteen minutes longer. On the request of Tri-Mark (who were Cannon's U.S. distributor for *Lifeforce*), Hooper was asked to cut down the runtime for American theaters, to which the director willingly obliged. Rather than trim from the areas one would expect like, you know, some of the nonstop full frontal nudity, the U.S. version mostly removes scenes from the space-set prologue. (In an even earlier, unreleased cut, the first 35 minutes of the film took place on the *Churchill* shuttle—many snippets of this footage were re-used to comprise Carlsen's flashback later in the film.)

Lifeforce gradually found its cult fandom on home video, and not just because Mathilda May's nudity lends itself to a format which can be paused and rewound. Divorced from expectations, *Lifeforce* is usually a big surprise to those who stumble across it unaware of just how crazy it is.

It's a grand showcase for the sort of top-level practical effects work that would soon go extinct as computer graphics overtook the film industry. Hailing from a decade that produced much of cinema's best science fiction, *Lifeforce* manages to stand out as one of the most gonzo examples of them all.

As for Cannon, however, *Lifeforce* wasn't the cinematic event of the 1980s that they had loftily hoped it would be. Instead, it signaled the beginning of the end. *Lifeforce* kicked off a misguided period of overspending on gigantic, ambitious movies, rather than focusing on the small-budget, big-profit pictures in which they excelled. The end wouldn't come for several more years, but *Lifeforce* can certainly be looked at as the moment where Icarus started his ascent toward the sun.

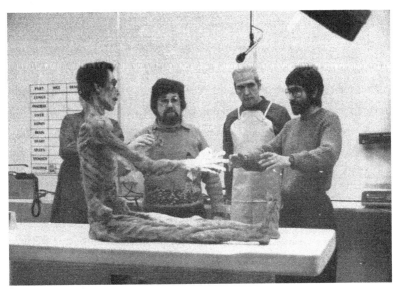

Nick Maley (center) demonstrates his animatronic corpse puppet for Tobe Hooper (right).

Interview: Make-up Effects Designer Nick Maley

When it comes to make-up effects artists of the 1980s, few have worked on as many big-name, science fiction spectacles as Nick Maley. Ever since he was a young man, Maley had a desire to work in film. Through dedication and persistence, he worked his way into the industry and was hired by make-up effects pioneer Stuart Freeborn. This led to Maley making contributions to classics such as *Superman* (1978), *The Shining* (1980), and *Clash of the Titans* (1981), and most notably *Star Wars* (1977), where he worked on timeless characters such as Chewbacca, Greedo, and Mos Eisley's Cantina Band. He returned for *The Empire Strikes Back* (1980), where he was part of the team that brought Yoda to life.

As Maley's reputation grew, he was brought on to oversee make-up effects on several '80s sci-fi classics. These included *Krull* (1983), *Highlander* (1986)—on which he handled the movie's many beheadings, the Kurgan's prosthetics, and devised the "quickening" effects sequences—and Cannon's *Lifeforce* (1985), for which Maley and his team created several of the most complex animatronic puppets ever seen on film to that point.

Known affectionately as "That Yoda Guy" by *Star Wars* fans, Maley is now semi-retired to the Caribbean island of St Maarten, where he runs a museum dedicated to his work in science fiction cinema. His book, *The "Do or Do Not" Outlook*, gives behind-the-scenes stories from his more than sixty-film career, and provides readers with self-empowerment tips that can be applied to their creative lives.

You were working under Stuart Freeborn when *Star Wars* came along and opened doors, not only for you, but for sci-fi and fantasy films in general. Can you tell me how you landed the job on *Lifeforce*, or Space Vampires, as it was called then? I imagine you were one of the top guys for makeup and animatronics at that time, especially in the UK.

Nick Maley: Yeah, I was by then. I basically got known as the guy who did all the jobs that everybody else thought was impossible. They paid me more because I worked ridiculous hours. It was common for me to do sixteen hours a day, six days a week.

I read the script, and it seemed so full of creature effects. How could I turn it down? I talked to Tobe, and he was very easy-going. The director and producers really are important, in terms of being able to get on with the job, or being blocked. Tobe was very open to suggestions and changes, and that led to me actually rewriting some of the sequences in the movie. When I say rewriting, I mean, I devised new sequences and then sat down with Dan O'Bannon to work them into the script.

Can you describe which of the scenes you worked on with Dan O'Bannon?

Basically, a lot of the creature effects sequences. In the script, every time we got to the demise of one of these infected people, it just said, "They crumbled to dust." Page seventeen, they crumble to dust, page twenty-eight, they crumble to dust, page fifty-two, they crumbled to dust. I said to Tobe, "You know, we're seeing the same thing over and over and over again. It costs just as much the third time as it did the first time, but it's going to have less impact because people have already seen it."

This was Cannon, so everything was budget-oriented. They wanted to keep the budget down to a minimum. They asked me to devise what the budget needed to be and I said, "Well, what the hell are we going to build?" It's a matter of being precise and economical. Obviously, if I'm going to devise how to do these scenes, I have to have control over what is happening there.

The pathologist [blowing apart in the cell bars], exactly how that happened and what happened, was one of the scenes that I devised. The demise of the pathologist, instead of just looking into a cell and watching him crumble to dust—after you've just left the guard, and he'd crumpled to dust, too—I said, "These have to be two different effects." So, the whole thing with the pathologist smashing into the bars and coming apart and getting stuck in the Home Secretary's teeth—that was my sequence. The sequence of the girl on the table coming back to life, and then struggling, and dying, and exploding, was my sequence. The whole thing with fire coming down and trapping Caine, the zombie coming out, and he shoots it in the head, that was my sequence. The sequence of the car stopping and the zombie sticking his arm through the window, and the arm coming off and then wrestling with the arm—those were all my sequences.

Over the years, you've talked about some of the technical difficulties you had with the Yoda animatronics. The creatures in *Lifeforce*—**the ones on the lab tables, especially—look like they were much more complicated builds. Can you describe some of the problems you had to solve to get those to look as good as they do on screen?**

Basically, on *Star Wars*, I was one of the two senior techs. There were very few of us there: there was my boss [Stuart Freeborn], there was his son [Graham Freeborn], there was myself, there were three trainees, and there was Stu's wife, who was basically looking after people on set. I should also say, they gave us ten months on that movie to build the stuff, and film it. On *Lifeforce*, they came to me and said, "You've got six weeks to prepare to shoot the transformation sequence with the pathologist."

Very often on movies, they will put the hardest thing the first week, because if it fails, they can still pull their money out of the movie and not have lost as much as if they had tried shooting it on the last day. That's okay for them, but it's a real aggravation for the rest of us. [*Laughs*] The thing about *Lifeforce* was that I needed a big crew. There wasn't any way that I could physically do everything myself, and to be quite honest, the animatronics that we were developing on that were more advanced than anything we'd done before. I really needed some specialists along the way to help me achieve that. One of the critical issues over trying to do the pathologist's transformation was, "What the hell do the characters look like?" I'm starting now, today, and I've got six weeks, and they haven't cast the actors yet.

Oh, wow! That's a critical piece of information.

Time started to tick by and they still hadn't cast the actor. In fact, they did not cast the actor until ten days before filming was due. I'd been through a few areas before where the same sort of thing happened. First and foremost, I just got a standard, medical skeleton, and I cast it so that we had the basic shape and the parts. I gave one cast to my animatronics guys and said, "You're going to have to figure out how to make this skeleton move." Then, I took the other one and gave it to my sculptors and I said, "We're going to sculpt a shriveled person on this skeleton." So, rather than sculpting something, and then fabricating it, and then giving it over to someone to make the mechanism, the mechanism was being built while it was still being sculpted.

As time went by, we sculpted up the basic body of what we thought a shriveled husk might look like, and part of that was based on Auschwitz photos, and part of it was fanciful. To be quite honest, we didn't think that the movie was going to be that serious at the time. If you look at our designs, they have a certain tongue-in-cheek quality that is just a little beyond reality. So then, I had eight sculptors, and I asked them to sculpt up eight different heads.

Now we've got eight heads sitting there, we've got our bodies sitting there. Ten days to go, they say "this is the actor." I got the actor to come in so we could lifecast him, so that we can make an animatronic of him for the beginning of that sequence. We looked at the eight heads and said, "Well, this one's the closest, I'll give you half a day to change the eyebrows, change the cheekbones, make it look more like him."

Of course, the mechanism had already been built for the skull of the skeleton that I started with. I needed to be very creative to hit these things in the time frame we were given. I did a lot of things on that movie that were not normal practices, to try and deal with the schedule. I had largely a young crew because the older guys would have told me, "That's not the way that we normally do it." I needed people that would just follow my lead. In that crew there were a lot of people who went on to acclaim in their own right. Bob Keen was my number two; he did *Hellraiser* (1987). One of the trainees that started with me on *Krull* (1983) was David White—he's the guy who is doing all the effects for *Guardians of the Galaxy* (2014). Another trainee, a junior in the workshop, Stephen Norrington, went on to direct *Blade* (1998).

Images from Maley's transformation sequences were heavily utilized in the film's advertising around the world.

You do all of this work on your end making these creatures, and the final product on screen would have lightning and other optical effects added to it by John Dykstra's team. Did you have to talk with those other departments ahead of time?

Not as much as you might think. John was there once we started filming, but then he'd be off doing other things. We did talk a little bit. The first of all the zombies we shot was the one that goes into the helicopter. He was filming that. When we got to the pathologist, you know, Tobe is directing the wide shots and the close ups of the actors, and I'm directing the animatronics crew. There were twenty-three puppeteers for that sequence.

In those days, computers were not what they are now. We devised a method to get a computer to operate eight channels of radio control. We had three computers that were operating preset reactions in the face, where each head had twenty-four radio control servos in them. Those were for things that were over and above the twenty-three puppeteers. It was very complex. Tobe kept on saying, "You're going to get an Oscar for this." But ultimately, they didn't get the acclaim at the time that they were hoping for, so they didn't shoot for the Oscars.

You directed Frank Finlay's death scene in the film. I've heard that his transformation had to be trimmed so that the film could avoid getting an X rating. Is that true?

I'm not 100% sure. The bubbling face is very much the way it was filmed. We did it in three takes, and that was it. I was surprised that I ended up directing that, because I was in my makeup room trying to get this makeup together. They got to the end of the shooting day, and everybody decided they were going home. So, there was just this little crew left waiting for me. When I got down there, Tobe wasn't there, so I filmed it.

I can't remember exactly how long it took us to put that makeup together, but it was extensive. It was certainly over four hours, because it had to have bladders and other things that were applied to the face before any prosthetics were put on, and before you could color it and do those other things. I think Frank was a little taken aback to find out that the makeup man was shooting his sequence, but it came out okay.

I had an extension of that sequence. After the spirit came out of his body and he had caught fire, we'd do a cutaway and when we cut back, the body sat up and it's completely on fire. The face kind of started to melt, the eyeballs fell out. Although it was live action, photographs of it in its final stage have been confused with the closing of *Raiders of the Lost Ark* (1981). But they did that in stop motion, and we did it in real time. I guess it was too gruesome. Probably the moment when the eyeballs fell out was what stopped it from going into the movie.

In the script for the helicopter scene, it just said that blood comes out of his mouth, and it forms into the blood clot girl. I mean, that was it, it was as simple as that. I added all the details that were in there, but what you see is only about a third of what we filmed. We had the blood clot grow an arm out of it, and then there was the shape of a head that moved up like a set of jaws and it had teeth, and the teeth withdrew. As what would have been the mouth was filling and the face formed in it, you realized that it was the blood clot girl. I don't know why they didn't include all of that, because it looked pretty good.

In that sequence, I had filmed the animatronic Patrick Stewart waking up. I was disappointed that they started with a scream and just jumped to it, because that head was very expressive. Basically, it woke up and started to look around and had a very demonic look that came on its face. And then, all of the blood and stuff started to come out of its eyes and ears and mouth.

These were hugely complicated, complex things that we were doing there. We've got animatronic figures that have blood coming out. The pathologist, for example, that sequence worked by pumping chemicals into the foam skin. You've got an animatronic head that's got twenty-four servos in it, and you're pumping chemicals through the same head. They came out through about thirty different holes in the skull that caused all of those bubbly, blistery things. Some we shot backwards, and some were shot forwards, so that you saw what appears to be something blossoming and something shrinking.

It's amazing. You've described this movie elsewhere as some of your best work. Is that because you were able to design such complex things and pull them off?

It's no good doing something really complex if someone else films it, and you don't get to see it on screen. That was what happened to the beast in *Krull*. We had an extraordinary character with lungs that expanded, and a heart that was on the outside, and veins where you could see fluid running through the body. The guy who filmed it, with the best intentions, felt that no one was going to believe a person in a suit. So, he put an anamorphic lens on the camera and put Vaseline all over the lens, and you never got to see the details that we'd spent a long time trying to make work. I wanted to be sure that didn't happen again. On *Lifeforce*, they let me just do what I wanted to do. Tobe would come in and say, "Okay, what are we doing today?"

It sounds like he might have been one of the easiest directors you've ever worked with.

He was very easy to work with and accommodating. So was Russell Mulcahy, who I did the Duran Duran "Wild Boys" video with. I worked with him on *Highlander* (1986). The problems on *Highlander* came, really, from the producers and the cinematographer. The cinematographer couldn't handle the idea that the guy with the makeup was telling the camera man to turn the camera over. It was those kinds of politics. You can't get past them.

You mentioned producers. Did you have any specific impression of Cannon at the time? When they made *Lifeforce*, they weren't really known for big budget movies. This was the first time they'd gone out and spent money on something this big.

That's true. What can I say? Cannon was well-known for not throwing money away. They wanted things to be done at the best possible price. You can't blame them for that. But it did have its impact on some of the things that we were doing there.

You also had to do makeup work on Mathilda May, giving her an almost inhumanly beautiful quality. What can you tell me about that?

The whole principle was that she was perfect. Normally when you're dealing with an actress, you're just trying to make them look good. But what they wanted was something like an untouched look. I don't know how happy Mathilda was with that makeup. I think there were times when there were other things that she would have liked to have done, but the truth of the matter is the body had to be perfect. All blemishes, all marks, all of those things had to be covered. I would have liked to have airbrushed her. I was doing airbrush makeup at that time, when nobody else was, and that gave a finish that looked just so perfect—it looked like it'd been retouched in Photoshop. I had gotten one of my assistant makeup artists to do that job. You also have to not overlook the fact that, maybe not half the time, but certainly 40% of the time that you see Mathilda naked in there, it isn't Mathilda. It's the dummies that we made of her, such as in the spaceship and when they first find her.

When you're working on a movie like this, I'm sure your nose is always to the grindstone. Do you get excited when you finally get to see your work put together with all of the editing, music, and other effects?

I get excited when something, especially a sequence that I devised, is there in its entirety, the way that I visualized it. The three sequences—the pathologist, the shriveled girl, and the pathologist's demise—I really liked seeing. I really liked the basic concept of the pathologist running up to the bars and coming apart, and getting stuck in the teeth of the Home Secretary. It really appealed to my sense of humor. That was just so entirely different. I know it's a little, throwaway thing, but I deliberately kept the demise of the guard more minimal, to be honest. Tobe liked things that were really over the top. The guard screaming as much as he does, I felt was a bit more than we needed. But the pathologist coming apart through the bars, I thought the timing was perfect.

You talked about how Finlay's death scene and the scene in the helicopter were shortened. I know a lot was cut from the movie's beginning, especially from the scenes in outer space. Do you recall if much of your work was removed when they trimmed the space sequences?

The only things of mine that were cut that come to mind are the sequence with Fallada on fire, the beginning of the blood clot sequence with the animatronic head, and the [Patrick Stewart animatronic]. I don't know whether it was all because it was considered to be too scary. That must have come out with an X rating, didn't it? What rating did it come out with?

It had an R rating in the United States.

Really? Well, then I guess that's why it was all cut down. There was a lot of nudity in it for that particular time, and too much blood and gore. I guess they just thought it was too far over the top. I would have thought that would have been ideal for Tobe, because he loved all of that stuff.

You run a museum in Sint Maarten dedicated to your work. I see there's a big display of *Star Wars* artifacts, obviously, because it's the most famous piece of science fiction of all time. Are there artifacts there from *Lifeforce* for fans to see?

Yeah. There were several versions of the shriveled girl. One of the versions is the dummy that you see in the field, and that was an articulated dummy. I have that here, but it's in very bad shape, because the foam latex basically disintegrates over time. I have the sword that goes through Mathilda May at the end as well, because that was another little insert that I did, which was the close up of the sword coming out of her back. I have the animatronics of several of those heads here as well.

Cannon, at the end of all of this stuff, having done things that had never been done before, the line producer suggested to me that he was going to sell my mechanisms to my competitors. I ended up actually buying a number of those things from them at the end of the movie to make sure that that didn't happen.

This videocassette copy of *Thunder Alley* was rented out by Hometown Cinema of Bridgewater, Virginia.

Thunder Alley

Release Date: August 1, 1985
Directed by: J.S. Cardone
Written by: J.S. Cardone
Starring: Roger Wilson, Jill Schoelen, Scott McGinnis, Clancy Brown, Leif Garrett
Trailer Voiceover: "If the dream is music, then the place is Thunder Alley … Thunder Alley, where music can make your dreams come true!"

I may be jaded—or I may just have seen *The Apple* (1980) one too many times—but when it comes to the music business, I know one thing: if you're a naïve, starry-eyed country kid dreaming of making it big with a guitar and a song, that dream is going to cost you your very soul. As soon as their fame level starts to soar, our good-natured starlet or honey-voiced heartthrob will give in to carnal temptation and/or the lure of narcotics, leading to a tragic fall. That's inevitably followed by a redemptive rise from the ashes, once they realize the good person they used to be isn't gone forever, but was inside them the whole time. It's a story that's been told over and again throughout the history of cinema.

Cannon's second take on this type of tale gives it only a modicum of an update—some posters for the film bore the spot-on tagline, "Sex, drugs & rock 'n roll, '80s style!"—but boasts a few, genuinely bangin' ballads, making it an enjoyable-enough entry in the genre of rock and roll cautionary tales.

Thunder Alley isn't set in any of the typical showbiz meccas like Los Angeles, New York, or even Nashville, but on a happening strip of live music bars in Tucson, Arizona. (If the establishing shot used for Tucson's rock clubs looks familiar to you, that's because the same shot was used for the downtown Los Angeles hip-hop club, Radiotron, in 1984's *Breakin' 2: Electric Boogaloo*.) Hundreds of local extras turned out for their chance to appear as rock and roll fans in the audiences of the film's many musical performances, with the larger crowds being paid for their time in hot dogs and soda.

Roger Wilson of *Porky's* (1981) and *Porky's II* (1983) stars as Richie, the hunky son of a farmer who spends his days picking cotton and his nights picking away at his electric guitar in the family barn. Everyone can see the kid has talent, none more so than his best bud, Donnie, played by Scott McGinnis of *Joysticks* (1983), *Star Trek III* and Cannon's own *Making the Grade* (both 1984). Donnie invites Richie to play as a fill-in guitarist for his pop-rock band, Magic. Their gig catches the attention of an evil music promoter who is surprisingly cool with being known only as "The Fatman," who signs them to a contract and schedules a dry run tour through some of the Southwest's seediest roadhouses and honky-tonks.

Before Richie can hitch a ride on the train to stardom, however, he has to overcome a few expected obstacles. Obviously, his pa would rather he take over the family business than toil his life away as a good-for-nothing musician. Plus, Magic's glam rock-y lead singer, Skip (child star, teen heartthrob, and grown-up train wreck Leif Garrett), really hates Richie's guts, regarding him solely as a country-western boy, as if that's a bad thing—and despite Richie's repeated demonstrations of his ability to shred just like Eddie Van Halen. And then there's the matter of Richie's brand new girlfriend, Beth (Jill Schoelen), whom he'll miss dearly while he's away on tour for just a few weeks.

Fortunately Richie's pop rolls over in his convictions pretty easily, and with Beth's encouragement Richie hits the road with Magic. Their catchy power pop is a hit at every stop along the way, leading Fatman to summon his new stars back home to play the hottest club in Tucson. To these bright-eyed kids, this headlining hometown gig is big-time. They've made it!

In most cases, this is where our hero would start sampling dangerous drugs and jumping into bed with big-haired floozies. However, our Richie is a straight arrow, poo-pooing his friends' cocaine use and even deflecting the advances of one particularly aggressive groupie—it's actually his bandmates who fall susceptible to the perils of fame. While Skip predictably grows jealous when their new guitarist begins singing his own songs and stealing the spotlight, Donnie in particular handles Richie's rise to stardom the hardest. He develops a nasty coke habit, which transforms into an addiction to speedballs—which he sort of blames Richie for driving him toward, by being so talented and making the rest of them look bad.

Of course, Richie is awoken by his mother in the very next scene telling him that Donnie had overdosed. Richie takes his best friend's death very hard, and it throws him over the deep end: he gets into a fistfight with his bandmate and then cheats on Beth with the groupie who'd been trying to get in his pants earlier in the movie. This poor hussy then makes the mistake of offering him drugs, and he almost kills her. When she tells him that Fatman was supplying Donnie's habit, he goes on the offensive and threatens Fatman behind his nightclub with a sledgehammer.

For Magic, the ride seems like it's all over: Donnie's gone, Richie's out of control, their contract's been ripped to shreds, and Skip is about to jump ship to become the new lead singer for Fatman's most beloved hair metal group, Surgical Steel. There's one, final glimmer of hope when Fatman's lead lackey (Clancy Brown) decides he's had enough of his evil boss, and approaches Magic with a scheme to sneak them into a surprise set at the big music festival they had been previously slated to open. The problem is, though, that

Richie doesn't want to do it: he's hit full blown asshole mode, going so far to dump his poor, sweet girlfriend when she shows up and begs him not to throw all of his talent and ambition away. The movie's finale comes during that big show, as the rest of Magic wait backstage, biting their nails and fretting (along with the viewers at home) over whether or not Richie's going to show up for their make-it-or-break-it performance.

You can probably guess what happens . . .

Richie (Roger Wilson) takes center stage in a sales ad for the film.

Writer-director J.S. Cardone based *Thunder Alley* on his memories of playing in a Tucson-area rock band in the 1970s. He returned to his hometown to shoot the movie on location at local venues, even employing one of the area's most popular, real-life metal bands, Surgical Steel, to play themselves in the movie. (Surgical Steel never released a full album, but it's worth noting to other metalheads that their demo tape was produced by Judas Priest singer Rob Halford.)

Cardone had previously written and directed an unconventional slasher film called *The Slayer* (1982), which had earned a spot on Great Britain's infamous Video Nasties list. When the more mainstream *Thunder Alley* failed to set the box office ablaze, Cardone turned back to the horror genre, where he built an admirable career directing, producing, and/or writing cult features like *Shadowzone* (1990) and *The Covenant* (2006).

Thunder Alley only received a small theatrical release from Cannon, but it developed a small niche following through rentals and frequent cable showings. Much of this late-come love is thanks to the movie's soundtrack, which surprisingly never saw a cassette or LP release. Many of the songs performed by Magic are covers of tracks previously released by other artists; others were written by *Thunder Alley*'s associate music producer, Scott Shelly, who'd been a guitar instructor to the superstar metal axeman Randy Rhoads. The instrumentals were recorded in a studio by Shelly and a group of studio musicians, but the vocals were shot live with Wilson and Garrett actually singing while the band pantomimed their other parts. To his credit, Wilson's playing looks pretty convincing, even during the complex solos. (Wilson was a musician in real life, and has played in numerous bands over the years.)

From discussions of the film in online forums, *Thunder Alley* seems to have inspired quite a few who saw it as youths to pick up the guitar themselves, which is nice to think about.

Thunder Alley sports supporting performances from several actors who would go on to bigger and better things. Jill Schoelen, who plays Richie's doe-eyed romantic interest, Beth, might be recognized by some who grew up in the VHS rental era for her part in the ensemble cast of *D.C. Cab* (1983), which also included Mr. T, Gary Busey, and The Barbarian Brothers, or possibly her appearance in the teen T&A comedy *Hot Moves* (1984). Following *Thunder Alley*, she landed her breakout role in the cult thriller *The Stepfather* (1987), and further solidified her scream queen status with roles in horror flicks like *Curse II* (1989) and *Popcorn* (1991). One of her slasher films of this era, *Cutting Class* (1989), is primarily remembered for giving Brad Pitt one of his first starring roles. Schoelen and Pitt were engaged for several months after the movie was shot, but she reputedly dumped him when he flew to Hungary to visit her on the set of the Menahem Golan-produced *The Phantom of the Opera* (1989), starring Freddy Krueger himself, Robert Englund.

Meanwhile, Clancy Brown—who played Magic's ballbusting road manager, Weasel, who the writer-director named after his own rock band from the 1970s—went on to become one of Hollywood's most recognizable character actors, as well as an extremely busy voice actor. *Thunder Alley* came after his appearances in *Bad Boys* (1983) and the superbly weird and wonderful *The Adventures of Buckaroo Banzai Across the Eighth Dimension* (1984). Some of his best-known roles include playing The Kurgan in *Highlander* (1986), a sadistic prison guard in *The Shawshank Redemption* (1994), a drill sergeant in *Starship Troopers* (1997), and the villainous pastor/devil incarnate of HBO's *Carnivale* (2003–2005). In the recording booth, he's most famous for voicing Lex Luthor in numerous animated Superman films and television shows, and Mr. Krabbs on *SpongeBob SquarePants*, from its premiere in 1999 onward.

Band member Butch is played by Phil Brock, who next appeared as the doofy third wheel to Michael Dudikoff and Steve James, Private Charley Madison, in Cannon's *American Ninja*, also released in 1985. (He'd return the following year for 1986's *P.O.W. The Escape*.)

Roger Wilson acted infrequently after *Thunder Alley*, but stayed in the public eye as the longtime boyfriend of supermodel Christy Turlington. In the late '90s, Wilson filed a $45 million lawsuit against actor Leonardo DiCaprio, after the future Oscar winner allegedly punched him in the throat, damaging his larynx, and ordered his buddies beat him up outside a Manhattan restaurant. The alleged altercation happened after Wilson confronted the *Titanic* (1998) star and told him to stop repeatedly calling his then-girlfriend, *Saved by the Bell* (1989–1993) and *Showgirls* (1995) star Elizabeth Berkley. The lawsuit was eventually dismissed.

The U.K. video release of *Thunder Alley*.

AMERICAN NINJA™

THE CANNON GROUP, INC. Presents a GOLAN-GLOBUS Production of a SAM FIRSTENBERG Film
"AMERICAN NINJA" Starring MICHAEL DUDIKOFF
STEVE JAMES • JUDIE ARONSON • GUICH KOOCK and TADASHI YAMASHITA
Music by MICHAEL LINN • Supervising Editor MICHAEL J. DUTHIE
Director of Photography HANANIA BAER • Story by AVI KLEINBERGER & GIDEON AMIR
Screenplay by PAUL DE MIELCHE • Produced by MENAHEM GOLAN and YORAM GLOBUS
Directed by SAM FIRSTENBERG

The first U.S. video release of *American Ninja*, featuring one of the most
badass and patriotic VHS covers of all time.

American Ninja
American Ninja 2: The Confrontation
American Ninja 3: Blood Hunt
American Ninja 4: The Annihilation
American Ninja 5

Release Dates: August 30, 1985 (I), May 1, 1987 (II) February 24, 1989 (III), March 8, 1991 (IV), 1995 [video] (V)

Directed by: Sam Firstenberg (I & II), Cedric Sundström(III & IV), Bob Bralver as "Bobby Gene Leonard" (V)

Written by: Paul De Mielche (I), James Booth & Gary Conway (II), Gary Conway (III), James Booth as "David Geeves" (IV), George Saunders & John Bryant Hedberg (V)

Starring: Michael Dudikoff, Steve James, David Bradley

Trailer Voiceover: "For two thousand years, the sacred art of the ninja has been guarded in the East . . . Now, it has come to the West!"

Sometimes all it took was the perfect title to kick off the next great action franchise of the 1980s. If "American Ninja" sounds like the Cannon-est of all

Cannon movie titles, that's because it came from Menahem Golan himself. Golan had a feeling it would be a big hit for the company—even before he had a script, star, or even a premise for the movie, beyond that it would probably feature a ninja who also happened to be an American.

When Golan first dreamed up the title—perhaps during the same, mad fever dream in which he came up with the phrase "Electric Boogaloo"—the initial thought would be that it should feature their newest action star, Chuck Norris, who had just scored them a legitimate hit with *Missing in Action* (1984). Norris had previously kicked a bunch of ninjas' asses in *The Octagon* (1980), and Golan figured this could be another great opportunity for their new, bearded hero to further show off his chops (and punches, and roundhouse kicks) as a martial artist. By this point in his career, however, Norris—now in his mid-forties—didn't want to be pigeonholed as a martial arts star, and was leaning toward action roles that let him carry a gun and called for slightly less kicking. (He also wasn't keen about having his face covered for much of the movie, which kind of threw a wrench into the whole "masked ninja" thing.)

Golan was insistent, though. He conscripted *Missing in Action* writer James Bruner to write an American Ninja script. In trying to please both Chuck and Menahem, Bruner penned a script in which Norris would play an anti-terrorist operative with the *codename* "American Ninja." Everyone involved loved the script, but thankfully came to the realization that they couldn't call it *American Ninja* if, well, there weren't any ninjas in it. That script—which already had Joseph Zito attached to direct—was re-tooled and sent into production as *Invasion U.S.A.* (1985), which you can read about in our next chapter.

The previous ninja on Cannon's payroll, Sho Kosugi, had left the company for greener pastures after wrapping up their first ninja trilogy, which included *Enter the Ninja* (1981), *Revenge of the Ninja* (1983), and *Ninja III: The Domination* (1984). Kosugi played totally unrelated ninjas in those movies, and served as the only link which connected all three. The rising action star handed in his walking papers after the company chose to make Lucinda

Dickey the star of the third film, downgrading Kosugi to a supporting role after he'd played the hero in *Revenge*. He quickly found work with other producers, who'd put his signature brand of ninja action front and center in post-Cannon flicks like *Pray for Death* (1985), *Rage of Honor* (1987), and *9 Deaths of the Ninja* (1985), and gave him a James Bond-like crack at non-ninja stardom opposite a then-unknown Jean-Claude Van Damme in *Black Eagle* (1988). When Kosugi proved he didn't need Cannon, Cannon had to scramble to find someone to replace him.

Director Sam Firstenberg was fresh off a pair of successful, back-to-back ninja features in *Revenge of the Ninja* and *Ninja III*, and so Cannon smartly brought him back for another smorgasbord of shinobi action. He was teamed with associate producers Gideon Amir and Avi Kleinberger, and the trio came up with the framework for the film's story. Aware that they would be shooting in the Philippines, they opted to set the film on an American military base, and so it became obvious that their reluctant, ninja hero would also be a soldier. Once a few ideas were in place, they tapped writer Paul De Mielche to flesh out all of the details and write the screenplay. (A former marine, De Mielche had not only studied martial arts himself, but been friends with Bruce Lee through actor James Coburn, whom he'd lived with and collaborated with on various projects.) As the pieces started to come together, Firstenberg and his team still had their most important task ahead of them: finding Cannon their American ninja.

An open call was put out in trade papers, to acting schools, and martial arts studios. More than four hundred young hopefuls answered the advertisement. The herd was trimmed down significantly by a physical test: any potential star had to at least *look* and *move* like they knew martial arts, even if in real life they didn't. After this there were around one hundred left to read for the part; those were culled down to a small handful of finalists that included the movie's eventual lead, Michael Dudikoff, and Chad McQueen (son of Steve). Firstenberg knew in his gut that Dudikoff would be their perfect hero from the moment he first met him: not only was he good-looking and athletic, but the director saw a bit of James Dean in the young star.

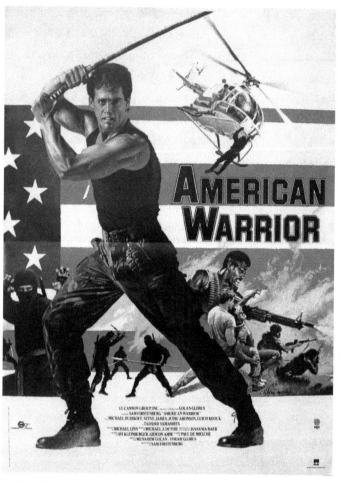

Michael Dudikoff stars as the *American Ninja*—or, *American Warrior*, as the movie was known in the U.K.

Born and raised on the California coast, Michael Dudikoff never wanted to be an actor despite growing up so close to Hollywood—his plans were to become a child psychologist. While waiting tables to put himself through college, he served dinner to an *Esquire* fashion editor, who asked him if he'd consider doing some runway modeling work. Before long he was appearing in a print ad for Adidas sneakers. Print begat commercial work for everything from Coppertone sunscreen, to Coca-Cola, the Army Reserve, and zit cream.

It was only a matter of time before he wound up on television, making his first splash in a two-episode appearance as Joanie's boyfriend on *Happy Days* (1974–1984).

Dudikoff became a busy actor, fast. He had small roles in *Bloody Birthday* (1981), *TRON* (1982) and *Uncommon Valor* (1983), and a lead role in *Radioactive Dreams* (1985) from future Cannon regular Albert Pyun. Most notably, though, he was cast as one of the leads on the short-lived Brian Dennehy sitcom *Star of the Family* (1982), and appeared as one of Tom Hanks' sidekicks in the raunchy hit *Bachelor Party* (1984). By the time he auditioned for Cannon, Dudikoff considered himself a comedic actor. No one would have guessed—not even him—that he'd become the company's next major action hero.

There was only one roadblock: Cannon was only going to pay scale for *American Ninja*, meaning that all actors would have to work for the minimum amount of money allowed by their union. Dudikoff, though still relatively unknown at the time, was too experienced for that—and his agent demanded double what they were prepared to pay him. Golan was taken aback when he heard Dudikoff wouldn't work for peanuts, and almost re-cast the role—but after some begging from Firstenberg, eventually gave in and agreed to pay the young man double the peanuts originally offered.

Thinking he needed a stage name that sounded more like a movie star, Cannon had the gall to ask him to change it to "J. Michael Girard." Dudikoff rightfully refused.

Private Joe Armstrong—a.k.a. the American Ninja—has one of those origin stories that's so badass it feels right out of a comic book. After his parents died at sea, the bouncing baby ninja-to-be washed ashore on a remote, Pacific island. He was found by Shinyuki (John Fujioka, later of 1992's *American Samurai*), a former Japanese soldier and full-time master ninja who's lived by himself for decades, unaware that the War was over. He takes the boy in as his own son, dubs him "Joe" (being the only American name he knows), and immediately sets to training him in ninjutsu, just as any other hermit ninja who finds an orphaned baby would do.

125

Joe Armstrong (Michael Dudikoff) rescues the panicking Patricia (Judie Aronson) from danger in *American Ninja*.

In a horrible stroke of bad luck, young Joe is effectively orphaned for a second time in his life when a construction crew unwittingly catches him in an explosion while they're clearing a path through the jungle. They send the little white boy—now rendered an amnesiac—back to the United States, where he spends his teenage years bouncing in and out of foster homes before he's arrested for accidentally killing a man in a brawl, and given the choice of jail or the military. He picks the latter, and that's where we find him at the start of the franchise: working as a truck driver at a U.S. Army base in the Philippines.

As it happens, the quiet loner isn't the most popular guy with his fellow troops. Their opinion of him plummets even further when their supply run is hijacked by gunmen, and the bad guys' manhandling of the colonel's lovely daughter unlocks Joe's secret ninja mode. He saves the supply truck and escapes with the colonel's daughter, but inadvertently gets several of his fellow soldiers killed by ninjas in the process.

It's in this opening massacre that we're first shown one of Joe Armstrong's greatest talents: turning seemingly harmless, everyday objects into deadly weapons. In this fight alone he kills a hijacker by throwing a screwdriver like a knife and stops an arrow with the handle of a shovel. Over the course of the film, he also incorporates a tire iron, garden hose, and bucket into his fighting arsenal. Talk about being resourceful!

Interestingly, our hero is nearly mute for the first fifteen minutes of the movie, waiting to utter his first significant dialogue when he's half-naked in the jungle with the Colonel's prissy daughter, Patricia. This inevitable love interest is played by actress Judie Aronson, who had already been killed by Jason Voorhees in *Friday the 13th: The Final Chapter* (1984), and played Hilly, one of the popular girls who inspired the geeks to cook up the woman of their dreams in *Weird Science* (1985).

For some reason everyone assumes it's our hero's fault that his army convoy was attacked by ninjas. The Colonel (Guich Koock of TV's *She's the Sheriff*, 1987–1989) threatens to court-martial him, and several of his fellow servicemen are asked to keep an eye on the good-for-nothing, amnesiac ninja. This includes the dorky Private Charley Madison (Phil Brock, last seen in Cannon's *Thunder Alley*, 1985), and Corporal Curtis Jackson, played by a true pillar of b-movie badassery, Mr. Steve James.

Born in New York City, the magnetic, martial arts-practicing Steve James built his movie career as a stunt man, doing lots of uncredited work in locally-shot productions like *The Wiz* (1978), *The Wanderers* (1979), and *Dressed to Kill* (1980). Some of his earliest on-screen roles included bona fide cult classics such as *The Warriors* (1979)—playing one of the Baseball Furies—and *The Exterminator* (1980), where he played sidekick to Robert Ginty's armed vigilante. James was muscular, athletic, and handsome, with weapons-grade charisma. James would have undoubtedly been a bigger star had he broken into the business a few years earlier. Unfortunately he missed the height of Blaxploitation cinema, and instead spent the '80s mostly playing second fiddle to other heroes and threatening to outshine the movies' stars. (James was struck down tragically young by cancer in 1993, at the age of 41.) Hollywood's loss, however, was Cannon's gain, as the studio hired the actor to appear in seven of their films, three of those—including this one, *Avenging Force* (1986) and *American Ninja 2* (1987)—opposite Michael Dudikoff.

In one of the '80s action's most memorable scenes of masculine bonding, Corporal Jackson approaches Joe Armstrong and essentially challenges him to a tough guy contest. The two men proceed, then, to beat the shit out of each other while the rest of the base stands around gawking at their knock-down, drag-out display of dick-measuring. It's evident that in any normal scenario, Jackson would have wiped the floor with a hundred men of Joe's size, but every time he tries to land a powerful blow, Armstrong is able to sidestep or deflect it as if he knew exactly when and from where it was coming. In a final confirmation of his mystical ninja abilities, Joe casually lowers a bucket down over his head, and continues to best Jackson in the fight—even while blind, and looking completely ridiculous.

Jackson finally submits, recognizing that his opponent's got game. The two immediately become BBFFs: *B*adass *B*est *F*riends *F*orever.

Meanwhile in villain-land, a bad dude named Victor Ortega (Don Stewart, of soap opera *The Guiding Light*) is training an army of ninjas to steal weapons from the American military so that he can sell them on the black market. His adorable ninja school—which looks like a deadlier version of a children's playground, and has a dress code that calls for brightly color-coded ninja uniforms—is run by a Black Star Ninja master, played by another real-life martial arts star, Tadashi Yamashita. (The black star tattooed on his cheek is to let other ninjas know he's turned to the dark side.)

Joe Armstrong does battle with the deadly Black Star Ninja in an Italian poster for *American Ninja*.

Born in Japan, Yamashita began training in karate when he was only eleven, and earned his black belt by the age of sixteen. He dedicated himself to training, reaching the seventh degree by the age of 26 and becoming the youngest-ever Japanese person to do so. He moved to Southern California in the early Seventies, where his skills were immediately recognized by many of the region's celebrated martial artists (including *American Ninja* fight choreographer Mike Stone, who recommended him for his role in the film.) It's said that he trained Bruce Lee in how to use nunchucks, and after the international superstar's passing, Yamashita was cast in several Bruceploitation films—sometimes under the memorable pseudonym, "Bronson Lee." He later appeared with Chuck Norris in *The Octagon* (1980) and Kurt Thomas in the b-movie classic *Gymkata* (1985).

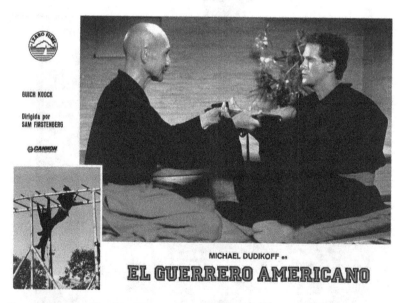

Joe Armstrong (Dudikoff) receives ninja wisdom from his adoptive father, Shinyuki, played by John Fujioka.

If you're looking for the movie's twist, here it is: the lowly gardener working at the black market kingpin's heavily-armed compound, however preposterously, happens to be Joe Armstrong's adoptive father—the one who trained him in the deadly art of ninjutsu right before he was bonked on the head and lost all memory of his past.

Most of the movie revolves around Ortega dispatching the Black Star Ninja and his army to take out Private Joe Armstrong, the only man who can stand in their way, as our hero, his girlfriend, and his new best bud try to figure out which crooked Army officers are secretly in on the black market weapons trade. It's almost nonstop action, save for a few tame, romantic interludes as our hero and the colonel's comely daughter get to know one another. Eventually Joe catches up with his long-lost dad, who switches on his super-ninja powers with a bit of special meditation. Those bad guys had better look out now!

Watching *American Ninja*, you can tell that director Sam Firstenberg spent his time off between ninja movies directing the hallucinogenic dance spectacle, *Breakin' 2: Electric Boogaloo* (1984). The evil ninjas in this film often move in tandem, striking rad poses and then moving again at the same time, almost as if they were synchronized swimmers. While it sounds silly on paper, it's pretty cool-looking on screen. When it happens, it can sometimes feel like you're watching a Busby Berkeley musical number . . . a Busby Berkeley musical number *OF DEATH*, that is.

Almost the last ten minutes of the 95-minute film are dedicated to an epic battle of good ninjas versus bad ninjas versus Army rangers. I won't spoil it with a play-by-play, but a few of the highlights include Corporal Jackson essentially shredding a dude's crotch with his bare hand, the evil kingpin opting not to escape in his helicopter because he (understandably) wants to stick around and watch two master ninjas fight to the death, and one of the best displays of bromantic teamwork between Joe and Jackson that you'll see in all of '80s action cinema—a combination of era and genre that was particularly well-known for its bromances.

For a movie that Cannon didn't pour a ton of money into, *American Ninja* looks fantastic. When filming abroad, Cannon rarely flew in more than the minimum number of cast and crew members needed, choosing instead to fill out their crew with locals wherever possible. This usually meant that more than half the people working on a film were relatively inexperienced:

obviously, Cannon selected most of these filming locations because they were cheap, and not for the size of their local film industries. *American Ninja* was the rare exception to this rule: most of the crew they inherited had worked on the infamously grueling, six-month long *Apocalypse Now* (1979) shoot, and thus were about as experienced as any crew that Cannon could have pulled together in Los Angeles.

Some of the cast and crew members that Firstenberg and his producers did choose to bring with them included fight choreographer Mike Stone, stunt coordinator Steve Lambert, stalwart Cannon cinematographer Hanania Baer, and actor John LaMotta as Lieutenant Rinaldo, who had starred in Firstenberg's debut feature, *One More Chance* (1981), had small roles in *Revenge of the Ninja*, *Ninja III: The Domination*, and *Breakin' 2: Electric Boogaloo*, and would soon be known in living rooms across the nation as nosy neighbor, Trevor Ochmonek, on TV's *ALF* (1986–1990).

Joe Armstrong fends off the Black Star Army in *American Ninja*'s epic finale, shown here on a Yugoslavian lobby card.

Outside of the sweltering, 115-degree heat, the production went about as smoothly as you could hope for on a Cannon movie—save for Michael

Dudikoff coming down with malaria. (If he looks a little unwell in some shots, that's because he was.) That, and stuntman Steve Lambert getting smashed up while doubling for Dudikoff in the movie's thrilling motorcycle leap—a moment which can be seen in the final film.

American Ninja opened over Labor Day weekend in 1985. It debuted in a very admirable fourth place at the box office, especially once you consider the movies ahead of it were *Pee-wee's Big Adventure*, *Teen Wolf*, and the money-making juggernaut *Back to the Future* (all 1985). Although contemporary critics weren't overly high on the film, the movie was a relative hit for Cannon, earning more than $10 million on a roughly $1 million budget.

The movie played very well abroad, too. In a funny turn of events, *American Ninja* had to be renamed "American Warrior" for its release in France and a few other territories, as another movie had already beat it to foreign theaters under the name "American Ninja." Known stateside as *9 Deaths of the Ninja* (1985), that movie's hero was played by Cannon's former ninja star, Sho Kosugi, and directed by Emmett Alston, director of their *New Year's Evil* (1980) and the man fired from *Enter the Ninja* (1981) when Menahem Golan chose to take over.

Not only did Cannon have a hit on their hands, but they'd found their newest star in Michael Dudikoff. Model handsome and athletic enough to do his own stunts, it is worth pointing out that he was also significantly younger than Cannon's other two leading men. (Dudikoff had just turned 30, whereas Norris was in his mid-forties and Bronson in his early sixties.) Paired as he so frequently was with the similarly-aged Steve James, Cannon suddenly had new demographics they could target with their action output.

With *American Ninja* turning out to be as big a success as it was, Cannon would of course require a sequel. That wouldn't happen immediately, though, because—as was typical of the company's breakneck speed of doing things—both of their stars had already been cast in their next Cannon productions before the popularity of *American Ninja* could really sink in. Steve James would next appear in *The Delta Force* (1986), and then he and Dudikoff would appear together again in *Avenging Force* (1986), the next feature from Sam

Firstenberg. Like *American Ninja*, *Avenging Force* had been assembled as a project for Chuck Norris, but when Chuck decided against the project, Dudikoff stepped in. As soon as the director and stars' schedules had freed up again, they all went to work on what would become *American Ninja 2: The Confrontation.*

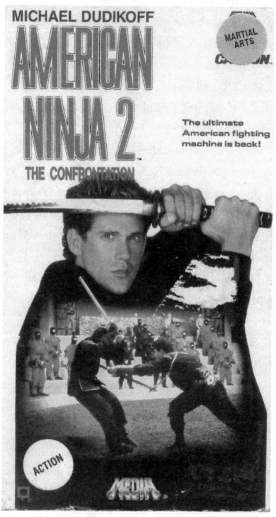

The U.S. video release for *American Ninja 2: The Confrontation*. An early working title for the film was "American Ninja 2: Re-Creation."

The script for *American Ninja 2* was penned by a pair of writer-actors. The original script came from Gary Conway, who had starred on TV's *Burke's Law* (1963–1966) and *Land of the Giants* (1968–1970), and had found semi-recent success producing and starring in the violent revenge film, *The Farmer* (1977). It was Conway who brought the early screenplay for what became *Over the Top* (1987) to Cannon, envisioning it as a star vehicle for himself. When Golan passed over Conway in favor of a bigger-name star—and made Sylvester Stallone the highest-paid man in Hollywood—the producers kept him close by to write the second and third *American Ninja* movies, and play the second film's primary bad guy, shady millionaire Leo "The Lion" Burke. Once Conway was cast as the villain, Firstenberg recruited his pal, British actor James Booth—who'd written *Avenging Force* and played Dudikoff's boss in that film—to handle rewrites so that Conway could focus on his role. (Booth would be given his own opportunity to play an *American Ninja* villain in the franchise's fourth installment.)

Michael Dudikoff and Steve James: the most dynamic duo of '80s action.

Where the first *American Ninja* shot in the Philippines during the reign of the corrupt authoritarian president Ferdinand Marcos, Cannon apparently tried to one-up themselves by having *American Ninja 2* shoot in South Africa during Apartheid. The segregation understandably made members of the cast and crew uncomfortable. On top of that, the local crews were not nearly as experienced as they had been in the Philippines. Compared to the smooth sailing that was *American Ninja*'s production, the sequel had significantly more hurdles to jump.

No longer viewed as military troublemakers, Joe Armstrong and Curtis Jackson are now essentially working as the Army's anti-ninja task force: a dynamic duo who are dispatched around the world at the first signs of ninja trouble. Soldiers have been mysteriously vanishing at a Marine base in the Caribbean, with an eye-witness reporting their kidnappers wore black suits. Enter our ninja.

Armstrong and Jackson are picked up at the airport in a convertible by a couple Marines, including Sgt. Charlie McDonald (Larry Poindexter), who will take over the role of their third wheel in this film. They're shocked to discover how lax the rules and dress code seem to be at the base, which is overseen by a blowhard Captain known affectionately as "Wild Bill." (He's played by Jeff Celentano, credited as Jeff Weston, who'd reappear in Cannon's *Journey to the Center of the Earth* [1988] and *Alien from L.A.* [1988].) It's revealed that the surfer gear is part of the unit's required uniform, allowing them to blend in as tourists. The Marines all turn up their noses at the two Army boys who were sent to save their butts, because it wouldn't be an '80s military thriller without some tension between our heroes and their higher-ups.

It's not long before a traitorous marine tries to lure the two of them into a trap on a remote, rocky island crawling with ninjas. The ensuing battle was filmed on the aptly-named Boulder Beach, a picturesque tourist destination outside of Cape Town which is now well-known for its large penguin colony, rather than the epic ninja smack-down that once occurred there.

Armstrong confronts the treasonous soldier, who tells him he's being extorted into leading his fellow servicemen into traps by a mysterious drug lord known as "The Lion," just moments before he's assassinated by ninjas in the back room of a seedy bar. Horror fans will want to take note during the numerous scenes where our heroes slap around thugs at the Blind Beggar Bar, as one of the movie's stunt men is none other than Kane Hodder, the only man to have portrayed all three of Jason Voorhees, Freddy Krueger, and Leatherface on screen.

Making the first movie look almost grounded in reality by comparison, *American Ninja 2* delivers a villain that's straight out of James Bond territory. From a distance, Leo "The Lion" Burke (Conway) looks like your average eccentric billionaire, living on a private island known as "Blackbeard Island," which isn't weird or suspicious at all. On closer inspection, though, we find out that he's kidnapped a local scientist who was on the cusp of curing cancer, and has instead forced him to engineer an army of genetically-enhanced, super cyborg-ninjas.

The Lion's ninja army is trained by master ninja Tojo Ken, who you know is evil incarnate by the scar on his face. Tojo Ken is played by karate champion Mike Stone, the man who introduced ninjas to Cannon with the script that eventually became *Enter the Ninja* —in which he had originally been cast to play the white ninja before being replaced by Franco Nero—and had worked as the fight choreographer and Dudikoff's martial arts trainer on the first *American Ninja* movie. Like Tadashi Yamashita's role in the prior film, the bad ninja here is played by a real-life badass: Stone went undefeated during his years as a tournament fighter and was inducted into the Black Belt Hall of Fame. Well-known within the Southern California martial arts scene, he was friends with both Bruce Lee and Chuck Norris, and had been considered for the latter's role in *The Way of the Dragon* (1972). Infamously, he was also the karate instructor with whom Priscilla Presley had an affair in the early 1970s, leading to her divorce from Elvis.

The Lion had the missing Marines kidnapped to use as physical specimens for his second generation of experimental ninjas because, frankly, his current ninja army kind of sucks. As Tojo Ken swiftly demonstrates for an audience of curious villains—and Armstrong unintentionally reiterates over and over again throughout the film—these are the easiest-to-kill ninjas in any of Cannon's movies. They break like knock-off, dollar store action figures. It used to be that only a ninja could kill a ninja, but I'm pretty sure a kindergartener with a sharp stick could kill the ones we see in *American Ninja 2*. Maybe even several at once.

Our heroes eventually get to the bottom of the marine-napping ring with the help of the scientist's lovely daughter, Alicia (South African actress Michelle Botes), and a streetwise urchin named Toto (Elmo Fillis). Along the way we get several very fun action sequences, including a classic Cannon bar brawl, complete with broken beer bottles, breakaway tables, and Steve James strategically ripping the sleeves from his marine dress uniform to show off his muscles. And speaking of good, ol' Curtis Jackson, we get several amazing moments of him storming the bad guys' compound, going into full Bruce Lee-mode complete with kung fu poses and threatening howls.

Rest assured, we get the obligatory showdown between good ninja and bad ninja when Joe Armstrong and Tojo Ken face off in The Lion's personal arena—and it's every bit as badass as we could hope. (For the location, the production team converted over a local stadium that was used for horse auctions.) Armstrong, now in full ninja garb and re-energized by a meditative flashback to his father's teachings in the first film, goes toe-to-toe with his evil counterpart. Save for a hot minute when Tojo Ken goes hog wild with a shotgun, we're witness to a pretty graceful sword fight: more akin to something out of an old samurai film than the explosive firefight happening between the marines and henchmen right outside.

There's a fun cameo during a scene where the good guys dress up like marines and attend a fancy gala. The elegant woman whom Steve James flirts with was model Nava Halimi, whom he'd met while filming *The Delta Force* in Israel and brought along with him on the *American Ninja 2* shoot. They'd be married soon afterward.

Released on the first of May in 1987, *American Ninja 2* was shot for a little more than a third of the budget its predecessor had, and brought home a little more than a third of what it did at the domestic box office. However, it did incredibly well abroad and on video, pushing it to become the most profitable of all of Cannon's ninja movies. Critically it fared about the same, but in retrospect *American Ninja 2* has picked up a great cult following, with a sizable number of fans citing it as their favorite installment in the series. (This author prefers the slicker look and more serious tone of the original, but that doesn't mean he loves *American Ninja 2* any less.)

If you've learned anything about Cannon in these books, you'd know a third *American Ninja* would be inevitable.

If these films were made by a normal Hollywood studio, the *American Ninja* movies would follow an upward trajectory. It's typical for each entry in a blockbuster action franchise to get bigger and ballsier, in an attempt to top the films that came before it. But, coming from a late-Eighties Cannon which was constantly on the verge of bankruptcy, they decided to do the opposite and wring all the remaining juice they could out of the series. The third film would go back to shoot in South Africa, and on a budget that was smaller than ever before.

This time there would be a changeover in the talent involved both behind and in front of the camera. Notably, Sam Firstenberg wouldn't be coming back. Cinema's premiere ninja movie director, who had been working for Golan and Globus since the 1970s, had little interest into stepping down into even lower-budget territory, and knew that he'd have a hard time following up his first two movies with the limited resources that Cannon was willing to put into their next one. To be fair, too, the young filmmaker had more than paid his dues, having directed six movies for Cannon in five years—four of them about ninjas. He'd temporarily step away from Cannon to direct the underrated *Riverbend* (1989)—an underseen starring vehicle for the *American Ninja* franchise's own Steve James—and the Israeli comedy *The Day We Met* (1990) before being called into emergency service by Cannon to take over the filming of *Delta Force 3: The Killing Game* (1991).

The mantle of *American Ninja* series director was passed on to South African filmmaker Cedric Sundström, who had previously worked as second unit director on both of Cannon's Allan Quatermain films. Gary Conway—part two's villain, "The Lion"—would again handle the script duties.

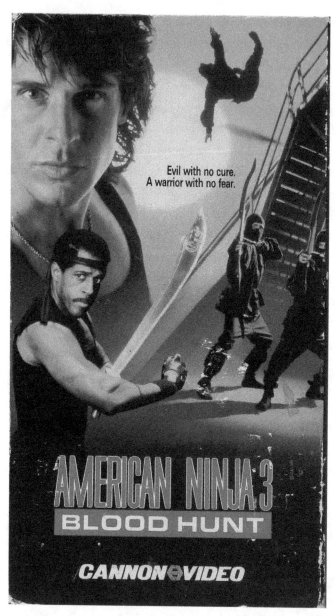

American Ninja 3: Blood Hunt on VHS.

Originally, the third *American Ninja* movie's plot was going to center on Joe Armstrong taking down a drug ring run by evil ninjas, but it soon became clear that franchise star Michael Dudikoff wouldn't be available to play the hero this time around. While Dudikoff wasn't totally opposed to coming back for another adventure as the American Ninja—as the fourth film in the series would soon prove—he was uncomfortable about continuing to shoot movies in South Africa under apartheid. On top of that, Cannon had double-booked him—he was already committed to *River of Death* (1988)—and the company wasn't ready to pump the brakes on their sequel train just because the franchise's star wasn't available. So, a new hero needed to be found.

Enter David Bradley, a first-time actor and second-degree black belt from Plano, Texas. The aspiring martial arts star was actually already known to his predecessor, Michael Dudikoff, who put in a good word for Bradley with his bosses at Cannon after meeting him at the Los Angeles car lot where he'd been working. (The role had initially been offered to Kurt McKinney, who'd recently faced off against a villainous Jean-Claude Van Damme in 1986's *No Retreat, No Surrender*, but he declined because he was worried about being typecast into a martial arts movie career.) Sundström admired Bradley's toughness and martial arts know-how, enlisting him to take over the franchise vacated by Dudikoff and launching a Cannon career that would include two more American Ninja movies as well as Cannon's own, officially-sanctioned knock-off of the franchise, *American Samurai* (1992).

How do you make an American ninja, anyway? Well, you start with an orphan . . .

American Ninja 3: Blood Hunt opens in Los Angeles in 1979. Two kids—awkwardly overdubbed by adults—are spectating a karate tournament as one of them, Sean Davidson, waits for his kung fu-trained father to step into the arena. Meanwhile, a group of gun-toting terrorists led by the wretched General Andreas (Yehuda Efroni) hold up the arena where the match is being held, and young Sean has the misfortune of walking in on the robbery. He's taken hostage, and his father is gunned down by their villainous leader while attempting to save his son.

Cut to a few months later, where his father's pal, Izumo, has taken the boy to Japan and begun training him in the ways of ninjutsu. (Izumo is played by

Calvin Jung, best known for his role as one of Clarence Boddicker's henchmen in 1987's *RoboCop*.) We make a quick leap ahead to the future, as full-grown Sean—now played by David Bradley—graduates from ninja school with a master's degree in kicking ass.

The third film in the series mimics the origin story from *American Ninja*, and shares a large number of plot elements with *American Ninja 2*. Our new hero, Sean, meets up with everyone's favorite badass best friend, Curtis Jackson, on the remote (and fictional) Caribbean island of Triana, which is playing host to an international karate tournament. (Watch for the referee at the tournament—it's none other than Mike Stone, who played the evil ninja in the last film and once again choreographed the martial arts sequences here.) Filling out the regular role of the duo's dorky third wheel is Dexter (Evan J. Klisser, previously of 1988's *Platoon Leader*), a goofball martial artist who fancies himself a ladies' man.

This time around the villain is once again a shady scientist nicknamed after an animal, conducting unorthodox experiments inside yet another laboratory compound that's heavily-guarded by ninjas. Known as "The Cobra" (Marjoe Gortner), he's working to develop a super-virus to be utilized in biological warfare by the notoriously evil General Andreas, who coincidentally killed Sean's dad in the film's opening. Before he'll buy the virus, however, the general needs proof that it will be able to kill even the baddest of badasses—hence, the convoluted plan to host a fake karate tournament, where the winner will become their final guinea pig.

The actor who plays this movie's villain, Marjoe Gortner, has one of the most interesting real-life origin stories you'll come across. He started his career as a child evangelist, of all things, making you wonder how he wound up playing the heel in an *American Ninja* sequel decades later. He was ordained in the late 1940s, at four years old, and preached on the revival circuit across America, becoming a religious celebrity when photographers from *Life* and Paramount Studios showed up to watch the preschool-aged child perform a wedding ceremony.

His family, who had trained him to preach, amassed millions of dollars on his preaching tours, which his father disappeared with when Gortner was a teenager. The young man soon grew jaded with his religious work and left it behind to become a hippie in San Francisco, eventually reviving and revamping his stage show to make himself into something of a rock star-styled preacher. As he grew cynical about taking money from true believers, he invited a pair of documentary filmmakers—Howard Smith and Sarah Kernochan—to film his final tour. Backstage and in hotel rooms, he was candid with the filmmakers about how easily preachers could take money from their followers in the name of religion. The resulting documentary, *Marjoe* (1972), was a scathing criticism of this style of evangelical ministry, and won the Academy Award for Best Documentary.

After torpedoing his preaching career in the most fantastic way possible, Gortner used his infamy to switch career paths, releasing a rock album titled *Bad But Not Evil* (1973) and eventually finding his way into film and television. He became a fixture of b-movies, landing roles in films such as *Earthquake* (1974), *Food of the Gods* (1976), Luigi Cozzi's spaghetti space opera, *Starcrash* (1978), and *When You Comin' Back, Red Ryder?* (1979), in which he played a crazed Vietnam vet who takes his fellow patrons hostage at a roadside diner. With the way he chose his projects, it was inevitable he would find his way into a Cannon film.

Back to the movie, in which Sean soon grows concerned that someone on the island, for some reason, has kidnapped his old sensei, Izumo. He and his pals soon abandon the karate tournament altogether, and embark on a three-man mission to infiltrate The Cobra's top secret laboratory. Standing in their way is not only an army of ninjas, but their leader, a female ninja—or "ninjette," as Jackson drolly refers to her—with the ability to change her face with the aid of lifelike masks, like a *Mission: Impossible* agent who also happens to know ninjutsu. She's played by actress Michele B. Chan, who'd previously been a regular on TV's *Danger Bay* (1985–1990), and eventually left Hollywood behind after marrying pharmaceutical billionaire Patrick Soon-Shiong, the inventor of a breakthrough cancer drug.

Steve James in *American Ninja 3*. Just how he hid those giant swords inside his skin-tight vest, we'll never know.

Beyond the numerous ninja-on-ninja beatdowns, one of the most memorable segments of *American Ninja 3* is when Sean and Dexter steal a couple of small aircraft and inject the film with a little bit of aerial action. The flight masks allow a pair of professional pilots to stand in while our actors dub

144

their lines; a contrived mishap results in Dexter having to land his plane—of all places—on the bed of Jackson's truck speeding down a roadway beneath them. The whole sequence is as exciting as it is ludicrous.

American Ninja 3: Blood Hunt is often considered the black sheep of the original American Ninja quadrilogy, primarily because this entry is Dudi-free. (Most overviews of the series don't bother to include the fifth movie, for an understandable reason—but we'll get to that shortly.) For his part, David Bradley does a fine job stepping into the empty tabi (ninja shoes) left behind after Dudikoff's departure. He's a strong martial artist, and a far better actor than, say, Chuck Norris. If the movie suffers anywhere, it's in its similarity to the prior films, and the way it recycles so much of their plots. Both the star and his director are given a better opportunity to shine with the fourth film, which strikes out in a more original direction.

It is a great send-off for Steve James, however. The musclebound actor is not only given ample opportunity to shine as a fighter, but is the source of the movie's best comedic lines —most intentional, and some perhaps not. Making his third straight stand against a mysterious ninja army, his character, Curtis Jackson, thankfully acknowledges how unbelievable it is that he finds himself in this same situation over and over again. When his new best friend confides in him that he's an orphan who was raised by his master in the way of ninjutsu, Jackson's nonchalant response is "You're a ninja? That explains a few things." (James' delivery is so dry and unimpressed-sounding, you can't help but laugh, even if the line probably wasn't intended to be quite such a zinger.) As the movie ends in its obligatory freeze-frame, he pleads with Sean that next time they're forced to fight, they try fighting something else:

"Now, look, if we're going to remain friends, can we fight other kinds of bad guys, like robbers, thieves, or muggers?" Jackson pleads. "I mean, does it *have* to be ninjas? Do you know how *long* I've been fighting ninjas? It's been a long time, pal."

There would be a next time, of course, but it sadly would not include Curtis Jackson. After a whirlwind Cannon career that included seven films in four years, sharing the screen twice with Chuck Norris and three times with

Michael Dudikoff, it was high time for the consummate sidekick to finally play the hero. Leading roles would come from other companies, but with a few familiar names: friend Sam Firstenberg would direct him in the underseen and underrated *Riverbend* (1989), and he'd play a heroic bounty hunter in *Street Hunter* (1990), produced by Menahem Golan's post-Cannon studio, 21st Century. Tragically, James was delivered a cancer diagnosis in the early 1990s, just as he was starting to establish himself as a leading man. He passed away in 1993 at the young age of 41. His funeral service was delivered by actor Sidney Poitier, a friend of the family.

American Ninja 3: Blood Hunt opened on the final weekend of February in 1989. Made for less money than its predecessor, it somewhat predictably made back less at domestic box office, failing to crack even $1 million—although video and foreign numbers boosted it more than enough to prevent the movie from being a failure.

Things would get better the fourth time around.

American Ninja 4: The Annihilation welcomes back Michael Dudikoff as O.G. American ninja Joe Armstrong. Well, at least it does for the second half of the film. Once again due to a scheduling overlap Dudikoff couldn't participate in a full shoot, and so we effectively get two mini-movies: the first half starring Bradley, the second starring Dudikoff, and culminating in a jam-packed finale featuring a team-up of American ninjas.

The film opens with an American Delta Force unit—if Cannon loved anything as much as they did ninjas, it was Delta Forces—being captured by an army of black-clad shinobi. The survivors are held for ransom by the wicked Colonel Mulgrew (James Booth), a British ex-pat and notorious arms dealer, and Sheikh Maksood (Ron Smerczak), who plans to blow up an American city with a suitcase nuke.

The last time we saw English actor James Booth on screen in a Cannon film, he was overseeing Michael Dudikoff's Matt Hunter character in *Avenging Force* (1986), which he also wrote. He'd previously penned and co-starred in *Pray for Death* (1985), one of Sho Kosugi's early post-Cannon adventures, and had been brought in by Sam Firstenberg to polish the

American Ninja 2 script. This time, he wrote himself into a gleefully hammy villain's role on *American Ninja 4*—which he penned under the pseudonym "David Geeves," to separate his on-screen role from his one off-screen. Before the *American Ninja* series, Booth was best-known for his parts in *Zulu* (1964) and *The Jazz Singer* (1980); after, his best-known work would be for playing Ernie Niles on the second season of *Twin Peaks* (1990–1991).

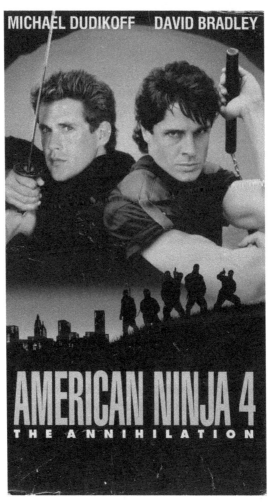

Both American Ninjas, together at last: the VHS edition of *American Ninja 4: The Annihilation*.

If we've learned anything over Cannon's last six ninja-related movies, it's that the best way to kill ninjas is with other ninjas, and so obviously it's up to our new hero, Sean Davidson (Bradley), to save the Delta Force and stop a terrorist plot. He asks his boss to recruit Joe Armstrong to assist him on the mission, but apparently Armstrong has retired from ass-kicking to join the Peace Corps. Instead, he's assigned the mostly-useless Agent Brackston (Dwayne Alexandre) to paradrop with him into enemy territory.

As in *American Ninja 2*, there's a local, streetwise kid who's integral to the American ninja's mission. Before the movie-quoting Pango (Jody Abrahams) can finish showing them around the island, Mulgrew and his minions are tipped off to their presence. With the help of an attractive Peace Corps doctor named Sarah—whose father, it turns out, was executed by Mulgrew—our heroes are able to elude the bad guys for a little while. They're eventually surrounded by their army of ninjas, however, and while Sean Davidson single-handedly whoops a respectable amount of butt, they're ultimately overpowered and taken hostage inside Mulgrew's impenetrable fortress.

If you're a horror fan and feel Doctor Sarah looks familiar, it's probably because the actress, Robin Stille, starred in the original *Slumber Party Massacre* (1982)—or, you recognize her from the ridiculously-titled *Sorority Babes in the Slimeball Bowl-o-Rama*, from 1987.

And now, the moment we've all been waiting for. With both the current American ninja and the Delta Force locked away in an enemy prison, there's only one man with the ninja training and smoldering good looks necessary to save the day. A high-ranking Special Forces officer approaches Joe Armstrong at a third world grammar school, where he's dedicated his life to teaching underprivileged children to appreciate nature. Joe is reluctant to return to his old way of life—"I told you last time it was the last time," he tells the operative, in a line that sounds like it could have been written for *MacGruber* (2010)—but he's convinced, once he's told just how many lives are on the line.

He makes his first appearance roughly 45 minutes into the 99-minute movie, yet Dudikoff still received first billing on *American Ninja 4*. That's the type of status heaped on Marlon Brando for his late appearance in *Apocalypse*

Now, which shows us just how much respect Cannon had for their blonde star at that moment in time. It's also understandable why David Bradley was said to have been somewhat resentful of Dudikoff during filming, having worked hard to make the series his own in the prior film, and then being asked to step aside and have his character be rescued by the series' original star.

A full-page ad from Cannon's 1989 pre-sales catalog advertising *American Ninja 4*.

Joe Armstrong reaches the island and enlists the help of the local resistance group, who look like they escaped from the set of a post-apocalyptic Mad Max knock-off. (They're led by Ken Gampu, last seen assisting Richard Chamberlain as Allan Quatermain's manservant, Umbopo, in the 1985 Cannon version of *King Solomon's Mines*.) The movie's lengthy climax is an all-out war inside Mulgrew's fortress, as multiple American ninjas, Delta Force commandos, and leather-clad rebels battle the baddies for control of an armed nuclear weapon.

American Ninja 4: The Annihilation has a lot going for it. Not only do you get double the number of American ninjas for your money, but fun stuff like a gratuitous bar brawl and an over-the-top, slimy villain with a whip fetish. There's also a steadier flow of action than the last time around, and it's better choreographed—Bradley, in particular, gets a handful of legitimately cool martial arts fights. On top of it all, there are some really awesome shots, like an aerial view of Mulgrew's ninjas training on a mountain. From top to bottom, this movie feels more polished than its predecessor.

Like the film preceding it, *American Ninja 4* only received a small theatrical release, but video and TV deals were enough to keep the increasingly low-cost series profitable. In fact, the *American Ninja* movies were such popular rentals that Cannon didn't even bother releasing the next one in theaters. Heck, *American Ninja 5* wasn't even meant to be an American Ninja movie at all.

Written under the hilariously goofy title "Little Ninja Man" and filmed as the more generic "American Dragons," Cannon re-named it *American Ninja 5* when they dropped it into stores on their own video label in the summer of 1993. Desperately hoping to cash in on their prior glory, they shoehorned the movie into a series with which it had no obvious link, save for the presence of star David Bradley and a smattering of pajama-clad assassins. With its pint-sized protagonist and an over-marketed appearance from actor Pat Morita, it's a movie more obviously indebted to *The Karate Kid* (1984) and its sequels than Cannon's own *American Ninja* films.

David Bradley doesn't reprise his role as the heroic Sean Davidson, but instead plays a guy named Joe—no, not Joe Armstrong, either—who works as a full-time karate instructor and a part-time ninja. His fellow instructor at the dojo is played by Tadashi Yamashita, the first movie's villainous Black Star Ninja, in case matters needed to be confused even further. (The martial arts legend also choreographed the fights here, and clearly plays a few of the ninjas that Joe later smacks around.) His master is the sage, old Tetsu, who hails from a long line of practicing ninjas, and is played by Pat Morita.

Having entered show business as a stand-up comedian, Morita first found himself in the spotlight as a recurring character on *Happy Days* (1974–1984), before briefly starring in the first Asian-American-led sitcom, *Mr. T and Tina* (1976), on ABC. He remained mostly a TV character actor until his breakthrough role as the wise Mr. Miyagi, Daniel's instructor in the smash hit *The Karate Kid*, for which he earned a nod for Best Supporting Actor, and its sequels. He became almost unbelievably prolific after this, with more than one hundred credits over the last twenty years of his life.

Near the beginning of the film, Tetsu—who is essentially Mr. Miyagi in everything but name—drops in on Joe at his dojo and tasks him with babysitting his orphaned nephew, his closest relative and the last of his ninja clan. Joe is reluctant to take on the wise-cracking tween, but Tetsu leaves Joe no choice after he uses his mystical ninja power to vanish in a puff of smoke . . . and away on a vacation.

Thirteen-year-old Lee Reyes played Hiro, the (appropriately named) hero of *American Ninja 5*. The son of legendary Tae Kwon Do master Ernie Reyes Sr., Lee had begun training with his dad from the moment he'd started walking, and was already a champion competitor by the age of ten. While his older brother, Ernie Reyes Jr., went on to a relatively prolific screen career which included the likes of *Teenage Mutant Ninja Turtles II: The Secret of the Ooze* (1991) and *Surf Ninjas* (1993), this was the younger Reyes brother's only major film role.

Joe begrudgingly drags Hiro along with him on his date with the lovely Lisa (Anne Dupont). Her father—played by Israeli actor Aharon Ipale, who had a role in Golan-Globus' early American effort, *The Happy Hooker Goes Hollywood* (1980)—is a brilliant scientist who, unfortunately, is being held hostage and forced to devise a nerve gas bomb for a terrorist general. (Stop me if you think that you've heard this one before.)

The Magic Power of the Ninja Is About to Reveal Itself...

David Bradley in

AMERICAN NINJA 5

Landing on video store shelves in 1995, *American Ninja 5* was one of the last Cannon films to hit VHS. This copy was rented out by Chief Vann Video Center of Chatsworth, Georgia.

To be honest, *American Ninja 5* suffers from having a glut of villains. There's the terrorist general (Marc Fiorini), an English arms dealer (character actor Clement von Franckenstein, who sometimes went by "Clement St. George" because he thought his real name might scare audiences), a traitorous American ambassador (Norman Burton, also of *Bloodsport* [1988]), and a mean, magical ninja known as Viper, played by prolific martial arts actor and stunt man James Lew, probably best known for his work in *Big Trouble in Little China* (1986).

The Viper dresses in a flamboyant, red outfit that looks more like the sort of cheap Dracula costume you'd buy at a pharmacy around Halloween than something a stealthy ninja assassin would wear. His ninja minions wear color-coded suits that aren't nearly as sharp as the shozoku worn by the baddies in the prior sequels, and look like they could have been purchased from a medical surplus warehouse. Anyway, the ninjas kidnap Lisa and whisk her away to Venezuela. Joe predictably does what any good ninja would do, and heads off to save her—unwittingly bringing the snot-nosed little kid along with him on his dangerous, international rescue mission.

American Ninja 5 was directed by Bob Bralver—under the pseudonym "Bobby Gene Leonard"—who had previously directed the Michael Dudikoff/ Mark Hamill thriller *Midnight Ride* (1990) for Cannon, and handled the second unit for their *Lambada* (1990). Bralver's most extensive background was as a stunt man, and it can at least be said that those are handled relatively well here: there are two pretty great chase scenes, one on a bicycle and in a van through the narrow Venezuelan streets, and another with poor Joe clinging for his dear life to the side of his own pickup truck.

This fifth movie has been considered a letdown for most fans, not only because it has nothing to do with the previous films in the series, but with its PG-13 rating—the others all received R's for violence—it's recognizably more kiddie-oriented fare. It might have a slightly better reputation today as a piece of occasionally enjoyable, family-friendly fluff, had there been no ham-fisted attempt to shoehorn it into a long-established and well-loved franchise. Shot in 1992, the picture languished on the shelf as "American

Dragons" while the remains of Cannon unceremoniously folded around it. Somebody eventually slapped the "American Ninja" name on it in hopes of milking whatever last cash they could out of a dying brand. The video release didn't hit rental store shelves until 1995.

In the years before his death in 2014, Menahem Golan made efforts to try and continue the series—both with and without Michael Dudikoff—but those never came to fruition, and so this is where the *American Ninja* saga ends.

While it's certainly an underwhelming and disappointing way to bring Cannon's prolific ninja oeuvre to a close, *American Ninja 5* makes a lot of sense when you consider the direction in which the ninja phenomenon had been trending. If you read the chapter on *Enter the Ninja* (1981) in the first volume of *The Cannon Film Guide*, you'll know that Cannon was mostly responsible for the ninja craze that dominated American pop culture from the early Eighties through the mid-Nineties. As unlikely as it sounds, Menahem Golan—via Mike Stone and Sho Kosugi—effectively brought ninjas to the West, putting them front and center in their own movie. From there they exploded into every imaginable facet of entertainment, and the traditional Japanese assassins suddenly could not only be found in countless, low-budget action movies—eight of those from Cannon themselves—but in comic books, video games, and on Saturday morning television. It's these latter developments that eventually brought us to *American Ninja 5*.

By the turn of the decade, ninjas had been so wholly co-opted by kids' entertainment—thanks, in no small part, to the massive popularity of the Teenage Mutant Ninja Turtles cartoon and toy line—that the primary audience for ninja movies had become children. (See: the live-action Turtles movies, *3 Ninjas* [1992], *3 Ninjas Kick Back* [1994], and *Surf Ninjas* [1993].) In a few short years, the best on-screen representation our favorite shozoku-clad assassins could muster would be getting slapped around by Chris Farley in the parody film *Beverly Hills Ninja* (1997). The ninja craze was dead.

At the start of the *American Ninja* franchise, Cannon made a defining entry into an action movie genre that they themselves had popularized. By the end of it, they were chasing a trend that was already arguably beyond its expiration date. I'll pose this to you, folks: could there be a more Cannon-appropriate coda to the series than that?

A press photo of Michael Dudikoff as Joe Armstrong, *American Ninja*.

Interview: Actor Michael Dudikoff

If one were to find a side of a mountain and carve a Mount Rushmore-like tribute to Cannon's biggest stars, Michael Dudikoff's face would be chiseled into the cliffside next to Chuck Norris and Charles Bronson's. Dudikoff arrived at Cannon at just the right time, when the company needed a young actor upon whom they could pin the fortunes of an all-new action franchise. In him, they found a new kind of hero.

Dudikoff was a California boy who had been studying to become a child psychologist when a patron at the restaurant where he'd been waiting tables recruited him as a fashion model. His attention soon turned to acting. As he worked hard to learn and improve his craft, he began to land roles in films and on television shows. With a background primarily in comedies such as *Happy Days* (1974–1984) and *Bachelor Party* (1984), his emergence as one of the great action stars of the 1980s came as something of a surprise. With the success of *American Ninja* (1985), Dudikoff became one of Cannon's go-to action heroes. He starred in the first, second, and fourth installments of that series for Cannon, as well as in *Avenging Force* (1986), *Platoon Leader* (1988), *River of Death* (1989), *Midnight Ride* (1992), *The Human Shield* (1992), *Rescue Me* (1992), and *Chain of Command* (1994).

American Ninja is the film that would forever change the course of your career. Is it true that you almost walked away from that audition before you even got into the room?

Michael Dudikoff: I remember riding my motorcycle up to the gymnasium where they were holding the auditions. Coming out of every orifice of that gym were lines that seemed to stretch on forever. I thought, "Oh gosh. This is going to be a crazy scene." Then once I walked up to one of the doors and went inside to look, I saw people doing flips. It was really crazy. I'm not a guy who does flips or backflips, or anything like that.

I started walking away when Mike Stone—great guy, great choreographer—came up to me and said, "Hey, where are you going?" I guess he thought, "This guy is interesting, so I'm going to go take a look at him." He brought me back in and he said, "Why are you leaving?" I just told him, "I don't know if I'm the gymnast that you need for this project."

When I started out in this business, it was all in comedy. So, here I am going up for some action movie, which was totally not my style. I'd never done an action movie. It was pretty different than what I'd done before. Once Mike Stone convinced me to come back, he said, "Can you do this?" He started doing a somersault, and came up to the heavy bag and started kicking it—a spinning heel kick and front kick, and hit it with a couple more strikes. I said, "Can I see you just do that one more time?" He stood way back—about five, six, maybe ten feet back—and he ran and did a somersault, rolled up to the heavy bag, kicked it and did the same old thing. Then I said, "Can I see it just *one more* time?" He did it one more time, and gave me a little look that was like, "Hmm, okay."

I did it. I had memorized it, and I did it the first time. He says, "I thought you said you couldn't do it?" I said, "Well, I didn't say I *couldn't* do it, but I would give it my best shot." He said, "Well, you did a really good job." I said, "Well, thank you very much." I shook his hand and left.

I got a callback. When I got the callback, they wanted to make sure that I knew how to act. I was in acting school every day of my life once I got into this business. I first started on *Happy Days*, and I put every penny I made into my acting career. I went to acting schools with Harvey Lembeck and Vince Chase—I went everywhere, studying and studying and reading and reading. I thought, I've got to be good if I'm going to be able to get job after job, and so I started studying like crazy. The next thing you know, I was getting one project after the other. It wasn't just action, it was everything—but Cannon really wanted me to have a lot of action projects.

Like you said, you weren't necessarily a gymnast or martial artist, but you were able to train with Mike Stone for *American Ninja*. Was it important to you to learn as much as you could from him?

Mike Stone is a legend—he won ninety-one straight fights, no losses. What a great man. Every day we'd jog and run. We would do a lot of stretching, because I had to throw those kicks and that wasn't part of my background. I wasn't really a martial artist, and he had to work really hard with me. I was always asking him things to make sure I knew every detail of a move. "Is it going to be a vertical punch? What kind of a downward sweep will I be doing?" I was very interested in making sure that I did everything right.

This was Cannon, so you have to realize we didn't have a lot of time to prepare before we had to shoot. They'd just go, "Here you go, do it." Gosh, I would be up late into the night in my room at the hotel, just stretching and doing everything else I needed to do to prepare, like going over my lines and practicing my movements.

I always memorized the whole script before I even got there, because I knew how Cannon worked. We may start with the end of the movie on the first day, and I better know what I'm going to do and what my character is feeling at the end of the movie. I was constantly making sure that I was completely prepared, no matter where they started. They could say, "Mike, is it okay if we start here?" and I could tell them, "We can start anywhere you want, just let me know where."

If I knew I was going to the Philippines, I would have that script read. Before I even got on the plane, I knew all of my lines. I'd have all my notes in there from the director. It was that way on every film—Africa, Israel, no matter where I went, I made sure the script was memorized so I could get in there and just be there with the director, with the stunt crew, and really give them all of my energy, so I could be the best that I could be. That's pretty much what I teach my kids, too. In order to be the best you can be, you've got to work hard.

A Yugoslavian lobby card featuring Michael Dudikoff in *Avenging Force*.

It seems that your devoted work ethic always paid off.

I think that's one of the reasons why Cannon liked me so much. Menahem used to say, "Michael, you're always so prepared. You come early, you know your lines, you work hard, and I like this. Thank you so much." He used to always just thank me for working so hard. He'd go, "You're going to be a big star. You're going to work with many people." He kept repeating that to me, "You're going to be a big star, Michael." He really loved me, and I loved him.

I loved Yoram, too. Yoram was the man behind the money and the finances. Menahem would just go to him and say, "Here, I want to do this," after he'd made a deal on a napkin. Poor Yoram was the guy who had to make it work, financially, and he always did. He was always gracious. I can tell you, I never had a bad moment with them. It was always good, even all the way until Menahem's last days. He was a special guy.

You were one of Cannon's biggest stars, and the only one whose action career initially blossomed at Cannon. Can you tell me what your personal relationships with Menahem and Yoram were like?

Menahem and Yoram were definitely a pair, two peas in a pod. I really enjoyed them. They were different, though: Menahem was way different than Yoram. Menahem wanted to do everything *right now*. He'd get very excited. The way that Menahem would do things was often like, "Forget about a contract. Let's sign on this napkin. Let's do it right now. I'll give you this much!"

Sometimes what he'd offer you was way too much money—he wouldn't slow down to see what the other guy was going to propose before shooting out numbers. I saw him shoot out numbers and people would almost be like, "Okay, let's do that right now. Like, yesterday." That must have driven Yoram a little crazy, because he was the money man.

I really miss those guys—I miss them a lot. They would call me in, and we'd have lunch in their office. We'd be telling jokes while eating. Menahem would say, "I'm going to put your picture on a poster. You're going to be the next Spider-Man." I'd go, "Oh, okay, that sounds good!" Then it was, "You're going to be the next Superman. You're going to be the next—" He wanted me to do everything. I mean, he really wanted me to do so much for them.

I was supposed to work with Charlie Bronson a few times. I really wanted to work with Charlie. I met him, and he was just a really neat guy. I was supposed to be in so many things that never happened, but it was fun. I mean, Chuck Norris was supposed to be the *American Ninja*, but he didn't want to cover his face, so they got me. [*Laughs*] I was fine with that. I just wanted to have fun and act. Acting is a lot of fun.

I was very humble. I was very thankful just to be in a position where I could work like this. I did everything I could to stand out, so that they would really believe in me and in my acting ability.

From _American Ninja_ through its first sequel and _Avenging Force_, you and Steve James formed one of my favorite action duos.

Oh my God, Steve James. He was my best friend. He was the most beautiful man. We had such a great relationship. We ate together, we worked out together, we talked, and we meditated. We were just two brothers. He used to say to me, "Hey, Mike, my brother from another mother!" He always had open arms. Just a great guy.

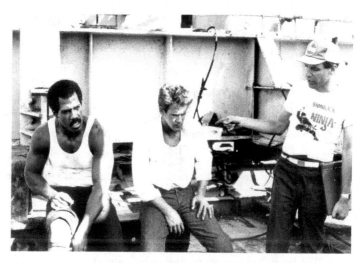

Sam Firstenberg (right) directs Steve James and Michael Dudikoff, on the set of _Avenging Force_. Photo courtesy of Sam Firstenberg.

I remember there was a scene where he had a shirt on and I was all dressed up, and we did some action. We came back out and we're in this hallway, and his shirt's gone. I go, "Steve, the continuity is not going to work here. Where's your shirt?" He goes, "Brother, I worked really hard for this body, and you know it. I don't give a damn about that shirt." [_Laughs_] I go, "Okay. I guess if it's okay with everybody else, continuity, shmontinuity." He was a wonderful guy. We really had a great respect towards one another.

It's clear you had a special relationship with Sam Firstenberg. He cast you in *American Ninja*, and you did several more films together after that.

Shmulik has always been a very creative guy, and he always knows what he wants. You want to work with a director who is prepared. No matter what changes come, he's got another option, or he's got other choices. What's good is that you can collaborate with him: Shmulik always just let me do what I needed to do. Sometimes we would collaborate on scenes to figure out how we should do them, and I liked that about him. He was always smiling, and always in a good mood, because he knew what he was doing. He was always prepared and that's the way you have to be.

Avenging Force came up, of course, and I did a lot of action in that. I even swam with the water moccasins in the bayous. There were times when I was in a boat and they were filming, and I had to get into the water, and there would be a water moccasin right there, looking up at me. Sam would say, "Michael, action on you." And I go, "Sam, I can't get in yet. There's a water moccasin looking right at me." He giggles a little then goes, "Okay, action when you're ready." I went ahead and got in, even though I knew there were tons of water moccasin snakes in that water. I went in and went across the bay and came out and did what I had to do.

There were a number of occasions like that where I went into different places where it was very dangerous. There was a place in Cape Town where we filmed *American Ninja 2*, where there was an inlet. There was a boat with a camera and I had to jump into the water. First, I had to make sure there were no pipes in the water, because I didn't want to get speared. I wanted to make sure there was nothing that was going to hurt me when I jumped in. Second, I needed to know how deep it was.

BJ Davis was the choreographer and a stuntman, and he said, "I've been in there with tanks, Mike. There's nothing in there." I really trusted him. He was very good, so I went ahead and jumped in. After I jumped there was a boat waiting for me, and I got into that boat so fast. As soon as I was in the boat, I looked back behind me at where I had left the water—there were sharks all over. [*Laughs*] It turns out this was actually a breeding ground for sharks. At high tide, this whole inlet filled and that's when the sharks would come in. I couldn't believe it.

You traveled to so many different countries and worked with so many people during your time with Cannon. Are there memories from those times that hold a special meaning for you?

I look back now at my life and what I went through, and I think about my experiences on all of those films and the people I met, from Israel to Africa to the Philippines. I am so fortunate to have had all of that time in those places and all those chances to meet such wonderful people. I'm so thankful for all of that, because through those people I met, the ups and downs of it all, it gave me so much substance. It gave me so much to build on, to be the man and the father that I am today.

I was in the Philippines during the Marxist regime. I was in South Africa during the apartheid. I was in Israel when a missile went over the Dan Hotel and I thought I was going to die. I was always where the action was, and through it all I was positive. I was with the right people. All of that helped me become who I am today. I am so, so thankful for all of the experiences that I had. I'm a very blessed person. I don't know what else to say. I'm really humbled by everything that I went through in my life with Cannon, and in the whole business.

Sam Firstenberg and Michael Dudikoff during the making of *American Ninja 2: The Confrontation*. Photo courtesy of Sam Firstenberg.

Interview: Director Sam Firstenberg

Having helmed eight films for the company between 1983 and 1992, Sam "Shmulik" Firstenberg is tied with J. Lee Thompson as Cannon's most prolific director. His time with Golan and Globus predated Cannon, however, by more than a decade, having worked in Israel with the filmmaking cousins—in every imaginable role, from courier to assistant director—since the early 1970s. He briefly stepped away to attend film school and make his debut feature, *One More Chance* (1981), but soon returned to them to direct his first action movie, the Sho Kosugi classic *Revenge of the Ninja* (1983), for their newly-acquired Cannon. Showing a special talent for delivering fast-paced, visually-exciting stories on budget and on schedule, he would find himself hired by Cannon on one project after another, including *Ninja III: The Domination* (1984) and *Breakin' 2: Electric Boogaloo* (1984) in rapid succession.

Although he never set out specifically to become an action director, Firstenberg earned his place among the living ambassadors of '80s action cinema. His films covered in this book include *American Ninja* (1985), *Avenging Force* (1986), *American Ninja 2: The Confrontation* (1987), and *Delta Force 3: The Killing Game* (1991). He also directed *American Samurai* (1992) in the company's waning years. Several of his projects away from Cannon include *Riverbend* (1989), *Cyborg Cop* (1993), and *Quicksand* (2002), all of which starred fellow veterans of the company's films. In total, Firstenberg has directed twenty-two feature-length films to date.

Detailed chapters on Firstenberg's early Cannon works can be read in this series' first volume. Anyone interested in further reading on the entirety of his illustrious career are encouraged to seek out Marco Seidelmann's massive book, *Stories from the Trenches*, which provides a wonderfully comprehensive examination of his filmography.

Breakin' 2 gave you a short break from ninjas. How did you feel about returning to them afterwards with *American Ninja*?

Sam Firstenberg: I didn't think twice about it. I'm a director. Those weren't my ideas or my scripts. Unless they told me to direct a porno, I wouldn't reject the idea. [*Laughs*] I thought, "Okay, let's go make *American Ninja.*" That's the profession of a director.

This time around you were working with Tadashi Yamashita, who along with Sho Kosugi is one of the premiere movie ninjas. What was he like?

Tadashi's a low-key person. Sho was more of a showman. Tadashi had made movies before, of course, it was not his first movie. He'd worked with Chuck Norris. But he was a low-key person. He'd come to the set and do what he needed to do. He was a very respectful and pleasant person to talk to. But he wasn't the star of the movie, anyway. The movie starred Michael Dudikoff and Steve James.

Tadashi just went along with everything. He had more contact with Mike Stone, the choreographer—they're both real martial artists. It was more their world. I didn't have to deal with him like I did with Sho Kosugi, who was the star of his movie. Tadashi was the villain, and he was a very professional and pleasant man to work with. We're still in touch to this day.

You've told the story about meeting Michael Dudikoff at his audition for *American Ninja* and instantly knowing he was perfect for that role. However, *American Ninja* was also a breakout role for Steve James. How did you find him?

There are many things I don't remember, but I remember Steve's audition. [*Laughs*] First the actors met with Mike Stone, just to check their martial arts before they came in to do their reading. In comes this guy, big-bodied, all muscle. He tells us right away, "I am a real martial artist. My style is Tiger Style," or whatever. He showed us some moves and did the reading, and in my mind that was it. We didn't have to see anyone else for the part. It was one of those rare, instant feelings of "Wow, you are the guy. If you're willing to do it, you can have the part." I also thought there would be good chemistry between him and Michael Dudikoff.

When you watch some of the other movies Steve did without him, including Cannon films like *P.O.W. The Escape* and *Hero and the Terror*,

164

Steve James always seems to outshine the primary hero. I think it says a lot about Michael that he was able to share the screen with him and hold equal footing. They had great chemistry.

Both Steve James and Michael Dudikoff have strong screen presence. Both of them, but in different ways. They don't compete. Steve shines on the screen and has a screen presence because of his body, and the outward energy and power he projects. Michael is exactly the opposite: he's the James Dean type. He grabs your attention *because* he's the underdog, *because* he's the guy with a chip on his shoulder. He's a James Dean-ish character. So, they didn't have to compete with each other because they had screen presences of different qualities, so to speak. It just so happened then that the chemistry between them was fantastic. They complemented each other and it worked. You believed the friendship that they forged in *American Ninja*.

When *American Ninja 2* came along, it felt to me like the tone shifted. It was a lot lighter, with things like the little kid and the bar brawl.

Yes, yes. Let's put it this way. Number one: it's not the same writer. *American Ninja* was Paul De Mielche, *American Ninja 2* was Gary Conway. When you have different writers, you get a different tone. For the first movie we went to the Philippines and we had this story of a reluctant hero who doesn't want to get involved. If you have a second story, he can no longer be a reluctant hero because we already know who he is. [*Laughs*] This time, we went to South Africa because there was some money there, or whatever. The money determined that we'd go to South Africa. We did not want to shoot a story about South Africa, so we turned it into an exotic island, and the fact that you're in an exotic island, vacation-type setting automatically sets a different tone for the movie.

Also, the idea for cyber-ninjas popped up somewhere. It really takes the whole subject farther away from reality. Where the first one was still anchored in a military environment, the second one had already moved into the territory of mad scientists, so the whole tone became less serious.

The German VHS cover for *American Ninja 2*, which featured artwork by the late, great poster artist Enzo Sciotti.

Mike Stone had been working behind-the-scenes on Cannon's ninja movies for years, but this was the first time he got to appear in one. Do you recall if he was happy to finally get his turn in front of the camera?

To the best of my knowledge, Mike Stone is the one who brought the idea for ninja movies to Cannon in the first place, with *Enter the Ninja*. He was going to be the hero of that one for a while—he wanted to be the next

Jackie Chan or Chuck Norris—but he didn't have any acting background or experience. For some reason, in the Philippines, Menahem Golan decided to switch actors. He'd met Franco Nero right there at a festival in Manila and decided to have him be the hero instead of Mike Stone. He stayed as the choreographer.

For *Revenge of the Ninja*, Sho Kosugi was the choreographer, so we didn't need Mike Stone anymore. With *Ninja III*, between Sho and Steve Lambert we didn't need Mike Stone. Also in the martial arts world, there are lots of rivalries. [*Laughs*] It was not good to have Mike Stone and Sho Kosugi together in the same place.

When we got back to do *American Ninja*, we no longer had Sho Kosugi. I was talking to people in the company and said, "How about we look for Mike Stone for the project? It sounds like he's very knowledgeable, since he choreographed the first movie and he's a master in martial arts." They thought it was a good idea, so we looked for him and found him. I told him, "I like what you do. We have this new idea for a movie about an American ninja, why don't you come?" We also had to train Michael Dudikoff. But, he said he didn't want to be in it. We almost cast him in the Tadashi Yamashita part, but he didn't want to do it. He said he knew someone that would be good for it, and brought in Tadashi. They knew each other.

For the next movie we went to South Africa, and for some reason he seemed to change his mind and said, "Okay, I'll play the villain." [*Laughs*] So it wasn't like he was waiting for his chance—he *agreed* to be in the movie. He was gracious enough to do it for us.

When you decided to walk away from the *American Ninja* series after the second film, was it solely because they wanted to go lower budget with them?

Absolutely. At this point, Cannon was here [in the U.S.] and the company that became Nu Image—it was called Nu Metro then—was in South Africa, and they worked together. There was some kind of money in South Africa, tax shelter, et cetera. Cannon had made those two *American Ninja* movies and they were very successful, but for some reason they decided to kill the goose that lays the golden eggs. They wanted to see how many golden eggs they could get for the minimum amount of investment. [*Laughs*] Basically they handed it over to Nu Metro in South Africa. They thought if you used less budget and a shorter schedule and mostly South Africans, they'd make more money. A studio would never do that. A studio would put *more* money into every sequel. Obviously it was the wrong approach, by what we know today, but that's what they decided at the time.

By then I was getting a lot of money to direct movies, about $100,000 to direct a movie. I was in the union and they had to pay my fees, my insurance, my pension, et cetera. And so turning it all over to South Africa, finding a director there—and not just the director, but almost everybody. Everyone except for a few of the stars came from South Africa. Labor was very cheap there at the time. It was an extremely cheap way to make movies, and they'd shoot them in only five weeks.

That sounds break-neck, even by Cannon's standards.

Yeah, they just gave them to Nu Metro. "Go ahead, make movies for us." It was like they were a subcontractor.

You also made *Avenging Force* for Cannon around that time. It's one of my favorite Cannon movies, and it sounds like it's one of your own favorites of the movies you've made. It started as a script called *Night Hunter* and was meant for Chuck Norris, but it was given to you and re-tooled as a vehicle for Michael Dudikoff and Steve James. Would you consider it the best screenplay you worked on for Cannon?

Not maybe. *Definitely*. It was written by James Booth and we didn't have to change one word in the script. The movie you see is exactly what we got in the script. Actually, there was only one change. When it was for Chuck Norris, it was supposed to be his daughter [who gets captured.] Michael was too young to have a daughter, so we changed it to his sister.

Usually in a movie we have to make all kinds of changes for budgetary reasons, or because of actors or locations. The finished movie is usually not the script we started with because so many things happen. In this case we did not have to change one word.

I had a big fight with Cannon. The script was written for New Orleans, but they didn't want to go there because it was expensive. I had many arguments with Menahem until he gave up. We went to New Orleans with a nine week schedule and a big budget—at the time, this was close to $9 million. For us, it was a tremendous, big budget movie. This was just a great script, and the feelings were so good. We didn't even have to fix anything in editing. Everything was as we shot it.

Do you know if James Booth's script was always meant for Matt Hunter, Chuck Norris' *Invasion U.S.A.* character, or if they changed it to fit him?

I'm not sure. The way Cannon operated, they'd find their scripts. James Booth probably brought them the script and they said, "Okay, but we need to squeeze it into this Chuck Norris series somehow." Maybe they changed a few things, but it was before I was involved. That's just how Cannon did things. They'd say, "Let's do this, let's do that." There are many posters for movies that never existed. Chuck Norris was supposed to be the American Ninja, but when it didn't work, they adapted.

A striking shot from *Avenging Force*'s rainy battle in the swamps of Louisiana.

Why the *Night Hunter* script didn't work for Chuck Norris, I don't know, but they gave it to me to see if we could adapt it for Michael and Steve and we made the movie. But I don't know the whole background with *Avenging Force* and Chuck Norris. In the Cannon history, that all ran parallel with *American Ninja*.

Can you tell me about working with John P. Ryan? No one plays a wild-eyed, crazy villain quite like he does.

When I got the script, we needed a villain. This time we were casting a little more seriously. It was easier to cast a script like this than a ninja movie, because not every actor wanted to be in a ninja movie. I'd seen *Runaway Train*, another Cannon movie where he was the villain, and I really wanted him. Moni Mansano, the makeup artist from *Runaway Train*, was working with us here, and I asked him to make a personal connection between me and John Ryan. A meeting was arranged for us. I wanted to take him to lunch but he insisted on doing it in our office. He said, "I don't want to do a lunch meeting, a coffee meeting. Let's make it a business meeting." He was a sweetheart of a man. In real life he was nothing like the characters he played. Nothing. He was a gentle intellectual!

It was a pleasure to work with him. He was a real actor's actor. He had this schizophrenic quality of being able to transform from John Ryan totally into his character. Until you said "cut," he was mentally and psychologically another person.

***Avenging Force* ends on a somewhat open note, with Michael Dudikoff's character reminding the Admiral that there's still a fifth member of Pentangle alive out there. The movie seems to imply that James Booth's character, the Admiral, was the fifth member. Am I right about that?**

That's right. It's from the script. When James Booth was writing it he hoped it would become a series, and was trying to arrange more acting jobs for himself. [*Laughs*] So, yes. But it was also the correct way to do it. It added tension.

It sounds like the Cannon offices were a hustling and bustling place in their heyday, with so many projects going on at once. I know you remain

friends with many of the actors and crew members you worked with directly on your films, but did you build any lasting friendships with anyone working on other projects at Cannon at the time?

Cannon was like a train station. It was unbelievable. At some time the madness and chaos was indescribable. They had a board with all of the movies they currently had in production, pre-production and post-production, and it was unbelievable.

Along the corridors there were many, many editing rooms. Now, the only time directors could meet other directors was during editing. Directing is usually a lonely job, the only time you usually met other directors was at functions for the Director's Guild. I was lucky enough, though, in the corridors I met Tobe Hooper and Joey Zito, and we became friends. Later on I was Tobe's second unit director on *Crocodile* (2000). I met Albert Pyun. We didn't really get to meet many other actors. One time I visited a set with Charles Bronson, but I didn't become friends with Charles Bronson. I met Chuck Norris a few times, and I met Aaron Norris many times—he was another director in the corridors at Cannon. The only actor I would see is Chuck Norris, because he had an office at Cannon. He was an exception.

It was nice that I became friends with Tobe Hooper, Albert Pyun, and Joe Zito. We were kind of a group. We were "the Cannon directors."

Interview: Actor and Martial Arts Choreographer Mike Stone

The Hawaiian-born Mike Stone is one of the most legendary tournament fighters in the history of karate. A famously aggressive fighter, he earned the nickname "The Animal" during a record-setting win streak starting in the 1960s that lasted ninety-one consecutive wins without a single defeat. As recently as the last decade, *Black Belt* magazine has speculated that Stone might have been the best karate fighter of all time.

Stone has the distinction of being the man who brought the idea for ninja films to Cannon, via his screenplay "Dance of Death," which eventually became *Enter the Ninja* (1981). As chronicled in the corresponding chapter in the first volume of *The Cannon Film Guide*, that film ignited the ninja craze of the 1980s—so, you could say that Mike Stone was directly responsible for the explosive popularity of ninjas throughout Western pop culture over the next two decades.

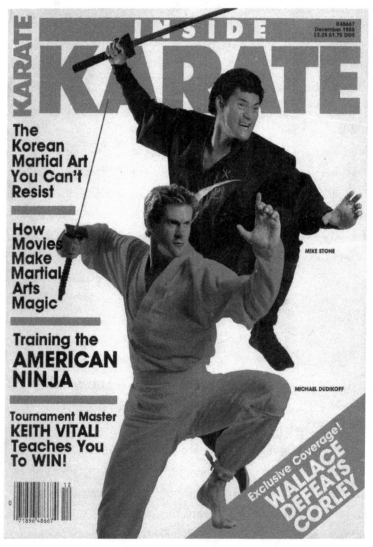

Inside Karate's December 1985 issue featured Mike Stone and
Michael Dudikoff on its cover, and contained an article on the
making of *American Ninja*.

Following *Enter the Ninja*, Stone worked with Cannon in numerous capacities throughout the *American Ninja* franchise, including as a trainer, fight choreographer, second unit director, and even actor—playing the evil ninja leader, Tojo Ken, in *American Ninja 2: The Confrontation* (1987).

You worked on *The Wrecking Crew* (1968), which utilized a legendary group of West Coast martial artists including yourself, Bruce Lee, and Chuck Norris. What was the karate scene like there at the time? Was there a friendly competition between you?

Mike Stone: The atmosphere was always friendly. I personally did not sense any feeling of competition with anyone. I was hired to be a stunt double for Dean Martin and I did what Bruce choreographed for me to do for Dean's character. It was great to be with martial arts friends, it made the experience so much fun and enjoyable to do.

After retiring as one of the greatest competitors in the history of the sport, it seems like you dedicated much of your time to promoting karate. Was Hollywood one of the ways you planned on raising public awareness of martial arts?

Hollywood, and particularly the movie industry, allowed for the greatest exposure to the general public. The normal avenues for getting exposure are limited, compared to what a movie can provide.

***Enter the Ninja* is widely credited for kicking off the ninja craze of the 1980s, as ninjas appeared in so many TV shows, comic books, cartoons, and movies afterward. Cannon often receives credit for introducing ninja movies to the West, but you introduced ninjas to Cannon. When and how did you first learn about ninjas?**

I was always fascinated with the mysticism of the oriental cultures and disciplines as a child, growing up in Hawaii. I love watching Japanese samurai movies in which ninjas were portrayed as the "bad guys." I was intrigued by stories of what they actually did in real life. The discipline, courage, persistence, and determination, but more importantly the simplicity, patience, and compassion they demonstrated and lived. I saw the potential for self-realization, and improvements in all areas and aspects of my life.

Can you tell me more about the inspiration that led you to come up with your "Dance of Death" script?

It was just a thought I had. I envisioned a movie made with a good story and physical precision in executing flawless, fluid, lightning-fast, yet powerful strikes and techniques.

Unless you have the [star power] of a Brad Pitt or Tom Cruise [behind you] when you sell your script, it is no longer your property. The people who control the money control what is seen, with major consideration for its budget, as it should be. I have no regrets. I was blessed with at least having an opportunity to participate, and for this I am truly grateful.

Did you approach Cannon with the idea yourself?

Yes.

Did you need to convince Menahem Golan that the idea would work?

No, allow me to explain.

Yes, I did approach Cannon, but not in a conventional way. I was walking past Cannon's office on Sunset, during lunch hour with script in hand. I went upstairs into their offices, there were very few people there. I lied to the receptionist when she asked if I had an appointment. She asked who I had the appointment with, and I said I had forgotten her name. Then she asked for my name, then repeated it loudly, as if to warn someone else in the office who may be expecting me. I heard a woman's voice from behind a partitioned wall. "Mike Stone, the real Mike Stone, the karate champion?" I said, yes, I was. Then the faceless voice said, "Have him come in." The voice belonged to Priscilla McDonald, a close friend of Menahem Golan.

We chatted a few minutes about her karate instructor, Gordon Duvasola, who ran a karate school a few blocks down from Cannon's offices. She said Gordon had posted several pictures of me in his school. Gordon and I were both from Hawaii.

Anyway, Priscilla said she could not promise anything, but she was on her way to the Canadian Film Festival to meet with her boss and would read my script, and if she liked it, would pass it on to Menahem. In a few weeks, I was contacted to meet with Menahem at Cannon. And, as they say, "the rest is history."

It was initially announced that you would star in the film, but that didn't happen. What changed?

I'm sure there were many considerations. In hindsight, there was no way I would ever be the leading man in any movie. I was naive enough to believe Hollywood bullshit. They really wanted and needed my knowledge and expertise to make it work, as there was no one at that time in the martial arts scene who knew enough about the subject matter, or had the physical abilities to do what was needed.

How different was *Enter the Ninja* from what you originally envisioned?

Very different.

Did many of your original ideas carry over to the film?

No, other than the basic storyline and what I imagined many of the fight and action sequences would be. Menahem was directing and rewriting the script daily as we shot.

You were also the one who introduced Sho Kosugi to Golan and Globus.

Yes. The guy I originally wanted to use as the "bad" ninja was one of my instructors, Tadashi Yamashita, but he refused, not wanting to be the villain.

Were the two of you friends?

Were we friends? Yes, I believe we were. Are we still friends? As far as I know, but you'd have to ask him that.

You returned to Cannon with their *American Ninja* series, working on the first four films in numerous capacities. How did they bring you back for those movies?

If they could have found another person to do what I could contribute, they might not have hired me. They apparently still needed my knowledge and expertise to make it work.

Michael Dudikoff was not a trained martial artist, but the filmmakers were confident enough to cast him because they knew you could teach him

enough to look convincing by the time it came to shoot. Can you tell me about training him for these movies?

I personally like Michael a lot. He was very open to learning and a good student. Before leaving for the Philippines, I trained Michael for a couple of months at Ed Anders' karate school on Ventura Boulevard, in North Hollywood. Ed was another martial artist I took to help with the fight scenes, and to double Michael in a few fight scenes.

What is the biggest difference between training someone for the screen versus training someone to compete?

Big difference, primarily in the mindset. It helps if the actor is physical and competitive, but the overall objective between the two disciplines are far apart. An actor can "get by" with minimum skills and abilities, along with the trained skills of a fighter or stuntman, which gives authenticity and quality to movements. It's just a different animal.

You have a memorable sword fight with Michael Dudikoff in *American Ninja 2*. It's a very elegant style of fighting, which almost reminds me of a samurai film. Can you tell me any memories you have from choreographing this climactic battle?

Yes, as I mentioned, I was strongly influenced by watching samurai and martial arts movies, and I trained in Kendo, so I think it's easy to see those influences projected on the scene.

You're working on your autobiography. You've led an incredible life. Would you ever want to see a movie about the life of Mike Stone during your lifetime?

I have been in the past, and am currently talking with two groups about that possibility. It would be nice, but I personally don't need to have it done for any particular reason. I'm good with who I have become.

Joe Armstrong restrains Patricia Hickock (Judie Aronson) from screaming in *American Ninja*.

Interview: Actress Judie Aronson

At the start of her career, actress Judie Aronson made three, rapid-fire appearances in a sort of holy trinity of '80s cult movie genres: the slasher, the John Hughes teen flick, and the action hero film. Her first role was in *Friday the 13th: The Final Chapter* (1984), where she was killed in an inflatable raft by an aquatic Jason Voorhees. She followed this up with a role in Hughes' *Weird Science* (1985), playing one of the cheerleaders who inspire Anthony Michael Hall and Ilan Mitchell-Smith to program the artificial woman of their dreams. Finally, she was cast as Patricia Hickock, the daughter of an American colonel, who becomes romantically entangled with Joe Armstrong (Michael Dudikoff) in the original *American Ninja* (1985).

Aronson remained very busy in both film and television for the next decade, which included a role in *Desert Kickboxer* (1992) for 21st Century Films, Menahem Golan's post-Cannon enterprise. The roles slowed as her attentions were drawn away by a series of business startups: first, gift shops, and then a chain of Pilates studios. For all of her success on screen, Aronson has achieved even greater heights as an entrepreneur.

You grew up in Los Angeles, so I imagine Hollywood didn't feel as far away to you as some actors I've talked to.

Judie Aronson: No, I grew up with a lot of people that were in the industry. Nobody in my family was, but a lot of people I went to school with. Then I was a theater major at UCLA, so I actually went to school with so many people that later became quite famous, like Mariska Hargitay, Daphne Zuniga, Tim Robbins. Lisa Wilcox. So many people. It was a fun time.

Then, going to acting classes outside of UCLA, I was in classes with so many people who have gone off to do phenomenal work. I remember when George Clooney had just gotten here, and we were in that class. He didn't even have money for a car. He only rode a motorcycle at the time. Brad Pitt was in one of my classes for a long time.

Can you tell me about your audition for *American Ninja*? Do you remember any details?

The actual audition was in Hollywood. I auditioned with several men for the role and one of them was Chad McQueen. He actually was one of the finalists to get the role, and he and I worked together. We became pretty good friends during that time. He was such a nice guy. We had a lot of fun together, and I really thought he was going to get the part. Then they put me with Michael.

I remember wanting to mention something to Menahem Golan about who I was, because I could tell he didn't realize how well he knew me. He didn't realize who I was. One of his daughters [Yael Golan] was one of my best friends in elementary school, when I was in fourth grade.

It's a small world!

Yes! I used to sleep at their house all the time. I remember him getting ready for the Golden Globe awards, and I was just totally enthralled. I remember I was at their house many, many, many times, and slept over many times. I just knew of him as being this man to whom everything was about film. He was very absent-minded, other than when something had to do with the film industry and movies. That's all he talked about. When I say absent-minded, I have this wonderful story: I remember Yael telling me that he had once opened up a can of what he thought was tuna and ate it, and realized that it was cat food afterwards.

He just didn't pay attention to everything. I wouldn't say that he was absent-minded about anything that had to do with film. It's just that it was always such a focus, that everything else was a little bit insignificant.

He was always working on so many films at once. I don't think my brain could process one quarter of the stuff he must have been thinking about at all times.

I picture him always coming into the rooms, and he was always doing something, always busy. I remember that. I had been there so much, and I remember being so excited seeing all his awards in the living room, but when I auditioned for *American Ninja*, he didn't know who I was. He had no idea. I remember calling Yael up and going, "I just auditioned for his movie and I got it."

Did he ever figure out who you were?

I don't know. I'd never once spoken to him. He was never around. By then, my friend didn't live with him because she was older, and I don't remember ever seeing him again.

Actually, this is funny. I just found a diary. Literally last week, I found a diary of mine, a journal that I wrote when I was, I think, in fourth grade, and it talks about the time that I was an extra. It was my first time in front of a camera, and my mother and I were extras in Menahem's film called *Lepke* (1975). Later on I found out that Shmulik [Sam Firstenberg] had worked on that back in the day. It was one of the first things he ever did working behind a camera. I think he was a PA only at the time.

My mother and I, because of being friends with the Golans, were asked to be extras in it, which just meant the world to me. I didn't know the difference between an extra, an actor, or any of that. It was just so exciting to be playing a role and be in front of the camera. It took place in the 1930s, and I remember the costumes and cars were just phenomenal. My mother had always wanted to be an actress, so it was really fun for her. She was given this long cigarette holder. I just remember dancing: it was a scene where I'm dancing at a nightclub or something like that, just a kid dancing on the chairs.

179

I was in my 1930s costume and walking around and people had asked me for my autograph, because clearly I was in the film, but I was just an extra. I remember thinking, "Oh my god." I felt so Hollywood-fabulous. It was really fun, as a kid.

In this diary it talks about how, on the second day of filming, I had to wake up and go back to the set. I was crying to my mother saying, "I don't want to go, I'm too tired." [*Laughs*] I went but I soon learned that being on camera wasn't everything that it seems. There's a lot of hard work, and it's very tiring. As a fourth grader, it was *exhausting*. It's funny, though, that ten years later I ended up starring in two of his films.

By the time you did *American Ninja*, you had some movies and TV shows under your belt, but you were still only a few years into your screen career. Were you ever nervous on the set of *American Ninja*? This was a leading role, after all.

I wasn't scared at all doing *American Ninja*. It all happened so fast. I was in the middle of finals at UCLA. I was studying, I had so much work to do. I got the phone call that I got *American Ninja* and I was so excited, but I was also told I had to leave immediately, basically. I had to finish up my finals and get them done really quickly. I was so excited because I was about to leave the country in a few days and go off to the Philippines. It was a blast—it was such a fun shoot.

I was the only female in the movie, but there were some females in the crew; specifically, the hair and makeup and script supervisor were females, who I'd become friendly with. Everybody else was male. We stayed at the Manila Hotel. It was an incredibly opulent hotel, and gilded to the brim. My room actually overlooked [President Ferdinand] Marcos' yacht.

At the time they were in turmoil, and Marcos was the ruler. Every time we walked into the hotel, we had to be physically body searched. *Every* time you walked into the hotel. Often, my room clearly had been gone through. I could see they had opened doors and cabinets and so forth, looking through things. I presume because my room was overlooking Marcos' yacht.

The hotel was such a wealthy, wealthy place, and there was a crazy juxtaposition the minute you walked out of those doors. We were in a very, very poor part of the country, in Manila, definitely third world. Yet, this was such an incredible hotel, but when you walked out the doors it was completely different.

I tan very easily. I was supposed to be the American girl in this, and so I was asked to try to stay out of the sun as much as possible, which is very difficult because on your days off—it was just so beautiful outside. It was very hard for me. Boy, we did some fun things, though. We shot in this one place called Pagsanjan Falls, which is where you can go rafting. It's where they filmed *Apocalypse Now* (1979). There was a time that we were all filming there, which was fantastic, and then there was a time when we were filming at a resort, and I remember windsurfing. I learned windsurfing and horseback riding. There was a cinema at the resort. I got stung by jellyfish there [*Laughs*], but it was a gorgeous resort. That's where we shot when [Michael] and I had our date in the movie.

Michael and I became very good friends during that time. Phil [Brock], Steve [James], Michael and I hung out a lot together. Michael was very focused all the time, though. He was *always* training. He wasn't trained in martial arts before that, so he took this incredibly seriously—and he did incredibly well.

I remember the scene where I'm jumping off the cliffs with him. Oh, my God. That was crazy. I was so scared. When my character was saying she was worried there were leeches and other things in there, I was *really* thinking that. I was like, "Oh, do not put me in there. Do *not* put me in there!" [*Laughs*]

Michael Dudikoff, Judie Aronson, Steve James, and Guich Koock in a press still from *American Ninja*.

Michael had mostly done comedies to this point, but this turned him into an action star. Did you get any sense that this movie would turn him into a big action hero?

Gosh, no. None of us had any way of knowing that at the time. To be quite honest, many people I knew never really gave much thought about what happens when the movies came out. Our fun was in filming them.

It's easy for an outsider like me to forget that most of you had already moved on to your next projects before the movies were released.

Yes. As a matter of fact, I had wrapped *Weird Science*, and then a few months later I landed in the Philippines and started filming *American Ninja*. Then I got a call that I had to go back to Los Angeles, because I had to do reshoots for *Weird Science*. They were trying to work this out; they were even talking about possibly flying me to Los Angeles and then back to the Philippines.

They ended up waiting. I went straight back to Los Angeles and did some reshoots for *Weird Science*. I had to wear a wig during the reshoot because my hair was completely different. It's funny, I notice it every time I see *Weird Science*. In the opening scene where we're at the gym, all I can think about is, "Oh, my God, my hair looks horrible." That was a wig. [*Laughs*]

Speaking of *Weird Science*, Steve James had a small part in that. Did you two meet before *American Ninja*?

No. We found out while we were filming *American Ninja* that we both had done *Weird Science*. We never worked together.

How do you remember him, as a colleague and as an individual?

He was a phenomenal man. What an interesting, deep, smart, loving man. Very serious about his work. He was great.

It was a good group of people. I got very, very lucky to be surrounded by such talent and kindness. We also got to rehearse a little bit, which is unheard of for small films like that at the time, but we were all away together, so it kind of became like summer camp. We were there for several months.

Also, there was a big earthquake while we were there. We were staying, like I said, in the Manila Hotel, and this earthquake happened and it was so big. I was in bed and when it happened, I literally could not stand up straight. I kept falling over—I couldn't stand up, it was so strong. I later found out that the reason why it felt that strong was because the hotel was on rollers. It was specifically built to move with earthquakes, so it felt so much bigger than it was, and it was already really big. I thought, "Oh my God, oh my God, I'm going to die. I'm going to die." [*Laughs*] We all did. We were all running down the stairs trying to get out of the hotel from the top levels.

There are a few other really great memories. Some of the crew members would climb up the palm trees and come down with coconuts for us. They'd hand us coconuts with a straw while we were sitting there, or cut up pineapples that they just picked. I loved that, it was just so cool. One time I was called in late in the day, and I had just missed the lunch that was being served. I asked if I could still get anything. I said, "Just serve me what you were serving at lunch, please." They gave me a plate and I went to sit down. I'm just about to put a bite in my mouth and somebody says, "No, no, no. That's dog." I'm like, "*What?*" It turns out that I was given the food that the crew members who were from the Philippines had. They ate different meals than the Americans did. There were dogs everywhere. It was so sad, there were so many stray dogs in the streets. I wouldn't be surprised if what I was about to eat was one of them.

It sounds like the whole experience was amazing. Can you recall a favorite single day on set?

There are so many. I loved every part of it for different reasons. The days that we were in the jungle running at the beginning of the movie, being chased by the ninjas. He cuts my skirt, and we're running and he's pulling me and all that. I really enjoyed all of that. I felt like I was in *Romancing the Stone* (1984).

Even being thrown off the cliff with him, and dragged around—just being such a little brat with him was so much fun. I really enjoyed those days because it was so much fun playing that role. I'm really feisty.

It was such a beautiful country. Like I said, there were beautiful bodies of water—everywhere you'd look, there was water. There were jungles, as you see in the film. It was an incredible experience. It was far more than just shooting the film *American Ninja*. It came as a whole package with a beautiful experience within it, and long lasting friendships afterwards.

Steven Lambert designed the stunts for several Cannon classics, including *Ninja III: The Domination.*

184

Interview: Stunt Coordinator Steven Lambert

Steven Lambert is an award-winning stunt coordinator and performer whose credits include such big Hollywood features as *Remo Williams: The Adventure Begins* (1985), *Pee-wee's Big Adventure* (1985), *Rambo III* (1988), *Indiana Jones and the Last Crusade* (1989), *Ghostbusters II* (1989), *Total Recall* (1990), and *Ocean's Eleven* (2001). A trained and dedicated martial artist, Lambert got his start fighting Chuck Norris in *Good Guys Wear Black* (1978), one of the future Cannon star's first leading roles.

He worked his way up through the industry, and was hired for his coordinating job on Cannon's *Revenge of the Ninja* (1983), where he not only designed and performed many of the stunts, but doubled the black demon ninja in his showdown with Sho Kosugi during the movie's epic rooftop finale. From there, he was one of Cannon's go-to stunt experts, working as a coordinator on *Ninja III: The Domination* (1984), *American Ninja* (1985), *Invaders from Mars* (1986), and *P.O.W. The Escape* (1986), and performing additional stunts in *Firewalker* (1986), *Barfly* (1987), and *Delta Force 2* (1990).

Lambert has published a memoir, *From the Streets of Brooklyn to the Halls of Hollywood*, which details his life and career and is full of incredible behind-the-scenes stories from his Cannon years and beyond. You can also read more about his experiences on his first two ninja features in an interview in *The Cannon Film Guide, Vol. I.*

You went from *Revenge of the Ninja* and *Ninja III: The Domination*, and then worked again with Sam in the Philippines on *American Ninja*. Can you tell me about working with Michael Dudikoff?

Steven Lambert: Sam Firstenberg picked Michael. At first, Menahem didn't want him, but there was something about Michael that Sam Firstenberg liked. That's how that evolved. There were all kinds of sons of big stars at the audition, like Steve McQueen's son, Chad McQueen. Chuck Norris's son was there, and a few others. Nicolas Cage was there.

Oh, wow—I can only imagine this movie with Nicolas Cage as the American Ninja.

185

I was in the office, and Nicolas Cage was there. I couldn't believe it. There were all kinds of people competing for this. Back then, nobody knew who Nicolas Cage was.

I was told by Sam that Michael Dudikoff was going to do it. I was in the Philippines already before I met Michael, because we were going to a foreign country and I needed to be there early. There was a lot more to *American Ninja* because it was shot in a foreign country, and there are things that you have to go the extra mile to get and make sure you have, because you're not in America anymore. Things aren't as easy.

I explained to Menahem and Shmulik [Sam Firstenberg] that I needed to go there before we began filming. They sent me off before anybody. I was there location scouting, setting things up, and talking to the set designer. I had to come up with an obstacle course, so that was big, and many action pieces. Tadashi Yamashita was in the film, and I doubled Tadashi, too. I doubled him, Michael, and a few others.

I didn't meet Michael until he came down. That's when we met and we sat down. I'll never forget: we were in the Manila Hotel, we introduced ourselves, and we started discussing the script. He had a lot of ideas. In order to come up with sequences, sometimes you need to know what the actor is thinking, and how he's going to play it. I'll never forget, he says, "I'm going to play it like James Dean." I said, "Okay." That's how I took it. Michael and I had some great ideas together.

Putting together the action sequences was very important to him, personally. I understand that as a stunt coordinator, I'm working for him, too. Certain things were very important to him. He came up with some ideas that we were able to work in, and we worked together wonderfully as a team. We hung out together, we became good friends. We hung out on the set and that's including Steve James, God bless him. Steve James and I became very close friends.

I had one little fight in there for Steve James. When he found out that I was putting it together, he was so excited. When he found out that he was going to make a grand entrance on an open bed truck, he came to me and he goes, "Steve, Steve, how are you going to write this? How are you going to bring me into the end sequence?" I looked at Steve, I said, "You're going to be the hero. You're going to come in the lead. Coming up on the stairs, shooting a machine gun, shooting fifty people." He was like a little kid, he was so excited. He had a wonderful personality. He got along with everybody there, and Menahem just loved him. It was sad when we lost him.

Michael and I got along really well. We had an understanding and we had respect for each other, and that's very important. I had a couple of trials and tribulations on that film, and Michael and I always respected each other, and always admired each other, and we always got along really well.

Looking back at all the movies you did with Cannon, which do you think was the most challenging, as far as the stunts?

There were a couple of things that were challenging. Sometimes "challenging" and "stupid" can be used at the same time. For instance, when I did the roof slide in *Revenge of the Ninja*, the way I had that set up wasn't too smart. I'm on the 28th floor going to the 25th floor with no safety, so to speak. Let's just say, there was a moment while doing that gag where there may no longer have been a Steven Lambert.

I did that because I felt invulnerable. I felt like Superman. Before then, I never came to reality. Everything I'd challenged myself on in the past, where most people would have been put in a hospital, I succeeded. Mentally I was in the wrong frame of mind. I didn't prepare things quite right for that action piece.

One of my proudest moments was on *American Ninja*. Michael Dudikoff was in the compound and Steve James brought him a motorcycle, and we jumped a bike over a wall. That was another exciting moment because in the stunt business, you have to be proficient in a lot of things. My number one was being a monkey [and able to climb things], and being physical in martial arts. But I was a novice at riding motorcycles. Originally, that stunt was given to two Filipino stunt people who said they could do it, but then they chickened out at the last moment. [*Laughs*] So, now I'm forced to do it!

187

There's a big difference between a novice and a pro when it comes to jumps. That was a sixteen, seventeen-foot jump over a wall onto solid cement. You usually give that to the pros. I had come up with that idea, but when it was time to shoot it, two people chickened out. [*Laughs*]

Sam's looking at me, and I go, "I guess I got no choice." That was a very scary moment, because the biggest jump I ever did before that was maybe a foot off the ground, four feet across, going over a little ravine. In a moment like that you need to use common sense. If you do what you're supposed to do, you'll make it. That's what I used, common sense. That was a scary moment, and a fun moment, and a proud moment in that picture.

Also, getting to double Tadashi Yamashita was exciting. Tadashi Yamashita, to me, is big time [in the martial arts]. Tadashi is the real thing. When I was a kid competing in tournaments here, I would watch many, many, many big martial art stars, including Tadashi Yamashita, perform, and I was always in awe. He's one bad mother.

The helicopter was very exciting too. If you remember when Michael Dudikoff's character, the ninja, comes up, it's like the matador and its bull. When I wrote that scene, I envisioned I was the matador and the helicopter was the bull. I'm standing in front of it, thirty feet away, and it starts rising up and coming towards me, and I grab on the front. It was like grabbing onto the horns of a bull. That's how I imagined it, and that's how I explained it to Shmulik, and he loved it. I said, "Picture it. Picture a helicopter's coming after me, and I grab its horns." I was very excited about that. That was a lot of fun.

Up until [*American Ninja*], I had never put together an obstacle course. In these situations, you always refer back to things that you've seen before. I always enjoyed old movies, I'm a big buff. All of these things, whether they're mine or somebody else's, everything comes from something. You just try to change it in a little way.

I had a great opportunity to put together the obstacle course [in the film], and I reverted back to the old Hong Kong movies that I used to see when I was a kid in Chinatown, in LA. The whole obstacle course that I designed and filmed there, it all came from things that I remembered from old movies. Every one of those props, those obstacles, came from an old Chinese movie that I saw.

That obstacle course was not the biggest or the most dangerous thing I've done. Sometimes it's as simple as that. Those Filipino stunt guys, acrobatics, and martial artists were just wonderful. There were very talented people out there.

Cannon flew you to a far corner of the world. Did you have any time to stop and enjoy yourself there, or was it just always too fast-paced, too busy?

You're talking to a punk kid from Brooklyn who left when he was thirteen years old and hated California because he didn't understand the people. Those were the only two places I'd ever been, other than spending a few hours in Tijuana. Going to the Philippines was the first foreign location I'd ever been to. The shock, the happiness, the things that were going on in my mind. I was thinking, "My God, I'm in Manila. What the hell is this place?" [*Laughs*]

The people were beautiful. But, there's good and bad. I spent ten months in the Phillppines, first on *American Ninja*, and then I did *Behind Enemy Lines* [a.k.a. *P.O.W. The Escape*, 1986] with David Carradine for Cannon Films. I got to really know the people. The country is beautiful, the people are beautiful. I thought I was in a fantasy world. I'm in Manila, the Philippines, I'm twenty-seven years old, and it's a beautiful thing, doing what I want, doing what I love.

I traveled through there and I saw things I'd never seen before. I hung out with wonderful people. Steve James, Michael, and Sam would come with us. We had a Filipino special effects guy, his nickname was Boom-Boom. He would take us to some wonderful places. It was a wonderful thing.

I tell a little story sometimes. You could say my three first pictures were *Revenge*, *The Domination*, and then *American Ninja*. That was at the beginning of my career. All the work I've ever done since, all the people I've worked for and worked with, I have never gotten the self-satisfaction that I've gotten from those three movies. Nor have I gotten that same amount of liberty but believe me, most stunt coordinators to this day, they don't get half of the liberty that I got on those films. God bless Menahem and Sam, all those guys.

Cannon's ninja movies played a major part in the explosion of popularity ninjas had in 1980s and 1990s pop culture, and that helped inspire a lot of kids—really, a large part of that generation of martial artists—to get into the martial arts. Do you feel proud having played a role in that?

You know, it sounds funny, but for many, many years after *Revenge*, after *The Domination*, after *American Ninja*, I had moved on and I never really thought about it. Then the websites started coming up, the computer world. I'm prehistoric, so to speak, when it comes to that kind of stuff, so I never really took to it. I would get calls from Shmulik every now and then, he would tell me about how the audience was growing, and what people were saying.

It never really clicked until years later, when I started diving into the computer age. Then all of a sudden, I'm realizing after all these years have gone by, when people list the top twenty-five martial arts movies, all three of those ninja films are still in there. You see all these fans of the movies that have become cult films, so to speak. I'm so proud now that I was involved in it. I sit back and say, "Well, listen, I did a picture that a lot of people remember." It makes you feel good, you know?

Interview: Actor Larry Poindexter

An actor best known for his roles in *S. W.A. T.* (2003) and the MTV comedy *The Hard Times of RJ Berger* (2010–2011), Larry Poindexter appeared in three Cannon films back-to-back near the start of his career. Two of these were small roles in *Invaders from Mars* (1986) and *Number One with a Bullet* (1987). The third role was the largest: playing Sgt. Charlie McDonald, Michael Dudikoff and Steve James' Marine sidekick, in *American Ninja 2: The Confrontation*.

Having accumulated nearly two hundred screen credits as of this writing, Poindexter continues to act in film and TV, but now spends much of his time producing theater in Los Angeles and New York.

MICHAEL DUDIKOFF

dans

The cover of the French pressbook for *American Ninja 2*. In France, the
movie's title translated to "The White Ninja."

You're the son of a lauded stage designer and an opera singer. Did it ever feel like becoming a performer was part of your destiny?

Larry Poindexter: Not really. I wasn't encouraged to be a performer. My father actually would have been happier if I'd been backstage, or behind a camera—which I actually have ended up doing, as a producer/writer.

Your role in *Invaders from Mars* wasn't a large one, but given all that was going on in that film, I have to imagine it was a memorable shoot. What do you remember of Tobe Hooper and your experience on the *Invaders* set?

It was very behind, and Tobe wasn't very approachable . . . I do remember reconnecting with Karen Black, whose ex-husband was a close friend of my parents. They'd even attended Karen's wedding.

It rarely seems like there was a long wait for Cannon movies: when someone was hired, they were usually expected to start shooting in just a few weeks. Was this your experience on their films?

Oh, yeah. But with the exception of stars who are attached early on, that's normal for the biz.

I've never heard a negative thing said about Steve James—everyone fortunate enough to have worked with him seems to have had a blast doing so. What are your memories of him?

I loved him! We continued to be friends up to his passing. Both of us went to the same YMCA. He was smart, talented, tough, and kind.

In *American Ninja 2*, you got to throw in on one of Cannon's famous bar brawls. There's a lot of fun, physical comedy in that scene, and I imagine it took a while to shoot all of the coverage needed for the stunt work and choreography. What do you remember of those shooting days?

It was great fun. They based it on the *Gunga Din* (1939) fight. I had a blast. There were a couple of scary moments in longer takes where a table didn't collapse correctly, and I was out of position for some throws. But it was just great fun, and BJ [Davis]—our stunt coordinator—was excellent!

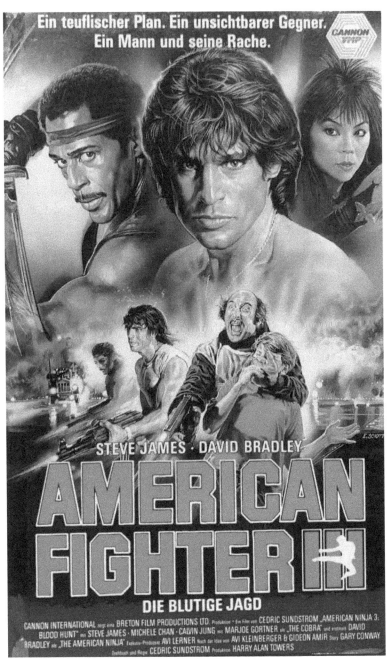

Another fetching German VHS cover with art provided by Enzo Sciotti.

It sounds like shooting dragged on a little longer than everyone expected. Did that extra time help you bond with your cast and crewmates? Any fun excursions off-set?

We did shoot quite long, for lots of reasons like weather, et cetera. It gave us plenty of time to bond. There weren't a lot of excursions for me, but other castmates had them.

Politics aside, how was shooting in South Africa?

It's the best place on Earth for me, to this day.

Most actors I've talked to have an "Only at Cannon..." story: something they saw or witnessed on a Cannon film that's unlike anything else they've experienced in their screen career, before or since. As someone nearing 200 credits to your name, is there a memory or experience from your Cannon pictures that you imagine will forever remain one-of-a-kind?

Only the fact that when we left for South Africa the producers had us check additional packages that contained props and more, because it was cheaper and easier to put it as "baggage" than ship it back.

Interview: Director Cedric Sundström

South African filmmaker Cedric Sundström has been a movie fan his entire life. At the age of thirteen he made his first films with local friends. By the early 1970s, he was already receiving attention for his underground shorts *Summer is Forever* (1971), *The Hunter* (1973), and *Suffer Little Children . . . (1976)*. When international studios began bringing their productions to South Africa, Sundström was frequently hired on as an AD or Second Unit director, working on films like *Killer Force* (1976) and *Zulu Dawn* (1979). Naturally, he found himself working on numerous African-shot Cannon productions throughout the 1980s, including *King Solomon's Mines* (1985), *Allan Quatermain and the Lost City of Gold* (1986), *Gor* and *Gor II* (1987, 1988) and both *Dragonard* films.

It would only be a few years before Cannon hired Sundström to direct their films outright. He took over the *American Ninja* series after Sam Firstenberg's departure, helming both *American Ninja 3: Blood Hunt* (1989) and *American Ninja 4: The Annihilation* (1990).

You were a teenager when you made your first 8mm movies. When you were that young, did you wish you lived in a country with a bigger film industry, or did that not matter to you?

Cedric Sundström: It mattered very much. South Africa at the time was not conducive to investigating film and the film culture, such as it was, was very small and insular. There were no film schools and I never considered that attending an international film school was an option for me. My early filmmaking on non-professional, standard film came entirely from the gut. I was certainly a child of cinema, and I was aware of that, but I was very much alone with no movement around me. The early films were made with casts made up of friends and family.

The official film industry was not small, and I did eventually get a job on industry productions: a film called *Stop Exchange* (1970) was the first, with Sid James and Charles Hawtrey of the *Carry On* team appearing in a South African production.

You were one of South Africa's original underground filmmakers, but also started working on many international productions that came to the country. Were you excited to work on those bigger, foreign productions early, or would you rather have been making your own films?

I felt that it was amazing to get work on an international feature as a second assistant director. The film was the *Diamond Mercenaries/Killer Force* with British director Val Guest and starring, for me, the iconic Peter Fonda, Telly Savalas and Christopher Lee. It was comforting to be doing something I loved, learning and getting to know the practical side of directing. I befriended Fonda and we were associated in setting up a futuristic story to be shot in South Africa called "On a Rooftop Waiting." Unfortunately all the pieces did not fall into place, and the production never happened.

From an international perspective, South African history at this time will be associated with apartheid. In what ways did that most affect what you were doing, as a local filmmaker?

From my perspective, working as I was on commercial productions, the apartheid monster was there but not overly intrusive. When there were international Black members in the cast, such as OJ Simpson in *Killer Force*, they were treated as well as the white international actors. This of course was all for show, as the South African government placed a lot of value on the creation of an international film industry presence. I found out later that certain members of the crew were, in fact, spies from the infamous security police. Local Black actors who I worked with (such as Simon Sabela and Ken Gampu) were treated with respect on set.

Your first Cannon gig was as an assistant director on *King Solomon's Mines* and then on *Allan Quatermain and the Lost City of Gold*. Can you share any of your memories of working on these two productions?

Sundström directing David Bradley during one of his two *American Ninja* sequels. Photo courtesy of Cedric Sundström.

I thought Sharon Stone was a brat, and she managed to rub most of the crew up the wrong way. Although these two films, after the magnificent epic *Zulu Dawn* (1979), were in their own way epics of a sort. I was excited to work with British director J. Lee Thompson, for whom I had a great respect from his films *Tiger Bay* (1959), *The Guns of Navarone* (1961), and *Cape Fear* (1962). I only discovered later that Sam Peckinpah's director of photography from *Bring Me the Head of Alfredo Garcia* (1974), Alex Phillips Jr., was on camera. On *Allan Quatermain*, I encountered a director, Gary Nelson, who next to Thompson was very lightweight—the less said about him, the better.

A few names from the earlier films in the *American Ninja* series, such as actor Steve James, writer Gary Conway, and choreographer Mike Stone, carried over to your film. Were you given much freedom by Cannon on *American Ninja 3*, or were many of the building blocks already in place when you were hired?

Sundström and Michael Dudikoff on the set of *American Ninja 4*.

Those building blocks were in place, but I was allowed to rewrite with others the script, as it was so close in essence to *American Ninja 2*.

With *American Ninja 3*, you were tasked with replacing the series' hero. I know casting was done in Los Angeles, but what can you tell me about discovering David Bradley?

The big pluses for me were his looks, vulnerability, and his martial arts expertise. He was a black belt in karate—what more can you ask for?

Steve James was a magnetic presence, and shone as brightly as the heroes in his many sidekick roles. What are your memories of him?

His presence could not be ignored. He had the one-liners and overcame the old chestnut of playing "the sidekick." He elevated himself into an indispensable part of the team. He was wonderful to work with and unfortunately, he was not considered for *American Ninja 4*. His absence was a great loss. He and David Bradley in *American Ninja 3* were the buddies that carried the concept through.

One of the most memorable action sequences in *American Ninja 3* was when the plane landed on the back of the truck. Do you remember where that idea came from?

In changing the script to update some of the action, I had the idea for Sean, with help from the other two, to swipe a microlight, and that's how he was able to get into the East Bay labs. I received a call from Menahem Golan, who asked me "Cedric, what are these microlights . . .?"

Were you immediately hired for *American Ninja 4*, or did some time pass before you know you'd be making another one?

I was not hired immediately, as Dudikoff was out of the picture. Then I got a message that they were bringing him back. He had been perceived as breaking the cultural boycott, so his only proviso was that the film be shot in a neighboring country: Lesotho.

What was your experience like directing Michael Dudikoff in this one?

I enjoyed the experience of having the *American Ninja* character who was the original, and tying him up with the new boy in town, although they weren't the bosom buddies in real life that they were meant to be on screen.

You're a man who clearly knows his cinema history, and seem to enjoy watching films perhaps as much as making them. Are there any tributes or homages to your favorite films hidden in either of your *American Ninja* movies?

As somebody brought up on and loving epics such as *Ben-Hur* (1959), *The Fall of the Roman Empire* (1964), and *King of Kings* (1961), those influences are intrinsic in my work. Also, overwhelmingly, *West Side Story* (1961), in the use of spectacle and choreographic vision. There are also, obviously, references to *Mad Max* (1979) and, look for it, Ken Russell's *The Devils* (1971).

The *American Ninja* formula had to be followed, wherein the American Ninja hero fights to ensure that good triumphs over evil. But for me, working within the confines of the formula, I took it upon myself to do it differently, and to bring some of myself and my own personal vision to the productions.

Invasion U.S.A. was a hit for Cannon, both in theaters and on videocassette. As the back cover reads: "America wasn't ready . . . but he was!"

Invasion U.S.A.

Release Date: September 27, 1985
Directed by: Joseph Zito
Written by: James Bruner & Chuck Norris
Starring: Chuck Norris, Richard Lynch
Trailer Voiceover: "They wanted a war. *He* gave them one!"

Terrorists have invaded the Southern United States, and the only person who can stop them is Chuck Norris.

Not the army.

Not the National Guard.

Not even the Marines.

Chuck Norris.

Released the prior year, Chuck Norris and Joseph Zito's *Missing in Action* had been an unmitigated success for Cannon, and so the studio was eager to reunite the director and their biggest star for an even larger-budget picture. Menahem Golan had dreamed up a cool film title, *American Ninja*, and imagined that it would be a perfect fit for Norris. The actor, however, wasn't interested in doing another martial arts flick, concerned about being pigeonholed as a sort of Western kung fu star, and aiming for a more well-rounded action career. He also didn't like the idea of wearing a mask over his face, which would have more or less been necessary in the ninja film genre. (And, hey, with a beard like Chuck's, who *would* want to cover that up?)

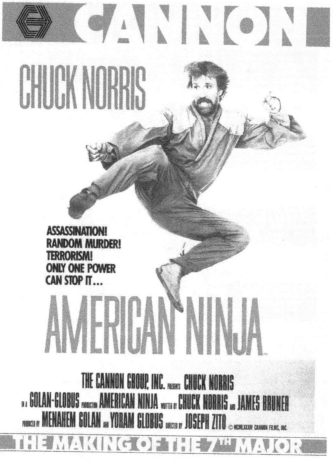

Cannon briefly advertised *Invasion U.S.A.* under the title "American Ninja." (Note the tagline.) For the image, Cannon's art team stuck Chuck Norris' head on the body of the evil ninja from *Ninja III: The Domination.*

Fortunately for the reluctant Norris, Golan had nothing more than a title at that point. That's when Norris's friend, *Missing in Action* (1984) screenwriter

James Bruner, had a clever idea to work around Golan's demands. Together, Bruner and Norris penned a screenplay about a CIA operative named Matt Hunter, whose *codename* was "American Ninja," but was in no other way an *actual* ninja. (Some ideas were adapted from an earlier story idea by Norris's brother, Aaron, about a sleeper cell of Soviet terrorists who spent two decades hiding in the U.S., waiting for word from Mother Russia to begin an uprising.) Menahem Golan loved the story that they presented to him, but he wisely realized he couldn't blow as sweet a title as *American Ninja* on a movie that contained no actual ninjas in it. And so, the film was greenlit under a new title: *Invasion U.S.A.*, to be released in 1985. (Despite a similar premise, this film bears no relation to the 1952 communist invasion film of the same name.)

Invasion U.S.A. offers an almost quaint, very Eighties portrayal of terrorism. Somewhat like the money-hungry, East German terrorists of *Die Hard* (1988), the bad guys in *Invasion*—a seemingly mismatched coalition of Russians, Cubans, and Middle Eastern militants—are led by a lunatic Soviet named Rostov (Richard Lynch), whose sole reason for leading an invasion onto U.S. soil seems to be that he wants to be the first person to try it in over 200 years.

Did you ever notice how, in many movies, the villains are given humanizing backstories, so that they seem somewhat sympathetic and the audience then feels a tiny bit bad for them when they inevitably meet their demise? Well, there's none of that shit here. There is zero grey area when it comes to *Invasion U.S.A.*'s bad guys. The first time we see them, they're disguised as members of the Coast Guard and rolling up on a boat full of illegal Cuban immigrants as they float somewhere off the Florida shore. These are families: women, children, and the elderly. At first, we worry that these destitute aliens will be deported back to Cuba—but, what happens next is far worse.

The villains' leader, Rostov (Richard Lynch), pretends to welcome them to the United States, and the boat erupts into cheers. He steps down onto their vessel, extends a hand to one old man, and then—*fake-out!*—he pulls out a pistol and executes the old guy, like a big, fat, evil dickhead. The rest of the faux Coast Guardsmen open fire with their machine guns, mowing down everyone on the watercraft. Afterwards, they bust open its hull and steal the load of cocaine hidden inside.

This massacre scene was shot from a barge off the coast of Florida with the cooperation of the Department of Defense. The Coast Guard, obviously, declined to participate, and you can't help but wonder if that had to do with the image of Coast Guardsman gunning down a boatload of Cuban families.

Hate those guys yet? Good, because in the next scene we meet the guy who is going to spend a good portion of the movie slaughtering those assholes in the name of sweet, American justice. We're introduced to our hero, Matt Hunter (Norris), as he speeds across the Everglades in an airboat, looking every bit the part of red-blooded, American badass. He's wearing an all-denim ensemble; his mullet and unbuttoned shirt flap in the wind, his billowing chest hair bared to all those who may conspire to do their fellow man harm. Matt Hunter has no lines here, but he doesn't need them: we can *tell* from Jay Chattaway's bold score that this, ladies and gentlemen, is our good guy.

Soon we're given further evidence that Rostov is a prime grade dirtbag when he drops by the office of a Miami drug kingpin and arms dealer played by Billy Drago, sticks a gun down his pants, shoots his pecker off, and then tosses his prostitute companion through a window. Afterwards, he makes off with the gangster's guns. (Between Richard Lynch and Billy Drago, *Invasion U.S.A.* had doubled down by casting two of the video era's best slimeball character actors.)

Although he primarily stuck to cheap genre pictures, Richard Lynch was one of Hollywood's truly great heavies. Lynch brought a wild intensity to even the silliest of villain roles. (See: the wicked barbarian-king, Kadar, in Cannon's 1987, Italian-shot sword and sorcery flick, *The Barbarians*.) The visible scarring on his face was due to an incident in 1967 where the young actor, high on "every kind of drug" as he told the Associated Press, doused himself in gasoline and set himself ablaze as a war protest. He underwent many skin grafts and years of rehabilitation, and eventually resumed acting. He died in 2012 with more than 150 credits to his name, including *Scarecrow* (1973),

Albert Pyun's *The Sword and the Sorcerer* (1982), and *Bad Dreams* (1988). He also appeared in the lambada-themed *The Forbidden Dance* (1990), the film made by Menahem Golan's 21st Century Film Corporation to compete with Cannon's own *Lambada* (1990), released on the same day.

Billy Drago would be given more screen time in Cannon's *Hero and the Terror* (1988) and *Delta Force 2* (1990), both also starring Norris. Regularly typecast as a villain thanks to his spindly frame and sinister smile—Drago often looked like a spider who wished upon a star to become human, and then did—Drago's breakout came a couple years after this film, when he played Frank Nitti in Brian De Palma's highly-acclaimed crime film, *The Untouchables* (1987). Drago also made appearances in Clint Eastwood's *Pale Rider* (1985) and *Vamp* (1986), and on numerous TV shows, including *The X-Files*.

Tough guys don't wear sleeves when they wrestle gators.

We'll now return to our feature presentation. As Rostov's men hustle off with the drug lord's cache of firearms, it seems like every part of the cunning terrorist leader's nefarious and vaguely-defined plan is falling into place. There's only one potential kink remaining that needs to be worked out. Rostov, you see, only fears one man, and that's Chuck Norris—*errrr*, Matt Hunter, the former CIA agent who thwarted one of his nefarious plots in the past, and to this day regrets not killing Rostov when he had the chance. (Rostov is so afraid of Hunter that he has *recurring nightmares* about him.) Now retired, Hunter lives a peaceful life in the Everglades, helping his Native American buddy, John Eagle, wrestle alligators, and riding around in that cool airboat we saw earlier.

Before launching his master plan, Rostov attempts to snuff out his old enemy by launching a sneak attack on Hunter's quiet cabin in the swamp, but only manages to murder Hunter's elderly pal and instigate his return from his early retirement.

Invasion U.S.A. featured a team of stunt people more than eighty strong, led by coordinator Aaron Norris, Chuck's brother. To avoid having any of his stunt men bitten by alligators or water moccasins during the movie's swamp scenes, Aaron would lower canisters of dynamite into the water to blow up any critters who were lurking nearby.

Having wrongly assumed that a dozen men with machine guns and rocket launchers would have been enough to kill Matt Hunter, Rostov launches his invasion. A few antique World War II U-boats—borrowed from a collector and shipped down to Florida—land on a Miami beach under the cover of night, and out pour a couple hundred armed guerillas of wide-ranging ethnicities. They load themselves into waiting semi-trucks and are dispersed to cities across the nation: Chicago, Detroit, Las Vegas, New York, San Francisco. (The movie only concerns itself with showing the attacks in Miami and Atlanta.) Rostov's plan is to wreak terror and havoc on the civilian population, using "their own freedom against them" to bring America to its knees.

Local bikers were cast as invading terrorists for this scene. As Zito remembered it, the police wanted to raid the shoot that night, since many of the extras had warrants out for their arrest, but the production declined to cooperate with law enforcement.

We see Rostov's dastardly scheme put into action in the most gratuitously evil way possible. He and his goons roll up into a wholesome, All-American suburb, where families decorate Christmas trees on their front lawns, children roller skate in the street, and grandmas take their poodles for evening walks. (For a little extra oomph, all of this is set to a saccharine rendition of the holiday carol "Hark! The Herald Angels Sing.") We watch in horror as the bad guys pull out rocket launchers and lay fiery waste to the surrounding homes. This scene is effectively terrifying, as we watch the (pretty literal) American Dream explode in sickening slow motion.

These weren't cheap facades being blown up, either, but real suburban homes. While scouting locations for the film, the *Invasion* crew stumbled across a housing development which was scheduled to be bulldozed in order to expand the Atlanta airport. The state government had purchased the houses and auctioned them off to local construction companies, who planned to salvage their building materials. One company wasn't able to make their payment on time, and so Cannon stepped in and bought the houses they destroyed in the film for around $7,000 a piece, obtaining permission from the local authorities to rig them with explosives. For a movie that mostly shies away from realism, this scene delivers it in spades.

Unfortunately, some of *Invasion U.S.A.*'s realism came at a cost. While filming a scene in which terrorists were supposed to collapse the entrance to an armored car garage with explosives, the charges instead blew apart the steel door, sending hot shrapnel towards stuntman Max Maxwell, seated at a desk almost sixty feet away. The impact fractured his forearm and caused multiple lacerations to his face and limbs. (The shot in which Maxwell was injured can be seen in the finished film.) In Florida, there was a five-car collision when the terrorists' convoy of trucks slid into each other while leaving the filming location, injuring one driver.

All of the movie's action and destruction are soundtracked by a strong score from composer Jay Chattaway, who also scored Cannon's *Missing in Action* and *Braddock: Missing in Action III*, as well as non-Cannon, maniac-themed cult classics such as *Maniac* (1980) and *Maniac Cop* (1988).

Meanwhile, in the movie, Matt Hunter does some investigative due diligence, dropping in on local low-life to see if they can help him pinpoint the terrorist leader's hideout. He tracks down one of Rostov's lieutenants in the back room of a seedy strip club, jamming a knife into his hand to painfully coerce some information out of him. When one of the club's burly bouncers pops in to find out what's going on, Hunter delivers one of the most Chuck Norris-y of Chuck Norris one-liners ever laid on film: "I'm gonna hit you with so many rights, you're gonna beg for a left." (Norris came up with this line himself, and was so proud of it that the filmmakers let him use it. It's cheesy, but also a perfect fit for him: no one but Chuck Norris could pull it off like he does.) When he's unable to wring any useful information out of him, Hunter leaves the terrorist lieutenant with one hand stuck to a table with a knife, and the other squeezing a live grenade.

Elsewhere, the terror train rolls on. At one moment, a pair of fake cops gun down a Latin dance party. One of them is played by Japanese-American actor James Pax, making his Hollywood debut—he'd most famously appear as a lightning-wielding sorcerer in John Carpenter's *Big Trouble in Little China* (1986), and less famously in Cannon's own *Kinjite: Forbidden Subjects* (1989), opposite Charles Bronson.

Another group of baddies attempt to blow up a crowded mall at Christmastime, only to have their plans foiled by our denim-clad superhero, Matt Hunter. What ensues is the most extravagant display of shopping mall destruction this side of *The Blues Brothers* (1980). As terrorists open fire on innocent shoppers, Matt Hunter drives his pickup truck through the building's glass entranceway. (How did he know the bad guys were there? How did he manage not to run over any civilians? We'll chalk it up to Chuck Magic.) After running over a few of the heavily-armed terrorists, Matt Hunter hops out of his truck to eliminate a few more with a pair of hip-fired Micro Uzis. While that's going on, the bad guy in charge of the operation manages to hotwire a display truck and tries to run Hunter over, but our mulleted man-o-war hops onto the side of the truck and clings to the door, punching the passenger's face in as they plow through mall kiosks and floor displays. (Yes, that's Norris doing his own stunt work here.)

ONLY MATT HUNTER
CAN STOP THE
SOVIET UNION'S
ULTIMATE PLOT

INVASION
U.S.A.

JASON FROST

NOW A MAJOR MOTION PICTURE
STARRING CHUCK NORRIS!

US/42669-0 • A CROSSFIRE BOOK • $2.95
CAN 43608-4 • $3.50

The official tie-in paperback novel for *Invasion U.S.A.*. "Jason Frost" was a
pseudonym shared by pulp authors Raymond Obstfeld and Rich Rainey.

Like the suburban development that was destroyed a few scenes earlier, the location scouts were able to find a nearby mall—the Avondale Mall, in Decatur—that was partially closed for renovation. As the mall planned to gut and redesign that whole wing of the shopping center anyway, the production gave them permission to destroy the main entrance, midway, and a bunch of the shops, including a closed-down Sears department store. As the mall had already been stripped down for construction work, the crew had to re-decorate the whole place—filling the empty stores with merchandise and building the gigantic holiday displays. Cannon initially objected to the film being set at Christmastime, as the cost of and additional time needed for set dressing—holiday lights, Christmas trees, and so forth—would go up, considering the film was shot during the summer months. The production team eventually won that argument, and the holiday decorations do make the villains' actions feel all the more sinister.

The fleeing terrorists manage to shake our hero off the side of their truck in the mall's parking lot, but Matt Hunter quickly commandeers a Mustang convertible owned by a freelance photojournalist (Melissa Prophet, a former Miss California) who fortuitously happens to be wherever anything terrorist-y is going down. He uses it to chase down the villains, and tosses a grenade through their driver's side window.

When Rostov's lieutenant informs him that Matt Hunter is still alive, the terrorist overlord executes his signature move and shoots the guy's dick off. His men move ahead with their orders to spread chaos across the nation. Unfortunately for them—but fortunately for America—Chuck Norris . . . *Matt Hunter* . . . is somehow several steps ahead of them, showing up wherever they are just in time to stop whatever evil, deadly hijinks they had planned. When they attempt to blow up a church, Matt Hunter pops over to rewire the bomb and hand it back to the terrorists. (He delivers a predictably sweet one-liner before tossing the suitcase explosive their way: "Didn't work, huh? Now it will." *BOOM!*) When they strap a bomb to a school bus full of children, Matt Hunter is there to pull it off and reattach it to the bad guys' vehicle. ("Lose this?" *BOOM!*) When they attack a crowd gathered outside a grocery store, it just so happens that Matt Hunter is nearby enough to pull over and wipe out the gunmen. (We have to assume that Hunter went back to the wrecked mall to retrieve his truck at some point, because he's driving it around for the rest of the movie.) Matt Hunter is a one-man terrorist-wrecking crew.

As terrible as their actions are, you almost begin to feel a little bad for these evildoers: they can't seem to pull off even the tiniest bit of terrorism without Chuck Norris instantly showing up to piss all over their plans. No matter how indiscriminate or nonsensical the deed, Hunter somehow knows exactly where the bad guys will be right as they launch their attacks. (How does he do it? Chuck Magic, once again.) However, a one-man super-army isn't enough to stop hundreds of them spread out across the entire nation, and Hunter acknowledges this. He hatches a plan. Later that night, as he lays in a hotel room bed, chewing gum and watching an over-the-air broadcast of 1956's *Earth vs. the Flying Saucers*, the FBI kick down his door to "arrest" him Rostov catches a news report on Hunter's arrest, which suspiciously includes the exact location where authorities are holding him—and diverts all of his remaining army there, to take Matt Hunter out once and for all!

The movie wraps up in downtown Atlanta, where the production staged what was—to that point, at least—the largest battle scene ever filmed in an American city. The scene was filmed with the full cooperation of the National Guard, who loaned Cannon six tanks, six armored personnel carriers, ten two-and-a-half ton trucks, and sixteen jeeps for their shots. They also loaned out *real* automatic weapons to equip the extras, who were required to hand over their drivers' licenses in exchange for the dangerous firearms. The sudden nighttime appearance of armored vehicles and hundreds of armed soldiers rolling into downtown Atlanta understandably distressed a few of the international guests staying at the adjacent Ritz-Carlton hotel, who weren't informed of the film shoot and thought they were witnessing a military coup.

In the scene, troops gather as helicopters drop leaflets down on the city, urging citizens to stay inside their homes and remain safe. In most cases, the production would have printed up flyers with a message along the lines of

"Cannon Films thanks you for letting us film in your fine city"—or, just left the papers blank. Someone in the prop department dropped the ball here, though, and had the leaflets printed up with the official-looking message we see in the movie, stating that "a dusk to dawn curfew is in effect immediately" during a "current state of emergency." Thousands of these were sprinkled all across downtown Atlanta, to a predictably disastrous effect. Radio and television announcements had to be released to clarify that the flyers were not real and only part of a movie shoot, and Norris himself was personally upset to learn about a pair of old ladies who hid from the invaders in their basement for *several days* after finding one of the fake warning sheets.

Soon, truckloads of terrorists swarm the downtown Atlanta compound where Rostov believes Hunter is being held, only to find it empty—and realize that they've been deceived. Instead of Matt Hunter, the bad guys find themselves surrounded and trapped by the National Guard. Soon the totally-not-imprisoned-at-all Matt Hunter squares off against a small team of elite baddies, led by Rostov himself. This whole action sequence—both inside and outside the building—is nonstop gunfire and pyrotechnics. For action fans, it's undeniably satisfying. The whole thing ends with Hunter and Rostov squaring off, mano a mano, with M72 LAW rocket launchers. Hunter wins, naturally, blowing Rostov's guts and body parts out of an office window. ("It's time." *Boom!*) The credits roll.

Invasion U.S.A. debuted in first place at the U.S. box office on the last September weekend of 1985, knocking *Back to the Future* (1985) from its nine-week hold at the top of the charts. It was even more successful as a rental tape, for a while becoming the second-most popular title in MGM's video library after *Gone with the Wind* (1939). The wantonly patriotic movie even fared very well in international markets, to boot.

All of this, despite the fact that contemporary critics pretty much *hated* the movie. The esteemed Roger Ebert called it "a brain-damaged, idiotic thriller, not even bad enough to be laughable." Many criticized Norris' stoic performance. "Though most of his face is obscured by a beard, it's possible to detect a complete lack of expression," wrote the *New York Times'* Vincent

Canby, oddly adding: "Even [his] eyes look empty and glassy, like the buttons on the face of a teddy bear." Others still criticized it for being episodic, or simply an excuse for nonstop violence. One *Pittsburgh Post-Gazette* writer, Duane Dudek, wrote: "There were so many fiery explosions that one could read a book in a darkened theater," and added a jab at the popular action star's devotees, "Not that Chuck Norris fans are interested in reading."

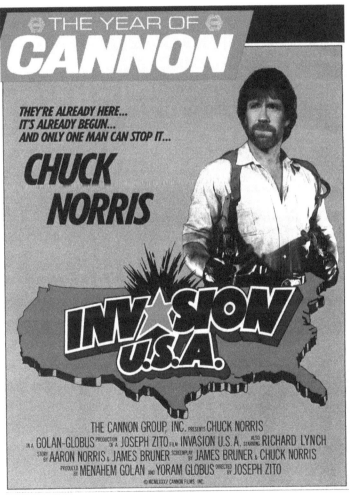

Cannon knew exactly how to sell their film: as a quintessential Chuck Norris movie.

As far as Cannon was concerned, it was another big hit from their hottest action star.

Cannon fans shouldn't care about those reviews, either. *Invasion U.S.A.* plays like a bigger, more violent, more fun *Red Dawn* (1984), without all of the unnecessary drama and teen angst. The filmmakers deftly crafted a film that forms perfectly to all of Norris' strengths and limitations. They knew that audiences flocked to Chuck Norris movies to see him kick ass—*not* to watch him unconvincingly mourn a partner's death, or stiffly romance a younger actress. Norris realized this by now, too, as evidenced in a profile interview for *Spin Magazine* published the same year:

"You get to know after a while what your audience expects from you. I go to all the theaters to see my movies and find out what they like and don't like," Norris explained. "I learned early on that they don't like me getting into sex scenes, for example. They want me to be a free spirit, to be a loner, a guy who deals with whatever odds he has to encounter. So that's what I try to give them, with a different twist each time. The whole thing is to try and find creative ways of dispatching characters, to take this bad element and dispose of it imaginatively. When you achieve that, you're entertaining the audience, and that's what my movies are for."

Invasion U.S.A. leaps from one exciting action scene to the next, as they find one new way after another for him to imaginatively dispose of the bad guys. Is it episodic? Sure, a little: Chuck drives his pickup somewhere, kills all the terrorists there, and then moves on (rinse, lather, repeat). But, why waste time trying to over-explain things? We know the movie's bad guys are *bad guys* from the moment they gun down a boat full of immigrant families, and those feelings are only reinforced every time they slaughter more innocent people. All the audience really wants is to see them die by Matt Hunter's hand. (Or by his feet, his Uzis, grenades, rocket launcher, etc.)

Writer James Bruner has explained that about half an hour's worth of the film was cut out, including backstories for the villains and scenes where Melissa Prophet's journalist character essentially narrates the terrorist strikes, connecting the film's many action sequences. Whoopi Goldberg had been

Norris' personal choice to play the reporter, and he suggested her for the role after he'd seen the then-undiscovered actress in a one-woman play. Zito and Cannon ultimately decided to go with Prophet instead. (Goldberg went on to appear in 1985's *The Color Purple* instead, and give a performance for which she was nominated for an Oscar.)

While the inclusion of those missing scenes may very well have made the plot of *Invasion U.S.A.* more cohesive, their exclusion makes it a better Chuck Norris movie. As released, the movie is a lean, mean 110 minutes: a full twenty minutes longer than the average Cannon movie, but without a slow moment to be found in the entire picture. It's easy to overlook plot holes when the action is so over-the-top, bombastic, and nonstop.

At its core, *Invasion U.S.A.* is a prototypical Chuck Norris action vehicle, but this one was made on a much larger scale than any of his films other than *The Delta Force* (1986). The practical and pyrotechnic effects still look fantastic, even by today's standards. The movie was filmed for $12 million—a sizable budget, for a Cannon feature. We know that $1 million of that went to the movie's bearded, 45-year-old star; from the looks of things, at least another $1 million was probably spent on all of the explosives and squibs. The team was able to stretch their production value even further through top-notch location scouting, and finding real-world buildings they could wreck and blow up. This gave the movie a realistic look that you just couldn't get from shooting on a studio's back lot.

The special effects team had come to *Invasion U.S.A.* direct from George Romero's *Day of the Dead* (1985) by the request of director Joe Zito, whom Tom Savini had previously worked with on *Friday the 13th: The Final Chapter* (1984). His team included future Academy Award-winner Howard Berger, who brought home gold for *The Lion, the Witch and the Wardrobe* (2005) and has worked on titles as varied as *Army of Darkness* (1992), *The Green Mile* (1999), and *Inglourious Basterds* (2009), and Greg Nicotero, best known for his work on the TV series *The Walking Dead* and its spin-offs. Savini, of course, had already earned his status as a horror legend, with credits on *Dawn of the Dead* (1978), *Friday the 13th* (1980), *Maniac* (1980), and *Creepshow* (1982).

He also worked on *Maria's Lovers* (1985) and *Texas Chainsaw Massacre 2* (1986) for Cannon, and directed the excellent 1990 remake of *Night of the Living Dead* for Menahem Golan's 21st Century Film Corporation.

Stunt coordinator Aaron Norris continued working his way up the production hierarchy, and went on to direct three Cannon films starring his brother: *Braddock: Missing in Action III* (1988), *Delta Force 2* (1990), and *The Hitman* (1991), as well as *Platoon Leader* (1988) without Chuck.

A sequel was written for Cannon by screenwriter James Booth, but Norris wasn't interested in returning to the character when he read it. That script was shot by Sam Firstenberg as *Avenging Force* (1986), with Michael Dudikoff in the Matt Hunter role, but outside of the name and its hero being a CIA operative, the two movies are otherwise unrelated. Meanwhile, Joseph Zito was rewarded for his success with *Invasion U.S.A.* by being assigned to Cannon's ill-fated, yet heavily-promoted *Spider-Man* movie—a film he worked on for roughly a year before dropping out, and which wound up never being made.

From where the author stands, *Invasion U.S.A.* is Chuck Norris at his Cannon-tacular best.

An Italian magazine ad for *Invasion U.S.A.* by artist Sandro Symeoni, complete with burning Statue of Liberty and levitating Uzi shells.

Interview: Screenwriter James Bruner

With *Missing in Action* (1984), James Bruner was the writer behind one of Cannon's all-time biggest hits. He'd follow that up with *Invasion U.S.A.* (1985), a movie that topped the box office the week it was released. He became one of Cannon's star writers, and in a flurry over the next few years was recruited to work on *The Delta Force* (1986), *P.O.W. The Escape* (1987), *Braddock: Missing in Action III* (1988), and several unmade Cannon projects, as well as to perform uncredited script doctor duties on a handful of other films, including *American Ninja* (1985).

Many of these screenplays were written for Chuck Norris, a friend whom Bruner had formed a collaborative partnership with while writing *An Eye for an Eye* (1981), one of his pre-Cannon starring vehicles. You can read about Bruner's early career and the *Missing in Action* saga in the first part of this interview, which can be found in *The Cannon Film Guide, Vol. I*.

Bruner continues to write screenplays, novels, and children's books with his wife and writing partner, Elizabeth Stevens. In more recent years, Bruner has worked as a film producer and director as well.

Cannon signed Chuck Norris to a big, multi-year contract after their first few films were big successes. Those sorts of studio contracts were normal in the '30s and '40s, but not by the 1980s. I imagine that news must have been good for you, considering the creative partnership you had with Chuck.

James Bruner: Yes. Cannon's history, from *Missing in Action* forward, was when a movie made money, they would make more movies like that one. Most of their movies originally made money because they had a really smart business plan, and when they stuck to that, they did well. But, they also wanted to compete with Warner Brothers and Paramount and so on, and when they went that way, they basically lost money, and Chuck's movies bailed them out. *Missing in Action* bailed out the company, *Delta Force, Invasion U.S.A.*, all of those did really help them—and then they would spend big money on awful movies, like *Over the Top* (1987) or something.

I had a good relationship with Menahem, too. I would get called in to script doctor things, basically without credit but getting paid. I'd come in and they'd say, "Okay, so here is all the footage we shot. We can shoot three more days with limited locations and actors. Can you make this movie make sense?"

How quickly did *Invasion U.S.A.* happen? If you were scouting locations when Chuck hadn't even seen *Missing in Action* yet, it must have been almost immediately.

Menahem had done several ninja movies, and he wanted to do another one called *American Ninja*, and he wanted Chuck Norris to be the American ninja. Chuck was like, "I can always do martial arts in a bigger action movie. I'd rather not be pigeonholed into just martial arts movies." I got hired to write *American Ninja*, and he basically said, "I don't want to do a ninja movie." I said, "Don't worry about it. I've got an idea."

Cannon was actually pretty good about letting you go off and write the script and not interfering too much. I had an idea where Chuck was a secret agent, whatever. His code name was "American Ninja," so we called all the drafts we turned in "American Ninja," but it was the story for *Invasion U.S.A.* Menahem read the script and liked it but said, "Of course, we can *not* call it *American Ninja*."

Chuck was really excited about the *Invasion U.S.A.* take on it. *Missing in Action* hadn't come out yet, but I think they had done such good presales and everything on *Missing in Action* that they thought they would be able to make money with him in bigger action movies, too. I don't think they knew *how* big it was going to end up being. At that time, they were being really smart about what they financed, and how much they spent. They looked at it and probably thought that they could make more money with a bigger action piece than they could on the ninja angle, but that's just my guess on it.

Was your original script significantly different than what was shot?

It was fairly close, although originally I had Chuck's dad living in a retirement trailer park in Florida, and he was a big character. They didn't like that angle, so they took that out, which I think would have been more humanizing, and given him less of a superhero kind of persona. That fell out pretty quickly, but the overall storyline was there really from the beginning.

A photograph more badass than even the best Chuck Norris Joke.

I was able to go location scouting with Zito. People always ask me regarding the action scenes, "Do you write everything out in detail?" I did that for *An Eye for an Eye* (1981), and they changed everything completely. [*Laughs*] From then on, especially for things with Chuck, I would leave lots of room. Menahem used to read the scripts and always say, "Take out all of this dialogue. He beats them! He beats them!" [*Laughs*]

On our location scout in Atlanta, we really hit some fortuitous things. We found this whole neighborhood that they were going to bulldoze to extend the Atlanta airport. All those nice homes that we ended up blowing up, where we see the bad guys driving through the neighborhood with their rocket launchers. Those were all real houses! It was the same thing with driving the truck through the shopping mall. That mall was going to be renovated, and they were going to tear all the stuff out. "Blow it up, do whatever you want," they said. We were able to write it into the script and incorporate things in there that added gigantic production value.

The ending really got ruined. I got a call while they were shooting that I was needed in Atlanta, because they had made some changes, shot some things differently, and needed a new ending. I wish I could remember what the original ending was—I remember being really pissed off. I went down and looked at the footage. They only had so many days left, and limited locations. I had to come up with an ending that compared to all the great action sequences in the rest of the picture, but without a lot to work with. I think the ending is weak compared to other things in the movie.

You're right—it does seem a bit strange that after seeing an entire neighborhood and a shopping mall blown up, the finale is basically set in a tiny office area.

It's not that satisfying—but the movie had bigger problems than that, unfortunately. It's one of those great "What could have been?" things.

I was still working on the script when Chuck called me from New York and said, "I came back to the hotel last night and somebody had left me tickets for an off-Broadway show." He said they had been an extra in *Good Guys Wear Black* (1978) or something like that. It was a one-woman show. He called me up, raving. He said, "It's fantastic. This woman's great! She should play your reporter in *Invasion U.S.A.*" It was Whoopi Goldberg.

Wow, that would have been interesting casting.

No one knew who she was. I thought, "Oh my God," because the characters didn't have a romance, and it really needed somebody strong in the role because the story was told through the reporter. It needed someone who could carry that. It would've been a great casting, but that got kiboshed. Melissa Prophet was a very nice lady and everything, but she wasn't strong enough to carry that part, and we ended up having to cut out probably twenty minutes of really critical information for her character and story, which had helped tie everything together. We felt really bad, because the performance was just not there and it would've been worse to put it in. I think the final movie is disjointed, because the interconnecting sequences are missing. Chuck's in one place, and then suddenly he's somewhere else. It's not tied together.

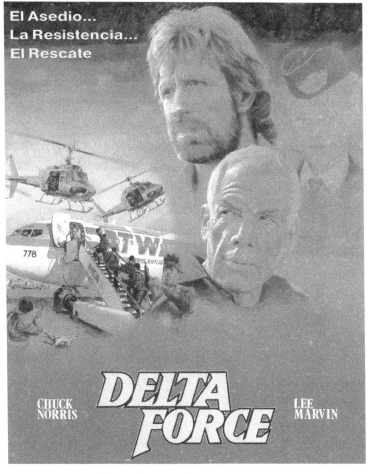

A Spanish poster for *The Delta Force.*

How did you and Chuck get from *Invasion U.S.A.* to *Delta Force*?

My friend and technical adviser, Jim Monaghan, was an ex-Green Beret. When we were working on *Missing in Action*, he told me about the Delta Force. He had helped train the original Delta Force that went into Desert One, when they had a disaster there. He told me about the unit no one knew about. I had pitched an idea to Menahem and at first he was like, "No, no, no." Later on he'd seen, like, a one-paragraph article in *Newsweek* or *Time* magazine about the Delta Force. He called me up, "Jimmy . . . Chuck Norris, Charles Bronson: *The Delta Force*. You want to write it?" I said, "Hell, yes, I want to write it! Are you kidding? Chuck and Charles Bronson in *Delta Force?* Oh my gosh, that's huge."

That would have been a match-up to see!

The final movie ended up okay, but I wrote the story for the Norris-Bronson *Delta Force*, and it would've been really spectacular. Those two guys at the top of the action game, I was so excited. I couldn't wait to do it.

Did anything from your Bronson-Norris version make it to the final movie? I know that their sudden decision to base it on the real-world hijacking that was playing out in the news kind of, well, hijacked the story.

It was going to be *Delta Force* with Bronson and Norris, and directed by Joe Zito. I thought, "Man, this is going to be the biggest one, for sure." It was going forward, and I don't know what happened. They couldn't make a deal with Bronson or something, and it ended up being Chuck and another one of my childhood heroes, Lee Marvin.

The whole story had to change because Lee's fantastic, but he's different from Bronson. Then the TWA hijacking happened and Menahem decided he would direct the film himself, and that it was basically a chance for him to remake *Operation Thunderbolt* (1979), which was his favorite film that he had made.

I always tell people, "Don't write anything current, because by the time you're done, there's going to be something else happening." I was following the events of the TWA hijacking as they were unfolding, and changing things in the script. Menahem had Elizabeth and I go to Israel for pre-production.

The script wasn't complete, there really wasn't an ending, because the hostages were still in the Beirut airport.

I would literally go to Menahem's office in the mornings in downtown Tel Aviv, we'd sit side by side and write stuff. I'd come back the next morning and he would have stayed up almost all night rewriting it, so it took half the day to fix his rewrite so we could move forward. Finally, one day he looked at me and said, "Jimmy, you will go to Beirut to the airport and we'll find out what is going on." [*Laughs*] I think, "Okay! I'm just this cheesehead from Wisconsin. I don't speak Arabic. I don't remotely look like I belong in the region, and I'm going to walk into the Beirut airport held by terrorists?"

Wow, wow, wow . . .

Luckily some of the other Israelis were like, "No, no." Then the hostages got released, and so there was really no rescue, no ending, and we had to come up with that. I thought we did a pretty good job. Menahem wanted Elizabeth and I to stay [in Israel] for the production and work on the script as it was going, but we had to leave because we were doing a little movie with Woody Strode at the time, so we couldn't stay.

Because of that, the silly stuff snuck in: Chuck on the motorcycle with the rockets, that goofy kind of stuff. There are some really, really good things in there because I got them to hire Jim Monaghan as the technical advisor. He used to battle with Menahem about, "The Israeli commandos do it this way, but Delta Force does it this way," and, "Let's do it the Delta Force way, because it's different." And Menahem would say, "No, no, we do it the Israeli way." Monaghan was able to give us some of the Delta techniques that weren't classified. They'd been used enough where bad guys would know it, so we could put stuff in the movie that wasn't giving anything away.

We had a scene where the hostages are at a school hall, and the Deltas come in to rescue them. Menahem took me on a location scout to look at this school in Haifa and, again, it's a building that's going to be demolished, so we can blow it up. That's always a good thing. We go into the basement of the school. The hostages are supposed to be on the first floor, but the basement's got a twelve-foot ceiling. Menahem says, "If you're going to blow a hole in the floor, I can't figure out how to get that last Delta up." He said, "There are two things we can do." I said, "Yes? What's that?" Because I had written it like the Delta Force would really do it—but he had his own ideas.

Menahem says, "Well, we have this mini-trampoline, and they run and they jump up through the air into the room." I said, "Okay . . . what's the other one?" He says, "Well, there's a teeter-totter, and one guy jumps from this end, and the other guy flies up into the room, but I can't figure out how to get the last guy up." [*Laughs*] We're trying to make a somewhat serious movie. Luckily I was able to talk him into doing it kind of like they would really do it: build a little platform, blow the hole open, and just stand up and boom, boom, boom—take everybody out. But I didn't know about the rocket launchers on the motorcycle or those other goofy things.

Can you tell me a little bit more what it was like writing that script with Menahem? You said he'd stay up all night changing it—did you come to expect that, and know that you were going to wake up in the morning with stuff to fix?

Yes. That's why I finally said to him, "Maybe we should share the writing credit?" In fact, now, thinking about residuals, I wouldn't have offered. He said, "Okay, but you get top billing." He was actually a pretty smart film-maker, but he would get certain ideas, and he was going to do it that way. The original version of the movie was almost six hours long, and they should have preserved that and put it out as a mini-series.

The script was really long. A lot happened. There were tons of characters, so it was challenging keeping up and keeping the story moving forward, especially without having an ending, too. Since we were following so much of the hijacking, basically recreating parts of it, it was very challenging.

There's another thing. There's a scene the night before the rescue. The Delta guys are sitting around, one guy is playing a guitar and singing a song about America. So, Menahem and I wrote this "hit" song about the stuff that made America so great, and there were lines in there about "little Brookie Shields." He *loved* Brooke Shields. That song was going to be a big hit and we were going to share the royalties. [*Laughs*] Never a dull moment.

I'll tell you, the exciting thing about the whole Cannon experience was that they made the movies. You didn't just develop the heck out of something and have it thrown out, or never see the light of day. Given all the flaws and everything in the different productions, it still was very gratifying. Most of them worked well and continue to have a pretty good audience to this day.

A Cannon pre-sales ad for an unmade version of *Delta Force 2*, which would have featured Chuck Norris and Lee Marvin taking down an international drug cartel.

You were briefly attached to *Delta Force 2* while Michael Winner was slated to direct. Do you recall why that version fell through?

Someone called me and said, "We want you to go to London. Michael Winner is going to direct *Delta Force 2*. We want you to go over and come up with a story that he's happy with, and then we'll go from there." I was going to go over for a week or ten days and hash out a story, and it was going to star Chuck and Lee Marvin. I actually had a story that I had worked on for the sequel, and I wanted Winner's input on it, so they sent me over to meet with him.

I'd never met him before. Of course I'd seen the original *Death Wish* and then some of the other Bronson movies, and I'd liked *Chato's Land* (1972). I wasn't really prepared for it—I knew nothing about him. This was before the internet, and you couldn't get much information about people. Now, you could easily look up Michael Winner and see all these interviews and go, "Okay, I know what I'm walking into."

I set up an appointment, and went to London to meet him. I walked up to the door of this beautiful, red brick Victorian mansion which was a Nationally Registered historic place—some really famous British painter had lived there.

I knock and this guy comes to the door, he's in his fifties, slender with glasses, and he's got this nervous kind of expression. He said, "Come in, Mr. Winner is expecting you." We went in and up the stairs and I saw a maid working, cleaning something, and she kind of had this nervous look, too, and I thought it was unusual. I go upstairs and Michael's got this beautiful study, with these big windows open. He's sitting behind his big desk with a cigar. "Hi, how are you doing?" We chatted a little bit.

It turned out that the butler guy was his roommate back in school. Winner used to pay him to make his bed and pick up his clothes, and the guy had been with him for, like, forty years. He yelled at the guy in front of me for something, I forget what it was about. He said something along the lines of, "Have you noticed the people that work for me are a little nervous?" I said, "Yes. Why?" He said, "It's because I treat them like that." He added, "What would you do if I treated you like that?" I said, "I'd pick you up and throw you right out the window." He looked at me, leaned back in his chair, and I was his best friend.

We finished our meeting, and he walks me out to the front door. Up through the front gate comes a beautiful, vintage Rolls Royce limousine. Out hops a chauffeur in full outfit, standing at attention. I thought, "Well, this is nice. He's going to send me back to my flat in style." Then Michael Winner says, "The bus stop is down the block." He just had this guy pull up to show off. [*Laughs*] I'm like, "This guy!"

He decided that he would have me stay and write the script, and they ended up paying me more to do that. The challenging thing was I was supposed to write ten pages a day, and then I was supposed to come over to his house every day at 11:00 AM, stay for lunch, and go over the pages. I'd write like crazy, and he would read it. "This is shit. This is shit. This is shit." He would rewrite everything. With Menahem, he changed stuff, but at least I got to do most of the typing. Winner had to do it, and the script just got goofier and goofier. I finally stopped fighting it. I tried to fix it where I could, but he was really stubborn, to say the least.

Finally, the company paid for my wife and daughter to come over. Elizabeth read Winner's script, and she said, "You got to tell them that you didn't write this." I said, "No, it's not that bad." She said, "No, you've *got* to."

I went into the story department the day after I got home and made an announcement. "Is there a script that was turned in with my name on? I didn't write it. That's Michael Winner's." The guy who was head of the story department at the time, he said, "Oh, my God. Thank God. We wondered what the hell happened to you."

You worked on a TV pilot for a *Delta Force* series. What can you tell me about that?

CBS was really interested in doing a *Delta Force* TV series. It would have been perfect for that time, when there were all these international, hour-long action shows doing really well all over the world. Jim Monaghan was hired to help me because of his expertise. I wrote a pilot script for an hour-long

Delta Force series and CBS liked it. This was right at the time when *Missing In Action III* was in the works. That was my last project for Cannon, which is a whole different story. I didn't know at the time that the company was in really bad financial trouble.

When Cannon had offices in the CNN building on Sunset, everything was cool. They had low overhead. The offices were funky, but it didn't matter. But then they built their headquarters in Beverly Hills, and unfortunately they put these big-budget movies out that didn't do well. They basically forgot about their financial model.

CBS wanted to do the *Delta Force* series, and Menahem said "no," because the deal they offered wasn't good enough for him. It would have put them in television with a big hit. That was hard to take, especially when the network wanted to go with it. I thought, "Oh, man. I can't believe you're turning this down."

Yet another ad for an unmade *Delta Force* sequel. For a while, the "Spitfire" version was shopped to buyers as a starring vehicle for Michael Dudikoff and Steve James, with Albert Pyun attached to direct.

As you just mentioned, *Missing In Action III* was where your time ended with Cannon. It sounds like by then they couldn't afford to pay people what they should have.

That was really disastrous. I wrote the [*MIA III*] script with Chuck Norris's input, and Joe Zito was going to direct it. I thought it was the strongest script that I'd written to that point, with the most emotional content, and a really good, strong story. Menahem called me into his office and said, "I want to pay you half of what we contracted for *Missing in Action III*." To be honest, they never really paid me that well. If I'd been at Warner Brothers or Paramount or somewhere like that, I would have done financially much better.

Menahem said, "I want to pay you half." I said, "Well, I already did all the work." He said, "I know, I know but I want to pay you half. If you don't take half, you'll never work for Cannon again." I said, "Well, you know, if you said something up front and you made up for it, maybe we could have talked, but I can't. I've already done all this work." He said, "With all due respect, that's it." That *was* it. It turned out that Aaron Norris had a deal where his payment was tied to whatever I got for the script, and Menahem didn't want to pay Aaron. If I took half, then Aaron would get half, and that's where they wanted to go with it.

After all this time, basically writing movies that saved the company more than once, it was hard to take. I couldn't believe it. They wanted to shrink the budget. They had four or five directors, I guess, attached to it. They did different rewrites. I don't know who did the final work on it, but it ended up with a goofy, over the top, World War II propaganda film bad guy, cackling and laughing. It was stupid. Probably some of it was budgetary, but it just didn't come together. It was disappointing to go out on a whimper with that one.

Mata Hari on VHS: "The bombshell of the '80s stars as the booby trap of World War I."

Mata Hari

Release Date: September 20, 1985
Directed by: Curtis Harrington
Written by: Joel Ziskin
Starring: Sylvia Kristel, Oliver Tobias, Christopher Cazenove
Trailer Voiceover: "The fate of nations was changed in her boudoir!"

Here are three words to assure you that Cannon's *Mata Hari* (1985) is a respectful, highly informative biopic which lifts a veil on one of The Great War's most intriguing, mysterious figures:

Topless women swordfighting.

Indeed, the only things being lifted in this film are the skirts of its femme fatale protagonist: quite often, and with great gusto. (And to be fair, her male co-stars doff their clothing quite a bit, too, as do many inconsequential background characters.) This World War I drama offers up sex, sex, and more sex, mixed with just enough ambiguous political maneuvering to upset and confuse any audience members who are in it purely for the wanking.

Did I mention the movie features a topless swordfight?

Mata Hari stars erotic cinema icon Sylvia Kristel, whose naked breasts serve as the audience's introduction to the real-life, historical character she plays. The film was Cannon's second attempt—following *Lady Chatterley's Lover* (1983)—to cast the famed *Emmanuelle* (1974) star in a movie that showed off slightly more than just her naughty bits. While the first was a literary adaptation, this was a costume drama ostensibly inspired by real-world events. The producers at Cannon were realists, however, and weren't about to make a movie starring the world's foremost softcore actress without displaying a healthy heaping of skin, and so this bewildering hybrid of history and humping was born.

Once again: this movie prominently features a scene where two women, bereft of covers for their breasts, have a swordfight.

We won't dwell much here on plot summary, as *Mata Hari* has a befuddling habit of making broad leaps in time and setting, as if the filmmakers were more concerned with checking off biographical boxes than threading the story together in a way that would make sense to the average viewer. As established by the opening (nude) musical number, Mata Hari is an exotic dancer. The movie then jumps ahead several years, to a three-way meet cute between Mata Hari, French military officer Georges LaDoux (played by Swiss actor Oliver Tobias, who was also in 1983's *The Wicked Lady*), and German officer Karl von Bayerling (Christopher Cazenove). These two bosom buddies become former friends when World War I breaks out, and they find themselves on opposing sides of the conflict. Mata Hari's role in this tumultuous love triangle lands her repeatedly in hot water, as does her habit of making any other man in a uniform who gets within ten feet fall madly in love with her.

One particular roll in the hay with a foreign soldier leaves poor Mata Hari—or as she's known formally, Lady MacLeod—in an especially compromising position, as her lover du jour is assassinated by poisoned dart while they're mid-boink. She's manipulated into spying for the Germans, and then the French, soon flipping back and forth at a rate that's dizzying to keep track of. Of course, the goodness in her heart shows through when she finally thwarts a plot by the evil German intelligence officer, Fraulein Doktor (Gaye Brown) and her right-hand murder guy (Gottfried John, a regular of Fassbinder's films) to blow up a cathedral full of Frenchmen. The French then repay her good deed by charging her with espionage and having her executed by firing squad, turning her into an unwilling martyr.

As you probably guessed, the majority of what happens in the movie is pure fiction. In all likelihood, her real life was less interesting than it's been made out to be, and far more sad. Over the century that has passed since Mata Hari's death, her legend has far outgrown the small role most historians agree she actually played in the Great War. We know that she *was* an exotic dancer, famous for dancing in "Oriental" styles and shaking her bare butt in music halls across Europe. She is also known to have been a high-end prostitute with a notably upper-class clientele. By the time the war broke out in 1914, she was aging and in a poor financial state. Historians can't seem to agree on the events that followed, with various accounts claiming that she was spying on Germany for France, that she was selling French secrets to the Germans, or that she was a double agent playing both sides.

In all likelihood, her contributions to either side's military intelligence were minimal, if she was even a spy at all. (It's unclear whether she had inflated her espionage role to make herself sound "cool," as the kids say, or if the French simply made her into a scapegoat when their war effort was at a low point.) In any case, she was arrested in Paris in 1917, put on trial, and then executed as an enemy spy.

The many retellings of her story have turned Mata Hari in to the ultimate femme fatale. Hollywood has certainly done its part in embellishing the Mata Hari story, going all the way back to Greta Garbo's 1931 portrayal of her in a film of the same name.

Cannon, as you might expect, used her tragic tale as an excuse to get down and *durrrr-tay*. They squeeze the most from their Kristel casting by inserting a steady stream of softcore sex scenes into a nearly-incomprehensible espionage plot. None of it is subtle: even in a moment of more tender, romantic lovemaking, a stroke of thunder and a flash of lightning punctuate the moment of orgasm. Much of the time, it's filthiness for filthiness' sake—i.e., Mata Hari masturbating as a pervy German officer peeps at her through a keyhole—or, worse, utterly nonsensical. Which brings us to that aforementioned, topless swordfight . . .

In one sequence, Mata Hari attends a decadent masquerade-ball-slash-orgy. It's the type of party where naked humans are hired to pose as living decorations. These fleshy statues are hand-selected by masked partygoers, and disappear with them to engage in some variety of crazy, rich people sex that's too wild for this movie to even show.

How did Cannon attempt to top their topless whip fight from 1983's *The Wicked Lady*? Why, with a topless sword fight, of course.

Dressed in an outfit that we'd describe as half buccaneer, half sexy Halloween Store version of George Washington—complete with a curly wig and tri-cornered hat—Mata Hari runs into her date's previous lover, who is also attending the party. For some reason that is perhaps only known to the film's screenwriter, we cut to the two women—now topless, but still wearing the rest of their ornate masquerade costumes—dueling with rapiers as a crowd of creeps in clown makeup leer at the spectacle. From the unamused looks on their faces, not one of them seems to think whatever is happening is the least bit strange, not even as Mata Hari calls the poor woman's mother a pig and stabs at her opponent's nipples with her sword. The fight ends when Mata Hari draws blood. Her prize for winning is a threesome with two of the hired sex slaves, while a clown and a bunch of old people just stand next to the bed and watch.

And, so, yeah . . . that's *Mata Hari* for you, more or less. That one scene completely overshadows the rest of the movie, for better or worse. It would feel weird if it were part of, say, a Federico Fellini movie, or *Eyes Wide Shut* (1999), but shoved into a World War I period drama? Bonkers. The rest of the movie pivots between sex scenes that stop short of being straight-up pornography, and sharply-dressed actors vaguely double-crossing each other in questionable French and German accents. If that's what does it for you, hey, no one's judging. Entertainmentwise, though, this one's a doozy.

Mata Hari played in its full-length version across Europe, in countries where Kristel's top billing was a box office draw and erotic films were regularly shown in mainstream movie theaters. In America, though, *Mata Hari* hit a snag with the MPAA, who took one look at the movie's plentiful sex scenes and threatened to slap it with an 'X' rating. Cannon capitulated and trimmed several minutes of the movie against their director's wishes. (Harrington's original desire was to release the movie under the full title, "Mata Hari: Erotic Adventures with a Spy.") Putting out what was essentially a softcore porn movie with most of the porn removed, however, proved as futile an endeavor as you'd imagine, and the movie face-planted during the theatrical run it was given in the United States.

This wound up being the final feature for director Curtis Harrington, who had come to prominence in the avant-garde film scene of the 1940 and 1950s, alongside filmmakers like Kenneth Anger and Maya Deren. After directing his debut feature, *Night Tide* (1961), starring Dennis Hopper, Harrington made a string of memorable b-movies that included such hard-to-forget titles as *Whoever Slew Auntie Roo?* (1972), *What's the Matter with Helen?* (1971), *Voyage to the Prehistoric Planet* (1965), and *Queen of Blood* (1966).

By the 1980s his career was in decline, and he worked almost exclusively in television. *Mata Hari* was his first theatrical film in almost a decade, but his experience with Cannon, it seems, was so bad that it led him to swear off Hollywood for good. It was bad enough for Harrington that he was forced to work on a low budget and shoot in a far-off location—Budapest, Hungary, which stands in (quite poorly) for both Paris and Berlin—with an inexperienced screenwriter. Worse yet, he was saddled with a leading lady who, in his own stated opinion, could not act. It's a testament to the director's consummate professionalism that he didn't throw in the towel before filming wrapped.

Kristel was briefly on the hook to appear in a sequel to *The Last American Virgin* (1982) which, like so many announced Cannon projects, failed to get off the ground.

One final piece of criticism which needs to be mentioned concerns the dance numbers themselves. If you can overlook their orientalist themes—it's highly doubtful the *real* Mata Hari's routines were any more culturally sensitive—it's hard not to notice how brief and uninspired they feel. There's a lack of commitment that's most bothersome. Mata Hari was one of the most legendary and notorious exotic dancers of all time—heck, there are some out there who attribute her as the inventor of the striptease. However, in the few minutes' worth of low-key dance routines we see in this film, Kristel appears listless and without energy. (And this was even during her period of heavy cocaine use!) Her Mata Hari doesn't even look like she *enjoys* dancing.

Considering that one of the film's taglines boasted, "When she danced, their secrets flowed like wine." If Kristel's interpretation is any indication of what her routines really looked like, we can't be sure her dances didn't put enemy soldiers to sleep.

A newspaper advertisement from *Mata Hari's* opening
weekend in Fort Myers, Florida.

Cannon's Allan Quatermain movies shared many similarities with the *Indiana Jones* films, down to their Drew Struzan-like poster art by Jacques Devaud.

King Solomon's Mines
Allan Quatermain and the Lost City of Gold

Release Date: November 22ⁿᵈ, 1985 (I), January 30ᵗʰ, 1987 (II)
Directed by: J. Lee Thompson (I), Gary Nelson (II)
Written by: Gene Quintano & James R. Silke (I), Gene Quintano (II)
Starring: Richard Chamberlain, Sharon Stone, John Rhys-Davies (I), James Earl Jones (II)
Trailer Voiceover: "The greatest treasure known to man is about to be pursued by the boldest, most daring hero ever to seek the thrill of adventure!"

Ah, Allan Quatermain. Like Sherlock Holmes, his longstanding residence in the public domain has made him a prime target for movie studios who need a recognizable, name brand hero, but don't want to pay anything to acquire their rights, or try to develop one from the ground up. Unlike Mr. Holmes, though, poor Quatermain hasn't enjoyed a 21st Century renaissance. There have been no blockbuster franchises, network television shows, or acclaimed

British miniseries to save this pulp hero from public domain purgatory. As his books have fallen out of fashion, so has their hero.

Nowadays, those familiar with the Allan Quatermain character are most likely so because of one of his many film appearances, two of which were made by Cannon in the mid-1980s. In fact, Cannon's take on the quintessential Quatermain adventure, *King Solomon's Mines*, was at least the fifth adaptation of the novel to hit the silver screen, with earlier versions having debuted in theaters in 1919, 1937, 1950, and 1979. (Later, Patrick Swayze took on the role in a 2004 TV miniseries version.)

Cannon presented this dynamic artwork to potential buyers to drum up
pre-sales for the film, even before it had been written or cast.

There was a time, however, when Allan Quatermain was more than just a royalty-free action hero for low-budget cheap adventure movies. From 1885 through the 1920s, Quatermain starred in a long series of best-selling books. Their author, Henry Rider Haggard, penned fifteen novels starring the British adventurer, occasionally crossing them over with his even more popular *She* series, about a powerful (and white, unfortunately) African queen. Their adventures resonated with Victorian readers, who were captivated at the time by the stories of the grand, archeological discoveries being made on the African continent during Britain's Imperialist expansion. Haggard himself had spent seven years in Africa and played a minor role in colonial efforts there, personally planting the Union Jack during the annexation of the South African Republic in 1877.

Haggard's Quatermain novels acted as one of the templates for the many adventure pulps and serials to appear in the first half of the 20th Century: the same ones that would go on to inspire the Indiana Jones franchise. Critics were eager to pass off Cannon's two Quatermain movies as knock-offs of the more successful Harrison Ford series. Their argument was, no doubt, helped by the fact that *Indiana Jones and the Temple of Doom* (1984) had been a top box office earner when the Quatermain movies went into production. (Also, by the presence of John Rhys-Davies in both franchises.) While their Indy-adjacency probably did help these movies along a bit, the less cynical truth would be that Golan and Globus grew up watching the same movies as George Lucas and Steven Spielberg—and Robert Zemeckis, whose similar *Romancing the Stone* (1984) and its sequel were also hits in the mid-80s—and they all took their inspiration from the same, old-timey reaches of popular culture. (Although, Cannon had the gall to use John Williams' famous *Raiders of the Lost Ark* score as place-holder music when they showed off an early *King Solomon's Mines* promo reel at Cannes.)

Notably, Cannon's version of *King Solomon's Mines* was released exactly 100 years after its source material. In 1885's *King Solomon's Mines*—the first Quatermain novel to be published, and the basis for the first of Cannon's movies—Quatermain describes himself as "thin and short and dark," weighing a scant 130 pounds, with a wiry beard and unkempt hair. Heroes of adventure films are rarely so jockey-like, though, so Cannon instead cast the blonde, 6'1" Richard Chamberlain, most famous as the heartthrob star of TV's *Dr. Kildare* in the 1960s. Chamberlain would make the leap from television to film stardom in the 1970s, when noteworthy turns in *Julius Caesar* (with Charlton Heston, 1970), *The Three Musketeers* (with Oliver Reed, 1973), and *The Towering Inferno* (1974) made him a familiar face among moviegoers. It was likely his starring role in the 1980 award-winning TV miniseries *Shogun* (alongside *King Solomon's Mines* co-star Rhys-Davies) that audiences of Cannon's day would have most recently seen him in.

Another thrilling pre-sales catalog illustration for *King Solomon's Mines*—this one listing *Kojak*'s Telly Savalas as Richard Chamberlain's co-star.

Possessing weapons-grade charm, Chamberlain gave Cannon an Allan Quatermain who was much more in line with the slick, matinee idols of classic Hollywood adventure films. He's cool under pressure, confident, and self-deprecating, yet quick-thinking and endlessly resourceful. He's the brand of hero who is addressed by last-name only, even by his fiancée and closest friends. (Oh, and remember, kids: it's pronounced QUATermain, which rhymes with "water main." Don't be tempted to add that extra "R" and turn it into *Quar*termain—even though many of the actors in these films do!)

Nowadays, though, Chamberlain's fresh-faced co-star is arguably the more famous of the movies' two lead actors. While she had played bit parts in numerous films and TV series, *King Solomon's Mines* was Sharon Stone's first lead role in a feature film.

As Menahem Golan spun the story in his typical fashion, he'd "discovered" Sharon Stone, but a popular legend about the producer paints it otherwise. The story goes that after reading the script, Golan had demanded they cast "that Stone woman." It wasn't until he was watching footage from the shoot that he realized they got the wrong actress: the "Stone woman" he had meant was Kathleen Turner, who had just starred in the similar, pulpy adventure film *Romancing the Stone*, a recent blockbuster. Sadly, as fun (and as Menahem-like) as that story sounds, it conflates the truth. Kathleen Turner *was* offered the role first by Cannon, but declined because the two franchises were too similar. Meanwhile, *King Solomon's Mines* director J. Lee Thompson had previously seen Stone's supporting performance in *Irreconcilable Differences* (1984) and was impressed, and had reached out to her to request an audition.

Cast intentionally or not, Sharon Stone's true big break wouldn't come until Paul Verhoeven's *Total Recall* (1990). In Verhoeven's follow-up, *Basic Instinct* (1992), she unwittingly exposed her naked crotch to movie-goers the world over and was transformed overnight into one of the '90s most iconic sex symbols. (*Basic Instinct* rode its controversy to more than $350 million at the box office, making it one of the biggest hits of its year.) Three years later she would earn a Best Actress nomination for her role in Martin Scorsese's *Casino* (1995).

Cannon doubled down on Allan Quatermain from the get-go, locking down their stars and shooting *King Solomon's Mines* more or less back-to-back with its sequel, *Allan Quatermain and the Lost City of Gold* (1987). The screen adaptation for *Mines* was written by two Cannon vets, James R. Silke (*Revenge of the Ninja* and *Sahara*, 1983, and *Ninja III: The Domination*, 1984) and Gene Quintano (*Treasure of the Four Crowns*, 1983, and *Making the Grade*, 1984). *King Solomon's Mines* was directed by J. Lee Thompson, himself no stranger to working for Golan and Globus, having already helmed *10 to Midnight* (1983) and *The Ambassador* (1984) for the cousins. (He would go on to direct five more movies for Cannon before his career was through.)

An oversized poster for the French theatrical release of *King Solomon's Mines*.

It was settled that the movies would be shot in Zimbabwe, not only because it would add a level of authenticity to Quatermain's surroundings, but because filming there was very cheap. This led to some friction from several organizations, who protested the mostly-Israeli and South African film crew, and the scant wages being paid to the locally-cast extras. The Zimbabweans were paid $6 per day for their work, much less than the $100 they would have been owed for the same work in Hollywood. Cannon— and the Zimbabwean Government, who fully sanctioned the production— defended this by arguing that their low pay was still much higher than the country's minimum wage.

Cannon spent more than $12 million on the production, a sizable sum for the company, which allowed them to not only construct an entire city set for the movie's opening scenes, but build up the infrastructure—bringing in electric and water—to the remote location where they would be doing much of their filming. They also hired thousands of locals to fill out the many crowd scenes; in typical Cannon fashion, they weren't equipped to feed such a large crowd. Instead of giving their extras meals, they paid them each a small per diem to provide their own, which led to a temporary market of food vendors cropping up around the filming site during the six months they were shooting the two movies.

Poor working conditions weren't the only controversy stirred up by Cannon's Quatermain films: their frequent portrayal of the African natives as cannibals, witch doctors, and paint-covered savages is what you might call problematic. (As was its portrayal of a few Turkish Arab characters, in particular the villainous Dogati, played by Welsh actor John Rhys-Davies.) Both Chamberlain and Stone came to the movie's defense during that same set visit from *The New York Times*, claiming the movie was poking fun at dated stereotypes to show how absurd they were, and then pointing out that their characters were the two biggest idiots in the film. (Indeed, the film's entire white cast play a coterie of nitwits.) Perhaps a stronger defense would have been to specifically point at the movie's most absurd character of all: Herr Bockner, an evil colonel who's such an over-the-top German stereotype that he's seen absent-mindedly munching wiener schnitzels and must be constantly accompanied by a gramophone playing a scratchy rendition of Wagner's "Ride of the Valkyries." He's played by the late, great character actor Herbert Lom, best known for his recurring role as Inspector Dreyfus, Clouseau's beleaguered boss, in the original Pink Panther movies. (Lom would appear in three more Cannon-produced films: 1987's *Going Bananas,* and 1989's *River of Death* and *Ten Little Indians.*)

Sharon Stone insisted on being photographed with her favorite leopard cub, which had doubled in size in the months between the film shoot and her posing for publicity photos. When it became spooked by the flashing lights, the leopard bit Stone—as *Prevue* magazine put it—on "one of [her] most prominent features." Interpret that as you will.

While it's obvious these films were vying for comic effect, and while the portrayals may be true to the pulp serials from which they took inspiration, it's difficult to completely overlook stereotypes that would have felt dated in a movie made in the 1950s—let alone, one made in the mid-'80s. Homages of this type aren't easy to pull off without appearing racist, even if it's accidental. (The script's use of a few ugly, ethnic slurs don't help its case, either, to be honest.) Even a director like Steven Spielberg ran into the same issue when he portrayed Indians as heart-ripping cultists and chilled monkey brain-eaters in *Indiana Jones and the Temple of Doom*.

If you're able to gloss over those elements as outdated products of another era, Cannon's Quatermains are silly, adventurous treats.

King Solomon's Mines wastes no time getting down to business. We meet our dashing hero, the big game hunter and all-around adventurer Allan Quatermain (Chamberlain), as he guides the beautiful American archeologist Jesse Huston (Stone) through the jungle on a paid mission to find her missing father, who disappeared while searching for King Solomon's fabled mines. (We see her father, played by the uncredited character actor Bernard Archard, kidnapped by scoundrels in the movie's opening scene.) They're accompanied by a native manservant named Umbopo, played by the respected South African actor Ken Gampu, who'd turn up again as a rebel leader in Cannon's *American Ninja IV* (1990).

Their journey takes them into the heart of Tongola, a nasty little city populated by robbers, con men, and slave traders. It's just the sort of home turf you'd expect to find a scalawag like Dogati, a murderous slaver hired by the villainous Colonel Bockner (Lom) to help him claim the wealth of Solomon's mines for the glory of Germany. (In a slight update to the source novel, Cannon's *Mines* are set in a WWI-adjacent era.) They plot to capture Jesse, thinking they can use her as leverage to get her tight-lipped, captive father to cough up the location of the mines.

Dogati is played by John Rhys-Davies, settling again into the role of a Middle Eastern character of questionable morals in which he'd been perplexingly type-cast over and over again, from *Raiders of the Lost Ark* (1981) and *Indiana Jones and the Last Crusade* (1989), and Cannon's own *Sahara* (1983). (He also appeared, but not as an Arab these times, in two more Cannon films: 1984's *Sword of the Valiant* and 1986's *Firewalker*.) While Rhys-Davies made a pretty good comic foil every time he was on screen, you do have to question how a white, Welsh man became Hollywood's go-to Arab character actor for the entirety of a decade.

After an unsuccessful kidnapping attempt which sees her rolled up in a rug, bounced off an awning, and dumped from a cartload of vegetables, Jesse finds herself in an antiquities shop owned by a shady dealer named Kassam, from whom they forcefully extract information about Jesse's kidnapped father before blowing him up with a stick of dynamite. Kassam's final words—"I've got it!" as he raises aloft a stick of dynamite with a near-extinct fuse—becomes a running gag throughout a movie in which Quatermain tosses around dynamite as frequently as Indy Jones utilized his bullwhip.

The wily Kassam was played by Cannon mainstay Shaike Ophir, an Israeli actor who also happened to be the country's most prominent mime. A regular in Menahem Golan's pre-Cannon directorial efforts, he also appeared in *The Delta Force* and *America 3000* (both 1986), as well as the 1987 Cannon Movie Tales rendition of *Sleeping Beauty*.

The Tongola set is one of the most impressive in *King Solomon's Mines*. The fake city was built from the ground up, and was to serve as the crew's location for the earliest weeks of shooting. An especially arid site was chosen so that it would resemble a city in the middle of the desert. While production was set to begin during what was projected to be a historic dry spell for that region of Zimbabwe, the skies unexpectedly opened up as soon as the cameras began rolling, forcing the crew to instead shoot indoor scenes that weren't scheduled for weeks. The set flooded, and the palm trees that were hauled in as decorations began to take root. For weeks, many crew members had little to do but race small, homemade boats down the currents that formed between the fake buildings.

And then as suddenly as it began, the rain stopped. In their marketing materials, Cannon chalked up the freak flooding to the set being built on an ancient burial ground, and its end being brought about by director J. Lee Thompson leading a prayer to appease the angry spirits. Whether there's any truth to that story, or if Cannon's marketing team had just ripped it off of *The Amityville Horror* (1979)—well, you can decide which of those two scenarios is more believable.

As the movie goes on, Jesse and Quatermain's adventures take them—by automobile, train, and biplane—deeper into the jungles of Africa. All of the action in *King Solomon's Mines* leans heavily toward the slapstick end of the spectrum. There's a thrilling action sequence that takes place on top of and beneath a speeding locomotive. Insanely, it ends with Quatermain rescuing Jesse's dad from being raped by his male, German guard (which is played for laughs, and feels so awkwardly out-of-place in this otherwise family-friendly adventure flick).

Another semi-infamous sequence involves our heroes stealing a German plane. Unfortunately for Quatermain, Jesse can't fly it and refuses to uncover her eyes while he hangs perilously from one of its wings. His situation grows even more dangerous when Jesse unwittingly engages in a dogfight with a German ace, who mistakes her lack of piloting skills as a challenge to a game of chicken. They narrowly avoid a mid-air, head-on collision, but as the German plane ducks under Jesse's stolen bird, the dangling Quatermain accidentally kicks the pilot in the head, sending his aircraft in a tailspin straight to the ground. It's almost laugh-out-loud funny enough to completely overlook the scene's shoddy green screen and obvious use of stock footage.

While no one was injured filming these particular aerial scenes, actor John Rhys-Davies was seriously injured during the shoot when a small Cessna he and two friends took for a weekend getaway hit a tree during takeoff, and then crashed. The damage he incurred to his leg required five surgeries to repair on top of a hospital stay. Yet, Rhys-Davies returned to the set as soon as he was able. Thompson reconfigured Rhys-Davies' remaining scenes to minimize walking, and framed them so that the actor's braced and heavily-bandaged leg would be covered or off-camera.

Once safe from "zee Germans," our heroes find themselves in the forests at the foot of the "breasts of Sheba:" twin mountain peaks that look, well, like a pair of boobs. Though you'd think this might be a crude joke inserted by the screenwriters, it's actually the informal name for two famous mountains in the small African nation of Eswatini (formerly Swaziland).

More than 1,600 locally-sourced extras were brought in to play tribesmen in
King Solomon's Mines' soup scene.

Over the next half hour of the movie they encounter one increasingly wacky tribe of natives after another. The first are unfriendly cannibals; they attempt to cook our heroes alive in a cartoonishly large pot of soup, but the good guys escape and make sweet love in a puddle of simmering vegetables. Next they're taken in by a friendly tribe of natives who live their lives upside-down, swinging from tree vines—and who conveniently and inexplicably assume the blond-haired, blue-eyed Jesse is their queen. The last tribe they encounter isn't as friendly: a large, armed congregation of cannibals led by the evil sorceress Gagoola. In a display of power so inefficient it would make any Bond villain proud, she has Quatermain strung upside-down over a pit of crocodiles, slowly lowering him in before Umbopo reappears for the first time since the first half of the movie, revealing to everyone that he's the true, exiled king of their tribe. (Once again, it's a highly convenient coincidence.) Umbopo's stunning deus ex machina almost works, save for the fact that Gagoola slips away with a captive Jesse, planning to sacrifice her in the volcano at the heart of King Solomon's mines.

The details that went into this movie's crocodile stunt are too wild not to repeat. While the filmmakers were fine with using fake-looking green screen effects in several scenes, the croc shots are, in contrast, very, *very* real. Richard Chamberlain's double, stunt man Andy Bradford was strung upside-down by his ankles between two fifty-foot trees on a wire cable held up by a group of strong locals on either end. Beneath him was a shallow, muddy pool filled with many hungry crocodiles. To ensure that the crocs would be active and opening their jaws, which would make for exciting shots, Bradford was smothered with what basically amounted to chum jelly, filled with meat byproduct and extremely smelly, so that the reptiles would be driven into a feeding frenzy. To get all of the coverage needed, Bradford had to hang upside-down for over *three hours*, smothered in raw meat sauce, in the African sun, while thousands of extras chanted. In case the unthinkable happened, the crew stationed local marksmen nearby to shoot the crocs before Bradford was totally torn apart. (And that is, if the sharp drop neck-first into six inches of mud didn't kill him first.)

In case anyone hadn't figured it out from the movie's title, it turns out that, yes, King Solomon's mines *are* more than just a fable. They're full of untold riches, but also an ancient, yet deviously-engineered series of traps to keep out all but the cleverest of treasure-seekers. Quatermain and the faithful Umbopo chase Gagoola into the caves, pursued closely by Colonel Bockner and Dogati, who by this point have lost or murdered every last one of their soldiers and hired hands. Without spoiling too many details, our heroes manage to escape numerous near-death scenarios, and our baddies are served their just desserts. All of this is at the expense of King Solomon's wondrous mines, which are collapsed in the process—forever burying the legendary treasures beneath the mountain.

Allan Quatermain and the Lost City of Gold on VHS. The illustrator, Jacques
Devaud, cleverly hid his signature in the rock carvings behind our heroes.

King Solomon's Mines was torn to shreds by critics, who largely missed the
point that it was meant to be a comedy. (Cannon's marketing did nothing to
clarify this, with trailers emphasizing the action over the humor.) In spite of

poor reviews from coast to coast, *Mines* opened at #1 at the box office and brought home more than $15 million over its first four weeks in theaters. Thus, factoring in the foreign sales, cable, and video rights, it was hardly a financial failure. The reported budget was $12.5 million, but this can be presumed to be an artificially inflated number, as per Cannon fashion: shooting in Zimbabwe, as we know, was cheap, and unless they grossly overpaid for their plentiful stock nature footage of elephants and crocodiles, it's hard to guess how that much money would actually have been spent.

After giving everyone a two-week break following the completion of *Mines*, Cannon rolled right into their regularly-scheduled production of a sequel titled *Allan Quatermain and the Lost City of Gold*. While most of the crew remained in Zimbabwe, director J. Lee Thompson departed to helm another film, *Murphy's Law* (1986), Cannon's latest vehicle for his favorite star, Charles Bronson. Thompson was replaced by filmmaker Gary Nelson, new to the Cannon fold but a longtime veteran of the industry, having directed live-action Disney classics such as *Freaky Friday* (1976) and *The Black Hole* (1979) and countless episodes of *Get Smart* and *Gilligan's Island*.

The sequel opens with Jesse and Quatermain preparing to embark on a freighter to America, where her parents have already scheduled for the two of them an elaborate wedding ceremony. Their plans, of course, are interrupted when an injured, feverish man drops half-dead on their front doorstep. He's carrying a mysterious gold coin and, it turns out, is a former companion of Quatermain's hitherto-unmentioned little brother, who disappeared as part of an exploration party hunting for a fabled lost city of gold. Adventure calls, and Quatermain answers! (Much to Jesse's chagrin.)

Quatermain's suspicions about his missing brother are confirmed by a turban-clad, Indian "Holy Man" named Swarma, played by lily-white character actor Robert Donner in embarrassingly dark makeup. (While Donner had funnier roles, notably as the deranged cult leader Exidor on TV's *Mork & Mindy*, his Swarma may be the worst thing about *Lost City of Gold*: not only is the character unbelievably grating, but his offensive performance sounds like a poor impression of *The Simpsons'* Apu.) The greedy Swarma joins Quatermain's rescue party, soon followed by an African warrior named Umslopogaas, played by the great James Earl Jones.

James Earl Jones' presence here is a major head-scratcher: he was not only a Tony-winning, Academy Award-nominated Shakespearean actor, but the voice of Darth Vader in the *Star Wars* franchise. (After John Gielgud, who was featured in 1983's *The Wicked Lady*, Jones is the second and last EGOT-winner to appear in a Cannon movie—that is, until Chuck Norris eventually wins an Oscar. And a Tony. And a Grammy. And an Emmy.) You'd think that Jones would have had better things to do than pull on a leopard-print tunic, spin an axe over his head, and speak in an implacable accent. He told press visiting the shoot that he'd taken the job so that he could visit Africa and explore his roots. From his periodically lethargic performance, you can sense that even he felt this material was beneath him.

Quatermain, Jesse, Swarma, and Umslopogaas blindly embark into the desert with five mute, expendable African manservants whose only job is to be killed off, one at a time, by each of the traps our heroes encounter. Those traps are frequent, and of varyingly (low) qualities of special effects. They include a horde of hand puppet snakes, a crevice that opens up in the ground beneath our heroes' feet, a spontaneous whirlpool, and a green screen canoe ride down rushing rapids, and straight into a pillar of fire. Compared to *King Solomon's Mines*, the SFX budget appears to have run out by the time they got around to shooting the sequel. While the first film was no *Avatar* (2009), it looked far better than its follow-up.

The four surviving good guys stumble onto The Lost City of Gold more or less by accident. They find the legends about it to have been true: the city is overflowing with riches, and a lost, white race has been peacefully living there for centuries in isolation. That is, until recently. An evil slaver known as Agon recently found the lost city and has installed himself as its High Priest, demanding frequent human sacrifices while smuggling the gold out of the city via an underground smelter. (He's played by the prolific villain actor Henry Silva, of 1962's *The Manchurian Candidate* and *Buck Rogers* fame.) The city is otherwise ruled jointly by two queens: the benevolent, blonde Nyleptha

(Aileen Marson) and the silent-but-wicked Sorais, played by Cassandra Peterson—who is better known as her iconic character, the TV horror hostess Elvira, Mistress of the Dark.

Italian maestro Sandro Symeoni did an excellent job capturing the cast's likenesses on the movie's local theatrical release poster.

The good news is that Quatermain's little brother, Robeson, is alive and well. (The character, not part of the original Haggard novels, took his name from actor Paul Robeson, who played Umbopa in the 1937 British production of *King Solomon's Mines*.) Whereas his fellow travelers met grisly fates, Robeson has simply fallen in love with the lost city's peaceful inhabitants and decided to live among them—he's "gone native," so to say.

Robeson is played by film producer and sometimes-actor Martin Rabbett, in his only big screen role. What wasn't public knowledge at the time was that Rabbett was *Quatermain* star Richard Chamberlain's real-life partner. Chamberlain had always maintained a very closed-off private life, concerned that his sexual orientation might adversely affect his Hollywood heartthrob image. (While a French magazine outed him in 1989, he didn't come out openly until publishing his autobiography in 2003.) The couple remained together for more than three decades. In *Lost City of Gold*, at least, the two of them certainly share a better on-screen chemistry than Chamberlain and Sharon Stone.

After Quatermain and Company topple Agon's sacrificial altar, the ousted tyrant gathers an army of hair-covered barbarians led by slapstick comic relief Nasta (Moroccan actor Doghmi Larbi) to retake the city by force. It's up to our heroes to lead these untrained, pacifist tribesmen against the attacking horde with nothing but a few makeshift weapons, and Quatermain's smarts. You can probably guess who comes out ahead in that one.

After several delays in its scheduled release—Golan reputedly considered the sequel bad enough to be almost un-releasable—*The Lost City of Gold* fared far poorer in theaters than its predecessor, bringing home only $3.7 million in total ticket sales, less than *Mines* had made in its opening weekend. Audiences may have learned their lesson the first time around, and it's hard to argue that *Lost City* isn't easily the lesser film of the two. Its script is less punchy, and the jokes are rarely (intentionally) funny. The adventure also eschews the exciting stunt work of *Mines* in favor of barely passable special effects, much to its detriment. Where the first one had that thrilling rescue atop a speeding train, the best *Lost City* can muster is having us watch a miniature canoe lackadaisically float toward an open flame—the excitement levels don't even come close.

A massive, painted poster heralded the sequel's release in France.

Much about *Lost City* feels rushed, and probably was: pre-production began only two months before shooting, which seems hardly enough time to scout locations in remote areas of a foreign country, fully test the special effects, and construct an adequately awe-inspiring Lost City of Gold. The movie's titular set looks like a run-down, mid-Century vacation spot, and that's because it was, in fact, built from the remains of a former resort hotel near Zimbabwe's famed Victoria Falls. The site had been repeatedly attacked by guerilla revolutionaries during the country's war for independence, and at one point in the 1970s was leveled by a heat-seeking missile. Cannon's production team came in, scribbled a bunch of cave paintings onto some rocks, and called it a day.

King Solomon's Mines had an original score by eighteen-time Academy Award Nominee Jerry Goldsmith, known for his composing work on *Planet of the Apes* (1968), *Chinatown* (1974), *Star Trek: The Motion Picture* (1979), and literally dozens of other classic movies. His *Mines* score is predictably fantastic. *Lost City* recycles Goldsmith's theme music for the first film, which would be just fine if it weren't reused over and over again *ad nauseum*—this little bit of music is recycled to a degree we haven't encountered since the "Torgo Theme" from *Manos, the Hands of Fate* (1966). Fortunately there is some new score inserted here and there from Cannon house composer Michael Linn (*Breakin' 2*, *Rappin'*, *American Ninja*) to break up the maddening monotony. (The only thing more grating than hearing the same song over and over again is Robert Donner's Swama character.)

If we're going to give it the benefit of the doubt, at least *Lost City* isn't as bad as it *could* have been: it's just extremely underwhelming compared to what came before it. The film remains just entertaining enough to endure its more cloying characters, and its laughable special effects need to be seen to be believed. At the very least, it's worth seeing Cannon's Quatermain saga through to its premature end: Menahem Golan was working on getting a third Quatermain film—tentatively titled "Allan Quatermain and the Jewel of the East"—up until he passed away in 2014.

Allan Quatermain (Richard Chamberlain) enters the city of Tongola: a location that proved far more troubling for the film's crew than its characters.

This ex-rental videocassette copy of *Fool for Love* was circulated by a Wesco convenience store location in Muskegon, Michigan.

Fool for Love

Release Date: December 6, 1985
Directed by: Robert Altman
Written by: Sam Shepard
Starring: Sam Shepard, Kim Basinger, Harry Dean Stanton, Randy Quaid
Trailer Voiceover: "Some people fall in love; Eddie tumbled. Some people live for love; May runs from it. Some people are wise to love; others are *Fools for Love*."

Following the releases of Jason Miller's *That Championship Season* (1982), John Cassavetes' *Love Streams* (1984), and Andrei Konchalovsky's *Maria's Lovers* (1985), The Cannon Group had earned a reputation not only for being the leading producer of Chuck Norris, breakdancing, and ninja movies, but a safe place where auteurs could realize their artistic visions with little studio interference. Over the next few years Cannon would ink deals with such highfalutin names as Jean-Luc Godard, Franco Zeffirelli, Roman Polanski, Barbet Schroeder, Norman Mailer, and Godfrey Reggio. Their final two releases of 1985 would be two such highbrow films: Konchalovsky's *Runaway Train*, and the Sam Shepard play adaptation *Fool for Love*, directed by Robert Altman, one of the greatest American filmmakers of the late-20th Century.

Robert Altman cut his teeth as a highly prolific television director throughout the Fifties and Sixties, shooting episodes of shows ranging from *Bonanza* to *Bus Stop* to *Combat!*, but in the following decade established himself as one of cinema's most consistently acclaimed filmmakers. His 1970 war satire, *M*A*S*H*, won top honors at Cannes, was nominated for five Academy Awards, and was spun off into one of the highest-rated shows in television history. Over the next decade he'd average more than a movie per year, the most notable among them being the classic anti-Western, *McCabe & Mrs. Miller* (1971), and the music-based, Best Picture-nominated *Nashville* (1975).

By contrast, however, the 1980s were not kind at all to Altman. He opened the decade with an infamous, major-budget flop that was the live-action *Popeye* musical, starring Robin Williams and Shelley Duvall. This was a film so eardrum-piercingly shrill that it turned many of the studios and critics against Altman for the next ten years. Following the *Popeye* debacle, the next four films Altman released were small, independent stage adaptations: these were *Come Back to the Five and Dime, Jimmy Dean, Jimmy Dean* (1982), *Streamers* (1983), *Secret Honor* (1984), and then *Fool For Love*. It was as if the director was actively trying to wash the taste of Hollywood from his mouth.

It took three consecutive knockouts—*Vincent & Theo* in 1990, *The Player* in 1992, and 1993's *Short Cuts*—for Robert Altman to fully earn back moviegoers' trust and critics' confidence. *Fool for Love* (1985) arrived smack dab in the middle of Altman's so-called "maligned period." It's said that numerous studios passed on *Fool for Love*, but Cannon—on their ever-constant quest for respectability—couldn't say 'no' to welcoming such a prestigious name as Robert Altman's into the family.

Having penned more than forty plays between 1964 and 2014, Sam Shepard was easily among the most celebrated playwrights of his generation. Three of those were nominated for Pulitzer Prizes, including *Fool for Love*, and Shepard laid claim to the award for 1979's *Buried Child*. (He was also the recipient of a record-setting ten Obie Awards, which are presented to the best Off-Broadway theater productions.) On top of his incredible success as a writer, Shepard was also a well-respected actor, having earned a Best Supporting Oscar nomination for 1983's *The Right Stuff* and appearing in more than sixty other films in his career.

Fool for Love stars Sam Shepard and Kim Basinger. Robert Altman's son, Robert Reed Altman, shot the film's gorgeous, black-and-white publicity stills.

Shepard was initially reluctant to have his play made into a movie, but gave in when it was Altman who approached him about bringing the Pulitzer-nominated script to the silver screen. Shepard would have preferred the lead roles went to actors Ed Harris and future *Street Smart* (1987) star Kathy Baker, who had originated the characters during the play's acclaimed theatrical run. Altman, though, insisted upon the playwright performing the words he'd written. Actress Jessica Lange was to play the May to Shepard's Eddie; the two decorated actors were a high-profile couple, and the idea of the real-life lovers playing such an incendiary ex-couple no doubt excited Altman. Lange, however, became pregnant, and bowed out before shooting began. Kim Basinger, best known at the time as a Bond girl from *Never Say Never Again* (1983), replaced her. She'd later be known for films like *9 1/2 Weeks* (1986), Tim Burton's *Batman* (1989), and *L.A. Confidential* (1997)—the latter of which won her a Best Supporting Actress Oscar.

The film opens with the beautiful, damaged May (Kim Basinger) hiding out in a dilapidated motel on the edge of the Mojave Desert. Eddie (Sam Shepard), a rugged cowboy-type, turns his pickup truck into the dusty parking lot, pulling a horse trailer behind it. He gets out and starts peeking in the windows of the rat-hole cottages. When he finds May's, he violently smashes through the door, and immediately kicks his feet up on her bed. May emerges from the bathroom in which she'd been cowering. Rather than flee, as one might expect in this sort of situation, she begins to verbally chew him out. It's the beginning of one long, nasty fight that spans the length of the entire movie.

As the movie rolls on, we're given some gradual insight into the characters' long, shared history. They were lovers—that, at least, is clear from the start. May left town after Eddie had a fling with a rich bimbo referred to only as "The Countess;" he's spent the time since trying to find May and bring her home. May insists she doesn't love him anymore, but by the way she breaks down each time he pretends he's going to leave, it leads one to believe that her words and her feelings don't line up. As the two lob accusations, scream at one another, and do a ton of property damage, a third individual—credited only as "The Old Man" (Harry Dean Stanton)—hovers in the near distance, observing their quarrel, offering the occasional bit of commentary, and pilfering their booze whenever they dare leave it unsupervised.

This goes on for much of the movie's 107-minute runtime. At various points Eddie's jilted lover, The Countess, shows up in a big, black Mercedes to fire a revolver through the motel's lobby windows and then drive off again. Early into the third act, Martin (Randy Quaid), a good-natured schnook, arrives to pick up May and take her out to the movies, only to be caught unaware in the middle of their high-pitched fracas and be relentlessly harassed by Eddie. It's at this point that we learn the dark secret that's keeping Eddie and May apart. The last half of this sentence should be considered a spoiler, although it seems to be the one thing anyone knows about the play (or this film) if they've heard of it: Eddie and May are brother and sister.

The last chunk of the movie feels like one giant, exposition bomb going off right in your face. After being trapped on the grounds of the old motel for more than an hour, Eddie and May's sordid backstories play out in front of us. As Shepard and Basinger narrate, young actors play teenage versions of their characters. It's revealed, too, that the Old Man—Stanton's character—is their father, by different mothers. By the time they figured out they were half-siblings, they'd already "fooled around" with each other, as Eddie so elegantly puts it. It was too late for them to stop.

The movie ends abruptly with more gunfire, an explosion, and the Old Man playing a sad tune on a harmonica as he wanders back into his rusty, old camper. The credits roll as the vehicle catches fire and burns up with the Old Man inside of it. (This isn't exactly a feel-good sort of movie; if that wasn't clear before, it will be once it burns alive an old man as a matter of punctuation.)

There are a number of problems with *Fool for Love*, but none of them stem from the casting: with three Oscar-caliber actors (Shepard, Basinger, and Quaid) joined by quintessential cult figure Harry Dean Stanton, the movie has one hell of an ensemble. As beloved as he is for playing the bothersome Cousin Eddie "Shitter's full!" Johnson in National Lampoon's *Vacation* movies, it's easy to forget that Randy Quaid is also a pretty great actor in serious roles, from *The Last Picture Show* (1971) to *Brokeback Mountain* (2005), to 1973's *The Last Detail* (which earned him an Academy Award nomination).

Meanwhile, Harry Dean Stanton, with his sagging features and down-trodden demeanor, was one of the best character actors to have ever worked in Hollywood. It's doubtful anyone's filmography is as jam-packed with cult classics as Stanton's, from *Alien* (1979), *Repo Man* (1984), *Escape from New York* (1981), *Twin Peaks: Fire Walk With Me* (1992), *Pretty in Pink* (1986), *Red Dawn* (1984), *Wild at Heart* (1990), and *Paris, Texas* (1984), to *Kelly's Heroes* (1970), *The Godfather: Part II* (1974), *The Green Mile* (1999), *Cool Hand Luke* (1967), and *Fear and Loathing in Las Vegas* (1998). If you had to pick *the* consummate cult actor, it would be Harry Dean Stanton.

The bulk of the issues with *Fool for Love* boil down to the source material just not being well-suited for the screen. The biggest element lost from the play's translation to film is its immediacy and assertiveness. Shepard's dialogue plays *very* differently when the two actors are punching walls, smashing bottles, and screaming their heads off at each other just a few meters in front of you on a cramped stage. Their explosive, love-hate relationship is thrown right in your face, and the experience can feel quite claustrophobic to the audience. On film, though, that's not the case. Not only is there a well-delineated fourth wall between the action and the viewers, but the setting is opened up to include not only the entirety of the motel's grounds, but the world around them. In the play, the actors are always confined to the space of the theater. In the film, they're able to spend a great deal of runtime pouting in a variety of different places. You can drive a horse trailer through the gulf this creates between them.

That's not to say the movie's set isn't absolutely outstanding: the entire motel was built from the ground up in the desert outside Santa Fe. (Drivers-by would regularly pull in and try to rent a room for the night, only to be informed that it was only a movie set.) The production offices were hidden inside the cottages not being used for interior filming, and dressing rooms were disguised as the broken-down trailers parked in the junkyard out back.

Harry Dean Stanton, one of the best supporting players to ever grace the movie business, in *Fool for Love*.

Altman made several other attempts to make the play more movie-like. As clever as they are, they don't quite work. In the play, the Old Man character is a spectral figure: a figment of Eddie and May's fissured psyches, who comments on the action somewhat like a theatrical chorus. (Martin isn't able to see or hear him, only Eddie and May.) In Altman's version, though, the Old Man is *very much* real, and living at the motel with May. It feels very weird, then, that Eddie doesn't seem to recognize him until the final act, even as he's chasing his deadbeat dad around the parking lot for stealing liquor out of his truck, like a Keystone Kop pursuing a mischievous hobo. Harry Dean Stanton is wonderful in the part, as he is in everything, but the choice to make his character a physical presence feels half-baked in execution.

The director also decided to film the characters' backstories as flashbacks. In the play, we learn about their sordid, incestuous past through intense monologues; here, those monologues become the narration, and the stories they tell play out on screen. Cleverly, the action and words don't always match up: the details they share are often different from what we see, as if the characters have chosen to remember the past in their own ways. As neat as the idea is, taking the audience out of the motel setting fifteen minutes from the movie's end torpedoes whatever remained of the play's claustrophobic atmosphere. The actors from the flashbacks also show up early on as other guests at the motel, which confuses matters more than anything.

Shepard was displeased with the final movie; he'd been under the impression that he'd have a hand in cutting it, only for Altman to piece it all together without him. He'd later refer to *Fool for Love* as a mistake, and famously tell a reporter that filmmakers like Altman knew nothing about actors. He'd backpedal on this later in his life and speak fondly of Altman after the director's death, but the experience soured Shepard on adapting further plays of his into movies.

One of the high points for the movie was actually its soundtrack, featuring country western songs written for the film by singer Sandy Rogers, who was Shepard's real-life sister. One of the songs, a title track called "Fool for Love," wound up not being used by Altman and left off the movie's soundtrack album. It wound up receiving far better exposure almost a decade later, however, when Quentin Tarantino resurrected the song for use in the film *Reservoir Dogs* (1992).

When they received the finished movie, it doesn't seem like Cannon was sure what to do with it. *Fool for Love* was given a tiny release in December of 1985, opening in only a few arthouse theater screens before appearing at the Cannes Film Festival the following summer, followed by a VHS release shortly thereafter. Critics were fair to it—praising the actors, mostly—but the movie couldn't have been helped by its hilariously misleading trailers and TV spots, which painted it as some sort of hillbilly romantic comedy. "Eddie and May are less than friends; *more* than lovers!" the narrator gleefully coos over a drawling country tune, glossing over the fact that this is a very dark and violent film about incest, fractured families, alcoholism, and suicide.

A strikingly illustrated poster for the Italian release of *Fool for Love*, with artwork by Piero Ermanno Iaia.

The American VHS cover for *Runaway Train*, the most acclaimed film in the Cannon library, with artwork by painter Richard Mahon.

Runaway Train

Release Date: December 6, 1985
Directed by: Andrei Konchalovsky
Written by: Akira Kurosawa (story), Djordje Milicevic, Paul Zindel, Edward Bunker
Starring: Jon Voight, Eric Roberts, Rebecca De Mornay
Trailer Voiceover: "They escaped together. They battled the elements. They achieved the impossible. But their train to freedom was out of control!"

As far as action-thrillers of the 1980s go, if it's possible for a classic to be overlooked, well, *Runaway Train* (1985) fits the bill.

Tense, unflinching, and featuring a pair of brilliant lead performances, *Runaway Train* is among the best films Cannon ever made. It's undoubtedly their most acclaimed feature, earning the studio its first three Academy Award nominations of the Golan-Globus era: Best Actor for Jon Voight, Best Supporting Actor for Eric Roberts, and Best Film Editing for Henry Richardson. While the film ultimately failed to take home an Oscar statuette, it did give Voight a Best Actor award from the Golden Globes, which was perhaps the loftiest prize the company ever received.

Runaway Train's path to the silver screen was a long and circuitous one, even by Cannon standards. The story came from an abandoned screenplay by the renowned Japanese filmmaker, Akira Kurosawa. Inspired by a riveting *Life* magazine article from 1962 about a locomotive that went out of control near Rochester, New York, *Runaway Train* was to not only be Kurosawa's Hollywood filmmaking debut, but his first color feature.

Kurosawa wrote a script in Japanese with his frequent collaborators, Hideo Oguni and Ryuzo Kikushima, and the translation was handed off to Sidney Carroll, writer of *The Hustler* (1961). The film was scheduled to begin shooting in the fall of 1966 with a budget of $5.5 million, a relatively massive sum for the era. Before the production could begin in upstate New York, however, Kurosawa had difficulties with his American producers and screenwriters due to language and cultural barriers making it impossible for him to work in the ways to which he was accustomed. Kurosawa first tried to postpone the production, then grew disinterested in favor of other projects. Rather than hire another director to take the wheel, Embassy Pictures canceled the film altogether.

The script languished for more than a decade, mostly untouched save for one aborted attempt by Japanese director Koreyoshi Kurahara to film it in Canada in the early 1980s. The company who held the rights eventually approached Francis Ford Coppola with the script, who suggested a young, Soviet filmmaker named Andrei Konchalovsky, who had been living in America but had been unable yet to make a movie there. The director of *Siberiade* (1979), which had taken home one of the top prizes from Cannes, had a deep admiration for Kurosawa, whom he'd considered to have had a major influence over his work. Konchalovsky flew to Japan to eat sushi and discuss the film with Kurosawa in his home, returning to the United States with the Japanese auteur's blessing to revise the script and finally make the film.

Even with such a renowned filmmaker's backing, Konchalovsky was unable to get *any* film greenlit in Hollywood until his friend, Nastassja Kinski, put him in contact with Menahem Golan and The Cannon Group, which led to his directing *Maria's Lovers* (1985).

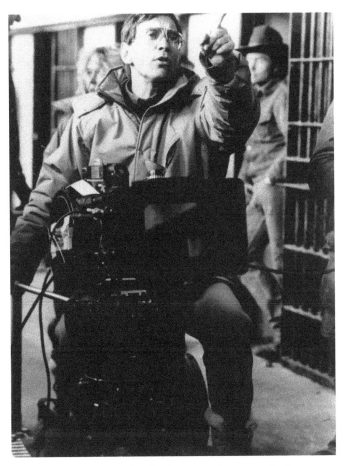

Andrei Konchalovsky directing *Runaway Train*.

While all of this was going on, the *Runaway Train* project was being developed independently by producer Henry T. Weinstein and his colleagues at Weinstein/Skyfield. They had the project re-written to better suit an American audience, and packaged it with headline stars. Once most of these major pieces were in place, they were able to seal a deal with Cannon to finance the film, and at long last get the project made.

Initially it was Robert Duvall who was considered for the lead role of Manny, the dangerous convict at the heart of *Runaway Train*, but the *Godfather* (1972) actor ultimately passed when he became too busy with other projects. This is when none other than Sylvester Stallone, one of the Eighties' biggest box office draws and future *Over the Top* (1987) star, expressed interest in the role. (For the full story behind his brief flirtation with starring in *Runaway Train* for Cannon, read the interview with development executive Brian Gendece which follows this entry.) Stallone didn't think the script felt authentically gritty enough for a prison film. To remedy this, the producers brought in a real-life ex-con by the name of Edward Bunker to punch up the screenplay, which had already gone through rewrites by Djordje Milicevic and Paul Zindel. Bunker had lived a hardened youth, bouncing in and out of juvenile halls, mental institutions, and hobo camps, before he earned the distinction of being the youngest-ever prisoner at San Quentin at the ripe old age of seventeen years old. He was paroled five years later, but was soon sentenced to a low-security prison for a misdemeanor—from which he promptly escaped, robbed a bank, and then was captured again following a high-speed car chase. He was released, and then incarcerated one more time in the early 1970s for running a drug racket and attempting yet another bank robbery. In prison for what would be his final stay, he soon turned his attention from crime to crime fiction, writing and publishing several novels from behind bars.

Bunker's first book was turned into the film *Straight Time* (1978), starring Dustin Hoffman, in which Bunker played a small role. Now able to support himself with both writing and acting gigs, Bunker no longer needed to rob banks to get by. He'd play Jonah, Manny's former partner, in *Runaway Train*, and appear again in the later Konchalovsky pictures *Shy People* (1988) and *Tango & Cash* (1989). Other cult film appearances by Bunker included *Miracle Mile* (1988), *Best of the Best* (1989), and *Reservoir Dogs* (1992), in which he played the fictional bank robber, Mr. Blue.

Many other actors were considered when Stallone passed on the project, before an agent called to pitch a three-actor, package deal that proved hard to resist: Jon Voight, Eric Roberts, and Rebecca De Mornay. Voight and Konchalovsky were already close friends. It was Voight who had helped Konchalovsky secure his work visa to come to the United States, being a fan of his prior work and having asked him personally to direct *Rhinestone Heights* for him at Columbia Pictures. (That feature was eventually canceled.)

Eric Roberts, Rebecca De Mornay, and Jon Voight in *Runaway Train*.

At first Voight was hesitant to play the hardened career criminal, admitting that the role initially "scared" him, and forced him to go to a dark place within himself. It was also casting against the All-American image he had at the time, following acclaimed performances in *Midnight Cowboy* (1969),

Deliverance (1972), and *Coming Home* (1978), for which he won a Best Actor statuette. Konchalovsky reportedly begged him to take the part, and Voight finally agreed. To prepare, Voight went to San Quentin and spent time with the prisoners there, doing his best to learn and understand what solitary confinement could do to a man's fragile psyche.

Nearly twenty years after it had first been canceled, *Runaway Train* began shooting in the spring of 1985. The film was initially going to be shot in Montana, but when an early thaw left the crew without any natural snow, the decision was made to pick up and move to Alaska, where the script was actually set.

The movie opens in the fictional Stonehaven Maximum Security Prison, where bank robber Oscar "Manny" Manheim (Voight) is locked—actually, *welded into*—his cell in solitary confinement. After two nearly-successful escape attempts, Manny has become an international celebrity and a folk hero to his fellow inmates. He's also earned himself an arch-nemesis in the form of the prison's sadistic warden, Ranken, played with wild-eyed intensity by John P. Ryan, one of the few actors capable of matching Voight's crazed performance.

A character actor who thrived in villainous roles, John P. Ryan became a Cannon regular after appearing in *Runaway Train*, later being cast as the baddies in *Avenging Force* (1986) and *Death Wish IV* (1987), and playing Chuck Norris' boss in *Delta Force 2* (1990)—giving him the rare distinction of having appeared opposite all three of Cannon's biggest action stars: Bronson, Norris, and Dudikoff. John P. Ryan began his screen career relatively late in the game, having served in the US Army before making his first film appearance at the age of thirty. The first decade of his career included memorable bits in *Five Easy Pieces* (1970) and *The King of Marvin Gardens* (1972), and playing the not-so-proud papa of a killer, mutant baby in the early entries of the *It's Alive!* (1974) franchise. By the 1980s, you could hardly spin around in a video store without accidentally knocking over a tape that he appeared on: from *The Right Stuff* (1983) to *The Cotton Club* (1984), *Three O'Clock High* (1987) to *Class of 1999* (1990).

When word that a prisoner has been welded into a cage reaches the outside world, Warden Ranken is forced by court order to release his favorite inmate from solitary confinement. Ranken dares Manny to attempt another escape, knowing that he can use lethal force to take him down if he does. Ranken forces the issue by hiring an inmate to shank Manny within hours of his release into the general population. Knowing that the Warden will have him killed if he stays, Manny is left with no other choice but to fly the coop.

Having been badly injured in the fracas, Manny's old partner Jonah (Bunker) passes on the chance to accompany him on his escape. Manny must enlist the aid of a younger inmate named Buck McGeehy (Eric Roberts), a boxer and convicted rapist, in his escape. Buck idolizes Manny, and wants nothing more than to partner up with his criminal hero.

One of the earliest advertisements from Cannon's sales catalogs, released while the film was still in production.

The older brother of *Pretty Woman* (1990) star Julia Roberts, Eric's was the first of the Roberts siblings' careers to take off. After getting his start in soap operas like so many other young actors, Roberts earned a Golden Globe nomination right out of the gate for *King of the Gypsies* (1978), his debut film appearance, and another for playing a murderer in Bob Fosse's *Star 80* (1983). These were followed by yet another acclaimed turn, this time in *The Pope of Greenwich Village* (1984), opposite Mickey Rourke, which cemented his reputation as an actor on the rise.

After earning his third Golden Globe nomination (and first Oscar nom) for *Runaway Train*, Roberts' career hit a speed bump following a high-profile drug arrest, and he did not make a new film for several years. He soon came roaring back with a vengeance in the cult martial arts film *Best of the Best* (1989), and then never slowed down: since the 1990s, Roberts has been one of the most unbelievably prolific actors in Hollywood, accumulating more than *six hundred* (!) credits to his name—a number which continues to climb. From 2013 through 2019 alone, Roberts made an average of *thirty* films each year.

In the film, Manny and Buck slip out of jail through Stonehaven's sewer pipe, and into the unforgivingly frigid Alaskan wilderness. Knowing they can't survive long while exposed to the elements—and that the warden is hot on their trail—the two men head to an industrial railyard and stow themselves away on a departing locomotive. As it's leaving the station, the train's engineer suffers a heart attack, which goes unnoticed by the fugitives. The train picks up speed as the miles pass, and it slowly dawns upon the convicts that they're trapped on the endlessly-accelerating vehicle as it heads towards an inevitable collision.

Saying too much more here would spoil the experience for those who haven't seen the film. To paint a broad portrait, much of the film details the many efforts made to stop the out-of-control hulk of steel, both by those trapped inside it and a crew of railroad dispatchers back at headquarters who are forced to do everything they can to thwart a fatal catastrophe.

The cast is top-to-bottom fantastic, Rebecca De Mornay of *Risky Business* (1983) and *The Trip to Bountiful* (1985) receives third billing as Sara, a railroad employee who finds herself trapped aboard the runaway engine, and who may be the key to the fugitives' survival. (Contrary to a popularly-repeated newspaper typo, Karen Allen was never cast in *Runaway Train*.) De Mornay would later star in the Cannon Movie Tales version of *Beauty and the Beast*.

Over at the railroad's dispatch station we have Kyle T. Heffner of *Flashdance* (1983) as Frank Barstow, the cocky programmer and engineer who designed the railway's foolproof (until now) electronics system, who has an unforgettable run-in with a seething Warden Ranken in the office bath-room. Kenneth McMillan plays the railroad's self-interested executive; fans of spectacularly misguided science fiction adaptations will recognize him as the icky Baron Vladimir Harkonnen in David Lynch's *Dune* (1984). They're assisted by a dispatcher named Dave Prince, played by T.K. Carter, formerly of Cannon's own *Seed of Innocence* (1980) and John Carpenter's horror classic *The Thing* (1982), one of the few films that, like *Runaway Train*, will make you feel chilly just watching it.

Stonehaven Prison is also populated by several great character actors—none more recognizable than Danny Trejo and Tiny Lister, both in their debut performances.

Action fans will spot the future *Machete* (2010) star's distinctive looks right away. Trejo spent much of his early adult life in California prisons for drug-related offenses. While doing time at San Quentin, he became the prison's lightweight boxing champion and well-known to his fellow inmates, including *Runaway Train* screenwriter Edward Bunker. Trejo was involved in a riot at San Quentin in 1969, which landed him in solitary confinement—an experience which inspired him to get sober and turn his life around. Once out of prison, he became a youth drug counselor, which in a roundabout manner led to his film career. One of his patients was employed by the film produc-tion, and asked Trejo for help staying clear of the cocaine which was report-edly plentiful on set. While there, he was recognized by Bunker, who helped Trejo get hired to fight Eric Roberts in the film's boxing match. Konchalovsky liked his look so much that he placed Trejo throughout the movie's prison scenes and the rest, they might say, is history. Trejo would make additional appearances for Cannon in *Penitentiary III* (1987), *Death Wish IV* (1987), and *Kinjite: Forbidden Subjects* (1989) before he became one of cult filmmaker Robert Rodriguez's favorite actors.

A towering character actor who also occasionally wrestled in the WWF, Tommy "Tiny" Lister had hundreds of film and TV credits to his name before he passed away in 2020. He was best known for playing Ice Cube's bully neighbor, Deebo, in *Friday* (1995), and for small-but-memorable roles in films such as *The Fifth Element* (1997), *Jackie Brown* (1997), and *The Dark Knight* (2008).

Two escaped convicts—played by Roberts and Voight—in *Runaway Train*. The film's title was wonderfully translated to "Hell Train" when it was released in Spain.

It's Jon Voight, however, who steals the show with his intense, terrifying performance: he's an absolutely dominant force with a grim philosophical outlook. To give himself a harder appearance, Voight wore fake teeth over his real ones, makeup to make his eye appear swollen semi-shut, and an apparatus to make his nose appear broken. He gave himself over to the role not only physically, but mentally: one of the film's most impactful moments comes when, after Buck openly fantasizes about blowing a load of stolen cash in Las Vegas, Manny delivers an impassioned speech about the courage and will-power it takes to walk away from a life of crime. It's a monologue that Voight himself added to the script, after hearing a similar one from one of the San Quentin inmates he spent time with while preparing for the movie. While Jon Voight did not win the Best Actor Oscar for *Runaway Train*—losing out to William Hurt in *Kiss of the Spider Woman* (1985)—he did take home the Golden Globe for his performance.

The film was shot on four real Alaska Railroad locomotives. While the railway requested that their logos not appear in the film, they did assist when it came to safety, keeping experts on hand at all times to make sure that no cameras could roll without all of the actors and crew properly har-nessed to the train. Part and parcel with shooting on an active rail line, the film crew and their engines would have to clear out each time a normal train passed through on its regular schedule. As a workaround to these time restraints, Konchalovsky had several cameras set up to shoot simultane-ously at any given time, getting coverage from different angles and packing more shots into every take. Using real engines and locations lent the film its cold, gritty realism. There are many incredible shots—from beneath, or hanging off the side of a moving train—that put the viewer right in the action.

Despite all of the safety precautions taken during the shoot, the produc-tion was struck by tragedy when helicopter pilot Rick Holley was killed, his aircraft crashing after it became caught in power lines while scouting loca-tions in Alaska. The film is dedicated to his memory at the end of the end credits.

Beyond Alaska, segments from *Runaway Train* also shot at the Old Montana Prison and a nearby railyard (where potato flakes were used to sim-ulate snow) as well as a soundstage in Los Angeles and the partially-burnt remains of the Pan-Pacific Auditorium, where larger-scale versions of the engines' interiors were constructed to allow for easier filming of those scenes.

Runaway Train received a limited, qualifying run in theaters in December of 1985 before opening wide the following month. Critics, for the most part, loved the film: even the hard-to-impress Roger Ebert gave the film a perfect, four-star rating, praising its inter-character dynamics and daring stunt work. It did fair business at the box office, and went on to an even better afterlife on the video rental market.

Konchalovsky had been granted relative creative freedom by Cannon while making this film, and it feels like a singular vision the whole way through (albeit a heavily Kurosawa-flavored one.) It's a cut above much of the studio's output in nearly every aspect, with perhaps the best ending in all of their filmography: an absolute stunner that's brutal, honest, and tragic all at once.

Brian Gendece with the screenplay for *Runaway Train*.

Interview: Development Executive Brian Gendece

Nowadays, Producer/Talent Manager Brian Gendece represents a roster of A-list choreographers and directors who have created world tour stage shows for musical artists such as Rihanna, Christina Aguilera, Madonna, Jennifer Lopez, Ricky Martin, Shakira, Prince, and Janet Jackson. The interesting path that brought him here, though, includes a decade working with Menahem Golan as an executive at both Cannon and then at 21st Century Film Corp.

Gendece's entry into the film business came under the mentorship of veteran producer Henry T. Weinstein, who was highly-regarded for his exceptional and literary-minded filmography. Weinstein/Skyfield Productions independently developed *Runaway Train* (1985), which was picked up by Cannon and led to Weinstein and Gendece's employment by the company. Gendece was named Director of Development, and later promoted to Head of Development, where he was involved with the bulk of Cannon's productions from 1985 to 1989. This includes major contributions to *Salsa* (1988), a dance film Gendece developed from the ground up—which will be covered in its own chapter in the third volume of this series.

Could you tell me a little bit about yourself and Weinstein/Skyfield, and how you got into the film business?

Weinstein/Skyfield Productions was a New York-based production company. Henry T. Weinstein—and it's very important to mention, *no* relation to Harvey Weinstein. Henry T. Weinstein was considered part of the New York intelligentsia, especially as it related to plays and films. He produced The American Film Theatre; for TV he produced *The Play of the Week* series (1959–1961); even Marilyn Monroe's last film, *Something's Got to Give* (1962). He worked with Paul Scofield and with Katharine Hepburn and was one of 20th Century Fox's big time, veteran producers who was known for having exceptional taste. After I graduated from college, I moved to New York and secured a job working as an office manager for him. I worked my way up to being his executive assistant, to a development executive for the company.

The Skyfield [of Weinstein/Skyfield] was the music arm of the company—run by Robert Whitmore, who is also credited as one of the executive producers on *Runaway Train*. I assisted on both sides, and learned a lot. They had a deal with Warner Bros. TV to develop children's programming, so we were going back and forth, West Coast to East Coast. Maybe a year later, like 1982, maybe '83, Henry had lunch with a major movie star. I begged to go along, but he wouldn't let me. He said, "Somebody's got to stay in the office." He returns from the lunch meeting and says, "The film star who gave me the script wants to remain anonymous and is a friend of the director, Andrei Konchalovsky, who won the Grand Prix at the Cannes Film Festival for *Siberiade* (1979)." I asked what it was called and he said, "Runaway Train" and he flopped it on my desk, and said, "Read it and let me know what you think." I looked at it, and the cover page reads "Akira Kurosawa." I'm thinking, "Wow, really?"

Henry adds, "I've already skimmed through it and there's little Western characterization, it's written like a foreign movie. I've really got to think about this one."

The draft of the screenplay we first saw, as best as I remember, there was no female character in it. There was no "Sara"—it was a male character. I remember Henry having conversations with Andrei saying, "You know, we've got to put a woman in this. There's also nobody really to root for. It's a hard film to make." Andrei had already met Menahem Golan at the Cannes Film Festival. While we were in development on *Runaway Train*, Henry and I went on location to meet with Andrei while he was shooting *Maria's Lovers* (1985).

I'm fairly certain that the rights to the project reverted back to Akira Kurosawa from AVCO/Embassy. I was involved with putting the paperwork together when Cannon Films got involved. We had developed the project independently, and Cannon paid Weinstein/Skyfield a reimbursement check for all of our development costs, paid to us with a non-negotiable check from Credit Lyonnais Bank in the Netherlands. It took a month for the funds to arrive. Every expense thereafter Cannon took on and financed, and [Golan and Globus] would become the producers. Henry became executive producer.

Cannon's advertisement for the movie from their 1985 catalog.

I've heard that Kurosawa's original script was three hundred pages long, which I figure has to be an exaggeration . . .

I would say that's probably true. I can tell you, with being a development executive you can take a script in your hand and do a flip-through and almost accurately guess the exact number of pages it is. [*Laughs*] My flip recollection is telling me it was about 286 pages in my mind. I don't remember for sure, but it was *long*.

Pre-Cannon, we were running low on development money. Henry came to me and said, "Can you help me raise money so we can hire Paul Zindel to do a rewrite on the script?" I accepted the challenge and ended up raising the money. That was my first foray into fundraising. Henry said, "Paul is a Pulitzer Prize-winning writer, he is so good at writing female characters, and so perfect to add an American sensibility to the dialogue." And then, Cannon came on board and said they would finance the film if we could get the appropriate cast. I believe Andrei was already talking to Robert Duvall to play the role of Manny, and he was interested, and then got busy and said he couldn't do it.

Menahem, who loved Sylvester Stallone, got very excited when the agent who represented Sylvester Stallone said that Stallone might be interested in playing the role.

Oh, wow!

So Stallone calls our office, and Henry places him on the speakerphone. That's how you learned: you listened to how these veteran filmmakers work. Stallone suggested we hire writers Miguel Piñero, or Eddie Bunker. Miguel Piñero wrote *Short Eyes* and was nominated for the Tony Award for it. He later wrote for *Miami Vice* (1984–1989). He had been in prison, so they thought that he could really flesh out the prison scenes.

I called Piñero's agent to check his availability, and was told that he'd just been arrested at the airport for cocaine possession. So, I believe that's when we hired Edward Bunker. If it weren't for Miguel Piñero, I don't know if Eddie would have been involved or not. Bunker is also in the movie.

Right, he plays Jonah.

Eddie really gave it the edge that the script needed. Stallone passed on the film. Henry and I were on the phone with every agent from ICM to William Morris, you name it, trying to put a cast together that would be acceptable to Cannon, which would assure them they could make their money back on this movie. As you know, Menahem and Yoram funded most everything through pre-sales at Film Markets. Golan wanted our film to start as quickly as possible. So, Henry offers the two lead roles to Sean Penn and Timothy Hutton.

Wow! Two more big names.

Well, it gets even better. They read the script, and said they would love to do it. But you know, it's a package of Sean Penn and Timothy Hutton, and the deal was being brokered by Sue Mengers—she was one of *the* biggest, most powerful agents of that time. She represented everyone from Barbra Streisand to Gene Hackman, Faye Dunaway, I mean, she was *it*.

Less than half a day had gone by since Henry had said to her, "Great, wonderful!" when we got a call from our agent, Marty Baum at CAA, saying: "We have Jon Voight, Eric Roberts, and Rebecca De Mornay. You have to take all three of them. It's a package. You don't get Jon Voight without the others. You don't get Eric Roberts without Rebecca De Mornay." I remember looking up Rebecca De Mornay's film credits for Henry.

She'd really only done one big role at that time.

Right. It made us very happy when we found out she brilliantly played the prostitute in *Risky Business* (1983). And, of course, Eric Roberts, I knew who he was, and Jon Voight. So Henry called Sue Mengers back and said, "We are going with Jon Voight, Eric Roberts, and Rebecca De Mornay."

Mengers sent a memo via fax to Henry and I was CC'd on it, and it said, "I will ruin your careers! I am going to tell *everyone* that you made a deal and backed out of it, and I'm going to let every casting director in town know." Henry wasn't fazed at all. But, I was concerned and I went up to Henry and I said, "Oh, my God, my career is ruined! My name is on this paper!" And he goes, "Are you kidding? Your career was just *made*! Everybody's going to know who you are now. You're not anybody unless you've been hated by Sue Mengers."

So, that's how the cast came about. We moved into Cannon's offices, and by the time the film came out, Henry was Vice President of Development for Cannon, as well as the executive producer on the film. And I came on board as Director of Development under Henry. Normally when you work at a major studio, if you work on two pictures at once, that's a lot. At Cannon we had over eighty film projects in various stages of development. At least twelve films a year were being greenlit, and it was the best experience of my life. Even as crazy as it was!

Yeah, I can imagine.

The critical success of *Runaway Train*, I feel, helped Cannon attract a higher quality and wider outreach of film projects, directors and producers.

The Japanese press book for *Runaway Train*. The film received additional attention there thanks to its Kurosawa connection.

Looking back, are there specific movies you feel like you were most involved with, or required more of your attention than others?

To many it seemed that if you could get a meeting with Menahem, there was a good chance you would get a deal. It was Henry's job and my job to take these scripts that people had written, or partial scripts, or story ideas that Menahem had come up with, and try to make them work. Menahem could come up with the story for *anything*. He loved doing this. We would then be given the challenge to develop an acceptable screenplay.

We would say, "Maybe we can get this writer or attach this director, maybe we can get this cinematographer." That's what we were doing. We weren't physically on set. The one production that I actually helped create from ground zero was the movie *Salsa* (1988). Menahem wanted another dance movie because of the monetary success of *Breakin'* and *Breakin' 2* (1984) and the appeal dance movies had to young audiences. I pitched him a movie about Salsa and Mambo dancing since it had been featured predominantly in Vestron's *Dirty Dancing* (1987). The *Salsa* storyline was based upon a very successful film in Israel called *Lemon Popsicle* (1973) co-written and directed by Boaz Davidson, who also directed *Salsa*.

Sometimes the art department at Cannon would create movie posters for screenplays that didn't exist—making movies to fit the posters. [*Laughs*] Interesting times!

Cannon was a mini-major at that time. I couldn't have asked for a better training ground. I think it was around the time of *52 Pick-Up* (1986), the film directed by John Frankenheimer, Henry became an executive producer on it, that's when they started telling him, "You know, why don't you just be executive producer on some of our films? That way you can be paid from the production budget rather than as an employee." Henry accepted the offer and left the company and went on to produce *Texasville* (1988), which was a follow up to *The Last Picture Show* (1971) by Peter Bogdanovich. Instead of hiring someone to replace Henry, they promoted me to head of creative affairs. Henry was very happy for me. I'm proud to have had him as my mentor in show business.

I'll have to look through my catalogs because they have executive rosters in some of them, with headshots. I might find you in there.

I don't think so. Cannon didn't want employees to get a lot of credit for what they did. It's just the way it was. But you didn't care, because you were learning so much. When Menahem left Cannon and opened 21st Century Film Corporation, he gave me a non-exclusive, first look housekeeping deal to develop dance films for him, because of my background in the dance and choreography community, including the work that I did on the film *Salsa*, which was a fairly decent hit internationally for them.

While I was there, Menahem said, "Well, while you're here, would you mind drafting deal memos for the different writers and directors that I'm hiring at 21st Century?" He said, "I'll pay you some extra money on top of what I'm giving you on your housekeeping deal, and I'll give you the penthouse suite." Done! [Laughs] I developed a dance film there called *Ballhouse Jam* but unfortunately the company went through various transformations and it never got made. My cast was Rita Moreno, David Charvet, and Julia Migenes, the famous opera singer who starred in the film *Carmen* (1984) with Placido Domingo. It was also going to be my directorial debut. I attended the Cannes Film Festival to promote the sale of it. The film rights were returned to me, who knows, maybe one day it will get made.

I was fond of Menahem's bigger-than-life-itself personality. If it weren't for *Runaway Train*, my relationship with Menahem would have never happened. And I would have never become friends and business pals with Karen Lee Arbeeny, Sam Firstenberg, Gideon Amir, and so many other talented Cannonites.

Did you have a working relationship with either Francis Ford Coppola or Tom Luddy at Zoetrope? I know they had some involvement in *Runaway Train* early on, and then again later with *Barfly* (1987), *Tough Guys Don't Dance* (1987), and *Powaqqatsi* (1988).

Just a couple phone calls with Tom Luddy. To the best of my recollection, Henry T. Weinstein knew Tom well, and also Francis Ford Coppola. There were always a lot of phone calls going back and forth. They wanted to help Andrei—they wanted to make this happen. Oddly, I remember that Henry asked me to research cappuccino makers, to buy one for Francis Ford Coppola and Tom Luddy's office. I think it was about $1800, which was a lot of money back then. [*Laughs*]

I know Jon Voight and Andrei were friends before making *Runaway Train*. Was Jon ever considered before they came to you with this package of him with Eric and Rebecca?

I don't know 100%, but my educated guess would be that he knew about the project, but the script was never there. With every actor, it's always about the script. Jon Voight attacked the character so perfectly. What strikes me the most is that opening scene when you first see Jon. Do you remember what he's doing?

290

He's doing push-ups, I believe.

Exactly. To show his strength. Andrei Konchalovsky is such a brilliant director. He took elements of the script and minimized the action to make it stand out more. When Buck silently draws the heart on the window? I mean, there are some really touching moments. And the paper swirling around in the train car. It's Andrei's artistic sensibility that really added depth to the film.

The Polish poster for *Runaway Train* was drawn by surrealist illustrator Jakub Erol. While the poster doesn't match the film's content, it certainly captures its tone.

I think it's easy to forget that it's a color film, just because of the way it uses so much darkness against the snow.

You know we had trouble finding snow, right? You read that, I'm sure.

How stressful was that? That set the production behind a little bit, but they were able to catch up.

We actually started production sooner than we thought we would. We were rushing to get started. Of course, before we even started filming, we had that horrible tragedy of losing Rick Holley, to whom the film is dedicated.

Yes—when his helicopter got caught in power lines.

He was doing recce (reconnaissance) work to find suitable filming locations. To hear this news before the start of Principal Photography--you have no idea how devastating that was to everyone. We felt horrible.

Shooting began in Montana, but I've heard there was so much trouble finding snow that Menahem made the decision to pick up and move to Alaska.

That's true. At least, that's the way I heard it—I wasn't on location. I was at the Cannon offices working on other films.

Here's another interesting story about *Runaway Train*. Before Rebecca De Mornay, I was friends with Laura Branigan, the singer who sang "Gloria." She was a major recording artist for Atlantic Records. She wanted nothing more than to be an actress. Agent Jonathan Trumper at William Morris said, "I really want Laura Branigan to audition for the role of Sara." She did a wonderful job, and I was pushing hard for her. I thought she'd be great for the soundtrack too. Of course, it didn't happen. I ended up putting Laura on the soundtrack of the movie *Salsa* to sing David Friedman's song "Your Love," which was later recorded by Diana Ross and went quadruple platinum in the UK.

I have an Eric Roberts story, too. Eric says to me, "I'll give you my phone number." I pull out a Rolodex card and I write down Eric Roberts and I say, "Okay, what's the number?" He replies, "I'm staying at my sister Julia's house" and gives me a West Hollywood phone number. I wrote on the card, Eric Roberts, the phone number, and underneath it in parentheses, "Julia's house." Julia Roberts wasn't a household name at that time. So about ten years later, I'm flipping through my Rolodex and I see that note and I just about died. [Laughs] Of course, I had to call the number. It didn't work, but it was amusing.

You would have been in the Cannon offices when *Runaway Train* started getting nominated for awards, which was a new experience for them. What was the reaction like there?

Opening night was in New York, December 6, 1985. I was there with Henry. I'll never forget Jon Voight was wearing a red winter scarf. We were happy that it opened at the Paris Theater across from the Plaza Hotel, an upscale area of Manhattan. Henry voiced concern that the film would struggle to find an audience because Cannon's distribution channels had been geared towards a different type of action film audience. Cannon booked this beautiful theater and the film received great reviews. Right off the bat, everybody said that Voight and Roberts would be nominated for Academy Awards and Golden Globes, and that all happened. Menahem and Yoram were overjoyed by the news. Henry and I were blown away by the news. [Laughs] We knew that it wasn't going to be a big commercial hit. For Henry, it wasn't necessarily about being commercial—it was about being *good*.

Kyle T. Heffner (right) with Kenneth McMillan and T.K. Carter in *Runaway Train*.

Interview: Actor Kyle T. Heffner

Kyle T. Heffner discovered his talent for acting very young, working in children's theatre and commercials as a youth. As a student at Northwestern, he was part of the university's improv comedy showcase, The Mee-Ow Show—famous for producing comedic actors such as Julia Louis-Dreyfus and numerous *Saturday Night Live* stars. Here he was spotted by Garry Marshall, who was already then a giant in the world of television sitcoms. Marshall cast

293

Heffner in his feature film directorial debut, *Young Doctors in Love* (1982), which became the young actor's first footstep into the movie business. Soon afterward he landed one of his best-known roles, playing short-order cook Richie in the surprise, runaway hit *Flashdance* (1983).

In Cannon's *Runaway Train* (1985), Heffner played Frank Barstow—the cocky, control room engineer who bears the brunt of Warden Ranken's rage in an unshakeable scene set in the train station's bathroom. In contrast to this dramatic role, Heffner is more often associated with his roles in comedies, including *When Harry Met Sally...* (1989), and for playing "Bizarro George" in a classic episode of *Seinfeld* (1989–1998).

Correct me if I'm wrong, but were you brought in as a last-minute replacement for another actor on *Runaway Train*?

Kyle T. Heffner: As far as I know, I replaced Wallace Shawn.

Oh, wow. That would have been quite different.

I got the call on a Thursday. They said there was this movie, *Runaway Train*, and an actor fell out. I didn't know who was at the time. I go to the set. At that point, I think they had shot all the exteriors up in Alaska, or wherever the hell they were. They were shooting in the burned-out Pan Pacific Auditorium, in this place called Pan Pacific Park here in LA. It's no longer there, I think this was the last thing that ever happened inside of it. Anyway, there they had the mockup of the train.

I remember walking onto the set. It was odd not being on a soundstage. It was basically kind of a shell of a building and they turned it into a soundstage. Then the mockup of the train is in there. I see this guy with the scar on his face and he's really scary and he's looking at me and I had no idea it was Jon Voight. I didn't even recognize him. I go in and I talk to Andrei Konchalovsky in his trailer. We talked about the character—I had read the script the night before. I think I went home and later they called and said, "You're starting work on Monday."

Does that mean you had a big cram session that weekend?

It was a cram session. I didn't have a lot of time to prep, but I got it in. I had told them I had tickets booked with my girlfriend to go to Europe for three weeks, so I think they shot me out fast. They had two cameras running all the time. They didn't have to change set-ups. It was like that. Andrei and I, we had a little bit of a thing. He likes things broad, and I had watched a couple of his movies over the weekend. He's an amazing director. I was trying to go small, he wanted me to go big. We had a little tussle there. It worked out. We got through it. It was really fun to work with him on it, and he had a really amazing vision. He just kept telling me, "Bigger, Kyle, more, more! Bigger! More of your face!" We came to a meeting of minds, and we ended up getting along very well.

You worked with, in my opinion, one of the great heavies of that period, John P. Ryan. How was he?

It's always those heavy, scary guys that are the sweetest, most kind people you'd ever want to meet. That was true with John. Sweet, kind, generous, but when he heard "action," he flipped the switch. That's how he was.

When we shot the bathroom scene, they told me, "Now, the toilet is cleaned up, but we're going to put a little apple juice in there to make it look like there's urine. But, it's perfectly clean. It's just water." It was all so controlled, and so perfect, that it allowed John and I to really do what we needed to do in that scene. Of course, he was scary as hell.

There's a little secret which many people don't know, but to give him a little extra ferocity, they reflected a butane torch in his eyes. That's a little secret I'll tell you, you can put in your book.

That's amazing.

This was pre-digital. They had a butane torch on hand for his close-ups. They had it so it was reflected in his eyes in the camera.

You worked with another great character actor too, in Kenneth McMillan, who passed away just a few years after *Runaway Train*.

Oh, yes. A lovely man. Absolutely lovely. Another kind, generous guy who's just there enjoying his job. He had great stories, because he had worked with everybody. We were shooting so fast there wasn't a lot of sit-around time to chat. Then the woman in that scene who played the secretary [Stacey Pickren], she was in *Flashdance*. She played the old flash dancer in *Flashdance*, and she and I are still friends. Also, the other guy, T.K. Carter, he's had a great career, and is still always working. T.K. and I became good friends, too. He's a terrific, super funny guy.

It was a fun shoot. It was really fast. My stuff was all in an old, silent film studio downtown. It probably doesn't exist anymore. They probably got it cheap or something like that.

A bold, French theatrical poster for *Runaway Train*.

Right around the same time you did a movie called *DC Cops* with Mario Van Peebles, who was doing a lot of Cannon stuff at that time.

It was a pilot for a series. Because *Runaway Train* opened a lot of doors, that year I did two pilots back to back. I shot *DC Cops* in DC, with Mario and Cotter Smith. Mario and I played homicide detectives. We were partners, and Cotter was the lead. We had a great time in DC. We were there for two or three weeks.

A couple of really fun things happened. They had a guy, Peter Greenberg, who was a big travel writer. I don't really know of him, but they hired him to keep us busy. One night he said, "You guys want to go to the White House?" We're like, "Yes." They said, "Well, be downstairs at eleven o'clock." Pre-9/11, right? We go downstairs. A van picks us up. They take us to the White House. We go in. Peter's walking through, flipping switches like, "Here's the Oval Office, here's this, here's that." We're just walking around. It's 11:30 at night. It was insane.

Then Mario and I were in the elevator going up to our room. Mike Nichols walks up, gets into the elevator. He's there directing a play at the Ford. Mario and I are standing there and he said, "Hello, gentlemen, you're two actors, aren't you?" We were like, "Yes, we are. Mr. Nichols." He goes, "Would you like to come to see my play?" We were like, "Yes. I would love to come and see your play." We got invited to the opening night of the play and the opening night party. It was pretty great.

Cannon was making more movies than anyone else in the mid-80s. Are there any other projects of theirs you auditioned for?

Yes. I auditioned for at least three Chuck Norris movies. [*Laughs*] I know I auditioned for one or two directed by Lance Hool.

That would have been *Missing in Action*—or, actually, what became *Missing in Action 2: The Beginning* (1985).

Yes, that's what it was. They were trying to get me in another one, but it never really happened for whatever reason.

They were on the verge of bankruptcy just a couple of years later.

They told me, during *Runaway Train*, they said we're going to spend all this money on promotion. "You're going to be going on all the shows." That never happened, but critically it was received quite well.

The Media Home Video release for *The Delta Force*, one of Cannon's most popular tapes.

The Delta Force
Delta Force 2: The Colombian Connection
Delta Force 3: The Killing Game

Release Date: February 14, 1986 (I), August 24, 1990 (II), March 22, 1991
(III)
Directed by: Menahem Golan (I), Aaron Norris (II), Sam Firstenberg (III)
Written by: James Bruner and Menahem Golan (I), Lee Reynolds (II), Boaz
Davidson, Andy Deutsch, and Greg Latter (III)
Starring: Chuck Norris, Lee Marvin, and Robert Forster (I), Chuck Norris,
John P. Ryan, and Billy Drago (II), Mike Norris and Nick Cassavetes (III)
Trailer Voiceover: "He's a gentle man with a soft touch, a mean kick, and his
own special brand of diplomacy!"

When Chuck Norris enters a room, he doesn't turn the lights on. He turns
the dark off.

Prisons don't keep citizens safe from criminals. Prisons keep criminals
safe from Chuck Norris.

There was once a street named after Chuck Norris, but its name had to be
changed because no one crosses Chuck Norris and lives.

"Chuck Norris Facts"—as they've come to be known—were a wildly popular Internet meme in the mid-2000s. The earliest Chuck Norris Facts on record appeared in the online forums of the humor site Something Awful in 2005. These ridiculous bits of "trivia" about the actor—and there are thousands of them—typically made outlandish statements regarding the then-65-year-old's masculinity, toughness, virility, or just general badass-ness.

Although it was adapted from a similar, existing meme centered on action star Vin Diesel, "Chuck Norris Facts" eventually transcended the web and went on to pervade larger popular culture, spawning T-shirts, calendars, and coffee mugs, and being referenced in TV shows, films, and even by presidential candidates. Yes, that's right: in 2007, Chuck Norris appeared in a campaign commercial for Republican presidential candidate Mike Huckabee, in which the former Cannon star and the Arkansas governor traded off telling facts about one another. Huckabee would recite one of the jokey Chuck Norris facts, followed by Norris providing a piece of straight-forward information about the conservative candidate. (The ad opened with Huckabee explaining his plan to secure the American-Mexican border: "Two words: Chuck Norris.")

Up until people got tired of them, part of the reason why these far-fetched Chuck Norris facts were so funny was that they fit so perfectly with the actor's cinematic persona. More often than not, Norris played a good-natured, no-nonsense patriot—usually a soldier or cop of some sort—who rarely had more to say than a stoic one-liner. His characters are invincible heroes who kick first and ask questions later, rarely miss and never, ever lose. (Of course, they take a lot of beatings, but those are only to demonstrate the level of pain they can endure in the cause of the greater good.) Chuck's heroes are equally as deadly with firearms, be they Uzis, pistols, or bazookas, as they are with their fists and feet. If Chuck's not shirtless or wearing camo, he's wearing all-black or, at worst, a denim button-down. And let's not forget that every single woman he encounters falls instantly in love with him, despite his usually being around twenty years their senior.

Chuck Norris almost invariably played a version of the '80s action archetype distilled down to its purest form, yet always seemed down-to-earth enough to be somebody's emotionally-barren uncle. Occasionally, his characters would deviate from these precedents, but usually to the detriment of the film. So, when someone explains how prisons don't keep society safe from criminals, but keep criminals safe from Chuck Norris—thanks to these movies, you can almost believe it.

While earlier outings such as *A Force of One* (1979), *Lone Wolf McQuade* (1983), *Missing in Action* (1984), and *Code of Silence* (1985) certainly contributed to Chuck Norris' ultimate action persona, it was Cannon's *Invasion U.S.A.* (1985) and *The Delta Force* (1986) which really cemented it.

If *Missing in Action* is the Alpha when it comes to Chuck Norris' action franchises, then *Delta Force* is the Omega.

Menahem Golan, behind the camera, directing *The Delta Force*.

The Delta Force was Cannon boss Menahem Golan's big return to directing action films five years after he unleashed *Enter the Ninja* (1981) upon the world. Quite lengthy by Cannon's standards—130 minutes—*The Delta Force* feels almost like two separate movies mashed together, starting out as a harrowing hostage thriller before turning into an over-the-top action flick, complete with Chuck Norris on a magical military motorcycle that fires missiles.

For anyone who isn't aware, the 1st Special Forces Operation Detachment-Delta, or Delta Force, is an actual counterterrorism unit with the U.S. Army. (Their Naval counterpart is SEAL Team Six.) Most of what they do is classified, but if you do some research you can read about a few of their real-world operations that have been made public. After this film, Cannon would start squeezing Delta Force operatives into whatever movies they could, just like they had with ninjas and break dancers before it.

The airplane hijacking that makes up the impetus for the movie was based (pretty exploitatively) on the terrorist takeover of TWA Flight 847 in June of 1985, much to the horror of its real-life survivors. Cannon reportedly pushed *The Delta Force* into pre-production as the events of the TWA Flight 847 hijacking were still unfolding in the real world. The movie opened in American movie theaters less than eight months after the hostages' release.

Instead of telling the story as it actually happened, though, Golan chose to play with history, and show how he thought the public would have *wanted* to see it happen—meaning, by having his biggest star, Chuck Norris, almost single-handedly wipe out every terrorist in the Middle East. With a large—again, by Cannon's standards—budget of $9 million, he gathered up an impressive cast and shuttled them off to Golan and Globus' home turf of Israel, where a large portion of the film was shot at the Ben Gurion International Airport in Tel Aviv.

Since the screenplay continued to change and evolve as shooting went on and both Golan and Norris thought of new ideas, Cannon put up writer James Bruner in a nearby hotel so that he could make nightly adjustments to the script and ensure that it would continue to make sense after each day of shooting. Bruner, of course, was among both Cannon's and Norris's most trusted screenwriters, having already penned *Missing in Action* and *Invasion U.S.A.* for the studio.

The movie has an exciting opening scene where Captain Scott McCoy (Norris) of the U.S. Delta Force goes against the orders of his commander, Colonel Nick Alexander (Lee Marvin), to mount a dangerous rescue of a comrade trapped in the wreckage of a downed chopper. After this valiant act of heroism, McCoy voices his distaste for the higher-ups who ordered this botched mission, and resigns from the Force.

This opening scene was clearly inspired by the historical Operation Eagle Claw, a failed attempt to bring an end to the Iran hostage crisis in 1980. The mission was aborted early when several of the helicopters procured for it were found inoperable; when U.S. forces prepared to leave the staging area, one of the helicopters crashed into a transport, and the resulting fire killed eight soldiers. It was to be one of the real-world Delta Force's first missions.

Seen here in his final screen appearance, Hollywood legend Lee Marvin was best known for his roles in war films such as *The Dirty Dozen* (1967) and *The Big Red One* (1980), in classic Westerns like *The Man Who Shot Liberty Valance* (1962) and 1965's *Cat Ballou* (for which he won the Best Actor Academy Award), and the musical *Paint Your Wagon* (1969). While his role as the Delta Force colonel had originally been written with Charles Bronson in mind, the gruff old soldier feels tailor-made for Marvin. Sadly, he was in poor health during the filming of this movie, and passed away just over a year after its release. From an interview conducted following the filming, it sounds as if Marvin and Golan had gotten along quite well, and the actor had been keen to appear in more of Cannon's films—most interestingly, as Geppetto in Tobe Hooper's unproduced "robot Pinocchio" movie.

The movie flashes forward five years to a Greek airport, where a terrorist has stashed a handgun and grenade in an airplane's storage compartment. Immediately after takeoff, two Lebanese men—the leader, Abdul Rafai, is played by Irish-Italian actor Robert Forster—hijack the plane, taking all 144 passengers and the flight crew hostage. The late, great Forster had many fantastic roles in his career that didn't require him to cross ethnicities, including ones in *Medium Cool* (1969), *The Black Hole* (1979), and *Alligator* (1980). He received a Best Supporting Actor nomination for his part in Quentin

Tarantino's *Jackie Brown* (1997), and was cast by David Lynch in both *Mulholland Drive* (2001) and *Twin Peaks: The Return* (2017).

Among the plane's crew and passengers are many, many admirable actors, and even a few Academy Award winners. George Kennedy—who won an Oscar for *Cool Hand Luke* (1967), but then went on to appear in Cannon's *Bolero* (1984)—plays a Catholic priest. Kim Delaney of *NYPD Blue* (1993–2005) is one of the nuns who accompanies him. Cult actor Bo Svenson is the plane's captain, and Hanna Schygulla—known in arthouse circles for her many collaborations with Rainer Werner Fassbinder—plays a German stewardess.

Martin Balsam, Shelley Winters, Rat Pack-er Joey Bishop, and Lainie Kazan play two pairs of vacationing couples. Balsam took home the gold for *A Thousand Clowns* (1965), but is probably better remembered for his roles in *Psycho* (1960) and *12 Angry Men* (1957). He was another Cannon veteran, having appeared in *Death Wish 3* (1985). *The Delta Force* was Shelley Winters' fourth film for Golan and Globus after *The Magician of Lublin* (1979), *Over the Brooklyn Bridge* (1984), and *Déjà Vu* (1985). She had won Oscars for *The Diary of Anne Frank* (1959) and *A Patch of Blue* (1965), and received additional nominations for *A Place in the Sun* (1951) and *The Poseidon Adventure* (1972).

One of the more incredible pieces of Cannon merchandising: *The Delta Force* Anti-Terrorist Attack & Rescue board game, for ages six and up.

The hijackers force the pilot to fly to Beirut, and then to Algiers. A *lot* actually happens on the plane over the first half of the movie. The Jewish hostages are singled out and separated from the rest of the passengers, and are taken to an alternate terrorist hideout in Beirut. The terrorists make demands to the U.S. government and, in one chilling scene, execute an American soldier and dump his body on the runway.

It's in the scenes on the plane where the film feels most exploitative of real-world events. In the TWA 847 hijacking by Hezbollah-affiliated terrorists, a German-American stewardess named Uli Derickson was forced to act as a translator, and was the basis for Schygulla's character. Unlike in the film, though, she protected numerous hostages when the hijackers asked her to help identify the Jewish passenger on the plane, and she hid the passports of those with Jewish-sounding surnames. Likewise, Robert Stethem—a 23-year-old Navy diver was beaten, tortured, and then shot in the head by the terrorists before his body was dumped on the tarmac at Beirut's airport. Rehashing those details in an action movie—one released only *eight months* after Stethem's murder—was tasteless, even for Cannon.

It's not long before all-purpose badass Scott McCoy is lured out of retirement to help the Delta Force mount a mission to rescue the hostages. In addition to Norris and Marvin, the movie's good guys include Robert Vaughn as a U.S. General. Vaughn is perhaps best remembered as Napoleon Solo on *The Man from U.N.C.L.E.* (1964–1968), and for his roles in *The Magnificent Seven* (1960) and *Bullitt* (1968). (He earned a Best Supporting Actor nomination for 1959's *The Young Philadelphians*.) The Delta Force itself is filled out by Cannon regulars Steve James—of the *American Ninja* series, *Avenging Force* (1986), and *Hero and the Terror* (1988)—and Bill Wallace, also of *America 3000* (1986) and *Avenging Force*.

With the aid of an Orthodox priest acting as a spy, the Delta Force is able to locate the hostages and mount their assault on the terrorist compounds. This is where the movie goes from "inspired by a true story" straight into "completely insane action fantasy." Where the real-world hijacking came to an end through negotiations that led to the release of the hostages, *The Delta*

Force opts for a purely action-oriented assault. There's even a point where one of the bad guys pleads for the Delta Force to negotiate, to which Chuck Norris responds by shooting the ham radio he's calling on.

It all begins with a high-octane car chase through the streets of Beirut, with Chuck Norris firing a Mini-Uzi through the back window of a van as the vehicles crash through a phone booth, other cars, a pile of trash, stacks of boxes, and of course the reliable car chase mainstay: a watermelon stand. They escape and link up with the rest of the Delta Force as they make a beach landing, and prepare for the rest of their attack, which mostly involves applying American flag stickers to their uniforms.

An officially licensed *Delta Force* Mini Mak toy submachine gun, for kids who want to act out their favorite scenes from the R-rated Chuck Norris movie.

As the bulk of the Delta Force cruises over to the first stronghold in a fleet of tricked-out dune buggies, McCoy and a few other elite soldiers stealthily scuba-dive into the enemy base. They pop up through a sewer lid like Ninja Turtles and set about slaughtering every terrorist there. The best kills come when McCoy puts a dozen bullets into a bad guy hiding under a bed, then tells his corpse to "Sleep tight, sucker." Another guy jumps his motorcycle over a terrorist *while the terrorist is on fire!*

The bad guys barely put up a fight—for the Delta Force, it's like shooting fish in a barrel. The overwhelming lopsidedness of these battles is almost weird. In any action movie, you *know* the good guy is going to win—but in the better ones, it always seems like there's a *chance* they can lose, especially in the face of seemingly insurmountable odds. In *The Delta Force*, the endless waves of bad guys seem like little more than arcade shooting gallery targets. Outside of one suffered casualty that's milked for emotional gravitas, the Delta Force totally wipe the floor with the villains.

As the rest of the squad evacuates the prisoners, McCoy and Bobby (Steve James) hang back to blow up the arriving reinforcements with synchronized bazooka shots. They high-five afterward as the stunned survivors watch, and it's pretty awesome.

We then move on to a scene where a caravan of terrorists is halted, not by the Delta Force, but by McCoy alone on a motorcycle. Their leader, Abdul, understandably thinks it's ridiculous that hundreds of heavily-armed terrorists would stop for one man on a bike, but he obviously hasn't seen prior Chuck Norris movies like his men must have. McCoy flips a switch on his handlebar and a rocket fires from the front of his bike, blowing the shit out of the lead jeep in the caravan.

The Badass-Super-Cycle that Scott McCoy rides throughout these scenes is a customized 1985 Suzuki SP600. The standard models did not include front-mounted rocket launchers or rear-mounted grenade launchers.

McCoy picks off some more baddies before the rest of the Delta Force show up and help him rescue the hostage servicemen from the back of one of the trucks—which involves McCoy hanging off the side of the vehicle as it moves, then wrestling the driver out of the front seat. This second part of the mission is a success, but once again McCoy has to stay behind to resolve some unfinished business. He jumps his bike through the window of the abandoned home that the lead baddie, Abdul, is hiding in, and then proceeds to beat him to a bloody pulp with a flurry of fists and boot-heels. This goes on for a while, but ends when McCoy climbs back onto his bike and pretends he's going to ride away, sparing Abdul's life—only to instead blow him up with what looks like a grenade shot out of his super-bike's tailpipe. Boom!

The rest of the Delta Force make quick work of the terrorists left to guard the hijacked plane, and rescue the crew inside. As they're readying for takeoff with the other hostages loaded safely onboard, McCoy catches up to them on his boom-boom bike, with the last surviving terrorists in hot pursuit. In one final, valiant demonstration of radness, McCoy pops a wheelie, *stands* on the seat of his bike, and grabs hold of a rope they've lowered down to him. They pull him onto the speeding plane, where the crew passes around cans of Budweiser and the soldiers and hostages share in a rousing rendition of "God Bless America." The hostages are reunited with their families back in Israel, and the Delta Force humbly file back onto their Lockheed C-130, a job well done. The crowd cheers as they take off for America.

The Delta Force might have been a better film had it not tried to straddle the line between being a serious hostage drama and a gonzo military action flick. Together as they are, the film's two angles mix just about as well as orange juice and chocolate milk. If you can separate them in your mind, though, it's possible to appreciate each for what they are. The hostage drama has its tense moments, even if it has the feel of a TV movie-of-the-week with some problematic portrayals of culture and race. These scenes were filmed on an actual Boeing 707 on lease from the local Maof Airlines. By all reports, it was extremely hot inside the vehicle—the Israeli sun and the airport's pavement combined to raise the plane's internal temperature to more than 100 degrees Fahrenheit—and you can see the sweat and discomfort on the faces of the cast members, which adds to the scenes' tension.

Delta Force 2 on American VHS, released under its "Operation Stranglehold" subtitle.

On the sillier side of things, the action—once the movie finally gets around to it—offers everything movie-goers could hope for from a Chuck Norris flick. There are one-liners, absurdly cool-looking weaponry, wild stunts, and even a good amount of martial arts combat squeezed in. It's all set to a really fantastic, energizing electronic score by Alan Silvestri, to boot—hot off his best-known work on *Back to the Future* (1985), he'd go on to compose for

Predator (1987), *Forrest Gump* (1994), and *The Avengers* (2012), among many, many others. However, it takes what can feel like forever—more than half the movie—before the Delta Force actually does any action-y stuff, which had to be disappointing to the audience members who came in hoping for nonstop bullets and explosions.

The Delta Force did okay for itself in theaters, but it wasn't the runaway, *Missing in Action*-level hit that Cannon had been hoping for. Despite a more sizable marketing budget than their average film, the movie only managed to double its $9 million budget in domestic receipts. Though negative reviews and poor word-of-mouth probably contributed more to the movie's failure at the box office—as well as Cannon's head-scratching decision to release it on Valentine's Day, typically a weekend reserved for more romantic fare—it probably didn't help that the film was protested nationwide by the Arab-American Anti-Discrimination Committee, who objected to the film's negative stereotyping of its vaguely Middle Eastern villains. *The Delta Force* certainly did well enough for the studio to greenlight a sequel starring Norris four years later.

If Cannon has taught us anything about sequels, it's that they only have to be nominally connected to their predecessors. While it wasn't the total departure that, say, *Revenge of the Ninja* (1983) took from *Enter the Ninja*, 1990's *Delta Force 2: The Colombian Connection* features a sharp tonal shift from the first film, as well as a rather significant makeover of the Scott McCoy character.

The stark contrast between the two films probably has something to do with the movie's circuitous production history. At one point, Albert Pyun almost directed Michael Dudikoff and Steve James in a version that would have been called *Spitfire: Delta Force II*, which would have involved action's most dynamic duo stopping terrorists from blowing up a nuclear reactor in Florida, but it never got off the ground. For a while, Michael Winner—of *Death Wish* and *The Wicked Lady* (1983) infamy—was attached to direct the sequel. The project eventually came back around to Chuck Norris, who had the screenplay heavily re-written to re-incorporate his character. Further revisions were made to bring the film's budget down into the cash-strapped Cannon's range of affordability.

An ad for *Delta Force 2* from Cannon's pre-sales catalog.

By the time *Delta Force 2* entered production, Menahem Golan had resigned from Cannon and thus wasn't going to return to direct the sequel himself. (Even when you're expecting it, it still feels strange to see "A Globus-Pearce Production" at the head of a Cannon film, rather than the friendly, familiar "A Golan-Globus Production.") The reins to the franchise were handed over to Aaron Norris, brother of Chuck, who had directed the thematically similar *Braddock: Missing in Action III* alongside *Platoon Leader* (1988) for Cannon over the previous two years. Lee Reynolds, whose only previous film credit was on the studio's own *Allan Quatermain and the Lost City of Gold* (1986), picked up script duties, although both Golan and Bruner received character credits.

The only meaningful link between the two films is McCoy himself (Norris), a Delta Force operative and martial arts expert. As far as any character Chuck Norris plays can be considered "grounded" or "realistic," the earlier version of McCoy at least had one foot in the real word. As over-the-top as his rocket-firing motorcycle antics were, it's not outside the realm of possibility that a well-trained special forces commando could pull off much of what he did in *The Delta Force*. In the sequel, though, he goes full Chuck Norris, turning into the sort of unstoppable, one-man super-army that we saw in earlier films such as *Invasion U.S.A.* and *Braddock*. Since the events of the first movie, McCoy has been promoted from Major to Colonel, and seems to have left behind his cattle ranch in order to dedicate himself fully to the Delta Force-ing cause.

The movie opens in Rio de Janeiro, where a carnival bacchanalia is taking place in and around a palatial mansion. Outside, a group of Drug Enforcement agents in a disguised van run surveillance on the film's Pablo Escobar stand-in, Ramon Cota, the "world's richest drug dealer," as one D.E.A. boss calls him. (A recurring Norris foil, Billy Drago had previously appeared in *Invasion U.S.A.* and *Hero and the Terror* with Norris.) When Cota arrives to the masquerade, he puts on a mask and enters the party. Inside, one of the agents attempts to make a sting, only to grab a costumed decoy planted by Cota. Outside, a quartet of goons in clown costumes open fire on the surveillance van with machine guns, killing its occupants. To hammer home just how evil its bad guy is, *Delta Force 2* cuts to Cota as he watches the surviving agent be ejected from his party, eats a maraschino cherry, raises his cocktail, and then flaps his cape across the frame, Dracula-style.

Billy Drago is one of the best things about *Delta Force 2*. As far as flamboyant, over-the-top evil Cannon villains go, his Ramon Cota is up there with *The Apple*'s Mr. Boogelow and *Enter the Ninja*'s Venarius. Typically clad in all-black clothing with slicked-back hair and a long ponytail, he speaks in a mumbled, vaguely foreign accent that isn't from any identifiable region, but lies somewhere between "Eurotrash vampire" and "pothead in a teen comedy." We're given a second demonstration of his almost cartoonish levels of heinousness in the film's first act, when he punishes a peasant woman for taking a break from harvesting coca plants to care for her newborn—by stabbing her husband to death and kidnapping her baby. For good measure, he then forces her to become his concubine. Almost every line he speaks is hissed, hammed, or sneered—it's pretty amazing. Really, all Cota is missing in this movie is perhaps a pitchfork or a waxed moustache to curl around his index finger.

We're soon re-introduced to his bearded badassness, Scott McCoy, over dinner at a moderately priced-looking Chinese restaurant. He briefly steps away from listening to his best pal Bobby (Paul Perri) and his wife make plans for their soon-to-be-born child to beat the shit out of—or, as McCoy puts it, to "deliver a motivational seminar" to—a trio of disrespectful punks giving the restaurant's owner a hard time. Back at headquarters, McCoy and Bobby are briefed on the Cota situation by D.E.A. agents, and tasked with capturing the dangerous drug lord. Not only do the U.S. authorities have no power to arrest him in his home country—the fictional South American nation of San Carlos—but he's protected by General Olmedo, the nation's most powerful military leader.

Here's a refresher: Chuck Norris' birth name is Carlos Ray Norris. So, you see what they did there? The fictional South American nation of San *Carlos*? At some point, someone at Cannon must have realized it was a bit silly that they subtitled the movie *Delta Force 2: The Colombian Connection* when it doesn't even take place in Colombia. (That was, unless they were more or less using "Colombian" as a synonym for "cocaine.") For some home video release, the movie was retitled *Delta Force 2: Operation Stranglehold*. The movie itself was shot in the Philippines, which stood in for the jungles of South America.

Mark Margolis, the long-faced character actor playing General Olmedo, appeared in many films and TV shows, but is probably best known for playing Hector "Tio" Salamanca—the bad guy in the wheelchair with the bell—on *Breaking Bad* (2008–2013), which was a TV show about the meth trade, and not a sequel to *Breakin'* (1984). He also appeared in *Scarface* (1983) and many of the films by Darren Aronofsky.

McCoy finds a workaround for the foreign diplomacy issues by coming up with a plan to arrest Cota while he's on an international flight and briefly passing over American airspace. He and Bobby make quick work of his body-guards and snatch Cota from his first class seat. When the drug lord refuses to play along by putting on his parachute, McCoy goes ahead and throws him from the plane without it. Using some sweet aerodynamics skills, McCoy eventually catches up with the screaming, tumbling tyrant.

Meanwhile, the heroic American General Taylor (John P. Ryan of 1985's *Runaway Train*, 1986's *Avenging Force*, and 1987's *Death Wish IV*) watches from a boat below and gives an incredible, running commentary. "Shit! Always the hard way," he chuckles, shaking his head and lowering his binoculars. "I need a drink!"

Like Billy Drago, John P. Ryan is one of this movie's unsung selling points. If you thought his wide-eyed, bellowing warden from *Runaway Train* was over-the-top, then hoo, boy, you ain't seen nothing yet. Half of General Taylor's lines are delivered as a gleeful bark, and he spends a lot of the movie smiling like a madman, even when it may not seem appropriate to his dialogue. It also seems like an odd choice to have your military movie's highest-ranking officer serve as comic relief—and it's hard to tell whether it was written that way in the script, or if that's just how Ryan chose to play it—but it somehow works. As out-of-place as his character feels in this film, you're always happy when he's on screen.

That is, except when General Taylor delivers what may be one of the most messed-up, misguided jokes in movie history. As McCoy is briefed on the local contact he's to meet with once he arrives in San Carlos, McCoy asks if she can be trusted. "Ramon killed her husband, murdered her sick baby, and used the baby's body to smuggle cocaine, and then he raped her," General Taylor explains, and then slaps an arm around McCoy and smiles. "It's probably not a good idea to bring it up when you meet. She may be a little sensitive." (Sweet merciful Moses, John P. Ryan. *WTF?*)

In Italy, *Delta Force 2* was released with a title that simply (and awesomely) translated to "The Massacre." Poster art by Sandro Symeoni.

Once on American soil, Cota is taken to court and immediately released on a paltry bail. (If the D.E.A. was ready to enlist the Delta Force to arrest a dangerous foreign criminal, you'd think they'd have spent a little more time determining how they would prosecute him.) In retaliation for being tossed from an airplane by the Delta Force, Cota murders Bobby's wife and teenage brother. This understandably sends Bobby over the edge, so he goes full Charles Bronson in *Death Wish 3* and goes on a one-man revenge mission— only to be captured and killed as soon as he sets foot in San Carlos. Cota then does something really dumb, and sends McCoy a video tape of Bobby's death. Any smart drug lord would have known that if you kill Scott McCoy's best friend, he's damn well going to head straight to your country and kill everyone in your entire cocaine operation.

After not one, but two, slow-motion Delta Force training montages, McCoy parachutes into San Carlos. The plan is that McCoy will first go in solo and single-handedly rescue three hostages held in Cota's compound. Two days later, the rest of the Delta Force will arrive to torch the coca fields and blow up the processing plants. McCoy infiltrates Cota's compound by scaling a steep cliff face near its rear entrance. He silently picks off much of Cota's security with an assortment of punches, kicks, and neck-snaps. (The mountainside estate used for Cota's lavish compound was built by former Philippines dictator Ferdinand Marcos as a guest house for President Ronald Reagan.)

McCoy frees the imprisoned Americans, but decides he'd like to pay respects to Cota despite having specific orders *not* to engage with him. (That's just *so* McCoy.) He manages to make it all the way inside Cota's personal palace and into his bedroom—which is as purple as anything you'd see in a Prince music video—before being captured by the drug lord himself.

As all of this is happening, the Delta Force are betrayed by the San Carlos government and their mission is canceled. The President of the United States personally gives the Delta Force permission to move forward on their destruction spree with or without San Carlos' cooperation, much to General Taylor's squealing delight. They fly around the country, straight up obliterating the coca farms and drug labs in an impressive display of pyrotechnics. General Olmedo (the evil general) sets the San Carlos military to red alert, and sends his own gunships to intercept the Delta Force chopper.

McCoy wakes up inside a gas chamber that Cota had custom-built inside his dining room. As Cota ruminates to him on the nature of death, the Delta Force chopper shows up just in time and starts blasting missiles into the compound. Not only does McCoy escape, but he escapes with the unconscious criminal mastermind hoisted over his brawny, brawny shoulder. He steals Cota's limousine and makes a run for it, only to be pursued by his hired men. By the midway point of this fun car chase, McCoy's limo is being pursued by a truck, two jeeps, and a San Carlos military chopper. They're eventually cornered by General Olmedo's personal helicopter, but good guy General Taylor's helicopter arrives in the nick of time to save the day. "Bye bye, asshole!" Taylor joyously screams, as he fires his missiles. (Is anyone more amazing than John P. Ryan?)

After a few more fist-, fire-, and machete-fights, McCoy hitches a ride with General Taylor and his crew. (Literally: he and Cota are hitched to ropes dangling from the bottom of the U.S. chopper.) As they flee San Carlos, Cota taunts McCoy about how he killed Bobby and his wife—just before his rope snaps, and he falls hundreds of meters to his death. The movie fades to black and the credits roll over the song "Winds of Change" by Lee Greenwood—the country singer best known for the hit 1985 patriotic pop anthem, "God Bless the USA." (If there was ever a singer qualified to compose an original song for a Chuck Norris flick, it was Lee Greenwood.)

While *The Delta Force* maintained a serious tone until its totally bonkers second half, *Delta Force 2* dives right into the insane action from the get-go. Like *Braddock* before this, director Aaron Norris—a stunt man and martial artist himself—instilled the movie with a good blend of gunplay and hand-to-hand combat, perfectly tailored to his older brother's skills as a performer. *Delta Force 2* completely tosses the first film's loose grasp on realism out the window, transforming McCoy from a stoic soldier into more of a wise-cracking action hero. Sure, the one-liners are cheesy and some of the characters are cartoonish, but the editing and action sequences are fast-paced, making this sequel a lot of fun.

Delta Force 3 on videocassette, featuring the sons of many far more famous movie stars.

Unfortunately, it's impossible to discuss *Delta Force 2* without addressing the tragedy that befell crew members on May 16, 1989. Shortly after take-off, the black SA 360 Dauphin—the helicopter portraying the Delta Force's chopper—unexpectedly veered to the left near the location used as Cota's compound, and suddenly dropped into a forty-foot ravine. It reportedly took the stunned crew a moment to realize that the crash wasn't part of a stunt, and that the helicopter had caught fire. A rescue team was able to extinguish the flames, but five crew members aboard the Dauphin were killed by the injuries sustained in the crash: pilot Jojo Imperiale, stuntman Geoff Brewer, cameraman Gadi Danzig, key grip Mike Graham, and gaffer Don Marshall. Production was shut down for a few weeks, and the film was dedicated to their memory.

Among the few survivors was John P. Ryan, who was hospitalized with injuries but made a full recovery. Ryan was said to have been leery about helicopters, especially after a pilot was killed in a crash during the production of *Runaway Train* (1985). This was after yet another helicopter crash had killed four Filipino soldiers who were hired to film aerial footage for Aaron and Chuck Norris' previous team-up, *Braddock: Missing in Action III*. In total, ten people were killed in three separate helicopter crashes on Cannon features in just five short years.

Following their second, deadly on-set helicopter crash, both Chuck and Aaron Norris had soured on the military action genre and bowed out of making a third *Delta Force* movie. From this point forward, Chuck Norris mostly stuck to playing cops.

While neither Chuck nor Aaron returned for the third film, the *Delta Force* franchise remained a Norris family affair. *Delta Force 3: The Killing Game* (1991) featured no actual movie stars among its cast, but it did include the children of several: Mike Norris (son of Chuck), Nick Cassavetes (son of John), and Eric Douglas (son of Kirk).

Delta Force 3: The Killing Game was released just as The Cannon Group was entering the final phase of its illustrious run. By this point, the cousins had more or less moved on—Golan having left years earlier to form 21st Century Films, and Globus having been named President of MGM—and the product, save for a few, rare winners, was getting pretty dire. For what it's worth, this was Cannon's direct-to-video era; not because *all* of the films went direct to video, but because most of them feel that way, quality-wise.

Delta Force 3 doesn't match the tone of either of its predecessors, and it feels like the "Delta Force" title may have been slapped on in hopes of cashing in on the earlier films' popularity. The movie's alternate title, *Young Commandos*, would have better fit the movie's theme, and helped remove it from the shadow of the Chuck Norris films.

While Golan and Globus' names were nowhere to be found, we do catch the names of a few of the company's stalwarts in the credits, including director Sam Firstenberg and producer/co-writer Boaz Davidson. Firstenberg was brought on after cult filmmaker Brian Trenchard-Smith was fired from the project, and a few scenes had already been shot. Handed the script and flown in on a redeye to begin shooting the very next morning, Firstenberg was amazingly tasked with directing parts of the film before he'd been able to read and digest the full screenplay.

The film opens on a beautiful, young Arab woman being slowly stripped nude and fitted with an explosive vest, marking one of the few (only?) times in cinematic history where anyone tried to make suicide bombings sexy. The explosives are detonated onstage during a peace prize presentation in Moscow. Terrorist leader Kahlil Kadal releases a video claiming responsibility for the deadly blast, and threatens to detonate a nuclear weapon inside an American city unless "all instruments of Western influence are removed from the Middle East."

This is where the Delta Force comes in.

In the third and final installment of the series, the Delta Force is tasked with capturing Kadal before he can set off a nuke in Miami. To complete this mission, they're forced to team up with their counterparts in the Soviet special forces—and, as you'd guess, egos clash as the bullets fly. (This was released before the Cold War had fully cooled off.)

The new Delta Force leader, Charlie, is played by Nick Cassavetes, the son of John Cassavetes and Gena Rowlands, whose last film together was the Cannon-produced *Love Streams* (1984). Although he's appeared in more than forty television shows and films, including *Face/Off* (1997), he's better known today as a director—most notably of the weepy date night staple *The Notebook* (2004), starring Ryan Gosling and Rachel MacAdams.

The core of the American team is played by fellow celebrity babies Mike Norris, Matthew Penn, and Eric Douglas, while the Russian group is led by Sergei, played by John Saint Ryan (sadly, no relation to John P. Ryan).

A German advertising card for *Delta Force 3*.

Mike Norris got his start with bit roles in his father's movies, but actually beat his dad to starring in their first Cannon movie by appearing in *The Young Warriors* (1983). These days, Mike Norris mostly directs and/or appears in low-budget Christian dramas with titles like *A Greater Yes* (2009) and *I Am . . . Gabriel* (2012). He's also the director of the bonkers right wing fantasy film *AmeriGeddon* (2016), in which the United Nations turns against the United States and a group of survivalist patriots use their Second Amendment rights to take their country back.

Eric Douglas was Kirk's youngest son, and the half-brother of Michael Douglas. An actor and stand-up comedian, his life in show business was overshadowed by his drug problems; sadly, he passed away from an accidental overdose in 2004. Matthew Penn is the son of *Bonnie and Clyde* (1967) director Arthur Penn. He left acting behind after *Delta Force 3* for a career in directing television.

As the Delta Forcers spend their time training and in-fighting with their Russian counterparts, one of Kadal's men manages to infiltrate the United States and plant the world's tiniest nuclear bomb inside the wheelchair of a Miami news producer, with the plan of setting it off on live television. Eventually the Delta Force gets around to invading the movie's fictional Middle Eastern nation, killing all of the generic terrorist types who get in their way.

The film's two story threads finally connect in the final scenes, when the Delta Force bring the captive Kadal with them to Miami in an effort to have him talk one of his followers out of detonating his nuclear device. That plan fails, but the Delta Force saves the day when an American commando stabs the terrorist in the foot while the Russian commando Sergei shoots him in the head, which should be seen as the ultimate example of what people can accomplish if they're able to put aside their differences and work together.

When you watch *Delta Force 3*, it's no wonder that none of the leads went on to major acting careers. None of them are terrible, but none of them have as much charisma as Chuck Norris, either—take that for what it's worth. The movie has some strong action sequences, but they're nowhere near as out-and-out crazy as those in the two previous movies. (Granted, it's hard to top a man leaping from the back of a motorcycle onto a moving plane, or a high-speed helicopter/limousine chase—the Delta Force craziness bar was set pretty high by the franchise's earlier entries.) The main issue with *Delta Force 3: The Killing Game* is that there are passages where it really crawls: time spent training, planning, and then sneaking around while the groundwork is laid for their mission. The payoff just doesn't quite match the amount of buildup there is to it.

Delta Force 3: The Killing Game brought Cannon's trilogy to a close, and the company itself would soon be defunct—but that doesn't mean Delta Forces would stop saving the world on-screen. Sam Firstenberg himself would direct *Operation Delta Force* (1997) for Millennium Films, a company founded by Avi Lerner, director of *P.O.W. The Escape* (1986) and a producer on many of Cannon's productions in Africa. This film would spawn four sequels. Later Yoram Globus himself would produce *Delta Force One: The Lost Patrol* (2000), a film directed by Joseph Zito of *Invasion U.S.A.* and *Missing in Action* fame, and co-starring Cannon vets Mike Norris and John Rhys-Davies.

Interview: Actor William Wallace

William Wallace is more than just the soldier he played in *The Delta Force* (1986): after the start of a screen career that included three back-to-back Cannon films, he joined the Army Reserves, where he served for eight years, including a nine-month tour in Bosnia. Afterwards, he dedicated himself to helping homeless veterans, first at the VA Hospital of West Los Angeles, and then running a non-profit in St. Louis known as the Missouri Veterans Endeavor.

In college, Wallace was on the path to becoming a professional soccer player, and his travels with the team allowed him to only participate in a few drama classes and the occasional reading. When this proved to be a bad time for pro soccer leagues in the U.S., Wallace pivoted after graduation and pursued an acting career in New York City.

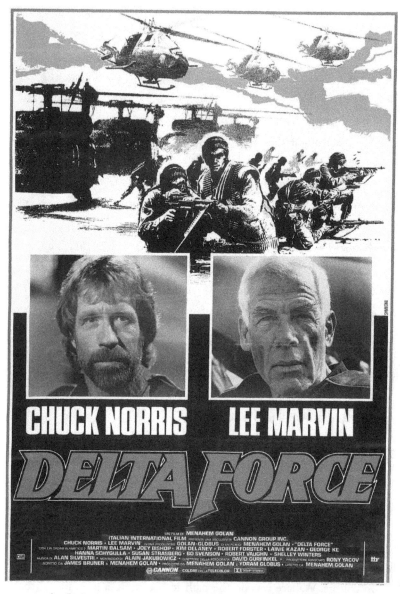

An Italian *Delta Force* poster designed by Sandro Symeoni.

Wallace's credits include three notable Cannon roles: Pete Peterson, one of Chuck Norris's top commandos in *The Delta Force*; the top hat-wearing sidekick to Chuck Wagner, Gruss, in *America 3000* (1986); and Wade Delaney, the villainous crony of John P. Ryan's racist millionaire in *Avenging Force* (also 1986). He can also be seen in *Beverly Hills Cop* (1984), *Troop Beverly Hills* and *Born on the Fourth of July* (both 1989).

How did your acting career begin?

I was fortunate to get a manager who would send me out on auditions. I did a lot of commercials and a couple soap operas in New York City, then went to California for the 1985 pilot season. It took me a while to get my feet on the ground. The first job I got was a small part playing a cop in *Beverly Hills Cop*: I had some lines, and I actually arrested Eddie Murphy with my partner when he gets thrown through a plate glass window.

Shortly after that, I auditioned for a movie called *America 3000*—at that time it was called *Thunder Warriors*. I didn't get the role. I didn't really think about it, then all of a sudden, I get this phone call from Cannon Films, and they wanted me to get on a plane and leave within days to go to Israel, because the guy that they had cast to play Gruss, the right-hand man to Chuck Wagner's character, Korvis, had apparently fallen and broken his leg and couldn't do it.

Once I was in Israel, I was there working on the film for, gosh, a long time. It was about four months because there were some delays, but it was the most fun experience I've had.

I know that the movie had troubles with production, and that it was unbearably hot there at the time.

It was *really* hot in the Negev Desert, but that was to be expected. One of the most fun things about it is we had horses and handlers that would take care of them. I grew up as a horseman and worked on ranches and farms all throughout high school into my college years, so I got to ride every single day. I'd just ride around the set, which was out in the countryside between Jerusalem and Tel Aviv, and it was a blast. I loved every second of it. My girlfriend at the time, who later I married and had my daughter with, came with me and had a nice part as one of the tribeswomen in the film.

Delta Force **would have put you back in Israel just a few months later after filming wrapped on** *America 3000***. Was there a connection between your casting in both movies, or was it just a coincidence?**

I think the director of photography and the production team liked me, and they thought I did a good job. Basically when I got back to America, the opportunity to do *Delta Force* was offered to me, and I was thrilled to go back.

I think I went there at the end of August and was there till early December. To be back with my friends in Israel and at that time of the year, it was spectacular. It's a very, very special place, and I just could not have had more fun getting to meet and work with the huge movie stars in *Delta Force*.

Chuck Norris said this was the best cast that he ever worked with—the movie is full of Oscar winners and nominees. Do you have any particularly fond memories with your co-stars?

I have fond memories with pretty much every one of them. We were all staying in one of two hotels right next door to each other. The guys who were part of the Delta Force ran as a pack. Chuck Norris is a big advocate for stunt guys and his brother, Aaron Norris, was a stunt coordinator at the time, and so Chuck knew all the stunt men. We loved to hang out with them.

One of the two guys I spent most of my time with was Steve James. He and I became really good friends on that film. Also, I was very, very close friends with Robert Forster throughout my whole time knowing him. We lived near each other in Hollywood, and we saw a ton of each other and really connected. He was such a generous guy.

Robert Forster invited me to go with him and some friends and his daughters to the premiere of *Jackie Brown* (1997). Afterwards I told him, "Robert, listen, you are so good in this film. I would not be surprised if you get nominated for an Oscar." He was always such a humble guy. He said, "Well, Billy, that would be nice, but I doubt that's going to happen." I ran into Roger Ebert that night at the premiere, and I said, "Listen, you're hearing this first. I think Robert Forster is going to get an Oscar nomination for his part in *Jackie Brown*. I will never forget what you and Gene Siskel said years ago in regards to *Delta Force*: you called it, 'Delta Farce,' which I didn't take offense to at all, because it was silly in certain areas, with rocket launchers on motorcycles. But, you pointed out that the best performance by far was delivered by Robert Forster as the terrorist, and you could not have been more spot on. You heard it here first, Roger. I think Bob is going to get an Oscar nomination." Lo and behold, he did. Bob Forster called me up the morning that he got the nomination. I was just so thrilled for him, because he was truly one of the old, Hollywood good guys. He just slugged it out and kept saying, "Keep it up. Keep trying, Billy."

Also, getting to sit around on the set with Lee Marvin was incredible. Now, Lee is one of the most highly decorated marines from World War II. He spent, I think, about three years on an island in the South Pacific, and he was taken off the islands when he got shot badly in the back. I think he was in a body cast for six or seven months. He told me that he was taken to Fort Dix and he recuperated there, which is in New Jersey. When he got out of the hospital and discharged from the army, he used his GI Bill to go to the Actors Studio and to learn acting with Marlon Brando and Lee Strasberg. Of course, Susan Strasberg was in the film as one of the passengers, and you had Shelley Winters, Martin Balsam, George Kennedy, Joey Bishop, all of these heavy-hitter and Oscar-nominated performers.

Lee, he was a guy's guy. Sadly, that was the last film that he ever did because he was pretty sick. One time, I was sitting on the set and I wasn't working that day, but he was, and I was about to do my scene where I get shot. I said, "Gosh, I just don't know what to do. I don't know what my process is." I think I was probably trying to be Method-y about it. All of a sudden, he took his big hand, and he winds up and comes down and hits me, not hard, but firmly in the middle of the back. He says, "Getting shot is like being hit by a two-by-four." That's when he told me the story of him being shot on the islands of the Pacific. It led into his talking about the Actors Studio, being in *The Wild Bunch* (1969), his friendship with Marlon Brando, *The Dirty Dozen* (1967), all of the stuff that he did.

What was it like to work with Menahem Golan as your director?

He was always a very fun guy to be on the set with. He wanted to get the shots and move the camera, which I guess was his producer side—he wanted to make sure that they were on budget. He loved shooting the action in that movie.

I love military history. Menahem was a fighter pilot for the Israeli Air Force. He fought in the War of Liberation. He flew what I think at the time were probably Spitfire prop fighter planes, but he may have flown some jets as well.

Bill Wallace (second from left) with Karl Johnson, John P. Ryan, and Marc Alaimo in a scene from *Avenging Force*.

He was a very fun-loving guy. He was also a big guy, so he was a little bit intimidating. I had known him from *America 3000* as the producer and had met him a few times, so when he became the director, I knew him and I felt comfortable around him and felt that we could joke around a little bit. He made sure that all of us had fun things to do in Israel. I remember when he took all of us on a bus up to Eilat, Israel, for a screening of *Invasion U.S.A.* (1985). There was a screening at a film festival and he surprised the crowd by saying, "And here are Cannon stars of the past, present, and future," and we got to go on the stage of this beautiful theater. He would have us out to his home on the ocean for weekend lunches.

You did this movie with Steve James, and then were immediately in *Avenging Force* together. Talk to me about him.

Steve was a very awesome guy. We had so many laughs together, because he and I loved to do impersonations of people. He was uncanny at being able to do impersonations. We would impersonate Bob Forster, and come up with these little things. We just laughed nonstop.

He would also exercise a lot, lift weights and do kicks, and he would teach me his martial arts. He was just a funny guy. He was also a historian of films; he loved Black films like *Shaft* (1971) and the movies of that era. He was very serious about how he wanted his characters to be portrayed. He didn't want them to be silly—he wanted them to be realistic.

He was a special guy. I last ran into him maybe six months before he died. He wouldn't let you know that he was sick. I ran into him at the post office, and it seemed to me he wasn't looking quite the same. Well, he had cancer, and died a few months later, but it was just like Steve to not tell anyone.

You went from playing heroes in your first two Cannon movies to playing a really bad guy in *Avenging Force*. As an actor, was it fun to switch sides to play Wade Delaney?

It was, but since Steve James and I were such good friends, I had a little bit of trepidation about the role. I didn't want to step over any boundaries. Sam [Firstenberg] understood that as well. If you look at the film, I never use the N-word in it. There were a couple of times I think that I was supposed to, but I asked Sam and James Booth if I could change it. I was not comfortable doing that. You could say that maybe I wasn't committing entirely to the role, but I felt that there was a different way to do it.

It was fun to play a guy who was evil. I was kind of looking at it as this guy is number one, exceedingly entitled, and number two, very, very racist. He's a sick guy. He's uninformed. He's spoiled, he's entitled, and he's allowed to get away with these things. I also played into it myself that he had a substance abuse issue. I would pretend that he would maybe take speed, then go out there and hunt guys down in the swamp. If you're going to be hunting people for four or five hours in a swamp, you had to stay up and do it!

I think Wade Delaney was just a very entitled, very racist, very spoiled guy who got a lot of attention because he was a Heisman Trophy winner, so he just naturally thought he could do anything he wanted and nobody was going to tell him he couldn't.

You spent a lot of time in the bayou to film your fight with Michael Dudikoff for *Avenging Force*. Would you consider that one of the hardest shoots of your career?

Well, it was pretty tough because it was so hot, and there were so many critters. There were leeches in the water. To be able to do the fight scene, it was tough, but it really was only for maybe two or three hours, the whole thing. It had to be incredibly hard for the art department and set builders because they had to anchor a plywood platform into the mud underneath the water, because if you stepped there, you would sink in these little sinkholes. The ground was so uneven they had to build a platform that we could fight on to actually do the sequence.

It was hard because you were in the water, and because of the leeches. I remember that they would come and set off charges every morning to scare away alligators or snakes that might be in the area, to get them away from the set. No snakes, no critters would want to mess with people but you had to clear the area at the beginning.

You worked alongside one of the great villain actors of the era, John P. Ryan. How do you remember him?

John P. Ryan was another guy I really became close with. Hearing his stories about working for Francis Ford Coppola, and working with Jack

Nicholson on *Five Easy Pieces* (1970) . . . I'd seen a lot of his films up to that point. We would go to movies together. Between him and Steve James and Marc Alaimo and Karl Johnson, we pretty much had every meal together.

I remember one time, John and I were walking through the French Quarter. It was a day that we were both off and we weren't working. It was a really nice day, and we see this movie set. He says, "What's that down there?" I said, "Oh, they're making some movie called *Angel Heart* (1987), with Mickey Rourke and Robert De Niro." He goes, "Bobby! Mickey!" and he marches right up to a production assistant and says, "Is Bob De Niro here?" "No, he's not here today." "Is Mickey here?" "Yes, Mickey's here." Next thing I know, we're knocking on the door of Mickey's trailer. Mickey opens the door and goes, "John, Bill, John, Bill," and he looks at me. What the production assistant said was, "You have John P. Ryan and Bill Wallace here." There was a martial artist named Bill Wallace back in the day. He was a famous kickboxer, and Mickey knew him. Mickey thought that it was John P. Ryan, his buddy from the Actors Studio, and Bill Wallace the kickboxer. He opened up and he went back and forth and he realized it was not Bill Wallace, the kickboxer, but Mickey invited us into his trailer. We spent probably three hours with him in the trailer, hanging out watching the Indianapolis 500, enjoying each other's company.

Interview: Stunt Man Jon Epstein

For nearly a decade, Jon Epstein served as the go-to stunt double for Chuck Norris. Any time Norris is blown up, thrown from a vehicle, or hanging from the back of a plane in a Cannon movie, you're probably watching Epstein at work. Specifically, he is the man responsible for all slick moves you see Chuck's character pulling off on the back of his souped-up rocket bike in *The Delta Force* (1986).

Epstein worked his way up the stunt ladder, and now coordinates films in addition to performing stunts. His Cannon adventures began on *Invasion U.S.A.* (1985), and continued onto *The Delta Force, Firewalker, The Naked Cage*, and *Allan Quatermain and the Lost City of Gold* (all 1986), *Braddock: Missing in Action III* and *Hero and the Terror* (both 1988), *Kinjite* (1989), and *Street Knight* (1992).

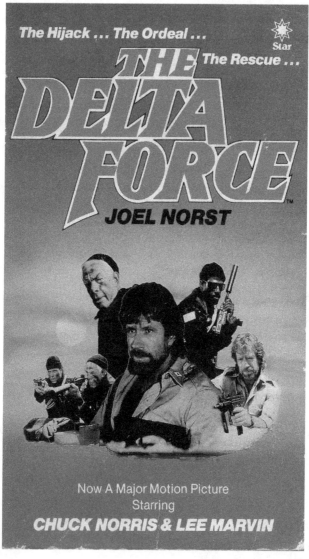

A *Delta Force* tie-in novel was written by Joel Norst—a pseudonym for speculative fiction novelist Kirk Mitchell. The audiobook version was read by George Kennedy.

Beyond Cannon, he's worked on more than 200 film and television projects, including classics such as *They Live* (1988), *The Abyss* (1989), and *Last Action Hero* (1991), and blockbusters like *Basic Instinct* (1992) and *The Avengers* (2012).

Were your motorcycle skills what helped you land a job on *Delta Force*?

Jon Epstein: I scratched my way into the business. I was lucky enough to get seen by people that were hiring, and I got on a Cannon movie called *Invasion U.S.A.* (1985). I was just sitting around in Georgia, at 2:00 in the morning at Peachtree Plaza, killing time, when the stunt coordinators Aaron Norris—he's Chuck's brother, and a badass himself—and Don Pike were walking around, and they stopped and looked at me. I'm just sitting there and I hear Don say, "He'd make a pretty good double for Chuck." Aaron is looking at me and goes, "No, he doesn't want to work eight months out of the year." [*Laughs*] Then he walked away, and I was just sitting there with my buddy, wondering what that was about. They came back, grabbed me, and brought me over to Chuck, who took a look at me. Next thing I know, I'm on that show, doubling him.

When *Delta Force* came up, the coordinator, Don Pike, said, "Hey, we're probably going to need a guy who can ride a motorcycle." I said, "I can ride." I didn't push my motorcycle work to get in the business. It's kind of funny: I wasn't a "bike guy," I was a great "fight guy." I could do fire. I could drive cars. Pike says, "Oh, really? Can you ride?" I go, "Yes, let me show you some pictures of some stuff I've done." You know, jumping through fire walls and stuff, and he's like, "Wow." Next thing you know, I'm on a plane and I'm heading to Israel. It was just completely bitchin'.

The motorcycle stunts are some of the most memorable parts of the movie. Can you tell me about shooting those?

It was really fun. Chuck was a racecar driver. He didn't ride a motorcycle, but he learned real fast. He's the kind of guy that does a lot of his stunts, but all actors have stunt doubles—even if they say they don't, they all do. Chuck would have done more stunts, so you'd have to hold him back, because he wants to do everything, and he *can* do everything. Very physical guy.

Remember the scenes at the airport, at the end, before I climb up that rope? I stand on the bike, climb up the rope to the plane? The first time we did that, I flipped over the handlebars and crashed.

Earlier in that scene, where I'm doing wheelies down the tarmac and stuff? I didn't even know they were shooting that. They were using a long lens. I think I was just rehearsing. They told me, "We've got the plane out there, Jon, just go out and get used to being around it." I didn't even know they were filming.

Menahem Golan was the director. He owned Cannon. Menahem, he was the greatest. He was crazy, wild, but he'd get his emotions across and was a really great guy. He's a family man, but when he directed, he went for it, you never knew what he was going to do. He was very unorthodox.

Well, the first time we did the rope scene, the bike stalled when I stood up on it and I flipped over the handlebars and landed on the ground. I hurt myself, but I got up and started chasing the plane, like I was still going to get on it. Menahem loved that. I'm thinking, "Oh, man, I just screwed that." He *loved* it. He thought, "I'm going to use that," but he didn't. Then he says to me, "Can you climb the rope, no feet, just hands?" I'm like, "Yes, I can do that. I think I can, yes." I could still climb the rope while I was hurt.

I remember Chuck's son, Eric Norris, had come to visit. He wasn't in the movie business yet. He was on the set and he goes, "Dad, you can't climb up that rope with no feet." Chuck goes, "I'll bet you I can." They made a bet and sure enough, Chuck climbed that rope, no feet. I'm telling myself, "I better be able to do this because I know if Chuck says he can do it, he can do it."

For me at that age, [working with Chuck] was the best job in the world because it was like a training camp. We worked out every single morning. We'd eat some kind of salads and get protein and all that stuff. It was a very healthy job. We would work out every morning five days a week, maybe six, and we'd work out *hard*. He was a great guy. I never saw him raise his voice to anybody, or belittle anyone. He always had good manners.

If you watch *Delta Force*, there was one motorcycle jump I did where it's over a guard shack or gate. There's a guy that for two seconds, he's on fire. He was really on fire, and I missed him and crashed myself, because I saw him and said, "Uh-oh." Somebody said "cut" besides the director, the effects guy. The guy walks back into the booth and—boom!—it blows up. I was on my way on my motorcycle and he was in front of me. If you look for two frames, there's a guy burning up. He went to the hospital. It was pretty gnarly, but that's stunts.

If I'm a stuntman, and I get hurt, I'm in charge of myself. It's not the coordinator's fault. It's not the producer's fault. It's my fault, because I'm a grown stunt person. I should be able to handle everything. If I don't like it, I say, "No." If the stunt guy gets hurt, everybody gets blamed. Well, sometimes, it's the stunt guy's fault.

When you double someone like Chuck Norris, do you have to study their physical mannerisms so you can match them better?

I look at them, yes. Chuck has a certain walk. I would pick up what he does mostly, and I would walk that way. If I was doubling Don Johnson, he has a different walk. This guy, Michael Paré, was one of the first guys that I ever doubled, I did *Philadelphia Experiment* (1984) with him and some other movies a long time ago. He would throw his feet out in front of him, do like a flop walk. Chuck had a really tight, straightforward walk, a square-hip walk, arms down. I doubled David Duchovny on *X-Files* (1993–2002), and he had more of a happier walk, a little bit of a carefree walk. Like, a little cosmopolitan kind of walk.

You worked as a stunt coordinator for Norris on *Hero and the Terror* (1988). Did you design the stunts with Chuck's skill set in mind?

Yes. I was young. I was in my twenties and I was coordinating a Chuck Norris movie and doubling him. It was a great opportunity. You know his skill set, so it's not that hard to design stunts for him. Anything physical, he can do.

Even on *Delta Force*, they stuck me on second unit to coordinate some stuff when the first-unit coordinator was working on something else. I mean, I wasn't the coordinator. It was just for the day, but that's how you learn and if you do a good job, then it's like, "You could do it on the next." It really helped my career. In hindsight, it helped my career a lot.

When you go into other countries, like I did with Cannon and Chuck Norris stuff, I would go with the effects guys in the Philippines and help wrap the bombs that they're going to set near us. At the end of *Missing in Action III*, they blow Chuck up in the air. You see me land on a street. It's a dirt street, but it was solid dirt. There was no pad there. They were putting two twelve-ounce bombs on my ass.

I wanted to know what those were, so I learned on that show. I would go into the trailer with them that night and wrap bombs with them. Four ounces, six ounces, eight ounces, how tight the wrap, how much the wrap, what kind of pot to put it in, pans, when it blows up, how the spread's going to be, how much gas you put on there. I learned all that through Cannon films. That was awesome.

I loved Cannon. I think everybody else did, too. They were paying money. It was great. It was good money. There were good people involved. There were maybe some not good people involved, but that's with any company.

Out of the films you made with Chuck, is there a stunt that you're most proud of?

No. I mean, I've been injured on a few. I've got hurt a little bit, but most proud of? I don't know. On *Firewalker* (1986) we jumped that car through a real palm tree out in the middle of Torno, Mexico. The sand, it was like fifteen feet high. I went straight through a palm tree into six inches of water with a hard-packed bottom under it. That stretched my neck out pretty far.

They put me in a CAT scan machine in Mexico City, and I had three broken vertebrae and got carted away. Wrecked that job, but it's nobody's fault. It's all me. I don't blame anybody for anything. It's stunts, and when a true stuntman gets hurt, he doesn't go suing everybody. You just recover and start working again, that's all.

There's no one stunt I'm most proud of. Some of them were easy, some were hard. I did an Allan Quatermain movie—and *Kinjite* (1989). Was that Cannon?

Yes, that was with Charles Bronson, and J. Lee Thompson directing.

J. Lee Thompson, yes. He was directing [*Firewalker*] when I got carted away in Mexico, right? I show up on *Kinjite* and I'm going to do some stunts—actually, you see me in there. I'm on a bus and I grab a guy that is molesting this chick, I think. He kicks me or something, and you actually see that.

I saw J. Lee Thompson. The last time I saw him, I was being taken out of Churubusco Studios on a stretcher. The coordinator says, "Yeah, this is the guy that's going to do this part." I go, "Hey, I know you," and I shake J. Lee's hand. He looks a little puzzled, like he didn't know me. So, I lie down on the sidewalk and go, [*makes awful, pained groaning sound.*] "Do you recognize me now?" Then he started laughing, because he remembered me from Mexico.

Aaron Norris would have stepped out from behind the camera to star in *Delta Force 4: The Deadly Dozen*, but Cannon didn't stick around long enough to make it.

The Naked Cage hit video store shelves with a salacious slipcover that no doubt helped rent out a few extra copies.

The Naked Cage

Release Date: March 7, 1986
Directed by: Paul Nicholas
Written by: Paul Nicholas
Starring: Shari Shattuck, Angel Tompkins, Christina Whitaker
Trailer Voiceover: "Even good girls grow up fast in . . . *The Naked Cage!*"

The women in prison genre has been around for a long, long time—long before *Orange is the New Black* (2013–2019) made it something acceptable for your mother to discuss while in line at the supermarket.

Hollywood has been sending its starlets to prison for almost as long as they've been making movies. The 1933 film *Ladies They Talk About* was one of the genre's first major features, in which Barbara Stanwyck was sent to San Quentin for bank robbery and had to learn the ropes from her fellow female inmates. Women in prison films—or "WiP" films, as they're often referred to—didn't really explode, however, until the Fifties, when they developed many of the tropes that are still associated with them today. This second wave of movies, led by 1950's *Caged,* starring Eleanor Parker and Agnes Moorehead (one of the few Oscar-nominated women in prison movies), *So Young, So Bad*

(1950), and *Women's Prison* (1955) with Ida Lupino and Jan Sterling, went a long way in cementing the traditional WiP formula.

Loosening regulations and the rise of the grindhouse circuit led to the type of women in prison flicks we most often think of nowadays: lurid exploitation features about young women forced into unwanted sexual arrangements by guards or other prisoners, or where the inmates are driven wild by their own unchecked lust. There is almost invariably an emphasis on the sexual possibilities presented by the premise of women behind bars, ranging from fairly straight-forward T&A—in most cases, group shower scenes—to more extreme scenarios such as bondage, sadism, and rape.

Silence of the Lambs (1991) director Jonathan Demme made his feature filmmaking debut for producer Roger Corman with *Caged Heat* (1974), one of the genre's more enduring pictures. (He also co-scripted 1972's *The Hot Box*, about American nurses thrown in an all-women's prison deep in a foreign jungle.) Blaxploitation icon Pam Grier played roles in four different WiP flicks in just three years: *The Big Doll House* and *Women in Cages* (both 1971), *The Big Bird Cage* (1972), and *Black Mama White Mama* (1973)—the latter, again, co-written by Jonathan Demme. The Eighties soon gave way to classic examples such as *The Concrete Jungle* (1982) and the *Chained Heat* series, which felt—and looked—tailor-made for VHS rental and late-night cable screenings.

Like they did with almost every other cinematic trend which showed even the slightest whiff of profitability, Cannon entered the women in prison arena with *The Naked Cage* (1986).

The film's director, Paul Nicholas, already had experience making women in prison movies, having written and directed the quite sleazy—but quite successful—*Chained Heat* in 1983, which starred Linda Blair and *Hercules* (1983) actress and all-around b-movie staple Sybil Danning. (Blair—of *The Exorcist* [1973] fame—became one of the WiP genre's most recurring actresses, starting in 1974's racy, made-for-TV juvenile detention flick *Born Innocent* before graduating on to even more exploitative WiP fare with *Chained Heat*, 1985's

340

Red Heat which co-starred Cannon favorite Sylvia Kristel, and *Savage Island* the very same year.)

Innocent Michelle (Shari Shattuck) is threatened by fellow inmate Rita (Christina Whitaker) in a publicity still from *The Naked Cage*.

Could Nicholas repeat the success he had with *Chained Heat*? In hindsight, the answer was "not quite," as the film didn't meet the same financial benchmarks despite checking off the boxes for almost every expected genre trope.

Does *The Naked Cage* center on a good girl wrongly imprisoned for a crime she didn't commit? Check. Doe-eyed Michelle (Shari Shattuck) is a young, wholesome, all-American girl who's never done a bad deed in her life. Her ex-husband, Willy, however, is bad news. We meet Willy (John Terlesky) as he's picking up a foxy hitchhiker named Rita (Christina Whitaker) in a stolen Corvette. We learn quickly that Rita's not the type of lady you'd bring home to meet your mother, as she gets the recovering Willy hooked back on drugs and then talks him into knocking over a bank. It just so happens that this is the same bank where Michelle works as a teller, and she gets caught up in their holdup—and mistaken for an accomplice by the police. She's sentenced to three years in the slammer when Rita lies about her involvement in the robbery.

Is the prison a lawless hell hole? Of course it is! The all-women's facility Michelle finds herself in has earned its nickname, "The Cage," because so few of its inmates live to see the outside world again. Prisoners seem to die left and right in gang fights, drug overdoses, and shankings, while no one in charge seems to bat an eye. The biggest bully in The Cage is Sheila (Faith Minton), an imposing gang leader who stands a foot taller than anyone else in the prison, and will kill any inmate who doesn't pay their protection fee on time. Fortunately for the new girl, Sheila takes a liking to Michelle because she respects her as a fellow bank robber. Michelle's taken in by Sheila's gang, who not only protect her from the vengeful Rita—who is also locked away in The Cage—but from the prison's nasty, sadistic staff. That brings us to our next check box . . .

Is the prison overseen by a corrupt, abusive warden? Yup! The warden (Angel Tompkins) treats her prison flock as her personal brothel. When she's not coercing the women into playing bondage games in her private quarters which look like the inside of Duran Duran's tour bus, she's covering up for the slimy prison guard named Smiley, her number one lackey, who also happens to be a serial rapist. (And seriously: the warden's bedroom is painted in a deep shade of maroon, lit by neon tube lighting, and filled with furniture that was definitely *only* manufactured between 1984 and 1987; it looks like a porn set designed by Patrick Nagel.)

An early pre-sales ad. While the prison in the film is referred to only as "The Cage," it's easy to guess Cannon's reason for adding the word "Naked" to its title.

Does the film exploit its T&A factor with little regard for any semblance of realism? Oh, you bet it does! The primary uniform worn by those locked in The Cage is a cotton nighty, either blue or peach in color, which hangs down just below the buttocks. Many of the women appear to have taken it upon themselves to cut a higher slit up the side of the dress, and rip the neck so that it reveals a lot more cleavage. The dress code doesn't seem to be too strict, anyway: other inmates wear sleeveless denim jackets, or daisy dukes and midriff-baring tees. The prisoners' ludicrous wardrobe has limited opportunity to become a distraction, though, as the female convicts spend an expectedly significant portion of the film wearing no clothes at all. Sure, this makes sense during the movie's plentiful shower scenes, but many of *The Naked Cage*'s background cast seem to forget to put their clothes back on once the showers are over.

(Note from the author: I haven't spent much, or *any*, time inside an all-women prison facility, but my guess is that everybody isn't hanging out naked all of the time for no apparent reason, like most '80s WiP movies asked us to believe.)

But, are there catfights in *The Naked Cage*, you ask? What a silly question, dear reader! Not only do the tensions between the gangs and the warden's stoolies cause nasty fights to erupt in the cafeteria and recreation yard, but Rita spends most of the movie trying to kill Michelle for telling the truth about her on the witness stand.

We won't spend too much more time on the plot, because it's pretty easy to figure out where things go from here. Michelle learns a bunch of quick, hard lessons about life in the slammer and before long she's one of the toughest girls behind bars. After too many bad things happen to her and her friends, she snaps, steals a guard's pistol and incites an all-out prison riot. The corrupt jailers get their comeuppance courtesy of the convicts, and Michelle goes free when Rita confesses to her innocence . . . just before being pushed into the prison's generator and fried to death.

The Naked Cage failed to perform as well as the director's prior hit, *Chained Heat*—despite being a very, very similar movie. It's a grimy, little film where nudity and rape scenes are played more for audience titillation than for plot reasons—but that's par for the course when it comes to the women in prison flicks of this era. Outside of Michelle, most of the "good" characters are actually pretty terrible people. Of Michelle's two main allies, Sheila is a bully who we watch murder a fellow inmate simply because she hasn't paid her protection money, and her best friend is a drug addict who sells out her cellmate for another hit of crank. Some plot threads feel rushed, while others seem cut short. Still, anybody interested in this type of movie knows what they're getting into, and it's better than many of the other, trashier women in prison films that came out around the same time. The film's reputation has only improved over the years, notably being championed by filmmaker Quentin Tarantino in various retrospective screenings.

All of that said, the cast is both game and more than capable. *The Naked Cage* was lead Shari Shattuck's first starring role. She'd later appear Empire Pictures' sci-fi spectacle *Arena* (1989) and Cannon's own *Number One with a Bullet* (1987), as well as a few other fun titles, including *Uninvited* (1987), about a killer cat let loose on a cruise boat; *Death Spa* (1989), which is about exactly what it sounds like; and Steven Seagal's *On Deadly Ground* (1994). She's now a novelist.

John Terlesky, who plays her no-good boyfriend, appeared in a few other movies of cult interest in the 1980s, including the b-movie classic *Chopping Mall* (1986). He was the titular warrior hero in the second entry of the Roger Corman-produced sword and sorcery series, *Deathstalker II* (1987), and also had a small role in *Appointment with Death* (1988), one of Cannon's several Agatha Christie adaptations.

Angel Tompkins, the movie's sadistic warden, earned a Golden Globe nomination for her film debut in the comedy *I Love My Wife* (1970), and is maybe best known for playing the student-seducing title character of 1974's infamous *The Teacher*. Many b-movie fans will remember her from the bizarre *Little Cigars* (1973), where she plays a mobster's girlfriend who teams up with a gang of dwarfs to commit their own crimes. She appeared in three more Cannon movies after this one: as a teacher in Albert Pyun's *Dangerously Close* (1986), as Charles Bronson's stripper ex-wife in *Murphy's Law* (also 1986), and *Crack House* (1989).

Other repeat members of the Cannon family include Lisa London—of 1980's *The Happy Hooker Goes Hollywood*—who plays Abbey, and also sings on the movie's soundtrack, and the six-foot, one-inch tall Faith Minton (Sheila), who had small roles in Cannon's *Number One with a Bullet* and *Penitentiary*

III (both 1987), and did stunt work for the Chuck Norris flick *Hero and the Terror* (1988).

The Naked Cage also features a bit of noticeably creative camerawork. There are a few, cool point-of-view shots, including one where Rita prowls the cafeteria, yanking back the hair of any blonde she comes across while hunting for Michelle. This scene feels like something from a slasher or giallo film, and is actually pretty tense.

In between her two Cannon film appearances, Lisa London (left) was a member of the pop group The Pinups.

Interview: Actress Lisa London

Across her filmography, actress Lisa London has appeared in both mainstream hits like *Sudden Impact* (1983) and *Dragnet* (1987), and unapologetically fun b-movies such as Andy Sidaris' *Savage Beach* (1989) and *Guns* (1990), and Gregory Hatanaka's *Samurai Cop 2: Deadly Vengeance* (2015), starring opposite Tommy Wiseau. London appeared in two Cannon films early in her career: *The Happy Hooker Goes Hollywood* (1980)—which we discussed in *The Cannon Film Guide, Vol. I*—and then *The Naked Cage* (1986), playing an ill-fated inmate who is forced into a sexual relationship with the warden (Angel Tompkins) so that she can pay protection money to a prison bully.

Looking at her credits, you'll find a few years' gap between roles in the early 1980s. During this time, London was a member of the CBS Records singing group The Pinups, who released three albums, toured the world, and were the first musical artists to wear lingerie on national television. London herself sang the vocals on "Heartbeat," the song which plays on *The Naked Cage*'s soundtrack during her character's love scene with the warden.

Prior to movies, London was a model who had been studying journalism on a full ride scholarship. When she began dating an older celebrity, his agent sent her on an audition for the campus comedy *H.O.T.S.* (1979), thinking he'd rid his client of a distraction. Unexpectedly, she won the role—which led to a long, fruitful career on screen.

The last time we talked, we covered how you got into the movie business. Back then you weren't ready to name this person, but since that time you've revealed that the celebrity they sent you on auditions to keep you away from was NFL quarterback Joe Namath.

Lisa London: I just started thinking that it was time—that it's no harm, no foul for anyone at this point. I was very protective of him during the initial onslaught of #MeToo because I didn't want to confuse any issues, or point a finger at him in any way, because of the age disparity. He was in his 30s and I was 17 when we first met. He has been nothing but a fabulous human being in my life. Basically, I never would have had a career if not for him, because his agent was the one that sent me on the audition for *H.O.T.S.* thinking I'd do terribly, and go home, and that would be the end of his dangerous

347

affair with this kid. History had other ideas. [*Laughs*] It didn't last very long. It lasted probably a couple years altogether, and we remained friends. We always speak extremely fondly of each other. He's just an incredible human in my life.

At the time I was following in my father's footsteps, going into sports casting and news journalism. It was because of my father I met Joe Namath; he was the announcer at the golf tournament he was in town for. Then, my little sister saw him at the spa at the Canyon Hotel and knew that I had such a mad crush on him and said, "Come down, come down." I literally rode my bike to the Canyon Hotel, and straight into the area where they were all seated and the rest was history. [*Laughs*] He literally just looked at me and said, "Hi," and I said, "Hi." It's funny to look back on.

After *Happy Hooker* you have a small gap in your filmography, which is when you became involved with The Pinups. Can you tell me about how that came about?

All my life I sang. I was always the lead singer in choir, or in Sunday school, or whatever. When I first moved to Hollywood, after I stopped dating Joe, I started dating a singer-songwriter named Randy McNeil, and I used to sing his demo tapes. One of my best friends was the casting director Craig Campobasso, and he would always hear the demo tapes and say, "You've got to audition for singing stuff, too." I'm like, "Mm-mm, no, I don't dance, really," and that sort of thing.

He heard about an audition—an international talent search—for a band called The Pinups. It was a major deal on CBS/Sony Records. I auditioned and thought I did so horribly that I ended up taking a modeling job in Mexico. I didn't tell any of my agents or anything, so they had to track me down to let me know that I was one of the girls who was picked to be in The Pinups. That was mind-boggling: it was four years of being a superstar in Europe. We recorded in Germany, so I got to live there. Then, in America, we were on every major show from *Merv Griffin* to *Dance Fever*. Our billboards were plastered everywhere, including the Sunset Strip. It was just an amazing four years.

Our song "Just About a Dream" was played during the Lakers and Bulls championship, because we had a line that was, "You're just about magic on a magic night." Of course, Magic Johnson was their star. That was my father's proudest moment, too, when my song was played during the Lakers game. That was amazing. Since then I've sung in a few movies. I'm actually on the soundtrack of *The Naked Cage*. I sing during my own sex scene, which is a bit bizarre.

Can you tell me a little about Paul Nicholas, your director on *The Naked Cage*?

We were actually very close for very many years. We had a few other projects that I was supposed to be in, that he was trying to get going, but he really didn't do much in Hollywood after *The Naked Cage*. I'm pretty sure he did some things in Europe, but nothing on the scale of *The Naked Cage*, which was a pretty big release when it came out.

Now, Quentin Tarantino has championed the movie so much for us. He screened it at his New Beverly Cinema in Hollywood right before *Once Upon a Time in Hollywood* (2019) came out. There was a huge Q&A. It was completely sold out. It was one of the most amazing moments of my career. To see a film last, and be even more important now . . . It was very much a female-empowering film. It was beautifully shot. I'm so proud of my work in it. It was ahead of its time—it had a lesbian scene in it, when nobody was really doing that, or at least not doing it realistically and well. Even though there's an element of tongue-in-cheek in its women in prison movie genre vibe, it's really a great film, and it really stands up.

You have that love scene in the film, which is almost staged like a piece of dance. Were the two of you involved with choreographing that?

A pre-sales advertisement for *The Naked Cage*, released before the film was cast. "Raw violence and hot rage explode behind bars!"

Yes. It was extremely choreographed. We rehearsed that a lot. They took days to shoot that, and it was very meticulously done. Then, Paul Nicholas and Chris Nebe, the producer, really fought with Cannon Films for me to have that song in the movie. I had a collaborator on that song, Rob Michaels, and he demanded a certain amount of money for it. Rightfully. He wasn't even asking for an extravagant amount, just a fair one. Cannon didn't want to pay it and Paul Nicholas said, "You have to. I love it. It's so perfect for my movie, and I've already started cutting the music into the scene." [*Laughs*] It was pretty amazing. It's a thrill to hear your music up there on the screen.

What was the shoot like? I know you were actually filming in a women's prison.

We shot at the Sybil Brand Institute, which was a gnarly place. In fact, there was a scene where I got down from my bunk bed and I'm walking through the prison. They were going to superimpose something that would bite me and I would scream, and they didn't have to do anything because a jumbo rat walked right in front of me when we were filming, and that was enough to get the scream out. [*Laughs*] I can't remember if that made the final cut.

Then, of course, my death scene was fun. How many people can say they've had a death scene where they get smothered by dirty laundry?

The Naked Cage **came out at the height of the video boom, when there were a** *lot* **of these women in prison movies lining the shelves. However,** *The Naked Cage* **is among the few that still have a following. In your opinion, what makes this one stand out from the crowd?**

I think it was the exceptional cast. I mean that in every sense of the word. All of the men in this movie, ironically, of course, were playing these misogynist characters, but they loved women, and all of us had such an incredible bond. There were lots of young actors who were just perfect for their roles, and had enough chops to bring them to life well. I think almost every single person in it did an incredible job.

The cast was so wonderfully diverse, too. There are so many Black, brown and white actresses in the movies—literally, almost every ethnicity, every type of female body and face was represented in the film. It was really

351

well-thought-out to be inclusive, and realistic, even though it was stylized. Even though the outfits are kind of like something from *Flashdance* (1983), and the love scene was done in this music video sort of way, there's something very real and authentic in the art of it. I think Paul Nicholas did an amazing job of directing the film.

Do you remember visiting the Cannon offices or meeting Menahem Golan?

I remember that they were very ostentatious—they were very much like, "We're in Hollywood and we're proud of it." Everything had an exciting, glamorous quality to it. Also, they gave the biggest, best parties. I think my favorite was the one they did in an airport hangar, and it was just incredible. Everyone was just dressed to the nines and drop-dead gorgeous. It was Hollywood glamour. Really, the last of it was in that era, I believe.

Did you ever interact with Menahem?

Yes. [*Laughs*] Look, obviously, there's a part of me that will respect and admire everything they accomplished—but, if they could get away with not paying for something, they would try. After I did *Happy Hooker*, my wonderful agent at the time was like, "I'm sorry, I'm sorry. I'm trying to get your check." So I stormed up there and I just walked into Menahem's office and demanded my check. They had all these excuses about why it was late, but within a few days I got my check.

Just a few years later you started working with writer/director/producer Andy Sidaris, a man whose work I know a lot of Cannon fans are probably very familiar with. How did you link up with him?

This is a wonderful story, too. One of my best girlfriends was Ava Fabian. She was asked to be in one of the Andy Sidaris films because Cynthia Brimhall couldn't do it. Ava was booked on something else and she said to me, "Look, I'm going to set up an audition for you." She goes, "Don't worry, it's at his house, but it's totally a S.A.G. job, and he's totally legit." [*Laughs*] I said, "Okay..."

I will never forget going up to meet with Andy Sidaris. He opened the door, looked me up and down, and said, "You're hired." I said, "Don't you want me to read?" Then he said, "Yes, come in." I became so close to Andy and his gorgeous wife who produced all the movies, Arlene Sidaris. I was lucky enough to be in *Savage Beach* (1989) and *Guns* (1990). Sadly, I was going to be doing another one, and then Andy passed away and that was that. You can't ask for anything more than to star in a film that shoots in Hawaii with Andy Sidaris. It was pure joy, pure fun. And, talk about it looking like it was a huge budget film—all of his movies looked gorgeous, even on their lower budgets.

"... there is no dream in Hell." A French poster for *The Naked Cage*.

The American poster for *America 3000* is nearly as wild as the film itself.

America 3000

Release Date: April 1986
Directed by: David Engelbach
Written by: David Engelbach
Starring: Chuck Wagner, Laurene Landon, William Wallace, Victoria Barrett
Trailer Voiceover: "It is 900 years after the great nuke and the roles of women have changed dramatically – much to the displeasure of men and mutants!"

If you asked someone to study the poster art for *America 3000* and then describe what sort of movie they thought it might be, you would probably get a pretty wide range of answers. If you haven't seen the film yet, try this experiment on yourself. Look at the poster, think long and hard about it, and then try to guess what the movie is about. I'll assume that your eyes were first drawn to the large, ape-like creature in the center of the art. Yes, the one wearing a satin jacket, holding aloft a very '80s boom box and waving a tattered American flag. Below him you'll spot a stampeding cavalry of armor-clad warriors; on closer look, you might note that they're all female. In the foreground is a man, either leading the charge or fleeing for his life—he's holding a dagger, and dressed in a prehistoric-looking tunic. Opposite him is an angry-looking lady with a music video perm, hoisting a bullwhip over her head, ready to strike. The two tag lines—"Back to the beginning" and "An outrageous post-nuke adventure"—almost seem to be at odds with one another.

Is this an action movie set during the Neolithic era? Is this a post-nuke comedy? Or is it some sort of man versus monkey, *Planet of the Apes*-style epic, like the ghetto blastin' gorilla might seem to indicate? Or could it be yet another cheap *Mad Max* knock-off, as the fact that it's an apocalyptic adventure made during the Eighties would suggest. The latter, of course, was how Cannon chose to market it—a choice which greatly annoyed writer-director David Engelbach, who had an altogether different vision for the film.

Post-apocalyptic films were all the rage among low-budget producers throughout the 1980s, thanks of course to the wild success of George Miller's cheaply-made yet immensely-thrilling Australian action flick, *Mad Max* (1979), and its progressively crazier sequels. Thanks to the subgenre's low cost of entry when it came to production design—all you really needed was some barren land, and a bunch of garbage strewn around the sand—you could make a science fiction movie set in a fantastic world without spending a fantastic amount of money. Post-apocalyptic movies began to flood the video store shelves, coming in from places like Italy and New Zealand, and from many of the cheapest American independent outfits. Over the next 20 years, *Mad Max* was responsible for spawning countless knock-off movies about desert wanderers exploring the wasteland, doing battle with radioactively mutated raiders wearing spiky bondage gear and riding around in souped-up muscle cars. A whole book could be written on just those films—and already has! (Seek out author david j. moore's encyclopedic *World Gone Wild: A Survivor's Guide to Post-Apocalyptic Movies*.)

With the subgenre being so popular at the time, it's a wonder that it took Cannon so long to dip their toes into the radioactive, post-apocalyptic water. *America 3000* (1986) was announced several times by the studio over the years, first as *Thunder Women* and, later, as *Thunder Warriors*, before the name was eventually changed again to *America 3000*, which was another point of frustration for writer-director Engelbach, who openly disliked the title—and voiced his frustrations with Golan and Globus to a reporter from *Cinefantastique*. "I'm fighting with the Golan/Globus Cannon Group on this film every step of the way," he told the magazine. "Menahem Golan doesn't have a clue what kind of product he's going to get."

One of several misleading advertisements Cannon used to pre-sell *America 3000* to potential buyers. Note that neither the artwork nor the tagline reflect the actual movie.

Engelbach entered the Cannon fold during the early 1980s, when Menahem Golan fell in love with his spec screenplay for the competitive arm wrestling film-slash-father-son bonding adventure, *Over the Top*, and became determined to bring it to the screen himself. (Golan's dream, of course, became a reality in 1987, when he helmed the film himself with Sylvester Stallone in the lead role—more on that, obviously, in the chapter on *Over the Top*.) During the interim years, Golan hired Engelbach to pen *Death Wish II* (1982), which was a big hit for Cannon despite the writer finding the nastier elements added by the movie's director, Michael Winner, to be gratuitous and appalling.

During their negotiations over his *Death Wish II* and *Over the Top* scripts, Cannon offered to produce Engelbach's directorial debut feature. Several projects came and went before Engelbach unearthed a script for a pulpy adventure-comedy set in a prehistoric, post-nuke future, which he'd written more than a decade prior. Cannon went for the concept, but not the title—*"Thunder Women"*—because Golan was convinced movie-goers would have no interest in seeing a film with the word "women" in the title. He couldn't be convinced otherwise.

Engelbach was handed a slim budget and the option to shoot his movie either in Israel or South Africa. Preferring not to cross into the African nation during the depths of Apartheid, Engelbach opted to fly eight American cast members to Golan and Globus' homeland, and shoot with a primarily local crew near the Dead Sea.

"Nine hundred years after the Great Nuke.

The world man created, he destroyed.

Out of the darkness and the ignorance of the radioactive rubble emerged a new order . . .

. . . and the world was woggos."

A product of Cold War anxieties (as so many post-nuke movies were), *America 3000* is set nearly a full millennium into the future. A tragic, *Dr. Strangelove*-esque nuclear gaffe led to the United States and the Soviet Union launching the entirety of their atomic arsenals in each other's directions, wiping out most of human life and leaving the Earth a radiated, lifeless wreck. After centuries pass, humans are born again free of mutations, allowing civilization to rebuild from the ground up.

The world as we know it is now run by loosely-interconnected tribes of Amazonian warriors, whose only purposes for men are to castrate them and make them slaves, or use them as "seeders"—which, well, you can probably figure out what they're for. (This movie is practically a reverse-*Gor* [1988].) Some of the men were lucky and resourceful enough to escape captivity, and compared to the women they live primitive lifestyles in small camps they've built out of the bomb-shattered ruins.

Korvis (Chuck Wagner) woos warrior queen Vena (Laurene Landon) in a publicity still from *America 3000*.

Of course mankind no longer speaks English as we're familiar with it—not after nine centuries of hard living and illiteracy. Their language is similar, yes, but a new lexicon of slang has developed within it. "Woggos" means crazy, "plastic" means "cool," "cold" means "dead," and so on and so forth. (Think: the language of *A Clockwork Orange* [1971], but more like surfer lingo.) You'd better try to pick up the language quick, because it's used heavily throughout

America 3000's dialogue and can become difficult to follow during the film's chattier sections.

Our hero is an escaped male of the species named Korvis, played by Chuck Wagner. The buff blonde was a Broadway-bound musical actor, but was best known at the time for starring in the title role of *Automan* (1983–1984), a technologically-impressive ABC series that only lasted a single season. On the show, Wagner played a super-powered, crime-fighting artificial intelligence brought to life in the real world by a dorky cop—played by Desi Arnaz Jr., last seen in Cannon's *House of the Long Shadows* (1983)—who essentially served as his partner on the show's thirteen episodes. The series used laser-lighting effects similar to the ones seen in *Tron* (1982), which made it too expensive to keep in production after it aired to middling ratings.

Korvis and his best buddy Gruss—played by frequent Cannon man William A. Wallace, also of *The Delta Force* (1986) and *Avenging Force* (1986)—lead a small tribe of men hiding out in the radiated wasteland of America. It's clear that Korvis is a special kind of leader, organizing raids on the women's camps, freeing slaves, and helping them survive for so long under the harsh living conditions. Most notably, he's taught himself how to read after finding an old phonics book in a pile of rubble.

It's actually the dopey Gruss who provides the movie's narration in an awe-struck, "aw, shucks" style of delivery that makes the movie feel something like a post-apocalyptic version of *The Wonder Years* (1988–1993). The voiceover is one of the primary contributors to the movie's bizarre tone. His matter-of-fact, pseudo-folksy commentary plays as comical, even when he's describing something horrible.

Over on the ladies' side of the desert, the leader of the local tribe is killed in an ambush by cavemen. This leaves her followers' fate in the hands of her two daughters: the more thoughtful Vena (Laurene Landon) and her jealous, ruthless sister Lakella (Victoria Barrett). Clearly, neither has let their hard life of survival prevent them from having spectacular, '80s music video hair styles.

An '80s b-movie staple, Landon made her first splash as a flight attendant in the dismal *Airplane 2: The Sequel* (1982) before co-starring as Officer

Theresa Mallory opposite Bruce Campbell and Tom Atkins in the cult classic *Maniac Cop* (1988). Her on-screen sibling, Barrett, will be recognizable by many Cannon fans; as a personal favorite actress of Menahem Golan's, she appeared as the object of Elliott Gould's fantasy in *Over the Brooklyn Bridge* (1984), had small parts in *Hot Resort* and *Hot Chili* (both 1985), and finally took on a lead role opposite Robert Ginty in *Three Kinds of Heat* (1987). Engelbach had Barrett's dialogue re-dubbed in *America 3000* because her West Virginia accent was too strong for the post-apocalyptic, Colorado wasteland.

Vena is crowned queen in a ceremonial bacchanal with neighboring tribes in attendance. As the ladies sleep off their hangovers the next morning, Korvis leads a raid into their fortress to steal food and supplies, and free the enslaved men to join their cause. They might have gotten away unnoticed had they not also freed Aargh the Awful, a mutant, seven-foot-tall ape-man presumed to be evolution's missing link.

Inside the suffocating Aargh the Awful costume was American-Israeli basketball player Steve Malovic, who bounced around the NBA during the 1979-80 season before relocating to Israel, where he played another 15 seasons. Despite constantly being on the brink of heatstroke inside the gorilla suit—temperatures near the Dead Sea rarely dipped below one hundred degrees Fahrenheit during the shoot—he appeared to be having fun with his part: Aargh's goofing around are some of the funnier bits of *America 3000*, in spite of the character being as awful to look at as his name would imply.

When the women wake up robbed of their food, wine, and slaves, the movie turns into a very literal battle of the sexes. The tribeswomen—as they in-fight over their leadership—vow to hunt down and exterminate these pesky males. As the tribe of men work to free more of their kind, Korvis hatches a plan to bring a permanent peace between the sexes. It helps that their two leaders—Korvis and Vena—have conveniently developed the hots for each other.

Along the way, Korvis stumbles into a long-hidden presidential bunker, where—had he made it there before the bombs fell—old Ronald Reagan would have waited out the apocalypse. It's stocked full of laser guns for some reason, as well a humongous boom box and several flashy, gold radiation suits. Luckily for the boys, the religion the women follow includes a prophecy in which a messianic being known only as "The President" will one day return to the land and lead them into a new age. With a gold spacesuit pulled on and a boom box tucked under his arm, Korvis proceeds to install himself as El Presidente.

Another early pre-sales ad for the film which doesn't look anything like the final product.

The production ran into myriad issues, many to do with the logistics of a shoot based at Golan and Globus' run-down Tel Aviv studios. Two of the main things Engelbach so desperately needed to bring the world of his

Thunder Women script to life proved to be in short supply in Israel: wide open space, and American trash. The crew had trouble locating spots where they could film and not capture a city skyline, military base, or another piece of infrastructure in the backgrounds of their shots. The script also called for the ruins of the United States to take the form of recognizable garbage. While scrapped Cadillacs, brand-name appliances, and other patriotic trash would have been cheap and plentiful at any American junkyard, they were almost nonexistent in Israel, and prohibitively expensive to have imported.

The troubles weren't limited to the set, either. Golan nixed Engelbach's preferred title, "Thunder Women," because he didn't think moviegoers would see a movie with "women" in the title. A compromise was struck and the film was shot as "Thunder Warriors" instead, before ultimately being changed to *America 3000*. The director discouraged them from marketing it as yet another post-apocalyptic action film—which were already over-abundant on video store shelves by the mid-1980s—but Cannon couldn't help themselves, taking out full-page advertisements with artwork that, in Engelbach's words, made it look like a "punky Mad Max ripoff."

It's clear through the whole process that the writer-director and his producers rarely saw eye-to-eye on the project. Rather damnably, the movie's associate producer in their Tel Aviv offices, Itzik Kol, implied that Golan didn't fully understand what kind of movie he was signing on for, because Golan couldn't follow the script's invented slang terms.

For Engelbach, the last surprise came *after* the film was released. The director had spent extra time overhauling the movie's soundtrack, having been unsatisfied with the one Cannon had inserted. When he pulled a rented copy of the tape out of its sleeve and inserted it into a VCR, he was horrified to find out that Cannon hadn't even bothered to use the music he'd prepared for them—instead, sending out the earlier version for wide release. This version with the incorrect audio is the one that's appeared on every home video release of the film to date. (Following *America 3000*, Engelbach was offered the director's chair on Cannon's aborted Captain America movie, but turned it down.)

There's enough to these known issues to wonder how much better *America 3000* might have been had it not been put through some of the worst parts of the Cannon wringer. Outside of the president's '80s glam bunker, the production design looks like something that was thrown together from whatever garbage the crew could get their hands on. The tone is all over the place—in one scene, Aargh the Awful will be doing Harlem Globetrotter tricks with a human skull standing in for a basketball; later, we'll get a sleazy rape scene between a hesitant tribeswoman and one of the "seeders." Many first-time viewers don't pick up all of the nutty lingo until the movie's half-over. On top of it all, the only thing more ridiculous than our heroine Vena's hair is her line delivery.

But, would it be woggos to say that the movie isn't *all* bad? Not in the least. There are some strong action scenes, and Chuck Wagner is a likeable hero, playing Korvis in the goofball way you might imagine Steve Martin would have played "Mad" Max Rockatansky, had he somehow been cast in that role instead of Mel Gibson. Acclaimed stage actress and dancer Sue Giosa makes a pretty good villain in her supporting role as the treacherous, rival tribeswoman, Morha. Other notable faces in the film include *Down Twisted* (1987) and *RoboCop 2* (1990) actress Galyn Gorg as Vena's bestie, and longtime Cannon veteran Shaike Ophir—here credited as "Shai K. Ophir"—as the creepy eunuch who takes care of the tribe's boy toys. Ophir appeared in at least nine Golan- and Globus-produced films, most recognizably as Father Nicholas in *The Delta Force* (1986) and as Kassam, the slimy antiquities dealer who Quatermain teases with dynamite, in *King Solomon's Mines* (1985).

Interview: Director David Engelbach

As a screenwriter, David Engelbach's name is attached to three separate Cannon projects, all big ones: *Death Wish 2* (1982), *America 3000* (1986), and *Over the Top* (1987). The first and last are projects that were taken out of his hands and re-written by other writers, resulting in final products that barely reflect his original screenplays.

The cover of *America 3000*'s videocassette edition, which was released with the wrong soundtrack on the tape.

His experience on *Death Wish 2*—a film from which he considered having his name removed—is recounted in this series' first volume, while the long, complicated history of *Over the Top* can be read about in the corresponding chapter in this book. The middle project was Engelbach's feature directorial debut, the post-apocalyptic action-comedy *America 3000*, and brought with it hurdles of its own for the first-time filmmaker to leap over.

Engelbach's studies initially began in theatre as an undergrad, before moving into film for his grad work. He initially pursued screenwriting as a path to becoming a film director. One of his student films was seen by none other than Steven Spielberg, who brought him on as an assistant on *Jaws* (1975). This gave way to TV work and, ultimately, his involvement in writing and developing *Over the Top*, which directly led to a relationship with Menahem Golan and Cannon that lasted through the first half of the 1980s.

Engelbach now teaches film and screenwriting at the Savannah College of Art and Design.

After graduating from film school, it sounds like you had a mostly typical couple of years for fresh film grads: making shorts, working on commercials, writing spec scripts. Then, your career took a turn when you somehow connected with Steven Spielberg.

David Engelbach: Yes, I had met Steven. I made a short when I was at USC that got some attention. Actually, I was very lucky. I had an agent who saw this film at one of the public screenings that USC would do. He contacted me, and he later introduced the film to Spielberg. I met Steven before he did *Sugarland Express* (1974). In fact, he wanted me to do a documentary on the making of *Sugarland*, which I was more than happy to do. At the time, we're talking about 1972 or '73.

I prepared a budget and everything, and submitted it to [producers] Dick Zanuck and David Brown, who said, "No, we're not going to spend the money on that."

I stayed in contact with Steven and when *Jaws* came up, we were going through the same thing. He asked me about doing a documentary on it.

Again they said "no," so he said, "Well, how about coming on as my assistant?" And I did.

After Spielberg, you worked in TV for a while.

After I worked on *Jaws,* Sid Sheinberg, who had been Steven's godfather, offered me the opportunity to direct television for Universal. I worked on a TV series called *The Night Stalker* (1974–1975) with Darren McGavin. I was a dialogue director on that. In fact, I was scheduled to write and direct the final episode of the season, which never made it to its production date because the show got canceled on the twentieth episode, since ABC wasn't going to pick it up and Universal was losing money on every episode. That went away.

It would have been during these years when you started work on *Over the Top*, which I gather was supposed to be a follow-up to *The Farmer* (1977) for Gary Conway and his partner.

I had been writing, focusing on low-budget action movies, since that seemed to be a better opportunity for me to get in as a director. I had dealt with Roger Corman, I dealt with Cirio Santiago, who was this Filipino producer who did a lot of stuff with Corman. As it turned out, I was developing a project to be shot in the Philippines about two American, Hollywood stunt women who were there in a movie, and witness a gang rub-out and they have to take on the gang to prevail.

A friend of mine was working at Columbia in distribution. He said that they got a script in from a company that they had released a very low-budget movie for a year or so earlier, and made a few dollars on it. The script was dreadful, but they had a hook that they thought they could sell about arm wrestling, and since they didn't have a director, would I be interested in looking at it if I could get the opportunity to direct it?

I read their script, from a guy named Gary Conway, who had been a former television actor. It was a pretty dreadful piece of script, but there was an idea in there. Gary was interested in arm wrestling, honestly, and so he had a lot of focus on the arm wrestling part of it. I saw it as a potential to make an interesting story about an estranged father and son, and that the relationship is paid off at the arm wrestling contest.

I said that's the movie I'd be willing to write, and Columbia approved the idea. I met with Gary. He approved it. We made a deal, and I went off and I wrote the script with the intention of directing it. As it turned out, Columbia really liked my script. They offered Gary and his company a really generous independent distribution deal, which included a first dollar break, which was unheard of at the time for independents.

Unfortunately after spending a year on the project doing pre-production, casting, et cetera, they didn't have the money to make the movie. We were about to lock in a cast and had to make offers, but it turned out they really didn't have the money. I had spent, I don't know, probably a year and a half of my life on that project. I only got paid minimum to do the script. I had pretty much been burned out by *Over the Top*.

There was a guy named Andrew Gatti, who was an exhibitor in Australia. He dealt with Menahem. When Golan-Globus had acquired Cannon, they were looking for material and apparently, Andrew knew Menahem, and he had given the script to Menahem without telling [us].

Menaham fell in love with the material, so I met with Menahem and it eventually ended up that the movie got made the way it got made.

That was very early into Golan-Globus' attempted takeover of Hollywood. What was your first impression of those guys?

I didn't know anything about them. Nobody did. I knew that Cannon had done the movie with Peter Boyle called *Joe* (1970). Blue-collar guy goes on a rampage. And I knew about—what was it, the *Hollywood Hooker*? They were a pretty moribund company. Andrew arranged a dinner for me to meet Menahem. I forget where it was, but I remember Menahem sitting in one of those corner booths in a restaurant and he took up most of the booth. [*Laughs*]

That was my first impression of him. He was very enthusiastic. He said, "I love your script, I love your script." "Well, that's nice to hear." Every writer wants to hear that. He said, "I want to make that movie." I said, "Great." He said, "But I have to direct." That was my first encounter with Menahem.

It sounds like once Cannon was involved with *Over the Top*, it was taken out of your hands.

They tried to make a deal originally with Gary Conway for my script. Gary was going to star in the movie, and they couldn't make a deal with him. Golan said we can't make this movie because Gary isn't a star, and Gary wouldn't back down from the project initially, so it didn't go anywhere. It just didn't happen at that point, but Menahem said to me, "I'd really like to *make movie* with you." I said, "Sure, fine, whatever."

Was that when Menahem called you about *Death Wish 2*?

Yes. I probably had talked to him, incidentally, one or two times, but we weren't staying in constant contact. There were some months where, if I remember correctly, I was working on two other projects at the time.

Menahem called me up and I remember his words, he said, "David, I want you to write a movie for me." He said, "We're going to make a sequel to one of the greatest hits of the 1970s." I said, "What are you going to do, *Godfather III*?" He said, "Close, we want to do *Death Wish 2.*" I laughed, then I found out he was serious. [Laughs]

I said, "Thank you, but no." He said, "No, no, we want you." I said, "Menahem, [*Death Wish*] had its time and place seven or eight years ago."

I'd always been a fan of Charlie Bronson. I grew up watching his movies, his action stuff, *The Magnificent Seven* (1960) and *The Great Escape* (1963), those films. I actually enjoyed his work as an actor for the kind of parts that he did, but I didn't want to do *Death Wish*. I didn't want to do that kind of film.

Menahem called me back later. He said, "David, I want to *make movie* with you." I said, "Great." He said, "But I want you to write *Death Wish* for me first." Since there was no deal in place for *Over the Top*, he actually had no obligation to me whatsoever to offer me a project.

That's what convinced you to write *Death Wish 2*.

I said, "Okay." I remember talking to my agent at the time, asking "Who's Cannon, who are these guys?" Nobody really knew who they were. They hadn't done anything to speak of yet. I knew Menahem had done *The Apple* (1980) because I remember he showed that to us when we first met with him in regards to *Over the Top*. We were thinking, "Well, it's got energy. I don't think this guy is Fellini, but it's got energy."

I remember I met with him at the offices they had in LA at the time. I had two questions for Menahem. I sat down and I asked, "One, do you have the rights to make this, and does Charlie Bronson's wife have to be in it?" He said, "Yes, we have the rights and no, she doesn't have to be in it." Both were wrong. They didn't have the rights and, as you know, she ended up in the film.

That was a movie that went through title changes. They had the rights, they didn't have the rights. They had a premature advertising campaign at Cannes, and Bronson's lawyers and agent slammed them on it. They weren't going to do the project because they announced it before he'd actually committed to it. [*Laughs*]

I know in the process of writing that movie, I got at least two phone calls telling me, "No, no, it's not a sequel anymore. No, it's a sequel again." Which, I think, really describes so much of their process at the time. It was still one of their first hits. They hadn't yet started making films by the kilo.

Their slates were still pretty trim at that point—in a couple years they'd be producing more than thirty films at any given time.

Yes. I compare them to a supermarket that only had one checkout lane.

We won't dig too deep into *Death Wish 2*, just because you've talked about that quite a bit over the years, but I know Winner basically rewrote your script into a near remake of the first movie, and added all of that gratuitous sexual violence himself.

Yeah, he made it a total Xerox of the original. I was very disappointed in that, to be honest. I knew what I was writing, but the script I wrote was a bit more sophisticated and really dealt with putting the character's actions into the context of the time. Anything that made it *not* a copy of the original, [Winner] basically took out.

There were apparently elements that I put into the character that apparently got used in some of the other Cannon films, but I don't know. I never saw any of the other ones. I had no interest in seeing three, four, five, six, seven, eight, nine, or ten, however many Death Wishes they did.

At least one of the movie's most famous lines—"Do you believe in Jesus?"—made it in there from your script.

Yes, that was one of the two times I went on the set. I had that line in my script: "Do you believe in Jesus? Good, you're going to meet him." I think they took the "good" out. Apparently people remember that line from the movie. God knows why, but they do.

For a time after *Death Wish*, you were involved with writing a Robert Mitchum movie for Cannon called "Déjà vu."

Yes, "Déjà vu" was supposed to be for Robert Mitchum and Yves Montand, about two old detectives who had been involved in a case years ago that ruined both of their lives. The femme fatale who they were both in love with came back years later to say that her daughter had been kidnapped, and the ransom demand was the [evidence] that they were never able to find from their first case. So, it brought these three characters back together again.

It was actually quite a nice script. It was a lighter Noir. It wasn't really a hardcore Noir, but played to the mythologies, Robert Mitchum in a trench coat, that whole thing. Only, he's a totally crapped-out private investigator at the time. When we first meet him, he's looking for a lost dog and can't find it. He gets a dog out of the pound, paints it, and tries to convince the owner that this is the dog he'd been hired to look for. That's about all the guy had going in life.

Did it not work because Mitchum didn't want to do it?

From what I understand, Mitchum liked the script. I don't know. I never talked to him about it. However, he had a woman who'd been managing him for years. She did not want him working for Cannon at the time, which is ironic because two years later he ended up doing *The Ambassador* (1985) and then a bunch of films for them. When Mitchum backed out, Yves Montand backed out. I mean, the two of them together would have been fantastic.

Later on, I put another cast together with James Coburn doing the Robert Mitchum part. Unfortunately, the agent who represented the actors wanted more for them than Cannon wanted to pay, so the project didn't happen. In one of those little bits of irony, the agent later told me that he made a big mistake, and it would have been good for everybody's career if they'd done that film.

It's the way things went. I believe that title was used by Cannon for another film.

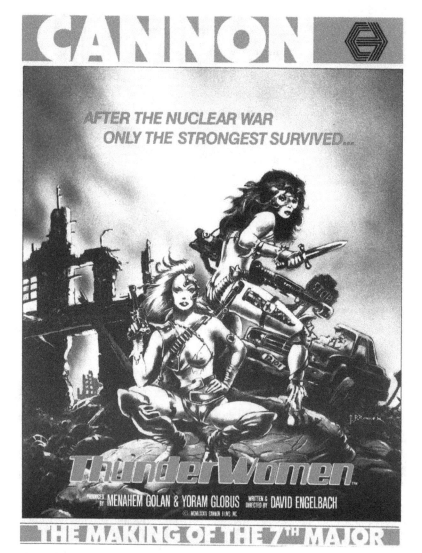

An early pre-sales advertisement for the film from Cannon's 1984 catalog.

When that fell through then, is that when *Thunder Women* became your next project?

Thunder Women was one of my very first script sales, to this independent guy. A friend of mine had done a low, low budget rewrite for him on a movie, and he made some money on it. He was looking to spend a little bit more on his next project. My friend said, "Look, let me give him the script." I said, "I just finished the first draft, no one's read it." He said, "Don't worry. He doesn't have any taste." I said, "Okay, fine, give it to him," and the guy bought it. [Laughs] That was actually my first script sale. Obviously, he didn't get it made, but I always liked the idea. I thought it was fun.

Menahem still wanted to do *Over the Top*, and they worked out some kind of deal with Gary Conway. I believe he did something else for them—they had to pay him off with another movie, as well. They still had an obligation to me, as a director on the project, from my original contract.

Thunder Women came up as an alternative. I bought the rights back from the original producer because I wanted the title. The irony, of course, is they released it under this horrible title, *America 3000*, that I was vehemently against. I had even paid for a title test out of my own pocket when we were in post-production. It was something like 87% of people said they were interested in seeing something called *Thunder Women*. It was under 30% for something called *America 3000*. I presented that data to Menahem, but he said, "Movies with 'women' in the title don't make money."

"America 3000" doesn't even make sense as a title if you actually do the math.

I said to him, "Is it a car race? What *is* America 3000? I have no idea what it is." At least "Thunder Women" tells you that you can't take it seriously. It's a little tongue-in-cheek. It's a wink and a nod. It sets the tone for what the material was, or at least the kind of film I was trying to make.

The early pre-sales ads that Cannon put out tried to sell it with a punkish, Mad Max vibe in their artwork.

I'll tell you what happened. When they agreed to do it, I had given this script to Menahem. I don't know if he read it, but I know his girlfriend,

Victoria Barrett, the blonde who plays the one who thought she should become the queen and challenges Laurene Landon for it, she read it. She was Menahem's girlfriend. I think she read the script to him in bed. [*Laughs*]

I met with Menahem and he said, "We're going to make this movie." I was living in Venice, and I remember when I got home about an hour later, a messenger showed up at my apartment. It was a list of credits and a headshot of Victoria Barrett. [*Laughs*] I figured, okay, this is Menahem's squeeze. I have to make a part for her. Originally I wrote a part for her that had no dialogue in it. They kept pushing me to give her a bigger part so that she could speak, which was not what I wanted to do.

But, I wanted to get the movie made. Menahem said we can make it in Israel. I went to Israel with my production designer, an American, scoped out the locations and came back. The original script was set in Colorado, which ended up in the radiation zone, but Menahem said, "David, desert is desert. I have already got a deal." So it was out of my hands.

He also gave me the option to shoot it in South Africa. This was in the Eighties, during the time of the apartheid regime in South Africa. I didn't want anything to do with that, unfortunately. If I had to do it again and it hadn't had that political environment, I probably would have shot it in South Africa. It would have given it a very different look. It wouldn't have had that desert look to it, which was a cliché in post-apocalyptic films.

I've heard some of the cast were surprised when they got to Israel and the budget was lower than what they had expected from the script they'd read.

[*Laughs*] I never saw a budget for that movie—or from these guys, to be honest. I never saw a Cannon budget. I had prepared a budget, independently, before I made the deal with Cannon. When I was trying to make the movie, I had another financing source. There was an alternative for me, at the time, to do the film as a low-budget movie in the States. I think my budget on my original script came out around $2 million, which is still not a lot but it wasn't $500,000, either.

[Cannon] made a schedule and I looked at it and thought, "I can't do it on that schedule. So, what am I going to do about it?" I thought the best thing I could do would be get Cannon pregnant, which is what happened. When we started to shoot, I knew how Cannon worked. I knew they made all their money on presales. As it turned out, my shooting began in the spring and it coincided with the Cannes Film Festival, which for Cannon was their supermarket. What I did first was shoot an action sequence. That was my first couple days shooting, and they'd rehearsed it very extensively. Alain Jakubowicz, who was my editor and had done a number of things for Cannon, did a really quick cut on it. We sent a tape off to Menahem at Cannes, and they pre-sold the film on the basis of that. Suddenly I didn't have a problem about getting more days on my schedule.

I remember once saying to Menahem that I needed more horses, and he said, "David, don't tell me how much you need. Tell me what you need, and I will give it to you." I said, "Menahem, I need more horses, but they have to be alive." [Laughs]

I know that getting something as simple as American trash to decorate your sets was nearly impossible in Israel.

I wanted a crapped-out American background, but it was way too sparse. What can I say? It was an ambitious project. If I had to do it again, I probably would have done something else instead of *Thunder Women*, because of the problems of trying to stage a big movie. The film does, I believe, have a little historical footnote as the only all-female cavalry charge in film history. [Laughs]

There's an amazing *Cinefantastique* article that was written on a set visit. It sounds like you were at war with Cannon over every aspect of this movie.

Not entirely. There was a constant battle going on in terms of cost. I had designed the main set, the women's camp, to be made out of lightweight fiberglass huts that could be moved easily to suit the camera. Well, they did everything in plaster in Israel, so these things—instead of being 125 pounds, which two grips could pick up and move—were like 800 pounds. They weren't going anywhere.

The construction coordinator who worked for Cannon paid no attention to anything my art director gave him, and so we ended up with designs and construction that did not fit what I wanted. I had a sequence in the beginning where we first see young Korvis and Gruss, when they're first brought in and they escape. For that escape scene where young Korvis hops on a horse, I designed a corridor that was getting narrower and narrower and narrower with a specific shot design.

You're watching this horse coming towards you, and you're watching this V-shaped corridor and going, "He can't make it. There's no way this guy can get through there." Well, the shot now looks like it's playing on the 405. It's a huge space, and it had none of the tension that I wanted because we couldn't get him to do things the way we wanted them. So, yes, that was a problem. I remember talking to Itzhak Kol, who was the Israeli line producer. They couldn't fire this guy, I don't know why. I still don't know why. If you have any information about that, I'd be curious all these years later.

I have no clue about that one.

My joke was that he must have had pictures of Menahem with sheep. I think one of my crew said, "That wouldn't be enough." [*Laughs*]

In spite of these issues and the limited budget, you got some exciting sequences in there. You mentioned the cavalry charge with all of the horses—I think that turned out pretty successfully.

They hired Spanish riders, horse people, who were my stunt people, and I have to admit, they were really good. It was a pleasure to work with them. They did hire an Italian—he always referred to himself as a Roman, not Italian, I can't remember his name—who was a very knowledgeable man. He was a real ally to me. We had a sequence, the culmination of the big fight with the big explosion. I wanted something that looked like a mushroom cloud.

He came up to me. He saw where I had placed extras, and he said, "I don't think your powder guy knows what he's doing. I'd be worried about that." So I moved people further back, away from the center of where the explosion was going to be. It turned out that he was absolutely right. You know how they do these contained explosions with charcoal and stuff? There was a metal top to this container. It went flying up in the air, and it landed exactly where I would have had an extra. It would have killed somebody, or seriously injured them.

If you remember what happened on the filming of *The Twilight Zone* (1983), I was very conscious about that, and the fact that I didn't want any animals or actors injured. I remember telling myself, "It's only a movie." That was one of those fortuitous things, and had I not listened to him and only gone for what the shot looked like, there would have been some serious injuries on that set.

Look, I liked the Israeli crew. I thought they were hardworking and industrious. David Gurfinkel, who was my DP, was helpful. I was a one-shot director coming from the United States to Israel. The crew were really working for Gurfinkel, because he was making a lot of movies for Cannon. He was my ally in many cases.

Shooting in the hot desert sun in Israel created real challenges, because I couldn't shoot masters between 10 AM and 3 PM, because of the sun. It would just bleach everything out and there would be no contrast to it. I ended up having to shoot coverage before I could shoot masters in some places, which is really strange.

Do you remember Menahem's reaction when he saw the finished movie?

When I showed him the rough cut of it, he was very excited about it. He was going, "Oh, we're going to do it in Panavision!" I'm like, "Menahem, we can't do that. It's not what the film is." I don't know what happened when he saw the final film.

I do know that I was disappointed with the soundtrack. I had actually hired Tony Berg to do the music, but I was very disappointed with Tony's music. I didn't like some of the voices on the actresses, and so I went to Menahem and I said, "Look, the picture's locked, but I really want to go back and redo the soundtrack."

He said, "Okay. I won't spend any more money, but anything we own in the music library, you can use." I'm pretty sure that what you probably saw is not correct. When Cannon went to release the VHS, they used the wrong soundtrack. I revoiced some of the actresses, including Menahem's girlfriend, to get rid of her West Virginia accent. I rewrote and eliminated some of the narration that Bill Wallace did on it. It made a big difference.

The French poster for *America 3000* made it look like a post-apocalyptic romance.

The theatrical release had the proper film soundtrack on it. When they went to VHS, they literally pulled the wrong soundtrack. It was like *Frankenstein*—they put in the wrong brain.

The right soundtrack exists, though, on theatrical prints? Hopefully that can be corrected for a home video release one day.

I would love to do that. I even said, "When you go to do the video release, I will come down and I will supervise the transfer because I want to make some color corrections and stuff like that." They never contacted me. I never heard from them. I didn't know it had even gone into video release until I literally saw it in my local video store back in Marina del Rey. [*Laughs*]

By that point, Cannon was moving around funds just to finish the movies they already had in production. They could only afford to give many of their films small releases.

They had pre-sold the film, so they already had profits on the movie. I had designed an advertising campaign. I didn't want it to go out into regular release. I wanted them to do a limited number of midnight screenings, to build some word of mouth, and then they could go into the normal release pattern. They paid no attention to that. They'd already made money on it, so they weren't willing to spend any money on the theatrical release. They were onto the next project.

At the time, they were robbing Peter to pay Paul. They were taking money out of distribution costs and putting it into pre-production for talent and stuff. They were pulling money from their left pocket and putting it into their right pocket.

Did you find out that *Over the Top* was moving into production when the news broke that they'd promised Sylvester Stallone a historically large paycheck?

I found out that they were actually making *Over the Top* when I was sitting in my apartment. I picked up a copy of *Variety* and went, "Oh, they're making *Over the Top*. Isn't that interesting?" I knew they were moving forward. I knew that they had approached Stallone, because I had heard from somebody who worked in the management or the agency.

Stallone really liked my original draft. It reminded him of his original *Rocky* (1976), because it was really much more heartfelt. It was really much more about the relationship between the father and the son. The kid had a real edge to him. He really thought his dad was a serious loser. The kid was the antagonist for the movie.

What I heard was that Stallone's people got a little nervous because Rambo, *First Blood* (1982), was becoming very popular. They said, "Look, you've got to keep some of that Rambo quality." So that, I understood, was what was driving him to add some of the stupid sequences, like where he drives the truck into the grandfather's house. My feeling about what they did with the script was that they didn't add anything to it. They just poured water into it. They made the soup brothier. They didn't really add anything essentially dramatic to the story. The arm wrestling contest at the end was pretty much, in many ways, what I'd written.

If you were to try to ballpark a percentage, how much of your original *Over the Top* do you feel made it onto the screen?

I say about forty or fifty percent. I know that Stallone and Stirling Siliphant did a rewrite. I don't know what order they did that in. Stirling Silliphant was a writer whose work I admired when I was a kid. He had created a very popular TV series called *Route 66* (1960–1964), with Martin Milner. It was actually a pretty nice show. It lasted for a few seasons on CBS.

I never had any connection with him or Stallone in terms of the changes to the script. My understanding was that they decided they had to add more action and pump that up, because they didn't want Rambo audiences to be disappointed with a smaller, more human-focused story.

That pretty much wraps up your association with Cannon, correct? Were any more projects ever discussed afterwards?

At one point, they had the rights to Captain America, and Menahem wanted me to direct it for them. To be honest, I read the script and it wasn't bad, but I didn't want to do another Cannon project. The boat was taking on water. It was clear that Cannon was extended beyond what was financially suitable.

They had bought a building and moved their facilities into it, and made a big deal of it. I was invited to the grand opening they had in the parking garage—a grand opening held on car ramps. That was very Cannon. [*Laughs*]

There's some footage of that party in the BBC documentary *The Last Moguls* (1986)—I laugh seeing all those movie stars in their fancy suits, hanging out in Cannon's parking garage.

That was the end of my Cannon period. I was involved with those guys probably from the time that they first contacted me, until after the release of *Over the Top*. I would say that it was maybe four or five years over that process. The thing is, I remember telling my agents at the time, "Look, you guys should pay attention to these guys. They've got money. They're going to give a lot of opportunities. You got a lot of actors, and up and coming directors who could probably get gigs making movies for these guys."

For all the hardship of dealing with them, I do remember a story. Something had come up, I may have needed more horses [for *America 3000*]. I called Menahem, it was one o'clock in the morning. He was in Rome and he answered the phone. I was like, "I need this. I need this—" This was like a Monday, and I said, "I need them by Wednesday." He said, "All right," and hung up the phone. And, I got them.

I had worked with the studios for ten or twelve years by that time. There was nobody at the studios who had that kind of passion for movies. Nobody. It reminded me of a throwback to the early founders of Hollywood—the ragamuffins who became the heads of Columbia, and things like that. I appreciated that about them.

Menahem made a statement to me. He said, "David, you're family to us." I said, "Menahem, I don't believe in incest." They were characters. I can understand, in terms of personality, they were the last of a breed. Their attitude was "Damn the torpedoes, full speed ahead."

Interview: Actor Chuck Wagner

Chuck Wagner is perhaps best-known for his starring role in the short-lived, cult favorite TV series *Automan* (1983), playing the computer-generated counterpart to Desi Arnaz, Jr.'s heroic police officer. Only thirteen episodes of the series were filmed, but the show remains beloved by fans as an early example of a special effects-driven superhero drama.

Korvis (Chuck Wagner) wearing his "El Presidente" guise in a press still from *America 3000*.

While the TV show made way for Wagner to star in Cannon's post-apocalyptic comedy *America 3000* (1986), the actor has been far more prolific as the star of stage musicals, including Broadway versions of *The Three Musketeers*, *Les Miserables*, *Beauty and the Beast*, and *Jekyll & Hyde*, as well as the Grammy-winning recording of Stephen Sondheim's *Into the Woods*.

Starting at the beginning: how did a boy from a big family in Tennessee develop a love for the stage?

Chuck Wagner: I was blessed to be part of a well-educated and well-traveled family, and when I was ten I was introduced to Broadway seeing the original cast of *1776*. I was hooked. That summer we visited Disneyland for the first time and I was totally inspired by Walt Disney's concept of Imagineering—that if you can dream it, you can make it happen. It would become my life's philosophy. I was encouraged by great teachers throughout my early school years, and I was given free rein to pursue my artistic interests, from drawing and painting to my early forays into the theatre.

From high school onward, it seems you were a lauded young actor in a number of prestigious programs and troupes. Was it always your intention to act on both stage and screen? And how did your transition to television happen?

I stayed very busy throughout high school, in the choir and the band—I was a drum major in 9th grade. I starred in *My Fair Lady* and *Carousel*. I also appreciated the theatrical spectacle of football as a decent, if not exceptional, player.

I started college at the University of Alabama Tuscaloosa, and my first show took me all the way to the Kennedy Center as part of the American Collegiate Theatre Festival. I was named Outstanding Freshman in Theatre. While there, I played Lancelot in *Camelot* for the first time. (I would later reprise that role opposite Broadway's original Lancelot, Robert Goulet's King Arthur.) During the summers I starred in *The Lost Colony*, America's longest running Outdoor Drama, directed by legendary Broadway director Joe Layton, who pointed me toward Broadway. I met my wife, Susan, there too. Those were magical summers.

After two years at Alabama, I transferred to the University of Southern California under the chairmanship of Broadway great John Houseman. My first show in Los Angeles was the lead in *Christopher!*, the first musical ever written by Frank Wildhorn, who would go on to become a Broadway staple—*Jekyll & Hyde, The Scarlet Pimpernel, The Civil War* and more. As part of the Troupe USC/USA, I toured the U.K., winning a prestigious Fringe First award at the Fringe Festival in Edinburgh, Scotland. After my four years of college, I was cast in a recurring role on ABC's *General Hospital*, a guest villain on *The Dukes of Hazzard* (1979–1985), and in various smaller roles on other soap operas, while staying busy in regional theatre throughout California. This led to my biggest TV role, as Glen Larson's computer-generated superhero *Automan*.

You starred in *Automan*, a superhero show that combined equal parts action, special effects, and comedy, which is similar to what many of the big superhero movie franchises do today. It only ran one season, but has a nice cult following. Do you think it might have been too far ahead of its time?

Automan was and is a blessing, and was certainly ahead of its time. It was a CGI concept before CGI was really a thing. It was TV's answer to *Tron* (1982), and was produced in part by two of *Tron*'s producers. What a treat to work alongside Desi Arnaz Jr. and Robert Lansing while working with some of the best SFX folks in the business. The effects were terribly expensive at the time, which is a major reason we did not run, but it was, to quote *Bill & Ted*, an excellent adventure!

Do you remember how you got involved in *America 3000*? Was there an audition?

Certainly we all had to audition, but thanks to *Automan* I had some notoriety. We all met with David Engelbach who gave us a very exciting script to explore. We all hit it off and were cast, and were very excited about the chance to shoot a real motion picture on location in Israel.

I've heard it wasn't an easy production—that it was incredibly hot the whole time, and that the crew in Israel was never on the same page with their producers in Hollywood. Hopefully you were spared of those frustrations. What were your personal impressions of the shoot?

First, once we got there we discovered that the budget was much smaller than the original script led us to believe. What read like a serious sci-fi adventure was downsized to a fairly primitive outing. The costumes were essentially rags, the sets were almost non-existent, and the makeup ranged from dirt to just plain silly. It was hot, but the thrill of being in the Holy Land with a great group of people made it fun.

The actual shoot was a grind, but getting to visit so many historical sites more than made up for it. We were graciously hosted in Menahem Golan's home, and my co-star Ari Sorko-Ram taught us volumes about life in Israel. I especially loved the view from Masada.

Did it take you long to learn the new lingo and slang words used in the script?

Not really. It is after all fairly simple and, let's face it, quite silly. It is certainly on par with the quality of my ABC book, with which I apparently taught myself to read!

How hot was it, wearing that gold suit in the desert?

That suit was made of gold lame and was not particularly durable, but was mercifully much cooler than an actual radiation suit. All I can say about it is that it was shiny!

Do any particular memories stand out with your fellow cast members?

Everyone in the cast was fun to work with. Laurene [Landon] was a bit mysterious, but game to attack the scenes with gusto in spite of having to deal with perhaps the oddest hairstyle I ever saw! The late, great Galyn Gorg was absolutely gorgeous and down to earth, and Sue Giosa was a dynamic powerhouse and very professional. Bill Wallace became a great friend. He really was the star of the film, and Ari [Sorko-Ram]—who we knew from *CHiPS* (1977–1978) on TV back home—was a true mensch.

The big attack of the Thunder Women—which was the film's working title—on Camp Reagan was a truly impressive set piece, and while shooting that we actually felt like we might be making a real movie. We had fun working with the horses, but I am pretty sure the horses did not feel the same way!

385

What do you think of the movie?

As a movie, it is not quite *Gone with the Wind* (1939), but we had fun. Production values were atrocious, sets and costumes were seriously primitive, and what was left of David's excellent script became diluted to the point of being nearly pointless. I still love it as a time capsule of that grand experience. (And, what can I say about Argh the Awful? Now, *that* was a hot costume!)

It wasn't long at all after *America 3000* that your Broadway career seemed to take off. Could you pick a favorite of your stage roles, if you had to?

I have been truly blessed with my stage career, and I love all of my roles. I made my Broadway debut as Athos in *The Three Musketeers*. Working with Stephen Sondheim in *Into the Woods* was amazing. My time in *Les Miz* was great and I treasure every moment as Disney's Beast. I like to think my favorite role is yet to come.

You spent several years as a Ringmaster for Ringling Brothers Barnum & Bailey Circus. Was that experience as fun as I'd imagine?

Of course it was. Sadly the circus is no more, but playing houses packed with tens of thousands of children of all ages was fantastic. Plus, how many folks can say they rode an elephant down 34th street to Madison Square Garden? It filled four amazing years of my life, living aboard the world's longest privately-owned passenger train. I really felt I communed with the spirit of P.T. Barnum. It was truly The Greatest Show on Earth!

You sound like someone who's learned from every life experience, and taken away lessons from every role you've played. Looking back at your career, is there something you learned while making *America 3000* that you still follow to this day?

I do try my best to meet all of life's challenges with grit, grace and gratitude. I often share a motivational message with my students. In life, everything we learn we learn by failing, but we must not see ourselves as failures. Celebrate the lessons learned, keep pursuing your dreams until you prevail . . . become a "Prevailure!"

As we learned making the film, work with what you are given and do the best you can. Treat everyone at every level with love, respect, and appreciation, and try to always leave the world a bit better than you found it.

And as for the crazy world we live in today, it may seem a bit "woggos," but if you look closely, you will see it is actually still "Hot Plastic!" Thanks for including me in this retrospective, and thanks to Golan and Globus for letting me be a part of this crazy legacy.

A publicity still from *America 3000*, which as of publication featured the largest all-female cavalry charge in cinema history.

P.O.W. The Escape on VHS. This copy was formerly rented out by The Movie Hut in Gilbert, West Virginia.

P.O.W. The Escape

Release Date: April 4, 1986
Directed by: Gideon Amir
Written by: Gideon Amir & Avi Kleinberger (story), Jeremy Lipp, James Bruner, Malcolm Barber & John Langley (screenplay)
Starring: David Carradine, Steve James, Charles R. Floyd, Mako
Trailer Voiceover: "The prisoner they couldn't hold is now the soldier they can't stop!"

By this point in their run, Cannon had already released their definitive film about a one-man-army leading an escape from a Vietnamese prisoner of war camp—the film was 1984's *Missing in Action*, which had been one of the company's all-time biggest hits, and had anointed Chuck Norris as a bankable box office draw. That movie's awkwardly-titled prequel, *Missing in Action II: The Beginning* (1985), followed a similar idea, but didn't bring home the same amount of box office bacon.

However, when *Rambo: First Blood Part II* (1985)—the second installment of another franchise with confusing sequel titles—made about a bazillion dollars for Tri-Star a few months later using the same premise, it proved that perhaps the well for P.O.W. rescue mission movies had not yet run dry. Thus, it's unsurprising that Cannon decided to take a third dive into this particularly niche action subgenre, and send yet another super-soldier deep into the Vietnamese jungle to bring home a few more of his enlisted countrymen.

This time around, David Carradine was recruited for the rescue mission. The eldest Carradine kid—son of John and brother of Keith, who had already made their Cannon debuts in *House of the Long Shadows* (1983) and *Maria's Lovers* (1985), respectively—was midway between his career highs of playing the hero of TV's *Kung Fu* (1972–1975) and the titular villain of Quentin Tarantino's *Kill Bill* movies (2003/2004). By this point, he was mired in a lull which saw him appearing in numerous, low-budget genre films throughout the 1980s. He was available when Cannon came calling.

P.O.W. The Escape (1986) marked producer Gideon Amir's first time in the director's chair. After receiving his degree from Tel Aviv University, Amir spent a few years creating documentaries and dramas for educational television. In 1975, he partnered up with co-producer Avi Kleinberger to start their own company, which produced a number of acclaimed Israeli films over the next decade. Eventually they offered their services to other companies looking to shoot films in Tel Aviv, which is how they hooked up with Golan and Globus and wound up co-producing *The Ambassador* (1985), on which Amir also served as First Assistant Director. That film's director, J. Lee Thompson, made an offhand compliment to Menahem Golan that Amir was the best A.D. he'd ever worked with—which Golan took very literally. This ensured that he fed Amir and Kleinberger a steady stream of work over the next few years.

Amir was sent to the Philippines to work on *Missing in Action* (1984) and then briefly to Zimbabwe to help J. Lee Thompson prepare for *King Solomon's Mines* (1985) before he was called back and then sent, again, to the Philippines—this time, for a movie to be called *American Ninja* (1985). It was Amir and Kleinberger who came up with that movie's premise and characters, which earned them a story credit on the film. (The only instruction that Golan gave them was the now-famous adage, "Only a ninja can kill a ninja"—apparently, that was all you needed to know before you were allowed to make a Cannon ninja movie.)

When Cannon sent Amir to the Philippines for a third time, it was as a director. Amir and Kleinberger had the idea to make a Western, but set during the Vietnam War. The idea for *P.O.W. The Escape* began as sort of a pseudo-remake of the Gary Cooper and Burt Lancaster Western *Vera Cruz* (1954), about a gang of gunslingers who are hired by the Emperor of Mexico to escort a Countess (and a secret stash of gold) to the titular city on the Gulf Coast.

A famously stoic individual, David Carradine feels like a natural stepping into the stone-faced super-soldier role, barking patriotic one-liners and assuming authority in increasingly lopsided combat situations. (Given that he's a Cannon hero, you can assume that when the bad guys outnumber him ten to one, it isn't a fair fight for the bad guys.) While most of his damage is dished out via guns and grenades, Carradine squeezes in one soldier versus soldier martial arts battle to show off a little bit of his old *Kung Fu* training.

Carradine plays Colonel James Cooper, a high-ranking army badass who specializes in special missions and whose personal motto is "Everybody goes home." Set near the end of the Vietnam War, Cooper is dispatched by the Pentagon to recover a group of American prisoners and send a message to the communists that his country is not one to be screwed with. Shit hits the fan, though, as soon as Cooper and his team touch ground in Vietnam. His vow that everybody goes home goes out the window when pretty much everybody is killed instead. Everybody, that is, except for Cooper, who is imprisoned alongside the P.O.W.s he was sent to save.

There are two unexpected elements which shake up the standard escape plot. The first is that the Vietnamese Captain Vinh, who oversees the prisoner of war camp, secretly wants to sneak out of the country to live with his family in Florida. He strikes a deal with Cooper wherein he'll help the POWs escape, so long as Cooper sneaks him out of the country with them. The *Vera Cruz*-ian twist arises when it's revealed that Vinh is smuggling with him a footlocker full of gold that he confiscated from American prisoners. It's a treasure that one slimy, American G.I. named Sparks will do anything—including sacrifice his fellow soldiers—to have all for himself.

A sales ad for *P.O.W. The Escape* under its alternate title. The movie was also released in some home video versions as *Attack Force 'Nam.*

Captain Vinh is played by the prolific Japanese-American actor, Mako, a recognizable face from both b-movies and blockbusters alike. Mako played a wizard in Arnold Schwarzenegger's first two Conan the Barbarian movies, and co-starred opposite Chuck Norris in both *An Eye for an Eye* (1981) and *Sidekicks* (1992), but long before any of these he'd earned a Best Supporting Actor Oscar nomination for his role in *The Sand Pebbles* (1966). Sparks is played by Charles R. Floyd, a favorite actor of Menahem Golan, who also found roles for him in *Rappin'* (1985, as Charles Flohe) and *The Delta Force*

(1986, as Charles Floye). He'd go on to appear in numerous soap operas under the name Charles Grant.

Cooper is forced to improvise when his escape plan falls apart, thanks in no small part to the traitors in their midst. His "everybody goes home" motto once proves a hard promise to keep, as more and more of his men are killed, but he does eventually replenish his forces with new POWs that he frees along their way. Meanwhile, a game of cat-and-mouse unfolds between the dastardly Sparks and the equally dastardly Vinh, who can't seem to sort out where the stolen gold has disappeared to. (Surprise, bad guys! Captain America Cooper has hidden it away, and plans to turn it in to the authorities once they get back to headquarters.)

Cooper and his gang of gung-ho patriots lay waste to innumerable Viet Cong as they hightail their way out of the country. It's the same sort of rah-rah America, high body count, pyrotechnic floor show that Chuck Norris would have been right at home in, had he not already been gainfully employed by Cannon elsewhere. At one point David Carradine removes a large machine gun from its tripod stand and mows down countless enemy soldiers on his way to rescue a tattered American flag, which he then proceeds to drape around his shoulder like a cape. As the POWs make their final escape in a U.S. chopper, it's scored to an electric guitar version of "The Star-Spangled Banner."

P.O.W. The Escape is a perfectly enjoyable piece of mid-tier Cannon action. Carradine does a lot of the heavy lifting, bringing a lot of charisma to his one-dimensional hero role. It's the sort of movie best watched on the Fourth of July, preferably with a cold can of Budweiser in your hand.

There are plenty more familiar faces for Cannon amongst the movie's many soldiers. Amir was allowed to bring with him two of his favorite *American Ninja* co-stars: the great Steve James—who plays Johnston, and whom Amir had invited to audition for Cannon after seeing him in a small role in *Mask* (1985)—and Phil Brock, who plays Adams (and also appeared in 1985's *Thunder Alley*). Daniel Demorest, who plays Thomas, would reappear in *Number One with a Bullet* (1987) and *Platoon Leader* (1988)—the same two films actor Tony Pierce ("Waite") would also return for. Meanwhile, for James Acheson ("McCoy"), this came as part of a run of four straight Cannon movies, which also included *Invaders from Mars* (1986), *Assassination* (1987), and *The Hanoi Hilton* (1987). The movie's many stunts were coordinated by the always-trustworthy Steve Lambert, by then a veteran of many Cannon productions.

Early in production, footage was shipped back to Los Angeles from the Philippines so that Cannon could get an early look at what they were paying for. Seeing these previews, Menahem Golan called up Gideon Amir to complain: "I ordered a Volkswagen. You're giving me a Mercedes Benz!" It was his way of ordering them to trim the budget.

When he saw an early cut of the full film, however, Golan was unhappy with Carradine's role. Apparently the character showed too much hesitation and depth, when what Golan wanted was a relentless commie-killing machine. He personally sat with Amir for several days in the editing room, making sure that all of these excess layers were removed from the movie's hero.

What remained of the film was more than a little disjointed. Screenwriter James Bruner—of *Missing in Action, Invasion U.S.A.* (1985), *The Delta Force*, and *Braddock: Missing in Action III* (1988) fame—was brought on late to rewrite the script after shooting was finished. He was tasked with filling in various plot holes, knowing that Cannon only had Carradine for one day of shooting new material in a single location which wasn't even in the Philippines.

Gideon Amir only directed one more film, but went back to television where he's worked as a very successful producer on many different television series. Two of the movie's screenwriters, Malcolm Barber and John Langley, would go on to create the long-running reality television series, *COPS* (1989–2020), for the Fox network. (As in, "Bad boys, bad boys, whatchu gonna do? Whatchu gonna do when they come for you?")

P.O.W. The Escape did well enough on video and in foreign territories that Cannon profited from it, but it didn't make anywhere near what a similar

Chuck Norris film would have. And of all the various titling conundrums in Cannon's catalog, this movie's may be the most confusing. Some early versions bear the title *Behind Enemy Lines*, not to be confused with the more famous 2001 movie starring Owen Wilson and Gene Hackman. More recent reissues have been put out under the name *Attack Force NAM*, presumably to avoid conflict with the 2001 film. For our purposes, we'll stick with *P.O.W. The Escape*, which was the film's video title, and was by far the version most people have seen.

The French poster for *P.O.W. The Escape*, or "In the Arms of Hell," with artwork by Jean Mascii.

Murphy's Law on VHS. "There's only one law Jack Murphy doesn't blow to smithereens: Murphy's Law!"

Murphy's Law

Release Date: April 18, 1986
Directed by: J. Lee Thompson
Written by: Gail Morgan Hickman
Starring: Charles Bronson, Kathleen Wilhoite, Carrie Snodgress
Trailer Voiceover: "He's a renegade cop. For years he's made his own rules. But now, he's been set up. The cops want him convicted, the mob wants him dead, and the only one who doesn't want him . . . is handcuffed to him!"

There's an old adage known as Murphy's Law, which famously states: "Whatever can go wrong, will go wrong."

Jack Murphy, an end-of-his-wire L.A. cop, doesn't believe in Murphy's Law. The only version he believes in is *Jack* Murphy's Law, which plainly states: "*Don't fuck* with Jack Murphy."

The venerable Charles Bronson teamed up with Cannon for the fourth time in *Murphy's Law* (1986), this time as a character not all that different from the homicide detective he played in the earlier *10 to Midnight* (1983). Jack Murphy's a lot worse for wear, however: a newly divorced and reckless alcoholic, Murphy spends his time off the clock drinking far too much and stalking his stripper ex-wife, played by cult actress Angel Tompkins, who appeared in both of Cannon's *The Naked Cage* and *Dangerously Close* this very same year.

It doesn't take long before things go from bad to worse for poor Murphy. Unbeknownst to him, there's a dangerous mystery woman on his trail. She holds a nasty grudge against the old, drunk cop for reasons we'll learn before the film is through.

The rampaging woman is named Joan Freeman, and she's played by Carrie Snodgress, a fine actress who'd earned an Academy Award nomination for her starring role in *Diary of a Mad Housewife* (1970). She left acting for much of the 1970s to care for the son she had with rocker Neil Young, whose song "A Man Needs a Maid" was written about her. The private eye she murders in *Murphy's Law* is played by Lawrence Tierney, a classic "tough guy" actor from Hollywood's golden age who'd have a bigger role in Cannon's *Tough Guys Don't Dance* (1987), but is perhaps best-remembered now for his end-of-career role as a crime boss in 1992's *Reservoir Dogs*.

This mean-as-nails woman guns down Murphy's ex-wife and her lover, then frames Murphy for the murder. Murphy suddenly finds himself not only behind bars, but handcuffed to the wonderfully-named Arabella McGee, a foul-mouthed car thief with a talent for conjuring up colorful slurs.

Although she'd previously appeared in a small handful of movies and TV shows, *Murphy's Law* proudly boasts an "Introducing . . ." credit for actress/musician Kathleen Wilhoite, who counts the bona fide classic *Road House* (1989) and a recurring role on TV's *E.R.* among her more than one hundred screen appearances. She'd soon return to Cannon again with a role in *Under Cover* (1987).

Murphy cunningly escapes from his jail cell and goes on the run from his former police colleagues, all while Arabella is chained to him by the wrist and hurling nonstop, nonsensical insults in his direction. By the time they reach safety, this previously-acrimonious odd couple have warmed up to one another, and Arabella decides to tag along and help him clear his name.

Murphy's Law was directed by J. Lee Thompson as his fourth feature for Cannon—his sixth with Bronson to this point—having recently high-tailed it away from the wilds of Zimbabwe on *King Solomon's Mines* (1985), having chosen to shoot this film over that movie's sequel. The screenplay came from writer Gail Morgan Hickman, who had been hired by Cannon to write multiple drafts of *Death Wish 3* (1985), all of which were ultimately canned. (Hickman did wind up writing 1987's *Death Wish 4: The Crackdown*, as well as that same year's *Number One with a Bullet* for Cannon.)

Charles Bronson finds himself handcuffed to foul-mouthed car thief Arabella (Kathleen Wilhoite) in *Murphy's Law.*

The movie's genuinely bitchin' musical score was composed by Marc Donahue and Bronson's stepson, Val McCallum: it's overflowing with unmistakably '80s guitar solos and synth tones, and may be one of Cannon's most criminally overlooked film soundtracks. The ending theme features vocals from co-star Wilhoite, who also penned the song's lyrics. It seems that having a dual threat actor-musician play the female lead opposite Bronson may have always been the filmmakers' intention for *Murphy's Law*: before offering Wilhoite the role, the producers had considered rocker Joan Jett, burgeoning pop icon Madonna, and Apollonia Kotero, who was best known for playing Prince's love interest in 1984's *Purple Rain*. (Jett was rejected due to lack of acting experience, and Madonna asked for a higher fee than Cannon was willing to pay.) It's hard to imagine that any of them could have consistently called Charles Bronson crazy names like "camel crotch" with as much gusto as Wilhoite was able to muster.

Arabella's bizarre potty mouth is one of the things that viewers often remember most about *Murphy's Law*. A large portion of her lines are punctuated with off-the-cuff slurs aimed at Murphy and other cops, which run the gamut from gross ("scrotum cheeks," "dildo nose," "jizzum breath") to goofy ("monkey vomit," "dinosaur dork," and "snot-licking donkey fart.") In early versions of the script, her character used more commonplace, sensible profanities, but for one reason or another the script was altered during shooting to the more colorful phrases we hear in the film. The results are a nonstop barrage of scatological gobbledygook.

Murphy and Arabella's adventures take them to several unexpected places, such as a hidden marijuana processing center in the California countryside. (One of the dope-dealing bikers is played by another of Bronson's stepsons, Paul McCallum.) They hide out with Murphy's former partner (jazz singer Bill Henderson), interrogate a vengeful mob boss (Richard Romanus), and eventually call in a big favor from Murphy's last remaining friend on the police force. (The actor, Robert F. Lyons, was hand-picked by Bronson for the role—he also appears in Cannon's *Death Wish II*, 1982, *10 to Midnight*, 1983, and *Platoon Leader*, 1988.)

All of this finally leads them to a big showdown at Los Angeles' landmark Bradbury Building, famous for its open design, wrought-iron railings, glass ceiling and M.C. Escher-like system of stairs and balconies. If it feels like you've seen the place before, you have: the Bradbury Building has been used as a shooting location in dozens and dozens of films and television shows since the dawn of cinema, most notably as the home of J.F. Sebastian in

1982's *Blade Runner*. It was an especially popular location for film noirs, and was also used in *Chinatown* (1974), *Lethal Weapon 4* (1998), and Best Picture-winner *The Artist* (2011), along with more TV shows and music videos than we can list. The building houses one of the most popular interior settings in all of Hollywood.

Among all of Bronson's eight Cannon films, *Murphy's Law* ranks somewhere in the middle of the pack as a more-than-competent thriller which lacks the individuality of *10 to Midnight*, and is missing the over-the-top action found in the better *Death Wish* sequels. Critics of the time weren't very fond of the movie, but they didn't particularly like *any* of Bronson's '80s movies, either—and bad reviews rarely stopped the films from making a fair amount of money. *Murphy's Law* did well enough at the springtime box office, bringing home almost $10 million in the U.S. and making it Cannon's third-biggest release of 1986, behind only *The Delta Force* and *Firewalker*.

Arabella (Kathleen Wilhoite) and Murphy (Charles Bronson) survive a chopper crash in *Murphy's Law*.

Interview: Actress Kathleen Wilhoite

Kathleen Wilhoite had been a singer-songwriter for years before acting became a focus of her career. She made her film debut in the teen sex comedy *Private School* (1983), which co-starred one of Cannon's favored leading ladies, Sylvia Kristel, before landing her breakout role opposite Charles Bronson in the Golan-Globus produced thriller *Murphy's Law* (1986). From then onward she became a regular player on our television screens, appearing in *Witchboard* (1986), Cannon's own *Under Cover* (1987), *Twin Peaks* (1990–1991), and *Color of Night* (1994). All the while, she continued to follow her muse as a musician, performing in the Patrick Swayze video classic *Road House* (1989) and releasing her first album, *Pitch Like a Girl*, in 1997.

Wilhoite remains busy in both mediums, as an actor and musician, and works as a professor of the dramatic arts through her own Wilhoite School of Drama, as well as CalArts and California State University Long Beach.

You were already a performing musician by the time you landed in *Murphy's Law*. I'm curious which passion you discovered first: acting, or music?

Kathleen Wilhoite: In Santa Barbara where I grew up, I did musicals in the summer, so singing was always intermingled with acting in my mind. In fact, I used to look at acting as just something you did between songs, and then when I was in high school I had an acting teacher named Rick Mokler who was a game changer for me. He basically taught me how to act and gave me the confidence I needed to pursue acting as a career. He also instilled a passion for the craft in my soul that I haven't quite been able to shake all these years.

You'd done smaller screen roles before this, but *Murphy's Law* was your first lead. Can you tell me about your audition process for the movie?

I remember it was between me and Apollonia—Prince's protégé at the time. I remember feeling very supported by Jill Ireland. I remember feeling joyful about the audition process. I loved playing tough "street" chicks.

I loved dancing around in my secret, tomboy world. I know "tomboy" is a bad word now, but for me it was how I identified myself. I was also on a bit of a roll at the time. I had an excellent manager who saw to it that I went from project to project, so my audition for this film was just one among many.

I remember feeling overjoyed when I got the role, and then I got the rewrite of the script. I definitely had some problems with the weird name-calling stuff. I wanted to be someone who had a horrible mouth in a very realistic way, but obviously they "went another way with it," and I had to do my best to make it work.

You were at the start of your career, while Charles Bronson had been acting for nearly forty years by this time. Was it intimidating to work with him?

I remember having to have a meeting with the director and producers before my first day of work, where they outlined for me how best to deal with Charlie. I remember them saying that I shouldn't try to make small talk with him; that if we had a conversation, it was best if he initiated it. They told me he didn't like it when people stared at him. Oh, and they told me not to try too hard to make him like me, or to try to be funny around him, that he doesn't like that.

So, on the first day of the shoot, we had a long car scene. I just kept my mouth shut the whole time. Eventually, and I would say rather quickly, he warmed up to me and was sweet as hell. We chitchatted all the time, and I can't help but be funny sometimes. I'm a goofy person. Unfortunately, most of the time I don't know when I'm being funny, which maybe helped in this circumstance.

J. Lee Thompson was another person who had nearly half a century's worth of experience working in film. How do you recall him, as a director?

J. Lee was amazing. Fun, smart, funny, a great director, generous. Here's a weird thing that I remember vividly: his wife had the softest hands I had ever felt. Staggeringly soft. Softer than the arch of my husband's foot.

I know that your character's language was originally written as more "traditionally" foul, and you found the re-written lines a bit tough to chew on. Can you tell me how you were eventually able to power through lines like "suck a doorknob" and "kiss my panty hose"?

I came from an acting school that taught me that I had to start to build my character by paying attention to what was written on the page. The writer was at the top of the heap in terms of the hierarchy of the work. I was disappointed by the rewrites, and was much more excited when the character was written as "traditionally foul" (nice way to phrase it, by the way)—but my job as an actor is to be a marionette. The script is the strings, and the director and DP are the guys in the rafters making the thing dance. I wasn't in a place where I could call the shots. It wasn't up to me. I did what was put in front of me.

What's one of your favorite memories from the set?

Carrie Snodgress taught me how to break down my script. That was a gift I will carry with me always. She was my friend. I loved her.

I adored it when Charlie was fed up with the futzing and puttering that goes on on a film set before a scene. He'd say, "Let's shooooooooooot," and it would crack everyone up. I had a blast with the guns and the squibs. I loved the crew, and we all hung out a lot after a long days' shoot.

Is there a scene you're most proud of?

Uhhhh, not much. Wouldn't say that it was my finest work. Ha!

You co-wrote and sang the movie's ending theme song. Can you tell me how that opportunity came together?

I'm a songwriter. I've written songs for years. Jill Ireland's sons were in charge of the music. I remember feeling like I got in the way of a sibling rivalry. Val [McCallum] is one of the best guitar players and singers I've ever worked with to this day. He's brilliant, but he was somehow on the other side of this competition as to who would land the coveted end credit song spot. We ended up getting it.

Uh . . . again, I wouldn't say it's the greatest song I've ever written. Also, they had us put all the lyrics up in front, and there was a lot of meddling with the structure of the song. I'm not a fan of non-songwriters giving their two dumb cents in on how a song should go. So, that was a drag.

Cannon made _Under Cover_ just a year after _Murphy's Law_. Was there any connection between your castings in these two movies?

No. John [Stockwell], the director, was my friend. We did _Quarterback Princess_ (1983) together. He cast me. I wasn't aware of the connection outside of getting a bigger break on landing the end credit song slot.

For Cannon, _Murphy's Law_ was a vehicle for one of their biggest stars, helmed by one of their most prolific directors. On the other hand, _Under Cover_ was a smaller thriller helmed by a first-time filmmaker. Did the two productions feel very different, from your perspective?

Again, I had an excellent manager at the time that enabled me to go from job to job, so I wasn't aware of any connection. To me, it was about taking the ride. _Murphy's Law_ shot in LA and _Under Cover_ shot in Slidell and New Orleans. I had an excruciating crush on an actor in that film, so, honestly, when I think about that, all that comes to mind was my endless pining and moping around the French Quarter, sobbing into my Hurricane, muttering about how no one was ever going to love me. It was a little pathetic, honestly. Thank God we grow out of those phases. That actor on that shoot is now a good friend of mine. My crush on him, in retrospect, seems ludicrous. Yaaaaaay for time and its ability to heal wounds.

Your role here was smaller than the one in _Murphy's Law_, obviously, but do you have any memories from working on it that you remain particularly fond of?

Again, it was a pretty pathetic time in my history. I was, as they say now, a "hot mess." I'm glad I lived to tell the tale of what an idiot I was.

I once saw you mention that you had a development deal with Menahem Golan at Cannon. Can you tell me what that entailed, and about any memories you have of him?

Oh, the opportunities I've squandered away. Opportunities are wasted on the young. At the time, all I wanted to be was a rock star. I remember they showed me movies all the time in their private theater. We saw *Breakfast at Tiffany's* (1961), we saw a bunch of Shirley MacLaine movies.

It seems like for many other multi-hyphenate musician-actors, one of those things eventually becomes secondary, but you've maintained a focus on both throughout your career. I look at a year like 1997, where you released an album while appearing in five different TV and film roles, not to mention voicing the main character on the cartoon *Pepper Ann* (1997–2000). How do you balance two creative passions?

Jack of all trades, master of none. Sad but true. I consider myself to be a blue-collar actress. I work when I can. I write music because I have to, and now I spend all my free time writing plays and movies. I haven't had a series of "wins" like I had back then. There just hasn't been the same amount of wind beneath my wings. Here's the good part about being an artist, though. That doesn't stop me. I just keep doing it, and I'll probably continue to chase down ideas until the day I die. It is what I live for. So, yeah, I keep hoping for the day I'll get to see some of my ideas up on the screen or stage—we'll see.

You built a resume that's more than one hundred film and TV appearances strong. In addition to your continued film and TV appearances and writing music, you also teach acting. Do you draw from your own experiences when working with your students?

That's all I do. I teach them what to do and what not to do from my experience. I come at teaching acting from the perspective that the only person that gets to tell you whether you can or cannot do it is you. As long as you continue to create, you win. It's nicer when you get paid to do it. It's incredible when you can make a living at it, but you're the only one who can quit, a.k.a. leave the party before the bus load of rock stars show up.

For a while, British movie-goers could get complimentary tickets to select Cannon cinemas with the purchase of beer. This promotion coincided with the U.K. release of *Murphy's Law*, meaning you could see it over and over again for free, if you drank enough.

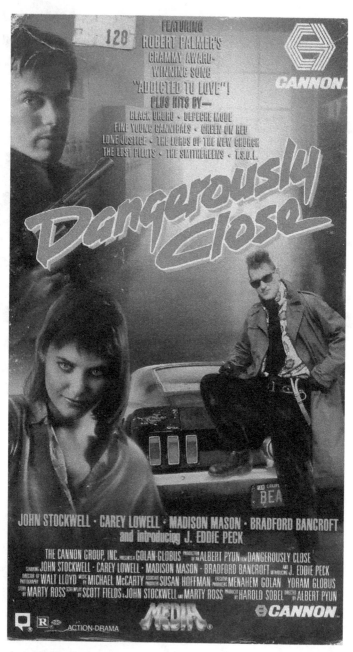

For their VHS release of *Dangerously Close*, Cannon heavily promoted the film on the strength of its soundtrack.

Dangerously Close

Release Date: May 9, 1986
Directed by: Albert Pyun
Written by: Scott Fields, Marty Ross, and John Stockwell
Starring: J. Eddie Peck, John Stockwell, Carey Lowell
Trailer Voiceover: "At Vista High, in the name of justice, some students are getting away with murder. He's searching for answers. Now, he's getting close . . . *Dangerously Close!*"

When the super-swanky Vista Verde high school launches a magnet program which introduces poor kids into the student body, the entire campus social order is thrown into chaos. A circle of preppy, rich kids take it upon themselves to form a vigilante group known as the Sentinels, who at night hunt down the outcasts and minorities among their classmates to teach them violent lessons about fitting in to their new, upper-class surroundings.

We all know the standard hierarchy of high school movies—where rich kids lord over the poor kids, and if ever the two dare mix, the clashing cliques come together about as well as fire and gasoline. *Dangerously Close* takes that old, standby setup and peppers in a dash of *The Most Dangerous Game* (1932).

Try to imagine *Pretty in Pink* (1986), but where Andrew McCarthy and his preppy pals hunt and kill Molly Ringwald and Jon Cryer for sport.

It's up to our hero, Danny, the first wealth-impaired student to cross over into the Sentinels' upper crust ranks, to blow the lid off their dastardly doings and find out just who among them is responsible for the disappearance of several of his classmates.

Dangerously Close is most notable for being the movie that brought film-maker Albert Pyun into the Cannon fold. A Hawaiian native who spent his childhood bouncing between military bases, Pyun moved to Japan at the age of eighteen and—thanks to some support from the legendary samurai movie star Toshiro Mifune—honed his filmmaking skills under the tutelage of Takao Saito, Akira Kurosawa's longtime cinematographer.

Pyun returned to the United States and made commercials until he was able to find financing for his debut feature, the appropriately-titled sword and sorcery film *The Sword and the Sorcerer*. The R-rated fantasy movie was a surprise hit, making a name for its young director as one of the most exciting new genre filmmakers. Next came the stylish *Radioactive Dreams* (1985), a post-apocalyptic film noir that included early starring roles for future Cannon stars Michael Dudikoff and John Stockwell. Pyun's unique vision, and his ability to craft compelling fantasy worlds from shoe-string budgets no doubt brought him to the attention of Golan and Globus, who made him into one of their most frequent collaborators. At Cannon, Pyun would direct *Dangerously Close*, *Down Twisted* (1987), *Alien from L.A.* (1988), and *Cyborg* (1989), and do a significant amount of uncredited work on the problem-plagued *Journey to the Center of the Earth* (1988) when its original director, Rusty Lemorande, was unable to finish the project. (During this time he was also the third director attached to their canceled Spider-Man project.) Pyun then followed Golan to 21st Century Film Corporation after his breakup with Cannon, directing *Deceit* (1990), *Bloodmatch* (1991), and the notorious Marvel Comics adaptation *Captain America* (1990) for him there.

Dangerously Close opens with a jarring and unsettling scene. In it several masked, armed men chase down a scrawny teenager, eventually ensnaring him in a trap that leaves him dangling upside-down from a tree. These scary, anonymous fascists make threats, hold a gun to his head, and pull the trigger—only to reveal that it's just a paintball gun. They cut him down with a warning (and a homophobic slur), but as they're driving away he tosses a rock at their leader's car. The shadowy figure hops out of the vehicle, chases the boy into a creek, and slashes his throat.

The next morning we're introduced to brainy senior Danny Lennox (J. Eddie Peck), who cleans swimming pools with his dad to help pay their bills. At school, he's a star student and the editor of the newspaper; unfortunately, he's from the wrong side of the tracks, which puts him solidly in the affluent school's lower social stratum.

His student newspaper has just published a scathing criticism of the Sentinels, a group of preppies and jocks who volunteer to monitor the campus grounds and clean up vandalism in the name of school pride. Their leader, Randy (co-writer John Stockwell), objects to being called a vigilante group, and submits a rebuttal, which Danny agrees to publish. This scores him some brownie points with the Sentinels, particularly Randy, who invites him over for dinner and a night on the town that involves drinking too much, thwarting an honest-to-goodness assassination attempt on Randy's life at a local nightclub, and then driving into the hood to exchange gunfire with a classmate who allegedly spray-painted the school's gymnasium.

Now, *that's* a night out.

Against his better judgment, Danny continues his new friendship with the school's cool clique because he's smitten with Randy's girlfriend, Julie (Carey Lowell, in her screen debut.) This is a big disappointment for Danny's punker best friend, Krooger (Bradford Bancroft), who drives around in a janky, customized Mustang. Jealous that his buddy is spending so much time with the rich "Twinkies," Krooger has the audacity to lash out at the

Sentinels, who in return make him the newest prey in their game—their *most dangerous* game.

Of course, Krooger turns up missing the very next day. Danny's forced to reassess his new friendship if he wants to get to the bottom of what happened to his old pal. Coincidentally, Julie's grown tired of her boyfriend's bratty, spoiled behavior and joins Danny in his mission to find out which of the Sentinels is taking their "game" too far. Is one of the gang members responsible for the murders? And just how involved is Mr. Corrigan—a school faculty member who is so close with the cool clique that he hangs out with them at night clubs, and throws down with them during their brawls with other students—in their crimes? As you'd imagine, things get more than a little hairy as Danny closes in on the secretive group, and it's not long before his own life is in danger.

Our heroes, played by J. Eddie Peck and Carey Lowell, in a publicity still from *Dangerously Close*.

That cast of *Dangerously Close* is well-stocked with actors who went on to big things. The nefarious Randy was played by John Stockwell, who as an actor is best known for his roles as Dennis in *Christine* (1983) and Cougar in *Top Gun* (1986). He'd soon transition behind the camera, making his directorial debut on Cannon's own *Under Cover* (1987), going on to a prolific filmmaking career that includes films like *Blue Crush* (2002), *Into the Blue* (2005), and *Kickboxer: Vengeance* (2016). He wrote *Dangerously Close*—then titled "Choice Kill"—as a way of fighting boredom during his downtime while acting in the TV miniseries *North and South* (1985).

Randy's girlfriend, Julie, was played by Carey Lowell, who next starred in Pyun's follow-up movie for Cannon, *Down Twisted*, and went on to fame as Bond girl Pam Bouvier in *License to Kill* (1989).

Our lead actor, J. Eddie Peck, went on to become a soap opera regular, but not before taking on another starring role in Cannon's *Lambada* (1990), not to be confused with 21st Century Film's *The Forbidden Dance is Lambada* (1990), co-written and produced by Menahem Golan and released on the same day. His punker buddy, Krooger, is played by Bradford Bancroft, who was one of Tom Hanks' chums (alongside Michael Dudikoff) in *Bachelor Party* (1984).

Randy's main cronies are the violent, unhinged Ripper and the more sensitive, wary Brian. Ripper was played by Don Michael Paul, who went on to have roles in Pyun's Cannon follow-ups, *Down Twisted* and *Alien from L.A.*, and is now a writer-director whose work includes the Steven Seagal vehicle *Half Past Dead* (2002). Thom Mathews, who plays Brian, is another Pyun regular and has appeared in many of the director's films, most notably as *Alien from L.A.*'s roguish Charmin'. Another Sentinel stooge, Lane, is played by Gerard Christopher, credited under the name Jerry DiNome, who would later don tights and a red cape to star in CBS's *Superboy* (1989–1992) for four seasons.

Anthony De Longis, who would soon play Blades in Cannon's *Masters of the Universe* (1987), returns here as Smith Raddock after appearing in Pyun's *The Sword and the Sorcerer*. Playing Ms. Hoffman we have Debra Berger, a Cannon mainstay—she can also be seen doing a sex scene with her real-life stepsister, Katya Berger, in Cannon's *Nana* (1983), and in movies such as

Invaders from Mars and *52 Pick-Up* (both 1986), and the Cannon-distributed *Lightning, the White Stallion* (1986). Her father was William Berger, the villainous King Minos in Cannon's two Hercules movies.

Despite a small handful of middling to fairly decent reviews, *Dangerously Close* was a non-starter when it hit movie theaters. You have to guess that there was some challenge in marketing a movie about high schoolers that, because of its R rating, most high school students wouldn't have been able to get into.

It also probably didn't help that the cast appeared to be pretty long in the tooth to be playing teenagers. While it has long been a standard Hollywood practice to cast adults in teenage roles, there's not a single actor in this movie who would have been asked for an ID if they tried to purchase a six-pack of beer and a fifth of Jack Daniels. Stockwell, the youngest-looking of the young men, was twenty-four years old when the movie was shot. Peck, our hero, was twenty-six but looked closer to thirty. (Most of the cast were also models, which only adds to a weird disconnect where no one on-screen looks anything like a real-world teen.) Given that *Dangerously Close* was released during the peak era of the brat pack and John Hughes comedies, audiences were accustomed to seeing teenagers played by actual teens.

Of course, Pyun was able to inject the project with some of his usual, high-end visual flair—the opening murder occurs as a stylish splash of slow motion and bold lighting set to opera music. The school hallways are frequently lit more like a classic film noir than any Eighties teen thriller you'll ever see.

It's worth noting, too, that *Dangerously Close* had a really rocking soundtrack album. The vinyl and cassette put out by Enigma Records was led by the single "Blood and Roses," from New Jersey power pop band The Smithereens. (The accompanying music video, featured on MTV's *120 Minutes*, cut together footage of the band with clips from the movie.) The record also featured tracks from punk acts T.S.O.L. and Lords of the New Church, reggae stalwarts Black Uhuru, alt-country predecessors Green on Red, and Deborah Hanan's Lost Pilots, who appear as themselves in the film during its nightclub scene. Also included in the film—but not on the tie-in album—are tunes by Depeche Mode, Fine Young Cannibals, and Robert Palmer. (The song, of course, being his ever-present '80s karaoke hit "Addicted to Love.")

With its eclectic pop soundtrack and cool looks, Pyun came close to crafting a classic thriller for the MTV Generation. Ultimately, the R-rating—crossed with the weirdness of watching full-grown adults pretending to be teenagers—was probably its undoing.

Interview: Actress Carey Lowell

Having begun her career as a successful fashion model, Carey Lowell spent the early Eighties modelling for Calvin Klein and Ralph Lauren, and appearing on the covers of such magazines as *Vogue*, *Glamour*, and *Mademoiselle*. When she crossed paths with Cannon, however, her attention shifted towards the silver screen.

After being cast in leading roles in two Albert Pyun features—*Dangerously Close* (1986) and *Down Twisted* (1987)—Lowell would next be seen opposite Griffin Dunne in *Me and Him* (1988) and then as Bond girl Pam Bouvier in *License to Kill* (1989), Timothy Dalton's last entry as the British spy. Later roles include a part in Nora Ephron's *Sleepless in Seattle* (1993) and playing attorney Jamie Ross on *Law & Order* (1990–2010) and its spin-offs.

You initially moved to New York for your modeling career, and there studied at the famed Neighborhood Playhouse School of Theatre. Do you recall an experience that drew you into acting?

Carey Lowell: I studied with William Alderson, who was a teacher at Neighborhood Playhouse, not at the Playhouse itself. I was modeling when I got an audition for *Club Paradise* (1986). They were looking for a girl in a bathing suit for Rick Moranis and Eugene Levy to hit on. My audition line was, "You got anything to smoke?" I got the part, ended up in Jamaica for many months on the shoot, had a ball and thought that this was something I wanted to do more of.

Carey Lowell in a publicity still for her second Cannon film, *Down Twisted*.

Our cast was amazing: Peter O'Toole, Robin Williams, Twiggy, Jimmy Cliff, Andrea Robinson, not to mention the hilarious Rick and Eugene. The wonderful Harold Ramis was the director. It was a wonderful introduction to Hollywood moviemaking.

Club Paradise shot before Dangerously Close but was released after, so at that point you might still have been considered "undiscovered" as an actor.

What do you remember of your audition and that process for *Dangerously Close*?

The audition was in Culver City, on a lot I can't remember the name of. There were a bunch of young people my age, and we were teamed up with a partner to read with for Albert Pyun. He was like a Hawaiian surfer dude, very kind and encouraging. I got the part and then I met John Stockwell, who was one of the writers and also the star.

Do you feel that your prior experience in front of cameras, as a model, made your transition to screen acting any easier? Were you nervous here, in your first big role?

I was nervous, but Albert made it all very painless. We shot a lot of nights, which was the hardest part.

Being in front of a camera as a model is almost harder for me, as you know it's there and you're usually required to look at it. In filmmaking you can ignore the camera and just act—or "lie truthfully," as it has been described.

What do you recall of working with Albert Pyun? How would you describe him, as a director?

Albert was very energetic, very engaging, fun, and light, but also very focused. He cared a lot about the music, and the mood of the scenes. He was very kind and supportive of me.

***Dangerously Close* seemed a bit ahead of its time, with visuals that were closer to what we'd see in MTV music videos than in other teen thrillers of the period. Do you remember what you thought of the movie when you finally saw it?**

I thought it was dark and menacing at times, and I was fairly awful. I was twenty-four years old playing a high school student. I think it succeeded in portraying a dark side of teenage-hood that most teen movies don't depict, and I know it was shot to look edgy. But, the storyline was incoherent. I think it got a 10% rating on Rotten Tomatoes, but it was helpful in teaching me the ropes.

The time between filming *Dangerously Close* and *Down Twisted* was quite short—about six months? Was it something you were already discussing with Albert during the first film?

Yes, Albert told me he was going to make *Down Twisted* in Mexico, and he offered me the role.

This was Charles Rocket's first leading role in his comeback from being fired from *Saturday Night Live*. Do you have any memories of him, as a co-star?

Charlie was the best: funny, self-deprecating, tall and lanky, and we had a lot of laughs. He was a devoted family man and very proud of his son.

We were all put up in this hotel in Puerto Vallarta, and we all had balconies. Charlie's was right next to mine, and one evening he comes out onto his balcony and looks over at mine and sees this guy, a peeping tom, standing on my balcony watching me through my window. Suddenly there was a big commotion outside. Charlie jumped onto my balcony and started chasing the guy—it was a big, outdoor balcony—who ran like hell. He was a hotel employee and didn't want to get caught and lose his job. It was creepy and somewhat hilarious, and Charlie was the hero. I was so saddened to hear he committed suicide—he was such a lovely guy.

What are some of your most vivid memories from either of these sets?

I met some great folks on that shoot. I met Trudie Dochterman, Linda Kerridge, Courteney Cox. Brad Pitt was actually one of the customers in the diner in the opening shot, where Courteney and I are waitressing. I ran into him years later at K-ROQ Christmas concert in LA, and when we were introduced he said something to the effect of, "I got my start in a Carey Lowell film!" and I said, "Well, look at us now, you are a huge star and I am a mom." It was a funny moment.

Just a few years later you would be co-starring in a James Bond movie. These two Cannon movies were much, much smaller in many ways, but do you feel that those little, action-packed movies helped prepare you in any way for the big league action of *License to Kill*?

I don't know if anything prepares you for the huge production that is a Bond film, but I was happy to have some experience under my belt and a bit more confidence. I will always be grateful to Albert for giving me a shot and believing in me.

"Registration is free, but dangerous. . ." A French poster for *Dangerously Close*, known there as *Campus '86*.

A sun-faded video copy of Tobe Hooper's remake of *Invaders from Mars*. The image of the fence and hill behind the family's house was a direct homage to the original film from the 1950s.

Invaders from Mars

Release Date: June 6, 1986
Directed by: Tobe Hooper
Written by: Dan O'Bannon & Don Jakoby
Starring: Hunter Carson, Karen Black, Timothy Bottoms, Laraine Newman, Louise Fletcher, and James Karen
Trailer Voiceover: "David Gardner just woke up to a nightmare in his own back yard, but no one will listen! No one will believe! And soon . . . no one will be left!"

In the mid-1980s, you have to imagine that producers looked at almost every family-friendly, sci-fi adventure script that crossed their desks and saw dollar signs. Films such as *E. T. The Extra Terrestrial* (1982), *Ghostbusters* (1984), and *Gremlins* (1984) were tearing up the box office year after year, while even next-tier entries in the genre such as *The NeverEnding Story* (1984), *The Last Starfighter* (1984), *The Goonies* (1985), *Flight of the Navigator* (1986), and *Short Circuit* (1986) did great business. Meanwhile, the *Star Wars* films continued to gobble up parents' hard-earned dollars thanks to the series' unprecedented level of merchandising and toy tie-ins.

It's no surprise, then, that when Tobe Hooper made a passing mention to Menahem Golan that he was interested in remaking *Invaders from Mars* (1953)—a movie about a young boy who helps thwart an alien invasion of Earth—Cannon would immediately jump on board to make it so. The fact that Hooper's 1982 blockbuster, *Poltergeist*, had been similarly centered on a child—and had made ridiculous amounts of money for Universal—probably gave them extra incentive to run out and purchase the remake rights for William Cameron Menzies' 1953 sci-fi tale while Hooper had his hands full shooting *Lifeforce* (1985).

The original film—produced independently, but picked up and released by Twentieth Century-Fox—was part of a wave of popular alien invasion movies that owed their success, in part, to the communist "red scare" that swept the era. Much of these movies' tension arose from the way normal people could be possessed and/or brainwashed by an invading force, much in the same way that sensationalist news reports scared Americans of the time into thinking that the communist invasion of their nation had already begun. (Think: "The enemy can be anywhere . . . in your town, on your street, *or in your very home!*") These films made for thinly-veiled but effective allegories, and resulted in some of the era's best science fiction cinema, including *Invaders from Mars'* better-known contemporary, *Invasion of the Body Snatchers* (1956). On release, the original film garnered acclaim for its special effects and for being one of the first science fiction movies to show aliens in color. It retained a cult following, and left a lasting impression on several future filmmakers who saw it—and were likely traumatized by it—as children, including Steven Spielberg, Brad Bird, and naturally, Tobe Hooper.

The 1986 remake of *Invaders of Mars* was to be the second film in Tobe Hooper's three-film deal with Cannon. Thanks to theatrical pre-bookings for the feature, the filmmaker didn't even have the chance to finish up post-production on *Lifeforce* before he was forced to begin working on his next movie for the company. Like that prior film, Cannon was determined to make a big splash with *Invaders* and to put out a product that could stand up next to its major studio competitors. They poured a higher budget and more production resources into it than the average Cannon cheapie, which usually came in well under $5 million. As is typical for most Cannon productions, locating a real budgetary figure for the film is difficult as they liked to inflate their numbers, but the cost of *Invaders* ranged somewhere between $7 and $12 million.

Hooper put that money to good use by hiring two of Hollywood's most brilliant special effects artists, John Dykstra and Stan Winston, to bring this alien tale to life. Dykstra, of course, is famous for leading the effects team on *Star Wars* (1987), designing the visuals for everything from its lightsabers to the movie's epic space battles; he had previously worked with Hooper on the visual spectacle of *Lifeforce*. Winston, by this point in his career, had become one of Hollywood's most sought-after makeup effects designers, following his groundbreaking work on *The Thing* (1982) and *The Terminator* (1984). With Hooper's permission, Winston himself departed from *Invaders* early and left his team in charge while he went to work on the stunning special effects for *Aliens* (1986), which won him his first Academy Award. Designs for the extraterrestrial creatures and spacecraft were handled by William Stout, an artist who had worked on both Conan the Barbarian movies, *Raiders of the Lost Ark* (1981), and *First Blood* (1982), and would later design costumes and sets for Cannon's *Masters of the Universe* (1987). (You can read his thoughts on designing this movie's Martians in the interview with Stout that follows this volume's chapter on *Masters of the Universe*.)

The massive, winding interiors of *Invaders from Mars'* alien spaceship were constructed inside the hangars at the former Hughes Airport in Los Angeles: the same one where Howard Hughes had built his gigantic H-4 Hercules prototype plane, more famously known as "The Spruce Goose." (This hangar was used again by Cannon during the initial, Rusty Lemorande-led production of the *Journey to the Center of the Earth*, which was later finished by Albert Pyun and released in 1988.) The family's picturesque home in the film is now the administrative building at Malibu Creek State Park, and had originally been built for use in the 1948 Cary Grant comedy, *Mr. Blandings Builds His Dream House* (1948).

423

KAREN BLACK
HUNTER CARSON
Directed by TOBE HOOPER

An early pre-sales advertisement for the film.

Work began from a script co-written by Dan O'Bannon, yet another '80s genre film legend, who had previously written or worked on *Alien* (1979), *Dead & Buried* (1981), and *Heavy Metal* (1981), and directed the punk rock zombie classic *Return of the Living Dead* (1985). He wrote *Invaders* with his *Lifeforce* partner Don Jakoby, who had also penned *Death Wish 3* (1985) for Cannon under a pseudonym.

After a lengthy credit sequence seemingly inspired by Richard Donner's *Superman* (1978), the movie opens on preteen David Gardner (Hunter Carson) as he watches a meteor shower with his father, George, a NASA scientist (Timothy Bottoms of 1972's *The Last Picture Show*). Later that night, David is awoken by thunder-like noise and flashing lights. He rushes to his window to witness a U.F.O. landing over the hill behind his house. Of course, nobody believes the imaginative, space-obsessed little boy when he tells them about it the next day. When his father goes over the hill to reassure his son that nothing's landed there, he returns . . . different. He's aloof, detached, and has a strange wound on the back of his neck. Most alarming of all is his fixation on taking David over the hill, to show him what he found there. The suspicious little boy declines his father's invitation.

That afternoon, his father goes missing. His mother (*Saturday Night Live*'s own Connie Conehead, Laraine Newman) assures him that nothing is wrong—she does this as David watches Hooper's *Lifeforce* on TV, making for a fun inside joke—but as the day goes on, David notices that others around town have started displaying the same peculiar behavior as his dad. First, it's one of his dad's colleagues. Next, it's a pair of cops who return from the crash site with similar odd demeanors. (Jimmy Hunt, who played the boy hero in the original film, plays one of the cops; he drops a humdinger line while walking up that familiar hillside: "Gee, I haven't been up here since I was a kid!") When little David's father eventually comes home, his first order of business is to take David's mother on a moonlit walk to the crash site. When she returns the next morning to eat raw hamburger by the fistful, David really begins to worry.

Arriving to Menzies Elementary—a sly nod to the original film's director—David finds his most hated teacher, Mrs. McKeltch (Academy Award-winner Louise Fletcher, a.k.a. Nurse Ratched of 1975's *One Flew Over the Cuckoo's Nest*) gulping down a frog as part of her alien conversion. As more of his classmates and neighbors are transformed by the Martian invaders, David finds a lone, adult ally in his school nurse, Linda, played by the actor's real-life mother, Karen Black—of *Five Easy Pieces* (1970), *Trilogy of Terror* (1975), and *Nashville* (1975) fame, among many others.

It's not until a third of the way into the film that you actually get to see any of the movie's spectacular alien designs, but when you finally do, that's when the film really takes off. The interior of the spaceship looks downright stunning, full of spacious, anthill-like tunnels and doors which open and close like valves in the human body. (Hooper had wanted the spaceship's walls to breathe and pulse as if they were alive, but the effects don't go quite that far.) The tunnels are dug by a humongous, tentacle-like spinning blade, which rears its gruesome head throughout the movie, sucking its victims down into the ground with sudden, whirlpool-like sinkholes which open up in the ground beneath them.

Ten-year-old Hunter Carson was the son of his *Invaders* co-star Karen Black and *Texas Chainsaw Massacre 2* screenwriter L.M. Kit Carson.

The best of all are the movie's grotesque monsters. The Martians' commander, The Supreme Intelligence, worms about the spaceship: a giant brain with a tiny face attached to the end of a long, snaking esophagus. During the movie's firefight between the Marines and the Martians, the alien throne room set caught fire and the puppeteer operating the Supreme Intelligence had to be cut out of his costume to be rescued. (He couldn't hear what was going on outside the puppet and assumed they were still shooting the battle scene; he went on acting, making the monster flail about while the cast and crew were evacuating the set.)

The alien soldiers, or drones, are grotesque, toothy mouths with tiny pincers and eyestalks atop a pair of skinny, chicken-like legs. These were each played by two puppeteers: one tall, muscular actor would be fitted into the suit backwards so that the monster's legs would bend forward, while a dwarf actor was strapped to his back to operate the creature's mouth and appendages. If *Invaders* has one crowning achievement, it's the movie's fantastic practical effects work.

Eventually David and Linda get around to recruiting the help of U.S. Marine Corps soldiers, who are stationed conveniently next to the NASA base and led by General Wilson (played by the great James Karen) and his trusted military badass, Sergeant Major Rinaldi (Eric Pierpoint of *Alien Nation*, 1989–1990.) Most horror fans will recognize Karen from *Poltergeist* and *Return of the Living Dead*, while some readers in certain parts of the United States may better know him as the spokesman for the Pathmark supermarket chain. He brings his trademark gusto to his role in *Invaders*. ("Marines have no qualms about killing Martians!" he barks at one point, dropping by far the film's best line—and arguably, one of the best in any movie ever.)

The second half of the movie is incredibly action-packed, as the Martians work to sabotage America's space program and the Marines lead an assault force deep inside the alien mothership. The military action is another one of the film's high points, as the production recruited real-life Marines as extras, who arrived in their uniforms and with real firearms to use as props. (The heavier weaponry, such as the tanks and rocket launcher truck seen in the film, were also on loan from the U.S. military.) A decorated Vietnam veteran, technical advisor Dale Dye—who has a one-line cameo, yelling "Fire in the hole!" while shooting an M40 Dragon missile launcher—went on to become Hollywood's premiere military consultant, having worked on everything from *Platoon* (1986) to *Saving Private Ryan* (1998), to the acclaimed WWII miniseries *Band of Brothers* (2001) and *The Pacific* (2010). His contributions to *Invaders from Mars* bring some added realism to the film so long as, of course, you overlook the fact that the military is battling big, toothy aliens.

Now, here's the big question. If *Invaders from Mars* is such a fun movie, with strong special effects, which pays loving tribute to a sci-fi classic, how did it face-plant so badly when it hit theaters? *Invaders* brought in less than $5 million at the box office, which is $2 to $7 million less than it cost to make, depending on which figures you believe. It's not like critics hated it entirely, either: both *The New York Times* and *Los Angeles Times* published positive responses to the film, yet it still opened in seventh place and only played in theaters for two weekends.

My guess? I think it was because, despite being marketed as a family-friendly feature, the movie is pretty damn terrifying. These Martians aren't the friendly beings of *Close Encounters* (1977) or *E.T.: The Extra Terrestrial*. This is a film where a kid's parents are turned into monsters, a mean teacher guzzles down frogs, and a peacenik scientist—played by Bud Cort of *Harold and Maude* (1971)—gets vaporized by aliens. Not to mention all of the other grossness, such as the whole consumption of raw, ground burger and the brain-like Supreme Intelligence, the hefty number of soldiers who get shot or mowed down by a spinning blade, the quicksand vortex, or a terrifying drill which plants telepathic screws in its victims' necks. Considering all of the above, it's easy to imagine why parents steered clear with their children. How the heck did this ever manage a PG rating? (Remember: this was a kids' movie by the director of 1974's *The Texas Chainsaw Massacre*.)

Chew on this: Tobe Hooper's original, desired ending would have had David running into his parents' bedroom only to find them no longer there—and one of the alien drone monsters slurping down their bedsheets. The only reason Hooper wasn't able to shoot this version was because the monster costumes had already been wrapped up and packed away by that point. (The movie instead ends on an ambiguous and sort of cheap-feeling "It was all a dream . . . or was it?" note, which is actually pretty faithful to the original film rather than a sign of laziness on the writers' parts.)

Holy super-grim ending, Batman! If you can, just think about that scene for a while, and then see if it's possible for you to ever fall asleep again.

General Wilson (James Karen, left) examines a piece of alien technology in *Invaders from Mars*.

Interview: Actor James Karen

When he was interviewed for this book, James Karen was among the last of a disappearing breed. He'd been working as an actor through eight different decades, having started on the New York stage before the bombing of Pearl Harbor. Karen put his career as a young thespian on hold to fight in World War II. Upon his return at the War's end, Karen went back to New York, appearing in some of the most famous productions and working with several of the biggest actors of the era.

He worked with Marlon Brando in Elia Kazan's original stage production of *A Streetcar Named Desire*, following that up with roles in the initial Broadway runs of *Who's Afraid of Virginia Woolf?* And *Cactus Flower*. He became close friends with Buster Keaton when they performed in a touring show together; the silent comedy legend would become the godfather of Karen's child.

Karen slowly transitioned from the stage to film and television, amassing more than 200 credits in his lifetime. He became, as he described it himself, an actor whose face everyone recognizes from somewhere, but don't necessarily know his name. Dedicated television viewers might know him from role on *All My Children* or as the villain in the series finale of *Little House on the Prairie* (1974–1982); movie-goers may have spotted him in *All the President's Men* (1976), *Opening Night* (1978), *The China Syndrome* (1979), or *The Jazz Singer* (1980). Shoppers up and down the East Coast may yet know him as the official spokesperson for Pathmark, a regional chain of supermarkets for whom Karen starred in hundreds of commercials over twenty years.

Horror fans, however, will immediately know Karen from two of his most famous roles. In Tobe Hooper's *Poltergeist* (1982), he played the sketchy land developer who built the cursed home on top of an ancient burial ground. In Dan O'Bannon's *Return of the Living Dead* (1985), Karen was the warehouse worker who accidentally unleashes the zombie apocalypse. It was his involvement in these two films that led to his casting as General Wilson in Cannon's *Invaders from Mars* (1986), which was directed by Hooper and co-written by O'Bannon.

Karen passed away in 2018 at the age of 94, not long after this interview was conducted.

If we may, let's go back to the beginning of your career, which started in New York, on Broadway. How did you get into film?

James Karen: That was after the War. I went to New York before the War, went to the Neighborhood Playhouse—Sandy Meisner's great school—and then I got interrupted by Pearl Harbor. I joined the Air Force. I enlisted on, I think, my 18th birthday. If you enlisted, you could choose your branch. I wanted to be in the Air Force. If you waited around to be drafted, they could put you anywhere they wanted. That's why I did it.

I went into the Air Force that December. I got out in November of '45, and immediately went to New York and had lunch with Sandy. That's where he said, "The best thing you can do for yourself is to pick up where you left off." I thought that was a great idea, so I went back to the Neighborhood Playhouse and had a year there.

I got out of the Playhouse and Willard Van Dyke, who was a documentary filmmaker, was doing a movie about the education of an American doctor. He was hoping to find a young doctor, and he couldn't. They didn't want to give up enough of their time to make a movie.

He had seen me perform a couple of things [at the Playhouse]. He hired me. I worked for almost ten months on *Journey into Medicine* (1947), which is a beautiful picture. It was photographed by Boris Kaufman, who later won the Academy Award for a Marlon Brando picture, *On the Waterfront* (1954). He was a wonderful man. I actually did two or three pictures later on for him. They saw *Journey*, which is how he got hired for the Brando picture, while I got hired for *Streetcar*.

Wow, everything's connected.

Yes. The best things in my life have happened through connections, people that you know or worked with or are doing something and somebody said to them, "Do you know anybody who could play this part?" and they mention your name. I am a believer in productive friendships.

You only made films occasionally through the first few decades of your career.

I lived in New York and I wanted to stay in the theater. I did very few movies. I think I did a picture in Puerto Rico, *Frankenstein Meets the Space Monster* (1965). I made a lot of little pictures. I did not plan to ever leave New York, but then in the mid '70s, everything in New York was English musicals. I found it to be very tough.

A guy that I knew, a director, Charles Dubin, came to New York from Hollywood to do a 90-minute special and he hired me for it. We were close friends. Charlie had just gotten a divorce. He was lonesome. My wife and I said, "Why don't you come and stay with us?" He did, and we had a great time. He was one of my best friends at the Playhouse. Then when he went back to California, he kept calling us, saying, "It's lonesome out here. Why don't you come out? I'll give you a job."

We got into the car and drove out, thinking we would stay a few weeks. We did the job, which happened to be shot in Hawaii, *Hawaii Five-O* (1968–1977). We had a great time. Got back to LA, and somebody else called and said, "Listen, I'm doing a television show. I'd love you to do it with me." We said okay, and we just never made it back to New York. Although, I went back almost every other Sunday night.

Was that to do your commercials?

For Pathmark, yes. We didn't know [our move to LA] was permanent, we really didn't know. What the hell, you're getting work. Why go back to New York, where there was very little work? We stayed. It was the best thing I ever did, because I got into a couple of hit movies. *China Syndrome* (1979), which was a big, huge hit, and I just began to work more and more. I was enjoying LA. It was fun. We kept our apartment in New York for about ten years, and then finally gave it up.

In the 1980s, you got into *Poltergeist* and, of course, *Return of the Living Dead*. Were you a fan of horror movies?

No, it was just being offered to me. I didn't turn anything down. Anything. I took every job that was offered to me and built up a library of films. I wasn't fussy. I tried to do the best I could when I took a role. I worked hard on the parts. I didn't take anything foolish. Although, I think all of my friends wondered why the hell I'd done *Return of the Living Dead*, but I loved it. I just thought it was wonderful.

We had a great time, and the cast was just all so friendly. We still get together a lot, which is unusual. I just loved doing *Return*. It was very creative. We were left alone. If you came up with a good idea, you could sell it, like my dénouement, my committing suicide. It came out of that. The end of the movie, I was wandering around in the rain like everybody else, and I decided I didn't want to do it. I came up with the idea of committing suicide. I went to

432

Dan [O'Bannon], the director, and said, "Listen, I've a great idea for a scene." The set was still set up, they hadn't destroyed it yet.

Dan said, "Yes, it's a good idea. Let's see if we can sneak it in this afternoon." We shot it that afternoon and it just worked out beautifully. It was good for me, it was good for the movie. We just improvised, really—the whole scene was improvised. I loved my taking off the ring and putting it on the toggle switch. I love that moment. Dan really was wonderful. He had never directed a picture. He took advice and if you came up with a good idea, he'd shoot it.

One of the things that saved that picture was Tom Fox, who produced it, had never produced a movie before. He was a bonds salesman. He made a lot of money for people when he was in Chicago. He bought the rights to the script. He went to the people that he had sold bonds to and said, "Listen, I have made a lot of money for you in bonds, I own a movie. There's a script. I'm going to make the movie, and I'll make you money if you invest in it." They did, and they made money.

Tom was a good friend of mine. I said to him, "You got a lot of kids in this movie who've never made a movie. None of them know each other, and they're all supposed to be great friends." I said, "I would advise you to pay them their salary and rehearse for a week." He agreed to do it. The kids all got to know each other and it helped them immensely. That's one reason why the kids all look great.

Because they were genuinely friends by that point.

Yes. We rehearsed for a week just the way we would do a play. We rehearsed it in sequence. They had a map of where they were, emotionally. It was so much fun to do. We had a great time shooting it.

Can you walk me through how you got involved then with *Invaders from Mars*? Did Tobe come to you after having worked together on *Poltergeist*?

Dan was not supposed to be the director [of *Return of the Living Dead*]. He'd written it, but it was originally going to be directed by Tobe Hooper, which is how I got into it. Tobe called me and said, "I want you to play in it." I loved working with Tobe, but Tobe couldn't make it back in time. He was doing *Lifeforce* (1985) in Europe. Dan became the director.

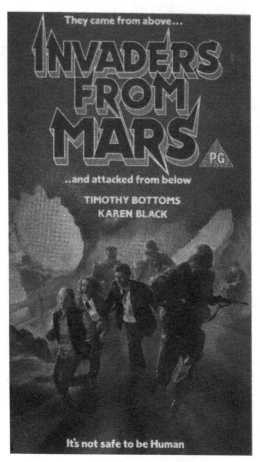

A magazine advertisement for the U.K. video release of *Invaders from Mars*.

For *Invaders*, I met with Tobe and he told me about the project. I said, "Sounds fine to me, but I'll do anything with you," which I would have done. I'm crazy about him. So we went and did it. It was a long, long shoot. A *long* shoot. I remember my agent kept calling me, saying, "When are you going to be finished with that movie? I've got another movie here waiting for you. I don't think they'll wait much longer." I said, "There's nothing I can do. I'm very happy working on this picture." I know it was the most financially remunerative job I've ever had, because we went on and on and on, and there was a lot of overtime.

We spent a lot of time in those sand tunnels. I noticed there were all these girls wearing masks. Then one day I saw they delivered some more sand. I was standing around with another actor, and I said, "No wonder they're wearing masks. Look at those bags—they're marked with double X's. It's poison." The stuff they were using as sand had sparkles in it. Very photogenic, but deadly. However, it did not affect me nor anybody that I know of, but it was alarming to see you're working in sand that arrives with poison warnings all over it.

Can you tell me a little bit about what it was like working with your primary castmates in *Invaders*, Karen Black and her son, Hunter Carson?

Oh, Hunter was a sweet boy, and Karen, I loved her. I'd done a few things with her, and she was just a warm, wonderful lady to work with. It was hard for her to have to look after Hunter and to worry about her own part. It's a tough position to be in. She was a very good mother to Hunter. I had a hell of a good time on the movie. I really loved working with all the people. It was a happy time for me.

Menahem [Golan] was out of the country. He didn't know we were still shooting until he got back. Most directors can't stop shooting. They want to continue. There's always more they want to shoot. Tobe certainly had that pull on this picture.

When Menahem came back, he found out they were still shooting. We were shooting in a Marine base. I know that around two in the morning, somebody just came over, ripped the lights out. I remember we were in the dark for a while, but that was it.

We'd been working there for a long time. There was a huge hanger made to lift up the sand. It looked like a desert. Every time there were whirlpools in the sand, it would drop down while we were trying to walk across it. When the scene was cut, they would have to go down with wheelbarrows and bring all the sand back up. It was a tough job for the crew. I had a lovely dressing room on a dock. I would swim between takes. The job's a lot easier for actors. The crew, sometimes, are killing themselves while the actors are off swimming. I really felt sorry for that crew. They really worked themselves hard.

Invaders was the longest shoot I've ever been connected with, by far. I remember crawling around in those tunnels all day, on our elbows and knees. I think I worked on that film for six months.

You've been making movies for roughly eight decades now. What do you feel are the biggest changes to the movie business that you've witnessed in your career?

The equipment is certainly made now so that you don't even notice it. There's someone walking around with a little camera. There's no reloading the film. The whole production is less intrusive, which I like. You still have the actors, the crew, but you just don't have all that machinery. Lighting is a lot easier. I have to tell you, I've been working in film all these years, I never tire of it. I like sitting around, waiting for the setup to be finished. I like the camaraderie with the crew. I really like the process.

Sometimes there are people you wish you hadn't gotten to know. [*Laughs*] For the most part, I've been very fortunate with the people I've worked with, both on stage and film. The process is very engaging if you keep alert to it, and are sensitive to it. On stage, of course, the joy is being there in front of a large audience and sensing the difference in an audience every night, which you don't have in film. What you have in film is an intimacy with the cameras, and the other actors. I consider it one of the great joys in my life, my profession.

Hunter Carson in a publicity still from *Invaders from Mars*.

Interview: Actor Hunter Carson

Only ten months old, Hunter Carson made his television debut on *Saturday Night Live* as his mother, host Karen Black, held him on stage while delivering her opening monologue. Less than ten years later, he'd star opposite his mother in *Invaders from Mars* (1986), Cannon's big-budget, Tobe Hooper-directed alien invasion film.

Carson made his acting debut playing Harry Dean Stanton's son in *Paris, Texas* (1984), after producer Fred Roos—a friend of the family—recommended him to Wim Wenders for the role. That film was co-written by Carson's father, screenwriter L.M. Kit Carson, who would begin preliminary work on *The Texas Chainsaw Massacre 2* (1986) while his son was shooting *Invaders*.

In addition to acting in them, Carson now writes, directs, and produces films.

You were more or less born into the film industry. Growing up in that environment, did becoming an actor feel natural to you?

Hunter Carson: Yes, you could say that. I was basically raised on a film set. In fact, my earliest memories are of being on movie sets. That was super comfortable for me, so there wasn't a whole lot to adapt to eight- to ten-hour days. As a nine or ten-year-old, that could be tough, but I was used to it. And *Paris, Texas* helped, obviously. It was very natural for me to get into acting. I was able to memorize scripts at a very young age. My mom and I used to run lines together for her auditions.

Also, Tobe had been a friend of my family's forever, and I grew up knowing Tobe. He was around, he was at parties. We would go to his house, he'd come to our house. It was a great relationship, and it was good working with a guy that I knew.

Tobe knew what you could do after seeing you act in *Paris, Texas*. How did he approach you about getting involved in *Invaders*?

He was in the process of doing *Lifeforce* (1985), and he just came over with it. He brought me the script, and we read it. I don't remember if there was some sort of a greenlight process, but having done *Paris, Texas* and it being so well received, there wasn't much of an audition for me. He just said, "Here's this," and we read the script. Then we watched the original one from the '50s, and I got jazzed about it.

I'm a big sci-fi fan and was back then, so I was really happy to be there. We went to his office, which was also where they were creating and building some miniatures that they were going to use later, on the set, and they had a lot of drawings up on the walls. He asked me if I wanted to do it and I said, "Yes, of course, I'd love to."

After that I did some screen tests with other actors, two of whom being Timothy Bottoms and Laraine Newman, and we got along phenomenally. Timothy Bottoms was just fantastic. I was like, "Wow, I don't know if I can act with this guy." He would say, "Just do your thing, man. You got it." He was a pleasure to work with.

Honestly, I don't know how my mom got involved. Obviously, she was there, and she was an icon at that point in her life, in the '80s. There was some sort of scream queen stuff that she was doing, so that worked out well with her fans. It all just came together.

What was Tobe like as a director? How much did your relationship play into how he directed you?

I think a lot, because he would just tell me to talk about the scene and read through it. It was very comfortable. He would scream a lot if stuff wasn't going his way. I'm pretty sure that wasn't unique to *Invaders*, he was just a screamer. But I was very comfortable on the set. If we had to work the scene, we'd all go back to the trailer and go through the script. By the time we were shooting, I had memorized the entire script, everybody's lines. In the read-throughs, if somebody forgot a line, I would tell them. [*Laughs*] A nine-year-old telling a grown actor their line was funny to me.

Tobe was great on set. He was a very hands-on director. He worked well with all of the cast. It was a fun time.

Paris, Texas **was a very heartfelt, symbolic movie, while *Invaders* was a huge production with a ton of special effects. Did that feel like a big jump to you?**

It felt like a huge jump. I think in the beginning, we were shooting in Malibu, at the house, and doing a lot of the scenes with just the family. Then, it would get bigger and bigger as we went along. We moved outside to the school and then, once we were at Three Mile Island, we had hundreds of extras that were all dressed in Army uniforms. We were shooting in a sandpit. It was the biggest thing I'd ever seen. That movie was probably one of the biggest movies made that year. It had huge production value, and big monsters.

You worked with James Karen on this film, who had been acting since the 1940s.

James Karen was an unbelievably kind man. He was very helpful to me with some scenes, especially inside the huge set they built on Three Mile Island. I was having some issues with the monsters, because when you're a kid and you look at them on the movie screen or on TV, they're scary, but when you're on a set and see the men inside the monsters, it's not scary. James Karen was giving me some pointers on how to behave fearfully, which was tough for me because I couldn't get out of my head the fact that these were puppeteers walking backwards inside giant foam creations. He's great and I loved him.

He mentioned that this was the longest shoot he'd ever been on in his entire career, and that was over fifty years of acting.

It lasted three months longer than it should have. [*Laughs*] That was a big deal. They kept going and going. I don't know, but I think it had to do with Menahem Golan wanting more, wanting it bigger, scarier, wanting more monsters. They were very much driving the fact that the monsters had to be *monsters*. Does that make sense?

Yes—they wanted this film to be *scary*.

I don't remember if we were reshooting on set, but we did the scenes several times more than I was used to. Tobe was very, very hard on himself about getting exactly what he wanted. He came from the world of maverick directors. They bucked the system. Tobe was one of the few that actually went and got *into* the system.

He was a perfectionist on the small scale jobs, and then once he got the big scale jobs, the perfectionism set in and he really wanted what he wanted.

Did you keep going until the plug got pulled? James Karen seemed to remember the lights just going out one day.

Yes. [*Laughs*] I think the entire generator blew up there on the island. We had to scramble and use flashlights. It seems because they had constructed it in old hangars, I remember there being generator issues, and they were having to power everything using this big, Panavision generator truck. Once one of those went down, we had some major issues.

That movie dragged on for a really long time. It just kept going. You'd think you were done and they're like, "No, no, we're going to shoot some more." It just kept getting bigger, and bigger, and bigger. By the time we expanded the ending, they had a helicopter flying around and I was like, "Wow, this is too cool!" It wasn't all CGI back then, so that stuff was really there, which was cool.

Louise Fletcher was really frightening in this movie.

She was fun, and super kind. I have really good memories of Louise. Years later when I watched her as Nurse Ratched [in *One Flew Over the Cuckoo's Nest*, 1975], I was like, "How could that be her?" She was so wonderful and kind! She would often have whatever meal they were serving with me. We'd go into her trailer, we'd eat and we'd talk. She was really nice. I think she'd known my mom through Jack [Nicholson]. They had a relationship because they were very pivotal actresses at that point in Hollywood, Louise and my mom. Louise was great—she was very encouraging to me.

Actors like Louise and James, everybody who had acted when they were younger, I think they understood that I felt a lot of pressure. There was a modicum of pressure put on me by Cannon itself, by their people and with their press. I had this feeling that it was important for me to do my best, and so it made me work harder. Louise had encouraged that. When we were shooting the scene where she was in front of the king monster, when she turned around and said, "I'll get you, David Gardner," it was very nasty. She took me into her trailer and she could tell that I was feeling the burn. Months had gone by and it was a lot of hours for a kid, and she just said, "You're doing a really good job. Keep on doing what you're doing. Just listen to Tobe. He's a good guy. Don't worry about the press. Don't worry about the pressure. Just do what you're doing." She was really wonderful.

Hunter Carson with his co-star (and mom), scream queen Karen Black.

How was it to work on screen with your mother?

It was cool. It was professional. Obviously, we were mother and son, but it was a professional relationship. We ran our lines together. We did scenes together. She had quite a bit of levity on there. She would do things on set to keep people laughing, and keep people joking, especially into the wee hours of the morning when we were shooting the biggest scenes. She was a very boisterous person. It was good for me to have somebody like that on set. We weren't always together because obviously, we had different stuff to shoot. When we were together, we had a good time.

What were your favorite scenes to shoot?

The military stuff and the monsters were the most fun for me. The very end scene, where we blew up the monsters, that was so much fun. I had my earplugs in and I was on set, and then they did that scene a million times, blowing stuff up. I was like, "This is cool." Blowing stuff up is fun. They don't do a whole lot of that anymore, but back in the day when they needed to blow stuff up, it was a lot of fun, pyrotechnics and all.

Your father worked with Tobe on his immediate follow-up for Cannon, *The Texas Chainsaw Massacre 2*. It's definitely not a kid's movie, but do you have any memories of that film being made?

It's not a kid's movie at all. [*Laughs*] They shot this in Austin, and it was the beginning of the film scene there. At that point, Austin was basically just a college town and Texas filmmakers would use it, and Tobe loved shooting in Austin. I was there on the set pretty much the whole time.

They shot it in the summer. I don't know why you would shoot anything in the summer in Austin, it was *hot*. [*Laughs*] They were shooting when *Invaders* came out and I actually went to go watch *Invaders* in the movie theater. When I first saw *Chainsaw*, it would've been at the premiere party. The cast and crew screening was later on that year. *Texas Chainsaw Massacre 2* is a great movie. It really makes a point, and it has a lot of deep character issues. Those guys, they really were fleshed out. Tobe worked in a sort of empathy—it was like the monsters had a heart.

When I was on the set when they were shooting *Chainsaw*, they would constantly be rewriting the script as they went along, because Cannon wanted it scarier. Then they would see the dailies and say, "Why are you making it funny? These are monsters." Tobe and my dad were working really hard to make it scary-funny, and then they would come back and say, "More scary, more blood, more guts."

My dad would be sitting there like, "How do I give them more blood, yet make it funny at the same time?" I think they wanted it to be gruesome, but they didn't want it to be mean. That was hard to do because they were dealing with cannibals, but there's still humor in there. Like, the reporter pulling a fingernail out [of the chili] and being like, "Oh, it's a hard-shell peppercorn." They would throw things in there that were funny but also gory, but they didn't want to get into the gruesome, mean edge. They wanted to eliminate that. Cannon really wanted a monstrous, mean, death, gore kind of thing, and that's definitely something that carried over from *Invaders*, which they wanted to be super scary.

Tobe and my dad were playing a game with Cannon. They were doing what Cannon wanted them to, but they were also doing what they wanted to do, and so it was a lot of back and forth. The execs would come down to the set, and they'd all sit there and watch the stuff and then say, "Yes, you guys are great." Then they'd go away and you'd get a phone call later being like, "The execs think it needs to be scarier and have more blood." It's like, "No, come on, man." [*Laughs*] "How much more blood can you do? Give me a break."

The poster for Cannon's incredibly small theatrical release of *Robotech: The Movie*.

Robotech: The Movie

Release Date: July 25, 1986
Directed by: Carl Macek & Ishiguro Noburo
Written by: Carl Macek & Ardwight Chamberlain
Trailer Voiceover: "See your favorite Robotech heroes, plus all-new characters, in the biggest action adventure ever!"

The rules of this book are being slightly bent to include *Robotech: The Movie* (1986) for two reasons: it was the studio's only foray into animated movies, and because the story behind its minuscule release is ridiculously entertaining. Although the movie wasn't produced in-house by Cannon, they—and specifically, Menahem Golan—*most definitely* had a hand in ruining it.

The company responsible for *Robotech: The Movie*, Harmony Gold USA, had been founded a few years prior to its release by Frank Agrama, a filmmaker and producer that we have to imagine was a kindred spirit to Golan and Globus. Prior to this, the Egyptian-born director had been responsible for a handful of rush-job knockoff films, including *The Godfather's Friend*, released only a few months after *The Godfather* (both 1972), *Queen Kong*, which hit theaters one week before the 1976 remake of *King Kong*, and *Dawn of the Mummy* (1981), a gory horror cash-in that lifted its title from *Dawn of the Dead* (1978) and had its gruesome mummies rise from the dirt and munch flesh just like the shambling corpses of Lucio Fulci's *Zombi 2* (1979).

Agrama's primary business was importing and exporting films and television shows to and from foreign markets. While doing so, his attention was eventually brought to Japanese animation, which provided a high-quality product that could be easily re-dubbed, re-packaged, and re-sold to English-speaking markets. (Agrama was later convicted by Italian courts for his role in a complex tax evasion and money laundering scheme, which involved the buying and selling of movie rights to bogus foreign companies, but that's a sordid story for someone else to chronicle.) To their credit, Harmony Gold played a significant role in expanding the fanbase for Japanese animation, or anime, within Western audiences.

In the early 1980s, Harmony Gold had acquired the rights to a very successful Japanese animated television series known as *Super Dimension Fortress Macross* (1982–1983), an epic saga tracking a war between humanity and alien invaders fought with giant, transforming robots. While assembling materials to market the show, Harmony Gold called up Carl Macek, a former college professor and anime super-fan who had been running an art gallery which sold animation cels. Macek was already familiar with the series, and so impressed the company with his knowledge that they invited him to their offices for a meeting.

Macek was soon hired to write and oversee their dubbed, Westernized version of the show. The issue they ran into while trying to sell it to American television was that there weren't enough episodes of *Super Dimension Macross* for syndication. This required a minimum sixty-five episodes, where the original Japanese series only ran for thirty-six. The solution they found was to combine the first series with two others they licensed that also featured transforming robots: *Super Dimension Calvary Southern Cross* (1984) and *Genesis Climber MOSPEADA* (1983–1984). It was Macek's duty to figure out how to mash together three separate robot shows with unrelated plots in a way that would make sense.

His results proved both influential and controversial. The combined shows became *Robotech* (1985), so named after a line of Revell model kits which licensed many of the same robot designs and were already on hobby store shelves. Macek rather ingeniously resolved the issue of merging the shows by repurposing each of them to portray a different generation of characters within the same universe. Thus, they could easily explain away the changes in casts, designs, and animation quality. While a sizable contingent of anime purists viewed Macek's alterations as a crass bastardization of its highly-regarded source material, the new *Robotech* quickly gained fans as soon as it entered syndication in the spring of 1985.

The show became notable for having an older-skewing audience at a time when—in the United States, at least—cartoons were still viewed almost strictly as kiddie fare. Yet, *Robotech* appealed to both teens and adults by taking its wartime setting very seriously. It dealt with adult themes. Characters were killed in battle. Cities were destroyed and, by the end of the first saga, most of humanity is wiped off the Earth. It's scary stuff, and decidedly not just for kids.

Enter Cannon, who somehow saw this as their entryway into the world of children's animation. (Of course.)

That summer, a Los Angeles news program ran a feature on Harmony Gold and the success they were having with their *Robotech* series. Menahem Golan saw this, and immediately placed a call to the company offering to distribute a *Robotech* movie if they could slap one together by the end of the year, which was a little under six months off. As the next *Robotech* series they were planning called for all-new animation—and would be far more expensive to produce than the dub jobs they'd previously released—a profitable movie could provide a quick cash influx. The team at Harmony Gold agreed.

Their Plan "A" would have been to simply re-dub the Japanese film *Macross: Do You Remember Love?* (1984), which was a feature-length reimagining of the first series from which *Robotech* had been adapted. When they couldn't secure the rights, they had to scramble for another film they could cut

447

up, re-dub, and repurpose into the *Robotech* storyline. They settled on the first movie in an entirely unrelated franchise called *Megazone 23* (1985).

This was given a new dub and sound mix, and references were added that would loosely link it into the established *Robotech* universe. Ten minutes of new, animated footage were commissioned to give the movie a more suitable ending. This version was taken to the Cannon offices and screened for Menahem Golan, who was extremely displeased with what he saw. According to Golan, it was *not* "a Cannon movie."

The problems Golan had with this cut of *Robotech: The Movie* were that it was too talkative, there wasn't enough shooting, and that it needed more robots. Another problem? It too easily passed what would become known as the Bechdel test, meaning that it contained scenes with female characters talking to each other while no men were around. In Golan's words, the film had "too many girls." They had to go.

Disappointed with what he saw, Golan sent the team from Harmony Gold away and reportedly gave them only *twenty-four hours* to come back with ideas for how they would fix the many issues he had with the film. Macek went back to the editing lab and hastily crammed all of the unused robot footage he had on hand—leftovers from one of the prior series they'd used, *Southern Cross*—into *Robotech: The Movie*. This created a host of new problems, including continuity conflicts and the fact that the two shows were done on different film formats, meaning the footage quality wouldn't match from one shot to the next.

Naturally, the integrity of the *Robotech* brand wasn't Cannon's priority. All they saw were transforming robots, which would no doubt appeal to the young boys who had made *Transformers* (1984–1987) a huge hit. (In Cannon's typically perfect timing, *Robotech: The Movie* would receive its limited theatrical release just two weeks before *Transformers: The Movie* [1986] hit theaters.)

Macek returned to Cannon with this new cut of the film the very next day. Being unable to record new sound during their marathon editing session, Macek was forced to act out all of the dialogue himself as the eighty-minute movie was screened silently on a television beside him. When the haphazardly slapped-together film ended and the lights came on, Menahem Golan arose from his chair, applauded, pointed a finger at the screen, and famously quipped:

"Now, *THAT* is a Cannon movie!"

The release date was pushed from Christmas of 1985 to the following summer, giving Harmony Gold time to polish up this version for its big screen release and promote the film to toy manufacturers and retailers.

Robotech: The Movie follows tubular dude Mark Landry, who's given a high-tech motorcycle that was stolen from the military by his soldier pal, Todd. It turns out this superbike—which transforms into a gun-toting robot, and is linked to the government's supercomputer by an artificial intelligence—is key to stopping yet another alien invasion, and blowing the lid off a military cover-up put in place by an evil clone of a top Army colonel.

That over-simplified synopsis might make the movie sound like it has a convoluted plot, but it's really not as bad as it sounds. The Earth-conquering aliens are bad. The murderous, cloned Army guy? He's also bad. The plucky kids with the sweet, robot motorcycle? They're good. If you can figure those things out, you should have no problem following the movie. For everything else you might need to know from the TV show, there's a lengthy, *Star Wars*-esque roll of expositional text to open the film, which summarizes the story so far.

Even if they weren't aware that *Robotech: The Movie* was made by taking two unrelated animes, cutting them up, and shaking the pieces up in a bowl like a big, mecha-flavored salad, many viewers would probably figure it out from watching the screen. Macek's fear of the footage not matching came true: most of the added robot footage from *Southern Cross* looks noticeably murky when spliced in with the brighter, more detailed material from the higher-budget *Megazone 23*. The characters from one set of footage hardly interact with the characters from the other; most of the stuff added at the last minute *feels* like it was added at the very last minute. Soldiers bravely sacrifice their lives attacking the alien marauders, but the audience is never told who any of these people are or given a reason to care. Rarely has humanity's last stand against total annihilation felt this random and inconsequential.

These war scenes are jarring in contrast with the ones centering on Mark Landry and his friends. Alongside the stolen superbike plot, these scenes also juggle side stories about his girlfriend Becky's burgeoning acting career; an independent action movie being shot by her roommate; and a mysterious pop idol. (This movie may have to battle 1984's *Ninja III: The Domination* for the Cannon crown of which one has the most dance aerobics scenes.) The film's upbeat soundtrack is quite good, though, with most of the songs performed by ex-Paul Revere and the Raiders member Michael Bradley. The central track, "Only a Fool," features guest vocals by Three Dog Night, and was written by prolific Motown songwriter Jack Alan Goga—who, ten years later, would die in police custody while awaiting trial for double homicide.

Perhaps being self-aware that they had no experience marketing an animated feature, Cannon opted to give *Robotech: The Movie* a rare, limited test run in Dallas-area theaters. If the film performed well with the desired audiences, they would proceed to send it nationwide. Carl Macek was sent to Texas to promote the screenings to the local media and *Robotech* fans, but that's roughly where Cannon's marketing savvy ended and they began repeatedly shooting themselves in the foot.

While they produced a cool-looking poster featuring Mark Landry jumping his sweet ride over a fisheye-lensed shot of a cyberpunk skyline, it wasn't used in most of Cannon's marketing materials. Instead, they went with a piece of artwork from the Comico comic book—which featured characters that did *not* appear in this film—and slapped on the misleading tagline, "The hottest family series—now a movie."

Cannon *was* gunning for a family audience, as misguided as that sounds, considering that this was based on a cartoon where most of the Earth's population is horrifically wiped out roughly one quarter of the way into the series. They bought up TV spots and ran commercials in the Dallas area, but *only* during the six a.m. weekday slot, when cartoons were running. On top of this, they only scheduled the film in matinee screenings, when most of the show's older audience was working or in school.

Many parents who *did* take their kids to catch the test run for the movie were likely horrified by what they saw: *Robotech: The Movie* is a rather violent animated film where more than one of the hero's friends is murdered, humans die in graphic ways, and the main female character comes seconds away from being sexually assaulted by her sleazy boss. (Come on in, kids!)

The craziest thing, though, is that the movie did relatively good business considering how high the odds were stacked against it. But, because the viewers who came to see it—mostly teen and adult *Robotech* fans—weren't representative of the children's audience which Cannon desired, they chose to shelve the movie after the Dallas run so that they could re-tool it into something which would appeal to a younger crowd. And thus, save for a handful of international VHS releases, *Robotech: The Movie* remained unreleased while Cannon's financial problems spiraled out of control, and the company seemed to lose any interest in salvaging their ill-managed foray into animated features.

As of this writing, *Robotech: The Movie* still hasn't had any official home video release in the United States, although bootleg versions are abundant. It's unlikely that will change, for several reasons. One, the original negatives are said to have been destroyed in a flood at Harmony Gold's offices in the early 1990s. Two, the various rights holders have disowned it over the years, blaming Cannon's interference for turning it into a nonsensical mess. Three, *Robotech* fans have long regarded it not a part of the series' canon, and so few of them are really clamoring for any sort of official release.

This is a shame, come to think of it, because while it may not be a proper *Robotech* movie, it *is*—as Menahem Golan succinctly put it—very much "a Cannon movie."

The U.S. video release for *Detective School Dropouts* came in one of MGM/
UA Home Video's oversized, book-style boxes.

Detective School Dropouts
Dutch Treat

Release Date: August 8, 1986 (I), 1987 (II)

Directed by: Filippo Ottoni (I), Boaz Davidson (II)

Written by: Lorin Dreyfuss & David Landsberg

Starring: Lorin Dreyfuss & David Landsberg

Tagline: "A couple of detectives without a clue ... out of place wherever they go!"

In the mid-1980s, Cannon produced two movies showcasing the new comedy team of David Landsberg and Lorin Dreyfuss. While their efforts failed to launch any sort of ongoing, on-screen careers for the duo, the two movies that Landsberg and Dreyfuss starred in together—*Detective School Dropouts* (1986) and *Dutch Treat* (1987)—are hidden gems within the Cannon canon, with the latter being particularly well-hidden for more than three decades.

By the time he got to Cannon, David Landsberg was likely best-recognized for co-starring as the Jewish Navy recruit, Skolnick, opposite Don Rickles on the short-lived WWII sitcom *C.P.O. Sharkey* (1976–1978). After that was canceled he went on to have small roles as a banker in *The Jerk* (1979) and in *Skatetown, U.S.A.* (1979), which is where he met his future writing partner and Cannon co-star, Lorin Dreyfuss.

The elder brother of *Jaws* (1975) star Richard Dreyfuss, Lorin Dreyfuss had co-written and produced *Skatetown USA*, the roller disco flick that launched the careers of Scott Baio and Patrick Swayze. Newly partnered, Landsberg and Dreyfuss co-wrote material for *Fantasy Island* (1977–1984) before landing a deal to write and co-star in a pair of movies for Cannon. The first of these would be *Detective School Dropouts*, shot primarily in Italy beginning in January of 1986.

Landsberg plays Donald Wilson, a down-on-his-luck New Yorker who can't seem to do anything right. The film opens with him being fired from job after job for self-inflicted idiocy, and a proclivity for daydreaming about dime store detective novels. Running out of options, Donald sees an opportunity to turn his interests into a career when he spots an ad for a private eye school, and makes the call. This brings him into contact with Paul Miller (Dreyfuss), whose dimly-lit office and cynical demeanor give him the outward appearance of an old-timey detective right out of the movies. The truth is, though, he's more con artist than investigator, and immediately gets down to business relieving Donald of his savings with phony lessons—all so he can pay his secretary's salary and keep the lights on in his office.

Meanwhile, on the other side of the Atlantic, a trio of mafia families wage a bloody war over, of all things, the Italian cheese industry. As the bodies pile up, there's a glimmer of hope for peace at long last when two young, star-crossed lovers from rival families—Carlo Lombardi (Christian De Sica) and Caterina Zanetti (Valeria Golino)—plan to wed, and consolidate their parents' cheese empires. This won't fly with the Don of the third family, the Falcones, who foresees himself being squeezed out of the industry after the merger. So, he orders his underling Bruno (George Eastman) to kidnap the Zanetti bride during her vacation in America, and then arranges for his own daughter, the bucktoothed Sonia, to wed Carlo instead.

Stateside, Paul needs Donald to pony up one more big check to pay off his debts, so he sells him a partnership in his sham detective agency. On their first case—trying to return a lost poodle for reward money—they turn up at the wrong address, only to find the home where mobsters are holding Caterina hostage by complete accident. The captive woman hands them a note and a necklace to give her bereaved beau, to prove she's still alive. Unfortunately for our heroes, Paul left the bloodthirsty gangsters his business card.

Their mission to deliver this message brings our two in-over-their-heads detectives to Rome, Pisa, and eventually Venice, in a zany series of madcap chase scenes set against as scenic backdrops as the Colosseum, the Leaning Tower, the Trevi Fountain, and the Venetian canals. Our ill-equipped heroes are pursued by gangsters who attempt to murder the duo along their entire adventure, which involves mistaken identities, a runaway Ferrari, Trappist monks, shenanigans in a confessional booth, and a dead body in an airport bathroom.

One of the funniest running gags involves a couple of older, American tourists whose photos of their European vacation are repeatedly ruined by our two dopey dicks, who always seem to be fleeing for their lives from someone whenever these fogies are posing for the camera.

Detective School Dropouts' humor ranges from lowbrow to ultra-lowbrow, and there's nothing wrong with that. Being a Hollywood-Italian co-production, it feels like a mash-up between the *Police Academy* movies and the Bud Spencer and Terence Hill comedies that were coming out in that era. We've got added "boing" sound effects and exaggerated punching noises, characters getting their pants forcefully removed, a sped-up chase scene, a drag disguise, and plenty of mugging for the camera. In between all of that, though, the movie's stars and co-screenwriters embedded a number of really clever, funny lines. (My favorite? When Paul voices his concern about bad guys shooting at Donald because "they might miss you and hit me.")

There's also a nice Cannon in-joke when our nincompoop protagonists find themselves stuck on an airplane and Paul complains, "I hope I like the movie." When it cuts to the in-flight television screen, we see that they're watching Sho Kosugi in *Ninja III: The Domination* (1984).

The Italian cast is composed of many decorated veterans of Spaghetti Westerns, post-nuke flicks, and grimy Video Nasties. The most notable among these guys is George Eastman, who plays the primary villain, Bruno, and had previously appeared in a pair of Django westerns and then starred in Joe D'Amato's *Anthropophagus* (1980), *Porno Holocaust* (1981), and *Absurd* (1981), before joining up with Cannon again in *The Barbarians* (1987). Cult fans may also recognize him from post-apocalyptic movies such as *The Bronx Warriors*, *The New Barbarians*, and *2019: After the Fall of New York* (all 1983), or *2020 Texas Gladiators* (1985)—Eastman was undeniably a fixture of the post-nuke genre.

The movie's star-crossed lovebirds are also semi-familiar faces. Christian De Sica (Carlo)—son of the famed Italian arthouse director, Vittorio De Sica—became well-known for making Italian holiday films, and has since become a well-respected filmmaker in his own right. Valeria Golino (Caterina) has won dozens of awards on the festival circuit for her Italian film work, but is probably better-known among American movie-goers for playing Pee-Wee Herman's acrobat love interest in *Big Top Pee-Wee* (1988), Tom Cruise's girlfriend in *Rain Man* (1988), and Charlie Sheen's therapist in *Hot Shots!* (1991). This was her first English-speaking role.

Detective School Dropouts was "directed" by Italian journeyman Filippo Ottoni, who is more notable for having co-written Mario Bava's *A Bay of Blood* (1971) than for any of his directorial efforts. (Most of the film's direction was actually handled by Landsberg and Dreyfuss themselves.) The endearingly cheesy synthesizer score is credited to a mysterious "Geo," which was actually a pseudonym for George S. Clinton, perhaps to make him sound more like a trendy Italo Disco producer rather than Cannon's house composer. He was responsible for the scores to *The Apple* (1980), *Avenging Force* (1986), *American Ninja 2* (1987), and *Too Much* (1987).

The movie was developed under a slew of different English titles, and some were arguably more fitting than the one they ultimately went with. These include "Private Defectives," "Defective Detectives," and my favorite, "Dumb Dicks." In Italy, the movie's title translated to "The Asylum Police."

Meanwhile, the suspiciously vulgar-sounding German title, *Die Klugscheißer*, literally (and hilariously) translates to "The Knowledge Shitters," although a more correct and closer English translation would probably be "The Smart-Asses."

For whatever reason, *Detective School Dropouts* received a very, very limited theatrical release, not even meriting a simple review in any of the large market newspapers. It was already in cable rotation by November, only three months after it premiered in theaters, where it picked up more of an audience. While it wasn't the best comedy Cannon made—it's arguably not even the best one they made starring Landsberg and Dreyfuss—there were certainly ones with fewer laughs that Cannon gave a much wider release.

In typical Cannon pacing, Landsberg and Dreyfuss had already shot a second film for the company before the first one ever hit theaters. *Dutch Treat* started filming less than two months after *Dropouts* had wrapped, and was released just five months after its predecessor. Not only did Cannon skip theaters entirely for *Dutch Treat* in the United States—opting instead to only release it around Europe and a few other foreign territories—but they didn't even bother to put it out for rental on videotape, which feels like an odd decision given that the movie is actually *very* funny.

Landsberg and Dreyfuss play roles in *Dutch Treat* similar to the ones they had in *Dropouts*: the former is a worry-wart loser who can't do much right, while the latter is an overconfident schemer always looking to turn a quick buck. They're named Jerry and Norm, respectively, and while their relationship isn't entirely clear, we glean that they're at least roommates and longtime friends. Let's say they're Bert and Ernie, all grown up.

The movie opens with Jerry in court for a traffic violation that was actually Norm's fault. When Norm talks him into pleading guilty in hopes that they'll get off with a slap on the wrist, Jerry lands himself a non-insignificant prison sentence. We fast forward to the day of his release, and Jerry's understandably bitter. He has even more reason to be upset when he learns that Norm's rented out their apartment to a large family of Jamaicans, and that his girlfriend dumped him for a boxer named Percy. *Oof!*

A collector's card advertising the German release of *Dutch Treat*. The film was not released on video in the United States.

Unfortunately, Norm's latest cash-grabbing scheme isn't going to cheer him up. The two men climb aboard a cruise ship as hired entertainment: Norm is "The Great Badir," an exotic knife thrower and Jerry is, obviously, dressed in drag as his "princess" assistant. Norm is of course *not* a trained knife-thrower, and this goes about as well as you can imagine. Our heroes are kicked off the boat in Holland, where they make the best of things and attempt to take in all that Amsterdam has to offer. One of the first things they happen across is a canal-side café, where they sit back and enjoy an open-air performance from the Dutch all-girl pop group, the Dolly Dots.

Now, if we're looking for a potential reason why *Dutch Treat* didn't receive a normal U.S. theatrical release, the Dolly Dots may be it. Formed in the dying dregs of the disco era in 1979, the Dolly Dots became a wildly popular all-girl singing group in their native Netherlands by the early 1980s. The six young women appeared on TV often, wearing coordinated outfits and performing simple, synchronized dance moves as they took turns singing lead. Locally they produced numerous hit records, and became something of a pop culture sensation: by mid-1984, the Dolly Dots not only had their own line of Barbie dolls, but their own Dutch television series. This is about the time Cannon entered the picture, when the Dolly Dots seemed poised to conquer the world with their distinctive brand of Abba-meets-the-Village-People pop sensibility.

Cannon made arrangements to shoot a cinematic star vehicle for the group, a proto-*Spice World* (1997), if you will, but it took several years to develop. The first project announced was a movie called "Give a Girl a Break"—named after one of the group's hits—and later changed to "Au Pair Girls." It would have had a different plot, but numerous similarities. (The fame-seeking girls would have come to America by posing as nannies, part of their scheme to play a gig at a big-shot Beverly Hills party.)

By the time Cannon finally got around to making the film, however, interest in the Dolly Dots had long since crested. One of the more popular members had left the group to have a child and launch a solo career. Worse yet, the band had made little noise outside of Holland, and completely failed to find any crossover success in the United States. By the time of *Dutch Treat*'s release, the group was on the verge of breakup and very few people west of Brussels had any idea who they were. Showing unusual financial forethought, Cannon opted to only give the movie a regional release in countries where the fading pop idols had once broken through.

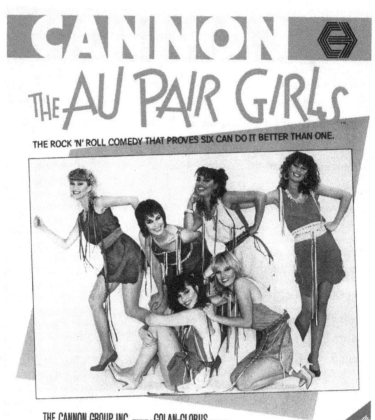

CANNON

THE AU PAIR GIRLS

THE ROCK 'N' ROLL COMEDY THAT PROVES SIX CAN DO IT BETTER THAN ONE.

THE CANNON GROUP, INC. PRESENTS A GOLAN-GLOBUS PRODUCTION
THE AU PAIR GIRLS STARRING THE DOLLY DOTS
WRITTEN BY STUART SCHOFFMAN PRODUCED BY MENAHEM GOLAN AND YORAM GLOBUS
DIRECTED BY JOEL SILBERG ("BREAKIN'")
© MCMLXXXIV CANNON PRODUCTIONS N.V.

CANNON'S FIRST MOTION PICTURE TO BE FILMED IN THE NETHERLANDS

THE MAKING OF THE 7ᵀᴴ MAJOR

Originally, the Dolly Dots movie—at first titled "Give a Girl a Break" and then "The Au Pair Girls"—was going to be helmed by Cannon's go-to musical man, Joel Silberg, director of *Breakin'* and *Rappin'*.

Back in the film, Norm attempts to smooth-talk the girls by posing as bigwigs from Capitol Records. They're personally invited to the group's gig later that evening at a leather bar, but on their way there find themselves engaged in hijinks in Amsterdam's famous red light district. (Of course, this means Norm and Jerry arrive at the club chained together and wearing nothing but skimpy, leather straps.) A bar fight ensues and much furniture is broken. This leads to our heroes being deported back to the United States in a private jet flown by a drunken woman and her dimwitted son. Before they leave, though, they make the girls promise to look them up if they are ever in Los Angeles, assuming that would never happen . . .

. . . and so, obviously, the Dolly Dots show up in Los Angeles almost immediately, instruments in hand, ready for Norm and Jerry to help them land their big break in America. The guys have to scramble to perpetuate their lie so that the girls don't find out they're really just a taxi driver and a busboy, even as the Dolly Dots run up an expensive hotel tab under their name.

This is where the movie turns into something akin to a screwball comedy, with the two men scheming their way into fancy gigs for the band, going way too far to maintain their lie about being big shots. There are a bunch of slapstick sequences, and more than one instance of mistaken identity. It's all actually very well-executed, with plenty of honest laughs to be had throughout. Even the songs performed by the Dolly Dots in the movie itself are catchy and well-staged. Had the band broken out beyond the Netherlands, it's easy to imagine the movie could have been a modest box office success. (One memorable musical number has the girls ludicrously disguised as Orthodox Jewish men so they can perform at an old rabbi's birthday party—only to strip off their robes and hats mid-song to reveal their model hairstyles and skimpy '80s fashion choices, much to the shock and delight of the audience. The whole scene's a hoot.)

The more straight-forward plot, gonzo humor, and upbeat musical numbers really benefit *Dutch Treat*, making it the more consistently entertaining of the two Landsberg-Dreyfuss Cannon movies. It's also helped by having a veteran director in Cannon regular Boaz Davidson, who directed this one in between *The Last American Virgin* (1982) and *Going Bananas* (1988). He gives the movie a slicker, more professional gloss than its predecessor, and his wife and longtime editor, Bruria Davidson, cuts the movie so that it consistently moves at a fast clip and ensures the punchlines land at the exact moments necessary.

One of the funniest moments is when Norm and Jerry first pull up to their apartment, and fail to register that they've stumbled into an over-the-top brawl centered on a roadside fruit stand. It's a throwaway scene, but it's spectacularly choreographed, and both actors deliver their lines perfectly while nonchalantly dodging flying fruit and swinging crowbars. It's comedy gold, and moments like these are why it's such a shame this movie's been so hard to find for so many decades.

Landsberg and Dreyfuss' on-screen partnership didn't continue into any further starring vehicles, but they both made cameos in the gambling comedy *Let It Ride* (1989). Dreyfuss continued working primarily as a voice actor, lending his talents to numerous cartoons throughout the 1990s. Landsberg made the occasional screen appearance but mostly moved behind the scenes, writing and producing for television series such as *Blossom* (1990–1995) and *Cosby* (1996–2000) before he passed away in 2018.

Interview: Actor/Writer Lorin Dreyfuss

In a partnership with fellow comedy writer David Landsberg, Lorin Dreyfuss wrote and starred in two movies for Cannon: 1986's *Detective School Dropouts*, and 1987's *Dutch Treat*. On screen and off, they proved an effective comic duo, mixing slapstick humor into a non-stop stream of over-the-top gags—and would have made more movies for Cannon, had the company not gone broke before they could do so.

The elder brother of actor Richard Dreyfuss, Lorin had his big screen break as a producer on *Skatetown, U.S.A.* (1979), one of the first roller disco films and the movie that gave Patrick Swayze his debut.

Your first credit came on *Skatetown USA*, which you produced and have a story credit on. Can you walk me down the path that brought you into the industry, to meeting David, and working with Cannon?

Lorin Dreyfuss: I was one of the rare show business guys that had right-brain and left-brain at the same time. I was a professor—I got my degree in finance—but my brother was already making a name for himself as an actor. I helped him from a business point of view, and then I got more involved with the creative aspect of the business, because I was reading a lot of screenplays and saying to myself, "I think I could pull this off. I think I could do this." Eventually, I left the academic world.

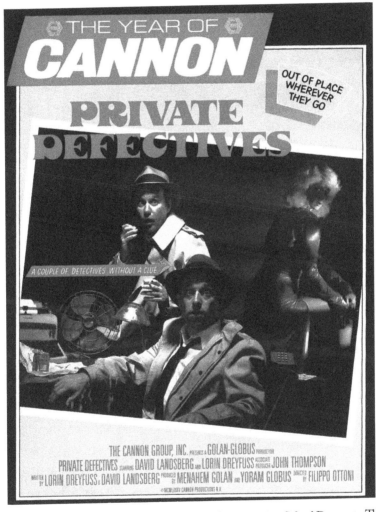

Landsberg and Dreyfuss in a pre-sales ad for *Detective School Dropouts*. The woman posed behind them in the red dress was the duo's personal secretary.

In the early '70s I had written a number of TV pilots that had not gone anywhere. It was very difficult to get in the door. *Skatetown* came about

463

through a friend of mine who knew a B-movie director named Bill Levy. He had this idea for *Skatetown*. We got along really well, and at the time I had access to Columbia Studios. I said, "Let me pitch this idea to the studio as a film." It would've been the first roller-skating movie idea. We pitched it. We sold it. We made the deal in July of '79 and it was released in September in a thousand theaters.

Wow, that's fast!

It was very fast. Our budget was $400,000. At the time the producer said, "No, we don't make $400,000 movies at Columbia. We make $4,000,000 movies." They gave us $4,000,000 instead of $400,000. [*Laughs*] They spent that and took, probably, half of it into their pockets, because I was pretty naïve at that time, but we made the movie.

During the casting is when I met David [Landsberg]. My wife and I were watching a TV show with Don Rickles called *C.P.O. Sharkey* (1976–1978). One of the actors was David, who I wouldn't know from a hole in the wall, but my wife knew him from Hofstra in Long Island. They were college drinking buddies. She said, "That guy, David, I knew him in school years ago, and he was very funny." I called David out of the blue and said, "Listen, my wife seems to know you and wants us to get together." Literally, he and his wife came over, we had dinner, and we fell in love with each other. We stayed partners for fifteen years, which was a long time.

The first thing I did is I put him into *Skatetown*, and then we formed a partnership, and out of that partnership we started writing television. We mounted two of our unsold pilots as one-act plays in Hollywood because we felt, as comedy writers, that the decisions in the comedy world were being made by people who weren't necessarily funny, and wouldn't know a joke if it fell off a shelf and hit them on the head.

Instead of giving them written material like a script, we said, "Why don't we put it on its feet and act it?" We invited all kinds of network people and friends, and through a series of different connections the people from Cannon found out about it.

Menahem Golan saw it. He called our agent and said, "Can you have those guys come and meet me?" We went to his office, he was just moving Cannon to LA—they were pretty much international schlockmeisters prior to that. We go to meet Menahem at his office and he says in his heavy Israeli accent, "I smell something in you guys." David said, "Well, that must be me."

Menahem said, "You're very funny and I watched the audience reaction to those plays." He said, "You make me laugh. I want you to do a movie for me." Now, if you could imagine what it's like for two young writers to be told, by a producer or an owner of a studio, that he wants to make a movie. To say that we were thrilled is an understatement.

We said, "What kind of movie?" He said, "That's not my job. That's *your* job." He says, "You go. You write a movie and you bring it back to me. You make people laugh." We said, "Oh, okay." He's, "Oh, and we're going to shoot it in Italy." I said, "Italy? Why Italy?" He said, "Well, we have a studio there that's vacant. It's going to need some production," blah, blah, blah. We literally walked out of his office smiling and shaking.

He was like the old-time moviemakers, the MGMs and the Harry Cohns of yesteryear. He was an instinctive guy. He didn't give a shit about art, or art craftsmanship, or business. He was just into making movies. He *loved* movies. He made a whole bunch of different movies and made deals all over the world.

I assume you went home and wrote the script. What happens next?

Menahem said, "You have to go find a director." We sent the script around and a man came to us through our agent. He said, "I've been acting and writing and producing stuff with my partner for a long time, and this is the first script that has intrigued me. I haven't done this for a while. I've been retired sitting on my money." He said, "I'll direct this movie for you guys." His name was Tommy Chong.

He had already stopped making movies with Cheech, but he knew a lot. He was very clever and he said, "I'll do this for you." He made a deal with Cannon for the director's fee. We all went to Italy to work on the script and to do a little preliminary casting, location scouting, and all that.

We had told everyone, "We're going to make this movie that's like a cartoon." David and Lorin would be like Heckle and Jeckle or the two Stooges, and we're going to fill it with laughs, as many as we can. Lots of gags and physical comedy, and we're going to shoot it in front of every famous place in Italy." We traveled all over Italy finding locations. The Colosseum, Venice, the Tower of Pisa. We said, "Instead of shooting an argument in a restaurant, let's shoot it in the Vatican." We had a crew that were guerilla filmmakers who didn't give a shit, and bribed all the cops and the guards.

We were there for about two weeks with Tommy, and he said, "You don't need me. I'm going to quit. You and David are just like Cheech and I. You don't need someone getting in your way. You know these characters, you know your timing, and you know your senses of humor better than anybody. Do it." He said, "I'll stick around and help you guys, but I don't need to get paid."

Literally, we were stunned, and the studio said, "No, no, no, you need a director." They promoted the first AD, an Italian guy, to be "the director." Really, all he was going to do was set the lights. We would tell him what we're doing: "He's going to walk in, I'm going to smack him in the mouth, he's going to fall in the canal. Let us know when you're ready to go." That's how we did it. We were supposed to be there three months, but were there for thirteen months, going back and forth, because we had to do everything— casting, location scouting, shooting. We had the time of our life. It was a riot, and we learned a lot. We laughed a lot. We made terribly good friends. We ended up making this cute, funny little movie that became a cult classic, in a way. It was a thrill.

I have a stack of sales ads for _Detective School Dropouts_ with similar art but different titles. Was it you guys switching the title around each time, or Cannon?

I think Cannon at one point came up with _Dumb Dicks_. We immediately said, "No fucking way." Then, they came up with _Defective Detectives_, or we all did. Then we realized that, "Hey, this had already been used before." I think it was a Jerry Lewis movie way back when. Then we came up with

Private Defectives, which still didn't click. Eventually it became *Detective School Dropouts*, and that's what stayed.

When the picture opened, it made some money. Canon didn't care about the money, because they would basically pre-sell their pictures using a one-sheet poster at the Cannes Film Festival. They get $20,000 from Fiji and $17,000 from Kenya, and raise enough money for them to pay off the previous movie that they made.

Every once in a while—and it's forty years later—I'll open up an envelope and there'll be $17.80 from Swaziland. [*Laughs*] It's better than opening it up and finding a bill from the IRS, but still, I get these residuals from God knows what. This was a movie that hardly made any money at all. It must have made substantial money for Cannon, even though they denied it. First of all, the budget, all in, including thirteen months there with a bunch of back-and-forth journeys to California and living expenses, was a million bucks.

By contract, you were given a salary and a per diem, living expenses. Our living expenses were 300,000 lira a month. That was to find an apartment and put the kids in school. We were given six million lira a month in cash, which was a box of money. When I left Italy, I had fifty million lira in boxes.

I'm picturing a pirate's treasure chest, overflowing with gold coins.

Right. I couldn't put it in a bank, I couldn't send it to the United States. I couldn't do any of that, because you're violating all kinds of laws. I gave ten million lira, which was like $5,000, to the costume designer, who was connected to all the major fashion houses in Rome. I said, "Buy me a wardrobe," because the clothing in Italy, especially then, was so beautifully done. She picked out a bunch of Armani, this, that, the other thing. I came home with stuff that I never would have bought on my own. Every time I put one of those suits on, someone would stop me on the street and say, "Where the hell did you get that fantastic suit?" The rest of it, I literally had to put in a suitcase and carry onboard, which was ⊠50 million, which converted to $50,000.

A French postcard advertising the release of *Detective School Dropouts*.

How did *Dutch Treat* come about?

We came back [from Italy] on Christmas Eve after being gone—our last excursion was probably two months. I walked in the door and the phone rang, and it was our agent saying, "Menahem wants to see you guys." I said, "We just got back." He had his office in Beverly Hills at the time, and our poster was on the roof of his building: a giant billboard of us. I'd drive by there every day, just to look up to the top of this building, at this giant billboard. Anyway, our agent says, "Menahem wants to talk to you about something. Can you get over here this afternoon?" It was December 24th.

Now, Christmas doesn't mean a lot to Menahem, because he's Jewish. David and I are also Jewish, so we didn't really care much about Christmas. Our wives, on the other hand, were not Jewish, and said, "Where the hell are you going? You just got back and it's Christmas Eve and we're putting up the tree." We went, "Fuck the tree. We're going to go to Cannon to see what Menahem has to say!"

We were walking into the Cannon offices and David and I said to each other, "What is he going to do? What does he want?" Our agent said, "I think he may want to do something else with you guys." I said, "Oh dear." Knowing Menahem, he's going to want us to put on animal costumes or something.

We walked into Menahem's office and he says to us, "You guys are great! You make me laugh. I enjoy your company. I want you to make another movie for me." David and I looked at each other and then he says, "I have an all-girl rock band that I signed in Amsterdam. I want you to go there. I have two more days on their contract, so I want you to go over there and convince them to extend their contract and make a movie with you guys." He adds, "If you want, just go over there and take them to dinner, you can fuck them if you feel like it."

We're looking at each other. Literally, David and I had feared that we were going to be dressed up as bunnies or something. We were stunned and thrilled. We said, "When?" He said, "Tonight."

He says, "You've got to fly the red-eye tonight and get there tomorrow because that's the day they're contracting. You have to go and meet them." We went home to our wives. My bags weren't unpacked. I said, "Hi, honey. Hi, kids. How's everything? Listen, I've got to go, I'll be right back." I start picking my suitcases and they're saying, "Where the hell are you going?" "Well, we're going to the airport. We're going to Amsterdam tonight." Of course, our wives loved us and were happy for us, but were a little upset about Christmas. We said, "We'll be back in a day. We'll go there, meet them. We'll sign the contract, and we'll get out of there." That's pretty much exactly what we did. I think we got back either the night of Christmas or the next morning.

Cannon started to fall apart pretty quickly over the next few years. Did you work on anything else with them?

We had a hell of a run with those guys. We had one more screenplay they wanted us to do. We created a story called *The Wrong Stuff*, because they had made this successful movie called *The Right Stuff* (1983), about astronauts. We wrote what we called *The Wrong Stuff*, where me and David and a group of misfits are inadvertently mistaken for green berets and dropped into the jungles of Mexico to kill a drug lord, or something like that. Of course, it's a complete mistake. There was a glitch in the computer. The FBI snagged us off the street along with about eight other idiots, and got us into an airplane that dropped us into the jungles of Columbia or somewhere.

We never got to make that movie because they went broke. They stopped making movies at Cannon. There was a falling out between the two cousins. Who knows what else was going on, but we never did make *The Wrong Stuff*.

That's a shame. It sounds like it would have been a lot of fun.

It was a great time and a wonderful experience. We learned a lot, I have to tell you. We enjoyed ourselves, we made a few bucks. It kicked off our careers. We then spent the next thirty years writing and working in television and movies. I was a script doctor for years and years. David went on to produce *Cosby* (1996–2000) and other things.

[Golan and Globus] were connivers. They were the Weinsteins without any real taste, the precursors. They would buy a script and make a Sylvester Stallone movie that went right into the toilet. They would do a Dustin Hoffman project, and it would go right into the toilet. They had no idea what they were doing creatively. They were just churning them out, dozens of movies at a time. They had a hell of a lot of success.

At one point, our movie went to the Cannes Film Festival as part of the Cannon slate, with Sylvester Stallone, Dustin Hoffman, all these people.

There must have been twenty or thirty pictures. For a while, they called it the Cannon Film Festival because they did so much marketing there. They were like circus barkers.

I enjoyed their company. As far as I can tell, they never bounced a check, they never lied, they always followed through with a promise. When they paid me that per diem for thirteen months instead of three, they were honorable about that. They didn't screw me or try to—as far as I know, anyway. I have nothing bad to say about those guys. They gave us a hell of a boost.

An Italian poster for *Detective School Dropouts*.

Cannon took misleading VHS covers to an all-new level with their videocassette release of *Salome*.

Salome

Release Date: August 14, 1986 (Italy)
Directed by: Claude d'Anna
Written by: Claude d'Anna & Aaron Barzman
Starring: Tomas Milian, Pamela Salem, Jo Champa
Trailer Voiceover: "The passion of an ancient kingdom comes alive!"

It's hard to guess who exactly this artsy-fartsy adaptation of a Biblical tale was made to entertain. It's a little too slow-moving and highfalutin to hold the attention of the hardcore perverts, but you have to imagine there were way too many exposed breasts and cast-iron dongs to earn it the endorsement of the religious crowd.

Cannon's *Salome* was "loosely adapted from" the 1891 play by Oscar Wilde. It wasn't the first film to explore this source material, nor was it the last—you need to scroll down through at least a dozen entries for "Salome" on IMDb before you land on this particular version—and like many others, it emphasizes the more titillating elements which Wilde read into the story, crafting the film into one, long tease for Salome's climactic, erotic "dance of the seven veils."

As might be surprising to some, the movie's title character doesn't play much of a role in the movie until well into its runtime. Instead, the story focuses on a Judean king, Herod, who seems to be neck-deep in a midlife crisis. *Nothing* seems to be going right for him. He has a handsome young prophet by the name of Yokanaan—referred to as John the Baptist in other texts—chained up in his castle's weird pit dungeon. He's imprisoned him there because he heard Yokanaan talking smack about his new wife, Herodias, who happens to be his brother's ex. Herodias is mad at her husband because instead of getting rid of the prisoner, Herod leaves him chained up where he continuously shouts mean stuff about them from the bottom of the pit. Oh, and she's also (understandably) pissed about the libidinous way Herod keeps blathering on about her hot-to-trot daughter, Salome—*his* niece and stepdaughter.

Things get even more awkward once Salome asks a guard to sneak her into Yokanaan's cell. The prophet hurls insult after insult at her and her family, but for some reason this seems to turn her on, and she falls mad with lust for the prisoner, who adamantly refuses her smooches.

Meanwhile, Herod tries his best to entertain the visiting emissaries from Emperor Caesar's army, who he has a sinking feeling may be there to remove him from power. He finally begs his sultry, young stepdaughter to perform a dance for the gathered men, offering her any reward she desires as payment. After Salome performs her long, elaborate striptease—dropping veil after veil until she's left in a single, see-through toga—she drops a bomb on her stepdad. Instead of asking for something sensible like, say, half of his kingdom, she demands the life of Yokanaan. Herod begrudgingly complies, the moon disappears from the sky, and Salome is soon found making out with the prophet's severed head, which she finds as unsatisfying as you'd expect. The movie ends with her being executed as punishment.

Sooooooo, yeah. The movie was shot at Cannon's Italian production facilities, re-dubbed into English, and premiered at the Cannes Film Festival in 1986, where it received little attention. Cannon forewent a traditional, theatrical release for the movie in the United States and dumped it straight onto video, where it was billed as a film about "The Most Erotic Woman in

History, and the Dance that Destroyed a Dynasty." In fact, much of the summary from the back of the videotape's box feels a tad misleading:

A pre-sales ad for the film from Cannon's 1984 catalog.

"Enter the decadent world of Herod's court—where savage lust and power reign supreme . . . the timeless story of a legendary temptress whose erotic dance fulfilled a prophecy and destroyed a dynasty . . . a thrilling glimpse at a barbaric dynasty and the raw sexual force of the single woman who wreaks its destruction."

Cannon's *Salome* sales catalog ad from 1985—now featuring nipples.

It's easy to see how Cannon's marketing team tried to spin the movie. It may also be closer to what they expected to get in return when they signed on to produce the movie, rather than this dry, talky drama that requires Cliffs Notes to fully follow. Sure, there are plenty of naked women lounging about Herod's palace, and not a single female character gets to keep her clothes on. (The men, meanwhile, get to cover up their wieners with . . . metallic, wiener-shaped cod pieces? That's what they appear to be, at least.) A few guys perform an interpretive dance in creepy animal masks, but it's Salome's infamous routine that comes closest to the sexual romp the back cover of the VHS promises, and even that's way artsier than any horndog probably figured they were bringing home from the video store on a Friday night.

For a premise that emphasizes its decadence, French filmmaker Claude d'Anna's version for Cannon seemed to take a minimalist approach to its production. Almost all of the film takes place in one large chamber of Herod's castle, which is decorated with little more than a few odd, blue-flamed torches—it sometimes appears as if the director was staging the film as a one-set play inside somebody's unfinished basement. (Whenever we get a glimpse outside the castle, it's always the same, murky shot of sand dunes that in all likelihood were just a crude matte painting.) The costume choices, at least, are interesting: d'Anna dresses up the emperor's visiting vassals in vaguely Nazi-like uniforms, invoking a style that the filmmaker described as a "science fiction fantasy set in the past," but looks more like they were trying to dress a *Dune* (1984) knock-off with a budget of just $100, and a trip to the nearest Army-Navy surplus store. The talents of Oscar-winning cinematographer Pasqualino De Santis (*Romeo and Juliet*, 1969) go grossly underutilized.

Salome herself is played by Jo Champa in her film debut. The fashion model would later play Steven Seagal's wife in *Out for Justice* (1991) and appear opposite Johnny Depp in *Don Juan DeMarco* (1994). King Herod is played by Cuban-American actor Tomas Milian, who appeared in many Spaghetti Westerns and cop films, notably *The Big Gundown* (1966) and *The Tough Ones* (1976). Actress Pamela Salem stepped into the role of Herodias shortly after playing Miss Moneypenny in the James Bond film *Never Say Never Again* (1983).

Golan and Globus appeared on the cover of the international edition of *Newsweek*'s May 26, 1986 issue—just in time for that year's Cannes Film Festival.

Intermission: On Highlander, Pirates, Cobra(s), and Other "Almost/Sorta" Cannon Movies . . .

Wow, Cannon sure did make a *lot* of movies in the mid-1980s, didn't they? Hoo, wee! This is a long, long book, and we still have a lot to cover in its second half. In true roadshow style, we're going to take a brief intermission here at the midpoint for a stretch break. So, get up, get yourself a refill at the snack counter. Hit the potty, if you need to. Take a smoke, if that's your thing. Just be sure to be back here in fifteen minutes.

Or, hang around here and listen to me clear the air on a few movies that some might expect to read about in this book, but won't. These include movies such as *Cobra* (1986), *Highlander* (1986), *Pirates* (1986), *Link* (1986), *Mannequin* (1987), and more, which are often believed to be Cannon movies, but the reality is more complicated than it seems.

Before you start audibly booing the book you now hold in your hands, please wait for the explanations. Trust me, *Cobra* and *Highlander* both rule, and I'm sad, too, that I'm not writing about them. The thing is, though, if I didn't draw a line somewhere, *The Cannon Film Guide* wouldn't be a trilogy, but somewhere closer to a nine-book, *Star Wars*-like saga. You'd be waiting longer for me to finish it than readers have been waiting for George R.R. Martin to put a bow on his *A Song of Ice and Fire* saga.

Hence, why I've chosen to focus on movies that were produced by Cannon in-house, or at least Golan and/or Globus had a heavy hand in their creation.

You see, by the mid-1980s Cannon had grown large enough to start spending money—theirs, and creditors'—to pick up independent movies for distribution, or purchase entire film catalogs. They also had numerous distribution channels around the globe, not to mention home video deals, which is how a lot of movies wound up at the rental stores emblazoned with a Cannon logo—including a few head-scratchers. Heck, my shop's copy of *The Evil Dead* (1980) was on HBO/Cannon Video, and insisting *that* film was a Cannon flick is a hill no '80s horror fan will be willing to die on.

Many of these came out of Cannon's purchase of Thorn EMI, including the kickass classic *Highlander* and the killer chimpanzee thriller, *Link*. When Cannon purchased the British company in the late spring of 1986, they were getting their full back catalog of films, a chain of movie theaters, the storied Elstree production facilities, and a handful of movies that were recently finished or in the final stages of completion. Finding themselves in debt again almost immediately, Cannon turned around and cut video deals for many of these movies after distributing them theatrically in a handful of territories. *Highlander* and *Link* wrapped up their shoots in July of 1985, nine months before Cannon took over. Another example of this was the John Cleese comedy *Clockwise* (1986), shot the same summer. (Anyone interested in reading a fantastic, in-depth history of *Highlander*, though, should seek out Jonathan Melville's *A Kind of Magic: Making the Original Highlander*.)

If you were browsing video stores in the late 1980s, this would have been even more confusing. Prior to their purchase by Cannon, Thorn EMI had a deal in place with HBO to release videocassettes from their combined catalogs. "Thorn EMI/HBO Video" would soon became "HBO/Cannon Video," though, and include a dizzying range of movies whose video rights were held by one company or the other, including *The Evil Dead*, *Raw Deal* (1986), *First Blood* (1982), *The Hills Have Eyes* (1977), *The Pee-Wee Herman Show* (1981), *Desperately Seeking Susan* (1985), *One Flew Over the Cuckoo's Nest* (1975), and countless others.

Occasionally when they picked up the distribution rights for an outside production, they would release it under the "Cannon Screen Entertainment Presents . . ." label. This included films like *Mannequin* and Nicolas Roeg's *Castaway* (1986).

When it comes to *Pirates*, this was an extremely expensive stinker of a movie that was tossed between studios like a hot potato for roughly a decade. When the music stopped, Cannon not only found themselves stuck with it, but paid a whole lot of money for that privilege.

Roman Polanski had spent decades wanting to make a swashbuckling adventure in the vein of the old Errol Flynn classics. He finished the initial script for what would become *Pirates* shortly after wrapping up production on his classic *Chinatown* (1974). Early versions were to have Jack Nicholson, with Polanski himself playing sidekick, and Isabelle Adjani, but plans were scuttled when in 1977, to put it as bluntly as possible, Polanski drugged and raped a thirteen-year-old girl while staying at Nicholson's Los Angeles home, then fled the United States to avoid imprisonment.

Although the likelihood of extradition prevented him from traveling to and working in many countries, including the United States and the United Kingdom, it didn't stop studios from lining up to work with the fugitive pervert and director of *Rosemary's Baby* (1968). Filmways, Paramount, Universal Studios, and United Artists were all announced as backers for the film at different points, as was Israeli mogul Arnon Milchan, before eventually dropping out. Finally it was Tunisian producer Terek Ben Ammar who started the ball rolling, investing millions of dollars of his own money to start construction of the massive pirate ship set and nearby studio facilities in his home country, before enlisting other producers and seeking additional assistance from MGM/UA to finance the movie's rapidly-ballooning budget. By the time filming was underway—and Walter Matthau had replaced Michael

Caine, who had replaced Nicholson—the budget, which had started out at $15 million, had blown out to a staggering $40 million.

Here's where Cannon comes in. When it became known that MGM felt they had a flop on their hands (rightfully so), producers Ammar and Thom Mount raised the money to buy out the studio's share. Urgently needing both a new distributor and to make back some of that money, they approached Menahem Golan, a man with a reputation for becoming a little starry-eyed around cinema's "great filmmakers." Eager to include Polanski's name on Cannon's roster, the company signed a multi-million dollar deal to distribute the film—but only in the United States and a few other countries, as most of the international rights had already been promised to other companies.

Pirates was a critical flop, and—unfortunately for Cannon—an even bigger commercial flop. Although it played on more than one thousand screens, the film opened in fourteenth place at the box office and barely crossed the $1 million mark in domestic ticket sales. Golan, at least, was quick to admit that they had made a very expensive mistake.

The boatload of money they paid for *Pirates* included use of the actual boat that was built for the movie, and Cannon planned for a time to recoup some of their losses with a pirate-themed TV show called "The Sea Hawk"— but that series ultimately never made it to television, no matter how many times Cannon announced it.

Cobra may be the most complicated case of them all, and is explained in more detail in this volume's chapter on the fellow Stallone-starrer, *Over the Top* (1987). When Cannon signed their exclusive deal with Sylvester Stallone to star in *Over the Top*, they made headlines by turning him into the highest-paid star in Hollywood to the tune of a cool $12 million dollars. The problem was that Cannon didn't have that sort of just money sitting around, and so in actuality they gave Stallone a half a million dollars as a retainer while they looked for investors to pay not only the rest of his promised fee, but for the movie's full, $25 million budget. This took a while, as perhaps few believed as strongly in their expensive father-son/truck-driving/competitive arm-wrestling concept as Cannon did. It was finally Warner Bros. who got on board to help finance *Over the Top*. Part of their deal, though, included Cannon's consent to let them bypass the "exclusive" stipulation in Sly's Cannon contract so that Warner Bros. could make *Cobra* while the former company got their act together and prepared to shoot *Over the Top*.

To help them look less foolish for advertising an exclusive contract with Stallone only for him to go and make a film for another company, Warners agreed to give Cannon Inc./Golan-Globus a hollow producer's credit. That's why their names appear at the top of the film, but not the Cannon logo. (Obviously they did not share in the film's $160 million worldwide box office, either.)

As someone who will eat pizza only after it's been cut up with scissors, trust me, I'm also disappointed that Golan and Globus' involvement in *Cobra* was little more than lip service. You know what's more disappointing, though? That they never made *Cobra Part II*, which both Golan and Stallone talked up to press during the production of *Over the Top*, and Cannon *would* have been directly involved with had they not almost immediately fallen into an immensely dire financial state, and far beyond the point where they could even entertain the thought of hiring a star of Stallone's pay grade.

And now, back to your feature presentation . . .

Tobe Hooper's *Texas Chainsaw Massacre 2* arrived on VHS more than a decade after its predecessor hit theaters.

The Texas Chainsaw Massacre 2

Release Date: August 22, 1986
Directed by: Tobe Hooper
Written by: L.M. Kit Carson
Starring: Dennis Hopper, Caroline Williams, Lou Perryman, Jim Siedow, Bill Moseley, Bill Johnson
Trailer Voiceover: "The *buzz* is back!"

Although it has found an adoring cult audience in the decades since it was released, it would be hard to fault any moviegoers who demanded their money back after seeing *The Texas Chainsaw Massacre 2* (1986) during its original theatrical run. Was it a bad film? No. Was it a total departure from the movie that preceded it? Absolutely.

The original *Texas Chain Saw Massacre* (1974), released twelve years prior to its sequel, is one of horror cinema's undisputed classics. Gritty, grimy, and suspenseful, the movie set the tone for a decade's worth of American horror films to come afterwards. It also birthed a wave of masked boogeymen, with the chainsaw-toting Leatherface cutting a path for psychos like Michael Myers and Jason Voorhees to become the true stars of their respective franchises. Director Tobe Hooper turned the independent horror film's low budget into an advantage, with the grainy film stock and a cast of unknown actors adding an extra layer of pseudo-realism to the feature. To top it off, *Texas Chain Saw Massacre* was marketed as being based on a "true story," fooling a lot of its early audience members into thinking that a murderous family of cannibals was still on the loose in the Texas countryside.

Texas Chainsaw Massacre 2, on the other hand, doesn't even pretend it takes place in the real world. This is a movie where Dennis Hopper plays an alcoholic, Bible-thumping, ex-Texas Ranger named "Lefty" Enright (pun intended) who, in the film's climax, engages in a chainsaw swordfight with the nefarious Leatherface. This is a movie where the cannibal Sawyer family lives under an abandoned amusement park, and runs an award-winning "barbeque" truck that serves up human remains. This is a movie about "teenage" Leatherface's sexual awakening. This is a movie where the theatrical one-sheet featured the grotesque cast in a pose which mimicked the iconic poster for *TheBreakfast Club* (1985)!

If you turned your head and squinted, there *was* a level of black humor present in the original *Texas Chain Saw Massacre*. (Very, *very* black humor.) But, it was nothing like the nonstop yuck-fest—both "yuck" as in funny, and "yuck" as in gory—which its sequel turned out to be. While *The Evil Dead* (1981) took itself more seriously than its remake-slash-sequel, *Evil Dead 2: Dead by Dawn* (1987), there were a number of laughs to be found in the first film, and the added humor felt like a natural progression on director Sam Raimi's part. *The Texas Chainsaw Massacre 2*, on the other hand, feels like a parody of Tobe Hooper's original film, which is more or less how he and screenwriter L.M. Kit Carson intended it.

"In a sense, the film is about Leatherface in love. This is Leatherface's coming-of-age picture," Carson told *Cinefantastique*. "It's a splatter satire."

A sequel to his low-budget smash hit, *The Texas Chain Saw Massacre*, was part of Cannon's contract with Hooper, which had already resulted in the films *Lifeforce* (1985) and *Invaders from Mars* (1986). Originally, Hooper was only going to work as a producer on *Chainsaw 2*, but finally settled on directing it himself when Cannon's constant budget-cutting made it impossible for him to hire anyone else to do the job.

Screenwriter L.M. Kit Carson was a fellow Texan and a longtime friend of Tobe Hooper's. Two decades earlier Carson had starred in *David Holzman's Diary* (1967), an influential piece of early, American independent filmmaking. A few years later, he co-directed *The American Dreamer* (1971), a compelling, druggy documentary in which he followed around his pal, actor-filmmaker Dennis Hopper, as he wrapped up post-production on his own film, *The Last Movie* (1971). A gig driving Jean-Luc Godard around Hollywood led to his being granted permission to pen the Richard Gere-led *Breathless* (1983), a remake that bore little resemblance to the quintessential French New Wave film. One of his best-known works came shortly before *Chainsaw 2*, when he spotted a despondent Wim Wenders on the set of his classic *Paris, Texas* (1984), who tasked Carson with re-writing Sam Shepard's earlier drafts of the screenplay.

L.M Kit Carson was also the father of *Invaders from Mars'* kidstar, Hunter Carson, so he and Hooper saw a lot of each other in the year leading into *Chainsaw 2*. Hooper asked him to handle the script for the sequel because he knew he could count on Carson to come up with something very different from the original film—which he very much accomplished. Part of it would be updating the setting for the 1980s. Where the first movie had the sadistic Sawyer family terrorizing hippies across the Texas countryside, their target this time around would be the vermin that Carson watched swarm the shopping malls in their pastel-colored sweaters: yuppies.

As legend has it, Hooper and Carson met with Cannon's Golan and Globus to discuss their ideas for a second Chainsaw film, but the producers didn't want to hear them. "You don't have time!" Carson recalled being told. Indeed, Cannon—in their typical, infinite wisdom—had already booked the movie into theaters before they had even talked it over with the filmmakers. The theatrical opening date of August 22, 1986, was already being touted in trailers and advertisements before a first draft of the script had even been completed. Hooper and Carson had to pull it all together at a breakneck pace if the film was to meet its advertised release date.

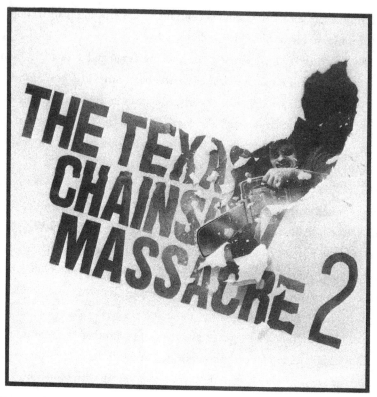

Cannon pre-sold *Texas Chainsaw Massacre 2* knowing little about the film, using catalog ads like this one—in which Leatherface looks more like an evil clown than the masked cannibal that horror fans know and love.

To put things into perspective: this was already the early, winter months of 1986. They didn't have a cast yet, and only a collection of loose ideas to work from. Carson wasn't going to have time to write multiple drafts of a screenplay—and in truth, wasn't even able to finish the first one before production began. The screenwriter had to remain on-set, writing new pages and revising scenes while shooting was already underway. (At one point, Hooper had to stop Carson from revising a scene late into the night—pointing out that they'd already shot it several days earlier.) Filming began in May and wrapped up on July 4th of 1986. The "final" shooting draft was dated June 28th.

The movie's eight-week schedule and $5 million budget were far less than what Hooper had been working with in recent years, including on his two earlier Cannon features and (obviously) the Steven Spielberg-produced *Poltergeist* (1982). The budget and schedule were, however, significantly larger than what Hooper had at his disposal when he made the original *Texas Chain Saw Massacre* in 1974. The lack of pre- and post-production time were where the crew of *Chainsaw 2* felt the real crunch. Hooper was forced to prepare for *Chainsaw 2* while finishing work on *Invaders from Mars*, eventually handing the latter off to Cannon editor Alain Jakubowicz so that he could turn his full attention to crash-prepping the next project. Meanwhile, gore maestro Tom Savini—who had recently wrapped up work on *Invasion U.S.A.* (1985)—was forced to design his special effects for the film in a makeshift lab hastily built near their filming locations, all without ever seeing a finished script. Despite the rushed conditions, Team Chainsaw barreled onward.

Filming took place in and around Austin, Texas, where a significant number of cast and crew members were hired locally. From the original film's cast, only Houston-based theater actor Jim Siedow—Drayton Sawyer, a.k.a. "The Cook"—returned for the sequel. Lou Perryman, a big, loveable Texan who had worked as an assistant cameraman on the original *Chain Saw*, was brought in this time to play L.G. McPeters, one of the movie's tragic heroes. For the rest of the cast, Hooper and Carson sought out fresh blood.

The role of the movie's heroine, disc jockey Vanita "Stretch" Brock, went to local Texas actress Caroline Williams, who made an impression on the filmmakers when she burst into the casting room with a blood-curdling scream, then proceeded to rip the chairs out from underneath them to barricade the door behind her. *Texas Chainsaw Massacre 2* turned Williams into a certified scream queen, leading to roles in many more horror films throughout her robust filmography, including *Stepfather II* (1989), *Leprechaun 3* (1995), and *Ten Minutes to Midnight* (2020)—as well as an appearance in the Tom Cruise racing film, *Days of Thunder* (1990).

A new scream queen is born: Caroline Williams as the terrorized rock radio DJ, "Stretch."

When Ed Neal's murderous hitchhiker did not return for the sequel—a big reason being that his character was splattered by a semi-truck at the end of the original film—he was replaced by a twin brother, whose backstory has him serving in Vietnam during the events of the first movie, thus explaining why he didn't make an appearance. This new character, Chop Top, was played by Bill Moseley, who had written and produced a short parody video titled "The Texas Chainsaw Manicure," which had made its way to Tobe Hooper, who got a kick out of it. Moseley co-starred in the parody sketch as a riff on Neal's hitchhiker character, leading Hooper to tell him that he'd keep him in mind if there was a sequel—a promise that Hooper obviously delivered on. Moseley became another fixture of the horror genre to emerge from this film, going on to appear in everything from the Golan-produced remake of *Night of the Living Dead* (1990) directed by Tom Savini, to *Army of Darkness* (1992), and to play the serial killer Otis B. Driftwood in Rob Zombie's films *House of 1000 Corpses* (2003), *The Devil's Rejects* (2005), and *3 From Hell* (2019).

When Cannon refused to pay higher than scale to an actor whose face would be covered by a mask, a replacement needed to be found for original Leatherface performer Gunnar Hansen. Bill Johnson was another local Texas actor who auditioned for the film, and ultimately won the role of the series' most famous bogeyman. A classical stage actor, Johnson was free to take a new approach to the character, playing him as much like a lovesick adolescent as a skin-wearing, chainsaw-waving psychopath.

Needing somebody to play the movie's half-crazy, revenge-obsessed sheriff, the filmmakers turned to no less than cinema icon Dennis Hopper. With their friendship extending back to the 1960s, L.M. Kit Carson viewed his casting of Hopper in the film as something of a "rescue mission." *Texas Chainsaw Massacre 2* was filmed at a point when many producers felt that the infamously unpredictable, drug-addled actor/director had become too unstable to work with. By the late 1970s, it was reported that Hopper's cocaine intake was up to three grams per day, which he would accompany with marijuana and wash down with a case of beer. In 1983, during an infamous appearance at Rice University, the very drunk and very high filmmaker went in front of an audience, attached sticks of dynamite to the legs of a chair and lit them, planning to perform a dangerous stunt known as "the Russian Dynamite Death Chair." He managed to survive the stunt by dumb luck alone. He followed this up by skipping out on a film shoot and disappearing into the Mexican desert on a lengthy bender. When he returned to the Mexico City airport, he climbed out onto the wing of an airplane before take-off, having convinced himself (with the help of lots of drugs) that it was a scene for a movie. After this, it was time for rehab.

Now sober, Hopper was finding it hard to secure the worthwhile work he'd been landing before going off the deep end. *The Texas Chainsaw Massacre 2* landed him right in the center of a career-saving upswing: it was shot directly after his unforgettable turn as the terrifying, nitrous-huffing villain, Frank Booth, in David Lynch's *Blue Velvet* (1986). He then went from the *Texas Chainsaw Massacre 2* shoot directly into *Hoosiers* (1986), for which he received a Best Supporting Actor nomination. To his credit, Hopper's cast-mates remember him as a consummate professional who spent his days off playing the links at Willie Nelson's personal golf course. Famous for being a method actor, Hopper took his role as "Lefty" Enright very seriously—he would rapidly spin in circles before Tobe Hooper called "action," so that his character would always have a wild, dizzy-eyed look.

The film opens with a brief scroll of text linking this sequel back to the events of the first film, and then we are treated to the movie's delightfully gory opening. Set to the sounds of Timbuk 3's "Shame on You," two preppy douchenozzles speed down a Texas highway, popping off revolver rounds into mailboxes and historical markers. These idiots choose to play a game of chicken with the absolute worst possible pickup truck: one driven by the Lone Star State's most notorious band of cannibalistic serial killers, the Sawyer Family. As they cross a ludicrously long bridge, the truck pulls up alongside their vehicle and out springs ol' Leatherface with his dead brother strapped to the front of him, doing a funny little dance and revving up his chainsaw, which he uses to cut through the roof of their car—and next, through the driver's skull.

The puppet-like corpse we see throughout the movie—and lounging so sexily in the movie poster's family photo—is meant to be Nubbins, the dead hitchhiker from the first movie. (The idea is that Leatherface scooped up his remains into a bucket after he was run over by the semi, and Chop Top sewed him back together when he got home from 'Nam.) To ensure there was a family resemblance, Tom Savini cast a full-body mold of actor Bill Moseley and used that to build their disgusting puppet.

It takes a madman to play a madman: Dennis Hopper as "Lefty" Enright.

Prior to having his head sawed off, this dead douchebag and his pal were making crank-calls to the local rock radio deejay, "Stretch" Brock (Williams), who overheard their gruesome demise. She takes this tape to a former lawman, Boude "Lefty" Enright (Hopper), an uncle of Franklin and Sally

Hardesty—two of the first film's victims—who has made it his personal mission to put an end to the family's serial murders. (Director Tobe Hooper makes a brief cameo here as the drunken partier wearing the horned helmet outside of Lefty's apartment.) Lefty convinces Stretch to air the horrific tape on her nightly radio show, with the hope that it will draw the killers out of hiding.

Unfortunately for Stretch, Lefty's plan works out *too* well. The broadcast is heard by the Sawyer family's ringleader, Drayton (Siedow), who by day handles the cooking at their award-winning barbeque truck. ("I've got a real good eye for prime meat," he admits, accepting a chili cook-off trophy. "It runs in the family!") Drayton dispatches his brothers to go out and get rid of the troublesome disc jockey. As Stretch ends her broadcast in the early hours of the morning, Chop Top (Moseley) and his brother Leatherface (Johnson) show up at the station, and turn her life into a living nightmare.

From this point on, the movie is pretty much non-stop chase scenes and cannibal craziness: a viewer's enjoyment will probably hinge pretty highly on how well they're able to stomach the movie's over-the-top levels of gore, and Leatherface's pervy advances toward the film's female protagonist. You see, the suddenly soft-hearted serial killer seems to have developed a crush on the leggy deejay—most infamously displayed in an uncomfortable moment where Leatherface rubs his chainsaw between her legs. (As Charles Bronson's character from *10 to Midnight* might surmise, "If anybody does something like this, his chainsaw has gotta be his penis!")

Stretch manages to escape the radio station with her life but her coworker, L.G. (Perryman), is not so lucky. Thinking she can still save her friend, she follows the Sawyers all the way back to their hideout, which is located underneath Texas Battle Land, an abandoned and incredibly spooky-looking amusement park. (The exteriors were filmed at the former Prairie Dell Lake Amusement Park, notable for its large, fake mountain that housed a family restaurant known as the Matterhorn, which was surrounded by Bavarian-themed shopping kiosks. The park had permanently closed its doors shortly before filming began.) From here on out the movie goes absolutely batshit, once Stretch is captured within the madmen's subterranean tunnel system, and especially by the time the crazy-eyed Lefty shows up hell-bent on bringing the Sawyer Family down with his own collection of chainsaws.

The movie's gloriously macabre production design is really given the chance to shine once the action moves into the villains' lair. The labyrinthine interior of the Sawyers' home was built inside the former printing facilities of the *Austin American Statesman*. Local artist Cary White was tasked with dressing this morbid locale, turning it into something out of an exceptionally baroque nightmare, resembling what an Applebee's might look like if decorated by Hieronymus Bosch. The seemingly endless, underground tunnels are illuminated with hoarded lamps and countless strings of holiday lights. The Sawyers' favorite decorations are, of course, human bones. When it came time for production to dress a set which called for dozens of skeletons, they were surprised to find it was cheaper to bulk order real ones from India than purchase ones made out of plastic. Most of these skeletons were posed in humorous dioramas throughout the Sawyers' home. (One prominently-placed skeleton straddles a bomb, in a nod to Slim Pickens' character in 1964's *Dr. Strangelove*.)

Lefty stumbles over the withered remains of his nephew, Franklin—the whiniest victim of the original *Texas Chain Saw Massacre*.

The Sawyers' furniture was built using animal remains sourced from local boneyards and slaughterhouses. The Texas heat—combined with some of the animal carcasses being, perhaps, a little too fresh—left the building with an awful stench early in the production. Being a former printing facility, the set builders would often walk out of the building with their hands and clothes dyed black from the ink dust that caked all of its surfaces.

After the tight schedule and budget, heat was the biggest issue the crew faced on *Texas Chainsaw Massacre 2*. Much of the film was shot inside an un-air-conditioned printing facility during the summer in Texas. Factor in the cramped quarters, the large number of crew, and the lighting, and it's no surprise that temperatures on set often reached 125 degrees Fahrenheit. The tunnels—lit by holiday lights and lamps purchased secondhand from thrift stores—would occasionally catch fire, filling the building with smoke and forcing cast and crew to evacuate. At one point, Cannon felt that the production was spending too much on *water*, and briefly cut back their supply—leaving some crew members at the brink of dehydration.

Seasoned horror fans will flock to *Chainsaw 2* to catch some top-tier special effects work by the genre's premiere talent, Tom Savini. The SFX trailblazer had worked as a combat photographer in Vietnam, and has said that the horrors he witnessed in wartime were a major influence on his cinematic gore effects. (The Pittsburgh native built his early resume acting in and designing the realistic, stomach-churning effects for numerous films by fellow Pennsylvanian George A. Romero.) The veteran of such gore masterpieces as *Dawn of the Dead* (1978) and *Maniac* (1980) didn't allow himself to be hamstrung by the fast-paced production schedule and penny-pinching budget. His handiwork is showcased here from the very beginning, when a yuppie's head—a fake head, of course, stuffed with real calf's brains—is sawed in half during the movie's opening scenes.

The Sawyer family puppet-corpse, Nubbins—nicknamed "The Muppet" in the script and on set—is a fun piece of floppy grossness, and the makeup work which turned a 34-year-old Ken Evert into the Sawyer siblings'

137-year-old grandfather is impressive. The film's pièce de résistance, though, is a showstopper dubbed "the L.G. effect," where the character is skinned by Leatherface—only to regain consciousness later, missing his face and much of his flesh. The effect required numerous prosthetics, and included a muscular structure that Savini's team made sure was accurate down to every anatomical detail.

One six-minute-long sequence that involved some heavy lifting on Savini's part—in which a parking lot full of yuppies was slaughtered wholesale by Chop Top and Leatherface—was sadly trimmed from the final film. Many of the film's deleted scenes (including ones starring cult movie critic Joe Bob Briggs and screenwriter C. Courtney Joyner) were released later, on home video, in rough form. Hooper cut them in interest of pacing, but also explained that Cannon was insistent upon the film running less than 100 minutes so that theaters could squeeze more screenings into each day.

As the film ran behind and the budget continued to climb, Cannon grew fed up with Hooper and tried to have him fired from the film and replaced by someone they could trust to finish the movie as cheaply as possible. In the end they weren't able to do this because the three-film contract they signed with him specifically prevented them from doing so.

Shooting on *Texas Chainsaw Massacre 2* wrapped up in the morning hours of Independence Day in 1986—just seven weeks before the film was scheduled to open in U.S. theaters. The last day of production was a marathon in which the cast and crew shot for twenty-four hours straight, as three different units rolled non-stop trying to get all of the shots they'd missed before Cannon cut them off. (The company had sent agents to watch over the set, standing by to literally pull the plug if they ran over the time they had been allotted.) Much of this final sprint was overseen by cinematographer Richard Kooris, as Hooper himself—like many cast and crew members, including Bill Johnson—had come down with pneumonia. Carson himself passed out at his typewriter midway through their all-nighter, only to be woken up and told that filming was finally, mercifully finished.

Two of the Sawyer siblings—Drayton (Jim Siedow) and Leatherface (Bill
Johnson)—antagonize *TCM2*'s heroine, Stretch.

When the film was first screened at the Cannon offices, Golan and
Globus were horrified—not because the movie was scary, but because it was
a comedy. The entire time they thought they were paying for a straight horror
sequel to Hooper's earlier masterpiece, and not an over-the-top parody of said
feature. To be fair to Hooper and Carson, it's something that Cannon would
have known in advance had they not blown off their pitch meeting for it, or
bothered to read the synopsis before they dumped millions of dollars into
producing the film.

Like it or not, however, it was crunch time—the movie was set to
debut in a few weeks, and Cannon had already been advertising the film
with trailers which featured close-ups of chainsaw blades (but no actual
footage from the movie.) Golan asked Hooper to cut most of an emotional subplot in which Stretch was revealed to be Lefty's daughter so

that they could get to the chainsaw action faster. The movie was then submitted to the MPAA, who returned it with an X-rating unless large portions of the film were cut out. Cannon balked—more likely because they didn't have time to re-submit it again before the release date, rather than out of creative principle—and decided to put the film into theaters unrated. When the BBFC requested a similar gutting—forgive my phrasing—of the finished product, Cannon abandoned their British release plans entirely.

Some critics got the movie, but most didn't. Roger Ebert called the film "a geek show," and alleged that it made the mistake of "[equating] screaming and mayhem with suspense." The *New York Times* were firm in their stance that *TCM2* was "not first-grade chopped steak" and called Hooper's direction "a little sloppy." Carrie Rickey, for the Knight-Ridder syndicate, wrote "if this cluttered, ugly movie is good for anything, it must be for making omnivores into strict vegetarians." Critic Edward Jones charged that even fans of the first film might find the sequel "hard to digest" and encouraged readers to "dine elsewhere." (Notice a running theme there? At least the critics had some fun writing their reviews.)

Taking into consideration the negative press and its lack of a rating, *Texas Chainsaw Massacre 2* actually fared pretty well in theaters. You have to imagine that any moviegoer who came in expecting something similar to the midnight movie classic that preceded it was likely blindsided by it being a comedy. On the other hand, those who approached it open to some level of silliness—lots and lots of silliness, to be exact—and an amped-up level of gore—loads and loads of gore—probably came away rather delighted by *The Texas Chainsaw Massacre 2*.

Nowadays, the film holds up a lot better than anyone would have believed, based on its contemporary reviews. *Texas Chainsaw Massacre 2* is an intentionally self-aware comedy poking fun not only at its predecessor, but other horror tropes of the 1980s, and it mostly works as such. ("We'll have the audience confused between screaming and laughing," Carson told *Fangoria* during a set visit.") If you like your horror on the goofy side, and aren't too squeamish—say, you're a big fan of *Re-Animator* (1985) or the aforementioned *Evil Dead 2*—then *Texas Chainsaw Massacre 2* might be right up your alley.

This was the last time Hooper directed a *Chainsaw* film, and when New Line Cinema produced *Leatherface: The Texas Chainsaw Massacre III* (1990) they pretty much pretended that this sequel never happened. It also soured Hooper's relationship with Cannon. After so much fighting over the budget, schedule, and content, the company removed him from consideration for their hopeless Spider-Man project, and canned his science fiction re-imagining of Pinocchio, which would have starred Lee Marvin as Gepetto. (Yoram Globus did work with Hooper again, though, hiring him to take over production on a film called *Night Terrors* [1993] to appease star Robert Englund, and that became one of the last releases put out by Cannon Home Video.)

Like Hooper, L.M. Kit Carson continued to work in Hollywood, producing and writing films for the next two decades. When the Wilson brothers' dad asked him over for dinner to talk his sons out of going into the movie business in the early 1990s, Carson instead took them to Sundance and helped them finance a short film titled *Bottle Rocket* (1993)—launching the careers of not only Luke and Owen Wilson, but their pal, filmmaker Wes Anderson.

Interview: Actor Bill Moseley

A far cry from the brain-fried cannibal that made him famous, Bill Moseley is likely the most well-educated person ever filmed eating their own skull-pickings. Before he became an actor, Moseley studied at Yale and worked as a freelance journalist in New York, writing for outlets such as *OMNI Magazine* and *Psychology Today*.

A fan of Tobe Hooper's original horror classic, he and his friends went to Staten Island and shot a no-budget parody short titled "The Texas Chainsaw Manicure," in which he played a hitchhiker character based on Edwin Neal's role from the first *Chainsaw* (1974). The short eventually found its way to Hooper, who enjoyed it so much that he cast Moseley in his first major screen role.

Dog will hunt: Bill Moseley as Chop Top in *Texas Chainsaw Massacre 2*.

Since making his blood-spattered debut as Chop Top, Moseley's been one of the horror genre's most familiar faces, appearing in cult favorites from Tom Savini's remake of *Night of the Living Dead* (1990) to Sam Raimi's *Army of Darkness* (1992). His other cult film characters include Otis B. Driftwood from Rob Zombie's *House of 1000 Corpses* (2003), *The Devil's Rejects* (2005), and *3 From Hell* (2019), and Luigi Largo from *Repo! The Genetic Opera* (2008).

You grew up in the Midwest, and went to Yale for journalism. How did you discover you wanted to get into film and acting?

Bill Moseley: I was always an actor. When I was growing up in Barrington, Illinois, my parents were part of something called the Barrington Play Reading Group, where the grownups would host a play reading every couple of months. The hosts would arrange the furniture in their living room as a set, and put out chairs. Even though the actors were in costume—the actors being the parents of Barrington—they would read from the plays, holding the books in their hand. I was drafted early on. Whenever they needed a kid, I was one of the go-to kids. I was in *The Lottery*. I was also in *Sunrise at Campobello*. I actually got a little Oscar for playing Nick in *A Thousand Clowns*, so that was an encouragement.

I always did the plays at school. I acted in Yale. I usually would do a play that rehearsed during the winter, because the winters were pretty bleak in New Haven. I did a little acting when I moved to New York City in 1976. For some reason, I had it in my head that acting was not a living, that it was just for fun. It was an *avocation*, versus a *vocation*.

I concentrated on writing for different magazines. Then in the summer of 1984, I worked on a ranch in Wyoming. I'd taken some time off from my hectic nightlife in New York. I was just a ranch hand, shoeing horses, digging irrigation ditches, basically the low man on the totem pole. I was working with a kid at the time, a sixteen-year-old who was a sugar freak, and he would have the Frosted Flakes and the Bug Juice and the Fudgesicles. When he started to do physical work under the hot Wyoming summer sun, he would go into what I called a "sugar delirium." He would start babbling and just foaming at the mouth, doing all kinds of cartoon characters and radio jingles and Top 40 hits. He would just blather. I would turn a deaf ear to it and just do my work. Then one day, he was going on and on about Captain Crunch or whatever it was, and then all of a sudden, out of this blather, he said "Texas Chainsaw Manicure". I heard that, and that got into my inner brain because *The Texas Chainsaw Massacre* (1974) freaked me out when I first saw it. It had stayed with me and disturbed me.

When I heard this kid say "Texas Chainsaw Manicure," I went out to the bunkhouse and I wrote out a five-minute scenario about a woman going to a beauty parlor and sitting under the dryer and wanting a manicure. That was the beginning of a change in careers.

That led to your short film of the same name. What did you plan on doing with that film once you made it?

When I did the "Manicure," my vision at the time was to sell it to *Saturday Night Live*. I really loved *Saturday Night Live*, and I wanted to get on the show. I had actually been rejected. I sent in an audition tape with a bunch of funny little skits, and I had been rejected. There's an actor named Harry Hamlin, and I was working with his half-brother Jerome, who was one of the few people way back when who had a video camera. There was still something called public access TV in New York City. Jerome had this little show called *Video Snacks*.

We were shooting these little skits and things and having fun doing it, but once I got my audition tape rejected by *Saturday Night Live*, I had this idea: "There must be lots of people who sent in tapes that had them rejected." We put an ad in *Backstage* Magazine for people who had gotten rejected by *Saturday Night Live*. That got picked up by *New York Magazine* as "The Not Ready for *Saturday Night Live* Players." We got a lot of tapes, so we ended up cobbling together these half-hour shows with a bunch of rejected skits.

We were having a fine old time. With the "Chainsaw Manicure," again, I had tried to get that on *Saturday Night Live*. They rejected it because it was too long for them, and it didn't have any *Saturday Night Live* stars in it.

I was basically stuck with "Chainsaw Manicure," which I had sunk some dough into. A friend of mine who had worked at Broadway Video, which was *Saturday Night Live's* production entity, had encouraged me and the director of "Manicure" to do the post-production at Broadway Video. He intimated that it would be free. [*Laughs*] We went over and did the editing, and then were presented with a very scary, large bill for it. It seemed like basically doing "The Chainsaw Manicure" had led to a bunch of dead ends and big bills. That's where I was. Like they say, though, it's darkest before the dawn.

That tape made its way to Tobe through a friend of yours, and Tobe loved it. Two years later, you got a call from L.M. Kit Carson asking if you're interested in appearing in the sequel to one of your favorite movies. What's going through your head?

The first thing that went through my head was, "Who is this, really?" It might have been the very night that I had just come back from an audition to play a dead body in an NYU student film. I didn't get the part. The address for the audition was a three story walk-up in the village. By the time I got to the top of the stairs—I was smoking cigarettes at the time—I was winded. I was told, "Great. Good to see you. Just lie there and be a dead body." I laid down on the floor, but my chest was heaving because I was winded from walking up the stairs. I didn't get the job. That was discouraging.

When the phone rang, I could tell it was long-distance because there was a sizzle to it. This must have been the winter, early 1986. It was this guy saying, "Is this Bill Moseley?" "Yes." "This is Kit Carson. I just wanted to get your address, so I can send you a copy of the *Texas Chainsaw Massacre 2* script."

I was thinking in my head, this is not a good time to be goofing on me. I'm about as discouraged as you can get when you can't get a job as a dead body. Anyway, I played along. I could tell it was long distance, as I said. If it were a goof, it was at least an expensive one. I gave him my address. A couple of days later, the script arrived in my mailbox. I was told to concentrate on the character [that became Chop Top].

I think Kit and Tobe had come up with this idea of this Vietnam vet with a metal plate in his head, who would keep scratching it with a coat hanger and all this kind of stuff. I think the character was originally called "Plate-Head." There was apparently some kind of a conflict with a *Masters of the Universe* character of the same name, so they changed it to Chop Top. I read it, and I just thought, "Damn, this is a big part." I thought that the script itself was hilarious. I called Kit back, and I told him I loved it. He was very happy to hear that. As with any writer, you hope that somebody gets it when they read your stuff.

We chatted about it. I said, "It's really funny and wonderful. I love the character." He said, "Great. We'll be in touch." I had no idea what that meant. The next call I got, maybe a day or two later, was from Cannon's legal department. They said, "Is This Bill Mosley?" "Yes." "This is Cannon Films' legal department. Do you have an agent or do you want to negotiate your own contract?" I was like, "What?" I was smart enough to say, "Let me get back to you," pretending that I knew what they were talking about.

I had met a William Morris agent at a Christmas party. I called her up and she took the call, which was nice. I said, "Look, would you negotiate a contract for me?" She said, "Sure, it's basically found money." She called up Cannon's legal team and had a discussion, and then called me back and said, "I've got some good news and bad news." I said, "Jeez, what's the good news?" "The good news is they want you for this part of Chop Top. It's eight weeks." I said, "That's great." She said, "The bad news is that they're only going to pay you SAG scale." I said, "Jeez, what's that?" She said, "Oh, I think it's $1,700 a week." I was like, "What? That's not bad news to me. That sounds pretty great!" As a writer, I was probably averaging about maybe $300 a week, at most. Fortunately, I had a cheap rent on the Upper West Side of Manhattan. You could still live on $300 a week back then.

She said, "Yes, but then there's something else." I said, "Oh, jeez, what?" "Because it's a character with prosthetics and this plate in his head, they're going to have to shave your head." She said, "I told them that you're a working actor, and that's going to put you back about six months, and they've agreed to pay $5,000 to shave your head." [*Laughs*] I was like, "Oh my God. That's *bad* news?"

You were clearly a big admirer of the first *Texas Chain Saw Massacre*. Did that weigh on you as you were stepping into your character, and that world?

The original had completely freaked me out. I'd seen it in Boston, I think in 1975 or 1976. It was on the end of a double bill with *Enter the Dragon* (1973). It was at the Combat Zone, which was kind of the Times Square of Boston, on a Sunday afternoon. I'd seen the title on a marquee at a closed drive-in movie theater outside of Boston. I just thought, "What the hell is that? What a name!" I knew I had to see it. I went to the theater, and it completely blew my mind. I came from rural Illinois, so I was all into night crawlers, bait shops, and mom-and-pop gas stations, everything "country." What that movie did was make everything that was rural frightening. Then, it was like "What is in those hot dogs—or *who*?"

I love horror movies. Everything about horror movies has always been in my blood. Yet, I was unprepared for *The Texas Chain Saw Massacre*. I determined that the only way to get over it was to see it a bunch of times, so that it became so familiar that it wouldn't be scary. That completely backfired. That was before even VHS, when it was very hard to find *TCM*. When I did, I would go see it. I probably ended up seeing it about six or seven times, just to try to make it so familiar, but it really pounded that thing deeper into my head instead.

I knew that this was going to be the sequel to a movie that had freaked me out, but there was something also wonderfully, giddily attractive about it. I wasn't really completely overwhelmed by it. For some reason, it didn't scare me so much. I tell you, what really turned the tide for me was when I was in the parking lot of the Brook Hollow Motor Inn outside of Austin, where we were all billeted. This car pulls up, and out gets The Cook, Jim Siedow. He drives up by himself, parks his car, and gets out of the car. I just went, "It's The Cook!" He looked at me and said, "Hey, kid, how are you doing?" In that moment, I think there was a transformation where I realized that instead of being frightened by these monsters, I really felt like, "Oh my God, I'm one of *them* now." It's like in *Freaks* (1932): "Gooba-gabba, one of us."

Now that I was one of them, that completely changed my mindset. It was like being accepted into a family that had just terrified me for years.

I've heard that from the moment filming began, you pretty much stayed in character as Chop Top. Many actors are trained that way, including your co-star Dennis Hopper, but other than perhaps a few acting classes it sounds like you found this method style on your own. Would you say that's true?

506

I would. What really got me into Chop Top more than anything, first and foremost, was Ed Neal's performance as the hitchhiker [in *Texas Chain Saw Massacre*], knowing that I was playing his twin brother. Of all the performances in the original *Chain Saw*, Ed's performance really struck me the hardest. He was my guy. He was my Virgil to Chop Top's Dante, through the world of the Sawyer family. He gave me a template, and that was really helpful.

Chop Top (Moseley) and Stretch (Caroline Williams) get acquainted in *Texas Chainsaw Massacre 2*.

What really did it for me was probably when they shaved my head. I never had my head shaved before. Like a lot of young males, I was worried about going bald someday, because my older and younger brother were already having some issues in that department. Then, to get my head shaved was incredibly liberating. For some reason, it really unleashed something else in me. I had such a great time with Tom Savini and the makeup artists in the

507

"House of Pain," what I called the makeup department. The whole thing was something I'd never experienced before. That also empowered me.

I wasn't Chop Top *all* the time. I'm not a method guy. When they said "cut," I wasn't still swinging a hammer at the craft service people. Although, I do remember one time, actually, there was a nicely-dressed woman with her little boy, and they were visiting the set. I was dressed and made up as Chop Top. I'd just been doing some work and standing there. The little boy took one look at me and was holding on, cowering behind his mother's skirt. His mother said, "Come on, Johnny. Don't worry, it's just an actor in makeup." I remember coming over to little Johnny, bending down, and whispering in his ear: "Don't believe it." [*Laughs*]

Tobe has been described as somewhat demanding, but that didn't mean he wasn't open to actors' ideas. Are there any moments you can point to, where perhaps you made a suggestion that was different from what was on the page?

I don't really think so. Basically, they would wind me up and say "action," and I would just do things. I certainly had technical experience. I would hit my marks and say my lines. It was actually good that the script was kind of incomplete. What happened was I ended up improvising the lines. Because what would happen, I would get into my Chop Top ... I won't call it a trance, really, because I was awake, but I would get into character. I would improvise and mix things up.

For instance, there was a scene where we're in the radio station. It's the introduction of Chop Top, where I'm banging on poor L.G. In that scene, Lou Perryman comes in with his coffees for Stretch, and Leatherface knocks him down. Then Chop Top jumps out of the record vault, starts banging on his head with a claw hammer. As I'm doing that, I'm saying things like, "Time for incoming mail! A one and a two . . ." It was like Lawrence Welk, and "incoming mail" was from the *Sgt. Rock* comics from my youth. I was making up all kinds of stuff. With each take, Tom Savini would wipe the blood off poor Lou Perryman's face. Tom was just off-camera with a blood pump—he had a gallon of blood, or whatever, and a tube that went across the floor up the back of Lou's neck and through his hairline, and it stopped right at the top of his forehead. When I'd be banging on poor Lou, Tom would be pumping the blood, and spraying it out of the little tube at Lou's hairline.

The set was very contained. Of course there were lights, and it was hot. It was a sticky, hot mess in there. We kept doing the scene over and over because the claw hammer that I was using was actually made of foam rubber. Sometimes when I would whack L.G., the hammer would bend. They'd go, "Cut." I'd look at the hammer and it would be like a wishbone. That wasn't working. It was take after take after take, and I was just making crazy shit up. Finally, we had done about at least a dozen takes. The last one we had done was good, and Tobe said, "That's great. That's great—oh, let's just do one more."

I remember looking at Tobe annoyed, but also wondering what was going on here. I said, "Tobe, am I doing something wrong?" He looked at me and said, "Hell, no, Bill, I'm just having fun watching." That's my kind of guy. That was one of the most encouraging moments I've ever had from a director. As an actor that kind of encouragement, even when you're hitting somebody on the head with a hammer, it's really food for the soul.

There was a lot of improvised stuff. Like, "Lick my plate, you dog dick." I made that up on the spot. When I was a kid, my parents encouraged us to eat up all of our food, my brothers and me. We had what was called the "clean plate club." That was where I got "Lick my plate." I don't know where "dog dick" came from—the whole thing just flew out of my mouth. It's funny that it has become one of Chop Top's signature lines, but I appreciate that.

I know it got up to 125 degrees on the set, that Cannon had you on a breakneck schedule, and there were long hours. This was a difficult shoot. Being one of your first movies, I imagine you walked out of there with a bit of dramatic scar tissue. Did it make your next few jobs seem easy by comparison?

It spoiled me, actually. I loved every minute of doing *Chainsaw 2*. A lot of people got the walking flu—or "the crud"—because a lot of the set was in the old *Austin American-Statesman* building, which was the old newspaper in Austin. It was like a big hangar, and there were great, big wooden beams in the ceilings. The beams had about a half-inch thick coating of printer's ink, just from years of it flying off the presses, carrying on the air and landing on the beams. There was a lot of dust. The conditions were also tough when we shot out at the Texas Battleground. That set had a bunch of dust. A lot of people were getting sick.

Bill Johnson got sick. I remember him coming into the makeup trailer one day. He had what looked like a big ball of hash. It was a dark green, and pungent-smelling. He said, "Here, eat this." I said, "What is it?" He said, "It's a Chinese medicine ball." So, I ate it. I don't know if that helped, but I never got sick. Billy did—he got *sick*. A bunch of people got the walking pneumonia thing, bronchial stuff, and I did not.

There was a paranoid connection between people getting sick and the fact that we were using real skeletons. Cary White, who was our amazing set decorator, was trying to get skeletons for the scene where Stretch is running through the tunnels, and there are all these skeletons sitting in beach chairs with Christmas lights, and all these different dioramas using human skeletons. He found that it was cheaper to actually get *real* skeletons sent over from Indonesia or India, I'm not sure which it was. He got a *ton* of skeletons from someplace where it was not a big deal to sell them. One of the rumors during post-production was that there was some kind of *Chainsaw* curse, because we were using real skeletons. But, I think it was just the conditions with the dust and the printer's ink. For me, though, maybe that Chinese medicine ball actually worked, because I never got sick.

There were times when we would work twenty-hour days because Cannon had said, "Look, we're pulling the plug on the Fourth of July." They had their goons around—I'm sure there's other, nicer words for them. Cannon had their muscle there, because they wanted to make sure that production ended right on schedule. We worked really, really hard. I'm so glad that I was in good shape, and I was able to not only endure, but really enjoy it.

What did it feel like when that marathon of shooting ended on the Fourth? What was it like for you, coming out of that world and that character?

On the Fourth, we worked literally for twenty-four hours to get it done. When we finally wrapped, I had had the prop guy make Tobe a trophy. There was a scene when Stretch comes into our lair, and we're banging on her head and trying to get that "slurpy booty" for grandpa. I had a ladle in my hand that I was supposed to put below Stretch's bleeding head. I think the ladle was going below camera frame or something like that, there was some kind of problem with the ladle that Tobe got mad about, like, "Damn it, get that ladle up." I commissioned the prop man to mount the ladle on a wooden frame rimmed with chainsaw chain. [Laughs]

We started at noon on July 3rd and worked around the clock. Somehow, we finally made it to noon on July 4th. The plug was pulled. All of us gathered to celebrate the conclusion of production. I came over, I think, probably still dressed as Chop Top, and presented Tobe with his ladle trophy. He said, "God damn it, that ladle." It was so funny.

We all went back, I got my makeup off. I remember I was in the honey wagon, just getting my stuff together. There was a knock on my door. I opened it up and there's Carin, Tobe's then wife, who was the wardrobe person, and she's carrying an open cardboard box with a bunch of stuff in it. She says, "Here, this is for you," and it was my Chop Top costume. I looked at it and I said, "You know what, thanks, but I would never wear any of this stuff." [Laughs] She went, "Oh, okay," and off she went. Eric Lasher, the set photographer, saw that and said, "I'll take it." He took it and hung on to it for, I think, at least fifteen years. One day he called me up and said, "I want to give you this costume." I think by then I had come to my senses. Eric gave me the costume, which I am very, very happy to have.

Do you remember where you were when you saw the finished film for the first time?

Yes, I was in Times Square. I was there with a buddy of mine. I remember just watching the movie and just thinking, "This is awesome." I loved the movie. The thing I remember most vividly was when the lights went up at the end of the movie, and people were getting up. My friend who was with me said, "Hey, everybody, here's Chop Top," pointing at me, embarrassing me. There was a guy sitting in front of us in a black leather jacket, and he turned around and said, "Nice job, man." He stuck out his hand to shake, and it was a hook. [*Laughs*] I remember my dad telling me as a little boy, "Take what's offered to you and shake it heartily." I grabbed the hook and shook it, but not *too* heartily.

I love talking about *Chainsaw 2*, because it was a labor of love. It changed my life. It gave me a career. It gave me Otis. It gave me Luigi Largo. It gave me all of my characters. I'm very grateful for it. It was more than a job—let's put it that way.

Bill Johnson (as Leatherface) and director Tobe Hooper pose for a promotional photo during the making of *Texas Chainsaw Massacre 2*.

Interview: Actor Bill Johnson

Bill Johnson has been a contributor to the stage for more than forty-five years, having originated roles by well-known playwrights in all varieties of venues. When Tobe Hooper sent out a casting call across the Lone Star State to fill the remaining roles in his horror sequel *The Texas Chainsaw Massacre 2* (1986), he found his new boogeyman in the Austin-based Bill Johnson. The stage actor was tasked with taking over the role of the near-mute Leatherface, *The Texas Chainsaw Massacre* series' marquee villain.

Among his many roles, Johnson can also be seen in *Future-Kill* (1985), *D.O.A.* (1988), *Paramedics* (1988), and *Talk Radio* (1988). Johnson remains active on both the stage and screen. He is also a co-creator of the Perspectives Enhancement Project, P.O.V. Gateway, which is researching the potential use of the Giza pyramids as a geo-magnetic climate control station.

You were trained as a classical stage actor. How did you find a way to connect to Leatherface, even while you were performing through all of the heavy makeup and mask materials?

Bill Johnson: Well, I just did sort of standard actor things. Typically, actors end up playing roles in the beginning where they don't have any lines. You know, "spear carrier," "second mate," that sort of thing. So, you find other ways to communicate. Taking a degree in this, you make quite a lengthy study of how to get the job done. It's evolved. Theater is the amalgamation of all the arts into one, so it's a pretty wide base of operations.

Is it true that you hadn't seen the original *Texas Chain Saw Massacre* until you auditioned for this film?

That's right. I had not seen it. I had, I think, seen some brief TV commercials for the film. But, I hadn't seen the film itself.

There was no dialogue in the script that they gave me [at the audition]. It was like, "Here's your relationship, go make it happen." They gave me a piece of a board that was maybe six, seven inches wide and about twenty inches long. "Go intimidate that girl." I thought, "What would you do in this parallel experience?" They liked what I did, and I got called back to audition for Tobe.

They had been doing a nationwide search. The production company was doing pre-production in Austin, so it was late into the process and they hadn't found anyone at all that they had liked. I got a call and I went in, and they liked me. We had one audition then a callback with the writer, Kit Carson, present. Then, another callback with Caroline [Williams] and Tobe. She ran through this scene, and she was totally committed and really had the attention of Tobe in the room. And she just says, "Do you want to see it again?" And Tobe kept saying "Yes," after question five, question ten, question fifteen. It was a lot, but she kept at it and he said, "Okay, no, I got it now."

That is sort of similar to what happened to Bill Moseley, as Chop Top, when he was hammering the head of LG, played by Lou Perryman. Bill was hammering his head to pieces, and Tobe just kept saying, "Do it again." This went on for at least ten or twelve takes. Bill was starting to doubt his prowess at being sadistic. He kept saying, "Can I do something different?" and Tobe would respond, "No, no, no, I like what you're doing, keep going. I like it." That's when I think he coined a phrase that I think was part of his *raison d'etre*. During the film, he called it "the cinema of excess." [*Laughs*] That theme was definitely repeated quite a bit throughout that movie.

This movie was a departure from the one that came before it. As an actor, did you find it freeing to be able to do things your own way, and not be forced into trying to continue a particular storyline or performance from the prior film?

Well, I may be one of the few actors that Tobe would have encountered who wouldn't have minded that. My early training in junior college was by a very seasoned director, Zula Pearson, who got her training at Northwestern way back when. She would give us incredibly detailed side coaching directions while she directed us in a scene, which is sort of like the antichrist of acting. Most actors think, "When I'm acting, you will remain silent, and I will guide the course of my great whatever-it-is that I'm doing." Most directors don't do much in the way of really doing *any* directing. They just say, well, you know, "action." If you start to ask for some kind of information, a lot of times they frown on that.

At any rate, during the scene that's the heart of the movie, in the radio station break room, where the clock on the wall was always "sex o'clock" . . . In that scene there, Tobe side coached me like he was the voice of Bubba, talking inside his head. That stuff's hard to get. Rarely is the director the writer, but he and Kit worked on this a lot, and Kit is so organic. You know, he and Tobe were like one on everything there was to say about the characters in this play. Tobe just showed me the way, and it made a lot of sense. Apparently, the audience liked it enough to keep watching it.

I've heard Tobe described as a director who had a clear vision of what he wanted, but was open to collaborative ideas.

We were working on a close-up, and I didn't know exactly what the hell was supposed to be going on. But, he told me how it was framed, and what he wanted me to do. He said, "Make your eyes do this, make your eyes do that, make your tongue and lips do this, that and the other." He left it up to me *how* to make that happen. Later on, when I saw it cut into a scene, it was amazing how he could see every single frame and where they shift and stuff. He would say, "Oh, you're moving too quickly. I need some time to get the scissors in there." You're getting used to each other's rhythm and tempo and how you want to tell the story, and at what kind of pace. What's the dance going to be, and how will it unfold in this particular variation of the seven basic master plots of the human race?

Bill [Moseley] would ask every now and then, "What do you want me to do?" Tobe would say, "Just do that crazy Chop Top stuff." [*Laughs*] He had a great sense of who he was working with. I liked working with him a lot.

There was one thing that Tobe requested: a chainsaw language. But, he was very impatient. I immediately started trying things, and he kind of flew into a tiff, "That sounds like Frankenstein," and he kind of shut it down. I don't think there would be a way to avoid sounding like Frankenstein and still sound like a chainsaw. We didn't really have enough time to explore chainsaw language, because that didn't seem to be a priority with him. I didn't get to see him all that much. In the beginning, he was really focusing on all of the action sequences that had to be there. They were behind schedule, I think, pretty much from the beginning. Cannon was giving him a hell of a time to get him to hurry up.

You were one of the local actors working on the film. Was it strange when you had to go back and forth between the world of the Sawyer family, and your regular home in Austin?

No, no. I mean, I lived in Austin, we were shooting in Austin, so it was like being in school. I would just spend all day and night rehearsing and then dragging myself home to get it together for the next day, to go do some more of it. It seemed like business as usual. What would have been unusual would have been going to a strange city and being put in a hotel with everyone else. I did miss that, because there were a lot of networking possibilities available at the hotel, because everybody was hanging together. But essentially, I was isolated.

I think Tobe isolated me on purpose in the beginning, to kind of drive me a little crazy. I got to know Gunnar [Hansen, the first Leatherface] through the years, which was quite a privilege. He's a brilliant person and very, very peaceful. I think he ended up being sequestered away from people for various reasons during the shoot of that movie. I think it bothered him a lot. I think [Tobe] was trying to wind me up. But you know, I'm an introvert. "You want to leave me alone, by myself? Oh, no!" It was like Brer Rabbit saying, "Please don't throw me into the briar patch!"

Was it true that Cannon cut back your drinking water at some point? While you were shooting in a hot warehouse during a Texas summer?

Let's go beat up on Cannon! Yeah. Mr. [Henry] Kline was the production manager, so all the money went through him. I don't know anything about his reputation, although I've talked to one person in the film business and they liked him, they thought he was first rate. Golan and Globus thought he was snazzy enough to take care of their money during the project. It was beastly hot—it was a *bad* summer. It was one of them summers like out of the movies, where the aliens come to hunt people. We were out in the middle of the woods with a light up above the treetops, lighting it up like some kind of a horrific, moonlit scene. The gypsy moths come in, looking for your blood. Being out there was pretty good, except, you know, being stuffed into the corner of an air conditioned trailer and waiting to get on.

You mentioned they were behind schedule from the very beginning, and I know that Cannon was always squeezing the budget. Were there places where it was really obvious that the tight budget was a restraint?

I really didn't know at that time. "Oh, that just looks like a $100,000 thing, and it should be a million dollar thing." I didn't know.

The French press booklet for *Texas Chainsaw Massacre 2*. "The Saw is Family!"

But, oh, the water thing. Let's revisit that. So yeah, it was 125 degrees inside the underground family hideout. We're going through stacks of cases of water on a regular basis, and it did stop for a while. I don't know the reason, but I'm thinking that if I wanted to send a message to a group on a nonverbal level that was intense, and felt sort of life-and-death, *that* might not be a bad way to do it. They were interested only in one thing: not being fined for not having the movie on the screen at the time that they were contracted to. I'm sure that bothered them a great deal. I have no idea what the penalties were, but I bet they weren't small. And Cannon did not pay them, because they got the movie out on time.

What can you tell me about the last days of shooting? I know it was a marathon: that you were shooting for over twenty-four hours straight going into the Fourth of July, and Tobe was sick with pneumonia.

Yeah, "the crud," he had it. A lot of us went down with it, including me. I was there just before Tobe. "The worst case of pneumonia I've ever seen in my life," the doctor said. I was taking meds every two hours for a week. That was a fairly tough time. I came back for the last week and a half, I think. There was a marathon on the very last day, but generally the chaos seemed to be about the same. It would be just more about, say, "Where is the tornado focused today?"

There was a twenty-four hour marathon at the end to get everything that they needed to complete the film. I've got to give huge credit to Dick Kooris, the cinematographer, and the assistant director who put together the shooting schedule with all they needed to do to get it done. That made a huge difference. Tobe had gone way over schedule on *Invaders from Mars*, and Cannon certainly didn't want a repetition of that one. I'm sure that's why they were more and more nervous as we got toward the deadline.

Bill had mentioned that you'd given him some sort of herbal remedy to help him avoid the crud. He said it was this crazy-looking thing, but it worked.

Yeah, Chinese herbs. Sometimes they're called yin yang balls. They're wrapped up in some form of paper foil or something, and it's a lot of herbs, and they're very powerful. Bill seemed to have an indestructible immune system. Everybody else other than him was falling ill, and he just sort of danced through it like Pinocchio. [*Laughs*] When you're in an artistic ecstasy,

I think your immune system goes up to Mach three or four. It really gets souped-up. He had energy until the cows came in.

The studio sent in a B-unit director. He was sort of like Bart Simpson: "Hi, how's it going? We're going to do a great job here. I'm in charge, we're going to get shit done." He was very cheerful, and not exactly in what I would call the mood of the film, but as a B-unit dude, he was behind his work. He started making problems for Tobe. I remember we were trying to get a scene started. We had just started rehearsing, and Tobe was getting ready to shoot and he said, "What the hell is all that noise out there?" And someone came in to talk to him. He said, "Well, shut it down, god dammit!" And the guy came back and whispered in Tobe's ear. Tobe leapt up and ran over to that door, which was like ten feet away, where the noise was coming from. He screamed. It was some *beautiful* sailor talk, lots of great blue language and rage, and shit shut down. He said "We're the A-team here, we're number one!" Which I think was a little comment for a would-be taking-over-the-film director guy, because that was sort of the vibe I got from working with this person. He was very, "Well, you're alright, everything's okay now, I'm here to take care of you and rescue you. Just do what I say and everything will be alright." All of it was verbally unspoken, but tonally hammered home.

I won't hold anything against Cannon for the pressure they applied, because it worked. Not only did they get their stuff in on time, but they knew that Tobe needed a strong hand. Richard Kooris said that Tobe makes a very personal film, which is very "filmmaker" and not-so-much Hollywood director-ish. And so, sometimes in making a personal film in the way that he does, he doesn't follow the carefully laid-out schedule made and agreed to beforehand. So, I can see why Cannon felt that they needed to bring him into focus. Everybody else got it.

Tobe was under stress, he got sick. We were so stressed with all the filth in that building. It was just astounding. You know, fifty years of crap being shaken down from the skies. The set even caught on fire briefly. The prop master, Michael Sullivan, who lived here in Austin, I had known since

1966. Brilliant guy. He had a big movie budget for that time, and he pretty much hired the entire art department from the University of Texas to work on the set design. All the bone furniture, and that bone sculpture from *Dr. Strangelove* of the skeleton riding his bomb down from the heavens waving his cowboy hat. There's a tremendous richness in the visual tapestry of this film. The color palette was like an erupting volcano, all those red and orange-y liquids spewing everywhere.

I sense there's a special camaraderie among the cast and crew who worked on this film, which I don't always encounter when I talk to people about other movies. What made this particular film such a bonding experience?

You ask about one of the most perpetual mysteries, and I always have the same answer: I don't know. It could be this, it could be that. Most movies are machines made to crank out a thing that will bring in some bucks. Hardly ever anymore will you find some bucks to crank out something that you hope will enrich someone's mind or spirit. That's typically what theater has been about. All of us in the cast had theater experience and the writer, L.M. Kit Carson, had done a lot of theater. He was excellent to speak with because he was also a performer.

This film is almost not a horror movie. Take out the killing and it's kind of like *Beauty and the Beast* or *The Hunchback of Notre Dame*, which I did model my character on the characterization by Charles Laughton. I really got it from him, about his relationship to her. And that was in this film: what the Firesign Theater called "the modifying spark of humanity." It got a hold of [Leatherface], and it changed him. That's not typical in your horror movie. Usually they're coming back to do something else more terrible than last time. The indestructible Jason: you can burn him, you can dissolve him with acid, he'll show up in about a year and a quarter on the big screen, all shiny and new.

There's a great quote from L.M. Kit Carson, where he describes this movie as Leatherface's coming of age.

Yeah, yeah. And he's thinking, "You raised me wrong! You told me everything wrong. Shame on you! Oh, god, and you made fun of me because I'd always eat my vegetables first."

A newspaper advertisement from the film's opening
weekend in Fort Worth, Texas.

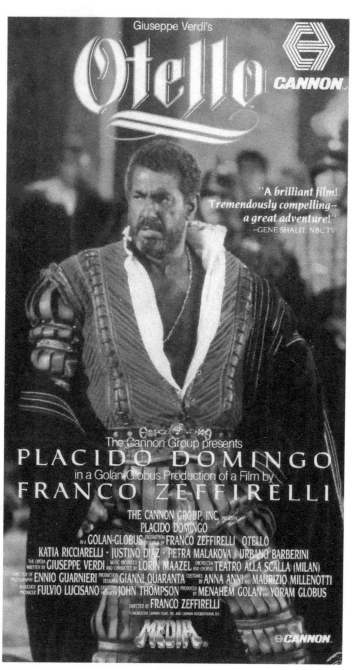

Franco Zeffirelli's *Otello* on videocassette.

Otello

Release Date: August 28, 1986
Directed by: Franco Zeffirelli
Written by: Franco Zeffirelli & Masolino D'Amico
Starring: Placido Domingo
Trailer Voiceover: "The deceit! The revenge! The triumph! Otello, the legendary Moor. His passion consumed his life!"

For the Cannon fans primarily here for the company's more action-packed movies, *Otello* may be a hard sell. It's a two-hour-long Italian opera without a single ninja, break dancer, machine gun, or rocket launcher assault. However, it's also among Cannon's most acclaimed releases and generally regarded as one of the better cinematic adaptations of an opera.

In 1985, Golan and Globus inked a deal with Spanish opera star Plácido Domingo to make a film out of one of his performances. This was at a time when Cannon desperately hoped to raise their stock with film critics—and in turn, awards committees—and few performing arts are more highbrow than opera. On top of that, Domingo was a superstar of his field, having risen up from his humble beginnings at the Israel National Opera in Tel Aviv in the

1960s—where Golan, no doubt, would have been familiar with his work—to becoming one of the art's most globally-recognized stars. He's won nine American Grammy Awards at the time of this writing (tying him with Frank Sinatra) and would become familiar even to non-opera fans as a member of the Three Tenors, a singing super group who made a pop culture crossover in the 1990s and were name-dropped on popular sitcoms such *Seinfeld*, *Frasier*, *The Simpsons*, and *Everyone Loves Raymond*.

At the time of his Cannon contract, Domingo was in preparations for a run of *Tosca* at the Metropolitan Opera. The show was helmed by the dual-talented director of stage and screen, Franco Zeffirelli, with whom Domingo had already made filmed versions of the operas *Cavalleria rusticana* (1982) and *Pagliacci* (1982). He talked his friend into joining him on this cinematic journey, which must have had producer Menahem Golan doing backflips with joy. Given how often Golan uttered Zeffirelli's name in the same breath as great filmmakers such as Cassavetes and Godard, it is clear that the Italian director was one that Cannon's chairman deeply admired.

Born in 1923, Franco Zeffirelli's backstory is chock full of crazy, little biographical nuggets. A grand-nephew of none other than Leonardo Da Vinci, Zeffirelli was born of an affair between a married fashion designer and a wealthy, womanizing silk merchant. In Italy at the time, bastards were given their surnames à la *Game of Thrones*, and so his mother took the term "Zeffiretti"—"little zephyrs"—from her favorite Mozart opera, which a clerical typo turned into "Zeffirelli." At the outbreak of World War II, young Franco Zeffirelli joined a resistance group in Italy. When he was captured by Mussolini's Fascist soldiers, he narrowly escaped execution when one of his captors just so happened to be a half-brother that he hadn't known about prior to the War. After the Allies invaded Italy, Zeffirelli re-joined with the British forces as an interpreter.

Following the War, Zeffirelli studied architecture and eventually met the great Italian director Luchino Visconti, who would become a global arthouse sensation with films such as *The Leopard* (1963) and *The Damned* (1969). Zeffirelli spent almost a decade as the great filmmaker's assistant, protégé, and lover. By the early 1960s, Zeffirelli had built his own name for himself as an esteemed stage director, soon overseeing performances of Shakespeare at venues as lofty as Stratford and the Old Vic.

It was when Zeffirelli applied his talent for adapting the bard's work to the silver screen that his name became a cinematic commodity. His first film was a movie version of *The Taming of the Shrew* (1967); stars Richard Burton and Elizabeth Taylor poured their own money into the project, which paid off in the form of a global hit. It was his version of *Romeo and Juliet* (1968) the following year that would become his enduring legacy: his decision to cast real, highly attractive teenagers as the star-crossed lovers resulted in Academy Award nominations for Best Picture and Best Director, and what's still considered by many to be the definitive film version of the play. As a filmmaker, perhaps he peaked a little early: none of the features he'd direct over the next 35 years would match *Romeo and Juliet*'s level of universal acclaim.

Zeffirelli spent the rest of his career with his attention divided between the screen and the stage. His attempts at a more mainstream Hollywood career were critically panned, yet box office hits: the Jon Voight boxing film *The Champ* (1979) was a top grosser for MGM, and the grim teen romance *Endless Love* (1981)—starring future *Sahara* (1983) actress Brooke Shields— raked in a cool $32 million dollars on its way to six Razzie nominations. It was during these years when Zeffirelli also became an eminent director of operas, staging productions at premiere venues such as New York's Metropolitan Opera and London's Royal Opera House.

As if he wasn't busy enough, Zeffirelli would later enter the world of politics, where he was somehow an even more controversial figure than he was in the world of art. Elected multiple times to the Italian Parliament, Zeffirelli was a devout Roman Catholic with outspoken, ultra-conservative values, despite openly identifying as gay. In 2004, he became the first Italian citizen to be awarded an honorary knighthood from the United Kingdom. Zeffirelli passed away in 2019 at the age of 96, leaving behind two sons—whom he'd adopted a few years earlier, when they were already adults.

Somewhere in the middle of all of this—well, late 1985, to be exact—Zeffirelli made a film version of Verdi's *Otello* for Cannon. While Domingo's initial discussions with Cannon had revolved around a movie version of Verdi's *Il trovatore*, the new arrangement presumably was an even better slam dunk. Not only were they getting the famous Zeffirelli to direct, but they'd have Domingo performing what had come to be considered his signature role: the tragic, Moorish general, Otello.

Filming was set to begin on the island of Crete in the fall of 1985. The production would be shooting at the real, Thirteenth Century Venetian fortress of Koules, in the city of Heraklion, which would have been historically appropriate for the setting of Shakespeare's famous play. Just before their scheduled start date, though, Mexico City—where Domingo had family living—was hit by an extremely destructive and deadly earthquake. The singer abandoned the production to check on his relatives in the city and found that four had perished in the collapse of an apartment building that had killed more than one thousand people. He chose to stay afterward for several weeks and lend a hand with relief efforts. This delay in shooting went on so long that Cannon was nearly forced to cancel the production altogether, but Domingo finally arrived on set and used the filming as a way to distract himself from the horrifying sights he'd witnessed in Mexico City.

There's not much that can be said about the story of *Otello* that hasn't already been greatly extrapolated on in the last several centuries. Although it's part of a second tier of works behind *Hamlet, Macbeth, Romeo and Juliet,* and *Julius Caesar,* Shakespeare's *Othello* still ranks among the most-performed of his tragedies. In the late Nineteenth Century it was adapted into an opera by the master Giuseppe Verdi—it became one of his best-known works, and a perennial favorite at opera houses. It's since been adapted for film at least twenty times across different industries and cultures. In short, it's been analyzed and written about to death, and so I won't dwell *too* long on giving a Cliff's Notes-style synopsis here.

Otello follows its titular hero (Domingo), a Moorish king who, as a child, was captured and made a slave, yet rose up the ranks of the Venetian military, having been promoted to general by the time our story begins. As Otello returns victorious from a naval battle, we're introduced to his treacherous subordinate, Iago (Justino Diaz), who is pissed off that Otello promoted his rival to captain over him. Iago executes some dastardly tomfoolery and convinces Otello that his smoking-hot wife, Desdemona (Katie Ricciarelli)—seriously, it's rare when someone *isn't* singing about how beautiful she is—is having an affair with his rival, the captain. Otello flies off the rails and murders his wife, only to discover that he's viciously been duped only after the deed was already done.

A big part of why *Othello*'s popularity as a play and an opera has endured over the centuries is that its messages—about jealousy and racism—are still relevant today. Although it's been debated by scholars of the Bard's work exactly what ethnicity Otello was meant to have been, his description as a "Moor" implies the otherness of a darker-skinned people, likely from Africa. Iago's hatred for his heroic general, and the way characters view Otello's marriage to the fair-skinned Desdemona as aberrant, only makes sense if interpreted as racism.

Placido Domingo and Justino Diaz as the classical frenemies Otello and Iago.

Zeffirelli's movie version of *Otello* chose not to leave any open questions about its hero's race by adding in flashbacks to the character's capture by slavers from a village in Africa . . . and by having Placido Domingo blacken his face with makeup.

If you're not well-versed in the world of opera and/or Shakespeare—and trust me, I wasn't—no one will hold it against you if your brain just exploded all over the page right there. What? Did Cannon *really* release a movie with its hero in blackface in the 1980s? They did, and at the time they viewed it simply as following tradition. For almost as long as the opera's been performed, it's been traditional for a white actor to wear dark makeup while portraying the title role; at any given time, it's been said that only three to four living singers possess the range to perform *Otello* at the highest level. Domingo wasn't even the first screen actor to "black up" (as it's called) for the role: scroll back through the decades and you'll find such esteemed stars as Laurence Olivier, Orson Welles, and Anthony Hopkins all darkening their skin to appear in movie versions of the play.

It wasn't until 2015 (!) that the Metropolitan Opera in New York finally decided not to have their lead "black up" for the part, making a leap of faith that their audience could imagine the character as African without the aid of dark greasepaint. Considering how easily opera fans can imagine that a portly, 45-year-old tenor is the teenage hero in Gounod's *Romeo and Juliet*, it was probably a safe assumption that the average audience member could pretend that a performer was of another race.

Otello was released in the late summer of 1986, where it served as counter-programming to box office juggernauts like *Top Gun*, *Aliens*, and *The Karate Kid, Part II*. Many critics praised Domingo's performance but were critical of the director's choice to cut nearly thirty minutes' worth of the opera out of the movie to get it down to a two-hour runtime. To opera fans—who, in all likelihood, composed the bulk of this movie's audience—chopping up Verdi's masterwork felt like a travesty. Someone must have seen this kneejerk reaction coming, as the movie's press notes included an explanation from Zeffirelli:

"Cinema is its own art . . . I only did to Verdi what Verdi did to Shakespeare." It's an excuse that feels totally fair, if more than a little bit egomaniacal.

Awards societies, on the other hand, were much warmer in their reception. The U.S. National Board of Review of Motion Pictures named it Best Foreign Film, despite it being produced by an American film company. It was nominated for Best Foreign *Language* Film at both the BAFTA Awards and Golden Globes, which makes a little more sense—although it lost in both venues. It was also nominated for the most hallowed of cinematic awards, the Oscar, in the category of Best Costume Design, and deservedly so: Anna Anni and Maurizio Millenotti's work is superb, and appears right at home in the beautiful castle in which the film had been shot. Once again Cannon didn't win, but hot off the heels of their three Oscar nominations for *Runaway Train* (1985), the recognition had to feel like another step in the right direction.

Cannon had hoped to adapt another opera with Domingo, reportedly either Franz Lehár's *The Merry Widow* or Johann Strauss II's *Die Fledermaus*, but the company's rapid financial decline over the following years cancelled those plans. Domingo went on, of course, to global celebrity as part of the Three Tenors. Zeffirelli returned to Shakespeare once again with a Mel Gibson-led version of *Hamlet* (1990) before turning out his heavily-truncated adaptation of *Jane Eyre* (1996) and the semi-autobiographical *Tea with Mussolini* (1999).

Matt Hunter (Michael Dudikoff) takes aim on the American VHS cover of
Avenging Force.

Avenging Force

Release Date: September 12, 1986
Directed by: Sam Firstenberg
Written by: James Booth
Starring: Michael Dudikoff, Steve James, John P. Ryan
Trailer Voiceover: "He's the only one who can oppose a deadly brotherhood. Now, in the ultimate form of pure, savage combat, they are the hunters—and *he* is their target!"

Matt Hunter not only has a mean right hook, but strong family values. Once one of America's top intelligence operatives, Hunter resigned from duty to care for his tween sister when his parents were killed in a terrorist explosion. He lives his life peacefully on the family ranch just outside of New Orleans until a secret society of evil, racist millionaires and ex-military martial artists attempts a hit on Hunter's best buddy, Larry, another former intelligence agent (and fellow badass) who is running for a Senate seat in Louisiana.

If the name of our daring hero sounds familiar, it's because Matt Hunter was the unstoppable, invincible, one-man anti-terrorist army played by Chuck Norris in *Invasion U.S.A.* (1985). Released the following year, *Avenging Force*

(1986) was intended to be a sequel to Cannon's hit action film. It's said that Menahem Golan, after attending a screening of *Pray for Death* (1985)—starring former Cannon hero Sho Kosugi—approached its writer and co-star, James Booth, to write a film for Cannon. Six weeks later, Booth returned to the Cannon offices with the script for "Night Hunter," which would eventually become *Avenging Force*. Considering how far removed the film is from the subject matter of *Invasion U.S.A.*, it wouldn't be surprising if it began as an original concept which Cannon later slapped Matt Hunter's name onto to cash in on the success of their prior film. In any case, Chuck Norris read the script and rejected it, opting instead to head off in a new direction from his usual on-screen persona and make the action-comedy *Firewalker* (1986). At best, *Avenging Force* could conceivably be considered a prequel to *Invasion U.S.A.*, tenuously linked only by the hero's name and his incredibly vague job description.

Here Matt Hunter is played by an actor fourteen years younger than Chuck Norris, Michael Dudikoff, whose *American Ninja* (1985) had yet to hit theaters and become Cannon's next successful action franchise when this one went into production. Excited about their new star, Menahem Golan presented the "Night Hunter" screenplay to *American Ninja* director Sam Firstenberg, curious to get his opinion on whether or not it might be a good fit for Dudikoff and his co-star, Steve James. Firstenberg immediately recognized the script's potential, and told his Cannon boss that it would be a perfect vehicle for the two rising action heroes. That's all it took for Golan and Globus to give the thumbs up and greenlight the project.

From right off the bat, it's clear that *Avenging Force* has a higher production value than most of Cannon's action cheapies. Most notably it's shot in the very recognizable setting of New Orleans—which would have been expensive for Cannon, requiring union labor and lots of location scouting. Golan and Globus pushed Firstenberg and the writer, James Booth, to change the setting of the film, and move it to somewhere cheaper—potentially, the Philippines—but the director stood his ground, pointing out that the story wouldn't make sense anywhere else but the American South. Given that this was early 1986, a period when Cannon was juggling nearly a dozen projects at any given moment, the producers gave in, and the crew was allowed to set up shop in the Big Easy.

By this point a seasoned veteran of martial arts filmmaking, Firstenberg injected lots of energy into the movie's action scenes, and squeezed a ton of extra production value from its (still) relatively modest budget. The charisma of *Avenging Force*'s lead actors carry it the rest of the way, going the distance to bridge over a few logic holes and make its frequently-used premise feel fresh again. And then there's John P. Ryan, whose wild-eyed, scenery-chewing performance as the movie's primary villain makes the crazed prison warden he played in *Runaway Train* (1985) look like a reasonable, mild-mannered individual. (Ryan makes a really, really, really great bad guy—it's almost sad he wasn't able to play the villain in *every* '80s movie.)

distribucija
CENTAR FILM
BEOGRAD

Dudikoff and James: the most dynamic duo of '80s action returns in *Avenging Force*.

533

Avenging Force is essentially another take on Richard Connell's 1925 short story *The Most Dangerous Game*, first turned into a film in 1932. Humans have been hunting humans on the silver screen ever since, with the premise being used again and again over the decades. The late Eighties and early Nineties were a golden age for humans-hunting-humans cinema, between Cannon's own *Avenging Force* and *Dangerously Close* (1986), Arnold Schwarzenegger's *The Running Man* (1987), David A. Prior's *Deadly Prey* (1987), *Death Ring* (1992) starring Mike Norris and Billy Drago, John Woo's classic Jean-Claude Van Damme vehicle *Hard Target* (1993), and *Surviving the Game* (1994), starring Rutger Hauer and Ice-T.

The film opens in the bayous of New Orleans, where a pair of ex-servicemen are being stalked as prey by the most flamboyantly-dressed rogues' galleries you'll find in an Eighties action flick—that is, except for maybe the playground gang from Firstenberg's own *Revenge of the Ninja* (1983). In this opening scene, our villains are only identifiable by their unusual combat uniforms: a kabuki ninja; a gimp; and what appears to be a Mardi Gras owl smoking a pipe. The two injured, hunted men—the blonde one is played by stunt coordinator B.J. Davis—put up a good show of defending themselves, but they're ultimately no match for this colorful gang of masked killers.

Once the last man standing has been strangled to death, the pipe-smoking Mardi Gras owl yanks off his mask to reveal that it's everyone's favorite bad guy, John P. Ryan! (Playing a racist megalomaniac named Elliott Glastenbury, that is.) He asks his fellow hunters to pay up the $50,000 wager they owe him for being the one to bring the man down, which explains the nature of the Most Dangerous Game they're playing.

Firstenberg sought out John P. Ryan specifically after reading the script, having seen his unforgettable turn as a madman in *Runaway Train*. A veteran of the *It's Alive!* horror franchise, Ryan would keep his Cannon streak alive with appearances in *Death Wish 4: The Crackdown* (1987) and *Delta Force 2: The Colombian Connection* (1990).

We learn that Elliott Glastenbury and his fellow, goofily-dressed hombres are part of a secret society named The Pentangle. They're a small club of right wing extremists made up of wealthy industrialists, world-class martial artists, and gun buffs. Their interests (besides hunting humans for sport) include sponsoring kendo exhibitions and, oh, no: assassinating Black politicians. These guys are *super-duper* racist. They're basically the Ku Klux Klan, but they've somehow found even more ridiculous-looking disguises than white sheets. At one of their posh, black tie events, Glastenbury gives an impassioned speech to his fellow xenophobes, warning them of the "dark times" their country is in:

"They call us paranoid because we love our country; because we want to survive the economic collapse of our lands. You know it's coming, don't you? Rioting in the streets of our cities. Civil disorder everywhere. Dope-crazed savages. Gangs of n***** rapists! Sniveling politicians trying to enforce gun control! Commie guerillas in Central America pointing their guns north, just waiting to cross the Rio Grande, just waiting to terrorize your mama and your children—in your neighborhoods and your churches!"

He goes on to warn of the millions of Mexican immigrants living in the Southwest, and their alleged plan to forcefully conquer the United States and hand it over to Mexico. According to Glastenbury, it's their "sacred" duty to utilize their Constitutional right to bear arms and defend their country from so-called "yellow-bellied liberals" who want to hand over the nation to communists. (The speech ends with the crowd giving a standing salute that's *just barely* not a Nazi salute.) The Pentangle's symbol is a five-pointed star, with each point standing for a member of the group's inner sanctum. We meet four of them: Glastenbury, the millionaire; Charlie, also a millionaire; Jeb, recent winner of the World Ironman Championship; and the youngster, Wade Delaney, "Harvard Heisman trophy winner, and the South's youngest Senator."

All of these guys probably look familiar. Charlie is played by Marc Alaimo, a character actor best known for playing Gul Dukat on *Star Trek: Deep Space Nine* (1993–1999). Karl Johnson plays Jeb, and had small roles in *Night of the Comet* (1984) and *Jake Speed* (1986). Playing Wade is William Wallace, a Cannon regular: he played Chuck Norris' brother-in-arms, Pete, who dies at the end of *The Delta Force* (1986), and the top-hatted Gruss in *America 3000* (1986).

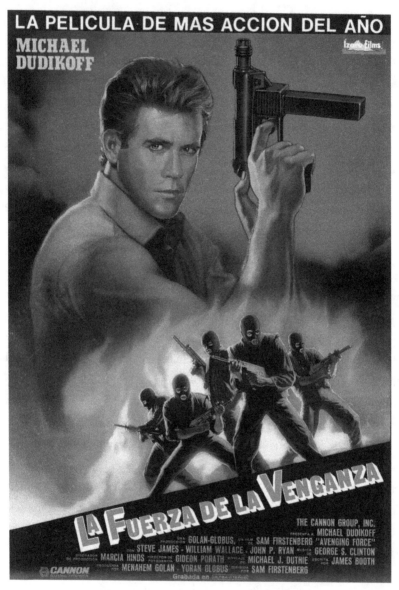

A Spanish poster for *Avenging Force*.

We catch up with our hero, Matt Hunter, as he's roping cattle on his family's spacious ranch, where he lives with his grandpa and 12-year-old sister, Sarah. (She's played by local child actor Allison Gereighty, whose voice was later overdubbed.) Through a bit of blunt-force exposition, we learn how Matt Hunter gave up his career as one of the government's youngest, deadliest special agents to watch over the farm and his family after his parents' death, which he blames on himself—even though they were murdered by terrorists.

Matt Hunter's best friend and old commando colleague, Larry Richards (Steve James), is running for a Senate seat so that he can help make the world a better place, but he's been receiving death threats from a mysterious group known as—you guessed it—The Pentangle. Steve James, of course, needs little introduction: this was his fourth Cannon role after *American Ninja, The Delta Force*, and *P.O.W. The Escape* (1986). He would continue on to *American Ninja 2* and *3* (1987 and 1987) and *Hero and the Terror* (1988).

It just so happens to be Mardi Gras in New Orleans, making it prime time for a politician to get his name and face out there in front of his constituents while taking a ride on a campaign float. This parade scene is a great example of Firstenberg's ability to squeeze a lot of production value from the resources given to him: with around 4,000 extras and some borrowed costumes and floats, he's able to stage a convincing Mardi Gras bacchanalia within just a few cordoned-off blocks of the French Quarter.

It's here in the thick of the celebration that the Pentangle launches their attack on the Senate hopeful. A handful of baddies open fire on Larry Richards' float using Uzis smuggled into the parade *literally* under babies sleeping in their buggies—which you have to admit is an especially nefarious method of hiding weapons. Richards and Hunter leap off the parade float and into action, dispatching the terrorists in a flurry of kicks, punches, and gunfire. Richards manages to escape the assassination attempt unscathed, but his son is killed in the crossfire. Of course, nobody tries to assassinate Matt Hunter's best friend and gets away with it, so he calls on his old boss, Admiral Brown—played by the film's screenwriter, James Booth—for help digging up information on the Pentangle. It turns out that the CIA has been after the group for years, with little success, which is why they need a badass like Hunter on the job . . . but he's put that life behind him.

Born David Geeves in South East England in 1927, James Booth changed his name early in his acting career because he thought it sounded too much like the fictional British butler created by author P.G. Wodehouse. At the Royal Academy of Dramatic Art he was classmates with Alan Bates, Peter O'Toole, and Richard Harris; an accomplished stage career eventually gave way to film roles, including his being cast as Private Henry Hook in *Zulu* (1964), his most celebrated role. Many expected him to be as big a star as his contemporaries, but Booth candidly blamed alcoholism and his dislike for self-promotion as the reasons why his career had stalled out by the 1970s. (It probably didn't help that he turned down the role that landed Michael Caine an Oscar nomination in 1966's *Alfie*.) Booth moved to Hollywood and became a character actor, but when producers stopped offering him roles, he transitioned into screenwriting. He wrote Sho Kosugi's post-Cannon feature, *Pray for Death* (1985); he followed *Avenging Force* with the second and fourth *American Ninja* screenplays. Later, TV fans would get to know him playing Norma Jennings' slimy, gambling addict stepfather, Ernie, on the second season of *Twin Peaks* (1990–1991).

The morning after the shootout at the parade, Matt Hunter accompanies Richards—who is taking his son's death in stride, all things considered—to an impromptu television interview, even though they've both acknowledged that it's probably a setup for a trap. Sure enough, they're accosted by agents of Pentangle (Pentanglers?) while en route to the studio. A thrilling car chase through an industrial section of New Orleans brings them to a massive shipyard, where the pursuit continues on foot. The ensuing battle makes fantastic use of a real, abandoned shipyard—how's that for low-cost, high-impact production value? The tide of battle turns in the good guys' favor, and they take out the members of the racist hit squad one-by-one with their deadly combination of ingenuity and punching.

When Glastenbury learns that his second attempt to knock off Richards was a flop, he is *pissed*. He decides that the only way to get his evil job done is to do it himself, and so he rounds up his inner circle of Pentanglers and creeps off to the Hunter family ranch, where Richards and his family are hiding out.

In the dark of night they make quick work of the armed CIA agents who are guarding the home, and set the farmhouse aflame. Richards is mortally wounded as he evacuates his wife and daughter from the house, but puts on one final, valiant display of badassery by limping back into the burning house to save his little boy, who is trapped in the attic. Hunter follows after him, and is by his side when he collapses over the rail of the balcony and falls to his fiery death one story below.

Outside the blazing inferno, the Pentangle assholes find and execute the rest of Larry's family. (Cannon had to heavily edit their death scenes, as killing an innocent woman and child on-screen would have caused the movie to be slapped with an X-rating.) Matt Hunter tries to be a hero, but then he takes an arrow to the knee and falls from the roof of the burning home. To his horror, he learns they've kidnapped his kid sister, and the only way he'll see her again is by playing their game . . . their *most dangerous game*.

Hunter tracks his sister down at a Cajun brothel, where she's been gussied up to be auctioned off as a sex slave. He rescues her, and escapes into the surrounding swamplands. The Pentangle Elite don their silly costumes once again, and follow them into the marshes. This is when Matt Hunter becomes Matt Hunt*ed*.

Avenging Force was shot over eight especially rainy weeks in and around New Orleans, with a good chunk of that time spent shooting these manhunt sequences in the bayous. To keep the alligators and deadly water moccasins at bay, the crew would toss grenades into the water to "scare off" any of the dangerous critters before filming. While the cameras rolled, crew members armed with shotguns would form a perimeter around the location and watch for incoming alligators. Despite all of these precautions, the actors couldn't be protected from all forms of predatory wildlife; namely, the leeches and mosquitoes, who regularly feasted on the *Avenging Force* team. (One crew member had an allergic reaction to a horsefly bite that made his arm swell to triple its normal size.) Each night when he returned to his hotel room, Dudikoff would douse himself with table salt to encourage the leeches he'd picked up that day to detach from his skin.

One at a time, Hunter squares off against each of the high-ranking Pentangle members. He narrowly comes away the victor of each battle, leaving behind only a dead bigot to rot in the mud. At last he faces off against Glastenbury himself; he manages to wound the jingoist society's leader, who crawls away into the nearby woods. Hunter allows him to escape, choosing instead to help his kid sister, who caught a bullet during the hunt and needs medical attention. He carries her to the medical staff at the CIA's secret headquarters, and tells them he's going after Pentangle's leader to finish him off. Admiral Brown urges Hunter not to act before he debriefs the committee. Dudikoff himself wrote Hunter's comeback line: "You can tell the committee to stick it where the sun don't shine."

Back at Pentangle mansion, Glastenbury dials his evilness up to eleven. Seated at the head of a swanky dinner table in a burgundy tuxedo and stroking a kitten, he pays *Adolph freakin' Hitler* a compliment: "I know the goddamn liberals scream 'fascist,' but the simple truth is Hitler was right. The man was a visionary. Forty years after he's dead, half the world is communists and we're defending our borders."

Thankfully, Hunter shows up to interrupt this Hitler-lovin' shitbag's party. He has Glastenbury's butler deliver him a photograph of Pentangle's (former) leadership, with each of the dudes he's already killed crossed out, which is s top-notch intimidation move on Hunter's part. The old racist coot excuses himself from the dinner table to confront Hunter in the foyer. He offers him money and a membership in Pentangle which, well, no shit, Hunter declines, so Glastenbury takes him upstairs to see his historical weapon collection, where he proposes a fight to the death. A staff, spear, mace, shield, cutlass, and scimitar are all wielded before their battle is through, but Hunter finally comes out on top—impaling old Glastenbury on a precariously-placed African statue.

For the scenes inside Glatenbury's posh home, Firstenberg and company rented a vacant mansion on New Orleans' historic St. Charles Avenue. The fully-furnished mansion had just gone on the market, so Cannon cut a deal to rent it for one month for shooting, on the condition that they were careful not to move any of the antique furnishings—which, you have to imagine, was probably difficult while filming the balls-out action finale. Dudikoff received a minor concussion during his sword fight with John P. Ryan, as well as a gash on his forehead which required stitches; shooting needed to be suspended for the rest of the day.

Avenging Force is left with an intentionally open ending, in which Hunter accuses his superiors of tipping off Pentangle as to Richards' whereabouts earlier in the film, and the audience is reminded that the mystery fifth member of their sinister inner circle is still at large. Who was the fifth member of Pentangle? (It was presumably Admiral Brown, in a case of James Booth writing himself into a bigger role in a potential sequel.) The movie ends with a freeze-frame on Dudikoff as he storms away from his boss with a look that says, "This ain't over." A sequel, of course, hasn't happened . . . *yet*.

The credits roll over a really sweet, guitar solo-riffic tune by frequent Cannon composer George S. Clinton—so sweet, in fact, that they recycled it for the end credits of *Journey to the Center of the Earth* (1989).

An *Avenging Force* poster from France, where the film was marketed as a follow-up to *American Ninja*—which was known there as *American Warrior*.

Cannon, who distributed *Avenging Force* themselves, didn't have the budget for a wide release or even much marketing. (For contrast: *Invasion U.S.A.* opened in 1,735 theaters a year earlier, while *Avenging Force* opened on only 500 screens.) Some contemporary critics lauded the film for the way it subverted the typical, '80s action movie attitude, by having the villains be the ones name-dropping their Second Amendment rights, rather than the hero. Over time, *Avenging Force* has grown a considerable cult audience, which is well-deserved: the action scenes and stunts are incredibly well done and, let's face it, there are few things more satisfying than watching Michael Dudikoff and Steve James beat the crap out of racists.

The rare, American VHS release of *The Berlin Affair*. "Before the war, there were conquests of another kind…"

The Berlin Affair

Release Date: September 26, 1986
Directed by: Liliana Cavani
Written by: Liliana Cavani & Roberta Mazzoni
Starring: Gudrun Landgrebe, Mio Takaki, Kevin McNally
Trailer Voiceover: "The seduction is so intense, so deadly, that it becomes their only reason to live. If they surrender, it can destroy them!"

Through their early years, Cannon supplied theaters with no shortage of middling erotic dramas set against distinct, period backdrops. *Lady Chatterley's Lover* (1982) gave way to *Nana* (1983), after which came *Maria's Lovers* and *Mata Hari* (both 1985), and finally the subject of our chapter, *The Berlin Affair* (1986). Shot by an internationally-infamous Italian director best known for a controversial, S&M-laced psychological drama, there was reason to believe that this film could have been both heady *and* hot. Instead, we're given the most poorly-acted, yawn-inducing, and pretentious-feeling picture on this list. (At least *Bolero* was never this self-important.)

The Berlin Affair—its European-language titles typically translate to "Inside Berlin"—is set in Germany at the brink of World War II. Louise

(Gudrun Landgrebe) is the bored wife of a Nazi diplomat, Heinz Von Hollendorf (Kevin McNally). She enrolls in an art class, where she meets—and is instantly smitten with—the daughter of a Japanese ambassador, Mitsuko (Mio Takaki). Their long walks and stilted conversations graduate to passionate lovemaking in fewer than 15 minutes of screen time. In spite of Louise having a husband and Mitsuko a slimy, art teach boyfriend named Benno, the women are flagrant about their affair.

Louise feels betrayed when she learns that Mitsuko's seduction was part of a half-cooked plan by Benno, in which he'd cover for his interracial relationship with Mitsuko by manufacturing rumors of an even more taboo affair between the two women. (The pivotal seduction scene comes when Mitsuko shows Louise a temporary tattoo of a rose painted on her left butt cheek, which leads to an awkward scene of literal butt-kissing.) Meanwhile, Louise's husband, Heinz, tries his best to break up the two ladies so that they don't endanger his Nazi career. The Third Reich is in the midst of what they call "house cleaning," and Heinz—conveniently, for this plot's sake—works with a group charged with outing suspected homosexuals among their ranks.

For a fleeting moment, Louise does feel some remorse for fooling around on Heinz, and tries to call it off with Mitsuko. This is where we learn that underneath her pretty kimonos and quiet demeanor, Mitsuko is batshit crazy, and will do anything to keep her lovers under her control, from threatening to kill herself if they leave her, to faking a pregnancy—and miscarriage—with Benno's baby. Ultimately, Louise decides she just can't quit Mitsuko. In a harebrained scheme to show Heinz how much they mean to each other, the ladies pop sleeping pills and fake a double suicide. Mitsuko wakes up first and, while Louise is still sleeping, puts the moves on her girlfriend's husband. Heinz immediately falls under the spell of the little sex-crazed sociopath. The audience sighs and goes along with it. Every other main character is already sleeping with Mitsuko, so why not him, too?

Both husband and wife find themselves so passionately obsessed with Mitsuko that they more or less adopt her as the world's creepiest third wheel.

Each night she comes to their home for dinner and, at the end of the meal, drugs them with sleeping powder so that they're unable to make love without her. We just have to accept that they're totally okay with this, because something about Mitsuko's cold stare and zombie-like delivery of dialogue is just too much for them to resist.

This unsustainable ménage-a-trois eventually comes to an end when the jilted Benno publishes a scandalous account of the aristocratic couple's personal life. All three are suddenly in danger of being arrested by the Nazis. Rather than flee Germany as Heinz sensibly suggests, Mitsuko instead convinces them to sip poisoned cocktails with her in a suicidal three-way. Louise wakes up later to find both of her beloved dead; it's ambiguous whether she survived the poison, or if Mistuko didn't poison her drink so that she could go on living.

The story is told through the framework of Louise recounting the full series of events to her old professor, who has also landed on the Nazis' naughty list for penning smutty books. (He's played by William Berger, an icon of the spaghetti western genre who Cannon fans will remember as the villainous King Minos in both of their *Hercules* movies.) Just as Louise finishes her tale and the story is ending, the Gestapo shows up and arrests her professor as she silently watches, which is presumably meant as a sort of final, clumsy statement about the rise of fascism.

The Berlin Affair has a boatload of issues, chief among them being its threadbare plot revolving entirely around tiny contrivances, which are little more than an excuse for its cast to take turns hastily mounting one another. The setting, at best, feels like a flimsy backdrop and, at worst, Nazisploitation.

For being a film built around secret, sexual encounters and breaking taboos, it doesn't even do the titillation all that well: there's a lot of loud huffing and groaning paired with stiff-jointed grappling, which too often looks more like a high school wrestling match than two lovers caught in the throes of ecstasy. With its R-rating, it's a little surprising that the most nudity flashed in the film is just that one half of Mitsuko's butt.

A pre-sales ad which recalls Cavani's prior film, *The Night Porter*, by shamelessly cribbing Charlotte Rampling's infamous "Nazi hat and no top" look from that movie.

Beyond all of the apathetic dry-humping, the performances are mostly serviceable. Gudrun Landgrebe was riding high as a darling of the international film scene for her performance in Robert van Ackeren's *A Woman in Flames* (1983), but there's not a lot more she could have done with the purple prose she was given as part of her character's incessant voiceover.

Kevin McNally has an easier time in his role as the cuckold husband, Heinz. The hardworking TV actor would eventually land his biggest role as Jack Sparrow's first mate, Gibbs, in the blockbuster *Pirates of the Caribbean* franchise. On the flipside, Mio Takaki, who plays Mitsuko, is something of a train wreck. A pop star in her native Japan, this Italo-German production of an English-language film perhaps wasn't the best crossover vehicle for her. (She only worked in Japan after this.) In any case, Takaki graces her role here with all the nuance of a cardboard cutout. It's hard to believe she's supposed to be this ultimate, sensual object worthy of throwing your life away for when the character is played like a demonically-possessed (and very horny) porcelain doll.

The film was met with a shrug at the Berlin Film Festival, and unfaltering derision everywhere else. Patrick Goldstein of the *Los Angeles Times* compared the movie to watching "a spectacular, 31st-story suicide attempt. While the spectacle has a morbid fascination, the end result is bound to be disastrous." (Ouch!) In their review for *The New York Times*, Caryn James felt the need to point out egregious continuity errors.

Cannon knew there was no salvaging this one. They opted to save money on prints and release the film in only a few theaters at a time, slowly, over the course of several years; some cities, such as New York, didn't get the movie until as late as 1988.

Director Liliana Cavani's output greatly slowed down after this, from a movie every few years to only a couple per decade. She'd earned international notoriety with her best-known film, *The Night Porter* (1974), about a holocaust survivor who, after the War's end, rekindles her sadomasochistic relationship with the former Nazi SS Officer who tortured her in a concentration camp. (Can you see why that one was so controversial?) Even as it receives periodic reissues on boutique home video labels, critics are still divided over whether *The Night Porter* is daring art or exploitative trash. As for *Berlin Affair*, it's gone more than thirty years in the U.S. years without anything but its original (now quite rare) VHS release. For what it's worth, it was one of the early films to portray an LGBT relationship between two women with more than just innuendo, but the movie is so poorly-executed that it only feels like it's done for taboo's sake. (Donna Deitch's landmark 1986 lesbian drama, *Desert Hearts*, was making its festival rounds at the same time as *Berlin Affair*, and is a far better treatment of the subject matter.)

If there was even the faintest bit of chemistry between the two main characters, then perhaps we'd be looking at *Berlin Affair* in a different light—although it's doubtful, considering how lackluster the movie is all around.

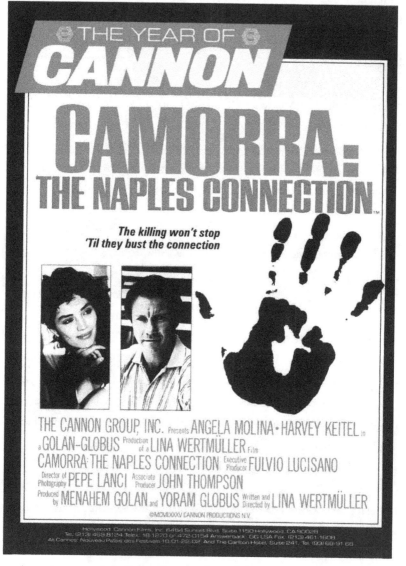

A semi-nonsensical ad for *Camorra* from Cannon's 1985 sales catalog.

Camorra (A Story of Streets, Women, and Crime)

Release Date: October 3, 1986
Directed by: Lina Wertmüller
Written by: Lina Wertmüller & Elvio Porta
Starring: Angela Molina, Harvey Keitel, Francisco Rabal
Trailer Voiceover: "One woman finds herself trapped in a brutal struggle between sides—a witness, a suspect, a victim."

Of all the films Cannon could have picked to barely release in the United States, 1985's *Camorra (A Story of Streets, Women, and Crime)* seems like an odd choice. Its director, Lina Wertmuller, was one of the surprisingly few international filmmakers whose name carried some box office weight beyond arthouse and repertory theaters. It co-starred Harvey Keitel, who was a relatively well-known commodity. And while that oversized, mouthful of a movie title might cause many to assume this film was a dry, gangster drama, it's very much not—*Camorra* is pretty wild, and very much in the Cannon vein. This is a film full of drugs, sex, murder, and chase scenes; it features a serial killer whose trademark is stabbing their victims in the balls with a syringe, a mobster with a harem seemingly hundreds-strong, a hero with a shady past as a criminal drag queen, a twisting-turning mystery plot, several out-of-nowhere dance numbers, and the stunning beauty of lead actress Angela Molina.

If *that* doesn't describe a movie Cannon should have been falling all over themselves to at the very least release on videocassette, I don't know what does.

Lina Wertmüller was born in Rome to an aristocratic family, of distant Swiss descent. After a childhood spent reading comic books and being expelled from numerous private schools, Wertmüller was drawn to the world of drama and performing arts, where she began writing plays and working as a puppeteer. In her early thirties she was introduced to filmmaking giant Federico Fellini, who took her under his wing and hired her as an assistant director on his masterpiece, *8 ½* (1963). Her debut feature, *The Lizards* (1963), followed the same year.

Her early career included several musical comedies, which she sometimes directed under a masculine pseudonym, and a rare, female-led Spaghetti Western, *The Belle Starr Story* (1968). The Seventies were when she truly came into her own, with films such as *The Seduction of Mimi* (1972), *Swept Away* (1974), and *Seven Beauties* (1975)—which were not only well-received in her native country, but were wildly popular internationally. The latter film led to Wertmüller's honorable distinction of becoming the first-ever woman to be nominated for Best Director, happening at the 49th annual Academy Awards ceremony in 1977. (There wouldn't be a second woman nominated until Jane Campion, for 1993's *The Piano*.) This granted Wertmüller a level of celebrity in the United States that many male, foreign auteurs never achieved. To give a sense of how well-known Wertmuller had become, she was recognizable enough to be impersonated more than once on *Saturday Night Live* by Laraine Newman, who would smoke cigarettes and wear her signature thick, white glasses. If that's not an indication of fame, what is?

Wertmüller's films usually revolved around women who defied expectations placed upon them, or marched to the beat of their own drummers. Although her films were often political, it was always in service of the stories she told. The Oscar nomination earned her a multi-film contract from

Warner Bros., but when her follow-up, the English-language film *A Night Full of Rain* (1978), was a box-office flop, the studio rescinded the contract, leaving Wertmüller a free agent once again. Her films of the early Eighties received a more tepid response in the United States compared to the sensations she'd brought forth in the prior decade, which explains how she found her way to Cannon in 1985.

Set in contemporary Naples, *Camorra* opens with Annunziata (Angela Molina), an ex-prostitute who co-owns a cheap boarding house, being assaulted by the lousy son of a local crime boss. She's rescued just in time by a mysterious protector, who shoots the attempted rapist dead and leaves behind no clues save for a hypodermic needle jammed through his shorts and into his testicles. Because she was the last person to see her attacker alive—and because she can't describe her rescuer's appearance—Annunziata becomes the primary murder suspect to not only the police, but the deceased gangster's blind, bereaved, mob boss father.

The daughter of famed Spanish actor, singer, and flamenco dancer Antonio Molina, Angela Molina was one of several siblings who followed their pops into show business. She rose to stardom as the young Conchita in Luis Buñuel's *That Obscure of Desire* (1977), and later went on to appear in Ridley Scott's *1492: Conquest of Paradise* (1992) and multiple films by Pedro Almodóvar.

The blind mob leader is played by the incredibly prolific Spanish actor Francisco "Paco" Rabal. Among the 215 screen credits he accumulated over his long career are several films by Luis Buñuel, as well as an appearance as Socrates, the strongman with the weak ticker, in Cannon's *Treasure of the Four Crowns* (1983).

As the days roll on, bodies begin to pile up in *Camorra*—the murders are clearly the work of a serial killer, with the victims linked by their involvement in the local heroin trade and, of course, the syringes left sticking out of their balls. Even as her guilt looks less and less likely, Annunziata is repeatedly questioned by the Naples homicide squad, as well as various gang bosses. The most memorable among them is "Tango," a smooth-talking don whose mansion is packed with dozens of infatuated women. (He's played by Paolo Bonacelli, best remembered as the star of Pier Paolo Pasolini's infamous 1975 film *Salò, or the 120 Days of Sodom*.)

Meanwhile, Annunziata is torn between two lovers. One, Toto (Daniel Ezralow), is a childhood admirer who sacrificed himself to protect her many years earlier, and was forced to flee to America, where he reinvented himself as a drag queen named Sophia, and got tied up in drugs and prostitution. Now returned to Naples, he applies himself as a dancer—which the film takes no half-measures in demonstrating to us with a surprising number of elaborate dance sequences, including one nearly-nude performance, for some reason, on a rooftop. Her other lover is her ex-boyfriend Frankie (Keitel), who used to smuggle cigarettes but now deals mainly in heroin. He's a sleazy son-of-a-bitch who slaps Annunziata around and regularly forces himself upon her, and is also a prime suspect in the mysterious needle-dick murders, as most of the deceased just so happen to be his rivals in crime.

Camorra came during something of a journeyman's period in Keitel's career. After starring in Martin Scorsese's debut feature *Who's That Knocking at My Door* (1967) and his breakthrough *Mean Streets* (1973), he frequently returned to work with the acclaimed director and played memorable supporting roles in *Alice Doesn't Live Here Anymore* (1974) and *Taxi Driver* (1976). Throughout that decade he was a very sought-after actor, also appearing in the debut films of Ridley Scott (*The Duellists*, 1977) and Paul Schrader (*Blue Collar*, 1978) before starting to drift into a more mercenary career as a hard-working character actor in the 1980s. His career turned around suddenly in the early 1990s, when a rapid-fire series of acclaimed roles—including *Thelma & Louise* and his Academy Award-nominated turn in *Bugsy* (both 1991), followed by *Reservoir Dogs* and *Bad Lieutenant* (both 1992)—allowed him to become more selective about his projects, and once again be sought-after by acclaimed filmmakers.

The plot of *Camorra* quickly comes to an exciting head when Annunziata discovers her pre-pubescent son is an aspiring heroin dealer, and the perpetrator of the scrotum-stabbings reveals themself to her. It's a surprise twist that we won't spoil, except to say that the movie shuts itself down quite abruptly before the audience is given any clue as to how all of these events will be resolved.

As a thriller, *Camorra* is sleazy and far-fetched, but entertaining. It played relatively well at various festivals, including the Berlin International Film Festival, where it was nominated for the Golden Bear award. Strangely though, it was given next-to-no screenings in the United States, except at various small, regional festivals, and for at least few days in Los Angeles—after which it was reviewed negatively by critics seemingly hurt by how it was shot in a true, Italian exploitation fashion, with actors speaking in different languages and being poorly overdubbed.

Harder to fathom is why Cannon didn't even bother to drop it into video stores as a rental tape, unless they somehow didn't secure the VHS rights from their Italian co-producers. Because it's gone so long without any official, English-language home video release in the United States, *Camorra* has become one of the tougher Cannon films to track down.

A videocassette copy of *52 Pick-Up* previously owned by rental giant Blockbuster Video.

52 Pick-Up

Release Date: November 7, 1986
Directed by: John Frankenheimer
Written by: Elmore Leonard & John Steppling
Starring: Roy Scheider, Ann-Margret, John Glover, Vanity, Clarence Williams III, Robert Trebor
Trailer Voiceover: "Harry Mitchell: Successful businessman, loving husband. A man who has become the perfect target. They're ruthless. Desperate. The only thing they didn't count on was Mitch having a plan of his own!"

The third time's the charm. That's what they say, right?

Golan and Globus attempted to make a movie out of Elmore Leonard's 1974 novel *Fifty-Two Pickup* three separate times, managing to complete films on their second and third tries. A book has to be pretty good for the same producers to adapt it over and over again, and *Fifty-Two Pickup* is a high-quality thriller by one of the most celebrated genre fiction writers of the 20ᵗʰ Century.

Born in New Orleans in 1925, Elmore Leonard's father—an employee of General Motors—eventually relocated the family to Detroit, a city where many of his future crime novels, including *Fifty-Two Pickup*, would be set. After serving in the Navy in the South Pacific during World War II, Leonard returned home and got a job as a copywriter at an advertising agency. It was during this time he got serious about writing short fiction on the side, submitting stories—Westerns, mostly—to pulp magazines and building up his name as a writer. These short works proved very popular with readers, and so full-length novels soon followed.

Leonard showed a talent for direct, unembellished prose and dialogue that read like it came from the mouths of real people rather than an author's typewriter. It took Hollywood no time at all to catch on to his work, and over the next twenty years several of his Western stories were adapted into full-length features starring big names, including *3:10 to Yuma* with Glenn Ford and *The Tall T* with Randolph Scott (both 1957), *Hombre* (1967) with Paul Newman, *Valdez is Coming* (1971) starring Burt Lancaster, and *Joe Kidd* (1972) with Clint Eastwood. In spite of his wild success as a writer of cowboy tales, Leonard's interests shifted toward crime thrillers starting with *The Big Bounce,* which was promptly adapted into a film starring Ryan O'Neal in 1969. He soon found himself being tapped to write the screenplays for many of his adapted works, including *The Moonshine War* (1970) with Patrick McGoohan, Richard Widmark, and Alan Alda, and the aforementioned *Joe Kidd.* For *Mr. Majestyk* (1974), which starred future Cannon superstar Charles Bronson, Leonard actually wrote the screenplay first and his novelization of it didn't come until afterward.

Golan and Globus snapped up the movie rights to Leonard's *Fifty-Two Pickup* almost immediately after its first hardcover publication in 1974. Golan's plan was to direct the film version himself, which would star earthy action hero Joe Don Baker. They were going to move the film's setting from Detroit (as it was in the book) to Israel and film it there, and got as far as flying Leonard out to Tel Aviv and having Sam Firstenberg drive him around the city while he worked on the new adaptation. Baker ultimately walked away from the project—we'd like to think it was to make his b-movie classic *Mitchell* (1975), but can't confirm the exact timing—and their plans to adapt the novel fell onto the backburner.

Although he was already quite successful as a fiction writer by that point, Leonard's popularity exploded in the 1980s. (The cheeky headline of a *New York Times* profile on the occasion of his 1983 novel *LaBrava* read, "Novelist Discovered After 23 Books.") *LaBrava* won the 1984 Edgar Award for Best Novel, but it was his next book, *Glitz*, which spent sixteen weeks on the Bestseller list in 1985, and prompted none other than Stephen King to pen what amounted to a gushing fan letter to Leonard as a guest reviewer for the *New York Times*. Each of his new books did very well, as did his robust back catalogue, much of which was being newly reissued for the mass market.

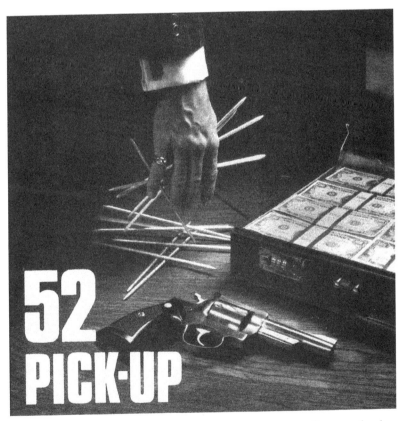

Based on this pre-sales artwork for the film, someone at Cannon clearly didn't know the difference between the prank card game "52 pick-up" and the similar-sounding game "pick-up sticks."

This was, of course, a good thing for Cannon: their option on his early thriller looked like a pretty fortuitous investment now that Leonard had become a literary superstar. Rather than adapt the movie outright with a big name actor and director, though, Cannon did a very Cannon thing, and instead slapped the novelist's name on *The Ambassador* (1985). To be fair, that film *was* loosely inspired by drafts of the Tel Aviv-set version which Leonard had worked on for Cannon in the mid-Seventies, but it was so far removed from his novel that you'd need to squint and tilt your head to see any major similarities. Shot in Israel and starring Robert Mitchum, Rock Hudson, and Ellen Burstyn, *The Ambassador*—which you can read all about in its own chapter—bore little resemblance to the *Fifty-Two Pickup* novel, save for a plot regarding someone being blackmailed over a sex tape. Anyone going into the movie because it was "based on" Elmore Leonard's novel would be sorely disappointed once they realized that the claim was mostly "based on" bullshit.

If you wonder how Leonard felt about Cannon using his name on *The Ambassador*, it's worth pointing out that it was the only movie he listed under the subheading "Disowned" in the filmography section of his personal website.

Fortunately for Cannon, it was around this time in the mid-1980s that filmmaker John Frankenheimer read the *Fifty-Two Pickup* novel and became enamored with the idea of turning it into a film. When he attempted to purchase the rights, he was surprised to find out that Golan and Globus had been sitting on them for more than a decade. So, he approached Cannon and pitched his services as a director for the film. Because there was no reason they *couldn't* adapt the same book twice in two years, a deal was made.

Like many of the directors Cannon hired, Frankenheimer was old school, having started out directing live television in the 1950s. Having earned five Primetime Emmy nominations before the end of the decade, his eventual move to feature filmmaking was inevitable. One of his early endeavors, the prison drama *Birdman of Alcatraz* (1962), earned four Oscar nominations; his best-known film, the Cold War political thriller *The Manchurian Candidate* (1962), came out the same year and was nominated for two more. More acclaimed films followed, including *Seven Days in May* and *The Train*, both in

1964, then cult favorite *Seconds* and racing hit *Grand Prix*, both in 1966. At this point the hits would slow, but still came: *The French Connection II* (1975) and *Black Sunday* (1977) were big commercial successes. While a struggle with alcoholism—leading to a stint in rehab—disrupted the quality of his work during this period, enlisting a known commodity like Frankenheimer was a feather in Cannon's cap, especially when many outside filmmakers were beginning to once again cast a wary eye toward the company as rumors circulated about their financial despairs.

Frankenheimer's version of *52 Pick-Up* was shot from a screenplay co-written by Leonard himself, and remained more or less faithful to the novel save for numerous surface-level changes. Originally set in Detroit, the adaptation was first planned for Pittsburgh before the setting was ultimately moved to Los Angeles so that it could be shot on a Cannon budget. Rather than being a successful inventor and businessman in the auto industry, Henry Mitchell (Roy Scheider) owns a facility where he bonds aerospace alloys with explosive force. Where his wife of twenty-three years, Barbara (Ann-Margret), was a housewife in the book, in the movie she's an up-and-coming politician. Their kids have been written out of the story. Rather than protecting his children from shame, Mitchell's primary impetus for hiding his indiscretion is to keep it from ruining his wife's political campaign.

52 Pick-Up, like the source novel, wastes no time getting started. After an opening montage set to some slick '80s music by composer Gary Chang—who also worked on *Firewalker* (1986) and would become a frequent collaborator of Frankenheimer's from here on out—Mitchell unlocks the door to an empty apartment, only to find the barrel of a gun jammed into the back of his skull. Masked men guide him to a chair in front of a television. They hit 'play' on the VCR, and a surprisingly friendly voice narrates the tape, which shows Mitchell engaging in extracurricular activities with a pretty, young woman who is most assuredly *not* his wife. They ask him for $105,000—an amount equal to one year's royalty on his explosives patent—to keep the affair hush-hush, allowing him some time to think it over before calmly showing themselves out the door.

561

Roy Scheider and Ann-Margret in a press still from *52 Pick-Up*.

Where his blackmailers went wrong was in assuming that their "perfect target" was the sort of easy rube who would roll over and give in to their demands. It turns out that's not Henry Mitchell at all. Rather than cash out and pay up, he confesses the dalliance to his wife, ready to accept the consequences, and tells the thugs to bugger off. Instead of backing away, they double down by murdering Mitchell's twenty-year-old lover and fudging the evidence so that it looks like he's the one responsible for her death. To keep them from turning their airtight "evidence" over to the police, his blackmail payment will now need to arrive in annual installments. It seems, for a moment, that Mitchell's goose might be cooked, but our bad guys have once again underestimated their victim—and overestimated themselves as crooks. Mitchell fights back, and one by one he turns his three extortionists against each other.

If we were to point at the biggest difference between the film and the novel, it's in its portrayal of its beleaguered protagonist. In the book, readers are made privy to Mitchell's inner monologue, full of self-doubt and more than a little bit of panic. With every move he makes, we get a round or two of second-guessing, and perhaps thoughts of giving up. In the film, though, we don't get any of that: Mitchell seems to act first and question himself later. Rather than being an everyman forced to deal with an increasingly terrible situation, Henry Mitchell as played by Roy Scheider is something closer to the well-equipped personification of vengeance that is Charles Bronson's Paul Kersey in the *Death Wish* sequels. This Henry Mitchell rarely feels like he's in real danger.

The most likely reason for this is Roy Scheider himself, who at this point was a star known for his Oscar-nominated roles in *The French Connection* (1971) and *All That Jazz* (1979), and of course for playing Brody in the blockbuster *Jaws* (1975). Cannon had been hounding Scheider to make a movie for them for years, but the actor didn't bite until he caught wind that the Leonard adaptation was in the works—like Frankenheimer, Scheider had been a big fan of the source novel. Don't get me wrong, Scheider is great in *52 Pick-Up*, but it's hard to fathom that the trio of chuckleheads attempting to blackmail him might actually be able to pull one over on him. Scheider seems too cool, too collected, and too resourceful for that. He's a hard guy to have doubts about. Scheider doesn't take away from the film, but he does significantly change the nature of the character.

The scene where Roy Scheider confronts his blackmailer in the projection booth of an adult theater was filmed in the screening room at Cannon's offices.

Despite her elevated public status, Mitchell's wife, Barbara, is actually given less to do in the film than she was in the book. (It's also hard to believe that, as grimy as this film is, what happens to poor Barbara in the book's final act is more graphic and awful than what we see in the film.) The role was well-cast with the two-time Oscar-nominated singer-turned-actress Ann-Margret, who by this point was far removed from the upbeat teen image she earned in early hits such as *Bye Bye Birdie* (1963) and *Viva Las Vegas* (1964).

Our "hero" is supplied with a rogues' gallery stocked with three excellent character actors. Alan Raimy is the trio's slimy mastermind: he's an amateur pornographer who speaks in an alarmingly friendly tone that drips with ooey-gooey condescension. (He's played by John Glover, who also had memorable parts in 1988's *Scrooged* and 1990's *Gremlins 2: The New Batch*.) His enforcer is a man named Bobby Shy, a quiet and unpredictable career criminal who's unafraid to kill when it serves his purpose. He's played with terrifying menace by actor Clarence Williams III, best known at the time as undercover cop Linc Hayes, one third of TV's *The Mod Squad* (1968–1973). (Eighties movie buffs might recognize him as Prince's father in 1984's *Purple Rain*, or from his small role in Cannon's own *Tough Guys Don't Dance* from 1987.) Their third man is Leo Franks, the nervous, hand-wringing proprietor of a peep show, played by Robert Trebor.

When we first meet our trio of sleazebags without their masks on, it's at a sex industry party hosted by Raimy. It's worth noting that the party scene was populated by Frankenheimer with a small army of real-life porn stars, including Tom Byron, Amber Lynn, Herschel Savage, Erica Boyer, Cara Lott, Randy West, Sharon Mitchell, Honey Wilder, Pat Manning, Jamie Gillis, and Ron Jeremy—the latter of whom served as an uncredited consultant on the film. It's at this party where we also (briefly) meet Mitchell's clandestine lover, Cini, played by a young Kelly Preston, seen prior in Cannon's *10 to Midnight* (1983) and best known later on for roles in *Twins* (1988) and *Jerry Maguire* (1996), and for being married to John Travolta.

It's scenes like this where the Los Angeles setting serves the film so well, and makes the slimy underworld that Mitchell must infiltrate look and feel believable. His quest to pick apart his blackmailers one-by-one takes him into a strip club, a nude modeling studio, a run-down porno theater, and into the apartment of a prostitute named Doreen, who helps him along his inquisition. It's a modest but very well-played role for singer and actor Vanity, who co-starred in this, *The Last Dragon* (1985), *Deadly Illusion* (1987), and *Action Jackson* (1988) over the course of just four short years.

Vanity's career was as a model up until the point she met the pop icon Prince, who gave her a stage moniker—her real name was Denise Williams—and set about crafting her into one of his musical protégées. Her pop star success took off at almost the same time as her acting career, but she was also famous for her high-profile romantic pairings with not only Prince, but Nikki Sixx, Billy Idol, Rick James, and Adam Ant. (She also spent one year married to NFL-player-turned-convicted-serial-murderer Anthony Smith.) In 1994, following a near-death experience at the end of a decade-long addiction to crack cocaine, Vanity gave up performing to become a born-again Christian evangelist, but died of kidney failure brought on by her longtime drug abuse at the age of 57.

Mitchell bribes Doreen (Vanity) for information. Believe it or not, her teddy bear winds up playing a significant role in one of the film's most frightening scenes.

Basically, what I've spent the last few paragraphs elaborating over is that there's really no weak spot in this cast, even if some of the actors changed the nature of the characters from how they were portrayed in the book. Some of the most memorable scenes come between actors with secondary roles, such as an encounter between Bobby Shy and Doreen after the former suspects the latter of betraying him, which leaves audiences—not to mention, Doreen—short of breath.

52 Pick-Up is also an uncommonly good-looking movie from Cannon, where even the oiliest, stickiest back rooms of Los Angeles are given a neon-lit sheen. That's thanks to a skilled German cinematographer by the name of Jost Vocano, who had previously shot *Das Boot* (1981) and *The NeverEnding Story* (1984), and then went on to become Paul Verhoeven's partner in crime, lensing *RoboCop* (1987), *Total Recall* (1990), *Showgirls* (1995), and *Starship Troopers* (1997).

Overall, *52 Pick-Up* is a tightly-wound thriller which ultimately ends in an abrupt but satisfying way. Without spoiling anything, this scene is also quite different from the novel. While the ending makes a lot more *practical* sense in the book, what we see on screen offers more over-the-top gratification.

52 Pick-Up received a significantly smaller release than many of Cannon's other high-profile films in 1986, but still fared okay at the box office. Critics were decisively split on the film in an interesting way, either praising it as a twisty little thriller which felt like a throwback to the old, studio b-movies from the '40s and '50s, or despising it for being predictable and full of unlikeable characters. One of the clearest displays of this dichotomy came from an episode of *Siskel & Ebert & the Movies* (1986–1999), in which the former found the movie too much for him to stomach, and the latter felt it was the best thriller he'd seen in years. The one thing that all critics, love or hate the film, seemed to agree upon was that John Glover made for a gloriously nasty villain.

Between their two adaptations of *Fifty-Two Pickup*, Cannon actually announced that they would be turning another Elmore Leonard novel into a film. That was going to be an adaptation of 1983's *LaBrava*, and would have starred, of all people, Dustin Hoffman—but, like oh so many projects that Cannon announced under Golan and Globus, it never came to be.

Media Home Video sent out decks of playing cards to promote the release of *52 Pick-Up* on VHS.

The award-winning novel followed the story of a Secret Service agent named LaBrava who gets caught in another blackmail plot. The film rights were immediately snapped up by producer Walter Mirisch, who had three Best Picture statuettes to his name and had been pals with Elmore Leonard going back to 1974's *Mr. Majestyk*, the Charles Bronson feature they'd made together. It was taken to Universal, who commissioned Leonard to turn it into a screenplay, but didn't get off the ground until Hoffman—fresh off *Tootsie* (1982)—expressed interest in playing the lead. With the renowned star of *The Graduate* (1967) and *Midnight Cowboy* (1969) tentatively attached, Mirisch was able to sign up none other than Martin Scorsese to direct the film. Just when everything seemed to be lining up perfectly, it all went to hell.

Hoffman, who was infamously difficult to work with, would skip meetings he'd scheduled to discuss the project, leaving the producer, director, and screenwriter—who flew cross-country multiple times to go over Hoffman's demanded rewrites—sitting in empty hotel suites. After this went on for almost two years, Hoffman finally committed to the role—but only if the studio paid him an astounding $6.3 million, *and* almost a quarter of the film's box office receipts. This was an absolutely staggering fee for the time, and too rich for Universal's blood, who bowed out of their involvement with the film. The project was then passed over by Disney and 20th Century-Fox, as well, based purely on Hoffman's colossal contract demands.

Enter Cannon.

The low-budget, independent company craved credibility. At the moment, they were flush with financing after the unexpected hits *Missing in Action* and *Breakin'* (both 1984) gave investors a feeling of confidence in their product. They'd just signed Sylvester Stallone to a contract that would pay him a record-breaking $12 million to star in *Over the Top* (1987)—a number they were reportedly ready to beat to get the highly skeptical Dustin Hoffman to agree to make a movie with them. Not only was Cannon willing to meet his absurdly high demands, but they reputedly counter-offered him *double* what he'd initially asked for to get him to sign on.

On the other hand, Scorsese flat-out refused to work for Cannon, and walked away from the project. Francis Ford Coppola showed tentative interest, but his schedule for the foreseeable future was blocked up by *Peggy Sue Got Married* (1986). The final replacement brought on was Hal Ashby, whose strong track record included *Harold and Maude* (1971), *Shampoo* (1975), and *Coming Home* (1978). Unfortunately, the marriage between Hoffman and Cannon barely lasted two months.

How angry do you have to make an actor to get them to walk away from what would have been the largest single-movie deal in history? Well . . .

Hoffman's big-time contract included a clause that gave him approval over all of the movie's advertising. Cannon, unable to contain their glee over landing Hoffman, couldn't resist taking out full-page advertisements featuring Hoffman's face, welcoming him to the Cannon family—*without* his approval. The first two times they did it, Hoffman was pissed but let Cannon off the hook with warnings. When they did it a third time, he had his lawyers write them a letter to terminate his whopper-sized contract. His reason was that if he couldn't trust them to do something as simple as not use his image to brag in the papers, how could he trust them to make a movie?

With that, *LaBrava*, the film, was effectively dead. Mirisch tried to repackage it at different points with different actors, including once with, of all people, *52 Pick-Up* star Roy Scheider, and another time with Al Pacino in the lead. Later on, the Coen Brothers separately developed their own take on *LaBrava*, which never came to be. As of this writing, the novel remains un-filmed.

Elmore Leonard wound up doing okay in Hollywood, though. He based his 1990 novel *Get Shorty* on his experience trying to make *LaBrava*, with the titular character—played by Danny DeVito in the 1995 film version—being a not-so-subtle dig at the diminutively-statured Dustin Hoffman. His works continue to inspire adaptations both critically and commercially successful, including Quentin Tarantino's *Jackie Brown* (1997), Steven Soderbergh's *Out of Sight* (1998), and the TV series *Justified* (2010–2015), based on the Raylan Givens character who appeared in several of his books and stories.

A previously-owned copy of *Firewalker* on VHS from Special Effects Video of Wellington, Ohio. Artwork by Jacques Devaud.

Firewalker

Release Date: November 21, 1986
Directed by: J. Lee Thompson
Written by: Robert Gosnell
Starring: Chuck Norris, Lou Gossett Jr., Melody Anderson
Trailer Voiceover: "In the proud history of adventure, no heroes ever have been more courageous, more faithful, or more optimistic than Max Donigan and Leo Porter!"

If cinema of the 1980s taught us anything, it's that you didn't need to be a great actor to be a major action star. If you accept that the bar for high-level action star acting ability was probably set by Sylvester Stallone, it paints a pretty dire picture of the rest of the competition. This doesn't mean that the Eighties' pure action heroes weren't right for their roles—to be an action star, you only had to be able to kick really high, drop one-liners, and not look silly when shirtless and holding a machine gun. (It also helped if you could make the veins on your forehead and biceps pop out on command.)

Of the big names, Chuck Norris was criticized for his acting ability as much as anyone in the bunch, and this includes guys like Van Damme and

Schwarzenegger, who could barely speak intelligible English at the time. In the entire spectrum of human emotions, you could count on Norris to convincingly convey two: stoic disapproval, and stoic patriotism. Beyond that, it got dicey. That's why everyone was surprised when Cannon put Chuck Norris in his first comedy.

Following *Treasure of the Four Crowns* (1983) and two Allan Quatermain movies, *Firewalker* (1986) was the company's fourth attempt to piggyback on the popularity of pulpy adventure films like the Indiana Jones series and *Romancing the Stone* (1984). Most savvy producers would have tossed in the towel after four tries, but in Cannon's defense, the idea didn't come from within the studio, but from their most bankable leading man, Chuck Norris himself.

After making a dozen mostly-serious action movies over the last eight years, the star was looking to stretch his wings a little, and *Firewalker*—which he presented to Menahem Golan and Yoram Globus with himself in mind for the lead—would be his first (intentionally) comedic role. Tired of playing dour-faced heroes who slow motion-kicked their way through opposition, Norris apparently liked the idea of playing a slightly less dour-faced hero who still slow motion-kicked his way through opposition, but also cracked a joke now and again.

Cannon greenlit the project and hired veteran director J. Lee Thompson, who had experience making this type of film after directing *King Solomon's Mines* (1985) just a year earlier. For a comic foil, Norris was paired with actor Lou Gossett Jr., who was only a few years removed from his Oscar win for *An Officer and a Gentleman* (1982).

We first meet fortune-seekers Max Donigan (Norris) and Leo Porter (Gossett) mid-dune buggy chase across an unspecified desert. Max fails to heed Leo's frantic pleas to turn and crashes their jeep into an oasis, leading to their capture. The men's hands and feet are tied to stakes, and a bad guy (Richard Lee-Sung) with facial scars—who they recognize as "the General," and clearly share a history with—leaves them to cook to death in the sun. Max, in a demonstration of wanton badassery, crushes a glass water bottle left by the general to taunt them in his bare hand, and uses a shard to cut them free of their ropes. This opening doesn't do much but establish that our heroes' relationship is built around exchanging friendly insults while in dangerous situations.

Soldiers-of-fortune Max Donigan (Chuck Norris) and Leo Porter (Lou Gossett, Jr.).

Back in Arizona, they return to what we assume has to be their regular watering hole—a run-down dive bar that has a reputation for being a place where adventurers and mercenaries hang out. A perky, pretty legal secretary named Patricia Goodwin (Melody Anderson of 1980's *Flash Gordon*) swings by and hires them to help her find a hoard of lost gold that she believes to be buried in a nearby mountain range. No one else has taken her seriously, because she claims that—get this—a *red cyclops* wants to steal her treasure map. Max and Leo laugh it up a bit, but take the job anyway and head off into the mountains.

It's deep in the heart of the secret cavern that Max and Leo encounter their first Problematic Native American Stereotype, bedecked in feathers and war paint, brandishing a spear and letting loose a battle cry. (The enemies they encounter look less like historically-accurate Native Americans and more like sports fans tailgating for their favorite racially insensitive sports team.)

"What is that?" Leo asks, shocked. "How the hell should I know?" Max replies. "Well, shoot it," is Leo's response, which Max obeys without question, firing several rounds and missing before Leo takes the gun away and drops the cave-dweller dead in his tracks.

The cave people that Max and Leo so nonchalantly murder raise several questions. Who are they, exactly? Are we to believe they're an uncontacted tribe that's been living in these cliff dwellings and guarding their temple for generation after generation? Or are they the temple's ancient guardians—their devotion to protecting their religious idols having kept them alive for hundreds of years—akin to the knight keeping watch over the grail in *Indiana Jones and the Last Crusade* (1990)? It seems no one will ever know, because Chuck Norris killed them all.

They proceed to massacre the rest of the guards as they try to defend their sacred temple from looters, further setting up the joke that Max is a terrible aim with firearms. This pays off in *Firewalker*'s most genuinely funny moment: Max takes a shot at one of the guards and misses. The bullet ricochets off the cave walls thirteen times—Max and Leo's eyes hilariously follow the bullet as it whizzes about the chamber, making "bing" and "boing" sound effects as it bounces off the stone—before eventually hitting (and killing) its target. Sadly, *Firewalker*'s Foley artist did not win the twelve Academy Awards he so clearly deserved for his work in this scene.

Once all of the ancient tribe is wiped out, the gang is bummed to learn that there isn't even any treasure in the cave. They snap a few photos of the murals, steal a ceremonial dagger, and head out.

The trio pays a visit to a local Native American shaman named Tall Eagle, and manage to take the film's racial insensitivities to another level by offering him a bottle of Jim Beam in tribute. (He's played by Native American character actor Will Sampson, best known for playing "Chief" opposite Jack Nicholson in 1975's *One Flew Over the Cuckoo's Nest*.) They show him the dagger, and he agrees to spill the beans about his culture's legendary treasure in exchange for a cut of their haul. He recounts a pointless-seeming myth about an Aztec priest named Firewalker who used his powers to fly away and live on the sun, but not before hiding a shit ton of gold somewhere in Central America. He also warns them to beware of "the Coyote," who is "treacherous and powerful." None of this makes sense until Patricia goes into a magical trance back in their hotel room, which points them to a location in the fictional banana republic of San Miguel.

After Patricia foils an assassin's attempt to drug and kill Max in his sleep, we're treated to a humongous bar brawl in a local dive. It's a scene that Norris was clearly proud of when promoting the movie's release, and it plays to his physical skills. It's a scene we've seen in plenty of Cannon movies before, but never with quite this much collateral damage. For those who can't be bothered to keep count at home: a grand total of *eighteen* boozed-up ruffians are punched and/or kicked unconscious, seven tables are smashed, a full shelf of liquor bottles is toppled over, two windows and one door have bad guys thrown through them, and a single mug of beer is chugged by Norris.

One painfully awkward Chuck Norris flirtation scene later, the three adventurers find themselves sneaking across San Miguel's closed border disguised as two priests and a nun. With the help of dumb luck and a Pig Latin prayer, they make it through a train ride deep into San Miguel's interior without being discovered. As soon as they step off the train, though, a group of soldiers sees through their ruse. They evade them in a nearby banana field, but wind up captured a few scenes later when a group of local freedom fighters finds their campsite. (This includes a scene where Patricia fends off a rape by a drunken soldier, which feels weirdly out-of-place in this otherwise family-friendly movie; it was trimmed from some foreign releases of the film.)

Just as our heroes are about to lose their heads on the edge of an executioner's blade, they're rescued by a deus ex machina named incarnate Corky, who it turns out is one of Max's old Marine pals. (Neither has Corky been mentioned to this point, nor Max's military service.) He's played with sociopathic bluster by Johnathan Rhys-Davies, whose prior Cannon appearances included *Sahara* (1983), *Sword of the Valiant* (1984), and *King Solomon's Mines*—although, obviously, he was best known for playing Sallah in the *Indiana Jones* films. At this point in cinema history, if you were making a treasure-hunting film and *didn't* find a spot for John Rhys-Davies to appear in it, you were doing something wrong.

Corky, it turns out, has gone native, and become the leader of an armed and dangerous jungle society, like a jollier version of Colonel Kurtz from *Apocalypse Now* (1979). He throws a fiesta in their honor, gifts them a Volkswagen, and sends them back off into the jungle. Our heroes set up camp next to a river, and Max and Patricia are given some alone time to swap spit and cuddle—only for Leo to disappear as soon as they wander off. He's presumably been eaten by crocodiles.

If you thought it was awkward watching Chuck Norris try to seduce a woman, you should see him try to mourn the death of his best friend. Rather than the world-shattering anguish one would probably feel if they were responsible for their closest friend's demise, he only musters the level of frustration one might have if, say, they opened their favorite box of cereal to find that someone had eaten the last of it and put the empty box back in the cupboard. "Damn you, Leo," Max pouts into the darkness of the jungle, fist balled at his side, looking like a grumpy five-year-old whose mother just told him it was time for bed.

Max and Patricia get over Leo's death relatively quickly, and decide to venture on without him. They find their way into the secret temple through a secret passage, and into a back room, where an eyepatch-wearing, Native American villain—the "red cyclops" Patricia warned Max about—holds Leo captive, suspended by ropes over a pit of boiling water. This is the evil "El Coyote," and he wants their ceremonial dagger. Max agrees to hand it over in exchange for Leo's safety, but El Coyote reneges on his offer, of course, because he's evil. Max attempts to rescue Leo as the chamber begins to flood, while El Coyote kidnaps Patricia and prepares her for an obligatory human sacrifice.

The movie was promoted in France with a nearly life-size poster of Chuck Norris.

El Coyote is played by Sonny Landham, a towering actor whose career began in pornography before he made his eventual transition into clothed films. His first mainstream breakthrough came playing a cop in the cult classic *The Warriors* (1979), followed by minor roles in *Southern Comfort* (1981) and *Poltergeist* (1982), and his breakout performance as Billy Bear in *48 Hrs.* (1982). His biggest cinematic splash came one year after *Firewalker*, when he played Billy Sole, one of Arnold Schwarzenegger's squadmates in *Predator* (1987). He was far less accomplished as a politician than he was as an actor. Hoping to find the same success with voters as his *Predator* castmates Schwarzenegger and Jesse Ventura, in 2008 Landham announced he was running for a U.S. Senate seat in the state of Kentucky. That same day he went on a radio show where he called for the genocide of Arab people while using several ethnic slurs in the process, and his party promptly withdrew their nomination. (That's a little something extra to chew on each time Chuck Norris slow-motion kicks him in the movie.)

In a finale that resembles that of another Cannon/Chuck Norris joint production, *Hellbound* (1994), Max and Leo arrive just in time as El Coyote prepares to sacrifice the unconscious heroine as part of a dark ritual that will grant him the Firewalker's powers. They defeat him in a battle that has both a fake-out death and, as expected, quite a lot of kicking. They find the treasure trove hidden underneath the sacrificial altar, and head home with overflowing sacks of gold and gemstones. The film ends with the trio celebrating in Fiji—actually, Mexico—and toasting to their futures of easy living. The camera then pans away to the bar, which—for some reason—is being tended by the scarred, Asian general who left them to die in the desert all the way back at the beginning of the film. He laughs villainously, and the credits roll.

Firewalker obviously sets itself up for sequels, which were never to be. The movie brought in $11 million at the domestic box office, making it the 70th highest-grossing film of 1986—which was decent for Cannon, but not enough to get them through the gauntlet of flops that would be their 1987 slate. (On its opening weekend, *Firewalker* barely beat out Disney's theatrical re-release of 1946's *Song of the South*—surprisingly making it *not* the most racist movie playing in theaters that week.)

Critics tore it apart, placing much of the blame on Chuck Norris. He honestly isn't terrible in this role, but he isn't exactly the roguish rapscallion that it calls for, either. Harrison Ford just oozed charm as Indiana Jones, and was able to deliver humor, romance, and excitement with aplomb; Norris, on the other hand, delivers karate and not much else. It didn't help matters, either, that *Firewalker* was an adventure film somewhat light on actual adventure: one of the most exciting set pieces involved Norris and Gossett swinging on a rope two feet over a puddle of dry ice. If you surveyed the average movie fan, they'd probably take Indy outrunning a boulder over Chuck Norris breaking chairs on the heads of drunks any day.

Melody Anderson and Chuck Norris in a publicity still from *Firewalker*.

Interview: Actress Melody Anderson

Having studied journalism in school, Melody Anderson worked in both newspapers and broadcasting for several years before she started appearing in guest spots on various TV shows. Soon came her breakout role: playing love interest Dale Arden in the cult sci-fi epic *Flash Gordon* (1980). She followed that up with a co-starring role in the horror film *Dead & Buried* (1981) and played opposite Jeff Goldblum in the biopic *Ernie Kovacs: Between the Laughter* (1984), while also starring in the short-lived science fiction series *Manimal* (1983).

After embarking on a heroic adventure with Chuck Norris in the Cannon action-comedy *Firewalker* (1986), Anderson received acclaim for her portrayal of Marilyn Monroe in *Marilyn & Bobby: Her Final Affair* (1993). Later, she would become one of the rare individuals to have a second successful career in a very different field: as a social worker specializing in trauma, addiction, and family therapy.

Do you recall how you landed your role in *Firewalker*?

Melody Anderson: It came after I had done *Flash Gordon*, so I was still up there—let's put it this way—in the file book of young actresses who had a certain amount of fame. [*Laughs*] Basically, I auditioned for the role and I kept being brought back, and brought back, and brought back, and then I finally met with Chuck and his people and it was a slam dunk. It worked out, and I got to work with two amazing people and actors. Those were Chuck Norris and Lou Gossett.

I just had a lot of respect for both of those guys, and it was really wonderful because I was able to watch Lou Gossett and how he worked. He was an Academy Award winner at that point. I think that whole concept of buddy movies was an attractive gig for him.

Of course, Chuck was amazing. Can you imagine? I'm going to go to my death bed saying, "I actually worked out pretty regularly with Chuck Norris and his team." Come on, who gets to say that? Unfortunately, Chuck moved to Texas and I lost track of him, but I run into Lou on occasion. I do still get to see him once in a blue moon, and we check in.

I know Cannon always moved very quickly, especially on the movies they did with Chuck. Were you given much time to prepare for the production, or was it pretty much "off to Mexico!" as soon as you were cast?

That's about right, but as an actor you're a journeyman, so you figure out what to do along the way. That was not a problem for me. It was last minute but as an actor, but a lot of your gigs are last minute, and you've got to pull it together. You get training in how to do that. You're just happy you have the job.

I'm a great believer of when you're in a country, get the regular food as soon as you can, so you can build up the bacteria. Chuck and Lou weren't able to come to work one day and were crawling around because of Montezuma's revenge. I never got it, because I was eating wonderful tamales off of the stand right outside of the studio in Mexico City. That was great.

The director [J Lee Thompson] had done some amazing movies in his day. He had a wonderful sense of humor. It was hot and there he was, this very light-skinned, tiny little British man, out there in the sun, and we've all got hats on and all that.

I've read that there was a lot of practical joking between you and Chuck. I'm wondering if you can elaborate on that?

Chuck Norris is just an ordinary boy in a man's body. He loved playing pranks on me, and of course the problem was that I loved playing pranks on him, too, so we kept feeding off each other. One time, he tried—oh, it's just so high school. He tried to put—seriously, how old was he at the time? Maybe in his 50s?—he came up with the idea to put a bucket of water on the door, so that when you open it, it falls on you. Of course, when he tried that with me, I got out of the way, and I didn't get too wet.

He would do things like put one of those plastic dog poops that you get from the back of comic books in your room. Nothing bothers me. I'm Canadian—we're used to a lot of weird things. I picked up the dog poop and I said, "Really? How old are you today?" I looked at him and I said, "You have no idea when or how, but one day, I'm going to get you so bad. I'm going to leave you in torture, waiting every day and wondering if today is the day I get you." I put the fear of God in him. From then on he was always looking at me from the side, just wondering what I was up to.

The days and the weeks pile up, and I still haven't pulled my prank yet. There were wonderful markets in Mexico City, and I got myself these lovely, wooden sculptures of some of the Christian saints. They were just beautiful, from the 1800s. I got them all pretty cheap, but I told him about this one I got of Saint Francis. I told Chuck it was incredibly old and that I had it appraised, and it's incredibly expensive. I kept telling him how much I loved it. Unfortunately, Saint Francis's head wasn't sticking onto his body too well—it was barely stuck on there. So I told Chuck I was going to bring it the next day so he could see it, and I was going on about its expense and its delicacy, and how this is the nicest thing I've ever owned in my life, that I grew up poor, whatever—which is not true. I handed the sculpture to him and the moment he touched the head, it fell off in his hand. I just looked at him with this devastated look, and started to cry. "How could you? I told you how valuable this is. I'll never be able to replace it." I was actually much meaner than he was. He honestly felt very bad about it, and I tortured him throughout the day. I would say to him, "I don't know if I can do this scene, I'm so upset about my Saint Francis." Then towards the end of the day, I started laughing. I said, "I told you I would get you one day," and I got him. I said, "I just want you to know, if you pull anything on me again, this is just the beginning of the war."

He was great about it. We just had so much fun. He was a real prankster and an incredible professional—as was, of course, Lou. I was just very lucky to work with the two of them.

You shot in some really cool locations around Mexico. Did you have any favorites?

Durango, I thought, was just beautiful. It was very, very much like those old John Ford Westerns. It was just a beautiful country. Then being in Mexico City, I loved it. I loved the art galleries. I'm a painter, so I really enjoyed all the arts, and the markets. Then we went to Puerto Vallarta, which isn't exactly a crummy place to have to go. Improving my Spanish was really, really important to me. I was pretty fluent by the time I left.

If you look back at the shoot, are you able to pick a favorite day? And on the flip side, what part was the most difficult?

I think the most difficult part of the shoot was when the Volkswagen sank down into the river. Physically, that was the most difficult because we had to be in the car and get out of the water. It was pretty tough. I think since I never got Montezuma's revenge, I didn't have the difficulties that either of the boys had, so it wasn't that hard.

Lou Gossett Jr., Melody Anderson, and Chuck Norris pose for a publicity photo on the set of *Firewalker*.

The biggest issue was making sure our film wasn't stolen when it went back to the United States for processing. We had to have somebody watch the person who was carrying it get through customs. It's the Wild West out there. In fact, one time, I think Chuck's van was taken aside by some questionable people, his dressing room RV. There was a sense that there were dangerous gangs out there.

For me, I had just such a pleasant experience with it all. As I say, I was very lucky to be with such really wonderful men. Lee was a very famous director. There were a lot of funny games, and a lot of room to play around, so it was fun. He'd let us improvise and things like that, which is always the most fun for an actor.

Did you spend any time in the Cannon offices, or meet Golan and Globus?

Yes, I did meet them, and they were just lovely . . . are they lovely people? I have no idea, but my contact with them was. Those guys, it was like nothing stopped them. They were, "Go, go, go, go, go," twenty-four/seven, and making seventeen movies at the same time. Really, I don't know how they kept organized with all the projects that they had, but they were very pleasant to me.

They came down a couple of times to Mexico, to the set, but there was no interference with me or Chuck or Lou, and I think probably not even with Lee. They would get a project, put it together, and then leave it alone. I sometimes wonder if that's the reason for some of the success they had on a popular level. Maybe not on a critical level, but a popular level with audiences, because everybody who was there got to do what they did best without feeling as if some hammer was on their head.

You continued to work in film for another decade afterwards, but you've said elsewhere that acting started to feel less rewarding as you went on. How did you discover your second calling in social work?

It's interesting. [*Laughs*] I had studied psychology as a minor in college, and I got my degree in journalism, and I was always fascinated by people. One of the things I liked about journalism—and also about acting—was that you're communicating with people, and you're changing their emotional states either by laughing, or crying, or whatever.

I started to see the writing on the wall that my ingénue days were becoming a part of the past. I was heading towards my mid-thirties. I was sitting there thinking, "Okay, five years from now, I don't want to struggle to do some crummy, crummy acting job just to keep a roof over my head." The answer to that was "No."

As things got quieter, I started taking some elective courses at NYU, in psychology and social work. Then I signed on and did the whole training, and absolutely loved it. For me, being able to be paid to tell people what to do was my dream job. [*Laughs*]. I have loved it ever since. The wonderful thing about this work is you can keep on training. Now, I specialize in trauma, addiction, and family therapy.

The other thing I liked about going into psychology is that the older, fatter, and grayer you become, the more they really think you know what you're talking about. It was a career that was rewarding, shall we say, my wisdom and "my aged phase." You can do it from a wheelchair. I saw it as a much more consistent way of making a living, and of course, much more satisfying. I continue to this day to train and study and read. I'm just so fascinated by how the human mind perceives the world.

Few people are fortunate enough to have one successful career, let alone two so different ones. I'm curious, though, has the acting bug completely left you?

Oh God, no. I don't think it ever does. It's an amazing experience to be on a set. It's like you're all on the Titanic, and your job is to keep the ship from sinking. There's this amazing camaraderie and instant family that's created on a set, because every day something crazy happens. That connection is almost as exciting as it is researching a role and becoming a character. I've played Marilyn Monroe and Edie Adams and got to work in all of these wonderful, wonderful roles throughout my career. That itself is exciting, but there is just this human experience in everybody being stressed to the nines on a daily basis; having to be on your toes, and not get stuck on, "Oh, yesterday was hard," because the next day could be even harder.

It's a very, very rewarding career. Now, if someone asked me to come in and play a therapist on a fun show, or be Mrs. Flash Gordon again, I would do it in two seconds, because I like going to Italy. One day, I'd like to buy myself a Tesla. With all that in mind, I certainly would take a job. But, it would have to be one that wouldn't interfere with my clients' perceptions of me, because my therapy is my primary interest and focus in life today.

An advertisement for *Firewalker* from Cannon's famous, sixty-page spread at the 1986 Cannes Film Festival.

Interview: Screenwriter Robert Gosnell

As a screenwriter, Robert Gosnell primarily had experience working on TV sitcoms prior to seeking work as a feature film writer for Cannon. While making a bid to rewrite *Number One with a Bullet* (1987) for the company, he submitted his spec screenplay for an adventure film then titled "Firewalking"—which was discovered by Chuck Norris, and would promptly become the martial arts actor's first foray into the realm of comedy.

Gosnell now instructs students in writing for film and television, and has penned a book called *The Blue Collar Screenwriter*, which provides guidance for aspiring writers.

You have TV credits before it, but *Firewalker* (1986) appears to be your first feature film. How did you get involved? Were you a writer for hire, or was it written on spec?

Robert Gosnell: The script was written on spec. I had written the screenplay, originally titled "Firewalking," as a straight-forward action piece, and afterward collaborated with Norm Aladjem and Jeffery Rosenbaum to turn the story into an action/comedy. My agent at the time, Dan Redler, learned that Cannon was looking for someone to do a polish on a screenplay called *Number One with a Bullet*, and sent "Firewalking" to Cannon as a writing sample. I was then called in to meet with a development exec, Susan Hoffman, and was hired for the job.

After completing the polish on *Number One with a Bullet*, I met again with Susan Hoffman to be considered for an assignment to write a comedy/action piece, "Kick and Kick Back," for Chuck Norris, which, as I understood it, was a concept of Chuck's. I then met with Chuck and was hired for that project. We met a few times to discuss the story, and Chuck then left for a promotional tour for another of his recently filmed projects, I can't recall which one.

While on his promotional tour, Chuck read "Firewalking" and was very complimentary of it. When he returned from his tour, I was called to a meeting, which I assumed was a story meeting for "Kick and Kick Back." When I arrived, I was sent to Menahem's office, where he, Chuck and several other executives had convened. It was then I was informed that the decision had been made for *Firewalker* to be Chuck's next project. They were already working on casting, and hadn't yet purchased the screenplay, but that deal was made soon after.

***Firewalker* was Chuck's stab at broadening the variety of films he could star in. Did you have to shape the character with that in mind?**

The character was already written. Nothing was written by me that was specifically tailored to Chuck.

The movie shares its pulpy, adventure tone with films like *Indiana Jones*, *Romancing the Stone*, and Cannon's own Allan Quatermain series. Were there any older films, books, or serials that inspired you when writing it?

Obviously, the films you mention above were instrumental in my choice. I was trying to cash in on a popular genre.

Cannon was famous for requiring screenwriters to do rewrites well into the shoot. Did you deal with any of that on *Firewalker*, or was it mostly shot as it was originally written?

I did some early polishes on the script before it went into production. Once it went into production, numerous changes were made for a variety of reasons, some logistical, some for time considerations, some that occurred in editing, and some were just changes made on the set. I was not involved in any of those changes. Additionally, it was Chuck's decision to change the title from "Firewalking" to *Firewalker*.

How close is the finished film to the one you imagined while writing it?

Most writers would tell you that the finished films often don't reflect their original vision. To quote Forrest Gump, "that's all I've got to say about that."

Chuck Norris wasn't the greatest actor, or the flashiest martial artist, but for a decade he could draw an audience to an action film. As someone whose writing was brought to life by Chuck Norris, what do you think gave him such broad appeal?

Chuck had a clear grasp of his image. He knew what his audience wanted from him, and he knew how to deliver it. He was adamant about not varying from it. He had a wholesome "hero" appeal to a broad audience. The closest I can come to describing it would be an action hero with a "John Wayne" appeal .On a personal level, Chuck always treated me with courtesy and consideration, and in the limited time I was around him, I never saw him treat anyone otherwise. He was simply a down-to-earth, regular guy; very approachable and very relatable. I think that translated into his characters.

You've said that every screenplay you write teaches you something new. Can you share some of the things you personally learned from the writing (and eventual production) of *Firewalker*?

At the risk of monopolizing your entire book, I'll try to hit on a few highlights. Much, if not most, of what happens to a screenplay once it goes into production is out of a writer's hands. When you become an "A" list, highly paid screenwriter, they might listen to you. Otherwise, get used to it and learn to live with it.

If I had the ability to go back and do things differently, I can think of several things. As mentioned, the part was not written specifically for Chuck. If it had been, I would have made every effort to fine-tune the character to Chuck's best qualities, but again, that was an option which was not available to me. It was the first crack at a comedy for Chuck, and put extra demands on him that he had no opportunity to prepare for. Had I been able to tailor it more to his personality, I believe it would have helped.

Another piece of advice would be to stay true to the genre. I enjoy dialogue; writing it, reading it and hearing it. Because of that, *Firewalker* was dialogue-heavy, which is not ideal for an action piece, and resulted in a great deal of it winding up on the cutting room floor. The result of that was that much character development, relationship building and story exposition was lost, which in my view ultimately hurt the overall story.

Some of the issues I recognized in the finished film can be attributed to the initial screenplay development. Looking back, I should have developed the characters more through action and less through dialogue. As mentioned, I should have relied less on dialogue, in general. I should have avoided some clichés that didn't play as well on the screen as I thought they would. *Firewalker* was my first film, and came early in my career, which had initially been confined to TV situation comedy writing. Over the years, I've learned a great deal more about screenplay writing than I knew then.

Finally: listen to everyone, but don't always assume they are right.

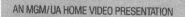

MV801117

A CANNON FILMS RELEASE

JULIE ANDREWS
ALAN BATES   MAX VON SYDOW

DUET *for* ONE ™

THE CANNON GROUP, INC. PRESENTS JULIE ANDREWS · ALAN BATES · MAX VON SYDOW
IN A GOLAN-GLOBUS PRODUCTION OF AN ANDREI KONCHALOVSKY FILM "DUET FOR ONE" ALSO STARRING RUPERT EVERETT
COSTUME DESIGNER EVANGELINE HARRISON ASSOCIATE PRODUCER MICHAEL J. KAGAN PRODUCTION DESIGNER JOHN GRAYSMARK DIRECTOR OF PHOTOGRAPHY ALEX THOMSON, B.S.C.
EDITED BY HENRY RICHARDSON, A.C.E. BASED ON THE PLAY BY TOM KEMPINSKI SCREENPLAY BY TOM KEMPINSKI AND JEREMY LIPP & ANDREI KONCHALOVSKY
PRODUCED BY MENAHEM GOLAN AND YORAM GLOBUS DIRECTED BY ANDREI KONCHALOVSKY

A VHS copy of *Duet for One* previously rented out by Yacolt Video of
Yacolt, Washington.

Duet for One

Release Date: December 25, 1986
Directed by: Andrei Konchalovsky
Written by: Tom Kempinski and Jeremy Lipp, Andrei Konchalovsky
Starring: Julie Andrews, Alan Bates, Max Von Sydow, Rupert Everett
Trailer Voiceover: "There are moments in life which can't be rehearsed. There are dreams from which you don't wake up."

Tragedy befalls the world's greatest concert violinist when the onset of multiple sclerosis leaves her reliant upon a wheelchair, unable to perform for the crowds that it's been her life's mission to entertain. And yet, that's only the first crack in her perfect, crumbling life: soon, her best student abandons her study for an unglamorous job in Las Vegas, her longtime accompanist dies unexpectedly, and her husband's affair with his pretty, young secretary becomes all-too-obvious.

No, *Duet for One* (1986) is not among Cannon's most upbeat films, if that's what you were wondering. It is, however, a superbly-acted downer from Andrei Konchalovsky, the company's most reliable director of arthouse-worthy fare.

The project itself came to Cannon several years earlier via actress Faye Dunaway, for whom starring in a film version of this lauded stage play had been a dream of hers. To win favor with the award-winning star—and, not to mention, a longer contract—following her appearance in *The Wicked Lady* (1983), Cannon picked up the rights to the play and wasted no time announcing their intentions to film it, with Dunaway in the lead and her then-husband, photographer Terry O'Neill, attached as a first-time director. Obviously that version never happened, although it didn't stop Cannon from turning *Duet for One* into a movie.

The original play debuted in London in 1980. It was the work of playwright Tom Kempinski, who had written the lead role for his wife, actress Frances de la Tour. The premiere run was massively successful on the West End—where Dunaway had seen it—and was brought to Broadway in short order, with a star-studded cast that included Anne Bancroft and Max von Sydow, and who were directed by *The Exorcist* (1973) filmmaker William Friedkin. This version, for hard-to-place reasons, flopped and flopped hard over its two-week run from the winter of 1981 into 1982, getting yanked after only twenty performances. Many critics unfavorably drew comparisons between it and the sad tragedy of master cellist Jacqueline du Pré, whose life had clearly inspired the play. (From early in her career, du Pré was considered to be among the world's best classical performers, but was forced to stop playing in 1973 after she was diagnosed with multiple sclerosis, aged only twenty-eight.) More recent revivals of the show have been regarded more favorably, thanks likely in no small part to audiences largely having forgotten about the real-life du Pré.

Kempinski co-wrote the screenplay for the film with Jeremy Lipp, who also had a credit on the *very* different *P.O.W. The Escape* (1986) for Cannon the same year. This is where "artistic differences" arose between Cannon and their presumed star, Faye Dunaway. In the interest of greater commercial viability, the script was vastly opened up for the screen. The play had featured only two actors, and consisted of heated conversations between its heroine, Stephanie Abrams, and her psychiatrist, in his office. The screen version, on the other hand, instead features eight characters with significant dialogue, and takes place in locations as varied as Stephanie's apartment, a concert hall, the airport, beneath a humongous tree, and even in a karaoke bar. Dunaway, who had been enamored with the intimate two-hander that was the stage version, got into a fracas with Cannon over their changes. Ultimately, she was able to use a script approval clause in her contract to bitterly pull out of the film altogether.

Cannon spent years using Dunaway's star power to pre-sell the film—only for the actress to leave over creative differences with their script.

By this point Andrei Konchalovsky had already replaced her husband, Terry O'Neill, as director, and was hard at work making his own additions to the script. (Konchalovsky was already neck-deep in pre-production for this film when he was informed that both of his stars had been nominated for Academy Awards for the newly-released *Runaway Train* [1985].) The final screenplay was far enough removed from the play that Cannon briefly mulled changing the title to "Gift of the Heart" or "Heart of the Tree," but ultimately stayed put.

Julie Andrews was cast as the film's new lead. The former *Mary Poppins* (1964) and *The Sound of Music* (1965) star took up violin lessons in preparation, and paid a visit to a hospice to interview people suffering with multiple sclerosis. The part of her psychiatrist, the other role retained from the original play, went to Max von Sydow, who had already done it on Broadway. Although the role was greatly reduced for the screen, it's still great casting—if you need an actor to broodingly ruminate over the paralyzing fear of mortality, who better to do it than the man who played chess with Death in Ingmar Bergman's *The Seventh Seal* (1957)?

Stephanie's husband, David—who was only talked about in the play—has the film's second-most screen time. That role went to celebrated English thespian Alan Bates, previously seen in Cannon's *The Wicked Lady* but far better-known for his Academy Award-nominated turn in *The Fixer* (1968) and performances in *Zorba the Greek* (1964), *Georgy Girl* (1966), *Far From the Madding Crowd* (1967), and *Women in Love* (1969).

There are two young faces in the film—relative newcomers, compared to their castmates—who nowadays are as recognizable as the film's stars, or more so. Liam Neeson plays a garbage man and gadabout named Totter, who makes a regular habit of sleeping with the lonely women whose trash he's been hired to clean out. This was after his appearances in *Excalibur* (1981) and *Krull* (1983), but a few years before he'd become a genuine star in his own right. (In a couple decades he'd begin the late-era Charles Bronson phase of his career, reinventing himself as a retirement-aged action hero.) Rupert Everett, on the other hand, had done less before *Duet for One*, in which he plays Stephanie's favorite pupil. In the next decade he'd also break out with roles in *My Best Friend's Wedding* (1997) and the wonderfully strange zombie film *Dellamorte Dellamore* (1994), also known as *Cemetery Man*.

The film starts after Stephanie's diagnosis, as she plans to play a series of sold-out London concerts that she knows may very well be her last. The action flits between her psychiatrist's office and her home life, making sizable leaps ahead in time so that the movie covers roughly one year of our heroine's life, bookended by birthday parties thrown under considerably different circumstances. Not only do we watch her physically degenerate over this time due to the disease, but her mental and emotional states take a beating as she seems to lose every person to whom she had ever felt close. Her only constants through it all are a devoted maid named Anya, played by Macha Méril of Dario Argento's *Deep Red* (1975) and Luis Buñuel's *Belle de Jour* (1967), and the sessions with her psychiatrist.

Cannon released *Duet for One* into theaters on Christmas day in 1986, sending it to a few arthouse cinemas in large cities before slowly moving those same prints into smaller markets throughout the following year. It was met with a mixed response from reviewers, with some leveling criticism against it for being heavy-handed in its symbolism, or for being overly talky, or for painting its portrayal of multiple sclerosis with so much hopelessness. Others liked Konchalovsky's dreamlike touches, and its characters who lashed out at their unfortunate situations in entirely believable ways.

Andrews' performance was the one element most consistently praised by critics, and ultimately won her a Golden Globe nomination for Best Actress in the Drama category. In a rare alignment of stars, she was also nominated for the same award that year in the Comedy or Musical category, for 1986's *That's Life!*, directed by her husband, Blake Edwards.

In *Duet for One*, Andrews pads her anger with elegant anguish—not to mention, there's an undeniable satisfaction in listening to Mary Poppins drop f-bombs. She brings a necessary softness to a character that's otherwise quite harsh; you can easily imagine that Faye Dunaway might have taken this into a "no wire hangers," *Mommie Dearest* (1981) sort of territory had she stayed on board.

The North American VHS release for *Field of Honor*, the grimmest of
Cannon's Vietnam films.

Field of Honor

Release Date: January 9, 1987
Directed by: Hans Scheepmaker
Written by: Henk Bos
Starring: Everett McGill
Trailer voiceover: "Left for dead, one man faces the ultimate challenge: survival!"

Holy shit, this movie is *dark*. Cannon made a lot of war films that were fantastical, over-the-top, or downright goofy. This is very much *not* one of them... although you might not get that impression from the first couple minutes of the film. When we first meet our hero, Sgt. "Sire" de Koning, he's fully nude and stumbling out of a whorehouse with a pink bow tied 'round his wiener. But, trust me, things get pretty grim from there on out.

Field of Honor (1987) is set during the Korean War—one of the more underserved settings in war films—and was a Dutch/South Korean co-production financed by Cannon. As if acknowledging that some of their viewers may not know or remember what the Korean War was about, the filmmakers open with a detailed, rolling text scroll that explains the events which led to the conflict between North Korea and South Korea. *Field of Honor* was inspired by the experiences of veterans of the Dutch Battalion; while the Netherlands were among the smaller forces supporting the South Korean war efforts, they suffered one of the highest percentages of casualties.

On the eve of deployment to the front line, Sgt. de Koning, or "Sire," as his soldiers address him out of both respect and affection, throws a "party" to build morale before his troops step out into the proverbial shitstorm. To do this, he's gone into town and procured whores and liquor. The prostitutes are, sadly, a mother and daughter; meanwhile, the little brother tags along to trade condoms to the soldiers in exchange for food. (I *told* you the movie was dark.) While the men get drunk and take turns with the mother, Chinese soldiers execute a sneak attack on their camp. Sire orders everyone to flee: "Every man for himself!" Many are killed, and their camp is completely destroyed.

Sire awakes the next day with gruesome injuries to his head and thigh. He's better off, though, than many of the men around him who are just barely clinging to life. He finds one of his boys screaming for him: he's blinded, his skin badly burned. Sire points his rifle at the man, who has just enough strength to grab the barrel and pull it into his mouth before Sire pulls the trigger.

Yeah. One hundred percent of this movie is f*cked up.

Sire finds one more survivor, delirious, with his innards hanging out of a hole in his gut. Sire binds a helmet overtop of the wound to prevent his entrails from falling out any further. Soon, the Chinese return. Sire hides under a nearby truck and plays dead, which seems like a good idea until one of the enemies tries to start it, and winds up backing one of the heavy wheels over Sire's boot—crushing his foot, and trapping him underneath. They leave again, and Sire is powerless to do anything but watch his friend die just meters away from him—and unable to scare away the rats which soon gather to feast on his flesh.

Damn.

Sire eventually wriggles out from under the truck, and is reunited with a dog that had once been his company's pet. The dog quickly becomes his closest companion, but as soon as he ties it up to go on a scouting trip outside of the wrecked camp, he looks back in horror to witness a young girl beating the dog to death. He's too far away for his shouting to be heard, and his leg injury prevents him rescuing his former pet—once again, all he can do is watch the horror unfold in front of him.

He goes back to camp, where he comes face to face with the younger of the two prostitutes who were at the fateful celebration. She and her younger brother survived the attack. Other than when they momentarily went out to bury their mother's body, they've been hiding inside a collapsed building. The brother is badly shell-shocked, only able to stare blankly into the distance. The girl had to kill his dog, she tells Sire, because she and her brother were hungry. (Its skinned carcass hangs in their hidey-hole.) When she can't get her brother to chew the meat, Sire does so himself, grinding down his own dog's flesh in his molars and then baby-birding it into the boy's mouth.

For a while, Sire does what he can to help them survive, and even kills a soldier who tries to rape the girl, but then there's another Chinese attack. He's able to protect the little boy, but not his sister, who is killed by a stray bullet. The enemies are eventually driven away by a Dutch counterattack. In the end, Sire walks the boy to safety, and promises one of his surviving underlings that he'll be back with the troops at the front line after a few days' recovery. The end.

Field of Honor is astoundingly grim from beginning to end. (Even the movie's first half hour, which I didn't detail here, primarily consists of the Dutch soldiers exploiting the local, impoverished Korean population.) The imagery ranges from gruesome to horrific. All of this, quite sadly, probably makes it one of the most realistic of Cannon's many war films.

You have to imagine this also contributed to *Field of Honor* becoming one of Cannon's more obscure U.S. releases. The movie received a less-than-stellar reaction at the Cannes Film Festival in 1986, which led Cannon to give it only the tiniest (contractually obligated) theatrical release before sending it on to video rental stores. It wasn't re-released on home video for the following three decades and, given the subject matter shown on screen, never went into cable rotation like so many other Cannon flicks.

The movie's only notable star is Everett McGill, who plays Sire. A veteran stage actor, McGill made the transition to screen playing a caveman in the well-regarded *Quest for Fire* (1981), and co-starred in Clint Eastwood's better-remembered *Heartbreak Ridge* (1986) the same year that *Field of Honor* premiered at Cannes. McGill is best-known, though, for his collaborations with director David Lynch, who cast him in *Dune* (1984) and *The Straight Story* (1999), and for whom he played lovelorn gas station proprietor Big Ed Hurley on *Twin Peaks* (1989–1991).]

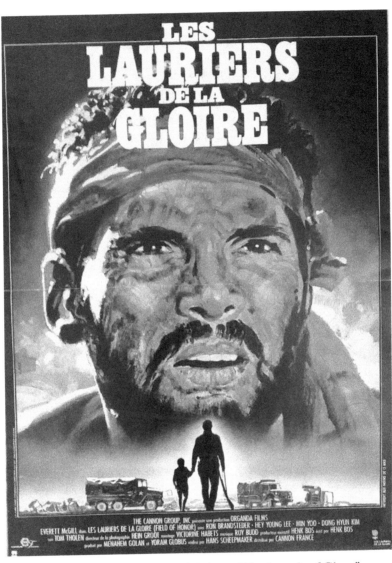

A French poster for *Field of Honor*, or "The Laurels of Glory."

An ex-rental VHS copy of *Assassination*, previously of the simply-named
Video Shop of Zanesville, Ohio.

Assassination

Release Date: January 9, 1987
Directed by: Peter Hunt
Written by: Richard Sale
Starring: Charles Bronson, Jill Ireland, Jan Gan Boyd
Trailer Voiceover: "Protecting the highest office in the land demands the toughest man in the business!"

Are you a bad enough dude to save the President's wife? If anyone is, it's Charles Bronson.

Having yet to see diminishing returns with the sequels, Cannon was ready to jump back into their profitable *Death Wish* series by early 1986. The franchise's stone-faced mega-star, Charles Bronson, knew he had some leverage over Cannon when it came to playing his iconic vigilante character. He agreed to appear in what would eventually become *Death Wish 4: The Crackdown* (1987), but only once they'd signed him to a new, six-picture deal that would pay him a cool one million bucks per film. The first of those movies would be the political action-thriller *Assassination*, which was first

603

called *My Affair with the President's Wife*, then *The President's Wife*, and briefly just *Assassin* before it settled on its final release title.

In the movie, Bronson plays secret service agent Jay "Killy" Killian, who returns from a six-month medical leave just in time for Inauguration Day. An agent of his seniority would normally be assigned to protect the President Elect, but his higher-ups have concern that he may be a little rusty and instead assign him to the new First Lady, Lara Royce Craig. Code named "One Momma" by the secret service, the First Lady has a reputation for being a spoiled rich girl, and a real battle axe. ("You're going to miss the hell out of Nancy Reagan," Killy's boss warns him.) She's played by Bronson's real-life spouse, Jill Ireland.

Ireland and Bronson had married in 1968. Together they raised five children from their previous marriages, and added two more. As an actress, Ireland had been working on-screen for almost as long as her new husband. After they wed she became a staple of his films, co-starring in sixteen of Bronson's movies. (She joked that she *had* to appear in her husband's movies because no other actress wanted to work with him.) Two years after appearing with Bronson in Cannon's hit *Death Wish II* (1982), Ireland was diagnosed with breast cancer. She fought the disease both privately and publicly, penning a high-profile book called *Life Lines* (1987), which detailed her battle against the illness. During these years she stepped away from acting, undergoing treatment while writing her memoir and co-producing two of her husband's movies, including *Murphy's Law* (1986) for Cannon. *Assassination* was meant to be her next job as a producer, with actress Jaclyn Smith (of Cannon's *Déjà Vu*, 1985) penciled in to play the female lead. When studio head Menahem Golan offered her the role instead, Ireland graciously accepted with the feeling that appearing on-screen again would be an inspiration to other women who were battling against breast cancer. After a mastectomy and chemotherapy, it was believed for a while that Ireland might have beaten the disease.

In the film, Killy and One Momma start their relationship off on the wrong foot when Killy accidentally gives her a shiner during the Inauguration parade. In his defense, he *was* protecting her during a botched attempt on her life, but everyone else assumes that the shady-looking "police officer" whose motor-cycle "accidentally" exploded near her convertible was only part of an unfortunate traffic mishap. Killy has a hunch that the fake cop was actually Reno Bracken (Erik Stern), an infamous terrorist holding a grudge against Killy for the time he led a Delta Force team that thwarted one of his plots during the Carter administration. (There's a distinctively Cannon touch for you.)

A postcard advertising the German video release of *Assassination*, with artwork by Enzo Sciotti.

605

No one believes Killy's hunch about the assassination attempt except his partners, Tyler (Randy Brooks) and Charlotte "Charlie" Chang (Jan Gan Boyd.) Brooks is best remembered for playing the detective who coaches Tim Roth's character about how to work undercover in *Reservoir Dogs* (1992). Boyd was a dancer-turned-actress whose only movie appearance prior to this was in Richard Attenborough's *A Chorus Line* (1985).

Proving excessively foolhardy, the First Lady sneaks out of the White House and boards a plane for her wealthy father's yacht, which is docked off the California coast. Killy and his team catch up with her and accompany her on the trip against her wishes. Just as they're readying to board the boat for an impromptu pleasure cruise with the First Lady, the ship is blown up by a mistimed explosives charge. (The impostor dockworker we see planting the plastic explosives on the boat's hull is played by writer Billy Hayes, who was charged with drug smuggling and sentenced to life in a Turkish prison from which he later escaped; his autobiographical book about the experience was turned into the 1978 film *Midnight Express*.)

It's not until Killy saves her life for a third time—when Bracken attempts to shoot down her helicopter with a rocket launcher—that the First Lady finally concedes that someone may actually be trying to kill her.

Despite there clearly being some sort of contract out on her head, the First Lady puts on another disguise and gives the White House the slip one last time. When Killy intercepts her, she reveals that even though she tried to have him fired on several occasions, he is the only person she feels she can trust. He promises to help her uncover the identity of whoever it is that wants her dead, and they embark together on an action-packed, cross-country road trip while posing as a married couple. Along the way there's a motorcycle chase, an exciting escape from a train, an exploding truck, and many attempts on their lives. Judging by the way would-be assassins lurk around their every turn, someone is indeed trying to kill them and that person is aware of their every move. Killy has another hunch: that it's the President himself who wants his wife wiped out of the picture.

Cannon's 1986 Cannes Film Festival ad for *Assassination*, pre-sold under its working title "Assassin."

Killy's hypothesis is all but confirmed when the First Lady admits she's been calling her husband each night from the road. She confides in Killy that their marriage is a sham, and that they only wed because they thought a wholesome-looking marriage would help his chances at being elected. Her "job" finished, she's now unhappy in their arrangement, revealing that an old war injury has left her husband totally impotent. (Including Bo Derek's paramour in 1984's *Bolero* and John Savage's traumatized veteran in 1985's *Maria's Lovers*, this is the third Cannon film with a plot that hinges on someone's non-functioning wiener.) The First Lady wants out of the marriage, but the President needs a cover for his impotence, which is the reason why the Executive Branch wants her dead. In their mind, a widowed war hero has a higher chance at re-election than a dick-less divorcee.

Needing a safe place to hide out while they make a plan, Killy and the First Lady head to her father's palatial estate in Lake Tahoe. Up until this point, *Assassination* functions as a pretty good, if predictable, action-thriller: a few of the set-pieces—particularly a memorable motorcycle chase over a rail bridge—are genuinely exciting. From the moment our heroes arrive in Lake Tahoe, however, *Assassination* seems to be in a sudden hurry to wrap itself up.

Behind the scenes, Cannon had drastically slashed the movie's budget during the shoot and the production essentially ran out of money. What was intended to be a month-long shoot for the movie's climax was hacked down to two weeks. Rather than several planned ATV chases and the exciting plane crash we were supposed to get in the film's final act, we received a rushed finale in which Bronson's unconvincing stunt double chases down the terrorist baddie on a jet ski. There's no big, final confrontation with the President, but instead a quick scene where Bronson tosses the slimy U.S. Senator who arranged the failed hit jobs out of a window. The entire last act of the movie feels slapped together at the last minute, which is because it was.

As a whole, *Assassination* is a mixed bag. It's a shame the last third of it feels rushed and unfinished, because up until that point the plot is more than functional enough to keep an audience wrapped up in trying to unspool the conspiracy. The script was adapted by screenwriter Richard Sale from his unpublished novel titled *My Affair with the President's Wife*, with the "affair" element of the story apparently dropped in favor of Killy being romantically involved with his fellow secret service agent, played by Jan Gan Boyd.

608

Sale had cut his teeth as a pulp fiction writer in the 1930s before breaking into Hollywood as a screenwriter. He'd previously written *The White Buffalo* (1977), a Western which had also starred Bronson.

When Bronson's favored director, J. Lee Thompson, had his hands full directing Cannon's Chuck Norris adventure-comedy *Firewalker* (1986), the studio turned to five-decade industry vet Peter Hunt. Hunt began his career as a film editor, with his big break coming when he cut the first five James Bond films in the 1960s, and then directed the sixth, *On Her Majesty's Secret Service* (1969). He'd worked with Bronson before this film, having directed him in 1981's *Death Hunt*.

Interestingly, it was announced that Golden Age Hollywood actor Joseph Cotten—of *Citizen Kane* (1941), *Gaslight* (1944), and *The Third Man* (1949) fame—had been cast as the father of Ireland's character. By the time the film was produced, however, the role had been reduced and was instead played by William Prince of *The Stepford Wives* (1975) and *The Gauntlet* (1977).

Assassination's score is mostly by Robert O. Ragland and Bronson's stepson, Valentine McCallum, but you might recognize the opening credit music being recycled from Jay Chattaway's fantastic *Invasion U.S.A.* (1985) soundtrack.

Charles Bronson and Jill Ireland in a publicity still from *Assassination*.

Up against the better entries in Bronson's Cannon canon, *Assassination* is ultimately a misfire. It's not all bad, however. It's always fun watching Bronson in films where he appears comfortable (which can't be said of every movie he made for Cannon.) He seems to be having fun playing a character that isn't as hard-edged or jaded as he was usually typecast. It's also one of the rare, PG-13 rated films in his later filmography, so it's not nearly as violent as his other Cannon pictures. Most of all, Bronson and Ireland have a good chemistry together, for obvious reasons, even if their relationship is more antagonistic than romantic in this film. It's heartbreaking that *Assassination* was the last movie they made together.

Charles Bronson and Jan Gan Boyd in *Assassination*.

Following *Assassination*, Ireland acted as a spokeswoman for the American Cancer Society, becoming a face of optimism for other women battling the disease. In 1988 she testified to a Congressional committee, urging for mammograms to be offered to women on Medicare, and was honored with the Medal of Courage by Ronald Reagan, and the Betty Ford Award from the Susan Komen Foundation. In 1989, doctors discovered that the cancer had returned, and had spread throughout her body. She fought until the end, keeping a brave face even as she received her star on Hollywood's Walk of Fame in the spring of 1990. Only weeks later she would succumb to the disease, passing away at the young age of 54, with her husband and family by her side.

Interview: Actress Jan Gan Boyd

Jan Gan Boyd began her career on stage as a dancer before she moved into acting. Her big screen break came in a dancer's role in Richard Attenborough's *A Chorus Line* (1985). Her next big screen appearance would come playing Charles Bronson's colleague and love interest, Charlotte Chang, in Cannon's *Assassination* (1987), alongside Bronson's real-life wife, Jill Ireland.

Following her Cannon role, Boyd co-starred in the action film *Steele Justice* (1987) and made guest appearances on the sitcoms *Sisters* (1991–1996) and *Cheers* (1982–1993). These days Boyd works in animation, as a voice actress.

You already knew director Peter Hunt because you were in talks to play a part in *A View to a Kill* (1985) before he had to leave that film. Can you walk me through your casting for *Assassination*?

Jan Gan Boyd: Peter Hunt and I met through *A View to a Kill*. They called me in to read for *Assassination*, and I just went straight to reading with Charlie. I didn't have to go through the rigmarole of the first audition, second audition, and so on. We screen-tested together, and they liked our chemistry a lot. Then I met Jill [Ireland], and they just really wanted me to do the film.

Charles Bronson had been acting for decades, but you were only a few years into your career. Was it intimidating to work with him, at least going in?

Oh, of course. I was so new. I think I was in the process of rehearsing for Michael Jackson's *Captain EO* (1986), and I got the *Assassination* job offer. I left *Captain EO* because dancers in those days were paid like $100 a day. It was nothing.

When I worked with Charlie, there were a few scenes where Peter and Charlie directed me, and told me how they would like me to change things. I'm really good at taking direction. When they asked me to adjust the way I performed, it was easy for me.

I was actually supposed to be naked in that movie, but I don't do nude scenes. I was talking to Charlie, and they were talking about my nude scene coming up and I'm like, uh . . . I was asked twice to do *Playboy* magazine and it was a lot of money in those days, but I turned it down because I knew I was going to have children someday and I didn't want them to have friends that go, "Is this your mom?" I have really strict moral rules. I had a really good moral compass about drugs and about sex and nudity and partying. I never believed in having sex to get a part or anything. I was just like, "It's not worth it to me. It's probably not worth it to them, either." [*Laughs*]

When the nude scene came up, I was telling Charlie and Jill that, "I don't want to do the nude scene." They said, "Okay. We will talk to them, Golan and Globus, so you don't have to do the nude scene. But just so you know, Jan, because you're new, if you sign a contract for a script that has a nude scene in it, you are required to do it or the people can sue you." I was like, "Oh my God." That was an eye-opener for me. My manager/agent was a newcomer at William Morris. He got me wonderful jobs and a ton more money than I would have with any other agent, but things like that slipped past him. Charlie talked to them, and they sat me down and they said, "Okay, we'll remove this from the script."

There were two places I was supposed to be naked. One was in bed, when Charlie calls me and I'm reading, and the other was when Charlie and I supposedly slept together. We toast with champagne and I'm supposed to just have, like, the bottom half of an apron on. I'd turn around, you'd see my boobs and my butt, and I was like, "No." [*Laughs*] Charlie really helped me there. He also gave me acting tips. I have a slight lisp, and it gets worse when I think about it. Charlie had speech issues, too. If you watch all his films . . . he does his S's out of the side of his mouth, sort of like—oh, God, who was the first James Bond?

Sean Connery?

Yes, Sean Connery, he did the same thing. They both studied how to remove their lisps through the same acting teacher, I think. He was telling me that the lisp can work for me in the film. Oh, you know who else had lisp like that? I was on *Johnny Carson*, and he had a different way of saying his S's, too. When I was interviewed [on the show], the first thing I was supposed to bring up was my lisp, but I got distracted. All the talk shows are scripted. You go in for an interview and then they write down what Johnny Carson, or David Letterman, or Arsenio Hall would ask you. Then they'd write down your answer. They would get your answers in a pre-interview and then they would script it out. I went off-script on *Johnny Carson*, because I was newly pregnant. Bob Saget was on before me showing pictures of his children When I came out, I brought ultrasound pictures of my daughter and it surprised Johnny, so it was funny. He worked with it. He did good improv.

Charlie and Jill told me I should study improv more than method acting, because my form of acting was more experiential, where you draw from your past experiences and/or imagination to form your character. Method acting was *"living"* the character. Sean Penn and Nicolas Cage were in my [acting] class. There were a lot of actors in my class, and I remember because they came from the Strasberg Institute over in New York and then came to LA and continued it with Peggy Feury and Bill Traylor. I had trouble with it. It's hard to be "living" a character. It's hard on all of the people around you, because you're a different person. Charlie told me to do improv at Groundlings, where Pee-wee Herman and all kinds of people came from. Mindy Sterling, who was one of my close friends, was my teacher. She's the one who played the Fraulein in *Austin Powers* (1997). She's hilarious.

Bronson made a lot of movies for Golan and Globus over the course of the decade, but something I love about *Assassination* is that he seems comfortable and relaxed in the role. I'm wondering if that was because he got to work with Jill, his wife?

A poster for the French theatrical release of *Assassination*.

We all just hit it off. Jill Ireland and I joined Charlie once at poker and, oh my God, there were these big actors there. George C. Scott, James Coburn . . . they were playing poker and smoking these big stogies and Jill said, "Come on, we're going to join them." She pulled up two chairs and they were like, "What are you doing?" Oh, we just played a few hands to screw around with them, but then the cigar smoke got to me and Jill and we were like, "Okay, we're out of here." [*Laughs*] That was an epic evening.

I can imagine!

I met so many people through him, and his connections. He just knew everybody. The one person he did *not* like and who did not like him was James Garner. He's a famous actor, too, but they did one movie together and Charlie was like, "I'm never working with that man again."

I was worried because I was only twenty-five, maybe twenty-four. I was young. Charlie was in his seventies and I was to play his girlfriend [in *Assassination*], so it was awkward. This is like one of those May-December relationships. But, it worked.

Like you said, the way he was just relaxed through that movie helped me not be so nervous. I loved him. I adored Charlie and Jill. Jill was suffering from breast cancer at the time, and Charlie just adored her, he loved her so much. He was so gentle, and kind, and open, and loving, but people would say, "Well, he's really mean. He won't give autographs," and that's not true. What people don't understand is what Charlie hated was somebody hiding behind a tree taking pictures of him. He would say, "If that guy over there just asked me for a picture, I'd take it with him, or if he wants an autograph, I'd give him an autograph." But doing that espionage-style, he hated that.

Charlie would read all the rags. He would read the *National Enquirer*, and I said, "I didn't know you read that." He said, "Oh, no, I just look through it to see if I'm in it." [*Laughs*] "What are they saying about me now?"

We talked about a lot of things. There was a scene where we came out of an Army helicopter, and they had all these rules about which way to walk out the door. They're like, "Turn right or straight, don't turn left." Charlie told me about a director who wasn't paying attention, who was looking at his script, and walked to the left and into the back blades. Charlie said the director got cut in half. I'm like, "I don't even want to exit the helicopter." [*Laughs*] "Please, let me just stay in the helicopter until they turn it off."

But, Charlie was kind and warm. The other thing he told me, and I believe this, too, is that when my films were out, people would look at me in a store and start following me, but not approach me. If I turned one way or the other way, they'd go down whatever aisle I was going down and just stare at me.

When you're having dinner with your family, and somebody walks up while you're taking a bite of food, it'll make any actor upset. It's like, "I understand you want an autograph, but now's not that time." People take that as, "Oh, he's unworkable," or "She's not a nice actress," or whatever. No, it's just that everyone values their privacy. We always got together for lunch or dinner, and people would walk up to the table, and he would dismiss them if we were in the middle of a conversation. Or, he'd sign an autograph if we were in between stories.

Jill was quite sick while she made this movie, but she put on a strong face and kept working. Can you tell me a little bit more about what she was like, as a person and a co-star?

She was more like me, just happy and upbeat. Charlie wasn't mean, but he was mellow, and she was the energy. They were one of those yin and yang couples. She would joke to him and he just laughed, or he would casually say something sarcastic and she'd go, "Charlie . . ." with her English accent. She was beautiful.

I learned a makeup tip from her. If you look at this film, she wears a lot of lip gloss. She told me lip gloss makes you look younger, and matte lipstick makes you look older. They had me in matte-colored makeup. Hers was shinier, really lip-glossy. It was cute. She wore a wig because she had lost her hair through chemo.

At their house, we were having dinner and Susan Komen was with us. Jill was saying, "Susan here is starting a foundation to benefit and teach women about breast cancer. I'm one of the spokesmen for her new foundation." That was a fledgling foundation at the time, and so I donated money, thinking "Oh, this is a great cause." Looking back now, it was unbelievable.

You have the rare distinction of playing Bronson's love interest in a Cannon movie, but your character actually survives through the film.

We were going to do a sequel, then Jill got really sick and she passed. That was really heartbreaking. Her funeral . . . Like I said, she was the energy, and she wanted [her funeral] to be a celebration of her life, which a lot of people want. She had music and drinks. Every table had a few bottles of champagne. It was like a wedding reception—it was huge. At the time, I didn't drink because I was pregnant, but I noticed that the family was suffering. Charlie was grieving, and then having to see people laughing it up and dancing and getting drunk was really hard for him. In your mind when you die, it's like, "Oh, this would be great," but in actuality, it's hard on the family.

Thinking back on happier gatherings, I hear you attended their holiday parties. Are you willing to share what Christmas with the Bronsons was like?

Oh, gosh, they were celebrities everywhere, from that era, like Jaclyn Smith. Oh, man, Shirley MacLaine was there and I was in awe because being a dancer on stage, she was one of my idols. There were a lot of people at his party, and it was festive, they had the whole house decorated. I remember Jill gave me this ring that was really pretty. It was a little gold friendship ring that I wore all the time, but I don't think they gave everyone presents. They had their parties catered, and there were people walking around with trays.

I think there were some people that were there for publicity shots. Blair Underwood was there. They took pictures of us together, and then it was in some rag with the caption, "Is Blair Underwood dating Jan Gan Boyd?" I'm like, "No, we were standing next to each other at a party."

Going back to *Assassination*, what was your most memorable day of filming?

I'm Chinese and a woman. I don't drive very well. In fact, I don't drive now because I'm a danger to everybody. There's a scene where I'm supposed to drive Charlie and myself in the car, and we're turning around this monument in the center of Washington. They showed me which way to drive, twice, and then Charlie and I parked and they said, "Now, we have to wait until it's dusk for the scene." This was when we didn't have cellphones, so we had a walkie-talkie in the car. They go, "Okay, and action."

I take off and I turn down the wrong street, and we end up on the freeway. I don't know if you've ever been to Washington DC, but it's laid out in a circle where everything ends up on a freeway to another state. We're on the freeway and I'm like, "Where are we?" They were like, "Where are you?" Charlie goes, "We took a wrong turn, we're on the freeway and we're pulling up in Virginia." They had to have a team come and get us, and I followed them back to where this shot was. They're going, "Jan, don't turn down that street, go around the monument." I'm like, "Okay, I got it." Then they go, "Action." I do the same thing: I get off the freeway and Charlie is like, "You do *not* know how to drive." I was like, "Yes, I'm establishing that right now."

We had to do the whole thing again. Charlie is fuming by now. They go, "Action." I do the shot right, and they go, "Good." It was one take, we're done. Charlie just jumps out of the car, he's so mad at me, and they go, "Okay, Jan, just drive to your trailer." I go, "No!" I'm screaming to the PAs, I'm screaming like, "I am not driving anymore." I'm throwing a full-on tantrum. They go, "Fine." One of the ADs gets in the car and we go, like, maybe half a block back to my trailer. I go, "Oh, thank you. Bye." [*Laughs*]

Another scene in Washington DC, I was supposed to drive up to the gates of the real White House with Charlie, and they said, "Okay, Jan, don't cross a certain line, because they will shoot you in order to protect the White House." I go, "Okay." They go, "Action." And I just gun it.

Oh, no!

As we pull up, Charlie is screaming, "You need to stop, they're going to shoot us, they're going to shoot us!" [*Laughs*] I think Charlie jumped out of the car with his hands up because the guards at the gate moved. I'm saying, "They're not going to shoot us." [*Laughs*] He was so scared. He goes, "You *definitely* can't drive." And I go, "Duh, Charlie, didn't you learn that from before?"

A Spanish lobby card for *Assassination* thatcaptures a relatively rare sight from this era: Bronson smiling.

Stallone comes to Cannon: *Over the Top* on VHS, with artwork by Renato Casaro.

Over the Top

Release Date: February 13, 1987
Directed by: Menahem Golan
Written by: Sylvester Stallone & Stirling Silliphant (from a story by Gary Conway & David Engelbach)
Starring: Sylvester Stallone, David Mendenhall, Robert Loggia
Trailer Voiceover: "The world has always bet against Lincoln Hawk—but a winner never listens to the odds!"

The story behind Cannon's big-budget, truck-driving, arm-wrestling, father-son drama—and likely the *only* big-budget, truck-driving, arm-wrestling, father-son drama that will ever be made—is a long one. Cannon's involvement with *Over the Top* (1987) dates back nearly seven years before it was released, to shortly after Golan and Globus took over the company.

Over the Top started life in the late '70s as a starring vehicle for Gary Conway, a tall, hunky actor best known for starring in the cult horror favorites *I Was a Teenage Frankenstein* and its follow-up *How to Make a Monster,* TV's *Burke's Law* (1963–1966) and *Land of the Giants* (1968–1970). He had recently experienced a middle-age career pivot when he starred in the violent, independently-produced revenge film *The Farmer* (1977), which was picked up by Columbia and met with some box office success. He and his partner on that film started cooking up their next project, coming up with an idea about a trucker who was also a competitive arm-wrestler. Needing help with the script, they enlisted a rising, young screenwriter by the name of David Engelbach, who shed a lot of excess weight from the screenplay to better focus on the relationship between the main character and his estranged, tween-aged son. Engelbach had recently worked as Steven Spielberg's assistant on *Jaws* (1975); in exchange for his rewrite, he was attached to the project as a potential director.

When the project ultimately stalled out at Columbia, Conway and his partner started shopping it around to other studios. The script eventually found its way to Cannon, which had recently fallen under the new management of Israeli cousins Menahem Golan and Yoram Globus. It was Golan who became personally enamored with the story, who went so far as to reserve it for himself as an eventual directorial effort. As consolation for being ousted from the director's chair, Cannon promised to finance a different film with Engelbach at the helm—that would become 1986's *America 3000*. In the meantime, Golan would also ask him to draft a script for *Death Wish II* (1982), which was re-written so heavily by director Michael Winner that Engelbach considered having his name removed from the movie entirely. (For that story, look to our *Death Wish* chapter in *The Cannon Film Guide, Volume I*.)

Cannon kicked around the idea of having Conway play the lead role, but soon decided to pursue someone with more star power. (Conway wasn't kicked completely to the curb; they'd hire him to co-write 1987's *American Ninja 2* and 1989's *American Ninja 3*, and he'd even play the villain in the first of the two sequels.) Cannon first considered Don Johnson for the lead—star of TV's *Miami Vice* (1984–1989)—before setting their sights on one of the biggest Eighties stars of them all: Sylvester Stallone.

So much has already been written about Sly Stallone's impact on—and continued contributions to—the cinematic landscape of Hollywood, so we'll be brief. Born Michael Sylvester Gardenzio Stallone in New York City's

Hell's Kitchen in 1946, a mishap during his birth left the newborn with a severed nerve that paralyzed part of his face, but gave him the facial expressions and speech patterns that became a signature element of his future performances. As a young adult, Stallone struggled while trying to make it as an actor, infamously filming a role in a porno flick called *The Party at Kitty and Stud's* (1970) for $200 while he was briefly homeless and sleeping in the Port Authority Bus Terminal. His luck eventually turned around, and he landed a series of very minor roles—often as muggers or goons—in a number of films before being cast as a lead in the greaser drama *The Lords of Flatbush* (1974). (He starred opposite Henry Winkler and, initially, Richard Gere—who supposedly left the movie after Stallone punched him for dripping mustard on his pants.) Stallone's real breakout would come soon afterwards.

In spring of 1975, Stallone watched a Muhammad Ali boxing match against underdog Chuck Wepner and was struck with inspiration. Over a frenzied, three-day writing marathon, Stallone banged out the screenplay for what would eventually become *Rocky* (1976). He shopped the script to producers and caught the attention of United Artists, who were enamored with the idea of casting a big-name actor like Robert Redford, Burt Reynolds, or Ryan O'Neal to play the role. Stallone put his foot down. He'd written the film for himself, and he wouldn't sell the rights unless he was attached as its lead. He gambled on himself, and won: the studio greenlit the project as a low-budget film in which Stallone would be the star. The movie went on to be a stupendous hit, bringing back more than $200 million dollars on a $1 million budget, and earning ten Oscar nominations. It won Best Picture, Film Editing, and Director; the latter for John G. Avildsen, who'd previously directed the early, pre-Golan and Globus Cannon hit, *Joe* (1970).

From that moment on, Stallone became a household name. Starring roles followed it, as did *Rocky II* (1979); this time he not only wrote and starred in the movie, but directed it as well. It would be his second franchise-launching role, playing shell-shocked Vietnam veteran John Rambo in *First Blood* (1982), which vaulted him to the top of the A-list. The movie was a box office smash, and like *Rocky* before it placed Stallone at the forefront of a series that would spawn frequent and reliably successful sequels throughout the 1980s.

Sylvester Stallone as Lincoln Hawk in *Over the Top*.

This brings us to 1984, the year when Cannon's courtship of Stallone would reach its apex. The year saw the company tie a couple box office hits under their belt, and establish themselves as more than just Hollywood pretenders, but legitimate contenders in the industry. At the time they had all the looks of a studio on the rise, but if they wanted to truly become "the seventh major studio," then they needed to book themselves a big-name star. In the 1980s, there were few stars bigger than Sylvester Stallone.

If you were to zoom out on the decade as a whole, only a small number of actors out-sold Stallone in total box office gross. Three of them were Eddie Murphy, Bill Murray, and Dan Aykroyd—all comedians—and the fourth was Harrison Ford, another actor lucky enough to star in two separate, wildly successful franchises. Meanwhile, Stallone was an *action* star, and came with a built-in brand that lined up very neatly with the movies that Cannon specialized in making. Major stars, however, weren't usually in the business of making the sort of low-budget films that Cannon traded in. To land their big fish, Cannon had to aim high and make Stallone an offer he couldn't refuse: an offer that, for a time, would make him the highest-paid star in Hollywood.

A deal was announced: Cannon would pay Sylvester Stallone $12 million to star in *Over the Top*, which was the most an actor had been paid to that point for a single film performance. As Stallone later remembered, Cannon just kept offering him more and more money until he could no longer say 'no.' The deal itself was so massive that the rest of Hollywood had no choice but to stop and take notice, which was probably Cannon's intention all along. A company that had spent four years being written off as wannabes and purveyors of schlock had not only aligned themselves with one of the industry's biggest stars, but had just written him a historically large check which reset the market for top-drawing actors.

The thing was, $12 million wasn't the kind of money Cannon just kept sitting around. They would usually use it to make at least two or three entire movies, rather than pay a single actor. The reality is that Cannon paid Stallone half a million dollars as a retainer for *Over the Top*, made their big announcement, and then went out to find investors willing to help them raise the approximately $25 million budget they'd need to actually make the film itself. (That would be $12 million for Stallone alone, and nearly the same amount to cover everything else in the movie.)

It was an amount many times larger than what Cannon was regularly able to assemble by pre-selling their low-budget, bread-and-butter flicks, which is one of the reasons for the two-year delay between their grand Stallone announcement and *Over the Top* finally getting made. In the end,

Cannon hopped into bed with Warner Bros., who in return for their financing received the movie's distribution rights along with a handful of other, yet-to-be-released Cannon movies.

Further funding came in the form of product placement, in which *Over the Top* serves as a master class: its credits thank more than thirty sponsors. It's difficult for even the most near-sighted viewers to miss the on-screen plugs for Pepsi-Cola, Duracell batteries, Pizza Hut and Carl's Jr., Trans World Airlines, Volvo-White Trucks, Brut cologne, and the many others who chipped in cash to see their products in the pictures.

In the meantime, Stallone appeared in *Rambo: First Blood Part II* (1985), *Rocky IV* (1985), and *Cobra* (1986). The latter film bears Menahem Golan and Yoram Globus' names as producers, but not the Cannon logo at the top, as the company actually had little to no involvement in its making. Golan and Globus were given producers' credits as a compromise by Warner Bros., who they allowed to bypass their exclusive deal with Stallone so that he could make *Cobra* during the long wait for *Over the Top* to come together. While it may look and feel a lot like a Cannon product, Cannon's ties to *Cobra* are essentially little more than a vanity credit.

For Stallone, the movie wound up coming at a time when it was helpful for him to soften his image. The star had been taking a lot of flak in the press for the on-screen violence in his movies. When asked about the topic during interviews, Stallone could deftly pivot the conversation away from the over-the-top violence of Rambo and *Cobra* by pointing at the wholesome, father-son story seen in *Over the Top*.

To play the preteen son whose affection Sly would be attempting to win back in this PG-rated adventure, the producers hired fourteen-year-old David Mendenhall, an actor who had spent much of his young career on the soap opera *General Hospital* (1963-present) and doing voice work, notably playing human Daniel Witwicky on the original *Transformers: The Movie* (1986). He'd later go on to star in two more Cannon-branded films: first opposite Dom DeLuise, Jimmie Walker, and Deep Roy in a chimp costume in *Going Bananas* (1988), and then in *The Secret of the Ice Cave* (1989). A few of his non-Cannon roles include a recurring character on *Taxi* (1978–1983) and lead roles in *Space Raiders* (1983) for New World Pictures, *They Still Call Me Bruce* (1987), and *Streets* (1990).

Sylvester Stallone, Magic Schwarz, and David Mendenhall in *Over the Top*.

Their main villain in the film would be played by Robert Loggia, a gravelly-voiced actor primarily remembered for roles as Al Pacino's drug lord rival, Frank Lopez, in *Scarface* (1983) and on *The Sopranos* (1999–2007), but also as the toy company executive who befriends Tom Hanks—and dances on the giant piano—in *Big* (1988).

By the time it entered production, the *Over the Top* script was substantially different from the one that Menahem Golan had been so smitten with when it was brought to Cannon. Stallone himself did a few major rewrites, as did screenwriter Stirling Silliphant, who'd previously penned the adapted screenplays for *In the Heat of the Night* (1967), *The Poseidon Adventure* (1972), and *The Towering Inferno* (1974). The changes to the screenplay were so wholesale that the movie's original writers, David Engelbach and Gary Conway, were only given "Story By" credits on the final product. Their original script took much more time focusing on the relationship between the father and the son; the Lincoln Hawk character was a man who deeply wanted to atone for his past mistakes, and was educating himself via audiobooks in his truck so that he could improve his lot in life. The son was also more confrontational toward his father. The rewrites by Stallone and Silliphant gave the story a more traditional antagonist, turning the grandpa into a dastardly villain—and upping the action quota in the form of hired kidnappers and a semi-truck being driven through the front of a building.

Filming began on *Over the Top* in early June of 1986. Both the movie's star and its director came into production with pre-conceived notions of the other, and understandably so. Stallone was hesitant to work with Golan because, frankly, despite his Oscar-nominated *Operation Thunderbolt* (1977), his résumé wasn't exactly stocked with many critically-acclaimed directorial efforts. Stallone clearly didn't feel that the Cannon co-chairman was up to the task of directing a movie of this magnitude. The story goes that Stallone had at first been willing to accept $10 million to star in *Over the Top*, but raised his asking price once Golan refused to give up the director's chair—to which Cannon responded by writing him an even bigger check.

From the other side of that equation, it's also easy to see why a filmmaker or studio in the mid-1980s might have had reservations about working with Sylvester Stallone. He was known for being a perfectionist, and had a reputation for butting heads with his directors. Everyone at Cannon was no doubt aware of how Stallone had recently left Paramount Pictures standing at the altar on their high-profile comedy, *Beverly Hills Cop*. After agreeing to do that movie, Stallone insisted on re-writing the script and removing all of its humor to turn it into a strict action vehicle. After the studio bent over backwards to try and meet some of Stallone's demands, the star proceeded to quit the movie two weeks before shooting was scheduled to begin. Eddie Murphy was recast in the Axel Foley role and *Beverly Hills Cop* (1984) went on to become one of the biggest blockbusters of the 1980s. It's safe to say that things worked out for Paramount in the end, but it understandably left some producers soured on the idea of signing big-money deals with Stallone. (He later changed the name "Axel Foley" to "Marion Cobretti," and Stallone's serious, non-comic revision of the *Beverly Hills Cop* script became the basis for *Cobra*.)

Both Stallone and Golan were known to be men with powerful egos. Neither was shy about voicing their wariness of the other, but Stallone and Golan managed to put aside their egos and work together long enough to make the film. This does not mean they weren't frequently at odds with one another. During a set visit by the *Los Angeles Times*, writer Pat H. Broeske noted that a few crew members had nicknamed the production "Warring Trailers," in reference to their director and star.

After some takes, Stallone would reportedly zip over to the monitors for immediate playback so that he could watch his performance, deliver Golan his own feedback, and then give his direction as to the lighting and camera operation for the scene. To Golan's credit, he was willing to hear his star out, likely acknowledging that the two latest, Stallone-directed *Rocky* movies had grossed more at the box office than an entire year's worth of Cannon releases combined. On that same note, it's worth pointing out that Golan probably knew he had left himself little room to put his foot down, and that his decisions didn't matter much, anyway, since his record-breaking contract with Stallone also gave the actor final cut on the movie. If they disagreed over how a scene would be done, they shot it both ways, and the actor had final rule over which would go into the finished film. Golan's wrists were effectively tied.

Over the Top follows truck driver Lincoln Hawk (Stallone), just a regular, American guy with an abnormally kick-ass name. Regular, except for the fact that he's a world-class arm wrestler known all over the country, especially amongst his fellow truckers. Hawk has little to live for beyond his big rig and the arm-wrasslin' ring, save for an estranged, twelve-year-old son, Michael (Mendenhall), whom he left behind at birth for reasons that are never explained within the movie.

Menahem Golan (center) directing Sylvester Stallone on the set of *Over the Top*.

Hawk shows up in the boy's life minutes after Michael graduates from a hoity-toity military prep school. The two haven't seen each other since the boy was a baby, yet it's important to his mother (Susan Blakely of *The Towering Inferno*, 1974)—who is in the hospital, dying of an unspecified disease—that her son gets to know his father, with whom she's still surprisingly friendly. She's about to undergo a dangerous surgical procedure, and she requests that it's Hawk who brings her son cross-country to Los Angeles to see her, rather than the exorbitantly wealthy grandfather (Robert Loggia) who raised the boy and bankrolled his fancy-pants education.

Their trip starts off on the wrong foot, with Michael disappointed in his truck-driving father's unrefined, blue collar existence, and understandably still holding a grudge against the man who abandoned him and won't say why. As they dine at greasy truck stops, sleep in the cab, and spend their mornings working out together, Hawk slowly melts his son's icy exterior with his earthy charms. Soon Hawk is schooling his son in the ins-and-outs of arm wrestling and letting the twelve-year-old drive his truck, and Michael is feeling full-on affection for his errant pops.

It's unfortunate that Michael's grandpa has such an outspoken hatred for the boy's dad, and hires goons to kidnap his grandson in the middle of their road trip. They evade capture, but sadly arrive in Los Angeles just a few hours too late, where they find that the boy's mother died during surgery earlier that day. Suddenly regretting that he spent those days riding cross-country in his dad's big rig rather than flying straight to his dying mother's bedside in grandpa's private jet, Michael tells off his father and returns to his grandfather's mansion.

Now, rather than attempting to make amends with his son in a calm, reasonable manner, Hawk acts out a bit irrationally and drives his semi-truck through the front entryway of his ex-father-in-law's mansion. (It's the same Bel Air mansion that was used for exterior shots on *The Beverly Hillbillies*, 1962–1971.) This goes about as well as any sane person would imagine, and Lincoln Hawk soon finds himself behind bars. The wicked grandpa sends in a slimy lawyer to make his son-in-law an unorthodox offer: he'll drop all the charges against him if he'll sign a paper promising he'll walk out of Michael's life forever. He's accompanied by Michael, who forgives his dad for making him miss his chance to see his dying mother one last time, but also persuades Hawk into thinking he'll live a more stable life with his millionaire grandpa than his homeless, trucker dad. (It's a pretty convincing argument.) Hawk signs his deal with the devilish grandfather and walks away from prison a free man.

Lincoln Hawk's focus then shifts from his son to the World Arm-wrestling Championship happening in Las Vegas. He drives straight to Sin City and pawns his truck—which is not only the entirety of his livelihood, but his home-on-wheels—to make a risky bet on himself as a longshot to win the competition at 20:1 odds. He's up against numerous champions in the sport, including rival trucker "Bull" Hurley, a man approximately nine times his size. Out of the five hundred competitors, Lincoln Hawk is a clear underdog.

The massive "Bull" Hurley is played by Rick Zumwalt, a real-world arm-wrestling champ who would also appear in Cannon's *Penitentiary III* (1987) and *Rockula* (1990). In the film, Hawk's competition is played by a mix of big-biceped actors and real life arm-wrestlers, including women's arm-wrestling world champion Lori Cole. The movie received wide support from the professional arm-wrestling community, who hoped Stallone's movie would do for their sport what *Rocky* did for boxing.

Meanwhile back at bad grandpa's house, Michael rifles through his mother's old belongings and finds a stash of letters that were regularly written to him from his father over the course of his lifetime, but presumably withheld by his grandfather. This is all the proof that Michael needs that his father actually *does* love him, and inspires an intrepid escape from his wealthy grandfather's clutches.

Michael knows his dad is just about to compete in a high-stakes arm-wrestling match, and that his father *needs* the support of his long-lost tween son. So, Michael steals one of his grandpa's luxury cars, drives it from the compound to the airport, and books himself a plane to Vegas . . . all while sneakily evading his pop-pop's henchmen. (Wait—could little kids actually book their own air travel in the 1980s?) When Grandpa figures out where his grandson is heading, he takes his private jet to beat him there.

At the Las Vegas Hilton Hotel and Casino, the stakes couldn't be much higher for Lincoln Hawk. The winner of the arm-wrestling championship takes home a grand prize of $100,000, plus a brand new semi-truck valued at more than that; the losers go home with nothing. (That's even truer for Hawk, who sold his truck and bet all of that money on himself.) Our hero expectedly makes it to the final round of the double-elimination tournament . . . and loses his first match, tearing an arm muscle in the process.

As he nurses his wound, he's surprisingly summoned by his one-time father-in-law to the hotel's swankiest suite. Despite Hawk already having signed away his custody of Michael, grandpa makes him one more offer: $500,000 and the best truck money can buy to never communicate with the boy again. This time, Hawk refuses.

Lincoln Hawk wrestles the heavily-favored "Bull" Hurley (Rick Zumwalt).

Before Lincoln Hawk can climb back into the arena, his son catches up with him at ringside. It's clear that Hawk has given up, considering himself—especially given his injured arm—as good as defeated. Now it's Michael's chance to turn the tables on his father, and deliver one of the tough-guy pep talks about never giving up that Hawk gave him earlier in the movie. Reinvigorated by his son's encouragement, Hawk readies himself for a single arm-wrestling match that will determine the course of the rest of his life.

One of *Over the Top*'s greatest achievements may be how exciting it makes arm-wrestling—a sport which, as snarky critics were eager to point out, essentially consists of two men holding hands and grunting—appear on screen. Stallone tried to recreate the feel of *Rocky IV*'s Las Vegas fight between Ivan Drago and Apollo Creed, and they largely succeeded. *Over the Top*'s arm-wrestling finale is a thrilling nail-biter.

Inspired by his son's words, the half-busted Hawk climbs back into the ring to do battle with an opponent four times his size . . . and, even when everything looks truly hopeless, ultimately wins. The movie ends with Lincoln and Michael Hawk climbing into their brand new truck, $300,000 richer, and talking about founding their own father-son trucking company together.

These happy, final notes weren't always the anticipated ending for the movie. Like he did with *First Blood*, Stallone re-wrote the last pages of the script to make the movie end on a more positive note. (In *First Blood*, John Rambo was originally supposed to have died, but test audiences recoiled and an alternate ending where he lives was inserted instead—paving the way for a lucrative series of sequels.) The *Over the Top* script initially called for Lincoln Hawk to lose the final match, but find a different sort of richness in the form of a rekindled relationship with his son. That ending was scrapped, and in the movie Hawk walks away with both the money *and* his boy's affection.

Cannon had inevitably set themselves up by releasing a movie called *Over the Top*: critics had a field day using "over the top" as their description for the movie itself. It's actually a reference to a specific arm-wrestling move, as well as the Over The Top tournament, a series of real arm-wrestling competitions which were held around the world in the months leading into the film's production. The finals were held in Las Vegas while *Over the Top* was filming, on the same stage, and a $250,000 Volvo truck was the tournament's grand prize. Arm-wrestler John Brzenk was the event's big winner but didn't receive the truck until nearly a year later, after Cannon had sent it on a tour around the country to promote the movie.

The promotion didn't stop there. There was a toy line by LewCo which included action figures of many of the movie's wrestlers, and a kid-sized arm-wrestling table. There was also a soundtrack album that featured the movie's omnipresent rock-and-roll tunes from the likes of Giorgio Moroder, Asia, Kenny Loggins, andFrank Stallone. We even got MTV music videos for Loggins' "Meet Me Half Way" and Sammy Hagar's "Winner Takes It All," the latter of which culminated in the Van Halen singer arm-wrestling with Stallone and somehow winning.

While this was an out-and-out marketing blitz by Cannon's standards, it wasn't enough to prevent the film from doing a massive belly flop when it hit theaters. *Over the Top* opened over a long Presidents Day weekend in early 1987, coming in behind movies like *Platoon* (1987) and *Mannequin* (1987) and bringing home just over $5 million in domestic ticket sales. That wasn't enough to recoup *half* of what they'd paid Stallone alone, let alone the roughly $25 million that was spent on the movie in total—not including the additional $5 million spent on prints and advertising. The box office reception was bad enough to drop Cannon's stock values by almost a quarter from the week before *Over the Top*'s release to the week after. While the movie's final numbers were helped by more eager international audiences, *Over the Top*'s grand take in North America was a little over $11 million in its theatrical run: a million less than Sly's much-publicized paycheck. Critics were just as underwhelmed as other movie-goers. The movie was nominated for three Razzie awards, and was the leading subject of Siskel and Ebert's "Worst Movies of 1987" special episode.

Before the film's release, Golan and Stallone had hinted at reuniting for a hypothetical *Cobra 2*—in which Marion Cobretti would have squared off against a drug cartel—but the poor returns on *Over the Top* (and Cannon's rapid decline into financial destitution) inevitably put the kibosh on that idea.

Arguably the movie's *largest* star—larger than Stallone, larger than armwrestler Rick Zumwalt—was Lincoln Hawk's trusty big rig, a vintage 1965 model A64 Autocar, which went on to have quite the notable movie career after *Over the Top*. Four of them were purchased for the film from a local logging company, and those same four were utilized again by Cannon in *Messenger of Death* (1988). The following year, one of the trucks made an appearance in the Fred Savage feature-length Nintendo commercial *The Wizard* (1989), in which you can still spot the "Hawk Hauling" logo on its door. Another was later re-painted silver and used in the science fiction movie *Tank Girl* (1995). Sadly, two of the original vehicles were scrapped after sitting unused in a junkyard for many years. The lone, surviving red "Hawk Hauling" cab was purchased by a fan in West Virginia, who hopes to one day restore it to its full *Over the Top* glory.

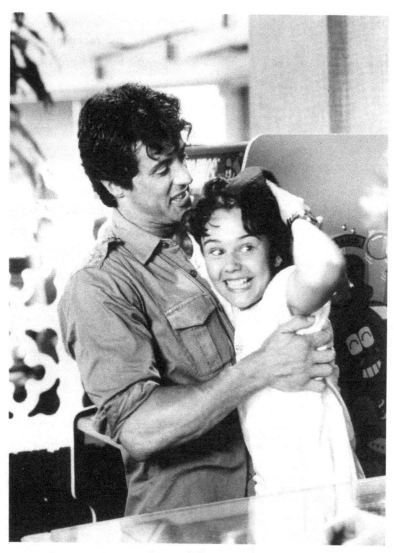

Sylvester Stallone and David Mendenhall in *Over the Top*.

Interview: Actor David Mendenhall

By the time he co-starred opposite Sylvester Stallone in Cannon's big-budget road movie *Over the Top* (1987), teenage David Mendenhall had already
been working in Hollywood for a decade. From 1980 to 1986 he appeared on
the soap opera *General Hospital* (1963-present), and had memorable roles on

episodes of *Taxi* (1978–1983) and *Diff'rent Strokes* (1978–1985), the latter of which also featured an appearance by First Lady Nancy Reagan. It was during these years when he also became a prolific voice actor, playing the Autobots' human sidekick, Daniel Witwicky, in both *Transformers: The Movie* (1986) and the animated series, and lending his voice talents to other Saturday morning staples.

After *Over the Top*, Cannon brought back Mendenhall for two more features: *Going Bananas* (1988) and *The Secret of the Ice Cave* (1989). Several of his roles outside of Cannon include *Space Raiders* (1983), *They Still Call Me Bruce* (1987), and *Streets* (1990).

What do you remember of your audition process for *Over the Top*?

David Mendenhall: I remember the process quite vividly. At the time, this would have been early 1986, I had been working as a regular on the soap opera *General Hospital* for six years. I believe when I was first called in to interview for *Over the Top*, it was to read with the casting director.

I actually don't know exactly how it came about, but Brigitte Nielsen was involved with the casting process for *Over the Top*. My first memory about the movie was reading for Brigitte Nielsen and [casting director] Ron Surma at their casting offices. Again, we're talking early 1986. I knew who she was, because she had starred in *Red Sonja* (1985). And I knew she was married to Sylvester Stallone.

I went back in and read for the part a number of times. My recollection has always been that it took seven interviews for me to get this job, if I'm correct. I know that a lot of others went out for the part, too. Then finally, the role came down to two of us. Ultimately, the two of us were brought in for a screen test at Culver Studios, where Stallone and the actor Brian Thompson were apparently doing some very last-minute reshoots for *Cobra* (1986) at the time—the screen test was at night, and it fit into their filming schedule. Both the other actor going out for the part and I did a final screen test with Sly, so we were each filmed on camera one at a time, and acted out one of the scenes with him.

This must have been one of your biggest productions, in terms of budget and size. I know you were already acting for a decade by that point, but were you nervous at all?

When I first heard about this role and found out it was to play the son of Stallone, I think I had a normal reaction. I mean, I was pretty excited considering that, at the time, there weren't many people more famous than Sylvester Stallone. He had the *Rocky* franchise behind him, and he had done a couple of *Rambo*s. If I recall correctly, right after we filmed *Over the Top*, he was going to start production on *Rambo III* (1988)—randomly, I remember that, because at one point during filming he said he was starting to grow out his hair for it. There was no bigger star in the world—people would be hard-pressed to find somebody more famous. Yes, I was certainly aware of *who* I was going to interview to play the son of. At the same time, I looked at it like any acting interview, like I would any other potential acting job.

I think the reality of it hit me once I found out I got it. As you said, I had been acting for ten years by this point in early '86, but I was still 14 years old. I didn't turn 15 until June of that year, after we had already started production. As a 14-year-old kid who had been a member of Screen Actors Guild since the age of four, I was comfortable going out and reading—as comfortable as an actor can be under the circumstances, if that makes sense.

Then, I'd say the nerves really kicked in when, after accepting the role, I was brought in to the Cannon Films offices, to the third floor. I went into a conference room along with the other cast members, and various production personnel, for a read-through of the script before filming was going to begin. That's when it really hit me that I was going to be working with Sylvester Stallone.

I think the nerves started to subside after about a week or two into film-ing. I had done other films before, and some big shows like *Taxi* and *Diff'rent Strokes*. I had met Nancy Reagan, for example, and worked with many stars before thanks to *General Hospital*, but this was a big film production, and I was certainly aware of that. I was able to ease into what was happening after a couple of weeks of filming. The filming took about ten weeks: two-and-a-half months.

What was Menahem Golan like? Both in the process leading up to the film, and then working with him as your director?

I loved Menahem. He was great. I just loved working with him, loved him as a human, as a person, as a creative spirit. He was passionate and had energy, lots of energy; *boundless* energy, not just on set, but at his office, any time I would see him. I got to form a good relationship and a bond with Menahem during filming. His daughter Yael also worked on the film, and other members of his family visited the set, so I got to meet them, too. I could tell how much family meant to him, which showed me the very human side he had.

I wasn't involved in doing business with him, per se. Instead, I got to work with him creatively. For me, that experience was fantastic. I saw him on multiple occasions during my life, not just during that film, but after the movie on multiple occasions, including prior to his passing. I did see him one last time in the 2000s—I want to say circa 2007. He was visiting Los Angeles and I believe, by that point, was living in Israel again. He was still energetic, still wanting to make films—he still had the bug, if you will, about filmmaking.

Menahem as a director? Here is my take. And if you were to ask Sly for his opinion, I'm sure he would have a different response, just like any other actor you'd speak with. To me, Menahem was *absolutely* directing us. In other words, he was in charge when it came to calling the shots, creatively. He was not a placeholder for someone else, or the director in name only. To put it another way in case there was ever a question, Sly wasn't the one directing us. Sly was acting. He was there to act.

Of course, from my perspective, Stallone nevertheless gave a lot of input about filming and other production issues. He was involved as a writer, and in many other aspects, creatively. As one of the biggest stars in the world, of course he had a lot of participation in the process. To me, filmmaking is a collaboration in general, anyway. When it comes to directing, there are a lot of technical things involved: choosing the angle, choosing the lens placed on the camera, the location, even reviewing the marketing materials. And the list goes on: wardrobe, makeup, hair. There are so many things the director has to weigh in on. From my vantage point, I witnessed Menahem involved in all of that. And, when it came to my acting performances, he was giving direction. He had a lot to say about what the actors were doing, it wasn't just, let's put the camera here and you go act! He worked with the actors, in my experience. My relationship with Sylvester Stallone on set was that of an actor working with a fellow actor. I never felt necessarily directed by Stallone. But that's not to say that his opinion didn't carry any influence. For example, when I first got the part in the movie, Sly had me go to a gym for a few weeks before filming to start working out, that sort of thing. He also brought in other crew he had worked with before to be part of the production.

There was one scene we were in together toward the end of the film, in Vegas, where my character gives Stallone's character a pep talk before his last match. We worked a lot to get that scene right, meaning Stallone, Menahem, and myself. In fact, as I recall, we shot that scene two different times. At first, like I had done for other scenes in the movie, I started playing it from an emotional place. But after a couple of takes, Menahem and Sly were in agreement and told me that, for this scene, Michael shouldn't cry. He's the one giving the pep talk here. And they were right, and that's how it ended up going, thank goodness.

There were a lot of other big personalities on the set behind the scenes, too. There was a producer named James D. Brubaker, who I believe still is a production executive. Duncan Henderson, the unit production manager, and the ADs Tom Davies and Josh McLaglen. And there were others involved up and down the line who, to this day, are still active in show business, big time. That's another one of the legacies some people don't think of when they see *Over the Top* or other Cannon movies. A lot of people who were part of the Cannon Films world went on to do some incredible movies.

One last thing about Menahem: working with him went so well that, ultimately, he decided he wanted me to work on another film for Cannon. Menahem had written the screenplay for a movie which eventually would be called *Going Bananas*. It was first titled *Ben, Bonzo, Mo, and Big Bad Joe*. That was the original name, which later became *My African Adventure*, and yet later was ultimately called *Going Bananas*. Menahem Golan adapted that screenplay from a series of children's books. We shot that in Africa right after *Over the Top*.

Michael gives his father a much-needed boost of confidence for his final match in *Over the Top*.

Can you tell me more about working with Stallone? He'd had other young actors in his prior films, but you were really the first young co-star he ever shared this much screen time with.

A lot of people have different opinions on what that film is. It's been referred to as a sports film, an arm-wrestling movie or, sometimes, a family film. I tend to think of it as a hybrid road movie. For quite a substantial part of that film, it's just him and myself in that truck, the characters working out their relationship, almost like a buddy film. We spent countless hours and days in the cab of that truck, going back and forth with the acting. In my experience, we formed a bond during the process. Not to mention, he was playing my father. That was a running motif in my early career, including on *General Hospital* and another movie I did, with Shelley Winters, called *Witchfire* (1985). A lot of the characters I portrayed in the 80s were dealing with a father-son relationship. Even the first movie I did, *Space Raiders* (1983), I'd arguably say, there was a father-son type relationship there. I was typecast in that role, somewhat. Beyond that, I also argue my character in the movie is the one that goes through a character arc. He's a different person by the end of the movie than he is at the beginning of the movie. Critics who decry my performance in the movie usually focus on what a brat I played. Well, that's what the character is supposed to be at the beginning. It was in the script. So I played him like that very much on purpose. Then by the end of the story, my character is very different, because he's been through this whole adventure, he knows who his dad is now, and he's happy the two of them have a real connection.

One of Sly's sons, Sage, was on the set for most of that summer with us. There were a few kids on set. The costume designer, Tom Bronson—his two kids, Corey and Toby, were there quite a bit. Of course, there was no school, since this was filmed during the summer. It felt like a family atmosphere a lot on set. Brigitte was also on set all the time.

I wouldn't say I had a father-son relationship with [Stallone] off-camera. It just felt like two actors working together, and I'd say we developed a good camaraderie. Working with him was very cool. What he did in that movie, acting-wise, was different than what he had done as an actor in any other movie prior to that point. His performance, in my view, is very understated—and also very underrated.

Sly talked about New York a lot with me. He told stories about acting in other movies early in his career—his experiences working on movies before *Rocky*, like *Lords of Flatbush* (1974)—as well as *F.I.S.T.* (1978), which he indicated he was particularly proud of. He told me stories about him growing up in Hell's Kitchen in New York, being a young actor, and some of his favorite experiences from his early years. That was very cool. And he was so funny.

He had a great sense of humor. On camera, we were just playing off of what the other was doing—textbook acting, in a sense. It wasn't phoned in. I knew he really wanted to show another side of his acting ability, and I will always argue that he accomplished that.

Critics will point to the arm-wrestling, versus what was happening with the father-son relationship, or the road trip parts of the film. Again, to me, it's a hybrid. It's a road movie, and then a sports movie at the end, which I think ultimately was difficult for Warner Bros. to sell when it came time to market the film. Some of us, on one hand, wished it was marketed as a family movie, but as you know from the posters, it was all about the action and the arm-wrestling. In my opinion, the posters didn't really convey the full story. A lot of people over the years—both men and women—have told me directly how much they loved the movie because it reminded them about their own childhood relationship with their father, and that kind of feedback from people who love the movie makes criticism I've heard sound somewhat trivial.

Stallone and Mendenhall in *Over the Top*.

Do you have a favorite scene in the film, or one that you're really proud of?

One of the first scenes we shot—I think in the first week of filming—is the scene where my character, Michael, is having a conversation with Linc and impulsively decides to jump out of the car in the middle of the highway and run to the side of the road. He's crying, he's very pissed off. After Michael runs out of the car and onto the highway, Linc chases him. They have an argument, and in the midst of it, one of Michael's jacket sleeves is ripped off. After that, Michael and Linc walk back to the truck. And there's a moment there when Stallone grabs ahold of my arm, and I intentionally pull my arm away from him. In defiance, I guess I would say.

That moment—pulling my arm away from him in defiance—made it into the film, and it's one of my personal favorites because it was so natural, from my character's point of view. Pulling my arm away like that happened completely naturally—it wasn't scripted or planned. At that point in the movie, the beginning, my character is rejecting this guy. To him, this guy is not his dad. This guy is awful, and he wants nothing to do with him. So in that moment as we were filming, when I pulled away from him, it was a natural reaction. We're walking back to the truck together, but I won't allow him to hold my arm. I really liked the result that ended up on screen. Sometimes, when unscripted things happen, they are some of the coolest things that end up in a movie.

I'm always impressed by how Menahem made arm-wrestling look as exciting as it did on the screen, especially during the final act in Vegas. Those were *big* scenes, between the number of extras in the crowds, the number of professional arm wrestlers they brought in, the lights, the set— it had to have been one of the biggest shoots Cannon ever did. What can you tell me about filming those final scenes?

As I recall, the Las Vegas filming took place over approximately three weeks. We filmed in the convention center in what was then the Hilton, it has a different name now. It's the same hotel where—if I recall correctly— Howard Hughes once lived, and Elvis Presley also resided up there in the penthouse. I think that penthouse is also where some of the scenes between Stallone and Robert Loggia were shot that happen toward the end of the film. In any case, it was a hotel with some Vegas lore attached to it when we went there for work.

The Convention Center had lots of people there daily for all of those scenes we were filming. It was quite an expansive space. I recall that people had to use their voices so much—including the background performers—they were losing their voices by the end because they had to scream so much. In fact, I think it's still in the film, but some of the actors who played the arm wrestlers, if I recall, by the end were losing their voices, too, because of how much yelling there was, and the vocals involved filming the arm-wrestling scenes.

When Stallone is arm-wrestling in the final competition with Bull Hurley, played by Rick Zumwalt, I'm on the sidelines yelling, "Over the top, dad, over the top, you can take him. Come on, dad!" I remember losing my voice by the end of that, because the direction was to just keep cheering him on for as long as I could. I think we shot that in one continuous take for about four minutes. Just lots of yelling, cheering him on, saying, "Over the top, over the top!" I was losing my voice by the end of that take.

Number One with a Bullet on VHS.

Number One with a Bullet

Release Date: February 27, 1987
Directed by: Jack Smight
Written by: Gail Morgan Hickman, Andrew Kurtzman, Rob Riley & Jim Belushi
Starring: Robert Carradine, Billy Dee Williams, Valerie Bertinelli
Trailer Voiceover: "Nick and Frank are special cops doing a dirty job!"

Buddy cop movies weren't invented in the 1980s, but it was the decade in which they were codified.

These films always revolve around two mismatched heroes who are forced to work together, typically against their will. Let's say that maybe one of them is old, the other is young. Maybe one's a straight-laced police officer, the other's a streetwise crook. Perhaps the first cop is strictly by-the-books, while the second one is a loose cannon with nothing left to lose. The pattern is easy enough to spot. Roger Ebert even coined a fun term for these, calling them "Wunza Movies." This was reserved for any film that's premise could be summarized beginning with the words "One's a . . .".

If there was one dynamic that was more prevalent than any other within the '80s buddy cop genre, it was that one cop would usually be a white guy, and the other would be Black. (Or occasionally a dog.)

This ebony and ivory buddy cop pairing craze in the 1980s was kicked off by Walter Hill's blockbuster *48 Hrs.* (1982), which matched up cop Nick Nolte with con Eddie Murphy to rake up one of the year's best box office totals. After that it was Murphy's turn to play a police officer, this time paired with Judge Reinhold in 1984's *Beverly Hills Cop*. Gregory Hines and Billy Crystal teamed up in the oft-forgotten *Running Scared* (1986), but it was the following year in which the buddy cop trope hit its zenith. *Beverly Hills Cop II* (1987) may have ruled at the box office, but it was the classic *Lethal Weapon* (also 1987) that went down as the quintessential buddy cop flick, pairing the young, erratic Martin Riggs (Mel Gibson) with the older, wiser Roger Murtaugh (Danny Glover) and turning the phrase "I'm getting too old for this shit" into the most overused line in the action movie screenwriter's toolbox. A major success, *Lethal Weapon* spawned multiple sequels and a television series.

Earlier that same year, Cannon pitched their hat into the ring with *Number One with a Bullet* (1987).

The script for *Number One with a Bullet* had originated with writer Gail Morgan Hickman, who had previously written the Dirty Harry sequel *The Enforcer* (1976). He sold *Number One with a Bullet* to Cannon several years before they eventually produced his scripts for *Murphy's Law* (1986) and *Death Wish 4* (1987), both starring Charles Bronson.

The project sat in Cannon's production queue for years, repeatedly getting bumped backwards as talent was attached and detached from it. William Sachs (*Exterminator 2*, 1984, and *Hot Chili*, 1985) was briefly in line to direct, and for much of that time actor Jim Belushi was set to star. The then-*Saturday Night Live* cast member took his own pass at the screenplay, and enough of his lines remained in the final shooting script that Cannon opted to give him a writer's credit. Belushi would have played the hotshot cop role, and he gave his character additional gags and wisecracks with the help of *SNL* writers Andrew Kurtzman and Rob Riley.

Other film projects managed to keep the younger Belushi brother away from his Cannon commitment, forcing the producers to replace him. The comedian instead starred in two other pseudo-buddy cop movies—*Real Men* (1987) with John Ritter, and *Red Heat* (1988), with Arnold Schwarzenegger—in the next eighteen months. If the fact that there were almost *three* different Jim Belushi buddy cop flicks in less than two years doesn't prove just how prevalent this genre was at that time, I don't know what will. (We won't even get started on Belushi's buddy cop dog movie, *K-9*, which followed a year later in 1989.)

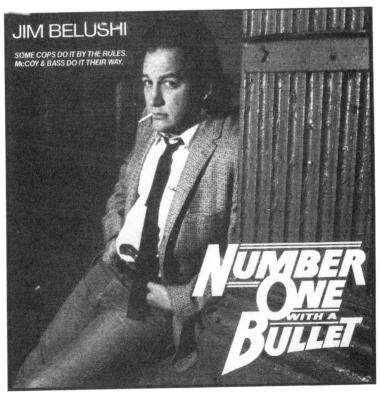

A pre-sales ad for the film from when Jim Belushi was still attached to play the lead.

The casting of Robert Carradine in an action-comedy is an odd one, even as a replacement for the lesser Belushi. Carradine was—and still is—best known as the alpha nerd with the unforgettably obnoxious laugh, Lewis Skolnick, in *Revenge of the Nerds* (1984), a role he went on to reprise in three sequels. Son of John, brother of Keith, and half-brother of David, it was once openly speculated that young Robert might have the finest acting chops of the entire Carradine clan, with lauded roles in *Coming Home* (1978), *The Long Riders* (1980), and Sam Fuller's *The Big Red One* (1980). It's his association with *Nerds*, though, that makes his casting here as a mean cop known for breaking rules and flying off the handle just a little too hard to swallow—even when it's being played for laughs.

Perhaps Cannon's main goal here was to check off the final box on their Carradine bingo card? They had already worked with John (*House of the Long Shadows*, 1983); Keith (*Maria's Lovers*, 1985); and David (*P.O.W. The Escape*, 1986). That would have put Robert next in line.

For the more level-headed—and Black—half of this buddy cop duo, director Jack Smight had originally brought in a budding, young actor named Denzel Washington. At this time the future superstar would have been known for his role on TV's *St. Elsewhere* (1982–1988) and little else. Menahem Golan reportedly blew off his meeting with Washington at the Cannon offices, and told Smight to come back with someone who had a little more star power. And, who did they find? Billy Dee Williams.

Now, that was no knock on Billy Dee Williams, as few could have predicted back then that Denzel Washington would someday be a winner of multiple Oscars. In 1987, Williams was the much bigger star. He'd earned an Emmy nomination while playing Gale Sayers in the classic TV movie *Brian's Song* (1971); was fresh off his role as ultra-cool cat Lando Calrissian in two *Star Wars* movies; he'd co-starred with Sylvester Stallone in *Nighthawks* (1981), and received his star on the Hollywood Walk of Fame in 1985. At the time he was cast in *Number One with a Bullet*, Williams had just begun a five-year national ad campaign as the suave spokesman for Colt 45 malt liquor. ("It works every time.")

The film's director, Jack Smight, had long worked in TV and was even responsible for a few classic *Twilight Zone* episodes ("Twenty-Two," "The Lonely," "The Night of the Meek"), as well as the sci-fi flop *The Illustrated Man* (1969) and the disaster movie *Airport 1975* (1974). The film's jazz-punctuated score was composed by Alf Clausen, who for twenty-seven years would oversee the music on *The Simpsons*.

Nick Berzak (Carradine) is a young narcotics officer with an ex-wife and a chip on his shoulder. He's got a reputation for enforcing the laws in his own way, earning him the nickname "Berzerk" from the slingers and thugs on the streets. He's the sort of guy who lives in a dirty apartment filled with empty beer bottles, and eats raw steak with a pocket knife straight from the Styrofoam tray. (Yeah, he does that.)

Berzak's ex-wife, Teresa, is played by TV's Valerie Bertinelli, child star of *One Day at a Time* (1975–1984) and dozens of television movies. It's his interactions with her—rather than the ones with criminals—that clue us in that Berzak might be somewhat unhinged. He repeatedly shows up at her house unannounced and demanding they get back together. He pays a neighborhood kid to spy on her, and at one point pretends to be her doctor so that he can lie to one of her suitors about her being riddled with STDs. Hold on, let's scratch "unhinged"—Berzak may be a sociopath.

The Murtaugh to his Riggs, Detective Frank Hazeltine (Williams) is Berzak's more even-tempered partner. He's a smooth-talking ladies' man who doesn't eat junk food. To make sure the audience understands just *how* smooth Hazeltine is, the movie opens on a scene where the cop is moonlighting as a jazz trumpeter at a swanky nightclub. Berzak interrupts him while he's chatting up a young lady following the show, and then proceeds to blow up his partner's spot by telling his date that he watched Hazeltine "go into a bar full of dykes and kick the shit out of them." He follows that tall tale by making up a story about how Hazeltine once "blew away a nine-year-old kid by mistake" because he was carrying a water pistol. (It's unclear which of the four screenwriters considered hate crimes and police brutality to be so joke-worthy.) But, yeah, that's how we're introduced to Berzak's character. He rarely comes across as the cool, unpredictable '80s action hero you figure they were going for, but instead appears to be a genuinely disturbed individual.

Berzak is obsessed with bringing down a local politician named DeCosta, whom he suspects of being the linchpin of the city's drug trade. DeCosta, though, has a clean record—and deep enough pockets to keep it that way. His bosses repeatedly tell him to leave DeCosta alone, but you know a loose cannon like Berzak isn't going to do something sensible like "listen to orders." The most recognizable of his superior officers is played by Peter Graves, best known for his role as Director Jim Phelps on TV's *Mission: Impossible* (1967–1973) and for playing the pilot in the comedy classic *Airplane!* (1980). Graves was a childhood friend of director Jack Smight, with whom he'd attended high school in Minneapolis in the 1930s.

When we finally get to see our heroes in action, they're carrying out an undercover sting at what appears to be a church bazaar. Berzak, for some reason, is wearing drag, which only makes a tiny bit of sense once we realize that the suspect they're tailing is *also* in drag, for some reason. (Billy Dee Williams, meanwhile, is disguised as a blind carnie.) Berzak corners the baddie in the basement of the church. The desperate man (in a dress) rips off his wig and takes a priest as his hostage. When he threatens to shoot the poor man of the cloth, Berzak one-ups him and threatens to shoot the priest himself—then suggests they may as well shoot some innocent bystanders while they're at it. Fortunately this unorthodox hostage negotiation method doesn't backfire in his face, because the crook, convinced Berzak is insane—quite reasonably—puts the gun down and gives himself up. Berzak and Hazeltine are heroes, yet again.

They're given a special assignment: protect an organized crime member as he's being transported to safety, so that he can snitch on his mysterious bosses. It doesn't go well. Their plane is shot down by an attack chopper, but Berzak manages to land it safely. He chases the bad guy into a nearby barn, where the escaped goon is shot dead by a farmer. Convinced that their deceased snitch would have fingered their arch-nemesis, DeCosta, as the city's drug kingpin, our two rogue cops go even more rogue, and shake down one of their informants: a petty thief named Casey, played by Mykelti Williamson. (That's Bubba from *Forrest Gump*, 1994.)

Can we talk about how odd this ensemble is? We've got a pair of loose cannon cops played by Lando Calrissian and Lewis Skolnick, one of which is married to a future Jenny Craig spokesmodel. They work for the pedophile pilot from *Airplane!*, and their main source of street intel is Bubba from *Forrest Gump*. Oh, and Berzak's mother is played by Doris Roberts, the mom from *Everybody Loves Raymond* (1996–2005) and *National Lampoon's Christmas Vacation* (1989). Her main function in the film seems to be to nag (humanize?) her psychotic son. It's hard to wrap your head around this cast in the 21st Century, and—well, maybe it didn't make a ton of sense in 1987, either. But, here we are.

Our heroes recklessly pursue their hunch about the drug ring's leadership, through a stakeout at a zoo and stings at a crematorium and an underground mud wrestling club, to a shootout in a local garbage dump and a torture session inside an unfinished skyscraper. (To its credit, *Number One with a Bullet* was shot in a whole bunch of visually interesting locations.) As you'd expect in this sort of movie, their actions get people killed and cause a lot of property damage. They get busted down to traffic, as rogue cops often do, and then sent on a two-week vacation to "cool down," which obviously frees them up to bring down the big boss baddie using their own, unauthorized methods.

There are a handful of very funny moments throughout *Number One with a Bullet*, such as when Berzak tastes the cremated ashes of a suspect's dead mother, assuming that there was cocaine hidden inside the urn. There's another sequence in which he infiltrates a drug lord's heavily-guarded compound while inexplicably quoting Edgar Allan Poe's "The Raven," which pays off in the movie's best one-liner when Berzak knocks out a guard:

SOME COPS DO IT BY THE RULES.
McCOY & BASS DO IT THEIR WAY.

NUMBER ONE WITH A BULLET

THE CANNON GROUP, INC. PRESENTS A GOLAN-GLOBUS PRODUCTION NUMBER ONE WITH A BULLET
WRITTEN BY GAIL MORGAN HICKMAN PRODUCED BY MENAHEM GOLAN AND YORAM GLOBUS DIRECTED BY WILLIAM SACHS
© MCMLXXXIV CANNON FILMS, INC.

THE MAKING OF THE 7TH MAJOR

Another pre-sales ad for the film. Note that the characters' names are different, and William Sachs is still attached as director.

654

"Quoth the raven, *asshole*."

I won't call this a spoiler as much as clichés playing out as expected, but our heroes eventually bring down the bad guy and flush out the corrupt cops who were working for him. What, did you think this buddy comedy would have a dark ending?

Let's talk about the good things in *Number One with a Bullet* first, because it won't take that long. As far as the action goes, *Number One with a Bullet* does it pretty well. In a classic case of a Cannon movie punching above its weight class, some of *Bullet*'s action sequences look like they could have come from a higher-budget studio movie. Cars get crushed by machinery during the junkyard shootout, there's some pretty sweet aerial work during the plane crash sequence, and the movie culminates in a high-speed chase with a big rig towing a trailer full of drug dealers. This is all really good, exciting stuff. And that wonky cast? Every one of the supporting players does a nice job in their secondary role.

The big issue with *Number One with a Bullet*, aside from its dated and predictable script, arises from its mismatched heroes—which, when it comes to a buddy cop movie, is probably the most important element to get right. While casting the king of the *Nerds* as an unhinged cop probably wasn't the best fit, it's hard to blame Carradine for the role's problems. It's obvious the writers intended for the character of Nick "Berserk" Berzak to be humorous, but he never comes off as a "ha ha" sort of funny—he gives off a more distinct "whoa, this guy seems like a danger to society" sort of vibe. Not only is he a loose cannon, but the ways in which he constantly harasses his ex-wife and cock-blocks his partner—at one point, by telling a woman that he's Hazeltine's secret lover—make him seem like an individual who's mentally unwell, rather than a likeable scamp.

It doesn't help that our cop buddies have little chemistry together. Where we'd normally have seen an unbreakable love-hate bond between two men of law enforcement, Hazeltine and Berzak are just sort of . . . two guys who do cop stuff together? The defining trademarks of their relationship is that Berzak repeatedly frightens away any woman Hazeltine communicates with, and Hazeltine frequently scolds Berzak about his lack-luster diet. That's it. Perhaps there's a more interesting way to read these two characters—given Berzak's extreme fear of Hazeltine having a relationship with a woman, as well as his unexplained drag scene—but the rest of the script doesn't seem clever enough to subvert the genre's expectations in any intentional way.

Another issue is Billy Dee Williams. God bless the man, but his performance here is a textbook case of coasting through a role. He's an actor for whom it normally takes very little effort to be charismatic, but he acts like that little bit of work wasn't worth putting into *Number One with a Bullet*. If he tried half as hard here as he did in his Colt 45 commercials of the era, we may have had a much better movie. Instead, he seems totally checked-out.

In the end, *Number One with a Bullet* is a middleweight action-comedy. It's not the classic buddy cop film that Cannon deserved, but it's at least one hundred times better than *Three Kinds of Heat* (1987).

The buddy cop genre endured, although producers would soon find it necessary to make wackier pairings in order to stick out in the crowd. Belushi teamed up with a dog in the aforementioned *K-9*, as did Tom Hanks in *Turner & Hooch* (1993) and Chuck Norris in *Top Dog* (1995). Burt Reynolds teamed up with a kindergartener in *Cop and a Half* (1993), while Sylvester Stallone took down an arms dealer with the help of his elderly mother in *Stop! Or My Mom Will Shoot* (1992). In the end, *Theodore Rex* (1995)—which paired Whoopi Goldberg with a wise-cracking dinosaur—may have been the ultimate in kooky '90s buddy cop movie pairings.

The deranged detectives of *Number One with a Bullet*: Robert Carradine and Billy Dee Williams.

A VHS copy of *Down Twisted* previously rented out by a Kroger supermarket in Dallas, Texas.

Down Twisted

Release Date: March 13, 1987
Directed by: Albert Pyun
Written by: Albert Pyun, Gene O'Neill, Noreen Tobin
Starring: Carey Lowell, Charles Rocket
Trailer Voiceover: "It was an easy set-up . . . with a deadly twist!"

Albert Pyun has always been a filmmaker with fantastic vision. His visions are often many times greater than his budgets allowed him, but he has a talent for eking out extra production value from the (usually) meager resources at his disposal.

It was Pyun's vibrant, violent breakthrough, *The Sword and the Sorcerer* (1982)—a richly imaginative entry in the sword and sorcery genre—that caught the attention of Cannon, who wisely signed on the talented, young Hawaiian's services. His Cannon debut, *Dangerously Close* (1986), was a teen thriller which felt like a tempered bid to woo mainstream, MTV-guzzling youth audiences. *Dangerously Close*, however, was a film that would only be considered tempered in comparison to Pyun's other output. Before his Cannon career could even begin, the prolific filmmaker had completed projects for two of Cannon's closest competitors, including *Radioactive Dreams* (1985) for the De Laurentiis Entertainment Group and *Vicious Lips* (1986) for Empire Pictures.

The former is one of the most far out entries in the post-apocalyptic genre—and that says a lot, given that post-apocalyptic films are rarely known for subtlety or understatement. *Radioactive Dreams* stars two young guys, Philip and Marlowe—future Cannon stars John Stockwell and Michael Dudikoff—who emerge from a fallout shelter fifteen years after nuclear war eradicates civilization as we know it. On the surface, they evade cannibals, bikers, and "disco mutants" while trying to keep the activation keys for the world's last nuclear missile out of the wrong hands. There's a lot of new wave music, noir styling, and even some tap dancing mixed in there—*Radioactive Dreams* is legitimately incredible, and recommended to all fans of fun, far-fetched cinema.

Vicious Lips, meanwhile, is part space opera, part rock video. The film was named after the all-girl rock group at its center, who need to get from one planet to another to play a star-making gig at a hot interstellar club, but crash land on a strange planet while en route to the show. It's packed with big hair, visually striking (and very '80s) spaceship sets, and Pet Benatar-esque musical numbers. While not on the same level as *Radioactive Dreams*, *Vicious Lips* is so unusual that (like much of Pyun's oeuvre) it begs to be seen to be believed.

Cannon would eventually let Pyun loose to explore wilder fantasy worlds with *Alien from L.A.* (1988) and *Cyborg* (1989), but before doing so he seemed to make one more appeal to the mainstream moviegoer with *Down Twisted* (1987).

From a distance, *Down Twisted* looks like a twisted take on *Romancing the Stone*, the 1984 adventure-comedy starring Michael Douglas and Kathleen Turner which netted nearly $90 million in ticket sales across the globe. *Romancing* centered on an out-of-her-element romance novelist (Kathleen Turner) who flies to South America to pay a ransom on her kidnapped sister, where she unwittingly links up with a handsome, roguish smuggler (Michael Douglas); adventure, hijinks, and romance ensue. *Down Twisted* shares some elements with this box office smash—both broad concepts and distinct, tiny details—and filters them through an unmistakably Pyun-y lens.

Cannon's 1986 Cannes Film Festival advertisement for *Down Twisted*.

Down Twisted begins with a relic heist gone murderously awry. As an opening block of text explains, an eccentric, evil billionaire has hired a team of six thieves to steal for him an ancient religious artifact that happens to be the symbol of the fictional South American banana republic of San Lucas. (The film was shot in Mexico.) When the delivery of the artifact turns out to be a set-up, bullets fly and one of the thieves winds up dead. This forces his blonde girlfriend to go on the run from his former cohorts, who believe she has a key they need to fix their botched heist.

This brings us to our heroine, waitress Maxine (Carey Lowell, returning from *Dangerously Close*) whose roommate happens to be the girlfriend of the murdered jewel thief. (Watch for the future *Friend* and He-Man sidekick, Courteney Cox, in her ninety-second big screen debut as Maxine's co-worker.) As she's walking home from work one evening, roomie Michelle pulls up and threatens to blow her own head off unless Maxine hops in her car. As they pull away from Max's home, they drive past a poster for Roman Polanski's *Pirates* (1986), a recent Cannon pick-up—how's *that* for cross-promotion synergy?

They head to an empty parking garage, where Michelle persuades Max to assist her with a drug deal. Max is barely out of the vehicle when it explodes into a tower of flames, presumably killing her low-life roommate in a grisly, fiery death. That's when Michelle's boyfriend's burglar buddies show up, and they assume Max was in on her double-cross. They drug and kidnap her, whisking her off on a boat bound for San Lucas.

All of this happens in the film's first few scenes!

Max escapes from her captors, jumps ship, and washes ashore in the fictional military nation. Now we've got an innocent girl unexpectedly wrapped up in criminal activities, stranded in a hostile, South American jungle nation. To complete the *Romancing the Stone* framework, she's joined by Reno (Charles Rocket), a handsome, sarcastic stranger with an illicit past. Usually cast as a comedic foil rather than a leading man, Rocket's *Twisted* character was a bit of both—and then some. Over the course of the film, Reno goes from bumbling nincompoop to tough-guy hero, to sly con man, and then wise-cracking romantic interest.

As an actor and comedian, Charles Rocket is perhaps most famous for being fired from *Saturday Night Live* for dropping an F-bomb during a live broadcast in 1981. Rocket was able to bounce back from this controversial moment in TV history, landing memorable parts in *Dances with Wolves* (1990), *Hocus Pocus* (1993), and *Dumber and Dumber* (1994); he also had recurring roles on *Max Headroom* (1987–1988) and *Moonlighting* (1985–1989).

Reno and Max become fugitives of the San Lucas military within hours of arriving in the country, and then begrudgingly work together as they do their best to elude both the army and the greedy criminals who are hot on their heels. (The thieves are played by Galyn Görg of 1986's *America 3000*, and Pyun regulars Linda Kerridge and Thom Mathews.) They're chased through locations varying from exotic to downright apocalyptic, and the plot takes twist after twist: new deals are struck, double-crossers are double crossed, and dead characters turn up alive, all while our poor heroine has little to no idea what's going on. (At some points, neither does the viewer.)

All of the various subplots wrap up quickly and violently as the surviving characters—along with the San Lucas military—converge on an airport concourse. Afterwards there's a short, ironic coda for our bad guy, and a happy ending for the heroes, but then that's it. If the denouement feels a little abrupt, well, it is *Down Twisted's* brief, 88-minute runtime includes nearly ten minutes of closing credits.

While the plot may be too complicated for its own good, there is still plenty to like about *Down Twisted*. As with even the cheapest of Pyun's movies, it has a distinctive visual style, from its bright pink and yellow opening credits to its travel animations—the obligatory dotted lines traced across maps—and its assortment of attractive shooting locations. Cinematographer Walt Lloyd, whose first film was Pyun's prior picture, *Dangerously Close*, went on to DP several acclaimed features, including Robert Altman's *Short Cuts* (1993) and Steven Soderbergh's career-making *Sex, Lies, and Videotape* (1989), and cult favorites such as *Pump Up the Volume* (1990) and *Empire Records* (1995).

The soundtrack, too, is very well-curated, in typical Pyun fashion: hip cuts from contemporary acts like Oingo Boingo and Fine Young Cannibals keep the movie bumping where it might otherwise drag. And while Pyun might have been confined to a mostly realistic setting—a fictional banana republic being more grounded, at least, than cyberpunk dystopias, apocalyptic wastelands, or foreign planets—a few actors from his stable of regulars are allowed to go wild. Thom Mathews, in particular, appears to be having a great time as a platinum-haired gangster in a crushed blue velvet suit and Norbert Weisser, a veteran of more than a dozen Pyun movies, makes a stupendously smarmy evil businessman.

Sure, *Down Twisted* may not be one of the wildest transmissions from the far ends of the Pyun-iverse, but lots of style and a game cast ensure that it's an entertaining one.

Reno (Charles Rocket) saves Max (Carey Lowell) from Damalas (Thom Mathews) in a publicity still from *Down Twisted*.

Interview: Actor Thom Mathews

With key roles in two classic franchises—*Return of the Living Dead* and *Friday the 13th*—Thom Mathews cemented his legacy within horror fandom. For fans of the work of filmmaker Albert Pyun, Mathews holds a similar position of reverence. As a young actor in the 1980s, Mathews embarked on a long-running collaboration with Pyun, appearing in twelve feature films for the Hawaiian-born filmmaker, including his essential cyberpunk actioner *Nemesis* (1992) and a starring role in 1991's *Bloodmatch*, co-produced by Menahem Golan's 21st Century Film Corporation.

Pyun and Mathews' first three films together were for Cannon: *Dangerously Close* (1986), *Down Twisted* (1987), and *Alien from L.A.* (1988).

I've heard that it was your high school girlfriend who talked you into being an actor. Is that true?

Thom Mathews: She suggested it, yes. I was just out of high school and not knowing what I wanted to do with my life. I've always been woodworking and doing things like that, some artistic stuff. She mentioned acting, and when she mentioned it, I had the weirdest sensation. It was literally like she took a pen and stuck it in my brain, and it just exploded in my head. I was like, "That's it." I really had a physical sensation when she suggested that. It was amazing. I started pursuing acting right after that.

You did some television and commercials before landing your break in *Return of the Living Dead*. Could you describe what your life was like starting out as a new actor during that era, trying to find your way into the industry?

I was taking acting classes for a couple of years. I didn't call myself an actor because, being pragmatic like I am, if I'm not making money doing it, then I'm not going to give myself that label. My plan was to go work at Lorimar Pictures when they were over on the MGM lot. I started working for them while I continued my acting classes. While I was there, I let the casting department know that I was pursuing acting. One of the casting directors gave me a walk-on role on *Falcon Crest* (1981–1990) and that's how I got my SAG card.

From there on, I was doing some print work and got a commercial agent. I did a bunch of commercials and that made the transition for me from my regular job into an acting job full time. Then I got a theatrical agent and started pursuing TV and films. Luckily for me, or not luckily, I started doing movies while my other friends were doing television. Then one thing led to another. My first role in a movie was in *The Woman in Red* (1984). I did a little cameo, and then from there I got *Return of the Living Dead* right after that.

Did you ever imagine that *Return of the Living Dead* would have the impact that it did?

Honestly, I played it straight. It wasn't a very fun, comedic movie. It wasn't really written like that. The beauty of *Return* is that the humor comes out of the situations and that's always the best calling for me. People can believe what they're seeing and what's going on because it's based in reality. I didn't really know if it was a comedy or we were playing it for real.

As far as it being a success and having the legs that it has, and the fact that it has now become part of pop culture . . . now, whenever you think of a zombie, you think of them eating brains. I just asked my twelve-year-old daughter's friend, I said, "When you think of zombies, what do they eat?" She goes, "Braaaaaaains." I said, "That's because of a movie that I did thirty years ago. It's because that movie said zombies, they eat brains."

I had no idea it was going to be such a huge success and have the following that it does. The music helps a lot. I think it's fantastic. The whole thing. Dan [O'Bannon] had everyone rehearse two weeks before we actually started the principal photography, which helped everyone gel together. Even looking back, and I've done a lot of movies since then, it was a great experience. I didn't really realize how special it was at the time. The more I work, the more I realize how special it was.

Low-budget productions tend to hire more young actors who are just starting out. Were you aware of Cannon, and watching what they were doing?

I would always watch what movies they had planned for their slates. I'd been watching them. I knew a guy who was a carpenter for the studios, and those are the guys who always get the green light first, because it takes them a while to ramp up. He knew what was going on. That was another tool that I used to gauge stuff. Basically, everything gets submitted to the casting director, and then next they call the agents. They look at everything and submit it to the client.

I happened to be in that ballpark and I did a lot of movies for Albert Pyun, which tied me into Cannon. He liked to use me over and over again. We worked on some really fun projects. He cast me in things that I would never have gotten cast for otherwise. He just really believed in me and liked my talent.

I remember *Down Twisted* was one of the movies that Albert directed. The guy was scripted as a 250-pound, dark-haired mass of a man. He said, "Do you want to do that part?" I said, "Okay." [*Laughs*] They had already gone down to Mexico. I had colored my hair black because it said the guy had dark hair, and the coloring never did really fit my skin color or anything, so then I went the other way. I bleached my hair white, and I didn't tell him. I went down there and stepped onto the set. I said, "Hi, Albert." He didn't even recognize me, but he loved what I had come up with. I came up with the silver cap on my tooth, all the jewelry that I decided I wanted to use for the character, and a blue suede jacket that I actually found. That was a lot of fun.

You worked with Albert many times over the years. What were your first impressions of him, as a director?

He's very easy-going, and he certainly knew what he wanted. He had a really clear sense of that. The first movie that he called me in on was *Dangerously Close*. He kept everybody there at the auditions for hours and hours. People did scenes together, he would mix and match people. He just kept us there for *hours*. He did that for a particular reason, and I asked him why. He said, "I just wanted to see how everyone's attitude would be once we started shooting. I don't want to have any problems with personalities if a shoot went on longer than what they had in mind." That's what he did.

What memories do you have of shooting *Down Twisted* in Mexico?

That was a particularly interesting shoot. We stayed at a great place in Puerto Vallarta. It was about a five-week shoot.

We would shoot out in the jungle. We went to have lunch, and there was this makeshift restaurant out there. I asked what was on the menu, and they said, "Well, whatever we caught out in the jungle this morning." [*Laughs*] That's what we had for lunch, and I have no idea what it was.

Your third Cannon feature for Albert was *Alien from L.A.*, with Kathy Ireland.

I think of Kmart now whenever I think of Kathy Ireland. [*Laughs*] That one had Bill Moses from *Falcon Crest* as the lead. Kathy Ireland was the female lead, and they were looking for a love interest. They hired me to play

Prince Charming—or Charmin'. I'm only in twelve minutes of the movie, but test audiences liked my character so much that they gave me a starring credit. That was fun.

The German VHS cover for *Down Twisted*. In parts of Europe, the film was released as "The Treasure of San Lucas."

Kathy actually had that voice back in the day. I improvised a lot about it, because you couldn't go *without* saying something about it.

The production value for that movie is really good, in spite of the tight budget.

There's one scene—and again, this is Albert's genius—where I have a lot of dialogue, where I'm talking to Kathy Ireland. It looks like we're going up a staircase, turning a corner, turning another corner, climbing the wall of a building. It was just one wall with a staircase. We'd take the stairs, say our dialogue, stop, go back to the beginning, and continue our dialogue. That way, it looked like we kept going and going. That's a filmmaker's trick.

A poster for the French release of *Down Twisted*.

Street Smart on VHS.

Street Smart

Release Date: March 20, 1987
Directed by: Jerry Schatzberg
Written by: David Freeman
Starring: Christopher Reeve, Morgan Freeman, Kathy Baker, Mimi Rogers
Trailer Voiceover: "Jonathan Fisher is a reporter with a deadline—he's about to get a dangerous idea. Now he's crossed the line between fact and fiction, and his lie has landed him in the middle of a murder investigation!"

For most movie fans, Christopher Reeve *is* and will forever be Superman. The actor played the classic DC Comics superhero in four films over the course of a decade, turning in what are generally considered the character's definitive big screen appearances. Like many actors whose rise to fame came from playing one of pop culture's most beloved characters, however, the adulation and global recognition that came with playing Superman was both a blessing and a curse. Reeve was *so* synonymous with The Man of Tomorrow that many people—fans and filmmakers alike—had a hard time accepting him in any other role.

How strong was his association with the character? In a 1987 appearance on *The Tonight Show* while promoting *Street Smart*, Reeve regaled Johnny Carson with a story about his bicycle being snatched during a ride around Central Park. When the actor chased down the bike snatcher, the thief recognized him and pleaded "Oh, no, Superman, I'm sorry!" When Reeve shared a controversial, same-sex kiss with Michael Caine in *Deathtrap* (1982), there were multiple reported stories of audience members shouting "Don't do it, Superman!" and similar lines at the screen.

The pigeonholing certainly wasn't lost on Reeve. A lauded stage performer who had been trained at Juilliard, Reeve appeared destined to follow a pathway into classical acting before a longshot audition for the lead role in *Superman* (1978) pulled him away from Broadway and forever changed the arc of his career. For the next ten years, audiences would largely see him as the Man of Steel and no one else, so popular were his performances in the Richard Donner-directed blockbuster and its sequels. Meanwhile, Reeve felt the comic book role led other filmmakers to not take him seriously as an actor. His non-Kryptonian performances came mostly attached to mediocre films (*Monsignor*, 1982, and *The Aviator*, 1985), or barely made it to theaters at all (the Merchant-Ivory production of *The Bostonians*, 1984).

Reeve wasn't shy about voicing his desire for roles that didn't require him to wear red underwear over blue tights. You can almost sense a bit of jealousy when he would point at an actor like Harrison Ford in an interview, and explain that audiences had no problem accepting him both in pop hits like *Indiana Jones* and in serious films such as *Witness* (1985). "I need one big, non-Superman commercial hit," he told interviewer Michael Blowen in a 1987 profile for *The Boston Globe*. "That's what it takes."

By the mid-1980s, that non-Supes commercial hit had yet to arrive. After *Superman III* (1983) failed to live up to its predecessors, both critically and at the box office, Reeve famously went on the record saying that he would never play Superman again. Not only did he desire to open a new chapter in his acting career, but Reeve—then approaching his mid-30s—felt he was physically aging out of the role.

Cannon touts their new alliance with Christopher Reeve at the 1986 Cannes Film Festival.

In early 1986, Reeve rediscovered a screenplay sitting on his bookshelf that he'd received years earlier but had never given a proper read. *Street Smart* had been written by David Freeman, and Reeve became enamored with the dishonest reporter at its center—a character defiantly at odds with the staunchly righteous newspaper reporter, Clark Kent, whom he'd played in the Superman franchise.

Cannon was well aware that helping big-name stars bring their pet projects to the screen was a surefire way to lure A-listers to work with them without having to write A-list sized checks. Reeve brought the *Street Smart* script to Cannon, who greenlit the film on the condition that he break his vow to never play the Caped Wonder again, and agree to star in a new *Superman* sequel for the company. (Cannon had bought the film rights to the DC Comics character after the third movie flopped—but more on that in the *Superman IV* chapter.) Reeve capitulated, contracts were drawn up, and *Street Smart* went into production.

The film revolves around journalist Jonathan Fisher (Reeve), a writer for a pompous weekly publication that's an obvious stand-in for *New York* magazine. Tired of penning reviews of cookware, ice cream parlors, and other puff pieces, Fisher pitches his editor (the titular Andre Gregory of *My Dinner with Andre*, 1981) an in-depth profile of a Times Square pimp. His editor bites, and he's given the weekend to bang out the story as a last-minute replacement for another article.

Here's the issue: when Fisher told his editor he was cozy with the pimp he planned to profile, that was a lie. (David Freeman's script was inspired by the screenwriter's personal experience, having penned an acclaimed feature titled "Lifestyle of a Pimp" for the May 5, 1969 issue of *New York* magazine—the subject of which, he later admitted, had been completely fabricated.) When Fisher goes out trawling 42nd Street for a subject, the pimps meet him with hostility and the prostitutes aren't willing to talk. Finding himself desperate and up against his deadline, Fisher does the journalistically unthinkable and fudges a story about a colorful, made-up pimp he names Tyrone. Thinking that it would be a quick, quiet way out of his predicament, Fisher never anticipated the story being a citywide hit—which it does become, once his excited editor makes it the magazine's cover story.

We'll break here, and talk about the film's second main character. Leo Smalls (Morgan Freeman) is a violent pimp who goes by the street name of Fast Black. Unlike the hero of Fisher's bullshit cover story, he doesn't live a glamorous life of cartoonish decadence. Instead, he appears to be doing everything he can to collect his take from a small stable of prostitutes, which doesn't afford him much more than a modest Bronx apartment, a decent car, and a driver/assistant. (It's far from the Hawaiian condo the fictional Tyrone owns in Fisher's story.) Not long after we meet Fast Black, he checks in on one of his girls and finds her being beat up by a crazed customer in a sleazy motel room. When he's unable to talk the john down, Fast Black diffuses the standoff with a swift kick to the man's chest. The man suffers a fatal heart attack, and Fast Black is arrested and put on trial for Murder One.

It's hard to imagine today, what with Morgan Freeman being one of the most recognizable actors—and possessing one of the most recognizable voices—of the last thirty years, but he was relatively unknown at the time he was cast in *Street Smart*. Prior to this, Freeman had been a cast member on the children's educational television show *The Electric Company* (1971–1977), but had spent the decade since making barely notable screen appearances in a variety of forgotten films and TV episodes. Approaching his fiftieth birthday and already a grandfather, Freeman was selected to play the terrifyingly erratic pimp, Fast Black—a role for which he would receive his first (of *five*) Oscar nominations. To this day, Freeman considers *Street Smart* to be his breakthrough; he'd go on to make awards-worthy performances in movies such as *Driving Miss Daisy* (1989), *Glory* (1989), *Unforgiven* (1992), *The Shawshank Redemption* (1994), *Se7en* (1995), *Million Dollar Baby* (2004), and so many more.

Back in the film, Fisher's bogus cover story makes him the toast of the town, much to the wary chagrin of his live-in girlfriend, Alison, played by Mimi Rogers. Rogers would have her own breakout role as the female lead in *Someone to Watch Over Me* (1987) just a few months after the release of *Street Smart*. She'd later appear in movies such as *Austin Powers* (1997) and *Lost in Space* (1998), but is almost as famous for her two-year marriage to Tom Cruise in the late Eighties.

As his star rises, Fisher is given bigger assignments, gets invited to fancy dinners, and is hired by one of the local news programs to be the on-screen host and producer of "Street Smart," a *Geraldo*-like TV investigation series about "life on the streets." It appears that Fisher may have gotten away with his lie until a district attorney comes banging on his door. It turns out that Fast Black bears a passing resemblance to Fisher's made-up Tyrone, who now happens to be the city's most famous pimp thanks to his high-profile murder trial. The prosecution wants to subpoena Fisher's notes—which don't exist—so that they can comb them for evidence.

SS4   Fast Black (MORGAN FREEMAN) threatens Jonathan (CHRISTOPHER REEVE).

street smart.

Morgan Freeman, former children's television star, in his breakout role as the pimp Fast Black.

While Fast Black himself thinks Fisher's story is hilariously off-base, his lawyer sees value in perpetuating the misconception. One: Tyrone is a folksy, likeable character, and might color both juror and public opinion of him, and two: the defense knows that a journalist is unlikely to give up his source and that, by asking for Fisher's notes, the trial could be caught up in a lengthy First Amendment battle. The defense, of course, doesn't know that Fisher's story is completely fabricated and that admitting so would ruin his career, which only plays in their favor.

The sticky situation Fisher finds himself in is further complicated by the unexpected relationship the two men have formed. After his story went out on newsstands, Fisher was put in contact with Fast Black by one of his girls. Initially the friendship looks very patronizing from Fisher's side, as the journalist uses Fast Black as a retroactive "out" for his lie, bringing the pimp to fancy social gatherings and asking him to pretend he's the Tyrone that he wrote about. As time quickly reveals, it's not Fisher using Fast Black, but the other way around. When Fast Black needs Fisher to forge story notes to provide an alibi, he manipulates the writer like he would one of his prostitutes: through intimidation, threats, and violence. Where Fisher had tricked himself into thinking Fast Black was actually the friendly, make-believe Tyrone he'd dreamed up, he learns that the real person is someone far more dangerous.

Fisher's world is flipped upside-down when the unethical reporter is imprisoned for contempt of court. Fast Black attempts to push him into falsifying an alibi by hurting not only Fisher's girlfriend, but Punchy, a prostitute from his roster with whom Fisher has grown particularly close. Punchy is played by Kathy Baker in yet another breakout performance. (She's now best known for her Golden Globe-winning role as Dr. Jill Brock through four seasons of *Picket Fences* [1992–1996], and had another memorable part playing the neighbor who attempts to seduce Edward at the salon in 1990's *Edward Scissorhands*.) When *Street Smart* was released, it's unsurprising that both Freeman and Baker were almost universally lauded for the supporting roles. There's a scene in which Fast Black threatens her character with a pair of scissors, and it's terrifyingly intense and intimate—and arguably among the finest displays of pure acting ability in any Cannon movie.

AMERIČKI FILM **NOĆ I DAN MAKROA** DISTRIBUCIJA ZVEZDA FILM

Kathy Baker and Morgan Freeman in *Street Smart*'s most harrowing scene.

Eventually Fisher is forced to make a hard choice, and take his fate—at least, as far as Fast Black is concerned—into his own hands. The ending is rather abrupt and perhaps too tidy, but the execution is clever enough. At least one of the two slimeballs at the movie's center gets what's coming to him.

Street Smart was filmed in the late spring and early summer of 1986. (The marquee of the former RKO Times Square Theater can be spotted through the window of the donut shop where Jonathan meets Punchy; it bears an ad for John Carpenter's *Big Trouble in Little China*, which was released in June of that year.) The crew shot on location for three weeks in New York before shifting production to Montreal, Quebec, where Cannon could skirt union rules and save some cash. (This was a point of contention for Reeve, a vocal union supporter.) The production team, to their credit, did a fantastic job disguising the Canadian city as New York, dressing up a historic theater as a 42nd Street peep show and covering up French phrases with English advertisements. Unless you're watching closely, it's hard to tell which scenes were shot where.

Street Smart's director, Jerry Schatzberg, was no stranger to telling gritty, New York tales: his prior film *The Panic in Needle Park* (1971) was about NYC heroin addicts, and had provided a breakout role for a young Al Pacino. A New York native, Schatzberg made a name for himself as a photographer— shooting portraits of The Beatles, Andy Warhol and, most famously, the cover for Bob Dylan's *Blonde on Blonde* (1966)—before moving into filmmaking. His other movies include *Puzzle of a Downfall Child* (1970), *Scarecrow* (1973), and *Honeysuckle Rose* (1980). On *Street Smart*, he worked with his frequent collaborator, cinematographer Adam Holender, who was best known for shooting *Midnight Cowboy* (1969). Composer Robert Irving III's score is punctuated with trumpet solos by none other than jazz legend Miles Davis; Irving was a member of Davis' band through the 1980s.

For the most part, the movie lives up to its pedigree. There are a few plot elements that feel hard to believe—such as Fisher's instantaneous emergence as a TV personality, and how easily the ending falls into place—and a couple strange stylistic choices. (When Fisher finally hooks up with Punchy in a seedy motel, their conversation is drowned out by Aretha Franklin's "Natural Woman," which would feel more at home, say, as the soundtrack for a woman's sexual awakening, rather than a one-off scene about a condescending journalist cheating on his sympathetic girlfriend with a hooker.) Otherwise, *Street Smart* is a very effective thriller, with a bunch of riveting performances.

The film impressed critics: *Street Smart* was Cannon's most universally-praised movie of the year. Reviewers gushed over Freeman and Baker, and often pointed out the film's similarity to the story of disgraced journalist Janet Cooke. (In 1981, Cooke won a Pulitzer for a heart-wrenching story she wrote for *The Washington Post*; she later returned the prize when it was revealed that she'd invented the eight-year-old heroin addict that the article profiled.) Both Freeman and Baker received Best Supporting Actor nods from the Independent Spirit Awards and the National Society of Film Critics. Freeman went on to be nominated for an Academy Award in the same category, losing out to Sean Connery in *The Untouchables* (1987). He wouldn't bring home an Oscar statuette until his fourth nomination, for *Million Dollar Baby*.

Unfortunately Cannon couldn't capitalize on all of this critical acclaim. Already stretched woefully thin, the company was cutting production budgets left and right just to get their movies finished. They provided only a small release and almost zero marketing support for *Street Smart*. This was definitely a sore spot for Reeve, who had high hopes for the movie and had no qualms about expressing his disappointment with Cannon while doing interviews for *Superman IV*. With little promotion, the movie barely registered a blip at the box office, cracking just over $1 million and then disappearing from movie theaters altogether.

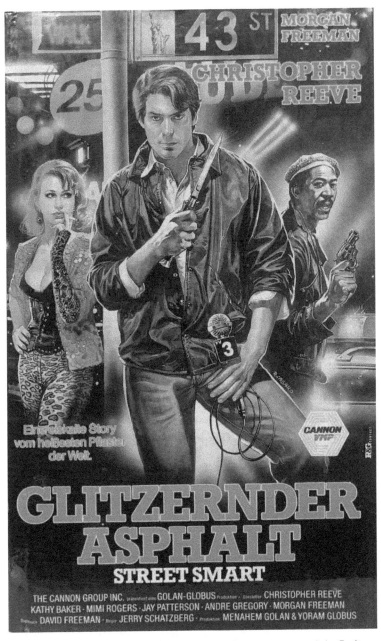

The German VHS release of *Street Smart*, featuring artwork by Italian painter Renato Casaro.

The Hanoi Hilton on VHS.

The Hanoi Hilton

Release Date: March 27, 1987
Directed by: Lionel Chetwynd
Written by: Lionel Chetwynd
Starring: Michael Moriarty
Tagline: "For Americans captured in Vietnam, one war ended. Another war was about to begin."

Think of *The Hanoi Hilton* as being a lot like *Missing in Action 2: The Beginning* (1985), but a half hour longer and without, you know, the part where Chuck Norris breaks out of the P.O.W. camp and takes his revenge by single-handedly blowing up most of Vietnam. This is *Missing in Action 2*, but missing the action. Consider yourselves warned.

Near the beginning of *The Hanoi Hilton* (1987), Lt. Commander Patrick Williamson's plane is shot down over Vietnam. He's captured and taken to the infamous Hoa Lo Prison, known colloquially to its inmates as "the Hanoi Hilton." This is the mid-1960s, and the prison's cells are still mostly empty. At this point, the hardest thing for Williamson to endure is the loneliness of isolation.

The prison is overseen by a wicked Vietnamese Major by the name of Ngo Doc, played by Aki Aleong, a prolific character actor who had a tiny role in Cannon's *Over the Brooklyn Bridge* (1984) and a far more notable one as the evil General Quoc in *Braddock: Missing in Action III* (1988). (Aleong was also a pop singer, scoring a top 100 hit in 1961 with the song "Trade Winds" after he was signed to a record deal by his friend, Frank Sinatra.) A sadistic tyrant, Major Ngo Doc uses a loophole in the Geneva Conventions to enact upon the soldiers whatever cruelties he sees fit, holding them as war criminals rather than war prisoners. As the conflict escalates, the halls of the Hilton fill up with new inmates, and the Major's torture becomes more savage.

By isolating the soldiers, feeding them cabbage laced with maggots, locking their ankles in irons, hanging them by their elbows with rope, and whipping and electrocuting them, the Major does everything he can to break these poor men. His singular goal is to force them to participate in propaganda that praises the Vietnamese and makes America look bad.

"The *real* war is not in the Delta," the Major explains at one point. "It's in the United Nations, Champs-Élysées, at Berkeley, California, on the Washington Mall. The cities of America. What we will not win on the battlefield, your journalists will win for us on your very own doorstep."

You see, the bad guys in *Hanoi Hilton* are not only the soldiers' sadistic Vietnamese captors (obviously), but also the hippies, journalists, professors, and other long-hairs back home. It's that sort of movie, where anyone who questions a war must do so because they hate America and are no better than Ho Chi Minh.

The movie chugs along as the years pass with no end in sight for the prisoners. Some men have been there for almost a decade. The only way they're able to endure it is by sticking together with an all-for-one, one-for-all attitude, and maintaining a chain of command according to their military rankings. When a senior-ranking officer is broken or killed by his captors, the next in line assumes his responsibilities.

If it wasn't clear from the summary above, *The Hanoi Hilton* is a thoroughly bleak and dismal movie: a nonstop parade of brave, red-blooded Americans being tortured and humiliated. The movie's hardest-to-watch scene—in which a soldier is brutally beaten and hung by prison guards, shown in complete silence—is the most memorable one, in a film that doesn't have many of them.

Outside of this, it's not a terribly well-written or well-directed film. *Hanoi Hilton* has a peculiar reliance upon using awkward background music and sound effects to prop up its many overlong speeches; for example, when one soldier wistfully remembers attending hockey games as a child, we hear arena music and a roaring crowd. When Major Ngo Doc delivers a villainous speech, the soundtrack plays generic, gong-punctuated oriental music, like he's Long Duk Dong in *Sixteen Candles* (1984). Writer-director Lionel Chetwynd is a co-founder of Friends of Abe, a secretive club for conservatives within Hollywood's elite, and made a career out of writing films mostly inspired by American historical events and Bible stories.

It's a shame the script isn't better, because the performances are generally pretty good. Being a movie about American war prisoners, it is chock full of tough-looking actors with recognizable faces, all wearing red-and-white striped prison uniforms. Lawrence Pressman, who plays Cathcart, the colonel who gets the resistance ball rolling, had significant roles in *Shaft* (1971) and *9 to 5* (1980), but is probably best known as Coach Marshall in *American Pie* (1999). The pious Major Fischer was played by Jeffrey Jones of TV's *Deadwood* (2004–2006), *Amadeus* (1984), *Ferris Bueller's Day Off* (1986), and several Tim Burton movies. Paul Le Mat ("Hubman") previously starred in *American Graffiti* (1973) and *Melvin and Howard* (1980), as well as *P.K. and the Kid* (1987), in which he plays a rough-edged father figure to a runaway teen played by Molly Ringwald as they're on a cross-country road trip to a high-stakes arm-wrestling competition. (Filmed five years earlier, that movie sat unreleased until just a few weeks before Cannon's similarly-flavored *Over the Top* hit theaters.)

David Soul plays Oldham, and was best known as the "Hutch" of *Starsky & Hutch* (1975–1979); he would return to Cannon for Michael Winner's *Appointment with Death* in 1988. And speaking of Cannon, this cast boasts several more repeat offenders. Ken Wright ("Kennedy") appeared in *Down Twisted* (1987) the same year as this film. Rick Fitts would return for a pair of Dudikoff movies, *Platoon Leader* (1988) and *Rescue Me* (1992). The stuttering Rasmussen is played by Jesse Dabson, also of *Death Wish 4: The Crackdown* (1987) and *Platoon Leader*. James Acheson ("Cummins") was in *four* Cannon movies: *P.O.W. The Escape* and *Invaders from Mars* (both 1986), *Assassination* (1987), and this one.

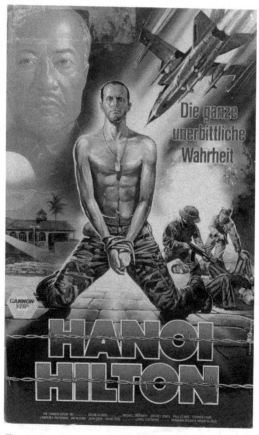

The German home video release of *Hanoi Hilton*.

A trio of actors with the smallest cameos have the most interesting backgrounds, however. The officers who arrive at the finale to bring home the surviving prisoners were real-life P.O.W.s who spent time in Hoa Lo Prison, and served as technical advisors on the movie. (Among those thanked in the movie's credits is Senator and one-time Presidential candidate John McCain, who was also imprisoned for some time in the Hanoi Hilton.)

The best performance, though, comes from Michael Moriarty, who—as Lt. Williamson, the closest thing this ensemble movie has to a main character—essentially carries the weight of this heavy, heavy film on his back. After roles in cult classics like *Q - the Winged Serpent* (1982), *Pale Rider* (1985), *The Stuff* (1985), and *Troll* (1986), he landed the role of district attorney Benjamin Stone on the landmark procedural *Law & Order* (1990–2010). There he was nominated for several Emmy and Gold Globe Awards before going a little nuts and being unceremoniously written off the show in his fourth season. Ask him the reason for his forced departure and he'll say it was because he threatened to file a lawsuit against Attorney General Janet Reno, who he was convinced tried to censor his TV show. Ask his colleagues from *Law & Order*, though, and it's because he would turn up at work in an unusual mental state, unable to get through his lines without laughing. (Which, we'd assume, isn't a good thing in a legal drama.) Moriarty fled to Canada as a self-described political exile, where he wrote and starred in an independent film called *Hitler Meets Christ* (2007). He's since published countless blogs about how the Clintons are alien invaders, and announced that he would run for the American presidency in 2008—inspired, as he claims, by Tom Clancy's fictional Jack Ryan character.

Michael Moriarty, obviously, did not become president in 2008.

Cannon took a chance on this movie when all of the larger studios spent nearly a decade turning it down, sinking between $4 and $5 million dollars into it. Nonetheless, *The Hanoi Hilton* was a critical and commercial flop, bringing in just over three quarters of $1 million in its very limited theatrical release.

Cannon entered the family section of the video store with *Aladdin* on VHS.

Aladdin

Release Date: April 1987 (Video)
Directed by: Bruno Corbucci
Written by: Mario Amendola, Bruno Corbucci, and Marcello Fondato
Starring: Bud Spencer, Luca Venantini
Trailer Voiceover: "When a Twentieth Century teenager rubs a Seventeenth Century lamp, he gets everything he ever wished for . . . and more!"

Six years before Disney sunk their teeth into the famous folk tale, unleashing Robin Williams' blue-skinned, motor-mouthed version of the character onto the world, one of Europe's biggest comedy stars had his turn playing the legendary genie of Aladdin's lamp.

Bud Spencer, the beloved, barrel-chested Italian actor with a booming laugh, was born Carlo Pedersoli on Halloween night, 1929, in Naples, Italy. By the time he was nineteen, the 6'4" young man had already set national records as a swimmer, going on to compete in the 1952 and 1956 Olympic games. His athletic renown and humongous frame—not to mention his familial relations, as the son-in-law of the esteemed, neorealist film producer, Guiseppe Amato—led him to be cast in bit roles in a handful of movies early on in his career, a time during which he also worked briefly as a songwriter for Italian pop stars and folk singers.

By the mid-1960s, director Guiseppe Colizzi was looking for a "giant" to co-star in his comedic Spaghetti Western, *God Forgives... I Don't!* (1967). The former swimmer, who weighed 240 pounds, was somewhat embarrassed by the idea of appearing in a cowboy parody movie, but needed the money. He grew out his beard in hopes that no one would recognize him. To complete the disguise, he did what many other Italian Western stars did, and adopted a more marketable, American-sounding name. "Bud Spencer" was born: "Bud," after his favorite brand of beer, Budweiser, and "Spencer," after his favorite Hollywood actor, Spencer Tracy.

The movie, which Spencer thought might disappear amidst the decline of Spaghetti Westerns in general, actually wound up being a huge hit. Spencer had stupendous chemistry with his co-star, fellow Italian actor Terence Hill, and the two instantly became a duo. They were signed up first for a pair of sequels, *Ace High* (1968) and *Boot Hill* (1969), and then another series of Westerns, *The Call Me Trinity* (1970) and *Trinity Is Still My Name* (1971). These movies were hits all across Europe, and Spencer and Hill's popularity continued even after they left the Western genre behind to star in cop comedies and adventure movies. The duo appeared in eighteen films together, up until their 1994 swan song, *Troublemakers*.

More than just an actor and Olympic-level athlete, however, Spencer held a law degree, spoke multiple languages, published a cookbook and a best-selling autobiography, founded his own airline (which survives today as Poste Air Cargo), and secured nearly a dozen patents for inventions, including one for a disposable toothbrush that dispensed its own paste. A true renaissance man, Spencer somehow found the time in his busy career to star in Cannon's version of *Aladdin* (1987).

The folk tale of Aladdin and his magical lamp has been around for centuries: it's one of the most famous stories from *The One Thousand and One Nights* (a.k.a. *Arabian Nights*), although it never appeared as part of that collection until an 18th Century French translation. It's been adapted for the screen more than twenty times dating back to the silent era, with the most famous version of course being Disney's animated musical from 1992. Cannon's version, released as "Superfantagenio" in Italy, only takes loose inspiration from the original tale, turning it into a modern story about a poor, unpopular teen boy's adventures with a powerful genie as his new best friend.

Aladdin is set in a modern-day Miami where many of the "American" characters speak with Italian accents. It centers on a fourteen-year-old boy, Al Haddin (get it?), played by Luca Venantini, the son of a prolific Italian actor Venantino Venantini, the man with the best name in the business.

Al Haddin's dad died when he was young, and his alcoholic grandfather (Julian Voloshin) gambled away all of the family's money, leaving them in insurmountable debt to a local mobster by the name of Monty Siracusa (Tony Adams). This has rendered Al's mother something of an indentured servant to the gangster, working for low wages and enduring constant harassment at his sleazy nightclub. (His mom is played by Swedish actress Janet Agren, best known for playing Brigitte Nielsen's priestess sister in *Red Sonja* [1985], and for her starring role in the second of Umberto Lenzi's three cannibal flicks, *Eaten Alive!* [1980].)

Doing his best to pitch in at home, Al earns five bucks a day working for a slimy antiques dealer. This is where he first comes into contact with a magical lamp, newly trawled up from the bottom of the Miami harbor after two hundred years on the ocean's floor. Al unwittingly summons the genie while polishing away the centuries' worth of sea muck. He is at first skeptical of the large, burly man who just manifested in the back room of the shop, but quickly becomes receptive to his new pal when the genie starts granting him unlimited wishes.

Cannon's *Aladdin* does a fun thing by giving its teenage protagonist a very small imagination. Rather than asking the genie for obvious stuff like, say, wishing away his enemies, or for the millions of dollars that would instantly make all of his family's problems go away, Al's wishes are surprisingly small. For example, when he can't afford to buy his date an ice cream sundae, he only asks the genie for ten bucks. Instead of asking the genie to make his crush fall in love with him, he asks him for a necklace that he can give her as a gift. The tiny scale in which Al's brain operates makes him seem endearingly dopey, and it also makes sure that his numerous problems aren't resolved too easily with magic.

Not all of Al's wishes are totally small potatoes, though. He transforms a pair of thugs who smash up his family's apartment into cockroaches. He magically learns karate to beat up his romantic rival. In one of the movie's most fun sequences, he walks onto his high school basketball team to put on a performance that would make both Michael Jordan and Lebron James bow down in appreciation. *Aladdin's* special effects are, well, nothing special—most are the sort of practical, in-camera effects you might see kids implementing these days in their YouTube and Tik Tok videos—but they're effective, particularly when Al is doing flips over his basketball opponents, or the genie's making their Rolls Royce levitate over a traffic jam.

Unlike many versions of the tale where the genie is only visible to his master, *anyone* in this version can see Bud Spencer's loveable wish-granter unless Al specifically asks him to turn invisible. Keeping his powers a secret, he enjoys dinner with Al's family and even gets fall-down, stinking drunk with grandpa. Clever Al repeatedly passes the big man off as his chauffeur, yet doesn't refrain from addressing him as "Genie." (It's "short for Eugene," you see.) The only apparent limit to the genie's powers are that they disappear from sundown to sunup, rendering him little more than a normal human during those hours. This fine print is used pretty well for dramatic purposes.

Most of Al's unlimited wishes are used to keep him one step ahead of his myriad enemies. (Seriously, this fourteen-year-old boy has a rogues' gallery as large as Batman's.) There's his rival, a standard high school bully. There's the police chief who doesn't want his daughter dating low-caliber riff-raff. There's his abusive boss, who wants revenge on Al for taking the lamp from his shop without paying for it. Of course, there's also that evil mob boss and his goons, who make it their job to ensure Al and his family are forever in their debt. Oh! There's also a shady government agent, who wants to dissect the genie and use his powers to shift the Cold War in his bosses' favor.

The German VHS release of *Aladdin*, with artwork by Enzo Sciotti.

Did I mention there's also a child trafficking ring, which Al and the genie single-handedly break up?

Yeah—in a movie full of WTF moments, there's a super-dark turn near the midpoint that makes all of those other WTF moments look pretty run-of-the-mill in comparison. Early in the movie, the genie asks Al whether he has any friends, and he mentions a buddy that's been missing for a few days and whose family fears for his safety. It's not mentioned again for the next half hour of the film, until Al is walking home alone after a date-gone-well and is suddenly snatched up by a passing car. He's dumped off at a scary orphanage overseen by a mean Nurse Ratched-type. He finds himself in a crowded room full of missing children, including the kidnapped pal that hasn't been mentioned since the start of the movie.

In another room, a grotesque man is making telephone sales pitches for his latest acquisitions, securing a deal for the newly-arrived Al—described as having dirty blonde hair and blue eyes—to be sold to a buyer overseas. (We have to assume it's for sex, right?) Before Al can be shipped off to his purchaser, he manages to snatch up the lamp and summon the genie, and has him transform the kidnappers into pigs. The whole child trafficking subplot only lasts a few minutes and barely impacts the rest of the movie, which only makes it feel so much weirder and darker. After the movie it leaves you thinking, "Hey, do you remember the part where Al Haddin was nearly sold as a sex slave? Wasn't that a really weird throwaway gag for a kids' movie?"

Everything wraps up pretty neatly by the film's climax, which supplies an unforgettable image of Bud Spencer and Al Haddin fleeing from a fleet of attack choppers on the back of a magic carpet. (That's just *so* perfectly Cannon, isn't it?) All of the good guys are given happy endings, even the genie.

From afar, *Aladdin* looks like a movie that *should* be terrible. The trailer doesn't do the special effects any favors, and the thought of a low-budget Italian adventure movie aimed at kids perhaps doesn't have the same appeal as Cannon's more over-the-top, grown-up fare. The big surprise, though? *Aladdin* is actually pretty darn good. Like, legitimately, *actually* good. The movie is charming and hokey, and totally entertaining—and you don't even have to be a Bud Spencer fan going in to appreciate it. When it comes to family-friendly Cannon movies, it's more entertaining to sit through this with your children for repeat viewings than most of the Cannon Movie Tales.

The movie is helped by its strong ensemble of character actors. None of the Italian cast is going to fool any viewer into thinking they're Americans, what with their barely-concealed accents, but there's not a bad actor in the bunch. Julian Voloshin, in particular, is able to endear us to Al's booze-fueled grandpa, when any lesser talent would have rendered the role annoyingly one-note. Al's crush is played by Bud Spencer's real-life daughter, Diamy.

Aladdin was directed by Bruno Corbucci, baby brother to the famed Spaghetti Western filmmaker Sergio Corbucci, who had helmed several of the comedies that made Bud Spencer a household name across Europe. Several of those films were penned by the younger Corbucci—including *Odds and Evens* (1978) and *Miami Supercops* (1986)—who was even more prolific as a screenwriter (146 movies) than as a director (54 movies and TV shows). The movie's cinematographer was Silvano Ippoliti, who'd previously shot some of Tinto Brass's films. *Aladdin*'s score comes courtesy of Fabio Frizzi, who is adored by horror fans for his collaborations with Lucio Fulci, including the soundtracks of *Zombi 2* (1979), *City of the Living Dead* (1980), and *The Beyond* (1981). This was, somewhat shockingly, his only Cannon work.

I'll give *Aladdin* my whole-hearted recommendation, with one word of warning: the theme song is perhaps the most inescapable earworm in all of the Cannon filmography. I'm hesitant to type any of the lyrics here as I'll run the risk of having the song embedded in my brain again for the next two weeks. Written by Eumir Deodato and sung by Bud Spencer himself in his gruff, heavily-accented English, "The Genie" is a song you'll find yourself humming for days after viewing the movie.

The American VHS release for *The Barbarians*, "a fantasy-adventure so outrageous it takes two heroes to handle it."

The Barbarians

Release Date: May 15, 1987
Directed by: Ruggero Deodato
Written by: James R. Silke
Starring: The Barbarian Brothers
Trailer Voiceover: "The internationally-renowned bad boys of body building: Peter and David Paul . . . The Barbarians! Feel the power!"

"Hey, remember *Conan?* Those two movies made a lot of money, right? People seem to like that barbarian guy. But, what if there were *two* of them? And what if, get this, *they were identical twins?*"

You have to imagine that was the thought process that went into *The Barbarians*, a low-budget sword and sorcery film released under the Cannon flag in 1987. But, don't let cynicism cloud your judgment: *The Barbarians* is a fun fantasy adventure, with some cool world-building, surprisingly high-quality production design, and a great cast that includes several members of b-movie royalty. There's a lot to enjoy here if you can get past our twin heroes' constant, dopey bickering.

Stars David and Peter Paul were born in Hartford, Connecticut in 1957. In the early 1980s, they rose to prominence on the national bodybuilding circuit, and it's easy to see their appeal: not only were they absurdly muscular, but they were *identical twins*! These two all-beef patties moved to Los Angeles with less than $100 between them, and would work out at the famous Gold's Gym—where *Pumping Iron* (1977) was filmed, and helped put bodybuilding on the map—sometimes in flannel shirts and work boots, billing themselves as "The Lumberjacks." This began to attract attention, as did the frequent sight of these two massively muscular identical twins riding around Hollywood on a single motorcycle.

Soon they started doing magazine photo shoots, and eventually landed small roles in Joel Schumacher's *D.C. Cab* (1983) and Garry Marshall's *The Flamingo Kid* (1984), along with an episode of *Knight Rider* (1982–1986). You might think that one of these is what brought the twins to Cannon's attention, but that wasn't the case.

What *actually* brought them to the attention of the studio was their photo spread in the July 1986 issue of *Playgirl*.

By this point, David and Peter Paul had already started billing themselves as "The Barbarian Brothers." From there, it must not have taken too much thought to connect the dots and make an *actual* barbarian movie starring these self-proclaimed "bad boys of bodybuilding." Cannon scooped them up for a sword and sorcery feature to be shot at their Italian production wing. Again, it was easy to understand the brothers' appeal: they had the same huge, jacked up physiques as Arnold Schwarzenegger, but you could get two of them for just a fraction of his price.

Schwarzenegger, of course, was directly responsible for launching a wave of sword and sorcery flicks that were extremely prevalent during the early video era. His star-making turn in *Conan the Barbarian* (1982) was a worldwide box office phenomenon, making an incredible $69 million in its initial theatrical run, and continuing to rake in the cash on video and cable. Like any major success—*especially* one made on a relatively low budget—*Conan* inspired many knock-offs of varying quality. This sword and sorcery genre, as it was called, separated itself from its closest relative, the sword and sandal epic, with a heavier emphasis on magic and fantasy and usually a darker, more violent tone. Where sword and sandal films typically found inspiration in mythology or Biblical tales, sword and sorcery movies were more influenced by pulp novels and Dungeons and Dragons.

Anyone old enough to remember roaming the aisles of their local, mom-and-pop video store in the Eighties and early Nineties can probably recall just how rampant the sword and sorcery genre was at the time. The box art was often painted, and stuck to a pretty consistent formula. You'd usually have a 'roided-out barbarian (or gladiator) standing front and center, typically clad in little more than a loincloth and fur-lined boots, holding a massive broadsword (or battle axe) poised to strike a malicious dragon (or griffon) while a model-gorgeous woman in a fur (or chainmail) bikini cowered behind him. Occasionally you would see a cover on which it was the woman in the armored bikini wielding the sword—while those were less common, you would tend to find more female heroes in the sword and sorcery genre than in many other action-oriented subgenres of the Eighties.

A few of the noteworthy sword and sorcery franchises of the era included the *Beastmaster*, *Deathstalker*, *Ator*, and *Gor* films, the latter of which were also Cannon products. Among the barbarian flicks with lady leads were titles such as *Sorceress* (1982), *Red Sonja* (1985), *Barbarian Queen* (1985), and *Amazons* (1986).

Once they dipped their toes into the cinematic adventures of burly, shirtless dudes on magical quests, Cannon turned to house scribe James R. Silke—author of two Ninja films, their first Quatermain movie, and *Sahara* (1983)—to handle the script, and Serbian filmmaker Slobodan Šijan to direct. After scouting locations and starting construction on some of the sets, Šijan was replaced by Italian director Ruggero Deodato, a filmmaker most infamous for the Video Nasty *Cannibal Holocaust* (1980). This fake "documentary" from 1980—about a lost film crew eaten by Amazonian cannibals—featured gory special effects that looked so real that they got their director in trouble. Within days of its release in Italy, *Cannibal Holocaust* was seized by authorities and Deodato was arrested on charges of obscenity. Later, a French magazine made allegations that the deaths shown in the film were real, and Deodato's charges were upgraded to murder. To clear his name, Deodato had to produce the actors—who had signed contracts not to appear in any media for twelve months after the film's release, to give the impression that the movie was real—and explain how he pulled off the special effects. Charges were dropped. However, while it was proven that no *humans* were harmed in the making of the film, the same can't be said for the animals. The on-screen deaths of a squirrel monkey, turtle, pig, snake, tarantula, and a coati are, unfortunately, quite real, and the primary reason why the film remains so controversial to this day.

From its opening credits, you get a sense that *The Barbarians* is going to be metal as all get-out. In the background is an imposing mountain range set against a flame-red sky; the foreground is a smoky battlefield, where armor and weapons are jammed atop pikes alongside human bones. It's exactly the sort of backdrop you'd see in a Frank Frazetta painting. (Pino Donaggio's chirping synthesizer score doesn't quite fit the imagery, but it certainly gets you in the mood for some '80s action.) A narrator welcomes us to a savage world "ruled by the sword," and holy shit this movie is off to a pretty kickass start.

Peter and David Paul in *The Barbarians*. (You guess which is which.)

As the titles wrap up, the camera pans across the battlefield and the narrator introduces us to the Ragnick people—a nomadic tribe of clowns, jugglers, dwarfs, knife-throwers and fire breathers—who are basically a traveling circus, but heavily armed. They dress like members of Adam Ant's backing band: a mess of colorful, glam rock makeup and poofy pirate sleeves, with lots of fur, braids, studded leather, gold jewelry, and feathers.

A long time ago, their king traded his entire fortune for a single, magical ruby that contained the secrets of music, laughter and kindness; because of this, they became their world's entertainers and storytellers, and are welcome to roam the land without fear of attack. They've recently adopted a trio of orphans—boys Kutchek and Gore, and a little girl named Kara—and given them tiny neck tattoos to mark them as members of their tribe. (If you need a name for your orphan barbarian baby, you probably can't get more metal than "Gore.")

Unfortunately this "nobody attacks the Ragnicks" rule seems to be on the honor system alone, because the Ragnick caravan is almost immediately ambushed by marauders. This band of warrior clowns prove fully capable of defending themselves, however, and we get to watch a surprisingly rockin' buggy chase scene. As the bad guys pursue them, the Ragnicks hurl knives, toss exploding crystal balls, and spit fire like human flame throwers. Their assailants—who look like antiquated versions of the villains from a movie, covered in hideous facial scars and wearing mismatched pieces of junk armor—eventually corner them in a valley. Their leader, Kadar (Richard Lynch in dreadlocks), demands they hand over the magic ruby, but the Ragnick queen, Canary, was wise enough to hide it during the chase.

The pint-sized twins make a valiant effort to defend their queen by rushing Kadar and biting off his fingers. (Damn!) He orders the boys' deaths, but Canary promises to be Kadar's slave if he'll spare their lives. He agrees, taking Canary, the twins, and the Ragnick women as his prisoners. They're all carried away to Kadar's fortress, where the boys are sent to work in the pits under the ever-watching eye of The Dirtmaster (Michael Berryman).

Let's pause to appreciate the actors playing two of our main villains. The last time we saw Richard Lynch in a Cannon movie, Chuck Norris was shooting him out of a window with a bazooka in *Invasion U.S.A.* (1985). (You can read more about his bio—and how he got his distinctive scars—in that chapter of this book.) Michael Berryman, meanwhile, is one of the most recognizable faces in genre filmmaking, with more than one hundred screen credits that include *One Flew Over the Cuckoo's Nest* (1975), Wes Craven's *The Hills Have Eyes* (1977), *Weird Science* (1985), and *The Devil's Rejects* (2005).

Kutchek and Gore are intentionally separated, and years pass by without them seeing each other. As they slave their young lives away hauling stones in the quarries, the twins grow from adorable pipsqueaks into gargantuan beefcakes. Every day, The Dirtmaster has each twin chained up and whipped; Kutchek's torturer wears a black helmet that covers his entire face, and Gore's tormentor wears a similar gold helmet. It may seem extreme, but it's all part of Kadar's long-term plan to exploit a loophole in the promise he made to Canary that neither he nor any of his henchmen would kill the orphaned twins. The boys are trained to hate the faceless torturers under their distinctive headpieces. Once they're of age, they're individually outfitted with the helmet of their twin's torturer, and sent to fight one another in the arena—where, Kadar hopes, they'll be cut each other to ribbons before a live audience. Luckily, Kadar's excessively long, drawn-out plan to kill off the twins doesn't play out as he'd hoped. Midway into the battle, the brothers' helmets come off and they're each met with a familiar face—literally, since they're identical twins. As if no time had gone by at all since they were separated, these two matching musclemen rip down the walls of the arena, hightail it out of the fortress and go looking for the remains of their tribe.

The moment the adult Kutchek and Gore open their mouths, the movie takes on a very different tone. For all of its spectacular world building and cool production design to this point, the twins undo much of that effort by sounding like stereotypical, dumb movie jocks, and acting like bratty two-year-olds. Where the Conan movies wisely limited how much their hero spoke, *The Barbarians'* barbarians, on the other hand, never stop bickering between themselves, or yammering about the size of their muscles. These two bumbling meatheads sound out-of-place in the film's heroic fantasy world. Sure, they're meant to be funny—but why wait to introduce humor into the film one third of the way into its runtime? It may not come as a surprise to anyone that most of the Barbarians' jokes were supplied by the twins themselves, who were reportedly allowed to ad lib because the director didn't speak enough English at the time to understand how dumb their jokes were. (And, hey, how many of us would have had the guts to tell these two, towering bodybuilders to stop talking?)

Back to the movie: Kutchek and Gore immediately find the remnants of their tribespeople living in a nearby forest. The Ragnicks, of course, don't believe that these two oiled-up lunks are the same little boys who were kidnapped from them all those years ago. (It's unclear just how many years have passed since the movie's opening—while the twins appear to have aged almost two decades, no one else seems to have gotten any older, or even changed their outfits.) The Ragnicks string up Kutchek and Gore to be hanged, even though it seems a little bit weird that the twins know all of the Ragnicks' names as well as intimate details about their society. One brother escapes the noose by flexing his neck muscles, which snaps the rope. The mystical clown people then do what they probably should have done before staging the execution, and check the twins' necks for distinguishing tattoos that would identify them as true Ragnicks after all. Once freed, Kutchek and Gore ask for weapons so they can go rescue Canary, but the peaceful tribesmen don't have any on hand. A mysterious lady thief named Ismena promises to help them locate an arms dealer in exchange for her own release from the Ragnicks' gallows.

The thief Ismena is played by actress Eva LaRue, making her screen debut. She'd go on to star on *All My Children* (1970–2011) and *CSI: Miami* (2002–2012), although genre movie fans may better know her from films such as *Ghoulies III* (1991) and *RoboCop 3* (1993).

Ismena leads the boys to a wholesome-sounding tavern called The Bucket of Blood. Here they meet a weapons trader named Jacko, who for some insane reason proposes that they arm wrestle him for his stash. (He's played by Italian exploitation staple George Eastman, whose previous Cannon appearance was in 1986's *Detective School Dropouts*.) Jacko loses the arm wrestling match, of course, which incites a brawl, and the boys flee the bar without any weapons.

A countertop standee was sent out to video stores to promote the VHS release of *The Barbarians*.

Unarmed, they go ahead and sneak into Kadar's fortress anyway. Fortunately for them, the guards are busy drinking and cavorting with loose women. (At one point, the twins pretend to make out with each other to fool a watchman—who falls for it, and assumes it's just one of his guards whoring it up with a ginormous prostitute.) With little effort they infiltrate Kadar's harem, where Queen Canary decides she'd rather not be rescued, but instead sends Kutchek and Gore on a series of fetch quests. They have to go to the "Forbidden Lands" to retrieve the magical ruby—which she's now calling "The Bellystone"—where it's guarded by a dragon named "The Gravemaker." But before they can fight the dragon, they need to go to the "Tomb of the Ancient King" and retrieve the "Sacred Weapons," which are the only things that can harm the dragon. (The quotation marks are there to emphasize how much her instructions sound like the words of a lazy Dungeon Master who couldn't be bothered to come up with original-sounding names for their campaign elements.)

Hokey names aside, this quest sounds like it could be pretty epic, right? Well . . . it only takes Ismena and the barbarian bros a few minutes' worth of screen time to find the ancient tomb. Queen Canary may as well have given them a quest to head to the corner store and pick up a gallon of milk—that's how truly un-epic this first leg of the quest feels. Once inside, they're stalked by a cave beast who looks kind of like Michael Jackson when he's only halfway through his werewolf transformation in the "Thriller" music video. Ismena simply plugs it with a single arrow and its head falls right off. She doesn't even shoot it in the head! (Or even aim her bow!) The monster's noggin just pops right off its shoulders. Fights don't get any more anticlimactic than this, folks.

Meanwhile in the Forbidden Lands, Kadar's evil sorceress, China, and The Dirtmaster are able to locate the ruby's hiding place before the twins do, but they're immediately and unceremoniously eaten by the dragon known as The Gravemaker. (This thing is hilarious: in wide shots, it moves stiffly like one of those animatronic brontosauruses you'd see in a touring dinosaur exhibit; in close-ups, it's a flabby puppet.) The twins arrive a little bit later and have zero trouble slaying the dragon. They crawl inside its guts—which are lit like a department store at Christmastime—and retrieve the ruby from the sorceress' cold, dead hand.

Out of nowhere, it's revealed now that the barbarian brothers have figured out that Ismena is actually Kara, the little orphan girl who mysteriously disappeared when the Ragnicks were attacked years earlier. (They must be smarter than they sound.) The trio emerges from behind the magic waterfall, where not only the ancient tomb was located, but apparently the entirety of the Forbidden Lands. They split up, with Ismena taking the ruby back to the Ragnicks, and the twins just wandering off to kill the bad guy or something.

As Ismena admires the ruby, it unleashes magic across the land which causes Kadar to lose his mind and accidentally murder Queen Canary. In turn, her death transforms the ruby into a regular, old rock. "We got the ruby!" Ismena proclaims to the Ragnicks, then opens her hand and frowns. "There must be a curse on it. It's turned into . . . a stone." (Her disappointment registers like Charlie Brown discovering he has a rock in his trick or treat bag.)

The Ragnicks realize this means that their queen is dead, and they must choose a new one from among the tribe's virgins—of which there are only two. (Cue sad trombone noise.) Their method of choosing a new monarch is pretty strange, to say the least: they line up the young women and test which one's bellybutton the ruby best fits inside, as if it were Cinderella's glass slipper. One by one, they stick the ruby—or "Bellystone"—into each of the young ladies' bellybuttons, only for it to slip right out. When they're about to give up, the stone begins to glow, and the village leader demands Ismena bring forth her own bellybutton for ruby insertion. Unsurprisingly, Ismena has little interest in being queen of the clown people who had imprisoned her only a few days earlier. But, they stick the ruby in her bellybutton anyway. When the gemstone enters her navel it begins to twinkle, and she's declared their new queen.

As the fair maidens' bellybuttons are being prodded with precious stones, Kutchek and Gore are wandering aimlessly through a valley when they're jumped by the nefarious Kadar. You might think a single, middle-aged dude missing half his fingers wouldn't stand much chance against a pair of offensive lineman-sized barbarians, but he actually holds his own for quite a while. It all goes to shit for Kadar, though, when he lines up one of the twins—not sure which, they look exactly alike—in the sight of his crossbow, but it misfires. The boys chuck their swords at him and he's run through by them simultaneously, making for a pretty sweet, *Mortal Kombat*-style fatality.

The Ragnick caravan picks up the twins along the side of the road. With Kutchek and Gore by her side, the new Queen presumably rules peacefully over the kingdom with her magic bellybutton gem.

Despite *The Barbarians'* cheap special effects and its boneheaded protagonists, it's an absolute blast to watch. If you're able to get over the Barbarian Brothers' brainless, unabated babbling, it's just the sort of crazy cinema that most Cannon fans crave.

As for the Barbarian Brothers, Peter and David went on to star in a trio of zany, straight-to-video comedies in which they played varying pairs of humongous guys who looked exactly alike. In *Think Big* (1990), the sibling duo starred as truck drivers who protect a young inventor from mobsters. In *Double Trouble* (1992), the brawny bros are cast as twins on opposite sides of the law, who join forces to bring down a smuggling ring. In *Twin Sitters* (1994), Peter and David play buff babysitters who are hired by a wealthy businessman to watch his troublesome twin nephews. It's more or less the same gimmick the Olsen twins had in their early film career, except with identical bodybuilders rather than identical ragamuffins.

Interestingly, one of the duo's most famous, post-*Barbarians* appearances was in a film they wound up not even appearing in at all. Oliver Stone cast the pair in *Natural Born Killers* (1994) as bodybuilders being interviewed by Robert Downey Jr.'s character; the scene was deleted due to their overacting in it. Sadly, David Paul passed away in 2020.

Eva LaRue as the thief Ismena in *The Barbarians*.

Interview: Actress Eva LaRue

A model and actress who would eventually become a star of both daytime and primetime television, Eva LaRue made her big screen debut playing Ismena, the female sidekick to twin bodybuilders David and Peter Paul in Cannon's epic fantasy film, *The Barbarians* (1987).

LaRue has been a fan-favorite cast member of the soap opera *All My Children* since 1993, playing Maria Santos at numerous points throughout the show's run. For seven seasons she appeared as agent Natalia Boa Vista on *CSI: Miami* (2002–2012). Prior to her rise to TV stardom, LaRue also appeared in VHS rental staples *Dangerous Curves* (1989), *Ghoulies III* (1991), and *RoboCop 3* (1993).

I imagine that out of all of your roles, *The Barbarians* might not be one of the ones you're approached about the most.

Eva LaRue: No, never! It's interesting, because it was my very first job. I had just won a county beauty pageant, Miss Riverside. I was supposed to go on to Miss California from there. The Miss California pageant was supposed to be at the same time as the role I had just gotten in *The Barbarians*, and *The Barbarians* shot in Italy. I'd never even been out of the country at that point.

I gave my crown up to the first runner up, jumped on the plane, and moved to Italy for three months. Even though the movie was a terrible piece of crap, it really was an amazing experience, at eighteen years old, to go live in Italy for three months. That was really cool.

It sounds like the casting must have happened pretty quickly, if you had to suddenly drop out of the pageant like that.

It literally all happened within a week or two. It was just, "Okay, you got the job and you're out of here next week."

Cannon wasn't big on giving a lot of time for pre-production.

None. You could tell.

One of the reasons I think this movie is so endearing, whether somebody likes it or not, is that the main cast looks like they're having fun. There are a lot of smiles in the film, even though it's set in this gloomy fantasy world.

We did. I have to say, [David and Peter] were such energetic forces to be reckoned with. They were their own battery packs. They would always seem to be in a good mood. They would squabble with each other all the time, but it was more like Laurel and Hardy. It was hysterical, a funny squabbling. There was one time where they were *actually* getting pissed at each other, and everybody on the set backed away because they're so large.

For the most part, they were constantly squabbling. It was hysterical, but they poked at each other constantly in a funny way. I will never, never forget when they were getting ready for a scene one time. They would pump up their muscles before the scenes so that they would have blood going through them, and they looked bigger. Somebody had their Volkswagen bug parked near the set. One of them walked over to the bumper of the bug, and started bicep-curling the bumper of the car. The car! It was crazy—that's how strong these guys were. They were literally bicep-curling the car.

Wow. Do you remember if this was an easy shoot?

When we were shooting, it was stunning. It was just gorgeous, all the places that we were. We got to shoot in Cinecittà Studios, which is super famous. It's like saying that you shot at Universal. It's a very huge studio lot. That was really cool. We also shot a lot out on location, in these beautiful Italian forests, and waterfalls, and countryside, which I still have never seen again, even though I've been back to Italy a bunch of times.

The director was a nightmare. He was a horrible, horrible little man. He just hated the women on the set. He was so berating and so condescending. He screamed at all of us because he couldn't scream at the boys. I don't know, he had to have been five-foot-four or something. He was this tiny dude, just this raging little Napoleon. He was really horrible to the women on set because we're all scantily clad. He would walk up to you and pinch your side and be like, "You expect me to put *this* on camera?" I was eighteen, without an ounce of fat at that point. He could walk up to me now and do that and I'd be like, "You know what? You're right, dude." He was just shitty.

He would get really frustrated on set because if the twins weren't ready, then they weren't ready. If they didn't feel sufficiently pumped up, or that their muscles looked good enough, you were going to wait until they found a car to bicep-curl. Or, if they were mid-argument with each other, you'd have to wait. It's not like they held up production—they really didn't. It was slower than I'm sure the director wanted it to be, because he was a little raging maniac, anyway, and didn't have patience for anyone. They really did not hold up production, they were just prepping, basically. But, this guy was so tightly strung that if anything was taking *slightly* longer than he wanted it to, then he would literally turn and take it out on everybody else around him, because he couldn't take it out on the twins. He wasn't going to touch them with a ten foot pole.

Visually, it's a very interesting movie. There are some amazing sets, cool action sequences, and neat costumes. Do you have any memories of wearing that armor, or getting to use a bow and arrow?

That was my first time at Cinecittà. I went into this massive costume department. The woman who did the costumes [Francesca Panicali], I thought she was awesome for the budget that she had—which was probably $4. I thought she did a great job.

I remember them building my—I can't say costume*s*, it was *a* costume. My little fur bikini. I thought it was very cool to be fitted for all those weird things.

When you think back on making this movie, are there any particular memories that come to mind?

I just remember being on set in that countryside. You're in some beautiful forest scene and you're like, "Wow. You know what? My job does *not* suck. I really love what I do. I'm riding a horse through a waterfall and into the country." And so many of the people I worked with were wonderful.

I didn't even know until just recently that David [Paul] died, which is heartbreaking. We stayed friends for a really long time after the movie, and then I lost touch with them when I moved to New York to do *All My Children*. [David and Peter] were so close. They did everything together. I can't even imagine Peter's anguish. They literally were inseparable.

Oh my gosh, Richard Lynch. I've never told this story before, but he's passed on now. Richard Lynch had been on the wagon for I don't know how long, who knows. I didn't know him well. He had come to Italy with his much younger girlfriend and they were staying in the same hotel as me. On set, he was in some scenes that were set in a tavern. I guess in Italy, they serve real wine in the tavern scenes. I don't know.

Anyway, he fell way, way, way off the wagon that day, and came back to the hotel and got in a very violent, scary fight with his girlfriend, breaking bottles and holding shards of glass to her throat, the whole crazy nine yards. I get a frantic knock at my hotel room door, screaming and crying outside, "Let me in, let me in. Oh my God, please let me in." I let her in. She tells me this whole story about how he'd come back to the room saying that she'd probably been there screwing guys all day. Drunk, drunk, drunk, and she'd never been with him drunk, because he'd only been sober in the months that they'd been together.

Not ten minutes later, [Richard Lynch] is banging on my door, "If you don't come out, I'm taking this door off the hinges and I'll kill you both." He's screaming outside my door that he's going to kill us both. It's raining outside. It literally feels like a scene out of a movie. It's storming. There's some girl in my room that I don't even know. I met her once on set when she came to visit, said, "Hi. Nice to meet you." I didn't know her. Now I've got her whole entire story and this dude screaming outside, saying he's going to kill us both. I was afraid to call security because I thought, "Oh my God, I have to work with this guy tomorrow. I don't want to cause an international incident." I kept thinking maybe the hotel neighbors would call hotel security. Finally, after half an hour of him sitting at the door and screaming, I finally did call down to security and they made him go away.

The next day on set, he acted like nothing happened. His girlfriend, of course, was on the next plane home. She was *out of there*. I don't know what happened after that. Honestly, all I know was that there were twenty-four hours of some chick I didn't know staying in my room. It was the weirdest, strangest nightmare.

It was just this weird incident that we never spoke of after that, and then when I started to hear the story of Richard Lynch—that he lit himself on fire in protest during the Vietnam War, and that he was a little not-on-the-sane-side to begin with, it all started to make sense, because I hadn't known him from Adam, either. All my scenes were with David and Peter. I didn't really have scenes with him.

That's horrifying, especially considering how young you were at the time. Talk about, "Welcome to the movie business."

Yes, that was my first foray into the movie business and I was like, "Yeesh." There was no internet then, so you couldn't really Google "What's the story with Richard Lynch?" When I told the boys the next day, they were like, "Oh my God. Do you not know why half of his face is melted like that?" I was like, "No, I don't know anything about this guy." They were like, "He set himself on fire. He's nuts."

There are so many actors I've spoken to who have taken every role as an opportunity for growth. Is that true for you? I would love to know if there

was something you learned on *The Barbarians* that you carried with you through *All My Children* or *CSI*, or any of the movies you've done since.

I learned a lot working with that director, and being away from home. Being a kid, really, it was my first time not being protected by parents or anybody. I guess I could have let that director really torpedo my security and my self-worth, but I learned to see it for what it was and go, "Okay. I'm going to do my work, stay in my lane, put up a little invisible buffer around myself and let you do you. I'll do me."

That was a really nice lesson early on. Collaborating in a healthy environment is great, but collaborating in a non-healthy environment is not a safe place to be. You just let them do them, and work hard to not be sucked down into somebody else's unhealthy environment, which is easier said than done sometimes, especially when you're away from your family and your friends. Especially on a feature film, and you're in this little movie bubble.

The twins were awesome. They were always upbeat. They were always positive. They were always in a good mood, except for sometimes with each other. They were just like a big, bright light. They really were. I loved working with them. I became their little sidekick. They were awesome, and they made the shoot really fun.

Interview: Actor Michael Berryman

With one of the most recognizable faces in genre filmmaking, Michael Berryman has built a screen career more than one hundred credits strong. The son of a US Naval neurosurgeon who worked in the Hiroshima fallout zone in the wake of the atomic bombing, Berryman was born with a rare condition that gave him his distinctive features—and left him without hair, nails, or the ability to produce sweat normally.

A chance encounter sparked his long career in the movies, which at time of this publication has stretched almost fifty years. His role as the slaver known as The Dirtmaster in *The Barbarians* (1986) was his only appearance in a Cannon production, but Berryman can be seen in countless other fantasy, sci-fi, and horror films. Some of his best-known credits include *One Flew*

Over the Cuckoo's Nest (1975), Wes Craven's *The Hills Have Eyes* (1977), *Weird Science* (1985), and *The Devil's Rejects* (2005).

Michael Berryman as The Dirtmaster in *The Barbarians*.

You have over one hundred screen credits, but it wasn't your initial goal to be an actor. I know part of your getting into the business is owed to George Pal, the great science fiction producer. What can you tell me about how you started out?

Michael Berryman: Before I met George, I had gone to the University of California. I was there for about five years, putting myself through college until I ran out of money. I wanted to be a veterinarian, so I had taken a few vet courses for the first year. My second year, I started to realize that the ends of my fingers, because of the birth defects, the dexterity was not present for me to be able to perform procedures on animals, even though I had the desire to do so. I had to go in another direction.

I worked at restaurants. I worked for a bail bondsman for extra money, picking up people to show up to court. A lot of odd jobs: I was a butcher, I was a taxi driver, you name it. I just struggled through until 1972, and it was time to regroup, so I went back to Santa Monica, my hometown. I shared an apartment with a friend. I had no idea what I was going to do

714

for a living. I have heat issues, so I lost a lot of work whenever I got warm. I really was at a quandary. My goal was to fill out paperwork and homestead in Alaska. It's a cooler climate, it would serve my needs better as far as my health, and I always loved nature and the woods. I bought a four-wheel-drive truck and got it all prepared to drive all the way to Alaska and do the paperwork.

In the meantime, in Venice Beach, California, there was a little house built in 1930-something. A friend of mine said, "Hey, look. I'm renting this place for a few hundred bucks a month. I have house plants. I let the local residents come by and they'll buy a plant here and there. The local artist put stuff up on consignment." It was cute, artsy-fartsy, kinda hippie, and just delightful. I said, "All right. I'll chip in a couple hundred bucks, and let's be partners. See if we can make a go of it."

After about four or five months, we weren't really making much money there. Across the street was a very well-established antique store. They sold antiquities—I'm talking Ming Dynasty, very pricey stuff. They were a very nice couple that ran it, a husband and wife. They told us one day that they were going to have an invitation-only sale, basically for millionaires. They were the only people that could afford these incredible items. They said, "If you don't mind, could you bring over all of the largest, most beautiful plants, whatever beautiful plants you have, and just distribute them around the room and make it look homey? Then we'll buy them all."

They ordered nice catering and really good wine. We called up a lot of our artist friends, and we all dressed up as fancy as we could. We were just going to hang out and enjoy the evening. That was the plan. We're just mingling around. Pretty soon, the wife of the owner of the store introduced me to her father, who happened to be George Pal.

Now, George looks at me, and he takes his left and right hands, angles his thumbs and pointer fingers, and makes a frame, and puts it up in front of his face. He goes, "You've got the face that I need for my movie. Are you an actor?" I go, "No, no, no. I'm not an actor." He introduced himself, and then I said, "Wow. Do you know who you are? You created *War of the Worlds* (1953) and *The Time Machine* (1960)."

He says, "Yes. I did, but I'm doing a movie called *Doc Savage* (1975)." I go, "Oh, I read those books." He goes, "Yes. I'm going to do as many as I can, starting with the first one. I want you to play the coroner of Hidalgo, Juan Lopez Morales." I go, "Sure. I think I can do that, but I am going to go homestead in a couple of weeks, so when are you going to do this?" He says, "About a couple weeks from now, we'll call you."

We shot the scenes out. Everybody was wonderful to work with. Everyone was great. I figured, "Well, that was the quickest film career anyone ever had." Then I just forgot about that. Anyways, the check came in the mail. I still didn't make anything of it, though—I still planned to go north and homestead, and be in a beautiful forest country.

The next phone call was for *Cuckoo's Nest*, ironically, because George had a casting director that happened to be casting for it.

You spent four months on *One Flew Over the Cuckoo's Nest*. That had to have been an incredible learning experience, being only your second film. What lessons did you take away from working on such an acclaimed production?

Like I said, I had no intention of trying to draw attention to myself. Growing up as a kid with a visual difference, being abused and dealing with bullies, I had hell of a temper. I had no patience for mean behavior or anything like that.

I was contacted by Fantasy Films and they said, "We'd like to meet you at Culver Studios." That was Saul Zaentz, Milos Forman, Michael Douglas, and some of the members of the production staff. I go there and I meet them, and they're great. I said, "What project are you doing?" "We're doing *Cuckoo's Nest*." I said, "Oh, wow," because I had seen the play, I read the book, I was familiar. When Michael Douglas told me that Jack [Nicholson] was going to play McMurphy, that created some interest to me.

I had no lines. It was just because I happened to have some scars from my skull surgery as a child. I told them about my father being a neurologist and brain surgeon in Hiroshima, and because of the bomb he came home radiated, and that's why I had birth defects. They said, "Well, you have the look. We'll put some lobotomy scars on you and we'll have a good time. We'll see you in the asylum."

You've said you weren't comfortable being cast for your looks. At what point did acting go from being something you were willing to do, to something you realized you had a talent for, were good at, and could turn into a career?

I didn't want to be on the screen forever. To me, it was a way to survive, make some money, pay some bills. I did have a minor in college in art history. I loved film and good storytelling, and used to read a lot of novels. It became apparent to me quite early in the production of *Cuckoo's Nest* that, number one, if you're going to be cast in a project, you have to have the right look, and then they look to see if you have the chops, if you have the ability and the talent.

Milos Forman turned me onto a book on cinematography. I said, "Hey, I know about storytelling, art, art history, what skills do I need to understand filmmaking?" because I was watching how they would do a master shot, then they'd cut in and do reversals, and then POVs and close-ups. At first, I said, "They already shot that. Why are they repeating them over and over again?" He let me look through the lens of the Panavision camera. I fell in love with the process of photography. That became a skillset that I was intrigued with. Even on my days off, I was on the set learning and asking. I drove people nuts.

I got $750 a week—it was a six-day, probably 80-hour week. I got paid to go to film school.

Your path crossed with Cannon's in the mid-1980s, in a movie called *The Barbarians*. What do you remember about getting involved with that project?

The Barbarians was just a lot of fun. I got to work with my dear friend, Richard Lynch. David and Peter Paul were charming to a point, but between the steroids and the raging, and the childish behavior, it sometimes got ridiculous. They were huge, they were fun, but it got out of hand on occasion.

I remember one day, we were on the set. We were sharing a motor home together, me and them. They would want to pump iron between every take. Ruggero finally got fed up with it. He goes, sarcastically, "Pump up, pump up. My God, you're fucking huge. What is wrong with you?" Then one day, they lost it. They completely lost it. I forget which one it was. They were upset about something, I forget what. I was tired, so I went into the big motor home that we shared and I noticed that there were syringes on the rug. They just threw them on the floor, and I almost stepped on one.

These guys were gigantic bodybuilders. It's a shame, because that stuff will kill you. I knew Lyle Alzado. I've known people that used steroids, and it can kill your kidneys. It makes all of your muscles grow, including your heart. Pretty soon your heart is compromised, it's gotten too big in the cardiac area. I see people have amputations because of that stuff. It's not a healthy lifestyle.

What happened was, David or Peter, I forget which one it was, was upset about something, and I heard him screaming. Now, we had the press corps from all over the world, Europe and other countries, there on the shoot. It's a Cannon production, in broad daylight, in public, with probably about one hundred people there. He starts *screaming*. They were so mad about something petty. He basically said, "I think I'll just kill everybody with my bare hands, I'm so upset." Now, I figure, "Wow, we need to do something or these guys are going to go to jail." I run outside and I grab each of them by the earlobe, and I yelled at them. I went, "You left your syringes on the carpet after you shot up your steroids, and I almost stepped on one. I am so pissed off! You march back in there and pick them up."

These guys are gigantic. Between the two of them, they're like 500 pounds. I was in good shape myself, but still, the point was I was upset with what they did, but also what they were saying. They were making a scene, and it was an embarrassment to the other actors. We were supposed to look out for one another. It calmed them down right away. I said, "You march back in there right now and clean that stuff up, but before you do that, you turn around so that everybody present hears what you say, and you apologize."

They did it. They just had a moment of rage—that stuff will do that to you. They both grabbed me from under the elbow and carried me back to the motor home so I could watch them tidy up their mess. [*Laughs*] It was one of those days where they took too many steroids and had a rage moment. It will do that. It wasn't personal, it was science.

The rest of the shoot was just wonderful. The dragon was remarkable. I got to ride one of the horses. Those horses were the descendants of horses from *Ben-Hur* (1959). I spoke to the trainer, and I said, "I can ride. I'm from California." I watched him so much, to see how he communicated with his babies. He put me on a horse, and he said, "No cowboy," and I go, "Okay." That means nothing on the bit, light on the reins. I said, "Is it pressure on the knees and legs?" and he goes, "Yes."

He scrunches his hands together in front of me and he says, "You are a sack of potatoes. I squish you, you go up. I move my hands, you settle down." I go, "I know exactly what you're talking about." I did exactly what he asked. The horse just said, "Okay, now we're in sync." I hardly touched the reins at all. It's just a little bit of leg pressure, a little bit of body movement, and the horse would run like a Cadillac.

Ruggero and his production staff, it's always a lot of fun to work with them. They're classy. *The Barbarians* is a great fantasy. The artistic talent of the Italians and Ruggero's people, specifically, is quite remarkable. For instance, in another Ruggero film [*Cut and Run*, 1985], I get shot in the hand. If we were in the States, it would take an hour to dress the hand wound. This guy did it on my hand with spirit gum, latex, Kleenex, snip, snip, open it up, dress the hole. He had it done in five minutes, and it looked really good. They have shooting solutions for scenes and situations. They get the shots, they get the day's work done, and they fly right through it, and the directors and producers are happy. And, we always got to go to some exotic location.

Richard Lynch was one of the great villain actors of that era. I've talked to people who've described him as intense, but you said he was your friend. What was he like?

Richard was extremely humane, intense, and intelligent. Richard Lynch was a dear friend. You do know how he became burned, is that correct?

I know he set himself on fire as a war protest.

He was on acid at the time, but he did it to protest the war. He said, "I give up my body as my forgiveness for what my country is doing in Southeast Asia." That's an incredible human being.

When we were in Guyana [filming *Cut and Run*] with Ruggero, Richard played the sinister character. We were at the hotel, and Richard had this look on his face at the bar. I said, "Where are you going, Richard?" He goes, "Well, I've got Saturday and Sunday off. If I'm not back at work on Monday, tell everyone I love them." I said, "I know that look. You're going on an adventure. What are you going to do?" He said he found The Dutchman, which would be Josef Mengele, but I don't know if it was him or one of his cohorts. He had a guide to take him up the Orinoco River to a camp where these ex-Nazis were still hanging out. He hung out with them and did a character study, because his character was very evil. That's Richard Lynch for you.

We had a shot of some really good scotch. We did a salute, took a shot, and off he went. Sunday night, there he is, around nine o'clock at night. He had a look like he had been on an adventure. I was sitting next to him at the bar of a beautiful hotel. The bartender says, "What do you want?" He says, "Half a shot of whatever he's drinking." I take a sip and Richard Lynch—he doesn't even look at me. He knows I'm sitting next to him. He takes a sip of his drink and goes, "He could have had me killed at any moment." I said, "Okay, well, that didn't happen, so how'd it play out? What did you do?" He said, "Well, I found him and he had his guards everywhere. We stayed up all night long and drank rum and talked about the human condition." [*Laughs*] Now, there's a story for you!

The U.K. video sleeve for *The Barbarians*.

An early ad for the obscure *Too Much*, initially intended as part of the
Cannon Movie Tales line but released independently of those.

Too Much: The Robot with a Heart

Release Date: June 1987 (VHS)
Directed by: Eric Rochat
Written by: Eric Rochat & Joan Laine
Starring: Bridgette Andersen, Morikiyo Bowhay
Tagline: "Little did Susie realize she would be embarking on the journey of a lifetime when she accompanied her parents to Japan!"

Runaway robots were a running theme throughout the 1980s, with films ranging from *Heartbeeps* (1981) to *Runaway* (1984) to *Short Circuit* (1986) and even *RoboCop* (1987) all dealing in renegade androids who discover some higher function beyond their programming. Heck, you might even toss *Blade Runner* (1982) into that category. The funny thing about this niche subgenre of cinematic science fiction was that its entries were almost evenly split between dark, violent movies aimed at adults, and sugary-sweet kiddie fare. Cannon took the latter route with their own bolting 'bot flick, dropping a popular child actress into the middle of a Japan-set robo-caper with the delightfully saccharine title *Too Much: The Robot with a Heart* (1987).

This being Cannon, their approach to this formulaic kids' movie was of course atypical—namely, in that it was written and directed by Eric Rochat, a filmmaker and producer best-known for his work in erotic films. Rochat had most famously produced the X-rated *The Story of O* (1975), starring Corinne Clery and Udo Kier and directed by future *Lady Chatterley's Lover* (1981) helmer Just Jaeckin. (The film was banned in many European countries upon its release.) Rochat later directed *The Story of O 2* (1984) himself. Other productions to his name included the documentary *Sex O'Clock U.S.A.* (1976) and Alejandro Jodorowsky's lesser-known film *Tusk* (1980). Despite having only previously directed a poorly-received porn sequel, Cannon went ahead and greenlit his children's robot adventure.

It's worth noting, though, that *Too Much: The Robot with a Heart* was actually shot in Japan. When you consider how many ninja movies Cannon filmed in the Philippines, South Africa, or Utah, it's surprising to see something Japanese-themed that was shot on location in the Land of the Rising Sun. The movie also features several upbeat pop songs written by Coby Recht and George S. Clinton, two of the musical minds behind Cannon's *The Apple* (1980), and robots designed by Studio Nue, a Japanese company behind several famous anime series, including the long-lasting *Macross* franchise.

Perhaps what's most surprising about the film is how often it places its young heroine in extreme danger. Onto the movie, shall we?

Little Suzie (ten-year-old Bridgette Andersen) travels along on an extended business trip to Japan with her parents. She finds herself bored at the Tokyo home of her dad's business associate, Dr. Tetsuro (Hiroyuki Watanabe), until she stumbles across a few of his robot appliances—a breakfast-making machine straight out of *Pee-wee's Big Adventure* (1985) and a prototype Roomba—and discovers his laboratory. The brilliant scientist sympathizes with her loneliness, and shares with her his secret plans for the most advanced robot he's ever built: one capable of learning and evolving, and being a child's best friend. Dr. Tetsuro's dream is that one day every child in the world will have one of his robots as a companion.

724

The next morning, a squat robot that looks like R2-D2 with Shop Vac tubes fixed to its shoulders rolls up on Suzie's doorstep. When it presents her with a Polaroid photo of a flower arrangement, the little girl comments, "Oh, you're too much." Her new, metal friend mistakes that statement for her giving it a name, and so "Too Much"—or "T.M." for short—is henceforth what it's known as.

Over the following months the robot is a constant companion, playing hide and seek, helping her reach cookie jars on high shelves, translating Japanese cartoons, and letting her win at Pong. T.M. becomes Suzie's best friend, but there's trouble on the horizon in the form of a rival scientist, the evil Dr. Finkel (Char Fontana), who wants to steal Dr. Tetsuro's invention so that he can use its technology in his own line of robots. He sends his slapstick, perpetually lollipop-sucking lackey Bernie—played by an actor credited only as "Uganda"—to spy on the little girl and her robot pal.

Suzie (Bridgette Andersen) embraces her robot pal "T.M." in *Too Much.*

The real trouble starts when it comes time for Suzie to go home to the United States. She doesn't realize until the last minute that T.M. won't be accompanying her. Heartbroken, she bolts from her parents at the airport. She manages to evade police by hiding behind some trash barrels near the runway, and calls T.M. to rescue her on her wristwatch communicator. While

T.M.'s primary mode of transportation is rolling along on his treads at around three miles per hour, he wastes no time getting to Suzie by latching himself on to the back of a car like he's a skateboarding Marty McFly in *Back to the Future* (1985). T.M. tries to return Suzie to her parents, but gets spooked when the airport cops shine spotlights on them. *This* is where the adventure begins.

T.M. takes off with Suzie in tow, fleeing into oncoming highway traffic. This scene is actually way more terrifying than you'd expect to get from the gently-paced, G-rated kids' movie that came before it. As T.M. slowly pushes Suzie on a luggage cart, automobiles swerve left and right to avoid plowing through them, leading to high-speed crashes, multi-car pile-ups, and presumably several deaths and grievous injuries.

Our intrepid heroine and her robo-buddy not only make it out of there alive, but they've somehow traveled *sixty-two miles* outside of Tokyo by the next morning. (This is downright amazing, considering that Too Much moves at about the speed of a lawnmower.) They manage to survive on milk—milking a cow is part of T.M.'s programming—and soda pop. Police finally spot the pair outside a gas station, but when Suzie slips free of one of the cops, he *opens fire* on the little girl and her sentient garbage bin, accidentally hitting a gas pump and blowing up the entire fuel depot in a big, fiery explosion. Golly! At least Suzie and T.M. are okay.

Early on in their misadventures the two are joined by a young, Japanese boy named Mata (Morikiyo Bowhay), who is able to help them navigate the area. The three steal a jeep to make a quicker getaway, leading the police on a highway chase which, of course, ends with the cop car flipping and nearly killing its driver. The whole time they're on the run we're given periodic updates on the national manhunt for the missing girl and her robot friend via radio news reports. The broadcasts also detail the rise of a mysterious-sounding "Children's Movement," in which the youth of Japan are rallying around Suzie and T.M.'s story and rising up to make a stand against adults who want to "suppress their free spirits." Are you wondering where this is going . . . ? It's impossible to guess.

Dr. Finkel and his goons manage to do what the entirety of the Tokyo police cannot, and catch up with the trio multiple times. At one point, Dr. Finkel attempts to cut open T.M.'s head to take a look at the hardware inside, using a can opener while poor T.M. screams in pain. (What possible, screwed-up reason did Tetsuro have to program his robot to feel physical pain?) They escape again and again, eventually holing up inside a shopping mall that happens to be hosting a robotics convention. This is where the police finally surround our errant heroes, triggering a final showdown.

The morning begins with riot police surrounding the shopping center, attracting a crowd of gawkers that includes Suzie's parents, Dr. Tetsuro, and Finkel and his henchmen. Suddenly a flash mob made up of tiny children in matching, brightly-colored outfits breaks through the line of riot shields and cop cars, waving banners and shouting their support for the runaways to the tune of an upbeat song called "We Are for Too Much." One little girl slaps an "I Love T.M." sticker onto the police captain's lapel; others rush the flagpole to hoist their own, newly-designed pro-robot flag.

Suzie and Mata lead a violent robot uprising in the Cannon children's feature *Too Much: The Robot with a Heart.*

Amidst the chaos, the front doors of the mall open and out pours a small army of consumer robots, remote controlled-toys, and even an animatronic band like you'd see at a Chuck E. Cheese restaurant. They're followed by Suzie, T.M., and Mata, who are met with cheers from the pint-sized crowd. The police make their advance, using cattle prods to electrocute the toy robots blocking their paths. (Some of the toys were rigged with explosives, making each one's "death" appear excessively graphic.)

Now here's the most messed-up part: Mata orders the robots to charge, leading them to start *shooting at* the police. These clearly aren't fatal bullets being fired from their teeny-tiny guns, but you still see police officers diving away from explosions—and you probably never guessed that a movie called *Too Much: The Robot with a Heart* was going to end with a large-scale police shootout. The evil Dr. Finkel enters the fray and gets close enough to T.M. to attempt to permanently decommission him with a cattle prod, but our robot hero reverses the charge and fries the mean scientist with his own electrical shock. The movie ends with Dr. Finkel being trampled beneath the mob of children, who rush to greet their heroes, and T.M. shouting "We did it, Suzie!" Just *what* they're so happy to have achieved isn't entirely clear. Killing Dr. Finkel? Surviving a firefight with Tokyo riot police? Inspiring a youth uprising? All of the above?

Too Much is perhaps one of the most mysterious entries in the entire Cannon filmography. Yes, it's obscure, with only a few 35mm prints known to exist alongside several international VHS releases, but it's not the least-known movie to be covered in these volumes. (Those who fondly remember *Too Much* tend to have seen it on cable in the late 1980s.) Rather, it is mysterious because of how seemingly little there is to be learned about it. No contemporary reviews of the movie can be found, nor articles about its creation. Most of the actors involved with the film barely worked again, if at all, or have long since passed away.

The most tragic passing of them all is, of course, that of the movie's child star, Bridgette Anderson. A child prodigy who told her parents she wanted to be an actress at the age of two, she made numerous appearances in TV shows and commercials before making her big screen debut in the cult movie *Savannah Smiles* (1982), playing a six-year-old girl who runs away from her parents and befriends a pair of on-the-lam convicts. Following her success there, Anderson kept busy for the next five years acting in movies such as *Fever Pitch* (1985) and *The Parent Trap II* (1986), and making many, many television cameos, from episodes of *Fantasy Island* (1977–1984) to *The Golden Girls* (1985–1992). She was also a popular interview subject, delighting newspaper reporters and Johnny Carson alike with her adorable, quick wit. In her lone appearance on the *Tonight Show* couch, she detailed for Carson her future plans to produce, direct, and star in her own movies when she grew up.

Sadly, *Too Much* wound up being her final released film. Anderson reportedly had trouble landing work as she entered her teen years, a period in which she also began a troublesome relationship with drugs. The former child actress died of a heroin overdose at her apartment in Santa Monica at the heartbreakingly young age of twenty-one.

Superman IV on videocassette. Artwork by Daniel Goozee.

Superman IV: The Quest for Peace

Release Date: July 24, 1987
Directed by: Sidney J. Furie
Written by: Lawrence Konner, Mark Rosenthal, & Christopher Reeve
Starring: Christopher Reeve, Gene Hackman, Margot Kidder, Mariel Hemingway, Mark Pillow, Jon Cryer
Trailer Voiceover: "The countdown has begun. The world is on the brink, and only one man can save us now . . . *Superman IV*: his greatest adventure!"

Look, up in the sky! It's a bird! It's a plane! It's . . . it's . . . it's . . . a poorly-photographed Christopher Reeve suspended from a visible harness somewhere in suburban London.

Sigh.

Let's talk about *Superman IV*.

Since Christopher Reeve made his debut as the definitive Man of Steel in Richard Donner's original *Superman* (1978), the franchise had been nothing less than a box office juggernaut. The first film was the largest-grossing movie of 1978, bringing in more than $300 million worldwide. Its sequel, *Superman II* (1980), broke records for single-day earnings on its way to an admirable $190 million across the globe. When the more campy *Superman III* (1983) stumbled into theaters, it brought home *just* $100 million, which is only an unattractive amount of money when you're speaking in blockbuster terms. Still, the disappointment led the movie's star and the series' producers, Alexander and Ilya Salkind, to assume the public's interest in Superman had waned, and that the franchise was on its way out. The critics largely agreed, widely accusing the third movie of recycling ideas and being over-reliant on slapstick gags.

Oh, they had *no idea* how much worse it could get.

While *Superman III* had been considered a financial let-down for its producers and studio, that $100 million disappointment made more than double what Cannon's most successful film of all time—*Breakin'* (1984)— had brought home. Once it was known that the film rights for the classic DC Comics hero might be up for grabs, Cannon got down to business and acquired them from the Salkinds for $5 million in June of 1985. (This was around the same time they snapped up the rights to Spider-Man and Captain America from Marvel, and made their He-Man deal with Mattel; Cannon clearly had their sights set on big-name pop culture properties.) Before they could jump into a fourth Superman movie, however, there was one problem they needed to work through first: Superman himself, Christopher Reeve, had announced that he would never play the role again.

In the years after *Superman III*, Reeve was quite vocal about his self-imposed retirement from the superhero world, telling interviewers that the movies had run their course, and that any attempts to continue the story would lead to rehashes and pale imitations of the prior films. In his mid-thirties and feeling like he was physically aging out of the role, Reeve even bowed out of his plan to make a cameo in the spinoff movie *Supergirl* (1984).

Although Reeve felt like he was finished playing Superman, others had a hard time seeing him in any other part. This is detailed more in this volume's chapter on *Street Smart* (1987), but like many other stars of incredibly successful movie franchises, Reeve found himself being typecast and had a hard time landing non-Kryptonian roles. Trained at Juilliard, Reeve identified as a serious, New York stage actor, which is something you're bound to be pulled away from when you star in a trio of big-budget, Hollywood blockbusters. In between Superman films, he tried a handful of dramatic movie roles. It largely turned out that if he wasn't wearing a cape, no one went to see them.

Reeve was desperate for a role that would make film critics and audiences take him seriously, and he thought he'd found it—in a reporter *not* named Clark Kent, in a script titled *Street Smart* (1987). As part of their bid to lure Reeve out of Super-retirement, Golan and Globus agreed to finance the actor's pet project, which wound up actually being a pretty darn good dramatic thriller, and made a movie star out of Morgan Freeman at fifty years old. (Again—you can read about that film in its own chapter.)

The second piece of Cannon's bid to woo Reeve back into his blue tights was to offer him a role behind the camera that was as big as the one he played in front of it. This included the promise to not only let him direct some of the second unit photography, but to come up with a story for the sequel. It was just the sort of offer Reeve needed to revive his enthusiasm for the Man of Tomorrow.

Reeve claimed his inspiration for *Superman IV*'s premise came on a sad day in August of 1985. The actor had been recording narration for a documentary when he learned that thirteen-year-old Samantha Small had been killed in an airplane crash in Auburn, Maine. Small had been a Cold War-era celebrity in both the United States and the Soviet Union. The precocious schoolgirl had three years earlier written an earnest letter to Soviet leader Yuri Andropov, asking whether or not he wanted there to be a nuclear war with the U.S., and pleading with him to prevent it. Her letter was published in a leading Soviet newspaper, and received a public response from Andropov. This kicked off a media flurry in both nations, as Small was interviewed on American talk programs and invited to tour Russia, eventually becoming something of a goodwill ambassador and authoring a book on her travels behind the Iron Curtain. Tragedy arose when a commuter plane carrying her and her father struck trees and crashed, killing everyone on board. Condolences arrived from far and wide, including comforting words from both Ronald Reagan and Mikhail Gorbachev.

Reeve, thirty-four years old at the time of filming *Superman IV*, wore a hairpiece to better match the Man of Steel's boyish hairline.

If you're already familiar with *Superman IV: The Quest for Peace*, then you can see how inspiration was drawn from Small's story. Much of the film's plot revolves around a letter written to Superman, care of the Daily Planet, from a concerned schoolboy, asking the Last Son of Krypton to do something to end the nuclear arms race. Convinced by this plea from an innocent child, Supes abandons his vow not to interfere in the follies of man, and promises in front of the United Nations to rid the planet of nukes once and for all. He does so, and pretty easily, it seems, by collecting all of Earth's missiles in a giant, netted bag orbiting the planet, then flinging it into the Sun. (A Cannon character hadn't thrown this much stuff into space since 1983's *Hercules*.) Of course that wouldn't be the end of mankind's troubles—or Superman's, for that matter.

To help transfer his idea to the page, Cannon brought in screenwriters Lawrence Konner and Mark Rosenthal—the duo responsible for *The Legend of Billie Jean* (1985) and *The Jewel of the Nile* (1985)—to take on screenplay duties.

Obviously, Superman's sequel rights falling into the hands of a company with Cannon's track record came with many trepidations, but there were also reasons for fans to be hopeful—at least early on. Not only would Christopher Reeve be returning to Metropolis, but so would two fan-favorite characters who'd been notably absent from the previous sequel: Gene Hackman as nemesis Lex Luthor, and Margot Kidder as love interest/sidekick Lois Lane.

Neither needs much introduction for movie fans, so we'll do this quickly. By this point in his career, 57-year-old Hackman had won an Oscar for his lead role as "Popeye" Doyle in the classic thriller *The French Connection* (1971), and been nominated twice more for supporting turns in *Bonnie and Clyde* (1967) and *I Never Sang for My Father* (1970). (He'd go on to win another statuette for 1992's *The Unforgiven*, following yet another nomination for 1988's *Mississippi Burning*.) After Marlon Brando, Gene Hackman's was the most prestigious name to appear in the credits of the original *Superman* film, and his performance as the Man of Steel's villainous foil was praised by both critics and fans. After the series' original director, Richard Donner, was unceremoniously fired from the second film, Hackman refused to act in the sequels in protest.

Canadian actress Margot Kidder also returned as Superman's long-suffering co-worker and love interest, Lois Lane, who somehow never recognized him when he put on glasses and became Clark Kent. Something of a scream queen in the early part of her career, Kidder spent the Seventies starring in horror films such as Brian De Palma's *Sisters* (1972), *Black Christmas* (1974), and *The Amityville Horror* (1979), mixed in with more mainstream fare, such as playing Robert Redford's love interest in *The Great Waldo Pepper* (1974). She'd become most closely associated with her character in the Superman movies, although her role in the third movie comprised only a few minutes' worth of screen time. (Her reduced role was rumored to have been because of her outspoken criticism of the movies' original producers.) Like Hackman, once the Salkinds were out of the picture, Kidder was presumably more eager to return.

Also among the returning faces: former child star Jackie Cooper as *The Daily Planet* editor Perry White—he'd appear in Cannon's *Surrender* (1987) this same year—and Superman's pal, Jimmy Olsen, played by Marc McClure, who played Marty's older (disappearing) brother in *Back to the Future* (1985).

Superman IV: The Quest for Peace hit a number of snags before Cannon could even send their newly-acquired superhero sequel into production. The biggest issue for everyone involved—and which can be most clearly felt on-screen—is the movie's budget, or lack thereof. The movie was initially announced by the studio with a budgetary figure hovering around $30 million, which would have made it Cannon's most expensive film ever. As the movie moved closer to its shooting date, that number decreased, and Cannon's financial woes piled up. By the time shooting started, that figure was nearly cut in half.

Cannon's money problems are chronicled throughout this book—and probably explained in the greatest detail in this volume's chapter on *Three Kinds of Heat* (1987)—but are more visible in *Superman IV* than any other movie. Golan and Globus had just blown $270 million buying Thorn EMI, an entertainment company whose holdings included a large back catalog of films, a chain of more than one hundred English movie theaters, and the legendary production facilities known as Elstree Studios. This massive production lot was where they filmed the first three *Star Wars* movies, *The Shining* (1980), *Raiders of the Lost Ark* (1981), and even Cannon's *Lifeforce* (1985)—and where much of *Superman IV* would be shot. The lines of credit used for this gigantic purchase had been earmarked for Cannon's upcoming production slate. When their increasingly expensive movies failed to turn profits, Cannon suddenly found themselves over $100 million in debt. This meant that corners needed to be cut: the biggest slices, arguably, came out of *Superman IV*'s budget.

For perspective, at $55 million, the first *Superman* film was the most expensive movie ever made when it came out in 1978. The next two sequels cost $54 and $39 million, respectively. Cannon was going to try to match the spectacle of the three prior movies, but spend less than $17 million doing it. That's like trying to buy a Lamborghini with a bucket of nickels and an expired coupon for puppy chow.

Reeve understandably became upset when Cannon informed him they didn't have the money to promote his low-budget pet project, *Street Smart*. If they didn't have the money to advertise a small film in a few markets, how the heck were they going to find the funds to shoot the *Superman IV* script as it had been written? But contracts had been signed, and the movie already had too much momentum to stop.

Likely knowing full well that it would prove near-impossible to pull off the most essential Superman effects on a shoestring budget, much of the lauded SFX team who were meant to carry over from the previous films instead handed in their notice. Left to do the heavy lifting was visual effects supervisor Harrison Ellenshaw, who'd worked on *TRON* (1982) and the Star Wars movies, and had his work cut out for him trying to pull off a script that called for more than 300 FX shots with very little money to work with.

It wasn't only the effects budget that visibly suffered, but the travel budget. Although the movie's script takes place in Metropolis, Smallville, New York City, Moscow, China, and outer space, Cannon couldn't afford to fly their cast and crew to different locations. It's a little ironic that because they spent all their money buying Elstree Studios, they had no choice but to shoot the movie almost entirely there and in various suburbs within an hour's drive of London.

Standing in for New York and Metropolis was the British "new town" of Milton Keynes, built largely in the late '60s and early 1970s. Although the city's concrete and glass structures weren't a bad stand-in for the fictional burg of Metropolis, trying to make suburban Great Britain pass for New York City was near-impossible: there were too many single-story buildings and wide open spaces. (It didn't help that the script and set designers treated Metropolis and New York as if they were interchangeable, making it hard to tell which city the characters are meant to be in at any given time.) Standing in for the front steps of the iconic United Nations building? A nondescript English parking lot.

Cannon initially approached Richard Donner to return and direct the film, who declined—he'd just wrapped *The Goonies* and *Ladyhawke* (both 1985), and was preparing to shoot *Lethal Weapon* (1987), and was clearly out of Cannon's league by this point. Part of Reeve's deal included his approval over the film's director—his first choice was Ron Howard, who had just released *Cocoon* (1985), but wasn't available to take on the project. When that didn't work out, the producers went outside the box and approached Wes Craven to direct the film. The horror maven, known for grimy, gory features like *The Last House on the Left* (1972) and *The Hills Have Eyes* (1977), had just come off a genuine box office smash with *A Nightmare on Elm Street* (1984). He already had a comic book adaptation under his belt as well, with *Swamp Thing* (1982). The director failed to hit it off with Reeve, unfortunately, and was removed from the project before he could even get started.

Finally, Cannon did what they had many times before and turned to an old, industry veteran. Director Sidney J. Furie's credits stretched back to the 1950s, and included the Michael Caine spy thriller *The Ipcress File* (1965), the Marlon Brando western *The Appaloosa* (1966), and the more recent military action movie *Iron Eagle* (1986).

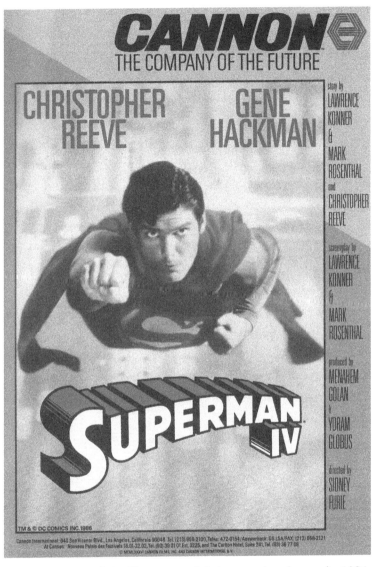

Cannon advertised the film as part of their upcoming slate at the 1986 Cannes Film Festival.

After an admittedly exciting opening in which The Big Blue Boy Scout saves a crew of Soviet Cosmonauts from a space station mishap, *Superman IV* starts with Clark Kent returning to his boyhood home of Smallville.

While there, he turns down offers to sell the family farm, and grabs a Chekov's gun in the form of a Kryptonian energy module—which the *Chicago Tribune* described as a "radioactive lime popsicle." Although the Kent Farm buildings from the first movie were still standing in Canada at the time the film was shot, it was cheaper for Cannon to build a reproduction facade outside of London than fly cast and crew members to rural Alberta.

It's revealed that Lex Luthor, America's most villainous businessman, has been working on a prison chain gang since Superman last foiled his nefarious plans. He's rescued by his punkish nephew, Lenny Luthor, played by *Pretty in Pink*'s (1986) lovelorn Duckie, Jon Cryer.

Lenny Luthor is probably the movie's most divisive character, but the filmmakers felt they needed to add younger characters so that kids would still be able to connect with a franchise that now starred a bunch of middle-aged actors. His relationship with Lex—whom he apparently idolizes—is a little weird, to say the least. Does he live with his uncle? Where are his parents? (Their relationship appears similar to the one that Scrooge McDuck had with Huey, Dewey, and Louie.) This movie came out the same year Cryer appeared in Penelope Spheeris' underrated *Dudes* (1987). For a time he'd become the second-highest paid actor on television, while starring opposite Charlie Sheen (and later Ashton Kutcher) on the CBS sitcom *Two and a Half Men* (2003–2015). He would graduate up to playing his on-screen uncle, Lex Luthor, in the CW television incarnation of *Supergirl* that debuted in 2015.

With his limitless funds and staggering brilliance, the best plan Luthor can come up with is to create an evil clone of Superman, which is easier to do than most would think. They steal a strand of Superman's hair from a museum exhibit and cook it up in a steaming vat of chemicals in Lex's apartment atop the Empire State Building. The Luthors' art deco penthouse is half playboy millionaire bachelor pad, half Frankenstein's laboratory—and was built inside the soundstage that housed the Millennium Falcon during the shooting of *The Empire Strikes Back* (1980). Why aren't the police or media covering the world's most notorious criminal's escape from prison? Who knows? In a few days' time, Luthor and Luthor have a super-powered embryo in need of one finishing touch: the radiation of the sun. Fortunately they know a guy in a cape and tights who's been spending a lot of time chucking stuff into it.

A contender for the most '80s image of all time: Jon Cryer as Lenny Luthor posing with a Nintendo Zapper in a publicity shot from *Superman IV*.

While Clark Kent has been busy dealing with the new management at his newspaper, *The Daily Planet*, which is rapidly turning it into a sleazy supermarket tabloid, Superman is busy gathering up the world's nukes and bringing the Cold War to an abrupt end. What he didn't expect was for one of the missiles he threw into the sun to have his wicked, fetus clone stuck to the side of it. Once it's enveloped by the sun's rays, it grows into a ripped, full-sized dude with a black cape and blonde mullet. His name is Nuclear Man, and he's played by former Chippendales dancer Mark Pillow.

The chiseled, first-time actor was represented by the agency where Sidney J. Furie's son worked, who passed his headshots along to his father. The look of the character—Pillow wore his costume to the Royal Command Performance gala of the film, where he was seated with Princess Diana and Prince Charles—was meant to include a radioactive glowing effect designed by makeup artist Stuart Freeborn, but that idea was dropped when the budget was cut. For inexplicable reasons, Nuclear Man speaks with Lex Luthor's voice, and Pillow was forced to lip-synch to Hackman's recorded dialogue.

Lex Luthor orders his new Nuke Boy to kill Superman, but instead the custom-built Man of Atom just flies around being a pain in Superman's Kryptonian ass. He smashes up the Great Wall of China, which Superman rebuilds with his Super Rebuild-o-Ray, a new power that was specifically dreamed up for this movie. It had been intended for Superman to rebuild the Wall with super speed, but Cannon's budget only allowed for them to include a few reversed shots instead. (Other new powers invented for *Superman IV* include telekinesis, teaching his pals to fly without assistance, making it so that humans can breathe in space without wearing special equipment, and the ability to erase Lois Lane's memory with a kiss.)

Superman has to follow Nuclear Man around the planet, cleaning up after him like a parent does a messy toddler, as he sets Mount Vesuvius ablaze and flies off with the Statue of Liberty. The bad guy eventually gets the best of our hero, as he delivers a radioactive cat-scratch to the Man of Steel's neck with a set of deadly press-on nails. Superman gets sick, and then better, and eventually gets a rematch with his atomic clone, which amounts to something more like a superhero slap-fight than a meeting of two of the most powerful beings in the universe. Fortunately, Luthor left his super-clone with a pretty dumb Achilles heel: the man-made demigod is solar-powered, meaning he deflates like a punctured pool toy whenever he enters a building or walks into the shade. You can bet Superman capitalizes on this dumb, dumb weakness.

Critics and audiences were quick to point out the film's many plot holes, which left the released product making little sense and raising more questions than it provides answers for. There are good reasons for that: namely, that the movie was hacked to pieces by Cannon before it could hit theaters. Roughly forty-five minutes' worth of scenes were cut or trimmed from the film to get it down under Cannon's preferred, 95-minute runtime. Remember: shorter movies mean theaters can squeeze in more showings per day, which theoretically means more ticket sales.

Superman squares off against a new, powerful enemy, Nuclear Man (Mark Pillow), in *Superman IV*.

Unfortunately, many of these scenes filled in gaps and helped flesh out the plot, detailing things like Superman's response to the little boy's letter; a King Kong/Fay Wray-like love connection between new *Daily Planet* publisher Lacy Warfield and Nuclear Man; Luthor's plot to sell nukes back to the disarmed superpowers; the United States and Soviet Union nearly blowing each other up when they mistake Nuclear Man for a missile; and some closure to the Clark-Lois-Lacy love triangle. A rarity in the Cannon catalog, *Superman IV*'s deleted scenes not only survived through the decades since the film's release, but many of them are readily available on home video editions of the film.

The longest scrapped sequence in the movie involved the Luthors' first, failed attempt to clone Superman, which resulted in a boneheaded, superpowered nincompoop played by Clive Mantle, who behaves like one of Monty Python's upper class twits. He gets into a slapstick tussle with Superman outside a nightclub before being destroyed, which sends Lex back to the drawing board. This "First Nuclear Man" was featured in the movie's pre-release marketing, but was nowhere to be found in the final movie. So much footage was cut from *Superman IV* that, for an ever-brief moment, Cannon considered re-editing those materials into a hypothetical fifth Superman movie, with new scenes filmed by *Dangerously Close* (1986), *Down Twisted* (1987), and *Cyborg* (1989) director Albert Pyun. Alas, the company's relative financial destitution ultimately put the kibosh on that idea.

Those desiring a more complete picture of what *Superman IV* might have looked like with a full budget and its plot intact should seek out the surprisingly good *Superman IV Movie Special* comic book published by DC Comics to promote the film's release. Based on the original script rather than Cannon's filmed version, it's a very fun take on the material—if a somewhat heartbreaking reminder of what the movie could have been.

While Cannon removed key plot points from Superman's battle against Lex Luthor and his evil creations, they left in a ludicrous scene where Superman and Lois Lane have a "double date" with Clark Kent and his new boss, Lacy Warfield. Taking place in a ritzy New York apartment, both Clark and Superman have to keep finding excuses to leave the room so that the other can put on or remove their glasses and make a brief appearance, only to find a reason to run off and switch again. (It's as if knowing full well how silly the Clark Kent "disguise" had become, the filmmakers decided to double down here on asking the audience to suspend their disbelief.) It's clear the screenwriters were going for the sort of madcap scene you'd see in a screwball comedy of the 1940s, but Christopher Reeve was no Cary Grant, and neither Kidder nor Mariel Hemingway were Katharine Hepburn. The scene is blocked poorly, and paced sluggishly—leaving viewers begging for Lex Luthor to do something, anything, that will make Superman have to leave so he can save the world, and get us out of this scene.

Mariel Hemingway was another new addition to the Superman cast. She plays Lacy Warfield, whose tabloid tycoon father David Warfield (Sam Wanamaker of *Raw Deal*, 1986) buys up *The Daily Planet* and sets about turning it into a gossip rag full of fearmongering headlines and photo spreads of bimbos in bikinis. While regarding Superman as a goody-two-shoes, she somehow develops a crush on her newest employee, the mild-mannered Clark Kent.

Twenty-five-year-old Mariel Hemingway was just a teen when she had been nominated for a Best Supporting Actress award for playing creepy old Woody Allen's underage lover in *Manhattan* (1979). Yes, she is one of *those* Hemingways—granddaughter of novelist Ernest, and sister to actress/model Margaux, who had already earned her own Cannon merit badge in 1984's *Over the Brooklyn Bridge*.

The official story is that, like Lenny Luthor, Lacy was written into the script because the filmmakers felt they needed more younger characters to appeal to kids. There were loud rumblings, though, that Reeve and Kidder did not like each other. Kidder thought Reeve was an egomaniac, and it's been said that Hemingway was brought in because Reeve thought Kidder had gotten too old to play his love interest. In an on-set interview with *Film 87*, Kidder—who seemed to barely conceal her contempt for Superman's off-screen alter ego—referred to the whole affair "a big, stupid mistake" on the filmmakers' part.

While Cannon's wholesale chop job on the film left parts of the movie's plot incomprehensible, most viewers were probably too distracted by the movie's truly awful special effects to notice. By Cannon's standards they were ambitious, but considering the first movie won a Special Achievement Academy Award for its visual effects nine years earlier, the massive downgrade in quality was an understandable letdown for fans of the series.

One of the most famous taglines for the original *Superman* was "You'll believe a man can fly." Except when it comes to *Superman IV*, you won't. Strapped for cash, Cannon chose to use a cheaper flying effect that had actually been rejected when it was tested for the original *Superman* film almost ten years earlier. *Superman IV* suffers from some very poor blue screen work, where the actors were frequently lit in a way that left them looking faded in contrast with their backgrounds. (It didn't help that the safety rigging was far more visible than it was in past films, either—at points, the rigging almost makes it look like Superman is wearing a diaper under his tights.) On screen, our heroes and villains fly and fall in ways that seem to defy the laws of physics. Worse yet, numerous effects shots are recycled throughout the movie: the exact same shot of Christopher Reeve "flying" directly into the camera is seen *nine times* in *Superman IV*. If you're wondering why they didn't just do more takes, well, money was of course a factor, but it doesn't sound like the wire system Cannon rigged up for the flight scenes was necessarily that safe, either. At one point, stunt man John Lees—who was doubling for Nuclear Man—fell twenty-five feet when his harness cables snapped, shattering his left ankle and both heels. Lees needed years of physical therapy to learn to walk again, and dealt with pain the rest of his life; he took Cannon to court, and was awarded $422,000 in damages for their part in the accident which nearly killed him. Nuclear Man himself, Mark Pillow, also suffered a broken bone in his foot during the filming of his battle with Superman on the moon.

Cannon, counting their chickens before they hatched, teased a sequel before anyone realized just how much of a disaster *Superman IV* would be.

The movie had one more hurdle to clear before it could hit theaters, in the form of a $45 million lawsuit filed against Reeve, Cannon, and Warner Bros. by screenwriters Barry Taff and Kenneth Stoller, who attempted to stop the film's release and alleged that the actor stole their idea to have Superman disarm the world's nuclear powers. Reeve, who had rarely spoken of the film without immediately reminding interviewers that the story had been *his* idea, took this accusation of plagiarism to heart. While waiting for his interview during a 1987 taping of *The Tonight Show*, Reeve was delivered a court summons for the lawsuit, and is said to have gone into such a rage that Johnny Carson and Ed McMahon had to halt recording so they could go backstage and console him while the audience sat in the studio.

Reeve cancelled the rest of his TV appearances for that week, and from that point on journalists and talk show hosts were warned that he'd walk away from any interview that brought up the lawsuit. According to an article in *Cinefantastique*, Warner Bros. and Cannon were prepared to throw Reeve under the bus if he was ruled against in court. It looked bad enough that the actor was said to have been in the process of safeguarding his personal assets in case the lawsuit results did not favor him.

While it's not unheard of for more than one storyteller to independently dream up similar plots, the similarities between *Superman IV* and the plaintiffs' story treatment—titled "Superman IV: The Confrontation," similar to the first American Ninja sequel—are hard to deny. Both premises involved Superman gathering up all of mankind's nuclear missiles in Earth's orbit and then specifically hurling them into the sun. Both open with Superman witnessing a space shuttle disaster. In both, Superman consults his alien ancestors for advice, and goes against their wishes that he not interfere in the affairs of man. Both had Superman deliver an address to the United Nations. Both even included a one-time use Kryptonian crystal that saves Superman from death.

The suing writers had registered their treatment with the Writers Guild in 1985, and sent a copy to Reeve. While it couldn't be proven in court the actor had read their full treatment, there was evidence that his copy had been signed for at his home address, and that Reeve had called up one of the writers to confirm its receipt before he signed on to make *Superman IV* with Cannon. While the case eventually fizzled out after years of arbitration and appeals, it resulted in numerous headlines along the lines of "MAN OF STEAL?," "Reeve Flies Off With Writers' Ideas," and "Lawsuit May Be Superman's Kryptonite"—all of which Reeve felt damaged his reputation in Hollywood.

None of this stopped *Superman IV*'s release in the summer of 1987, of course. How bad was it? The movie opened in a meager fourth place at the domestic box office, and had fallen out of the top ten entirely after three weeks. The would-be blockbuster failed to even crack the top fifty-grossing releases for the year, bringing home fewer ticket sales for Cannon than *Over the Top* and *Masters of the Universe*. (At least it finished exactly one spot ahead of *Ishtar* [1987], a movie that's title became a synonym for "box office flop.") *Superman IV* made under $15 million in the United States, and while the international grosses pushed it well over recouping its $17 million budget, the total was still less than half what *Superman III* had made, and that had been considered a dismal failure. While *Superman IV* was considered a major miss for Warner Bros., it was downright cata-clysmic for Cannon, who were running out of last hopes for financial salvation.

Critics were as savage as you'd expect, but in spite of all the derision the movie only received two Razzie nominations: Worst Supporting Actress (for Hemingway) and, obviously, Worst Special Effects. Reeve referred to the movie as a "catastrophe," and later called it "a huge blow to [his] career." It was arguably an even bigger blow to Superman's movie career: as *Boxoffice Magazine* succinctly put it, "Cannon has apparently done what even Lex Luthor couldn't do. They've killed the Man of Steel." Attempts to make another movie around the character repeatedly stalled out for the next nine-teen years. Cannon's efforts effectively K.O.'d America's mightiest superhero for the next two decades. When Superman finally *did* return to the screen in *Superman Returns* (2006), the movie conveniently ignored the events of *Superman IV* like they had never happened.

Lex Luthor (Gene Hackman) explains his latest plot to destroy Superman to the first Nuclear Man (Clive Mantle), who was deleted from the film.

Masters of the Universe arrives on VHS with art by the great Drew Struzan.

Masters of the Universe

Release Date: August 7, 1987
Directed by: Gary Goddard
Written by: David Odell
Starring: Dolph Lundgren, Frank Langella, Courteney Cox
Trailer Voiceover: "From a distant galaxy, they have come to Earth. Dolph Lundgren as He-Man! Frank Langella as Skeletor! Only they have the powers to be . . . Masters of the Universe!"

Long before the Transformers movies were tent poles of the summer block-buster season; before the G.I. Joe team starred in a PG-13 action franchise, and before the classic Battleship board game was turned into a $220 million alien invasion flick, there was a time when making a movie based on a toy line was generally looked down upon by Hollywood. When a toy did find its way to the big screen, it was almost always as a purely animated affair that did its best to translate a Saturday morning cartoon into an 80-minute theatrical experience. (Except for 1986's *Transformers: The Movie*, that is, which only existed to crush children's dreams, murder their favorite heroes, and squeeze

751

a final, gasping performance from Orson Welles as a planet-eating robot—all to the tune of a head-banging hair metal soundtrack.)

The truth was that movie studios didn't view toy lines as potential cash cows, but as kiddie stuff. They didn't see a market in turning action figures into big-budget, live action spectacles. Hoping to prove everyone wrong, however, toy manufacturer Mattel teamed up with Cannon for *Masters of the Universe* (1987): a special effects-filled, live action movie based on one of the hottest toy lines of the 1980s.

First, a little background on the action figures. In the mid-1970s, an unproven filmmaker by the name of George Lucas—you probably haven't heard of him—shopped around the license to make a line of toys based on his upcoming science fiction movie, *Star Wars* (1977). No one could have predicted how big and industry-changing that movie would be, and Mattel—the toy company best known for producing Barbie dolls—was one of several major manufacturers to shoot Lucas down on his offer. While their rival, Kenner, spent the next decade essentially printing money with a steady stream of four-inch-tall Vaders, Skywalkers, and C-3POs, competing companies such as Mattel were left scrambling to find their own way into the lucrative boys' action figure market.

Of the several ideas developed in-house at Mattel, Masters of the Universe won out. The figures stood almost six inches in scale—a full head taller than the market-leading Star Wars and G.I. Joe figures—and combined the popular science fiction and sword-and-sorcery genres in almost equal parts. Their leader was the valiant He-Man—a joke placeholder name that ultimately went to market—who looked like the blond Dutch Boy paint mascot had grown up and gotten totally ripped. His arch nemesis was the evil Skeletor, a skull-faced baddie with designs on ruling their home planet of Eternia. The toy line, launched in 1982, was composed of their many colorful allies, vehicles, weapons, and playsets.

The He-Man concept was an instant hit with children, who begged their parents into buying them millions of Masters of the Universe toys over the brand's first five years on store shelves. Like all of the best-selling toy lines of the decade, these sales were fueled by media tie-ins such as a daily cartoon and monthly comic book, where new characters and costumes could be introduced at a rapid pace. As He-Man, Transformers, G.I. Joe and the Teenage Mutant Ninja Turtles proved time and time again, if you wanted to sell your product to kids, the best way was to get them hooked on your half-hour, animated commercials. The syndicated cartoon, *He-Man and the Masters of the Universe*, debuted in 1983 and proved as popular as the toys themselves. At its height, it was appearing on more than one hundred American TV channels and airing in thirty countries.

While these days a movie tie-in would seem inevitable, the idea was somewhat novel when it came to Mattel around the launch of the toy line. Enter Edward R. Pressman, a movie producer who was no stranger to the toy world, with his father being the man who founded the Pressman Toy Company. Mattel and Pressman had briefly worked together on a proposed line of action figures based on his film, the Arnold Schwarzenegger-starring *Conan the Barbarian* (1982), an idea which Mattel ultimately dropped when they deemed the movie too violent for children. (This was a few years before competitors successfully marketed toys inspired by R-rated properties such as Rambo and RoboCop to kids.) An independent producer with films as wide-ranging as *Badlands* (1973), *Phantom of the Paradise* (1974), and *Das Boot* (1981) under his belt, Pressman was granted permission to start shopping the idea for a He-Man movie around Hollywood.

Word got around, including to Gary Goddard, who called up Pressman's office and pitched himself as the movie's director. Goddard had not directed a film before, but was already established in both the entertainment and toy industries. He'd began his career as one of Disney's famed Imagineers, helping design attractions at Disney World, Disneyland, and the brand new Tokyo Disney. After leaving the House of Mouse, Goddard was hired by Universal Studios to oversee their Conan the Barbarian live show, which essentially worked in Goddard's favor as an audition for *Masters of the Universe*. At the time, Goddard was also the head of his own new company, Gary Goddard

Productions, who had been hired by Milton Bradley to update their *Candy Land* board game, adding many of the iconic characters we associate with it to this day. Since Goddard had also done similar work for Mattel, he seemed a natural choice for the job.

By this point there was already a first draft of the script, which Pressman had commissioned from screenwriter David Odell, a writer on *The Muppet Show* (1979–1981) who had gone on to script Jim Henson's far more grim fantasy film, *The Dark Crystal* (1982). They both understood that a science fiction feature like *Masters of the Universe* would be expensive no matter how tight they tried to keep the budget, and so the decision was made early on to set the action on modern-day Earth, rather than on He-Man's home planet of Eternia. (Besides cutting down the cost of production design, the thought was that the story would be more relatable to audiences if their musclebound hero co-starred alongside two average, American teenagers.) Once Goddard was on board, he pushed for the movie's beginning and ending to take place on Eternia, figuring that it would add considerable production value to the film while only raising the cost by that of a single set.

The final piece of Pressman's package was its star, Dolph Lundgren. Perhaps the only human on the planet as blonde and as musclebound as the fictional He-Man, Lundgren was still a very, very fresh commodity in the movie business. With only a minor role as a Bond baddie in *A View to a Kill* (1985) under his belt before his star-making turn as Ivan Drago, Sylvester Stallone's Soviet foil in *Rocky IV* (1985), playing He-Man was a career U-Turn for the strapping Swede, who went from playing a near-mute villain to being a heroic leading man.

Although the role of He-Man is certainly not a great indicator of his intelligence, the truth is that not only is Lundgren ridiculously good-looking and incredibly jacked, but he is usually one the smartest men in any room he enters. Born and raised in Stockholm, Lundgren studied chemical engineering at Sweden's Royal Institute of Technology before bouncing around the United States on various scholarships. He went on to get his Master's Degree and graduated at the top of his class, earned a prestigious

Fulbright Scholarship, and began working toward his Ph.D. at the revered Massachusetts Institute of Technology.

MU7   He-Man (DOLPH LUNDGREN) views the battle-scarred face of the planet Eternia.

There was perhaps no human being on Earth in the mid-1980s more appropriate to play He-Man than Dolph Lundgren.

Eventually, though, the handsome, six foot five inch-tall chemical engineer took a break from his studies to earn a few extra bucks modeling in New York City, where his career path would change forever. He met actress, supermodel, and singer Grace Jones at a club, and the two became an item. With Jones, Lundgren was something of an NYC scenester, palling around with icons such as Andy Warhol, David Bowie, and Michael Jackson by night, and taking acting classes by day. It was Grace Jones who encouraged him to audition for his debut role in *A View to a Kill*.

His next screen performance was the sort of breakout that most aspiring actors dream of having. Lundgren beat out many other actors for the chance to fight Sylvester Stallone in *Rocky IV*, even though Stallone initially wrote him off as too tall to play Ivan Drago. The movie wound up becoming the franchise's most successful sequel, and Lundgren its most recognized villain. This was even after Lundgren nearly killed one of the '80s biggest stars while making the film.

During fight rehearsals for *Rocky IV*, Stallone had egged on Lundgren to hit him harder and harder, seeking that extra bit of realism in their performance. What Stallone either didn't know, or tragically forgot, was that the Scandinavian stud that he was sparring with had a black belt in karate to go with his degree in chemical engineering, and had once been a European martial arts champion. One of Lundgren's fists crashed into Stallone's ribs, sending Stallone reeling. The impact was hard enough to make Stallone's heart swell inside his chest, and the actor had to be flown to an intensive care unit where it took him five days to recover. This sort of injury is most commonly seen in car accidents—not boxing matches.

A few months later, Mattel would happily sign off on Lundgren playing He-Man, who you have to admit was a perfect physical match for the action figure. Not only was he built like a Frank Frazetta oil painting come to life, but he had the blonde hair as well. With a script, director, and star attached, Pressman and Mattel only had to find a studio willing to gamble on their big-budget toy movie. A couple major studios, reportedly Warner Bros. and MGM, got over their reservations enough to make modest bids for the project. Needing all the money they could get to bring their interstellar adventure to the screen, Mattel finally brought the package to Cannon, who outbid their major studio competitors by $2.5 million. Contracts were signed.

It's doubtful many outside Cannon knew just how bad the company's financial future was beginning to look at this point, but *Masters of the Universe*'s bed was made, and there was no choice but to sleep in it. On the flipside of that coin, Cannon probably wasn't aware that the toys' popularity had already started to decline after almost half a decade, and that Mattel was hoping the live action film would be the thing that would save their Eternian cash cow.

David Odell's *Masters of the Universe* script opens in a really cool way. On the planet of Eternia, a war between good and evil has long ravaged the land—and evil stands on the brink of winning. The wicked Skeletor and his minions have captured Castle Grayskull, the seat of all power in the universe. Its divine guardian, the Sorceress (Christina Pickles of TV's *St. Elsewhere*, 1982–1988), is trapped within a mystical prison. The resistance to Skeletor's evil empire has been all but crushed by the desiccated despot's robot armies. Only their leader, He-Man, and a pair of his most trusted soldiers stand in the way of Skeletor's subjugation of their beloved planet. Things look downright bleak for our heroes at the beginning of the film, but this opening instills the movie with a properly epic, Star Wars-ian scale.

Anyone who's seen *Masters of the Universe* will likely agree: Skeletor carries much of this film. Frank Langella acts the hell out of his role, and does it through several inches of prosthetics and skull makeup. Every monologue is delivered as if Langella were performing Shakespeare's *Henry V* at Stratford, lending his part far more gravity than you'd expect from someone playing a mean space skeleton. Even his movement is almost dancer-like in its grace and intent. Frank Langella is so, so, so good as Skeletor that even if everything else had gone wrong with the movie, *Masters of the Universe* would still have been worth watching for his performance alone. There's a perceptible weariness in Skeletor's pursuit of evil, and it arguably set a template for how actors would play world-conquering villains in the superhero movies that would sweep movie theaters more than twenty years later.

Primarily viewing himself as a stage actor throughout his career, Langella made his Broadway debut in the mid-1960s. It wasn't long, though, before the talented thespian was offered film roles, soon appearing in Mel Brooks' adaptation of *The Twelve Chairs* (1970) and the critically-acclaimed *Diary of a Mad Housewife* (1970). He earned a Tony Award while appearing in Edward Albee's Pulitzer-winning *Seascape* on Broadway, and then was nominated for another while starring as the titular vampire in a celebrated theatrical adaptation of Bram Stoker's *Dracula*. His passionate performance as the undead count was brought to the screen in the film *Dracula* (1979), co-starring Laurence Olivier and Donald Pleasence, and it became his signature role.

Frank Langella brought Shakespearean drama to his role as Skeletor.

Langella continued to prefer the stage over cinema, which is where director Gary Goddard had seen him in a 1982 Broadway run of *Amadeus*. When Goddard approached the lauded theatre actor with the offer to play celebrated cartoon villain Skeletor, Langella surprisingly didn't blink an eye. It turns out Langella's children were He-Man mega-fans, and so he couldn't resist—and prepared for the role by asking his kids how Skeletor would react in different scenarios, and learning from them what exactly made their favorite interdimensional skull wizard tick.

Two of Skeletor's better-known henchmen from the toys and cartoon joined him on the big screen. Most notable among them is the sorceress

Evil-Lyn, played in the film by Meg Foster, whose penetrating blue eyes can also be seen in cult classics such as *The Osterman Weekend* (1983) and *They Live* (1988). The second was a redesigned Beast Man, played by bodybuilder Tony Carroll.

Most of the action set on Eternia takes place in and around Castle Grayskull, represented by some eye-catching matte paintings and what, at the time, was the largest movie set built in Hollywood since the Golden Age. *Masters of the Universe* filmed inside Culver City's Laird Studios, former home of RKO, and the one-time shooting location for classics such as *King Kong* (1933) and *Gone with the Wind* (1939). To construct Grayskull's massive throne room set, production designer William Stout had the wall knocked out between two of the facility's largest soundstages.

Knowing that the throne room set would be the film's biggest source of production value, Stout was allowed to pull out all the stops to make it look as cool as possible. An experienced illustrator, underground comic artist, and movie poster designer, Stout had been pulled head-first into the film industry. While working on designs for *Conan the Barbarian* and its sequel, Stout was recruited to create storyboards for *Raiders of the Lost Ark* (1981) and Rambo's debut movie, *First Blood* (1982). Horror fans can thank him for designing the many undead nasties, including the iconic Tarman, for the classic zombie comedy *Return of the Living Dead* (1985). Following that, Stout was conscripted by Cannon to draw up the aliens for *Invaders from Mars* (1986). On *Masters of the Universe*, Stout was tasked with taking the characters from the cartoon and toy line and translating them to the real world, coming up with new heroes and villains, and designing every set, from Castle Grayskull to Charlie's Music Store. To assist him on some of these tasks, Stout hired French comic artist Jean "Moebius" Giraud, best remembered for his design work in *Alien* (1979) and *Tron* (1982).

Outside the castle, He-Man leads what little is left of the resistance forces against Skeletor's troops. (The Vasquez Rock Formations stand in for the Eternian desert—thanks to their otherworldly look and close proximity to Hollywood, they're one of most-used and most-recognizable shooting locations in film history.) He-Man runs into two of his most trusted allies, Man-At-Arms (Jon Cypher) and his daughter Teela (Chelsea Field), both highly skilled soldiers. Responding to his distress cries, the trio rescue a brilliant dwarf inventor named Gwildor (Billy Barty) from an enemy trap, and our movie's heroic quartet is formed.

Both Man-At-Arms and Teela are characters that kids would have already known from the cartoon, but Gwildor was newly created for the film. A lifelong professional actor, the three foot, nine inch-tall Billy Barty had been working in Hollywood since the 1920s, having appeared in a Marx Brothers movie (*Monkey Business*, 1931) and two Busby Berkeley musicals (*The Gold Diggers of 1933* and *Footlight Parade*, both 1933) and *The Bride of Frankenstein* (1935) with Boris Karloff, all while still a child. As an adult he would appear in numerous fantasy films, including *Legend* (1985) and *Willow* (1988). Additionally, he appeared in two Cannon Movie Tales: *Rumpelstiltskin* and *Snow White* (both 1987). He brought the sort of professionalism gained over two hundred film and TV appearances to the role of Gwildor, acting under a heavy amount of makeup and prosthetic work. His makeup job wasn't among the movie's most convincing examples, and was perhaps a little more grotesque than it needed to be.

The gross, little Gwildor—who is no doubt a cousin of the similarly disgusting Aughra from *The Dark Crystal*—invented a "Cosmic Key," which utilizes musical tones to open portals to anywhere in time and space. (In practice, this is done by randomly mashing on the buttons.) The original cosmic key, which resembles a tower of spinning sporks, was recently stolen by Evil-Lyn, which explains how Skeletor's armies were able to get a jump on the resistance forces. Fortunately for Team Good Guys, Gwildor had a second, prototype Cosmic Key hidden away. He-Man and his friends try—and fail—to use it to save their beloved Sorceress, and accidentally find themselves on mid-1980s Earth after making a hasty escape from Grayskull. Worse yet, they dropped their Cosmic Key somewhere on their way through their portal and have no idea where it is.

Dolph Lundgren with Billy Barty as Gwildor, a character newly created for the *Masters of the Universe* film.

This is where most of *Masters of the Universe* takes place: in the wholesome-looking Los Angeles suburb of Whittier, California. We're introduced to the movie's Earthling heroes, Julie (Courteney Cox) and Kevin (Robert Duncan McNeill), high school lovebirds who stumble across the alien, interdimensional travel device while visiting the graves of Julie's parents. We learn that Julie's folks died in a plane crash, which she blames herself for, and she feels that the only way that she'll be able to shake her grief is by skipping town immediately after graduation. Before they say goodbye to each other, Kevin—a somewhat thick-skulled aspiring musician—asks her to stick around for his band's sound check. While they're at it, they'll try out the Cosmic Key, which he believes is some sort of sweet, Japanese synthesizer.

Courteney Cox made her big screen debut in another Cannon feature, *Down Twisted* (1987), but it would be another seven years before she broke out as Monica Gellar on *Friends* (1994–2004), one of the most successful sitcoms of all time, and then co-starred in the successful *Scream* slasher franchise. It took roughly the same amount of time for her on-screen boyfriend, Robert Duncan McNeill, to land the TV role he'd be most associated with:

Starfleet Lieutenant Tom Paris on *Star Trek: Voyager* (1995–2001). He'd eventually shift the focus of his work to behind the camera, directing television and serving as executive producer on the series *Chuck* (2007–2012), among others.

Meanwhile, He-Man and his posse have a limited amount of time to track down the Cosmic Key before Skeletor permanently robs the Sorceress of her powers. (This doesn't stop them from exploring Earth's native wildlife and sampling the best fried chicken and ribs in the area.) Nearby, Kevin can't help himself from noodling around with the Cosmic Key, which allows Evil-Lyn and Skeletor to triangulate its coordinates and send lackeys to Earth to hunt down the renegade Eternians. This is what turns the He-Man crew's fish-out-of-water adventure into a battle to save Earth from alien invaders.

The Skeletor Squad includes the aforementioned Beast Man, plus a few new characters designed by William Stout for the film: a skilled warrior named Blade, the reptilian Saurod, and Karg (Robert Towers), a small, ape-like monster with a big, Eighties hairstyle. Blade is played by Anthony De Longis, one of Hollywood's premier weapons masters, who trained Dolph Lundgren to wield He-Man's sword, as well as Harrison Ford and Michelle Pfeiffer to crack a whip in *Indiana Jones and the Crystal Skull* (2008) and *Batman Returns* (1992), respectively. The short-lived Saurod was played by puppeteer Pons Maar, who was the main Wheeler in the nightmare-inducing *Return to Oz* (1985), and the voice of the Noid in the old Domino's Pizza commercials.

Finding himself mixed up in this whole interdimensional mess is one of the 1980s' go-to authority figures, James Tolkan, playing hard-nosed cop Hugh Lubic. He's known for playing an FBI agent in *WarGames* (1983), Commander "Stinger" Jardian in *Top Gun* (1986), and Marty McFly's no-nonsense principal in the *Back to the Future* movies. (Here's a bit of trivia: the scene where Tolkan calls Marty a slacker was filmed at Whittier High School, just down the road from where most of *Masters of the Universe* was shot.) Charlie, who owns the town's ill-fated music store, is played by Barry Livingston, also known as Ernie from *My Three Sons* (1960–1972).

Masters of the Universe's special effects were overseen by Richard Edlund, who had been part of the Oscar-winning teams behind *Star Wars* and *Raiders of the Lost Ark*, and had worked on *Poltergeist* (1982) and *Ghostbusters* (1984). Many of the effects come off very well, but some clearly suffered from Cannon's penny-pinching as production ran over schedule. The most ludicrous-looking effect is when He-Man hops on a flying disc to pursue his enemies. This involved locking Lundgren's ankles into ski-like boots on a platform, which was then driven down the street on the back of a truck at forty miles per hour as the actor admirably did his best to keep his balance and not break his ankles. This looks even sillier once poor He-Man is inserted into some very suspect green screen work.

As time wore on, Cannon's rapidly-decaying financial state became more and more apparent to the crew. There were mornings when payroll checks never arrived, and Goddard had to plead with his team to keep shooting while a producer drove to the Cannon offices to find their money. This continued until filming was underway on the movie's grand finale, which took place once again in Castle Grayskull's humongous, opulent throne room. Cannon, who had over-extended themselves with several ill-advised real estate purchases and "big" budget features, was just about broke. Before they could film the ultimate battle between good and evil that the whole film had been building up to, Cannon literally pulled the plug—shutting off the lights at Laird Studios, and sending everybody home.

If production had truly stopped here, *Masters of the Universe* would have ended in one of those most anti-climactic finales in cinema history. Our hero, He-Man, and villain, Skeletor, poised to do battle with the fate of the universe hanging in the balance. Their weapons collide, sparks fly, and . . . the credits roll. The audience wouldn't even have seen who won! It would have been the worst possible ending for the movie, but for Cannon—who were already in the process of liquidating their assets to stay alive—it was considered "good enough."

For the cast and crew who had poured their energy into the movie, this of course wouldn't stand. Goddard begged Menaham Golan to let them finish the film. As a final compromise, they were given the permission and budget to wrap up the movie's finale, which would normally have entailed lots of choreography and numerous effects shots, in a *single day.*

Needing to get creative, Goddard returned to the Grayskull set with a skeleton crew. Because they'd trained together and could quickly come up with convincing fight choreography, Goddard had Anthony "Blade" De Longis put on Frank Langella's Skeletor makeup and gold armor to spar with Lundgren in this final scene. (Their battle was shot in dim lighting because it was the best look they could come up with given the limited crew members and equipment on hand.) The fight ends, of course, with our hero victorious, knocking his foe over a ledge and into a pit of lava. The end . . .

. . . or, was it?

After the credits roll comes to an end, the screen brightens again with a shot of lava. Langella's Skeletor rises from the muck and teases the camera: "I'll be back!" This is an early example of a post-credits sequence, which had previously been reserved for blooper reels or gags, such as Ferris Bueller or The Muppets' Animal telling the audience that it's time for them to go home. It's arguably the first to directly tease a sequel—something that the Marvel Cinematic Universe later turned into an essential piece of the movie going experience. In *Masters of the Universe*'s case, obviously, a sequel never happened, although that doesn't mean Cannon didn't try for one. (More on that in a bit.)

It's up for debate whether or not audiences would have had any interest in a second He-Man movie by the late 1980s; box office returns on the film's late summer release in 1987 were a disappointment. The most likely culprit was that the movie had spent too many years in development. By the time Cannon pushed it into production, the toy line had already entered a decline. Like any fad, interest in He-Man had moved on. Where it had been their top seller a few years earlier, Mattel was losing money on the action figures and were pinning their hopes of the line's survival on the movie being a huge success. The cartoon had already gone out of production almost two years before the movie was released; the toy line was put on ice just a few months afterward. In all likelihood, many of the little boys who'd grown up on the character had grown out of him by the time Cannon's presumed blockbuster hit theaters.

A Japanese flyer advertising the release of *Masters of the Universe*.

The critical lashing the movie received probably didn't help things, either. While some reviewers were willing to admit the movie offered up a family-friendly, escapist romp, others were far harsher. Some of the hokier special effects were a frequent target, but more so was Dolph Lundgren's thick accent. Although his line delivery improved dramatically as his career continued, he can be hard to understand over *Masters of the Universe*'s sound effects and Bill Conti's score. (Remember: in his biggest pre-He-Man role, Ivan Drago, Lundgren only spoke a handful of short, scary lines, like "If he dies, he dies," and "I must break you.") Goddard hoped to re-dub Lundgren in post-production, but contracts—not to mention, there being zero budget left over—prevented that from happening.

Like so many of Cannon's higher-concept features, though, *Masters of the Universe* fared better in Europe, and went on to be a cult hit when it was made available for rental at video stores. Thinking they might turn a bigger profit on a smaller investment, Golan went to the Cannes Film Festival and announced that *Masters of the Universe 2* would soon enter production with director Albert Pyun at the helm. The sequel would be a much lower-budget feature at only $4.5 million, less than a quarter of what was spent on the first movie.

Having felt embarrassed by *Masters of the Universe* and not wanting to get pigeonholed into b-movies, Lundgren had already expressed that he had no desire to return for a part two. Cannon made plans to replace him as He-Man with pro surfer Laird Hamilton. (The proposed sequel would have sent He-Man back to Earth, disguised as a high school quarterback.) Just as Pyun was set to begin filming it back-to-back with Cannon's similarly-unrealized Spider-Man movie, Cannon missed a payment to Mattel and lost their rights to make a He-Man sequel.

Not wanting to waste the costumes and sets that had been prepared for the *Masters of the Universe 2* and *Spider-Man* shoots, the ever-resourceful Pyun quickly banged out a script using those existing materials, and re-purposed them into a low-budget, post-apocalyptic adventure which would

766

utilize Cannon's newest star, Jean-Claude Van Damme. That movie became *Cyborg* (1989), and it's a story for *The Cannon Film Guide Volume III* . . .

Director Gary Goddard overseeing the production of *Masters of the Universe* from Skeletor's throne. Photo courtesy of Gary Goddard.

Interview: Director Gary Goddard

Throughout his long and varied career, Gary Goddard has worked in almost every imaginable facet of the entertainment industry. He got his start as one of Disney's Imagineers, getting to work side-by-side with several of the company's most legendary animators, and working to create attractions for their parks. Ever since, Goddard has remained among the most sought-after theme park consultants and designers in the world, with his handiwork on view in such well-known attractions as Universal Studios' *Jurassic Park: The Ride*, *Terminator 2: 3-D*, and *The Amazing Adventures of Spider-Man*, and in theme parks across North America and Asia. It was his live stage show at Universal, *The Adventures of Conan: A Sword and Sorcery Spectacular*, that essentially served as his audition to direct the Cannon film *Masters of the Universe* (1987), which is the only feature directed by Goddard to date.

Prior to taking on He-Man's live action movie debut, Goddard's company was hired by Mattel to redesign their bestselling *Candy Land* board game, adding the theme and characters still associated with the game today. He is also the creator of the television shows *Captain Power* (1987–1988) and *Skeleton Warriors* (1994).

Masters of the Universe wasn't your first exposure to Cannon—before that, you had helped John and Bo Derek write the script for _Bolero_. What can you tell me about that experience?

Gary Goddard: I had met the Dereks originally through Maxine Goldenson, daughter of the legendary Leonard Goldenson, founder of ABC. I had just left Disney Imagineering and landed at Paramount pitching a project called *Against the Gods* to Frank Yablans. It was essentially "*The Ten Commandments* in Space," and I had developed the concept with Claudio Mazzoli.

We sold the concept, and Paramount engaged me to write the screenplay, which got me into the WGA. I had an office on the Paramount Lot, in the historic Producers Building. Maxine had an office there and we met, and she was looking for a writer. It turns out, she had the rights to a new Marvel Comics title that did not yet have a story, only a name. It was called "Dazzler." She had met the Dereks, and Marvel had said "If you can get Bo Derek to play Dazzler in a movie, we will make the story work for a comic," whatever that is. So Maxine said, "They want a superhero story of some kind, can you do that?" I said "sure"—but after thinking about it, I had a different idea.

I wrote a short pitch treatment for Dazzler. I thought it was a bit too on the nose to cast Bo Derek, as she was the biggest female star in the world at the moment . . . So, my idea was to create a kind of fantasy epic in a post-holocaust world, with swords, sorcery, and science, and "Dazzler" was a legendary sword created by science that could, essentially, destroy anything in the right hands. Bo would be a "Joan of Arc" figure who would rise to wield that sword: a kind of Arthurian spine, but with a female protagonist. Maxine wasn't sure that is what Marvel wanted, but they said "If Bo agrees to do it, we are in." Bo and John loved it; I had written a brief, six or eight page treatment. John and I hit it off well, and we were working on the story. This was when they were in pre-production on *Tarzan the Ape Man* (1981) at MGM.

In the midst of working on Dazzler, John and Bo called me over to their home and said, "You know we are working on *Tarzan*, yes?" I said I knew that. John said, "Well, we don't like the dialogue, but we like your writing. Would you consider doing a dialogue polish on *Tarzan*?" I said *yes*. This meant I would be working on an MGM movie that was already in pre-production. So, YES!

In two weeks' time, I had about 75% of the dialogue polish done, and John and Bo called me over once again. This time John said, "We like what you're writing, but we don't like what it's based on. We want you to rewrite the entire script," and then said, "We are leaving for the Seychelles in five days, and we want you to fly with us so we can write it there."

To make a long story short, I lived in a mansion on a hill in the Seychelles with Bo and John, where I completely rewrote *Tarzan the Ape Man* three times, on an IBM Selectric, using a lot of Wite-Out. Essentially eating, drinking, sleeping, and working with Bo and John during those three weeks kind of bonded us.

Bo was getting all kinds of offers, but they elected to stay a team, and so whatever was next would be something John would write and direct. They asked me if I would "ghostwrite" John's next idea, which was *Bolero*. They were very upfront saying I would not get a credit, that John would be the writer and director, but they would pay me handsomely for a first draft. I said "no problem," and off we went.

Working on *Bolero* was fun; most of it was written at John and Bo's new home, a small horse ranch in Santa Ynez. They had a guest house there, separate from the main building, and I would stay there and write. Essentially I would meet with John in the mornings, much as we had done on *Tarzan*, and he would tell a story and I would take detailed, hand-written notes. Then I would head to the new computer that IBM had given them, and I would write out the scenes, plan them, try to enhance John's basic verbal narrative, and create the pages. We would review them later that day, and would work into the evening. Then we would repeat it again the next day. In about a week, we had a first draft.

I have to imagine there couldn't have been a better audition for He-Man than your Conan show at Universal Studios. Were you essentially able to point to that when pitching yourself as the movie's director to Ed Pressman?

Yes, that had a lot to do with it. I had heard, or perhaps read, that Ed Pressman was looking for a director for the *Masters of the Universe* motion picture he was planning. At that time there was no studio—it was Ed Pressman, who had the rights from Mattel, and a script he had commissioned from David Odell, and Dolph Lundgren was set as the star, hot off *Rocky IV* (1985).

I called him up and I said, essentially, "I'm your director." I rattled off my screenplay credits. That led to a meeting with him and David, and during that meeting I told them I had just finished directing, designing, and producing the *Conan Sword & Sorcery Spectacular* at Universal Studios, and I invited them to see it. They went, probably with low expectations as that is kind of what people thought of theme park live shows. But, they were blown away at the scale of it all, and the level of staging and design details. I think that cemented it. That, and the fact that Mattel had director approval, and I said that I didn't think that would be an issue for them, since I was already consulting with them on toy design. They would know that I understood the importance of keeping the "brand" in mind when making the move. It all kind of came together quite well.

Howard Kazanjian was on as the producer for about nine months. At that time, the project was going to be done with Warner Brothers. Ultimately, Howard said the movie would cost $22 million as written, and Warner Bros. said they would not spend a penny over $15 million. Howard worked with me, and we got the budget down to $17.5 million, but Warner Bros. wouldn't budge.

When we started on *Masters of the Universe*, the toy line was just beginning its descent. Mattel wasn't completely worried at that point, but they were concerned. In the nine months of trying to get Warner Brothers to up their budget, the MOTU line started a more rapid descent, in terms of sales. When Pressman pulled it from Warners once Cannon agreed to the $17.5 million budget, Mattel was now *very* concerned about the toy line's sales.

Meanwhile, Howard was concerned, given the delays and the fact that I was going to try and make a movie with great production value—and with the addition of Richard Edlund and his new BOSS Effects Studio—that his original budget of $22 million was actually the right number. (As it turned out, he was right.) Anyway, Howard elected to walk away from the project after meetings with Cannon and the $17.5 million budget. Elliot Schick was brought in at that point.

Gary Goddard (center) at work during one of *Masters of the Universe*'s night shoots in Whittier, California. Photo courtesy of Gary Goddard.]

Do you remember what your first sign was that there was trouble at Cannon? That they might not have enough money to finish the movie as planned?

I remember it well. There were issues going on behind the scenes before the moment that I became aware of it all—I think everyone was trying to protect me as the director. But I showed up on the set one morning, probably around 7 or 8 A.M. Elliot rushes over to me and says, "We have to talk," in a very urgent tone. Essentially, the checks were not delivered for the week, and the crew wasn't going to work. The heads of the different trades wanted to talk to me. Elliot seemed very worried. I said, "Well, let's meet with them." By nature, I try my best to be the calm in any given eye of any given storm, and we had been through *many* such challenges on this shoot, though the magnitude of this one was greater than most. Still, it was just one more hurdle in my mind.

So, I met with the heads of the crews and they said, "We're not going to work without our checks." And I said something to the effect of, "I completely understand, but—can I suggest that we consider another option?" I pointed to Elliot and said, "Elliot is going to the Cannon offices now, and it is my understanding that we will have the payroll here by the end of today's effort. Since everyone is here, and since we are already pushing a hard schedule, is it possible that we work through the day, and not lose this time? If Elliot fails, we are none of us the worse off—and I understand no one will show up tomorrow. But we're here—and I am very confident that Elliot will get the payroll checks today. And if he does, we all keep working and live to fight another day."

I essentially begged them to see the day out, since everyone was already on set and ready to work. They said they needed to talk about it. Ten minutes later they came up and said, "We'll do this for you."

Obviously I was relieved. And Elliot *did* go, and he *did* get the checks. I never knew until *years* later—Bill Stout told me—that what happened was *Mattel* stepped in and covered that payroll, and that happened two other times during the course of the shoot.

If I had any doubts about Cannon, this was the morning I realized just how bad things were. It was a motivator, as well, to keep pushing forward as fast as humanly possible.

I know comics were a big influence on this film—in particular, the work of Jack Kirby. Your Production Designer, Bill Stout, had a long history in comics before entering the film industry. How was it, working with Bill?

I knew Bill before *Masters of the Universe* and I asked him to come on board for the initial concept work. We had another Production Designer initially, but his work was quite off-putting. Very abstract. I kept telling him that there is a "visual vocabulary" that we needed to be aware of, and that creating a believable fantasy world required that we not get too abstract. Anyway, one day he flipped out and stated that he hated comic books, and all of this kind of thing. Whether he quit or was fired, I don't remember. But, Bill had been doing *fantastic* work on character designs, costume design concepts, settings, and so on. So, I asked Bill if he would consider coming on board as Production Designer, and he said yes. We both had a common language and we both intuitively understood the fantasy/real world ideas that were at work on this project.

I was furiously working on adding things like the God Transformation, the Air Centurions, the arc of the He-Man/Skeletor relationship, and creating new characters for the movie—rather than trying to do strange, make-up versions of Trap Jaw or Man-E-Faces, or other characters that Mattel was pressing for, which would just have come off terribly because there was no digital/CGI to use in those days.

Bill is a genius in his own right, understanding film design, production design, character design, and costume design—and, he knows epic fantasy world building. We could meet and talk for fifteen minutes, back and forth, and in an hour or two he would have sketches. We'd have another meeting and a few hours later he'd have a final design. He also had a strong team of other designers working with him as well: Ed Eyth, Claudio Mazzoli—and he even brought in Moebius at one point.

Dolph was already cast when you came on. Physically, I don't think there could have been a better person to play He-Man, but as an actor he was still really green, having not yet played a lead role in a movie. What was it like to work with him on this film?

Actually it was pretty good, overall. Dolph had a "can do" attitude and was always ready to give it his all. I had an issue with his acting coach at one point, and I had to have him removed from the set when I saw him coaching Dolph on the side—and coaching him to do the opposite of what I was trying to get from him.

Of course, Dolph had one line in *Rocky*, and in the original [*MOTU*] script, he had a *ton* of lines. Another decision was that I would make the villain the driving character in the movie, not that this was unusual. The antagonist generally drives a movie, but in this case, when rewriting, I was giving as much of the exposition and set-up to the characters that surrounded He-Man, and letting other, more experienced actors carry the dialogue-heavy scenes.

Dolph really looked up to Sylvester Stallone and Clint Eastwood, and other actor/directors who were action heroes. I argued that in most, if not all such situations, the hero was often strong and silent. A hero does not go around talking all the time. More is said with a gesture, or with a nod. It was better that Teela, or Man-At-Arms, or Gwildor discuss the details of a plan, to which He-Man would approve or not, and so on. Dolph bought into that. Whether he believed me 100% or just was practical and knew he had a heavy accent, and figured out that I was doing what was best for him and for the movie—I don't know. But he went along with it.

It's public information that I tried to get an actor in to dub him prior to the release—and I found a guy who did a perfect version of Dolph, keeping just a slight accent. But Menahem wouldn't hear of it: "I paid for Dolph Lundgren—I want Dolph Lundgren's voice!"

The other funny story is—at one point—to justify Dolph's accent, I thought "Well, they are Eternians—what if they *all* speak with Dolph's accent?" Clearly that was something I discarded sixty seconds after considering it.

With the casting of Frank Langella, you were able to land the first actor you envisioned for Skeletor and shape the movie around him. I read

774

that the two of you discussed Shakespeare and Moliere while developing the role. How much did the character or his lines change, once Langella was on board?

I only had three people in mind, but Frank was my first choice. All three were classically trained actors with both stage and screen experience, and all of them had done Shakespeare and other classic roles. They all knew "how to wear the cape," and to carry themselves.

The interesting story about Frank Langella is, although I knew him from appearances in movies that included Mel Brooks' *The Twelve Chairs* (1970), John Badham's *Dracula* (1979), and the Michael Pressman's *Those Lips, Those Eyes* (1980), among others, it was seeing him live on Broadway in *Amadeus* that stuck with me. He played Salieri, the nemesis of the young Mozart, and he played it well. A noble villain, vain and not without his own talents, but nothing compared to Mozart. It was an amazing performance. Chilling. And I thought that Frank would bring the right amount of nobility, of intelligence, and of jealousy—along with menacing intentions, of course. The jealousy of Mozart that so drove Salieri was *exactly* the kind of jealousy that I felt Skeletor would have for He-Man, but many times over. He-Man is everything Skeletor not only wants to be, but in many ways thinks he already is. In Skeletor's mind he is *already* He-Man's superior—he just needs everyone *else* to understand it.

Now, none of what I just described was in the script that Frank read. We had a very good talk on the phone, and then I went to New York to meet him in person and to talk through my intentions. We did indeed talk about Shakespeare, Moliere, and I think a bit of Ibsen and Pinter as well. Within a very short time we were on the same page, and I think the fact that I was familiar with theatre and the great playwrights helped to put him at ease. I told him of how I saw the role, and how it would be rewritten; that I needed an actor with the power to play "though the facial appliances," and one that could carry himself as a king, as an emperor, and ultimately, as a God. I told him I intended that Skeletor would drive the picture, and that I needed an actor who could do that.

Frank signed on. I learned later that the fact his son was into He-Man helped him to make the decision to do it, as well. We worked closely on the development of Skeletor's character and dialogue. I would be doing dialogue rewrites the night before his scenes, using bits of Shakespeare and others, based on conversations and little notes that Frank and I would compare between scenes, and sometimes between takes. It was a collaborative process.

With Skeletor, I knew from the start: he does not see himself as the villain. He sees himself as the wise and all-knowing ruler who is doing everything he believes is *best* for his people—for his world.

Gary Goddard working with Gwildor (Billy Barty) on the set of *Masters of the Universe*. Photo courtesy of Gary Goddard.

Billy Barty had been in the business for more than half a Century by this point. Do you have any memories of him you can share?

Billy and I became pretty good friends through the course of the film. He also came to visit me at my office at Landmark Entertainment Group after the film was over and actually provided some input on a few theme park projects, from the perspective of a little person.

In addition to my love of theatre, films, comic books, pulp novels, sci-fi, and epic fantasy, I also love Broadway and Vaudeville. Billy was around and part of the old Vaudeville circuit, so I would always want to hear about his adventures, and he was a great story teller. He also told great jokes—and did so on the set often—but I don't think any of those jokes would be printable.

I will say this: Billy had to have three to four hours of make-up every day he was on set, and he had to wait quite a lot as we would set up shots. He never complained. He was a total pro, and always ready when needed. I never saw him lose his sense of humor. A great, great guy.

Muhammad Ali hung around the *Breakin' 2* set on occasion, but the *Masters* set was supposedly visited by the King of Pop, Michael Jackson. Is that true?

As it turns out, Michael was shooting on one of the soundstages next door to our stage. He was shooting the now classic "Smooth Criminal," though no one knew it. It was very hush-hush, I guess.

A bit of backstory first . . . to get the Throne Room to have the epic scale that I was looking for, the guys came up with the idea of opening the huge stage doors between two soundstages and building the set *through* them, to create the massively long throne room that I wanted.

On the Sunday prior to what would be our first day on the set, I was meeting with the DP, the Production Designer, and a few other key crew leads on the set. The final stage of set preparation was a clear varnish on the entire floor, to make it shine like marble. The stage had to be totally empty for twenty-four or forty-eight hours, to let the varnish dry.

Yellow tape was up at every entrance to the stage, and the entire throne room was built up on platforms off the floor. To enter at any point, you had to go up stairways to reach the entry arches. Signs were on tape that blocked all entrances, saying "NO ENTRANCE." We were on the stage discussing set-ups for the following morning, and I see someone peeking over the tape on one of the upper levels. As soon as I see the mask on his face, I know who it is. So I called out, "Michael?" and he kind of freaked a bit, and backed away with a kind of "Oh, I'm sorry . . . "

I said, "No, it's okay—I'm the director. You are welcome to take a look around, just take off your shoes first." We were all in socks, so as not to get any scuff marks on the shiny "marble" floor. So, Michael walked onto the stage and into the Throne Room—and he *loved* it. It was quite massive, and in fact many professionals in the industry would drop by over the next few weeks, having heard about this giant set that hadn't been seen in decades.

Anyway, Michael then invited me to visit him on his stage, which I did over several days, during breaks in our shooting. I happened to be there on the day they "machine gunned" the set, and also on the day that they did the famous "extreme lean" choreography. Michael snuck onto the set several other times during shooting, usually in one of his "disguises"—which, as you might know, were not all that great. It was Michael with a moustache, or Michael with a funny hat and glasses.

Did you personally have to engage in most of your battles with Menahem Golan, or did you have a producer assisting you with that? What was your personal impression of him?

Elliot Schick did most of the battles, I think. For the most part, I think everyone was trying to protect me and keep me focused on getting the film made. It was a challenging project. When I looked back I realized it had been a baptism of fire. My first film—and we had creature make-up, contact lenses, major wardrobe requirements, over one hundred 70mm effects plates that needed to be "locked down" to shoot, pyrotechnics, fog, animals, tons of action sequences, wire work, mattes, miniatures, mechanical props and weapons. I mean, it was a textbook for everything a film could possibly require.

As a director, you have to plan to the greatest degree possible, but you also have to be able to improvise on a constant basis, because most of the time none of the mechanical props or special equipment work as they are supposed to. All of the stunt sequences and wire work and other complex scenes—they always take longer than anticipated or planned for. The best thing for the director is to try and stay focused on the movie. That being said, by the time we were on the night shoots in Whittier, once or twice a week, for a week or two, I would be told, "You have to meet with Menahem tomorrow at 8 AM," or whatever ungodly hour. We were on night shoots, so I was usually going to bed at about that time. I would reply, "How about 3:00 in the afternoon?" I was cleverly planning such meetings knowing that I would have to leave by 4:00 to be back in Whittier by 5:00, to begin prep for the shoot that night.

So, I would be driven to the Cannon offices on San Vicente Boulevard in Beverly Hills. I would get to Menahem's office and be told to wait. Then, I would be brought in and Menahem would be there waiting, and with that booming Israeli accent, it would go something like this: "MY GOD YOU ARE DRIVING US BANKRUPT WITH THIS MOVIE WHAT THE FUCK ARE YOU DOING? YOU HAVE TO CUT PAGES YOU HAVE TO MAKE IT FASTER YOU ARE KEEEELING US KEEEELING US YOU ARE BANKRUPTING US DO YOU KNOW THAT YOU ARE KEEEEELING US KEEELLING US!" And then he would take a phone call, and talk for thirty or forty seconds on the phone about some other issue, and then look back to me: "YOU ARE FUCKING US YOU HAVE TO CUT PAGES WHAT THE FUCK ARE YOU DOING OUT THERE GODDAMMIT YOU HAVE TO CUT PAGES AND GET ON SCHEDULE!"

I would say, "Menahem, it was crazy to do a night shoot in Whittier— they make us break up everything at sunrise, and we have to set everything up all over again every night. We start at six, and we are ready to shoot at ten or eleven, and then we *maybe* get a scene done, and then its dinner break, and then we are back at 1:00am and we shoot for another four hours, maybe five—but we have to have all the equipment off the street by 6am." And Menehem would scream again, "FUCK THEM JUST SHOOT THE FUCKING MOVIE YOU ARE BANKRUPTING US!" And I would say, "Okay, well, I have to get back." Menahem would suddenly shift gears, look at me, and in a calm voice say, "Okay, well, do good tonight." I would say "I will," and off I would go.

These sessions would last about twenty to thirty minutes—him yelling and cursing, and blaming me for Cannon's financial issues. And then it would be, "OK, do good tonight." Sometimes there would be another director waiting outside his office, and I figured he was about to get the same spiel.

The dark lord Skeletor goofs around with his director, Gary Goddard, between takes on *Masters of the Universe*. Photo courtesy of Gary Goddard.

Cannon notoriously pulled the plug before you could film the finale, and you had to convince them to let you go back with Dolph, Anthony De Longis, and a skeleton crew to shoot the battle we got. Do you have any idea of what you'd have done if you had not been granted that extra day? Was there a backup plan?

I was told the night before, "Tomorrow is the last day, and the shoot will end at midnight." Knowing we had the entire choreographed sword fight to get and much more, I realized that we needed a Plan B. I really had to rethink things fast.

The direct answer to your question is "no," there was no other backup plan—the backup plan *was* getting the extra day, and doing what was necessary to tee up that day, assuming we would get it at some point.

Actually, that extra day included flying Frank out from New York. That was *Frank* and Dolph for all that last bit. What Anthony did was equally important. When I was told at around 6pm—the start of our last day on the Culver City Throne Room set—that we would stop at midnight, Elliot was very clear that he would literally *stop* the shoot *at midnight,* as he was under strict orders from Menahem. There was no way we could do that.

I spoke to Bill Niel, the 70MM cameraman from Boss Films—who had been told by his boss, Richard Edlund, to only shoot the shots on the storyboard. I told Richard I needed *one* shot, because I had an idea of how to save the night, but to do it I would need one framed shot of He-Man and Skeletor as the staff and sword met. What I would do would have him roll the 70MM film, and when the sword and staff met, we would kill all the lights on the stage for a "fade to black," but that I would need BOSS to animate the glow and sparking of the two weapons, to create a moment that made it seem that they were sucking all of the power and light out of the Throne Room. By doing that, we could then cheat the sword fight between Skeletor and He-Man, in the dark, using backlit color wheels and a hand held camera. I remembered such a scene, martial arts-style, from *Big Trouble in Little China* (1986) and I thought we could do something like that. I had the team go out and get a color wheel, and prepared the Camera Operator for doing some handheld work.

Bill agreed, the Camera Operator agreed. Anthony would step in for Frank, as Anthony and Dolph were going to have to kind of improvise some staged battles as the cameraman and color wheel guy tried to stay aligned.

So we got the final 70mm shot that I needed, with me promising to explain to Edlund that I required it, and promising to get additional funds for the "transition" from light to dark. And when we got that shot, barely, Elliot shut down the production. Everyone left but the color wheel guy, Anthony and Dolph, and myself, and a very few others. We stuck around and got up on that stage and we shot all of those moving camera shots in the dark with the color wheel. We shot about twenty or thirty minutes until Elliot freaked out, and we stopped. But, I felt in my head I had everything we needed now to create a finale up to the moment of impact where the sword breaks the staff, and Skeletor is defeated. I knew that I would have to come back and shoot that at some point down the road, but I assumed Menahem would understand. Sure enough, the 70MM shot worked to get us into darkness and working with Anne Coates, she really pulled together a pretty decent finale "fight" that got us up to that final moment.

Now, we still needed to shoot that final bit with the lines, with the breaking of the staff, with the moment when God Skeletor returns to loser Skeletor, pulls *his* sword out and tries one final trick, smashing the sword out of He-Man's hand—then He-Man grabbing it just in time, blocking Skeletor's final smash, and sending Skeletor over the edge and into the endless pit. All of this was shot in *one day* at the Boss Studio stage. I wrote the scene, shot for shot, and assured Menahem it could be done in one day.

By the way, once we had a very rough cut of the scene up to this moment, I showed [Menahem] *why* we needed to have this last scene, to give the film its necessary ending. And I will never forget this. Menahem said, "You don't need to shoot anything else, this is fine." I said "But, there's no ending—they're just fighting, and there's no winner—" And Menahem said, "You don't need it—just fade to black!" I was taken aback. "Fade to black?" I said, and he said, "YES! YES! JUST FADE TO BLACK!" I couldn't believe it.

Anyway, cooler heads prevailed and they made me this offer: it was going to cost $150,000 for the day, I believe—and they said if I would contribute half of it, they would put up the other half. They said, "If it's so important, then you put up half!" Which I did. But, I also got Frank to get in that vat of bubbling liquid, so that I could get in the moment that I wanted *after* the end titles.

I will never forget Frank looking at me, in baggy swim pants, but with the mask on and the hood and the shoulder part of the cape. "This is what you have brought me to," he said to me, and I laughed. I think I said, "Anything for your art, Frank." But, we got it, and over thirty years later, someone at Marvel clearly liked the idea of the teaser after the credits.

Even with the shortened production, there are scenes that were trimmed from the initial cut that was shown to audiences, and ones that were cut from the script along the way. What do you recall of those? Are there any you wish had stayed in the film?

There were some, yes, but most I think were probably for the best. However, the one cut we did that I think hurt the film was at the very end.

When Julie says goodbye to the Eternians, we shot a very "*Wizard of Oz*" kind of farewell, and Bill Conti scored it *perfectly*. The music hit the right emotional note and swelled at the exact right moment—it really was nice. After she says these goodbyes, she and Kevin head into the Portal as the music swells yet again, and then as they are disappearing we see and hear Julie say, "No, wait! Send us back to—" and we fade to black.

Well, at the first preview, people were getting a little teary-eyed at the farewells—you could hear some sniffling, which was great. The problem was that the moment after we faded to black for those few seconds before she wakes up in her room, well—people at the preview, some of them got up and started to leave *thinking the movie was over.*

Menahem and the execs thought it was because no one wanted to sit through to the end. I explained what I thought had happened, and tried to tell them "Didn't you hear people sniffling and crying?" But they didn't, because they were way in the back. Anyway, I fought it, but they kept hammering me, and that was the one thing I gave up on and have regretted ever since. I think it changed the ending, and we lost an emotional hook that existed.

Walt Disney always said, "I want people to laugh in our movies, but I also want them to cry." And of the two, he considered the tears more important. If people cry in your film, they are affected by it. So, I hated losing that and I think—in fact, I *know*—they made the wrong call on that.

One of William Stout's many tasks on *Masters of the Universe* was designing the massive set that served as Castle Grayskull's throne room—the largest set of its kind built in Hollywood since the film industry's Golden Age.

Interview: Production Designer William Stout

Since the late Sixties, artist William Stout has been leaving his thumbprint all over American pop culture. After receiving his Bachelor's Degree on a full scholarship to the Chouinard Art Institute, Stout received his first professional work as a comic illustrator, working with famed artists such as Russ Manning on the *Tarzan of the Apes* newspaper strip and Harvey Kurtzman and Will Elder on the *Little Annie Fanny* strips for *Playboy* magazine. Soon afterward, he would become one of the first American contributors to the influential sci-fi and fantasy magazine *Heavy Metal*. At the same time, Stout gained a reputation in the rock and roll scene, illustrating forty-five bootleg album covers and working as the art director for *Bomp!*, the rock magazine that launched the writing careers of Greil Marcus and Lester Bangs. He also became well-known for his collaborations with the Firesign Theatre.

Of course, the movie industry—or "The Biz," as Stout refers to it—would soon come calling. This began in the late Seventies, when Stout was hired to create the movie posters for the cult classics *Wizards* (1977) and

Rock 'n' Roll High School (1979), and was enlisted to work on the *Buck Rogers* (1979–1981) television show. He was responsible for much of the world-building for the genre-codifying *Conan the Barbarian* (1982), and drew storyboards for the blockbuster action film *First Blood* (1982) as well as Michael Jackson's landmark "Thriller" music video. Around this time he also created storyboard illustrations for the 1981 classic *Raiders of the Lost Ark*—for which, like his creature design contributions to 1987's *The Predator*, he went uncredited.

Stout became the youngest production designer in Hollywood when he was hired on *Return of the Living Dead* (1985) to dream up its gruesome zombies and create the movie's infamous Tarman. This was shortly before his path crossed with Cannon's, and he was hired to do similar concept and design work on the Martians for Tobe Hooper's *Invaders from Mars* (1986). He'd follow that up as the production designer on the sci-fi spectacle that was *Masters of the Universe* (1987). To date, he's worked on more than thirty feature films.

Across a career that includes work in video games, animation, as a Disney Imagineer, and as a theme park attraction designer, Stout has perhaps been most celebrated as the world's foremost illustrator of dinosaurs. Since the release of his acclaimed 1981 book *The Dinosaurs: A Fantastic New View of a Lost Era*, Stout's paleontological artwork has been featured in museums and exhibitions around the globe. This same volume of art was acknowledged by Michael Crichton to be one of the inspirations for his 1990 novel, *Jurassic Park*.

As a kid you went to see monster movies with your mom and science fiction with your dad, and that was a big influence on your illustration work later on. Would I be correct in guessing that made the opportunity to update *Invaders from Mars* an engaging prospect for you?

William Stout: There were several factors involved in deciding to take on designing *Invaders from Mars*. Back at that time, the film business usually shut down for the holidays, beginning in November or late October. In January, The Biz would open back up. In the first two weeks of January I would typically have about five films offered to me. I would consider each one. First, I'd read the script. Then I would find out whom I would be working with and check their reputation in The Biz and with friends who had worked with them. I would look at whether or not the budget and schedule for each film was realistic.

The original *Invaders from Mars* (1953) was directed and designed by one of my big cinematic heroes: William Cameron Menzies. He was the very first production designer, [having worked on] *Gone With The Wind* (1939). His *Invaders from Mars* is practically a textbook on low-budget film making. We both began as illustrators. I studied his career and what he accomplished very carefully.

As it had been a Million Dollar Movie, I had seen *Invaders from Mars* many, many times. (The Million Dollar Movie ran one film each week, screening it twice each weekday and three times each on Saturday and Sunday.) I loved that the story was told from the kid's point of view.

As far as the crew, initially *Invaders from Mars* had two things going for it: a Dan O'Bannon script and Tobe Hooper as director. I loved Tobe's horror masterpiece *Texas Chain Saw Massacre* (1974). And I loved Dan O'Bannon's screenplays, especially *Alien* (1979). We were friends and had worked together on his directorial debut, *The Return of the Living Dead* (1985). He directed *Return of the Living Dead*, and I was his production designer. I was curious as to what Dan and Tobe would do with *Invaders*.

Dan and I had lots of projects we were going to do together. It would have been thrilling to have collaborated more with O'Bannon. One thing we shared a love for was comics. We planned to do several comic book stories together.

Dan collaborated with Moebius on one of the great sci-fi comic book stories, "The Long Tomorrow". The look of that story is the basic design template for *Blade Runner* (1982).

Dan could be difficult, but that was usually because of his goal of making our movie the best that it could possibly be. Dan was not only brilliant as a writer, he also had a strong visual sense. I learned a lot from him.

Tobe Hooper had a similar origin story to yours—making *Invaders* was paying homage to the sci-fi and monster movies he'd enjoyed in his youth. How was your experience working with him?

Tobe was a low-key, warm and friendly guy. Our storyboard artist, Keith Crossley, had worked with Tobe on other films. He confided in me as to a lot of Tobe's "tells," to use a poker term. For instance, if I presented an idea for the film to Tobe and he wasn't going to do it, he'd say, "Could do, could do." But if he liked the idea and decided he would actually include it in the film, he'd say, "Can do, can do."

There are two distinct monsters that fans associate *with Invaders from Mars*: the alien drones, and the brain-like Supreme Intelligence. Would you mind telling me a little bit about your ideas that went into each?

Sure. One of my first friends in the movie business was Rick Baker. We entered The Biz at roughly the same time. We talked a lot about creatures and creature design—it was Rick who brought me in to design the *Predator* (1987). Rick always felt that an audience could tell right away when there was a guy in a suit, because the creature had the same bodily configuration as a human. But, Rick suggested, what if the monster suit was designed to be worn *backwards*? The legs would no longer look like human legs—they would be bending the wrong way.

I took (stole) Rick's idea and used it to create the Martian drones. Then Stan Winston added a little person inside the suit, sitting inside in a backpack, facing forward and operating the drones' arms.

In regards to the Supreme Intelligence, I came up with about a dozen different designs. The one that made it to the screen was conceived by one of Stan Winston's crew.

I ended up sort of being the Martian Production Designer, designing All Things Martian for the film: the ship, the drones, the machinery, the ship interiors, the weapons, et cetera.

You worked with a couple fellow legends here, in SFX maestros Stan Winston and John Dykstra. Was the job more attractive, knowing talents like theirs would be bringing your designs to life?

Young David flees from his body-snatched teacher and two alien drones in the William Stout-designed mothership from *Invaders from Mars*.

Not necessarily. I was suspicious of both gentlemen for various reasons. Had I been the production designer on *Invaders*, I might have hired someone else. I was close to a lot of people in their two arenas that I knew would deliver for me without any political bullshit or any other baggage. They both worked out OK, though, with pretty much a minimum of sand and grit in the machine.

Part of your job on *Invaders* was similar to things you did on *Conan the Barbarian*, in having to conceptualize the culture and technologies of a fictional civilization. These are things that weren't necessarily fleshed out in the scripts, but would ring false on screen if someone hadn't taken the time to think them through.

For me, it's important for everything in a film to have a backstory or a sense of history, whether that ends up on the screen or not. It helps the actors to believe in their characters; it helps the believability of the film itself.

As a designer, I'm a hands-on, detail-focused kind of guy. On *Invaders*, for example, I even went so far as to design a Martian alphabet and typeface.

What was your process like for coming up with the Martians' environments and technology?

Everything starts with the script. That's my Bible. After I read the screenplay for the first time, I re-read it, noting everything I will have to design and its function within the film. That tells me a lot. And, as most good designers know, form follows function.

Once I deliver some designs the director is happy with, I expand upon that design path so that the film's look has some consistency.

You recommended James Karen for his role in *Invaders*, after working with him on *The Return of the Living Dead*. Sadly, our conversation for this book wound up being one of his final interviews. I found him to be one of the warmest and funniest people I've spoken to. Were you good friends?

Yes, we were. Jimmy was amazing. He brought Jason Robards to the set of *Return* one afternoon! Jimmy would even show up on the days he wasn't working, just to keep the cast pumped up. I wanted James Karen in *every* movie of mine. He was one of the most generous, positive and funniest guys I've ever met. The world is poorer for his absence.

This was the first of two movies you worked on for the company. What were your initial impressions of Menahem Golan, Yoram Globus, and Cannon? Did those change at all over the course of these two films?

I thought those two guys were a riot; absolutely hilarious. The stories our First Assistant Director told me about working with Menahem in Israel were sidesplitting.

But as I got to know them, I also found them crucial to the business. It's very hard for a young person to break into the film business. But if you were a young filmmaker, you could get an audience with Roger Corman or Menahem so that you could pitch your film. No working up the long chain of command at a big studio that would eventually end in "No." Roger or Menahem would give you a "Yes" or "No" on the spot after your pitch. If either of them said "Yes," you'd get your chance. You wouldn't get much money to make your film, but you'd at least get a shot at actually making a movie. That was very, very valuable. We don't have opportunities like that anymore for young filmmakers.

Plus, those two guys were producing *lots* of movies. Back when I was on *Invaders*, the highest number of films in production at the big studios was at Warner Brothers, who had eight. Cannon had over *sixty!*

You came from a background in comics: first as a fan, and then as an artist. You've drawn many storyboards in your career, for everything from *First Blood* to uncredited work on *Raiders of the Lost Ark*. Did comics prepare you, in any way, for those jobs?

Yes, indeed. One of the great things about comics is that you learn how to draw *everything*. Plus, you learn how to draw the human figure out of your head; there's no time or budget to use models.

Are there any similarities in their storytelling skill sets?

There are two main differences in storytelling between comics and movies. In comics, you can change your panel format all you want. You can have a page with a square panel, a rectangular panel, a horizontal panel and a vertical panel. In movies, that screen format stays the same for the entire length of the film.

The other difference is screen direction. In comics you can place your "camera" anywhere you want. But in film, if a character is running from left to right, you can't suddenly place your camera on the other side of your character—it will look like he's running back to where he had just come from. In The Biz, that's called "crossing the axis"—a cardinal cinematic sin, and very confusing to the audience.

Is it true that you initially turned down the production design gig on *Masters of the Universe*?

No. I was hired from the very beginning to do storyboards on *Masters*. Having worked as a production designer on some other films, though, I knew what *Masters* needed. So, sometimes I would dash off a character design or a design for a set; just trying to give the film a good "look." Plus, director Gary Goddard loved what I was doing, both storyboard-wise and non-storyboard-wise. We really hit it off. It was production designer Geoffrey Kirkland, though, who recommended I take over his job on *Masters*. He and Gary did not see eye-to-eye.

The brain-like Supreme Intelligence from *Invaders from Mars*.

Obviously, the Dutch Boy haircut had to go if anyone was going to take He-Man seriously in a live action movie. What were your biggest hurdles

in taking a cartoon world and making it so that viewers would believe it in a live setting?

The biggest hurdle was Mattel. They fought against making He-man and his world real. You can't just take the toy as it is and put it up on the screen. You won't sustain the audience's interest. The toy costumes, for example, won't be believable as the clothes and armor your character would live in. There's not enough depth or texture to them. They'll bore the audience after a minute and look cheap.

First and foremost, you as the filmmaker have to believe in the story you're telling, and that the characters that are in it are real. If you can't believe it's real, you can't expect your audience to believe in it. Plus, you have to sustain your audience's attention and interest in the story. You add all kinds of little bits along the way to keep the story you're telling exciting.

It sounds like the decision was made relatively early to move most of the movie's action to Earth.

Not *too* early; we didn't have that much time in our schedule. Making most of the film happen on earth was due to budget. I knew that was going to happen. On nearly every film I've worked on, about a third of what was planned has gone into the trash without being filmed.

How much design did you do for Eternia that went unused?

Originally about a third of the film took place in Eternia. I designed several Eternia sets and more Eternia characters who never made it to the screen, including She-Ra.

You hired the great Jean Giraud, also known as Moebius, to assist you in some design work on the film. Can you describe your working relationship on *Masters*, and how you decided which design tasks you would give him?

Fortunately for me (and for the film), my dear friend Jean "Moebius" Giraud was living in Santa Monica while I was making *Masters*. I asked him if he'd like to do some work with me on *Masters*. He was excited to do so.

Knowing Jean's brilliance, I threw the toughest problems his way. I wanted to see what he would come up with.

I assigned him four tasks: re-design He-man; take a stab at designing the throne room; design the Sorceress; and design the flying disc men. He came through with flying colors on all four, even though his designs later got filtered or compromised.

I loved Jean's thought process. In redesigning He-Man, Jean designed a guy who had been in this world civil war on Eternia a long time. He-Man was someone who could improvise on the battlefield. In the course of the war, He-Man had lost much of his body armor. So, he would take bits of machinery he would find on the battlefield and strap those pieces to his body as an improvised armor substitute. Brilliant! And visually interesting! I fought hard for this concept but couldn't convince Mattel.

Jean's throne room design had giant statues lining the path to the throne, inspiring me to expand upon that concept. The throne room was the seat of power for all the universe. Power is neither good nor bad—it's what you make of it. So, in opposition to Giraud's Space Gods, as I called them, who represented the good that can be done with power, below the surface of the walkway were demonic gargoyle figures, representing the dark side of power. The yin and the yang of power, so to speak.

Instead of seeing the Sorceress as an adult woman, Giraud came up with a thousand-year-old Sorceress who looked like she was but twelve years old.

The disc riders were in more of Moebius' typical wheelhouse; very cool designs where everything about them looked functional. I had Ed Eyth do his interpretation of Jean's designs. Ed came up with almost all the cool, techie-looking stuff in *Masters*. Great designer!

One of the regrets you've talked about in regards to this film is that they couldn't use the entrance you'd designed for Evil-Lyn. Can you describe what that would have been?

I think entrances are one of the most important scenes a character can have. The way the audience first sees a character should be indelible; it should tell the audience just who this character is and what they're all about.

I designed Evil-Lyn's entrance so that she looked like she was coming up from the depths of the underworld. She was going to meet Skeletor, so I gave her some steps she had to ascend. You saw her head first, then her shoulders as she scaled the steps, until finally you saw all of her. That also established Skeletor as a power you had to climb to meet. *He* was on top—not you. Our writer, David Odell, went nuts when he saw those storyboards! It renewed his passion for the film.

Dolph Lundgren wore re-designed armor for his portrayal of He-Man in the *Masters of the Universe* movie.

I was also disappointed that Evil-Lyn was given a haircut. Hair on a young woman is power. The longer and thicker the hair, the more Power she seems to have. Meg Foster came to me in tears when she found out that her character's hair was going to be cut. I had designed Evil-Lyn to have a big, thick black mane studded with pearls all throughout. I based her look and attitude on Gloria Swanson's Norma Desmond character in Billy Wilder's classic film, *Sunset Boulevard* (1950).

Were there many additional characters you designed for the movie, but didn't make their way into the film?

A lot. That's mostly because we were shooting in the dark—and Mattel was hoping we'd revitalize the franchise and come up with new characters for their *Masters* toy line. The entire art department spent a week or two coming up with new characters. Most were duds. You gotta have a lot of luck and smart design sense to come up with characters that everybody loves or at least finds interesting. Plus, as a designer, you need to know what is possible in a practical sense.

In the decades since *Masters of the Universe*, the movie's drawn comparisons to some of Jack Kirby's work, particularly his Fourth World saga. Your connection to comics runs miles deep, and director Gary Goddard was a huge Kirby fan who collected comics since childhood. Do you remember there being a conscious Kirby influence when you were preparing the film?

Yes; mostly on Gary's part. I was attempting to come up with something that was visually unique, yet certainly Kirby-influenced, as that was Gary's particular bent and what I thought was a very appropriate visual influence for the film. Both Gary and I knew Jack and were his friends. I ghost-inked an issue of Jack Kirby's *The Demon*.

I understand Frank Langella had a lot of say in his wardrobe, and that Dolph Lundgren perhaps tried to have more. Can you talk about any changes that were made (or almost made) to the costumes, once you were working with the actors?

Frank was a consummate professional. He took an interest in everything that involved his character. We tried cape after cape with him until we got a cape with the proper weight that flowed magnificently when Skeletor walked or made one of his grand, dramatic gestures.

Dolph was very different from Frank. He didn't have Langella's confidence. Julie Weiss, my costume designer, came to me one day with a problem. Lundgren had become fixated on wearing these kickboxing boots as He-Man. I didn't design them that way. I felt that kickboxing boots were much too short on the leg, very unattractive. Julie invited me to Dolph's costume fitting. He wanted to show me how cool the kickboxing boots were on him. He did a few turns and gestures.

"Well, what do you think?"

"I think they look *fantastic*, Dolph—but very gay."

The next day those boots were nowhere to be found.

The throne room set was one of the largest built in Hollywood since the Golden Age. Do you recall your feelings when you first walked in there and saw your work realized on such a large scale?

When you design a set of such size and scale, you can feel quite a bit like God.

It was gigantic. I took two soundstages and knocked out the wall between them. Everybody in the business had visiting this set on their must-do list. And they all wanted their picture taken on the throne, the seat of power to all the universe.

It looks like there was some stuff underneath the throne area that we don't really get a good look at. Was that intended for the finale that was infamously cut short?

If the cool stuff under the throne area wasn't shot, it wasn't because there was nothing there. I wish that more of that netherworld had made it to the camera—but it didn't.

You've worked on many, many films since that pair for Cannon. Is there anything you learned on either *Invaders* or *Masters* that you've carried with you through the rest of your film work?

Every film that I work on—especially the bad ones—teaches me something new about filmmaking. Because I had such a key position on those films and the attendant responsibilities, I learned loads on those two films. Working on *Invaders* gave me the confidence and drive to go back to being a production designer. By the time I designed *Masters*, I knew I had my own special tastes and a design sense that was unique, even if informed by the past. Both films taught me how to fight more effectively in getting what I wanted for the film to make the movie better.

Kevin (Robert Duncan McNeill) and Julie (Courteney Cox) stumble across the Cosmic Key in *Masters of the Universe*.

Interview: Actor Robert Duncan McNeill

Robert Duncan McNeill has contributed to science fiction films and television on both sides of the camera for more than three decades. As a young actor, McNeill played the earthling Kevin Corrigan, who mistakes the Cosmic Key for a synthesizer but winds up saving the day in *Masters of the Universe* (1987). The following decade, he'd be cast as a regular on *Star Trek: Voyager* (1995–2002), playing Starfleet officer Tom Paris for all seven seasons of the show.

Although McNeill continues to act, his focus has moved to directing and producing. Among his many behind-the-camera credits, he has executive produced shows such as *Chuck* (2007–2012) and the Marvel series *The Gifted* (2017–2019), and directed episodes of *Star Trek: Enterprise* (2001–2005), *Dead Like Me* (2003–2004), and *Supernatural* (2005–2020).

This wasn't your first role, but it was your first big one—and this was a massive production. What was it like for you as a young actor, to walk on to something of that scale?

Robert Duncan McNeill: I was about twenty when I got that role. I'd had a bit of a whirlwind for the three years before that: I'd moved from Atlanta to New York City. I thought I was going to be a waiter, and maybe get into the chorus of a touring show. I had an old Hollywood idea of what being an actor in New York might be like. Things changed very quickly. I did some musical theater and some tours, and then I ended up going to school at Juilliard. All of a sudden I got a TV show, *The Twilight Zone* (1985–1989), then I was on *All My Children*, and then I was on *Masters*. In three years, I'd gone from getting off a bus from Georgia, to doing a big movie. It was quite overwhelming, but it seemed to fit the path that I'd been on for a few years.

The cast was so tight—it was such a great group of people. Courteney Cox and I hit it off right away. We were like brother and sister. We were very close. I stayed at her house all the time. I'd go over and end up sleeping over there. She had a lot of friends. She had an open door policy. She loved being the hostess, coordinating everything. There would always be people around. That was fun.

Everybody was wonderful. Jon Cypher was great. James Tolkan, I loved him. He was a New Yorker and I lived in New York at the time, so Jimmy Tolkan and I would connect over New York life. Chelsea Field was a dancer who had just gotten one of her first big roles. I had come out of musical theater, and I had been a tap dancer as a teenager. There were a lot of people in that cast that I really connected to and bonded with. It was exciting, and it was a little surreal.

For me, I was doing two jobs at once. The original shoot was supposed to be six and a half weeks or something like that. I was doing a soap opera, and I'd gotten permission to take four weeks off completely from the soap, then the other two weeks, or two and a half, whatever it was, they agreed that they would work with the movie to schedule around whatever conflicts there were, so I could do the soap in New York and the movie in Los Angeles, which was quite crazy and ambitious for me.

It was immediately clear that this movie was falling behind schedule. We had the original DP, who I really loved, but was replaced after a few weeks because we were dropping so much work and falling behind schedule. So that six-week shoot turned into seven, eight, nine weeks—much longer than originally scheduled. The soap opera in New York was like, "Well, you've got to come back to work. We gave you your month off and we worked with them for a couple of weeks, but now we're in first position and you've got to do this."

Masters then scheduled a lot of stuff around my soap opera schedule, but it was tricky. Sometimes I'd find myself in New York, going to the soap opera at seven in the morning, getting that done by six o'clock or so in the evening, jumping in a cab, going to the airport at Newark, jumping on a plane, getting off and going to a night shoot. Because of the time difference, I'd gained a few hours. I'd show up at a night shoot in Whittier or something after working in New York and trying to sleep on the plane. It was a crazy, disorienting time for me when it got into that phase—I was twenty, twenty-one years old. I was not sleeping. It was too much.

It's funny. When I see the movie, I can see some scenes where I'm like, "Oh yeah, I remember that." The very last scene of the movie, when the sun comes up and Courteney and I are running in the neighborhood, wondering "Did that happen?" "Was that real?" That was one of those nights where I had flown on a red-eye, or some late flight, and then didn't shoot until the sun rose, so I'd been up for twenty-four hours. I can see it in that last scene. [*Laughs*] I can see it in a number of scenes, but that one, in particular, it's like "Oh, I wish I had just been able to be on the California schedule and not try to work on both coasts at the same time."

You went on to work on many other science fiction and genre shows, not just acting on *Star Trek*, but with many of the series you've directed. Did *Masters* prepare you in any way for those future jobs?

Robert Duncan McNeill and Courteney Cox discuss their scene with director Gary Goddard during the shooting of *Masters of the Universe*. Photo courtesy of Gary Goddard.

Yes. We spent nearly a month in downtown Whittier, shooting only nights. That's the first time I'd ever experienced anything like that. That was an extreme version of it. I think the way that I didn't manage my rest and sleep very well during *Masters* has made me a little more mature in the way that I try to rest now when I direct. I take naps at lunch, even if I'm directing. I go into my trailer and make myself lay down with a meditation tape on, and I get fifteen minutes of sleep. I didn't do any of that back then. I was just go, go, go. I think now I've got a more mature approach to night shoots.

The makeup on *Masters*, Mike Westmore and that whole department, looking at *Masters* and the characters they created, on every level they were phenomenal. A lot of young people got their start in their makeup careers with Mike Westmore on that movie.

The movie started as non-union—Cannon was low-budget, non-union. That's how they made their money, by shooting cheap. The actors were union, but the crew was all non-union. The crew was approached by the union during the middle of a shoot early on, I think, and at one point we shut down because the crew struck to go union. I remember when that happened. I was very naive about a lot of things back then. I didn't quite understand what was going on.

A lot of those people in Mike Westmore's makeup department, and electricians and grips, I ended up working with on *Star Trek* years later. A lot of them had gotten into the union and began their careers on *Masters*.

Did you have the idea that you would eventually want to work behind the camera, even back then? Were you watching the director, or the other people working on the set?

Absolutely. When I was doing *Masters of the Universe*, we had an editor named Anne Coates who had won an Academy Award for *Lawrence of Arabia* (1962). She was an A-list editor, which is ironic, because she was working on this cheesy little Cannon Film at the time. This is when there was no Avid or digital editing. She cut film. She physically *cut* the negative and hung it up, and had it on a Moviola or whatever it's called. She'd cut the film and splice and tape.

We shot at a place called Laird Studios—it's now called Culver Studios. Before that, it was originally the Selznick Studios where they filmed *Gone with the Wind* (1939) and *Batman* (1966–1968). A beautiful, tiny little studio in Culver City. Small, not a lot of stages, maybe six or eight, tops. Anne Coates had an editing room up above some of the bungalows in this cool, old editing space where they may have cut *Gone with the Wind*. I would go up there when I wasn't working and got to know Anne and her son, who was assisting her, and the other editors. I just watched them cut the film and that process fascinated me.

That was the first time I remember realizing how many people it took to make a movie or a TV show. It wasn't just some camera operators and actors out on the stage, but there were so many complicated layers of putting that project together. They felt like the grown-ups on set. Sometimes, as an actor, you feel like you're the kids playing around and having fun. It doesn't feel like grown-up work. When I went up there to Anne's editing suite, I was like, "Oh, these are smart people and they're grown-ups and they're doing a grown-up job." You can see they are physically putting something together and building something that, when they're done, they can go, "Look what I've built," and point to this thing. Sometimes as an actor, you don't feel that same sense. It's a little abstract.

Chelsea Field as Teela in *Masters of the Universe*. Image courtesy of Jérémie Damoiseau.

Interview: Actress Chelsea Field

Like fellow Cannon starlet Lucinda Dickey, Chelsea Field transitioned into film after working as a featured dancer on the TV variety series *Solid Gold* (1980–1988). She made her first big-screen appearance in the John Travolta-Jamie Lee Curtis romance *Perfect* (1985), but '80s action fans are more likely to remember her other very early role, playing the flight attendant on the receiving end of Arnold Schwarzenegger's classic one-liner, "Don't bother my friend, he's dead tired," in *Commando* (1985).

After playing the heroic soldier Teela in *Masters of the Universe* (1987), Field is best known for co-starring in *Harley Davidson and Marlboro Man* and *The Last Boy Scout* (both 1991). More recently, she appeared as a series regular on *NCIS: New Orleans* (2014–2021), playing attorney Rita Devereaux.

Masters of the Universe was near the very beginning of your screen career. What were your earliest days in Hollywood like?

Chelsea Field: I think it was my first feature film. The reason that it was a big deal was because I had only had little, teeny tiny parts. I had been a professional dancer for ten years before I transitioned into acting. I remember I had so many auditions for *Masters*, it was insane. I found out later, from the director, that the reason was because the producers were worried about giving it to me because I didn't have enough experience.

They just kept having me back for call back after call back, and it was so silly because there were hardly any scenes to read. It was such a physical part. I would be in their office running around and hiding behind the couch, pretending I had a laser gun in my hand.

I do remember when my agents called and told me that I got it, I literally felt like it was the last five seconds of the Super Bowl and I had run in the winning touchdown. It just was the best feeling ever.

Gary Goddard had mentioned that he had remembered you from an audition for his *Conan the Barbarian* live show. Do you recall that?

Yes, I do. The story was I had been a dancer and done a lot of great dance work, and then I went on the road with a band as a singer and came back to

LA, and decided to take a break from the band and just get some work. I had been auditioning and I hadn't gotten anything.

That week I had three auditions. One was for the *Conan* show at Universal, one was for an NBC affiliate show, and then the other one happened because a choreographer for the NBC affiliate show was also choreographing *Solid Gold*, and then later that week I had an audition for *Solid Gold*. I ended up getting all three of them.

I remember the week before I had those auditions, I was running out of money. I didn't want to hit up my parents for anything and I literally said a prayer. I was like, "Okay, God, either send me some work or I'm going to put the band back together and go back out on the road." Literally. Then I had three jobs and I said, "Okay, that's enough." When I auditioned for the *Conan* show, I was in one of those states that, I think, artists get to where you're just questioning everything about your choices and saying, "Am I any good? Maybe I'm talentless, I don't get it".

I was doing great, I had a ton of work, and then I was trying to make this transition and the universe didn't seem to be supporting me. At the time I was pretty impatient. I remember just saying, "Please, I'll do anything, I'll do anything." They said, "Can you do gymnastics?" I said, "Sure." They said, "What can you do?" I said, "An aerial." So I did an aerial.

They're like, "Oh, can you do a back handspring?" I said, "Yes." I had not thrown a back handspring since I was like fifteen, and I was like, "Sure", and I literally threw a back handspring. I'm sure I almost broke my neck but that's what you do when you want a job and your adrenaline is flowing.

When they were making *Masters*, He-Man was one of the biggest toy and cartoon properties of that era. Did you have any young nephews, neighbors, or friends' children, who were excited by your casting?

No, I had no idea. Mattel was always around the shoot—they were always there, having meetings and talking to us, and getting ready to do different dolls. I was completely clueless to all of that. I had no idea that it was a big thing. I didn't have kids at the time and I don't even think my nephews were born yet. I came into it totally blind, so to speak.

The Grayskull throne room set was one of the biggest built in Hollywood in decades. What was it like stepping into such a big production as a relative newcomer?

It was fantastic, because there was so much wonderful support. Gary was fantastic. All of the actors became very close and a lot of us have remained friends. Jon Cypher, who was an absolute doll, that I worked a lot with—Jon and I both did a lot of broadsword training, which they didn't end up using in the movie but was all in the prep. We would go down onto one of the soundstages to take lessons and practice.

Then when we went onto the set, it was just—it was unbelievable. I didn't have a reference because I hadn't been on a lot of sets. I'd done a few little things, and maybe a couple of guest stars on some TV shows that were happening at the time, but I just was flabbergasted. We felt like tiny ants when we walked onto that set.

You mentioned Jon, and I'm wondering if you can share any memories you have of your co-stars. I hear Billy Barty was fun to be around.

Yes, he was great. Such a great attitude and always positive and super—just a wonderful spirit to have around. We did a lot of night shooting in Whittier for that whole sequence when we're in the town, and it just seemed like we shot there forever. When you're shooting nights, you're driving out at three or four to get to the set and get your makeup done, so that when the sun's going down you're blocking your first shot.

Then you work from sundown, and you're usually racing because everyone's like, "Oh God, the sun is coming up. We've got to get this shot. Hurry up." Then you're driving back to your house when the world is waking up. In a weird way, it really bonded everybody because for weeks we weren't in the regular world, we had our own little nighttime world going on. There were some really amazing actors in that movie: Jon, James Tolkan, and of course Frank Langella, who was unbelievable.

Jon was this very dramatic person, along with being a great dramatic actor, and he has this amazing, booming voice. We'd be sitting around for hours waiting for a shot to be ready, which is typical when you're doing big action movies. People would be yelling at Gary, "Come on, we got to go." He would say, "Gary, what are we doing? We're sitting around, let's shoot." He just used his huge, booming voice that was actually frightening and all of us—me, and Courteney [Cox], and Robbie [Duncan McNeill] . . . our eyes would be as big as lemons.

He'd be in front of us and he'd be yelling at Gary, and when he turned around he had this ridiculous grin on his face like he was joking, and poor Gary's running around like, "Okay, we're ready, come on, let's shoot." He would just do that kind of stuff all the time, and then we were in on the joke because then we knew, "Okay, he's not serious. He's pulling Gary's leg." But poor Gary thought he was serious. That's one of our fun stories we had.

Do you remember when you first saw the finished movie, and what you thought?

I probably didn't really see the movie until years later because I was so nervous about it being my first film where I actually had something to do. For many years I was super self-critical. I think every time I came on the screen, I was like, "Oh my God, why did I do this? I could have done that. Oh, what about this?" Like a typical actor, thinking of a million other things I could have done or said, or the different ways I could read the line. I probably never really looked at the film until many years later, when I was able to watch it.

There was an anniversary screening, and I went with my youngest son. It was a blast. I had kept saying to him, "It's really a stupid movie. It's so silly. It's nothing like the superhero movies that they have out now. We didn't have those special effects." Then the movie finished, and I looked at him, and he's like, "Mom, that was good." I said, "Yes, it holds up." The special effects are not what they are today, but the story holds up.

I know many of you became friends while making this.

We had so many dinner parties. It would either be at my house, or at Courteney's. James Tolkan would be there and Anne Coates, our amazing editor, may she rest in peace. Gary and Frank Langella would be there, Jon Cypher, Robbie. It was a great group of people.

That was an experience that made such an impression and, of course, I never had it again. I never stayed friends with anybody from any movie the way I had with all of them. It holds a dear place in my heart.

Are there lessons that you learned on this set that you've carried with you into other roles?

I think I marveled at the way Frank Langella could deliver his monologues, through that costume and through that mask. It was quite unruly, the mask that he had to wear. There was very little of him—you couldn't even really see his eyes. It was such an overwhelming mask that he wore. I really marveled at his ability to deliver these scenes and these monologues with such amazing integrity to the character. I think that that was a wonderful example for me.

Also, James Tolkan is an amazing actor, and of course Jon was. I really learned from those guys, Meg Foster, and Christina Pickles. They were these deeply talented actors, and none of the scenes were really scenes that you could bite into. They were all these very—how do you describe them? You had to pack a lot in with very little dialogue. They did it so beautifully, and I think that's probably what has stayed with me.

My part was very physical and I had very little lines, so it was a challenge. It was actually a perfect first film for me. Coming from a very physical field such as dancing, it was probably a good introductory role for me.

Interview: Actor Anthony De Longis

Actor, stunt man, fight director, choreographer, and weapons specialist Anthony De Longis has earned his reputation as one of the most skilled swordsmen in the film business. It's a talent he was able to put to good use not only playing the villainous Blade in *Masters of the Universe* (1987), but by training Dolph Lundgren in how to wield the Power Sword, and doubling Frank Langella as Skeletor. For Cannon, he also appeared in 1986's *Dangerously Close*.

Although best-known for his recurring roles as Jal Culluh on *Star Trek: Voyager* (1995–2001) and for trading blows with Patrick Swayze's Dalton in the classic *Road House* (1989), some of De Longis' highest-impact contributions to pop culture have come from off-camera. De Longis trained Indiana Jones himself, Harrison Ford, how to use his bullwhip for *Indiana Jones and the Kingdom of the Crystal Skull* (2008). He provided similar instruction to Michelle Pfeiffer when she chose to perform her own whip stunts as Catwoman in *Batman Returns* (1992).

Blade (Anthony De Longis) and Evil-Lyn (Meg Foster), two of Skeletor's most dangerous allies in *Masters of the Universe*.

Among De Longis' many screen credits are *The Sword and The Sorcerer* (1982), *Far and Away* (1992), *Almost Heroes* (1998), *Highlander: The Series* (1992–1998), *Secondhand Lions* (2003) and *Jet Li's Fearless* (2006). While he continues to work in front of and behind the camera—he's also a prolific voice and motion capture actor—he runs a training center at his home, Rancho Indalo, where he helps visitors improve their skills with weapons and horses.

When you came on board for *Masters of the Universe*, was it as an actor first and then choreographer/trainer, or vice versa?

Anthony De Longis: It was just as an actor at first. I don't really remember my audition. I'm sure I had one, but no, I was hired as an actor. I was given a choice by the makeup artist on it. She said, "Well, we can either do a bald cap, but with as much activity as you're going to be doing, it's not going to stick. Or, you can shave your head." I said, "Let's shave my head." My wife at the time said, "You didn't have a contract yet?" I said, "Well, it was implied." [*Laughs*]

After I was already playing Blade, [stunt choreographer Loren Janes] was going to be training us and he looked at me and said, "You know more about the sword stuff than I do. You train Dolph." That was fine with [stunt coordinator] Walter Scott. That was how I ended up training Dolph, and I gave him a foundation. Then I didn't see him for a month, because he was busy filming.

I kept asking Walter, "When can I see the location for where we're going to do the fight and show you some ideas?" He said, "We're going to have plenty of time when we get down there. Stop bugging me here." "Okay." We had six weeks of nights at Whittier which is down towards Orange County, which meant I had to get rush hour traffic both going to and coming from the location. I would sit in the car with an electric shaver they'd given me and I'd shave my head.

What do you think was the first thing we shot when we got to the location? The first day was the fight scene. I said, "Okay, Dolph, remember that thing that I taught you with the sword? Okay, that's what we're going to do."

At one point during that fight, they go, "Okay, now here he's going to grab Saurod and throw him at you." I think, "Oh, great. I'm essentially going to be his stunt pad." He was up on the top of a loading dock and He-man turns around and then he throws Saurod into my chest, and I catch him and I tumble back and basically, I'm his stunt pad. He tweaked his back while doing that, actually.

I should be grateful because after that, I worked for Walter on *The Magnificent Seven* (1998–2000). It was a TV show. I remember once when

809

we were walking across the Melody Ranch, where they had been shooting Westerns since the '50s. He said, "You know what's wrong with this show? There's about four heroes too many." [*Laughs*]

Blade was among a group of characters developed for the movie, rather than coming from the He-Man toys and cartoon. Was there room for you to shape the character yourself, or bring your own ideas?

Lots of room. I don't really remember ever getting any direction from Gary. By that point in my career I realized the director is busy, he has a lot to think about. He's the captain of the ship. If he wants something different, he will say so. Don't go looking for an "Atta boy." Basically, he pretty much left me alone. I don't recall Gary ever saying anything to me like, "Oh, don't do that." I really appreciated the freedom he gave me. One of the things that I'm proudest of was that I got to create a new character to the *Masters of the Universe* universe. [*Laughs*]

Blade and Evil-Lyn interrogate Kevin (Robert Duncan McNeill) in *Masters of the Universe.*

There's a funny, funny sequence with Robert Duncan McNeill, the boyfriend. I loved working with Meg Foster, too. I'd been a huge fan of hers for a long time. She's a stunningly beautiful woman, and I thought she did a terrific job in this. When we break into the kitchen and put the Collar of Truth on [Robert], there is a piece of direction Gary gave me. He said, "Can you scare him a little?" [*Laughs*] I said, "Yes." Now, normally I wouldn't do this without telling an actor I was going to do it, but Robert knew me, and I had a safety factor built into the distance. However, the knives I had on my wardrobe were Gerber knives, and they were *sharp*. When we got to that part with the Collar of Truth, I pulled the knife out and I slammed it into the table next to his hand. It was about ten to twelve inches away. It was plenty of room because I knew where I was, what I was doing, and how I could keep him safe. He wasn't going anywhere, but yes, his reaction is very organic. [*Laughs*]

Wardrobe? Let me give you a quick little thing. I was wearing surgical rubber. It was lined so I could get in and out of it. Basically, I'm wearing a wetsuit. I had on the gloves and I had the thing over my eye. When they originally gave me the eyepatch, I said, "I'm not going to have any depth perception. Will you please drill pinholes in it?" If you've ever had an eye exam, you can see through a pinhole and it'll give you depth.

The Power Sword, I called it "Buick Slayer," because it was enormous. It's not well-balanced. It was visual. It's like the weapons you get in video games. It says a lot for Dolph's athleticism, and then also the technique and the instruction that I gave him. The sword balances in your hand if you allow it to. He wields the sword really well. It was not easy. It's a workout.

I'm going, "If I'm going to be fighting him, I need both eyes. I need to be able to see." They did that, and most of our time was spent trying to re-glue that thing to my head as I would sweat a lot. They originally had me in long sleeves and I got them to cut the sleeves off, but I still had the gauntlets and I had the gloves, and I had the boots, and I had the surgical rubber. Then, over the top of that came the chainmail.

Julie Weiss was the costume lady. A lovely lady, very famous. Unlike today, where you go to all kinds of ren faires and people make chainmail—which is still very heavy—you have people who were actually making it. Or, what's usually done in movies is they knit it and then they spray it, and it looks like chainmail from a distance. That wasn't for Julie. Apparently what they did was they took ten six-foot lengths of pipe and cut them into quarter-inch pieces. I'm wearing around fifty feet of pipe and it would be on my shoulders, and then over top of that was the chest piece with the spikes sticking out of the shoulders. The first time they put that on, it's like football shoulder pads. I'm going, "Well, I guess I won't be doing any shoulder rolls." [*Laughs*] At the end of the day, when I would peel myself out of that, I would literally pour more than a pint of sweat out of my boots. I kept expecting a fish to come out.

Were you aware of all the problems that Cannon was having at the time, and the effect they had on the movie's budget?

The cast, at least as far as I know, had no idea that any of this was going on. We were over at Laird Studios, and we had taken over two soundstages. It was such a magnificent set, but they had a lot of trouble getting all of those epic master race sort of figures into the camera lens.

Cannon wanted to pull the plug and I guess Gary talked them into one more half-day, and he's got this spinning light wheel like you'd have in a bowling alley. He did this color wheel and some bright lights behind it, and a couple of rather primitive effects. Before that, I think it all stopped with them clashing together. Menahem Golan apparently said, "Yes, yes, just wrap it up. Just end it." Gary knew that wasn't very satisfying, so he bought us that extra time and we got that scene.

Then after the change, there was the little bit of where I'm back as regular Skeletor, and suddenly whip out this sword. He knocks the Power Sword towards the edge of the abyss, and he goes after it and He-Man manages to send me over the abyss.

When they had rehearsed it the night before, they put me in the harness, but didn't quite lock off the cables. They pulled me up. I'm only about six feet off the floor, and one of the cables snaps. It's a good thing I know how to tuck and roll, or I would've broken my neck on that.

A German advertising postcard with art by Renato Casaro. Part of De
Longis' job was to train Dolph Ludgren how to wield the Power Sword.

Frank [Langella] had wanted to do more action, but we just didn't have time. When everything is being thrown together, Walter says, "You're going to be doubling Frank." It was okay, because Dolph knew me and trusted me from our training. Dolph could do his performance because he knew he wasn't going to hurt me. They put me in [Frank's] boots, which didn't fit. They were really tight. They also had smooth leather soles. First thing I'll do when I get a pair of boots is I'll put dance rubber on the bottom, so I've got a grip. Then they're using this smoke that leaves an oily film on things. I've got leather soles and kind of an oily film on the floor. *Then* I've got his mask on.

At first when I put the choreography together with the power staff and stuff, I asked, "Now, this is before the transformation, right?" They said, "Yes, before the transformation." I had the staff going around my head and doing a couple of things that were kind of fancy. It's a little more imaginative than the choreography that's in there, a little bit more dangerous-looking. Then the day we're going to shoot, they say, "Oh, no, no, no, this is after the trans-formation." I went, "Ohhhhhhh. . ." If you recall, that helmet is like the New York skyline and elk antlers combined. I knew there wouldn't be any of those over-the-head passes, that's just not possible. This is, of course, all at the last minute.

And then when I get that headgear on . . . take and put your hand right under your nose with the palm flat. How much can you see? [*Laughs*]I can't see my feet, which are slippery as hell. It's like being on an ice rink. I had no peripheral vision. Then I've got on the cape and everything else. It's like, "Here, you're moving way too well. Let me shoot you in the leg and poke you in the eye, too." But you have no choice. If you don't shoot it, you don't have it. We had apparently wrangled just a couple hours with a crew and a camera and a swirly light. We got done when we got done.

I keep going, "Okay, [Skeletor] says he's going to be back when he comes up out of the blood pool." Blade's not really dead—he just kind of gets tagged with the butt end of the gun and disappears. So . . . if they make another *Masters* movie, I'd love to be in it. [*Laughs*]

Skeletor's evil henchmen pose for a photo with their director.

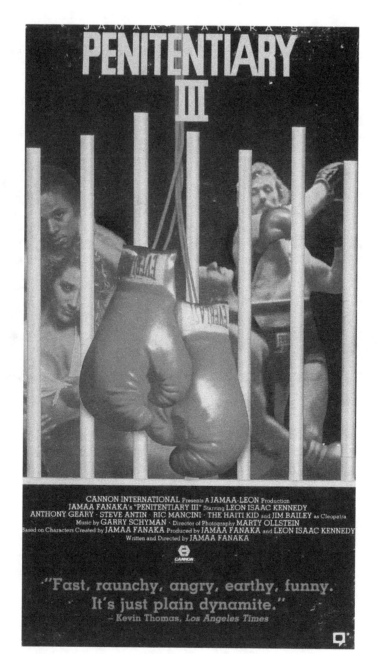

Prizefighter "Too Sweet" Gordone returns to the ring in *Penitentiary III* on VHS.

Penitentiary III

Release Date: September 4, 1987
Directed by: Jamaa Fanaka
Written by: Jamaa Fanaka
Starring: Leon Isaac Kennedy, Steve Antin, Anthony Geary
Trailer Voiceover: "In here the fighting has no rules, and the only winners . . . are losers!"

Penitentiary III may be one of the wildest films covered in this book—which, I'll remind you, is the volume that contains chapters on *Lifeforce* (1985), *America 3000* (1986), and *Tough Guys Don't Dance* (1987).

Like *Death Wish II* (1982),*Exterminator 2* (1984), *Texas Chainsaw Massacre 2* (1986), and *Superman IV* (1987) before it, *Penitentiary III* (1987) was a later entry in a franchise that Cannon didn't originate, but was more than eager to continue. A series of boxing-driven prison films that had turned huge profits on low budgets, Cannon had already made one boxing movie— *Body and Soul* (1981)—with the franchise's star, Leon Isaac Kennedy, so it was probably only just a matter of time before they picked up the *Penitentiary* ball and ran with it.

Much was written about Leon Isaac Kennedy's impressive career in the *Body and Soul* chapter of *The Cannon Film Guide Volume I*, but it's worth summarizing again here. By the age of sixteen he was already "Leon the Lover," America's youngest nationally-syndicated disc jockey. His popularity on the radio translated to television, where the teen prodigy wrote, produced, and co-hosted a pair of variety shows—*Teenarama* and the nationally-broadcast *Outta Sight*—by the time he was eighteen years old. The charismatic kid then pivoted to the film business, where he made appearances in a string of Blaxploitation flicks while opening and running a chain of successful disco joints. His movie work eventually culminated in *Penitentiary* (1979), a gritty independent film that was a roaring hit, both with critics and at the box office.

Penitentiary was the brainchild of filmmaker Jamaa Fanaka. Born Walter Gordon in 1942 in Jackson, Mississippi, the future Fanaka was accepted to UCLA film school, where he became a prominent figure within the film movement known today as the L.A. Rebellion. The movement included fellow African American filmmakers who came out of UCLA, such as Julie Dash and Charles Burnett. By seeking out private investors and government grants, Fanaka was able to write, produce, and direct his first three independent features—*Emma Mae* (1974), *Welcome Home, Brother Charles* (1975), and finally *Penitentiary*—before he graduated from film school. The latter of these became Fanaka's calling card, especially as it grossed more than $30 million dollars on its $600,000 budget. MGM/UA, and later Cannon, would hire him to make further *Penitentiary* sequels over the next decade.

The *Penitentiary* series follows the pugilistic exploits of Marten "Too Sweet" Gordone (Leon Isaac Kennedy), who was given his sugary nickname because of a weakness for candy. The first movie begins with the hitchhiking Too Sweet being picked up in the California desert by a friendly prostitute on the way to service some clients. When bikers start harassing her, Too Sweet steps in to defend her honor. A fight breaks out, one of the bikers dies, and Too Sweet is wrongfully pinned with the murder. The peaceful Too

818

Sweet is forced to defend himself in jail, or else become the prison boss's new sex slave. It turns out he's a damn good fighter. He joins the penitentiary's boxing tournament, where the prizes that can be won include conjugal visits, or potentially a prisoner's freedom. Standing in his way, though, is a beastly opponent named Half Dead, who would not stop short of murdering Too Sweet in the ring.

Released three years later, *Penitentiary II* (1982) follows Too Sweet during a brief time outside of prison. The evil Half Dead escapes from behind bars and murders Too Sweet's girlfriend, and so our hero has no choice but to climb back into the ring with his enemy to get his revenge. The second movie is neither as good as the original nor as wacky as the third, but it *is* notable for its fortuitous casting: future Ghostbuster Ernie Hudson plays the wicked Half Dead, and Mr. T makes his big screen debut as Too Sweet's trainer—a full month before his breakout role in *Rocky III* (1982), and a year before the debut of *The A-Team* (1983–1987).

By the mid-1980s, Leon Isaac Kennedy had been meeting with Cannon about a potential follow-up to *Body and Soul*. Some of these discussions involved a movie which would have teamed Kennedy with Chuck Norris. The two had appeared together in *Lone Wolf McQuade* (1983), which Norris made just before starting his lengthy series of collaborations with Cannon. When those talks stalled out, Menahem Golan suggested they do a third *Penitentiary* movie instead. Kennedy agreed and took the idea to Fanaka, with whom he collaborated on the story, and *Penitentiary III* was born: a direct sequel to the two prior hits, but with a distinctly Cannon flair.

In *Penitentiary III*, Too Sweet finds himself behind bars once again and forced to fight in yet another prison boxing ring. After training with Mr. T and avenging his girlfriend's death in the prior movie, Too Sweet has established himself as a pro boxer in the mainstream sense of the sport, only to have his ringside mouthwash unwittingly spiked with a drug that turns him into a supercharged, murderous maniac. In a blind, drug-fueled rage, he accidentally beats his opponent to death—much to the horror of the audience—and punches himself a one-way ticket back to the penitentiary.

Too Sweet's cellmate is the youthful Roscoe, a good-natured kid in the slammer for brawling, who likes to lull his fellow prisoners off to sleepytime with a few soothing toots from his saxophone. Roscoe should look familiar to Cannon fans—this movie is chock full of Cannon alumni—as the actor, Steve Antin, played Gary's slimy, crush-stealing best friend, Rick, in *The Last American Virgin* (1982). (He's otherwise most famous for playing the bully jock, Troy, in 1985's *The Goonies*.)

There are some people at the prison who are excited about Too Sweet's arrival. It turns out the entire power structure of the facility is built upon an underground boxing tournament. When the warden (Ric Mancini) approaches the new arrival with an invitation to join his boxing team, Too Sweet rebuffs him, having vowed to never step into the ring again after he accidentally killed an opponent that he had once considered his friend. When the resident crime lord, Serengeti (Anthony Geary), comes calling, Too Sweet declines his offer, as well. The thing is, Serengeti doesn't consider himself a guy to whom you just can say "no."

If it wasn't clear from the incarcerated singing group or the dry ice fog that fills its corridors, this isn't your normal prison. Having racked up insurmountable debt by losing bets on the convict fighting league, the warden long ago surrendered control of the jail to Serengeti, who wears the real pants in the institution. Not only does Serengeti have the prison guards in his pocket, but he's allowed to wear embroidered kimonos instead of his issued uniform, keep his girlfriend Cleopatra (Jim Bailey) as a cellmate, and import a French chef who rolls his meals into his cell on a silver cart. Even his cell is enclosed by red, velvet curtains and filled with furniture, fresh flower arrangements, and other décor that can only be described as "funeral parlor chic."

Serengeti should be recognizable to anyone who watched network television on weekday afternoons from the 1980s through the 2000s. Anthony Geary is best known as the Emmy-winningest actor in all of soap operas, a distinction he earned for his longtime role as Luke Spencer on *General Hospital* (1963-present). In that role, Geary formed one half of "Luke and

Laura," daytime TV's first super couple, whose hour-long wedding special on November 16, 1981 was viewed by more than thirty million fans and holds the record for earning the highest TV ratings for any American soap opera episode. By this point Geary had already put in six years on *General Hospital*, having left the show in 1984, and was so desperate for non-soap roles that he purposefully sought out bizarre parts to distance himself from his uber-famous daytime persona. That's how he wound up playing the snakelike Serengeti in *Penitentiary III*, starring opposite rappers The Fat Boys in *Disorderlies* (1987), and playing the mad scientist Philo in "Weird Al" Yankovic's cult comedy, *U.H.F.* (1989). Unfortunately he found himself still being pigeonholed by filmmakers, and returned to *General Hospital* in 1991, where he appeared almost daily until his retirement in 2015.

The most dangerous weapon at Serengeti's disposal is *Penitentiary III*'s most bizarre and memorable element. "The Midnight Thud" is a prisoner so deranged and dangerous he's kept in solitary confinement, save for when Serengeti has him dragged into someone's cell at night to enact his twisted punishment. He's called The Midnight Thud because that's the only warning you get before he attacks: an audible "thud" next to your bunk just before the clock strikes midnight.

The Midnight Thud is a dwarf in a bondage suit who growls like a T-Rex, fights with ferocious abandon, and may or may not have the ability to fly. Oh, and if you can't defend yourself from his attack, he'll bite your dick off.

Yeah.

To be fair, it's never *explicitly* stated in the film that The Midnight Thud bites the dicks off his victims, but multiple characters describe his finishing move as "flushing their manhood down the toilet." That particular, peculiar phrasing is too widespread to just be a metaphor. Maybe The Midnight Thud only rips off their dicks with his bare hands, but in either case, there's no choice but to interpret what he does as physically removing their junk and flushing it down the toilet.

When Too Sweet turns down Serengeti's offer to join his boxing team, Serengeti turns The Midnight Thud loose on him.

Penitentiary III's Too Sweet wrestles with The Midnight Thud, who Cannon's marketing materials described as "a four-foot-two homicidal mini-monster with a taste for dismemberment."

The Midnight Thud is played by wrestler Raymond Kessler, credited here under his stage name: The Haiti Kid. He wrestled for numerous organizations through the 1970s, eventually working his way to the World Wrestling Federation during its mid-1980s boom. His most notable appearance would be at WrestleMania 2 in 1986, where he appeared in Mr. T's corner in his

822

match against "Rowdy" Roddy Piper. Kessler occasionally wrestled as "Little Mr. T," with his hair cut into the Eighties icon's signature Mohawk style. (Did you guess you'd be reading the name "Mr. T" so many times when you started this chapter?)

At the stroke of midnight, guards usher Roscoe out of his cell and lock The Midnight Thud in there with Too Sweet. Their claustrophobic, savage, knock-down drag-out fight lasts for more than six thrilling moments of the movie's runtime. It's every bit as crazy as you'd imagine our hero fighting for his life (and genitals) against a growling dwarf wrestler in a gimp suit would be. There's blood—*lots* of blood—and plenty of moments where it genuinely feels as if the fight could go either way. Our hero pulls through, of course, but Too Sweet's prize is a trip to solitary and a round of shock treatment.

While Too Sweet's chained up in the basement and drooling all over himself, chipper young Roscoe works his way up the brackets in the prison's boxing league, competing for the warden's team. Thinking this may finally be his year and that he has an ace in the hole, the warden sneaks Roscoe downstairs to receive secret training from Too Sweet. The pair share an excellent training montage, and Roscoe adopts the fighter name "Sweet 'Nuf" as a tribute to his mentor.

As a thank you for training his prizefighter, the warden smuggles Too Sweet in a gift from the lady's prison next door. Her name is Sugar, and she's played by Mindi Miller (credited here as Ty Randolph)—an actress known for cult movies such as *Body Double* (1982) and *Amazons* (1986), and for being Elvis Presley's girlfriend for a couple years near the end of his life. (Savvy Cannon fans will briefly spot her as one of the two scantily-clad lady wrestlers in 1984's *Seven Magnificent Gladiators*.)

While Too Sweet is . . . otherwise indisposed, Roscoe's title match against Serengeti's toughest fighter is unexpectedly moved up and—oh, shit! It's Danny Trejo. After making his screen debut in Cannon's *Runaway Train* (1985), Hollywood's most killed man made another appearance here as a prisoner in a Cannon movie. He'd go on to appear in *Death Wish 4: The*

Crackdown (1987) and *Kinjite: Forbidden Subjects* (1989), making four of his first six screen appearances in Cannon movies. (At the time of this writing, he was at more than four hundred.)

Trejo's *Penitentiary III* fighter is named See Veer, as in "severe," because that's how he fights. Get it? Before their match is through, See Veer pops a little bit of the maniac drug which Too Sweet was slipped at the beginning of the picture, and he nearly beats poor Roscoe to death. By the time Too Sweet wraps up his lovemaking and finds out what happened, it's too late.

Too Sweet puts two and two together and realizes it was Serengeti's drug that made him accidentally kill his sparring partner and landed him behind bars. Once again, he's left with no choice but to fight for revenge and honor. He promises to fight any one of Serengeti's men—gloves off, no holds barred, kicking and biting allowed—for control of the prison. What he wasn't anticipating was that the gangster's gigantic flunky, "Hugo the Hulk," would be the one to step up to the challenge.

The massive Hugo is played by Magic Schwarz, an actor, wrestler, bodybuilder, and celebrity bodyguard who describes himself as a "professional bad guy." He made his acting debut as "Mad Dog" Joe DeCurso in *Grunt! The Wrestling Movie* (1985) before facing off against Sly Stallone on the armwrestling mat in *Over the Top* (1987), Jean-Claude Van Damme on a racquetball court in *Lionheart* (1990), and Brian Bosworth on a motorcycle in *Stone Cold* (1991). He stands a full head above Too Sweet and makes for a formidable-looking opponent.

Too Sweet is in no shape to take on a fighter twice his size, especially with his brain half-fried from the shock therapy. This is where the movie takes its craziest twist. The Midnight Thud suddenly speaks up from behind the heavy, steel door of his cell, where he's been hanging out and casually smoking crack since he and Too Sweet last beat each other to a pulp. Not only can he speak clear English in a remarkably deep voice, but he reveals that his real name is John Jessup, and that he wants to train Too Sweet in the mystical arts he uses to take on much larger opponents. (No, not the dick biting part—but his takedown strategies, and the ways in which he channels his energy.) Much of the training involves breathing exercises, but there's a part where the Thud repeatedly slams a doorknob into Too Sweet's stomach while screaming "You've got to beat Hugo with your guts!" over and over and it's unintentionally hilarious.

The big match between Too Sweet and Hugo lasts for more than ten minutes, and is legitimately exciting. It looks a lot more like pro wrestling than the boxing featured in the prior movies. At one point, Hugo brutally slams Too Sweet into the floor *ten consecutive times*, and throws him so hard against a cement wall that it leaves a bloody mark in the shape of a crucifix smeared behind him. The fight is downright savage, and really a lot of fun. I won't spell out the ending of the movie, but it plays out how you expect.

Penitentiary III is bonkers, campy fun. It's memorable for a pair of lengthy fights, a cadre of noteworthy villains, and its leather-clad, crack-smoking dwarf martial arts guru. Its secondary cast is filled out by familiar faces, too, particularly the laid-back security guard played by professional arm wrestler Rick Zumwalt, best known for playing Sylvester Stallone's ultimate opponent in Cannon's *Over the Top* (1987). Serengeti's personal attendant, Cleopatra, was played by Jim Bailey, a celebrity drag performer who was famous for his impersonations of Judy Garland and Barbara Streisand. The lady boxer who steals a smooch from her opponent is none other than Raye Hollitt, who a couple years later would become "Zap" on the original run of *American Gladiators* (1989–1996).

Somewhat surprisingly, *Penitentiary III* received strong reviews from critics, including a few of the stuffy ones who almost never went for Cannon's fare. Unfortunately, though, Cannon botched the movie's release, slowly tricking it out across the United States, a city here, a city there, for almost a year rather than sending it out wide. The east coast got the movie in the fall and winter of 1987, while Los Angeles—where the first two movies made their biggest box office splash—didn't get it until the spring of 1988, killing the movie's chance to build up any word of mouth. It wasn't long before the movie was relegated to video store shelves and late-night HBO broadcasts.

Following the third film, Kennedy's last, notable big screen appearance was in the Harry Alan Towers-produced war film, *Skeleton Coast* (1988). He made a couple more TV appearances before leaving the acting world behind to become an evangelist minister in the 1990s.

Meanwhile, Jamaa Fanaka also only made one more film—the little-seen gang movie, *Street Wars* (1991)—but he did not disappear quietly into the night. Throughout his career, Fanaka was critical of how few opportunities had been offered to Black filmmakers by Hollywood. He pointed out that even after his wildly successful independent feature, *Penitentiary*, had made millions back on a minuscule budget, he hadn't been snapped up for mainstream studio work like similarly successful, white indie filmmakers. Instead, studios were only interested in having him make sequels to his prior hit. He brought a lawsuit against the Director's Guild of America over what he deemed discriminatory hiring practices, which he believed led to him being blacklisted by Hollywood for the rest of his career. At the time of his death in 2012, Fanaka had been working on a script for an independently-produced *Penitentiary 4*—we can only imagine how that movie would have brought the series to a close.

Interview: Actor Leon Isaac Kennedy

From his youth in Cleveland, Leon Isaac Kennedy felt destined for the spotlight, and worked incredibly hard to get there. When he was just sixteen years old, he was already the youngest-ever disc jockey to work in a major market; as the radio persona "Leon the Lover," his show was soon syndicated across the country. At eighteen he hosted a TV variety show called *Teenarama*, which was followed by *Outta Sight*, which he wrote, produced, and co-hosted. This was the first African American television series to receive national syndication, just beating *Soul Train* by a thin margin. He was still a teenager.

The natural next step was obviously a film career. In the 1970s he wrote, produced, or starred in an assortment of low-budget Blaxploitation films, and then in 1979 came his star-making turn in *Penitentiary*, Jamaa Fanaka's brutal, prison-set boxing film. The small, independent feature was a massive success, becoming the biggest-earning indie film of that year.

Producer, star, and uncredited co-screenwriter Leon Isaac Kennedy at "Too Sweet" Gordone in *Penitentiary III*.

A sequel, *Penitentiary II*, would arrive via United Artists in 1982, followed by *Penitentiary III* in 1987, produced by Cannon. This was actually the second boxing film starring Kennedy to come from Cannon, following *Body and Soul* (1981), which he had written, produced, and starred in with his then-wife: actress, model, and sports broadcaster Jayne Kennedy.

Kennedy's other credits include a role opposite Chuck Norris in *Lone Wolf McQuade* (1983), *Hollywood Vice Squad* (1986), *Knights of the City* (1986), and *Skeleton Coast* (1988). In the early 1990s, Kennedy left Hollywood behind to enter the ministry.

How did you connect with Cannon? Golan and Globus were still a fairly new presence in Hollywood when you made *Body and Soul*.

Leon Isaac Kennedy: Jerry Gross had a fast-talking person working for him in marketing named Billy Fine. He was a great Hollywood character. I loved him. My first introduction to Billy was after the opening weekend of *Penitentiary*, and I got this call at my hotel: "You don't know me, but you *will* know me. My name's Billy Fine. You broke box office records in the city of Detroit. You're going to be bigger than Billy Dee Williams and we're going to do a lot of good business together. I'm sending you to Cleveland next and, by the way, Leon, I just fired the PR person in Cleveland, so you're on your own. I know you can handle it!" [*Laughs*]

Because of the first movie's success, they wanted to do a *Penitentiary II*. In the interim, there were some contractual delays, and Billy was no longer with Jerry Gross—he'd taken this job with Cannon Films, to be in charge of distribution. Billy called me and said, "Leon, I've got some people who want to do a movie with you. I'm going to take you to a meeting. All you have to do is be quiet and answer a few questions and you'll have a movie."

I go in, and I meet with Menahem Golan and Yoram Globus. They spoke with a dialect, and some broken English, to an extent. They say, "Well, our demographics show that if you have your shirt off, and you're fighting, and you make love to women, it's going to be a hit movie. So, that's what we want from you. We want a strong 'R.' We want fighting, we want violence, and we want a *lot* of nudity. We're going to give you over a million dollars to make it." I said to them, "Well, thank you, I would look forward to that. However, I want to write it." They said, "No, no, no, you're not a writer." I told them, "You don't really know my background—I've written a lot of things. I've written television shows, I've written other movies. I want to write it, and you'll be happy with the script."

I loved Menahem, because he was a filmmaker and he had a heart for other film people. He says, "Okay, okay, we'll try it. If we don't like it, we'll hire our own writers." I said, "Fine, okay."

I said, "Well, if I'm going to write it and star in it, then I've got to protect the baby. I've got to produce it." Menahem says, "No, that's way too much money for you to have." I said, "Well, I've produced things in the past." "Well, you haven't produced with this much money." I said, "First of all, how much could I possibly go over budget: ten, twenty percent? I'll tell you what I'll do. I want to produce this. You can hold on to my salary as the star, the writer, and the producer, and you won't pay me until I turn the movie in. If I'm over budget, then you take it from me."

"You're going to bet your own money?" Menahem says. I said, "Yes, I'm betting on me." "We'll take that bet." That's how I ended up being the writer, producer, and star of *Body and Soul*.

Then I said, "If I'm going to be involved in the film like this, then as the leading lady, I want to put my wife in it." They said, "Who is she?" I said, "That's Jayne Kennedy." They said, "Well, who is she? We haven't heard of her." I said, "Well, she's a very beautiful lady. She's on CBS Sports right now. A lot of people know who she is. She would be perfect for the part that I'm going to write for her." I worked that out, and so Jayne was the leading lady.

I was very happy when I left Cannon that day because now, I had reached my dream. I like to have goals. My goal for myself and Jayne was to be like Douglas Fairbanks and Mary Pickford. He was the top leading man, she was the top leading lady. They later had their own production company. That's what I wanted for us. I floated out of there that day, very, very happy with the deal that had been made.

I know you're a big movie historian. Was making a contemporary update on the 1947 John Garfield movie something you wanted to do?

Originally, this was never supposed to be a remake—it was never supposed to be *Body and Soul*. It was supposed to be a movie where I was a young boxer based upon what they had said to me when I originally sat down with them: "Our research shows that if you have your shirt off and you're fighting and if you're making love to women, it's going to be a hit. That's what we want." I had my own idea as to the movie. Then, as I started writing it, Menahem came up with the idea, "Since it's going to be about boxing, we'll do a remake of *Body and Soul*."

I didn't want to do a remake. Any time you do a remake of a classic, you're going to be butchered by the critics. They just don't like people tampering with something that is revered. That's number one. Number two, especially, this is going to be a Black film, and we didn't have as much money as a major studio. To the critics, they're going to think this is a smaller-budgeted Black version of a classic. You're setting yourself up for disaster. I begged Menahem, "No, I don't want to call it *Body and Soul*." "It'll have prestige."

He called whoever had the rights. He said, "They want $75,000 for the title. I'm going to pay it." I said, "Menahem, I could use the $75,000 extra in the budget. We could call it many other things than *Body and Soul*." I didn't win that argument. I wrote it in such a way that even after it was done, with some simple editing, I could have changed things. In other words, I only used maybe two different sentences out of the original *Body and Soul*, which was, "Oh, what are you going to do? Kill me. So what? Everybody has to die. What matters is how." That's the only line I used. I shot that two different ways. I shot that scene using that line, and I shot that scene not using that line, just in case I could win my argument with Menahem not to call it *Body and Soul*.

Muhammad Ali had a small role in the film. At the time, he was one of the biggest stars of any type—sports, movies, anything—in the world. The two of you were friends, but how did you work it out for him to have a part in the movie?

Leon Isaac Kennedy with Jayne Kennedy in a pre-sales advertisement for Cannon's *Body and Soul*.

That has to do everything with the generosity and the big heart of the great Muhammad Ali. We were friends. I called him and I said, "Ali, I'm doing this boxing feature. The same way that you taught me how to box for *Penitentiary*, I now want to put your character in this movie playing yourself, and you're going to teach this character how to box." Then, I just read him some of the part. He said, "I like it. I like it."

At that time, he was the biggest star in the world. Any money that I had to give him would not have been enough. I had very little money to give. He says, "Don't even give me any money. I'll do it for you." He did it for me, for free. I put some of his people in the film, and gave some of them some money. That's how Ali was in the film. He did a personal favor to me.

When I screened *Body and Soul* [for Menahem], at the end of the screening, he and Yoram both applauded. We were the only ones in there. It was for them to see. They both applauded. Then, Menahem came over to me and hugged me and kissed me on the cheek. He said, "You are a really good filmmaker." That meant a lot to me.

A couple of years later, after *Body and Soul*, you did *Lone Wolf McQuade* with Chuck Norris and Steve Carver.

They were interviewing all the top leading Black men at that time to be in that film. They interviewed Carl Weathers, OJ Simpson, Howard Rollins. Anybody else who was a leading Black man, they had interviewed. Then, I get the call from my agent, "Well, Leon, they like you the best, and they want you to have the part." I was elated to be able to star opposite Chuck.

I've been on lots of different sets, and some sets are chaotic, and some sets have a lot of screaming and hollering from the director or the 1st AD. That set, no one ever raised their voice. Everything went like clockwork. It was the easiest-going set that I've ever been on. They turned out a tremendous product on time. Everything was just superb.

Chuck and I would work out in the mornings. As we worked out, we talked. His hero was Muhammad Ali, while my hero was Bruce Lee. Chuck had worked with Bruce, and of course, I knew Ali quite well. I would tell him Ali stories, and he would tell me Bruce Lee stories.

When people ask me, "What's Chuck Norris really like?" I say, "He's one of the nicest guys in the world. Very, very nice, always a lot of fun." One outstanding memory when it comes to *Lone Wolf McQuade*, we had to rappel down a mountain, and they had to train us for that. They trained us on the side of a mountain, which would have been the size of a forty-story building. We trained for two days to learn how to rappel. Now, on the day of shooting, they're going to work down at the bottom of this mountain, but this mountain was like eighty stories, not forty. That makes a big difference. We're talking way, way up.

Chuck's wife is saying, "Honey, you shouldn't be doing this. You don't have to do this. This is why they have stuntmen. Let the stuntmen do it." I'm thinking, "If he has the stuntmen do it, then I don't have to do either." [*Laughs*] Then bravado kicks in and Chuck says, "No, I think I can handle this."

Now, there's a helicopter and the three of us up there. Robert Beltran, he looks down, and he says, "No, I can't do this. I can't do it." Then, Steve [Carver] says, "Well, I can still make the shot work if the two of you do it. If only one of you is going to do it, then the shot's not going to work." Chuck looks at me and says, "Leon, what do you think?" I say, "Chuck, I'll do it if you do it." Chuck looks at me and the bravado kicks in, and he says "Let's do it." I said to myself, "Oh, crap." [*Laughs*]

The ironic part is the way this thing was shot, you wouldn't know how treacherous it was or how high it really was. They used, not the close-up camera, but for impact they used the faraway view. You wouldn't have known who it was. All that drama for nothing. I just decided I was going to come down the wall real quick, so I just came down with big, big leaps, boom, boom, boom, long arcs, just going as far down as I could with each one. I get down, and it's like, "Okay, well, that wasn't too bad." You know, I dreamed of that for about three nights. It did have a traumatic, rippling effect.

Before you started developing *Penitentiary III* with Cannon, you and Menahem had discussed doing another project in which you and Chuck would have co-starred together. What can you tell me about that?

That was called *Strikers Force*. I wrote that with a guy named Sheldon Lettich. Sheldon wrote *Rambo III* (1988) [and *Bloodsport*, 1988] and then ended up being a director. We would go to his office because he was the best typist. After we'd made our comments and so forth, Sheldon would be the one that wrote things up.

Sheldon and I had a history. He and I wrote *Strikers Force*. It was almost like a sequel [to *McQuade*], but not really a sequel, but it had the same buddy-type thing between Chuck and myself. It would have really done great. A lot of films, it's all about timing. With Cannon, they were interested, but Chuck was tied up. At another time it was like, "You can do it, Leon. You don't have Chuck, but let's see who else we can find for you." It was very close, but it didn't get done.

How did the discussion shift to doing another *Penitentiary*? Was that something you'd already been discussing with Jamaa?

No. That's the thing about projects: you just never know what's going to happen. I used to come down to Cannon quite a bit because I love movies. There was always a lot of action going on, as far as them casting things or whatever. I liked Menahem, and so I would spend time just with him.

Long story short, we're sitting and talking one day, and I'm pitching a couple of different ideas to Menahem. He doesn't really bite on the ideas that I pitched him. Then he says, "What about *Penitentiary III*?" I say, "I don't know. *Penitentiary* did good. *Penitentiary II*, they didn't market it as well as it should have been marketed at United Artists. I don't know what the market could be." He said, "*Penitentiary III*, I like the title. I like the title. Let's do that." I called Jamaa and I said, "Get ready. We're back in business." [*Laughs*]

I brought Jamaa and introduced him to Menahem. I really negotiated the deal. The nice thing about Cannon was that you weren't in what I call development hell, like at the studios. You're not just sitting around waiting for nine months, or a year, or longer in development. You make a deal with Menahem, you have an office, and you are in pre-production within a month. Once you get out of pre-production, you're shooting within another two months. They moved very quickly.

I don't believe you're credited as a writer on *Penitentiary III*, but it incorporated elements from a draft that you'd written yourself. What made it into the film from your version of the script?

The German VHS cover of *Penitentiary III*.

The part played by Anthony Geary and Jim Bailey, the famous female impersonator—those characters were mine. What we really did is we took my script and Jamaa's script, and then I spliced them together, so half of it was mine. I ended up not taking a writer's credit because Jamaa said to me, "Leon, you're the star. We're both producing this. I'm the director. You don't need the writer's credit." [*Laughs*] I didn't really care a lot about different credits. I just wanted to get work done.

Cannon probably expected you to have it finished in a big hurry.

Yes. Oh, here's another great story about Menahem. We're ready to shoot. We're about five days away. Now, Cannon had gotten a little more sophisticated so that now they had script readers that read the scripts. Now, I've got to tell you, I've never had a lot of faith in script readers because usually they bring in college kids to read a script and give their [thoughts] on a script. Guess what? They've never written a script. They've never directed a script. They've never done a movie. How valuable is their input? They're just going to go by the book and what they've learned in so-called writing schools. I've never had great faith, even to this day, in the script readers that studios have. As a matter of fact, I tell a lot of studio people, "I'm only giving you the script if you read it. I'm not interested in what a script reader has to say."

Anyway, long story short, he's got the script reader sitting in there, and Jamaa and I are there. Menahem says, in front of the girl, "The script is not ready. It has some holes in it. What do you say?" Jamaa said, "I like the script." Then, Menahem looks at me, and he trusted me more because we'd worked together before. He says, "Leon, what's your opinion?" I said, "This script is ready to go. If it weren't ready to go, we would have extended pre-production. It's ready to go." Then, he looks at the girl, and he says, "I trust the filmmakers more than the script reader." He says to us, "You start next week."

What are your memories of working on *Penitentiary III* once production began?

Penitentiary III was a hectic set. We started off being a whole day behind from the very first day. Jamaa wanted to do a scene with the Midnight Thud, which was going to be a flashback. I think the Midnight Thud was supposed to be a tunnel rat in Vietnam or something. They are shooting that, which was really a throwaway. You see, as a filmmaker, I believe in grabbing the hard stuff first. Get the meat of the film, and if time permits, then you can go out and shoot the incidentals, things that are not going to make or break the story. This really had nothing to do with the story or anything else. I would have wanted to have done it the last day of the shoot, not the first. Anyway, the main cast and crew are all at the Lincoln Heights Jail where the majority was to be shot. They didn't get back until five in the evening from probably a seven o'clock call. The day was already gone. We never did catch up.

The other thing that Cannon had at that point were these production people who would keep up with your pages if they thought you were behind schedule. They started coming down to the set, and Jamaa, being the director, never appreciated them being there. Sometimes he would get irritated with them, and I'd do my best to be the peacemaker.

Then, Menahem would say to me, "Leon, you're three days behind. You got to speed things up." I would say, "How can I speed things up? You speed things up when you are controlling the director. In this case, the director is my partner. It's very difficult to speed anything up." Long story short, some of the major fight scenes, we had to cram them all into three days to get the film done on budget, when it should have been like a whole week and a half.

I literally was putting in twenty-hour days, and I slept on the set. I didn't have time to go home—driving all the way home and then turning around to come all the way back, I couldn't afford the time. All I did was sleep for about five hours. I had two different crews going to help me get it done. I was really beat up and worn out. It was very different than *Lone Wolf McQuade*.

I was friends with Menahem till the day he died. He would come back to America every now and then. It's interesting how Avi Lerner and Danny [Lerner] picked up and continued to do what Menahem and Yoram did.

Menahem was trying to make movies, I know, up until his final days.

One of the last things he said to me, he came into town and we were having dinner. [My wife] Maureen and I brought him a present. He took the present and he said, "Oh, Leon, this is nice but you know the real present I want from you?" I said, "What's that?" He said, "Bring me a movie deal."

A videocassette copy of *Tough Guys Don't Dance*; or, as the back of the box describes it, "the most daring film noir murder-thriller ever filmed!"

Tough Guys Don't Dance

Release Date: September 18, 1987
Directed by: Norman Mailer
Written by: Norman Mailer
Starring: Ryan O'Neal, Wings Hauser, Debra Sandlund, Isabella Rossellini
Trailer Voiceover: "America's most controversial author, Norman Mailer, brings his bestselling novel to the screen."

Oh man. Oh God. Oh man. Oh God! Oh man! Oh God! Oh man! Oh God, oh man! Oh God!

Tough Guys Don't Dance may be one of the strangest movies to wear the Cannon logo, up there with movies like *The Apple* (1980), *Ninja III* (1984), *King Lear* (1988), or anything directed by Tobe Hooper. Perhaps more so than any of those other films, *Tough Guys Don't Dance* defies explanation.

From a safe distance, *Tough Guys Don't Dance* may look like little more than a vanity project for its director: two-time Pulitzer Prize-winning author Norman Mailer. The movie was widely panned on release for its bizarre performances, far-fetched, hole-filled plot, and wildly scattershot tone. It's easy to assume that it was directed by a man who had few qualifications to make a Hollywood film. Fortunately, *Tough Guys Don't Dance* is a supremely fascinating sort of weird. It's the sort of oddity that's worthy of repeat viewings and close examination: a sublime train wreck that's undeniably compelling to look at.

Now, whether it became this masterpiece-level train wreck by accident or by design is something film scholars will no doubt be pondering and debating for centuries to come. (It's also one of my favorite movies included in this volume.)

Regardless of whether or not he was qualified to shoot a 1980s Hollywood thriller, there's no denying Mailer's position as one of America's literary giants of the 20th Century. Published in 1948, his debut novel *The Naked and the Dead*—inspired by his time in the US Army during World War II—spent more than a year on the *New York Times* best seller list. In 1968, he won the Pulitzer Prize for his non-fiction work *Armies of the Night*, and then again for his novel *The Executioner's Song* in 1979. Over six decades, Mailer penned eleven best sellers, and was further known for his essays and social commentary. He was a key figure in the style of writing known as New Journalism, and a co-founder of the New York weekly paper *The Village Voice*.

During his life, Mailer was a literary celebrity. Almost as much as for his writing, he was well-known for having famous friends, for his six marriages and other romances, for his outspoken misogyny, his love of boxing, and for being involuntarily committed to a hospital psych ward after stabbing—and almost killing—his second wife at a party in 1960. (She didn't press charges, but they did divorce two years later.)

Mailer was notorious for doing exhaustive research while writing his books, which makes this movie's source material something of an anomaly within his body of work. After whittling away years in the process of researching and writing his mammoth historical novel *Ancient Evenings* (1983), Mailer felt he'd earned some time off. He spent the next ten months relaxing, away from his typewriter. His publisher, on the other hand, felt they deserved a bit of writing in return for the rich stipend they were paying him on a monthly basis.

Realizing he was contractually obligated to pound out another book and only had a month to write it, Mailer scratched his longtime itch to pen a hardboiled crime novel in the vein of Mickey Spillane or Dashiell Hammett. Understanding he had no time to research new locations, Mailer set the story within Provincetown, Massachusetts, a Cape Cod vacation destination where Mailer spent much of his time and owned a nice home, where he just so happened to write the novel. The hurried results of his month-long writing session, a novel titled *Tough Guys Don't Dance* (1984), were what many consider one of the author's lesser written works, but was nonetheless a bestseller.

While he was banging away at his keyboard, a thought occurred to Mailer that *Tough Guys Don't Dance* might make a good movie: one he wanted to direct himself. He dropped a hint to his friend, producer Tom Luddy of American Zoetrope—the film company founded by Francis Ford Coppola—who pitched the idea around Hollywood and was met with little interest. It was Cannon, of course, who finally bit.

Mailer had held a longtime interest in filmmaking that went all the way back to the earliest years of his career, when he followed up the success of his smash hit *The Naked and the Dead* with a couple fruitless years in Los Angeles during which he tried his hand as a screenwriter. When the 1960s rolled around and his reputation as a literary figure had grown significantly, Mailer independently produced, directed, and starred in a trio of mostly improvisational, avant-garde movies: *Wild 90* (1968), *Beyond the Law* (1968), and *Maidstone* (1970). All three were commercial failures that came out of Mailer's pocket and nearly bankrupted him.

The latter of the three films, *Maidstone*, became somewhat infamous for a real, on-screen fight that happened between Mailer and his co-star, actor Rip Torn. During one scene, Torn attacks Mailer with a hammer, striking a blow strong enough to open up a gash in the author's scalp. As blood pours down his head, the two men brawl on the ground: Mailer bites off a piece of Torn's ear, while Torn attempts to strangle the Pulitzer-winning novelist. The fight is finally broken up by crew members and Mailer's own wife and crying children, but the cameras continue to roll as the two men exchange heated barbs and cool their tempers. Despite the two men breaking character and shouting at each other using their real names, the footage—real blood and all—was used in the final film, and makes for a highly uncomfortable ten minutes within an otherwise forgettable feature.

In spite of his ignominious track record as a filmmaker, Mailer's desire to be a movie director remained very much alive. Never one to pass up a name that carried an air of prestige with it, Menahem Golan agreed to purchase the film rights to the novel and to let Mailer direct the movie himself. There was one condition: in return, Mailer would pen the screenplay for Jean-Luc Godard's adaptation of *King Lear*, a film for which Golan had famously scribbled out a contract on a napkin at Cannes. While Mailer carried through on his word, Godard tossed the renowned novelist's script in the trash—but, more on that in the *King Lear* chapter in our next volume.

Because of his incredible renown as a writer, word quickly got around Hollywood that Mailer was adapting one of his novels for the screen. Ryan O'Neal was attached to the project early on, as was actress and model Isabella Rossellini, for whom Mailer re-wrote the role to better fit her qualities. Tanya Roberts, Alana Stewart, Cathy Moriarty, and Ali MacGraw—the latter of whom would have been re-uniting with Ryan O'Neal almost two decades after their hit *Love Story* (1970)—tried out for the role of the duplicitous wife, Patty Lareine, but lost out to newcomer Debra Sandlund. The same role had earlier been offered to Anjelica Huston, who expressed interest but backed out when she learned that it would require her to star opposite O'Neal, with whom she'd had a relationship in the 1970s—one that she later wrote, in her memoir, had ended with him beating her in a bathroom during a party. Charles Cyphers and Mickey Knox were seen for the role of the *Tough Guys'* maniacal police chief. Interestingly, monologist Spalding Gray spoke of having a small part in the film during a speaking tour just two months before shooting started, but ultimately did not take part in the movie.

Production began in Provincetown during the late autumn of 1986, after most of the restaurants and attractions had closed up for the season and the crowds of tourists had long gone home, and continued through almost the end of the year.

Writer-director Norman Mailer on the set of *Tough Guys Don't Dance*.

Tough Guys Don't Dance is the story of an aspiring writer, ex-convict, and beach bum by the name of Tim Madden (Ryan O'Neal), a man who was just left by his wife and who has spent the better part of a month attempting to drink away her memory. After blacking out during one of his regular, alcoholic benders, the last thing Madden remembers is making love to a former porn star while her companion sobbed nearby. He discovers he has a new tattoo of his ex-girlfriend's name on his arm, that the front seat of his jeep is soaked with blood, and that there's an unidentified severed head tucked away in his secret marijuana stash. The local chief of police—a self-described maniac—wants to pin him with a pair of murders. Tim believes he's innocent, but he can't be sure of that.

It's a perfectly noir-ish setup, sure, but there's so much wrong with the execution that it's uproariously comical. The movie opens with a battered and bruised Madden receiving a surprise visit from his estranged father Dougy (Lawrence Tierney), who is dying of cancer. Chronologically this occurs near the end of the storyline: most of the movie unfolds in flashback, as Madden recounts the story so far to his no-nonsense, tough guy pops.

A heartthrob best known for his starring roles on TV's *Peyton Place* (1964–1969) and in films such as *Love Story*, *Paper Moon* (1973), and *Barry Lyndon* (1975), Ryan O'Neal's career was on a downturn when he was cast as Tim Madden in *Tough Guys Don't Dance*. A series of flops in the early Eighties had reduced him to being viewed, not as a top leading man, but as the slightly less famous half of a glamorous, celebrity couple, the other half being Farrah Fawcett. (The two were something like the Brangelina or Bennifer of their time.) Having not made a movie in two years, O'Neal agreed to appear in the film for just above scale: the union equivalent of minimum wage.

Like the novelist-turned-filmmaker behind *Tough Guys Don't Dance*, however, O'Neal was an avid amateur boxer. The two kept many of the same friends from the ring; O'Neal and Mailer had actually sparred together numerous times over the years at a gym they both frequented in New York. When it came time to cast his film, Mailer's boxing buddy was one of his first choices—after Warren Beatty, who had already turned Mailer down.

A former contract player for RKO Pictures during Hollywood's Golden Age, Lawrence Tierney was a classic tough-guy actor known for starring in gangster movies and film noirs such as *Dillinger* (1945), *Born to Kill* (1947), and *Bodyguard* (1948). Tierney's heavy drinking and frequent brawling led to many arrests over the decades, and had nearly got him run out of Hollywood entirely. He wound up doing jail time on several occasions, and by the 1970s was working in construction, bartending, or driving a horse-drawn buggy in Central Park to make ends meet. He finally gave up alcohol in the 1980s and made a return to acting. His performance in *Tough Guys Don't Dance* was one of the only consistently-praised elements of the film, and it helped rejuvenate his career. These days, though, most film fans recognize him as Joe Cabot, the old gangster who organizes the diamond heist in *Reservoir Dogs* (1992).

The events in *Tough Guys Don't Dance* unfold wildly out of order. Each morning, the hungover Madden rolls out of bed and uses shaving cream to write out the number of days it's been since his wife left him on his bathroom mirror—this is how viewers track time in the film. Patty Lareine, the runaway wife he's strung himself out over, is played by Debra Sandlund, whose only prior on-camera experiences had been on the TV beauty contests *Dream Girl U.S.A.*(1986–1987) and *The Miss Hollywood Pageant* (1986), and a single episode of *The A-Team* (1983–1987). She does *not* play a very nice woman here. As we learn, Patty Lareine is skilled at using men for her own personal gain. Prior to Madden, she was married to his former school buddy, the enormously wealthy Wardley Meeks III (John Bedford Lloyd). Before running away to Provincetown with our hero, Patty Lareine asked Madden to murder her husband, but he couldn't bring himself to off his old pal. Instead, Patty Lareine weaseled her way into a lucrative divorce settlement.

This wily bad girl isn't the love of Madden's life, however, nor is she the woman whose name he finds tattooed on his arm after that fateful blackout in which he may or may not have murdered several people. That would be Madeleine, a beautiful Italian girl played by Isabella Rossellini, whom Madden had lived with for several happy years. That was until one truly cataclysmic weekend in which he drove her down to Florida and pressured her into a spouse swap with a swingin' preacher (played by magician Penn Jillette) and his wife—who so happened to be professional gold digger Patty Lareine. Not only is poor Madeleine humiliated by the whole affair, but Madden crashes their car on the drive home and leaves her with injuries that render her barren. It gets worse: Madden is immediately busted for cocaine possession, landing him in jail for the next couple years.

Fast forward again to the near-present, after Patty Lareine has left Madden (presumably) for their chauffeur. Her primary reason for dumping our hero was a scary premonition she had during a séance, in which she and her junkie friends attempted to make contact with the dead pirate hookers whose ghostly voices have been haunting her ever since she moved to Provincetown. (For real.) Madden is now the main suspect in the murder of two tourists who were last seen drinking with him at a local watering hole. The last thing he remembers is having sex with the woman while her male companion wept nearby and pleaded with them to stop. His hazy memory causes further issues when he finds the severed head of a blonde female wrapped in a garbage bag and stuffed in his top secret drug stash.

Madden's main antagonist would appear to be the town's new chief of police. As Chief Alvin Luther Regency, actor Wings Hauser commits to such an intense, crazy-eyed performance that mid-'80s Dennis Hopper might have watched it and been impressed. In one memorable scene, Regency explains to Madden that "Both sides of [his] nature are obliged to express themselves: the enforcer, and the maniac." When Madden asks him which he currently has the honor of addressing, Regency leans really close into his face and whispers with a huge smile, "You've never met the maniac." Hauser's performance in this movie is so crazy that it's brilliant.

Regency newly arriving in town and putting the heat on Madden comes with a twist: it's revealed that he's married to Madden's ex-girlfriend, Madeleine. Regency may also be in cahoots with Madden's ex-wife, Patty Lareine, who in turn might be working with her ex-husband (Madden's former school pal), Wardley Meeks, to pull off a drug deal employing the two out-of-towners that Madden may or may not have killed. It all gets *very* convoluted, *very* quickly. It's almost impossible to keep track of who's slept with who and who's backstabbing who—because this is a movie where everybody's fucking everybody, and everyone is fucking everyone else over.

Now, overly complex and hard-to-follow plots have been a tradition within the crime genre going back to *The Big Sleep* (1946), and likely farther. Plus, *Tough Guys Don't Dance* certainly wasn't the first—or last—movie of its kind to tell its story out of order: *The Killers* (1946) and *Out of the Past* (1947) are two classic examples of nonlinear crime movies, as are the more recent *The Usual Suspects* (1995) and the aforementioned *Reservoir Dogs*. The problem with *Tough Guys Don't Dance* lies in its execution, or lack thereof.

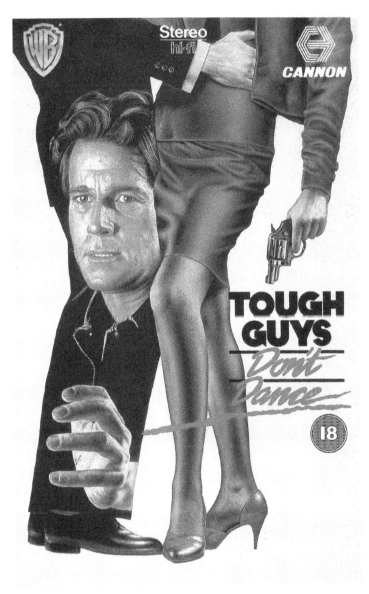

The U.K. video artwork for *Tough Guys Don't Dance*.

Mailer himself admitted often that he had a hard time adapting his own novel for the screen, which is perhaps the reason why respected screenwriter and script doctor Robert Towne—at that point, a four-time Oscar nominee, and an Oscar winner for *Chinatown* (1975)—was brought on to advise before filming began. (Towne had known Menahem Golan for decades, having served with the future Cannon boss on the crew of Roger Corman's 1963 picture, *The Young Racers*.) Towne clearly couldn't save the script, however: the way the mystery unfolds is a *mess*.

Any great mystery withholds information from the audience, but *Tough Guys Don't Dance* has a habit of holding back simple facts that would make the movie easier to follow. For example, Madden refers to his dad as "Dougy" in the film's opening scene, and some time passes before they bother to divulge that they're father and son. Why? We're not even told that Madden is a failed writer until forty minutes in, making the audience question just what it is he does besides drink and duck murder charges all day. We hear little about Patty Lareine's second ex-husband, Wardley Meeks—who turns out to be a major character—until almost the halfway mark, when it's revealed that not only was he coincidentally one of Madden's former school pals, but helped Madden get back on his feet after his recent release from prison. It's never even mentioned that Madden has a dog until twenty seconds before it's stabbed to death in a knife fight. ("Your knife is in my dog," Madden seethes at his assailant, leaving the audience to wonder: since when did he have a dog?) Films that utilize a nonlinear style typically do it so that they can answer questions or make bombshell revelations at dramatic moments. In *Tough Guys Don't Dance*, it feels like Mailer was repeatedly forgetting to mention things we should already know. It's arguable that more essential plot points of *Tough Guys Don't Dance* play out *before* the movie begins than during it.

The movie's absurd, over-the-top macho-ness is also a factor in how hokey it is, but that was probably to be expected of Mailer, whose words and actions—such as that time he stabbed his wife—made him a regular target of feminist criticism throughout his career. Hard-drinking, mean-talking tough guys are part and parcel of the crime genre, but the level it's taken to here can sometimes feel like a comedian had decided to bang out a particularly mean-spirited parody of Mailer's trademark style. It's all too clear, though, that Mailer took his own words dead seriously.

The few women in the film fall into one of two categories: foolish angel, or devious whore. If they're not manipulating one of their fawning lovers into doing their bidding, they're being fucked and passed along to the next guy. (Or worse, murdered.) Comically, nearly every woman in the movie has had sex with Madden and at least one of the other male characters. There's literally only one named female character in the movie who *hasn't* slept with Madden, and her only significant line of dialogue is expressing disbelief that she and Madden haven't made it in the sack together yet. (We're surprised, too!)

Meanwhile, the men in the movie converse almost exclusively in the form of pissing matches meant to exert their supremacy over one another, or to question the other's so-called masculinity. The most obvious example is when a drunk Madden goads one of the future murder victims into having sex with him while her partner—a bisexual man—is forced to watch. Regency never wastes an opportunity to remind Madden that his ex-girlfriend now belongs to him. Only minutes into the film, Madden's dad belittles his son's choice in women. ("Certain dames ought to wear a t-shirt that says, 'hang around, I'll make a cocksucker out of you.'") Within the same exchange of dialogue, Madden must defend his masculinity from his own father, and announce that he made it through three years in the slammer and "no one made [him] their punk." ("You always worried I'd turn out queer!" he accuses his pops.)

Tough Guys Don't Dance has an especially low regard for its queer characters, who serve as the movie's most gullible patsies. There are two bisexual males in the film: when they're not being manipulated by women for their wealth and social status, they're being bullied by duplicitous men. The language used is especially tasteless. While interrogating Madden about the suspiciously-vanished "tourists," Lonnie and Jessica, Regency refers to the former as "a swish" and a "flaming faggot." Before their murders, Lonnie and Jessica fight over her cuckolding him with Madden earlier that evening. He calls her a slut, to which she spits back, "I'm no more of a slut than any faggot." (The blonde ex-porn star, Jessica, is played by Frances Fisher, who co-starred with onetime husband Clint Eastwood in *Unforgiven* [1992] and went on to play Kate Winslet's mother in *Titanic* [1998].) At one point Regency casually admits Madden, "I'm just a country boy, Tim, I like to kill homos," which Mailer seems to have intended as a joke. *Oof.* The ugly homophobia is probably the main thing preventing *Tough Guys Don't Dance* from becoming a bigger staple of the cult movie canon.

That awfulness aside, is *Tough Guys Don't Dance* worth watching? Absolutely. There are many bad movies out there, but few of them are as deliriously bizarre as this one. It's easy to get caught up in the mystery plot, as nonsensically as it unfolds and as far-fetched as it ultimately winds up being. Mailer may have failed at imitating the hard-boiled crime stories of Raymond Chandler or Dashiell Hammett, but he somehow managed to squeeze a half-decade's worth of soap opera subplots into one violent, smutty little movie. There's entertainment in that.

Patty Lareine (Debra Sandlund) and Jessica Pond (Frances Fisher) in *Tough Guys Don't Dance.*

Every single one of the actors in this movie is given plentiful opportunity to overact. We've already mentioned Wings Hauser, whose highly impassioned, totally bonkers performance as a psycho cop is one for the ages. Equally wild is John Bedford Lloyd's Wardley Meeks the Third, a spoiled rich kid whose every line is spoken with a thick, Southern twang that sounds like he's trying to channel Foghorn Leghorn and Scarlett O'Hara at the same time. "Lonnie is dead, Jessica is dismembered, Patty Lareine is off on some kind of toot, and I'm about to go into business with you two unspeakable sleaze-os," Wardley drawls in the middle of a lurid drug deal. "I know I'm out of my mind, but I've never felt more alive!" (If you close your eyes as he says it, you can almost picture his character fanning himself while gazing out over the plantation.) You can't help but love his characterization choices.

The actor responsible for *Tough Guys Don't Dance*'s most well-known piece of scenery-chewing, however, is Ryan O'Neal. It's not so much his performance as a whole—which is fine, considering he was rarely tasked with anything more than stumbling into every scene as if his character had just woken up with a hangover—but for one, particular moment that has gone down in infamy.

Near the midpoint of the movie, Madden drives out to a secluded beach to read a letter from his former lover, Madeleine. In voiceover, she informs Madden that his current wife, Patty Lareine, is having an affair with her husband, Chief Regency. "I don't think we should talk about it . . . unless you're prepared to kill them!" Cue loud, dramatic chords in the score, and a slow zoom in on Madden's face:

"Oh man. Oh God. Oh man. Oh God! Oh man! Oh God! Oh man! Oh God, oh man! Oh God!"

O'Neal's voice increases in pitch and ardor, but his face barely registers the moment. Instead, it's the sudden, overbearing score and the camera work—which whips around in circles, as if Madden's world is spinning out of control around him—that tell us this is supposed to be a Big Important Moment for our hero. It's the movie's most unintentionally hilarious twenty seconds, and was uploaded—free of context—to the Internet under the title "Worst Line Reading Ever." While I'd venture there are worse ones out there, that title is mostly apt. The clip went viral and accumulated millions of views, and was seen by far more people than have ever watched *Tough Guys Don't Dance*.

Ryan O'Neal begged Mailer not to use the take, and even his editors and cinematographer asked him to remove it, or at least tone it down. Yet, it remained in the movie as we see it, for unknown reasons. It's the single element of the movie that Mailer ever expressed any regret over in the years after its release. It soured his friendship with O'Neal, who called the director a jerk for having left that take in the final film, although his career as a top leading man was effectively over even before he did *Tough Guys Don't Dance*. (It's unlikely that "Oh, man, oh, God" was solely responsible for that being the case, but it probably didn't help.) Speaking about the movie on a DVD featurette recorded fifteen years later, Mailer referred to that scene as "the one disaster in the film." As if there were *only* one!

The film was shot with a reported budget of around $5 million, and to Mailer's credit the movie was completed under budget and ahead of schedule. Like John Cassavetes on *Love Streams* (1984), Mailer saved money by shooting big portions of the film in his own house. He shot almost entirely in places that were familiar to him, and gave bit roles to locals he knew from around town in exchange for use of their businesses as shooting locations.

Tough Guys Don't Dance bombed in theaters, making back less than $1 million at the box office. Perhaps more damning given its prestigious pedigree, the movie received a reception from critics that was lukewarm on its best days, and positively obliterating on its worst. Many reviewers seemed unable to process what it was they'd just watched, which is understandable considering the movie's confounding overabundance of flashbacks within flashbacks, ring-around-the-rosy romantic pairings, and unidentified severed heads.

Tough Guys Don't Dance tied with *Jaws 4* (1987) for the most nominations at the Eighth annual Golden Raspberry Awards, including Worst Director,

Actor, Actress, New Star, Supporting Actress, Screenplay, and Worst Picture. The only "award" it took home was the Worst Director trophy for Mailer, which he shared that year with Elaine May and *Ishtar* (1987): a movie that's title has become a synonym for a big, Hollywood flop.

Several critics compared the film unfavorably to David Lynch's *Blue Velvet* (1986), perhaps due to the close proximity of their release dates and the shared presences of both Lynch's favorite composer, Angelo Badalamenti (*Blue Velvet* and later *Twin Peaks*, 1990–1991), and actress Isabella Rossellini. Both movies suggest a seamy underworld lurking on the fringes of "normal" life, but *Blue Velvet* successfully contrasts those dark places against its artificially pleasant suburban setting. In comparison, *Tough Guys Don't Dance* seems to take place entirely within Frank Booth's social circle. We never see a lighter side to *Tough Guys'* picturesque, oceanside locale.

The only moments of (clearly intentional) levity come in the form of several very, very bleak jokes near the movie's end. We don't want to spoil the movie's denouement—because, if you've made it through the movie's first two acts, you at least deserve that much—but there's some banter around the disposal of human remains and a line involving "small potatoes" that are very funny, but also come completely out of nowhere.

Could the movie have been meant to be a black comedy, and just wasn't able to hit its landing? Could *Tough Guys Don't Dance* have been this weird .. . *on purpose*? Perhaps, perhaps not. I have a theory.

In reading the copious amounts of press he did for the film while shooting was underway, it's abundantly clear that Mailer thought—*hoped*—that he was making a masterpiece. He mentions again and again how tired he's become of the novelist's life: the long hours of isolation that go into the research and writing process. The dream he mentioned to almost every journalist he spoke to was having dual careers as a writer and a filmmaker, where he'd take turns writing a book one year and directing a movie the next. He even suggested he might walk away from writing entirely to become a full-time director, abandoning his Pulitzer-winning career "in exactly the way a man who is happily married for many years will run off with a floozy." The key in all of this is that Mailer desperately wanted to make *more* movies.

A 1986 Cannes Film Festival advertisement for *Tough Guys Don't Dance* that lists Norman Mailer's name four times, in case anyone missed whose movie it was.

You know what I think? I think that no one with a desire to ever work in the film industry again would willfully compose a disaster on the scale of *Tough Guys Don't Dance*.

I think Mailer set out to make a dark, edgy thriller with some elements of black comedy. (Think: *Blue Velvet* again.) He frequently described the film he was making to his cast as "a horror movie of the mind." Flipping to the first page of Mailer's own screenplay, we're met with the following statement from the author:

"*Tough Guys Don't Dance* is a horror film in the form of a tough guy murder mystery. It is built on the premise that off-beat characters, a brooding landscape, edgy humor, and violence let loose in a town builds terror as effectively as huge special effects. If a strange and sinister fever is loose in the pleasure-loving classes of America, this film looks to be the embodiment of that fever."

Sure, the "edgy humor" leaves some room for levity—but that really sounds like the description of something far more serious than what we see on screen, doesn't it?

I think that things went wrong, starting with a script that couldn't effectively tell its story. I think Mailer pushed his actors for performances that wound up being too over-the-top. By the end of an eight-week shoot plagued by weather issues—the movie was shot during a frigid New England winter—it also seems like he'd lost the faith of many in his cast. When reporter Joseph Gelmis visited the set seven weeks into production, Frances Fisher called Mailer "a dictator, not a director." In that same article, Wings Hauser tells the journalist straight up that "I hate him," and accuses Mailer of being a tyrant who treats his actors like children. Even O'Neal, his longtime friend, admits they've had their problems on the film, and mentions that he's had to refuse some of the requests Mailer was making of him.

What seems likely to me is that Mailer figured out that he had a clunker on his hands, either well into the shoot or possibly not until it reached the editing room. At that point he pivoted, and began to approach the movie as if it had been *intentionally* campy, implementing a form of damage control by pretending that the parts that were silly or bad were *meant* to be silly or bad all along. From there, he inserted some of the stranger takes to make the movie appear more consistently campy, but came up somewhat short. That could explain the movie's wildly inconsistent tone, and is the only fathomable (to me) reason why Mailer would insist upon using the version of the "Oh, man! Oh, God!" scene that made it into the finished film, despite his collaborators pleading otherwise.

The movie's remarkable theatrical trailer would seem to support this theory. In it, Mailer himself reads from several comment cards supposedly left by audience members after a test screening of the film. The comments alternate between slurping adulation and jeering insults. "Bold, innovative, wonderful." "Stinks!" "A movie not to miss." "A giant death orgy with lots of maniacs." "One of the best and most original films I have ever seen." "The worst ever—my grandmother could have done better." "Quick turns of plot, I enjoyed having to think." "Whoever wrote this has never read a good book." (He tosses away the comment card.) "The devil made this picture." (After that last one, Mailer smugly winks at the camera.)

This later attitude about the movie is a far cry from the one he displayed during production, when he consistently told reporters he was working on a "very good" film. In retrospect, the best shot he probably had at covering for himself—especially once it was clear *Tough Guys* was a flop—would have been by making it seem as if the schlock that unfolded onscreen had been his plan all along.

If that *was* his ploy, it was almost brilliant. If that *wasn't* his ploy, and this is genuinely the film he'd planned to make all along, then there was clearly a different sort of brilliance at play—one that bordered on madness.

In any case, Norman Mailer never directed another Hollywood movie.

Interview: Actor Wings Hauser

If one was to catalog the cult actors of the video store era, Wings Hauser would land near the top of almost any list. From his breakout as the sadistic pimp Ramrod in *Vice Squad* (1982) and onward, Hauser's name was a fixture on VHS rental sleeves. The actor appeared in dozens of low-budget genre films over the next three decades.

Wings Hauser as Provincetown's acting chief of police, Alvin Luther Regency, in *Tough Guys Don't Dance*.

Gerald "Wings" Hauser is the son of Dwight Hauser, a screenwriter who was blacklisted as a Communist during the McCarthy era. Earning the nickname "Wings" for the position he played on the high school gridiron, young Hauser left sports behind to follow his creative ambitions. At first this was music, rather than acting—Hauser recorded two albums in the 1970s. After moving to Los Angeles, Hauser turned to acting as a means of putting a roof over his head when he found himself homeless and raising an infant on his own. After years as a regular on the soap opera *The Young and the Restless*, his performance in *Vice Squad* opened up a floodgate for offers to appear in a wide variety of low-budget action films, thrillers, horror, and sci-fi movies being shot in all corners of the world. From *Mutant* (1984) to *Nightmare at Noon* (1988) to *Champagne and Bullets* (1993), *Tales from the Hood* (1995) to *The Insider* (1999) to *Rubber* (2010), fans could count on Hauser giving an engaging performance. This was regardless of whether or not the film around him lived up to it.

Tough Guys Don't Dance stands out in his filmography during this period: a presumptive prestige picture directed by Pulitzer Prize-winning novelist Norman Mailer. In it, Hauser plays Alvin Luther Regency, Provincetown's unhinged police chief. He was nominated for the Independent Spirit Award for his performance, which was widely lauded by critics as one of the best elements of the movie.

Tough Guys Don't Dance is a film I've watched quite a few times now. Every time I watch it I think I've enjoyed it even more—or, at least understood it a little more.

Wings Hauser: I was confused about it. I'm not kidding. I still wonder who kills who. I read the book. I've seen the film and read the scripts, and still I have some questions like, "Who killed who? Whose head was there?" It's a confusing piece of writing.

Your career exploded in the early '80s. All of a sudden you went from *The Young and the Restless* to *Vice Squad*, and from then on you were making a lot of movies. Can you tell me what your feelings were about your career in the years leading into *Tough Guys*?

It was really strange. I was raising a daughter by myself. I arrived in Los Angeles in 1972 with a box of Pampers, $30, a suitcase, and a 13-month-old baby daughter. No mother, no father, no nothing, just me. We were homeless in Downtown LA.

We were really homeless for about a week. Then we found this garage that this guy would rent us for $1 a night or something. It was an actual, working garage. It had a Volkswagen Bug in it. The motor was out of it, and the backseat was my daughter's bedroom. That's where we started from scratch. Basically, I was playing music, and ended up cutting another album, my second album for RCA. I was just scratching—I would do anything.

My whole life was putting a roof over this kid's head and giving her an education and trying to be the best father I could, and still get what I want in life.

I ended up in this acting class. I was making $50 a month working for one of the acting teachers. I got an interview on *The Young and the Restless* and I got the role. The first thing he said was, "Can you get out of it?" I'm like, "No! Are you fucking crazy? I got money! My God, I got food!"

I was on that show for about four years. I got a lot of confidence there as an actor, just doing mountains of dialogue because I had a photographic mind. I could memorize anything, and then I would forget it an hour later. I can memorize anything, like a telephone book. It's just a muscle that you nurture.

Along comes *Vice Squad*, and it was a really despicable role—but it was so the opposite of the role that I was playing on *The Young and Restless*, which was basically a Ken doll.

I got this film. In those days, the video market hadn't really taken off. Basically, if you were doing these kind of low-rent films, they went European and the United States never got them. It was really a happy existence: you could make a few bucks and you wouldn't have these shit films out there in America. You could still go around pretending like you were some kind of no-nonsense actor, an elitist.

Then all of a sudden, *Vice Squad* hit the theaters and just went nuts. People just couldn't get enough of this. That kind of set my ways. When you do something good in this town, that's how they see you, and that's how they see money, and that's what they want you for. That's basically what I was getting at. I was really scratching hard to get films like the Richard Pryor thing [*Jo Jo Dancer, Your Life Is Calling,* 1986], *A Soldier's Story* (1984) and pieces like that. I was trying to do good stuff.

At the same time, someone would come in and go, "We'll give you $250,000 to go down to Atlanta and make this stupid film." You go, "Well, this means my daughter can get an education. This means we can have a house. This means we have cars, insurance, my God." A lot of actors, I think, will tell you that they hold out for the good roles, and all this and that. I was basically in it for the money at that point. I knew I had talent but it was like, if they don't want to use it, fuck them. What am I going to do? Force it on them, beat them up?

When I say "they," I mean the powers that be, the white men. Fucking white men. [*Laughs*] They rule. It's funny when you see actors going, "I did this and I did that." The only reason why *anybody* makes it in this town is because they were allowed to make it. They got a break. They were given those roles. I was given *these* roles, and I ate them up and made enough money to survive. I think it's always been that way since I had a daughter and my wife didn't want her. Everything has been about survival. Now, as an older man, I can do what I want to do, which is very little acting, and playing a lot of music, working on my third album.

In the midst of doing all these films, you also wrote the original script for *Uncommon Valor* (1983).

Yes, I did.

Within a few years, a bunch of other movies were made in that same vein, about someone going back to Vietnam to save the guys left behind. Cannon alone made several of them with Chuck Norris. Could you tell me where the inspiration for that story came from?

I grew up in this place called Lake Sherwood, California. My next-door neighbor two doors down was a guy by the name of Paul Watkins, who came from a very Christian family. He was the president of the high school. The next year he was Charles Manson's right-hand man. He procured all the women for Charlie. The women got the men to do the dirty work through sex. That's how that whole thing went down. I ran into Manson a couple of times, he was just chilling. He just looked like a little rat to me, but to these people—after they had taken enough drugs—he was everything.

That was one of my next-door neighbors. My immediate neighbor, right next to me was Bob Denver, who played Gilligan, who had a huge cheetah run right on our property line, with a chain link fence that went all the way up and around.

He had two cheetahs that lived in his house, constantly just laying around, and a chimp. Like a teenage chimp. When my sisters got their periods, this chimp would just go fucking nuts and start screaming. The only door that locked in our house was the bathroom door, and they'd go in there and hide from it. They were so scared of this thing. It was just rattling the cage. You'd go down to Bob Denver's house and you could barely see Bob sitting in a chair, because the smoke from the marijuana was so thick. It went on and on and on. We were surrounded by an array of very eclectic people, child molesters and so on. [*Laughs*] It was a community of only ninety people, it was really small.

My other next-door neighbor was Gary Dickerson, who has been my dearest and oldest friend, and still is. My father had his dealings in the Fifties with the [House Un-American Activities Committee] people and all that. We were pretty left wing. We were all opposed to the war in Vietnam. We saw no sense in some drunk in the White House sending boys off to the slaughter house without Congress's approval. We didn't agree with it.

Anyway, Gary shows up and he goes, "I joined the army." Gary went and he did damage over there, not only to a lot of people but to himself. When he came back, he knew about four or five words and they all started with "F." I looked at him and I couldn't contact the guy, he was so blown away.

In 1978, '79, I got him drunk and I asked him a question. I said, "Would you ever go back to Vietnam?" He said, "Fuck no, I would never go near that fucking place." I said, "What if people were still there? What if somebody had been left behind, or whatever?" and he'd go, "I'd be there in a minute." I thought, well there, Jesus, God, what a story that would be. I just kind of thought about it, and then I started talking to other vets and I'd ask them the same question. They wanted nothing to do with Vietnam, but if somebody was left behind, in a minute they would go back.

That was the beginning of it, and then what I did is I went around and I interviewed P.O.W. wives. I saw this woman on, I think, *The Mike Douglas Show*, talking about P.O.W.s and MIAs, and I started contacting the P.O.W.

861

wives. They were just the most beautiful people in the world. They were saying that they still didn't know where their husbands were.

That's what led me to write [*Uncommon Valor*]. When I wrote it, it wasn't the comedy that it turned out to be. It was a real heavy look at people who were all fucked up, and they somehow unfucked themselves, to a degree, by going back and doing this, and getting their integrity back, and that's what it was about. The whole thing was about returning. The original title of the film was called "Youth in Asia." [*Laughs*] They didn't like that, of course.

What happened was, to put the thing in a better screenplay form, my agent had a young writer who he was pushing off on me. I paid the guy $2,500 to put it in a screenplay form, and he put a couple of ideas in. Then I sold it to Paramount. One day they wanted it and I refused them, and so they doubled everything they offered and I took it. [*Laughs*] I signed on to be an associate producer and everything was great. I was going to play the role of Blaster, and then they said, "Go get John Milius to direct this."

I went and met with John Milius, who was just the worst person I've ever met in this business. Just fucking horrible. The first thing I noticed as I walked into his house was there was nothing but Nazi paraphernalia, and I just kind of went, "Well . . . this is not a place I want to be." [*Laughs*] The second thing was his friend, this guy Darrell Fetty, I had an affair with his girlfriend—so life was not looking good for me there, and I got out of there as fast as I could. He ended up producing, and as soon as he took that on, he got rid of me. That's what happens to writers.

He hired this guy, Joe Gayton, who I had hired to do all the rewrites. He wound up with the credit after I went through several arbitrations at the Writers Guild, and because Milius was a member of the Writers Guild, he had a lot of pull, and that was the end of that. I walked away with the money and an associate producer credit, which I didn't do anything for, and ended up without the writer's credit. Or "Story By."

That's crazy.

Yes, it was, and it hurt like hell. Right out of that, I got this call: "We'll give you $200,000 to go to Atlanta and do this film called "Night Shadows," which is about toxic water. It all sounded great, but it turned into this film called *Mutant* (1984), with slow motion ghouls chasing me around. I'd be running, and I'd have to stop and let them catch up to me. [*Laughs*] It was so bad.

Some French moviegoers were given promotional matchbooks for *Tough Guys Don't Dance*, presumably so they could light up cigarettes afterward and try to sort out what the heck they had just watched.

What did you think of the *Tough Guys Don't Dance* script the first time you read it, and what potential did you see in the role of Regency?

Well, the thing was I'd just come off of a TV series called *The Last Precinct* (1986), which was a comedy. Then I went to Greece, Africa, and Texas, and did three films back-to-back, so by the time I met with Norman Mailer and read the script I was pretty full of myself, pretty big-headed. "Look at me, aren't I something?" I read the script, I didn't quite understand it on the first reading, but I'd read Norman Mailer and he was like an icon to me. To tell you the truth, I was more interested in meeting him than getting the role, because I didn't think I would end up with the role. I gave it my best.

As an actor you really don't put too much gold on that part of the scale, you'll end up totally depressed. It's like you almost have to walk in there with a "Fuck you, you're not going to hurt me." attitude. "I'm going to put the best foot forward and that's all I need out of this. If you want more, call." I read the script, I didn't quite get it the way I was supposed to get it. I read the book, and the book was kind of bizarre. [*Laughs*] I was like, "What the fuck is this?" It was a mish-mash of stuff.

I get a reading, I go in, I blow them away, and we just hit it off. I go home and think he's going to call, and they do, and they want me to read again. This went on I want to say six times, probably five times, then I'm called in, and the fifth time, my agent calls me and I go, "Fuck this guy, fuck him. I just came off three films and I'm fucking doing great, I don't need this fucking idiot." He goes, "Just do one more reading and it'll be okay." I go, "Well, fuck him. God dammit, what's it take? I've done everything. I've cried, I've yelled, I've screamed. I've pissed my pants, what else does this fucking clown want?"

I go in, and Ryan O'Neal is there. We do the reading and Ryan stops and just goes, "You know, the only actor in this room is Wings Hauser." I'm just thinking, "Whoa, that's too good. That is very nice." [*Laughs*] I leave.

Tanya Roberts read it with me and I thought she was phenomenal for this role. I know she got a bad rap for *Charlie's Angels* (1976–1981), but I thought she was perfect for this role and I thought, for sure, she's doing this. So, we did it and I got the role. They finally gave it to me. I was off to the races, off to Provincetown.

I doubt that he'll admit it, but Ryan is the reason why [I got the role]. He slammed the door on the process. He finally just said, "That's your guy." By the way, Norman didn't want me. Norman wanted this friend of his who wasn't an actor to play Regency. I think Fred Roos, one of the producers, and Tom Luddy were going, "No, you've got to go with Wings." I think he went with me as long as they went with Debra Sandlund.

He didn't want me, and it was obvious for the first week of rehearsals. We did not get along. We were seriously enemies.

One of the local Cape Cod papers profiled most of the cast during filming, and some actors spoke very positively of working with Mailer but others—like yourself and Frances Fisher—sounded fed up with him.

Oh, yes. Here's the thing. He wanted somebody else. This is the wonderful story of my life. The first week was horrible. From rehearsals he was on me. If I said "uh" instead of "a," he was like, "Don't rewrite my shit, what the fuck is this?" That kind of stuff. Coffee cups were bouncing off the walls—you can imagine. Ryan is known for having a bit of a temper. Norman certainly had one, and I've got one. [*Laughs*] With the three of us together, it got pretty intense for a week.

Then, the first day comes along, right, and its magic time, man. The cameras are on, and I lay down my first scene. Two days later after he's seen it, he comes up to me and he goes, "You're fantastic in this role. I had no idea." I look at him, basically, with a "fuck you" look on my face, like "How dare you doubt me?" [*Laughs*] That kind of thing. I've been offended. I've got the vapors. I show up on the set and every now and then he'd come up to me and just belt me in the stomach. I'd go, "Man, you are so lucky. You're so lucky because when I go, I'm going to go all over you."

It was just *hell*, and I would say probably three fourths through this film, I'd finally had it. I walked up to him and I said, "Look, I don't like you. You don't like me. Write this end scene and let me get the fuck on a plane tonight, and fuck you." He looked at me like he had no idea what I was talking about. Was this guy missing everything? So, we went upstairs—we were shooting in his house. We go upstairs, and we spent about twenty minutes together, and I must say—I've made Richard Pryor laugh, and Norman Mailer cry. Well, there were tears.

When we came down after that meeting—and I very seldom talk about what happened in that meeting—he got the whole crew together and he said, "I want to apologize to all of you for the way I've treated Wings Hauser. I thought this was the way you direct, and it's not. Wings, I apologize for that." I was just like, "Wow." When does Norman Mailer apologize? It's like getting Donald Trump to apologize. It was like, "This is not happening" I'm sitting there and I feel like a complete asshole, of course. I've got Norman Mailer apologizing.

Anyhow, we became close. Oh my God, we're doing all sorts of shit together. He takes me to the Eugene O'Neill Men's Club, which is this dark, dirty, filthy fucking hole in the wall. We go in. The dishes are in the sink. It's just horrible. We go upstairs and there's the most beautiful pool table. I was smoking a cigarette and I remember going, "Is there an ashtray?" He goes, "Interesting you should bring that up. In 1932, an ashtray initiative was introduced and it was voted down. Use the floor." [*Laughs*] I just went, "Okay." I was there with my scotch, and he was there with his marijuana, and we just got along great.

Until the day he died, we were writing letters back and forth. He sent me etchings. In my opinion, we became really good friends, and he was so proud when we were nominated for the Independent Spirit Awards. I don't know if he was nominated, but I was nominated and so was Debra, and he was sitting right next to me, his arm around my shoulder. It was like, "You wanted to fire me. Isn't that right, buddy?" [*Laughs*] "Here we are and we're getting awards, motherfucker."

That's a turnaround. Wow.

It was a complete turnaround. It was a one-eighty with skid marks.

Ryan O'Neal and Wings Hauser in *Tough Guys Don't Dance*.

866

Now, shooting in Provincetown, in Mailer's house, you were very much on his home turf. What are your memories of the location? Did you get to go out and enjoy the town?

Oh, God, we ruled the town. [*Laughs*] Are you kidding? We were there in the winter. The only people there during the winter were fishermen. Except, when I arrived, there was a week-long convention, and here's the thing. I was out walking, I think it was maybe the first or second night, and I was all bundled up because it was freezing. I wasn't used to this shit at all. I'm going from these cabins where we were staying, which were wonderful, and walking down Commercial Street, which is the main drag.

This beautiful, beautiful, tall woman was coming towards me, and I was going to give my line. I'm thinking, "Jesus, look at this." As she got closer and closer, I went, "Hi, good evening. How are you?" and this voice goes [*in a low register*], "Oh, I'll be fine once I get out of these fucking heels." [*Laughs*] I forget what the convention was called but it's where men came and dressed like women. Men came with their wives and things, and they all crossdressed for a week and they were just everywhere, but I had no idea.

We ruled the town. It was a small, little town. We tore it apart. We had a good time. We were out every night. What can I say? [*Laughs*]

What is your favorite part of *Tough Guys*? What do you feel is your best work in it?

Jesus, I really don't know. I've never thought of what's my favorite thing. First of all, I don't watch that much of myself. When I do, I want to go into real estate, basically, I think, "Oh, fuck. What am I doing?"

Many of the critics, even ones who hated it, agreed that your performance was one of the best things in the movie. I'm wondering where it stands for you, personally, among your roles? Is it one of your favorites?

Oh, yes. Yes, yes, yes. I would say it was definitely in the top ten, maybe in the top five. It was so hard working with Norman in the beginning, so that was very uncomfortable. That was a hard, hard shoot, until it got easy.

Oh—I know my favorite scene. My favorite scene was with Ryan, in the house, when I was in my uniform. I got right in his face—we were sitting at the table, I believe. It was right before I had the stroke. I really liked that scene. I liked doing that. That was good. He was good to work with. The guy's got a rap. He's got apparent issues, I guess, okay, but I got to tell you, the guy was nothing but great around me. This guy was kind, and giving, and fun. He's just a great guy to work with. I never saw anything detrimental about the guy. He's just a great guy.

With as many movies as both you and Cannon were making during the '80s, it's surprising to me that this was the only time you crossed paths.

Well, no.

No?

Well, I was in this acting class with Cheryl Ladd, who thought she wasn't pretty. [*Laughs*] Every guy in there was like, "Oh no, you're beautiful. You're absolutely fucking beautiful. Let me tell you how beautiful you look. Let's go out." It was me, Cheryl Ladd, Anne Archer, Tom Selleck, Bob Urich, Priscilla Presley. These real babes. We thought we were the cat's meow. When it came to Cannon Films, we looked down on them—only because Cannon wouldn't hire me. I couldn't get near them. It was all Chuck Norris [movies], so I hated Chuck Norris for a while until I worked with him. He turns out to be the nicest guy in the world, which was just disappointing. [*Laughs*] He's just a great fucking guy, you know? Right wing and all. He's just a really good guy and gives it up to you as an actor, and lets you do your thing. He makes you feel good doing it. It's such a surprising business.

But, no, no, Cannon wouldn't let me in the door. I had a bad taste for them. Which, as an actor, that's what you do. It's hard not to be bitter at some people, you know? When they won't even give you a chance. That was, until I got *Tough Guys Don't Dance*. Then I really liked them. It was like, "Oh boy, they're my best friends now." [*Laughs*] Menahem who?

My Academy speech is going to go like this—if I ever get an Academy Award, it's going to be like, "I'd like to thank Steven Spielberg, such and such, George Lucas. I'd love to thank them, but they never did anything for me. I couldn't even get an audition, so fuck them." [*Laughs*] "Now, here are the people I'd *really* like to thank . . ."

Wardley Meeks (John Bedford Lloyd) threatens Tim Madden (Ryan O'Neal) at gunpoint in *Tough Guys Don't Dance*.

Interview: Actor John Bedford Lloyd

John Bedford Lloyd played Wardley Meeks III, a key player in the mystery that unfolds in Norman Mailer's *Tough Guys Don't Dance* (1987). While it's not among his best-known roles, it's one that he cherishes as much as any in his career.

Standing six foot, five inches tall, John Bedford Lloyd is always a formidable presence whenever he appears on screen. Originally, Lloyd never planned to become an actor—but his involvement in a school production of *One Flew Over the Cuckoo's Nest* while studying pre-med forever changed the course of his career. He later studied drama at Yale and started acting on the New York stage, but it wasn't long before he was working in film and television.

Prior to *Tough Guys Don't Dance*, Lloyd had a leading role on the TV series *Hometown* (1985). Later roles include appearances in *The Abyss* (1989), *Super Troopers* (2001), *The Bourne Supremacy* (2004), and *Ozark* (2018–2020).

What do you remember of your audition for *Tough Guys*?

John Bedford Lloyd: Oh, God. It was one of the most truly out-there audition experiences I ever had. [*Laughs*] I originally was reading for the role of Regency, the part that Wings Hauser played. There's a scene in which Officer Regency of the Provincetown Police Department has what you could call a complete breakdown. That was the scene I was asked to read.

The feeling in the room was, "Just go for it," which I did. I won't get into the particulars but it was . . . well, I hope the tape has been burnt and the ashes scattered far, far out to sea. It was one of the most bizarre pieces of acting—and I hesitate to use that word—that I think I've ever done, because it felt comfortable. When actors feel comfortable in a room during an audition, especially when they're younger, they go, "Well, fuck it. I'll try this." I still remember some of the things I did and I just go, "What were you thinking?"

Then, for some reason, and I still don't know why, Norman said, "Okay, why don't you play the cocaine-dealing, landed gentry, Tampa, Florida, gay, homicidal, decapitating, prep school friend of the lead character?" [*Laughs*] I was very glad he did, because it was a delightful experience.

It's interesting casting because the character, just based on his name alone, Wardley Meeks, sounds like he'd be a small, weak guy, and you're a tall, imposing presence. Do you think that was intentional?

I was always surprised, because I was ten to fifteen years younger than Ryan [O'Neal] and we were supposed to be school buddies, or peers. It didn't matter in a movie like that.

The most fun we had, I'll tell you, other than doing certain scenes in the middle of the night when it was five degrees out, and watching a life-sized figure of Debra Sandlund covered in milk get pulled, headless, out of a barrel—the best part was sitting around with Norman and his dramaturg, and the other actors, reading through the script for about two, three, four days before we started shooting and just saying, "Norman, what's this mean?" "Norman, if I kill him here and I end up over there in Truro and I take a walk on the beach, how did I end up . . .?" All what the actors call "table work." Doing table work with Norman Mailer is something I will never forget, and I'll always be grateful for.

Can you tell me a little bit more about what he was like, as a director?

I don't think anybody in the cast except Ryan knew him—I think Ryan had boxed with him at some point. Is that true?

Yes, they were sparring partners.

I don't know if any of the rest of us knew Norman. We all knew him by reputation, because of all the very press-worthy stuff that he had done. Other than the fact that he was a brilliant writer, what we knew of the man he was, was some of the crazier stuff in his youth.

You meet him and you feel like going, "Norman, why are they saying these things about you?" He was the mildest, most—in some ways, he was like the grandfather that I never had. I had them, but they all were dead before I knew that they had even existed. He was the sweetest, most accepting, most supportive presence on the set. I think that came because of who he was. If he said something, everybody just got real quiet and listened.

He had a great support system around him, like John Bailey, who was the cinematographer and I think billed as the visual consultant. John Bailey is one of the most famous directors of photography in the world, and was very helpful. Whenever Norman needed some help realizing his vision for whatever scene we were doing, he was just delightful.

We would hang out with [Norman's] family, Norris Church, his wife, and John Buffalo Mailer, who was just a little kid at the time. As crazy as the movie was and as crazy as the characters were, it was a delightful family experience.

There are some fun, campy moments in the film, which I think are a big part of the reason why fans love it so much to this day. Do you think that was all intentional on Mailer's part?

[Laughs] What particular moments are you referring to?

John Bedford Lloyd and Ryan O'Neal in *Tough Guys Don't Dance*.

There are some lines in there that feel intentionally campy, at least to me. I think of your "two unspeakable sleaze-os" line.

That's just a great line! That's not campy. That's just a great line. "You unspeakable sleaze-os." What a great line. That's not campy—that's just good writing.

What about Ryan's famous "Oh God, oh man moment", with the spinning camera?

It was just a choice that somebody made. They did that, and it is what it was.

You've described this film as a cult movie without a cult following, which I feel is pretty accurate. I'm surprised it's not part of the midnight movie repertory now.

Oh, yes. It's true. The people that know it just absolutely adore it. Some of the writing was the most delightful, wonderful words I've ever spoken as an actor, and certainly ever in front of a camera.

You've had so many better-known movies and TV roles. How often are you approached, besides by myself right now, and asked about *Tough Guys*?

Never. Every once in a while I'll run into a guy who was on the crew, and we'll talk about it. I don't know if you know this, it was a non-union crew. Do you know about this?

I know that Cannon tried to avoid unions wherever they could.

We stopped for a while. There was this person, a shop steward, I think, and they got together and said it was freezing cold.

I don't know how badly they were being treated, but they weren't getting union [pay]. It was not a union shoot, so there was a period of time during which they shut down. I remember the crew and the actors met, and there was a meeting for solidarity's sake. We all elected, because we were all in the Screen Actors Guild, and said, "We're with you." It wasn't a particularly courageous move on our part. It just made so much sense. I believe they made it a union shoot before the crew went back to work. That was for Golan and Globus, right?

Yes, that's correct.

Well, that's what they did. What was your original question?

873

It was about how often you're approached by fans about *Tough Guys Don't Dance*.

Very infrequently. I did a movie called *Super Troopers* (2001). I will get approached for that movie more than any other thing I've done. It still amazes me because it was a stoner comedy that we made in the '90s and everybody remembers it—usually boys or men, policemen, security folks, ex-state troopers. It always surprises me. It's always fun. Now, *there's* a cult movie with a cult following.

I saw Norman, once, very close to the end of his life, at a tribute at Lincoln Center. They showed *Tough Guys*, or parts of it, and maybe parts of his other films. I'm so grateful that I got to see him again. I did a play by Arthur Miller called *Resurrection Blues*. It was the world premiere of that play, and Arthur was at the rehearsals for about a week. It was a brand new play and he was messing around with it, and he and Norman, I have to say, were the most muscular, powerful brains that I've ever been anywhere near.

You sat there, and you just couldn't believe that someone was that brilliant, and could put words together on the page, and were also just communicating with you about whatever we happened to be talking about. You spent a lot of time in their presence simply awestruck by their intelligence, and the power of their ability to communicate, and the beauty of the way they communicated so differently.

Norman was more pugilistic, almost in the way he spoke and the way he expressed himself, and Arthur was a little more, I guess, learned. Being with Norman, listening to him talk, exchanging ideas, and talking about his script—I never experienced anything like it before, and certainly not after.

The only thing I want to add [about *Tough Guys Don't Dance*] is that it was truly the most extraordinary role I've ever played, and the most extraordinary words I've ever gotten to speak. It was very, very special to have been in it.

A deleted scene, shown here in a Spanish lobby card for *Tough Guys Don't Dance*, included a musical performance by Wings Hauser, who sang an original song co-written by Norman Mailer and Angelo Badalamenti.

A VHS copy of *Surrender* formerly rented by Hill's Video Center of Florence, Alabama.

Surrender

Release Date: October 9, 1987
Directed by: Jerry Belson
Written by: Jerry Belson
Starring: Michael Caine, Sally Field, Steve Guttenberg, Peter Boyle
Trailer Voiceover: "A comedy for everyone who's sworn never to get roped into another relationship again."

Sean Stein (Michael Caine) is a wildly successful writer of mysteries, but that's about all in his life he can manage to do right. When he's not celebrating his latest bestseller, he's making uniformly terrible decisions in regards to women. A divorce settlement left him paying alimony plus twenty percent of his earnings to the ex-wife whom he left for a game show hostess (played by supermodel Iman, the longtime Mrs. David Bowie.) A few years later he finds himself paying palimony to the second woman, along with *fifty* percent of the proceeds on his latest books. When he brings home a prostitute for a round of no-ties lovemaking, she locks him in his bathroom, empties his wallet, takes his keys and speeds off in his Mercedes. With that, Sean swears off ladies altogether, and makes plans to sell his Beverly Hills mansion and move to Kuwait—because, as he puts it, "they flog [women] there."

In another part of Los Angeles, aspiring painter Daisy Morgan (Sally Field) is treading water in her own life. During the day she works on an artwork assembly line, banging out hundreds of identical acrylic landscapes to be hung in hotel rooms. (It's obvious she's unhappy when her boss reprimands her for painting a drowning woman into one of the idyllic, Bob Ross-like lake scenes.) At home, she's in a long-term, dead-end relationship with a younger, wealthier man named Marty, her corporate lawyer sugar daddy. He's dopey, devoted, and harmless, but uninterested in making any serious commitment to their relationship. Feeling like her biological clock is ticking down with each day that passes, she's open to the idea of starting a new romance.

Surrender's meet cute is undeniably unique. Our two leads find themselves dragged to a fancy-schmancy, black tie fundraiser—Daisy by her boyfriend, and Sean by his attorney/best friend, Jay—which is crashed by armed robbers shortly after their arrival. All of the guests are stripped of their clothes and valuables, then tied together in pairs. If you guessed that our two heroes would find themselves tied together, face to face and totally nude, well, you've either seen *Surrender* before or have a twisted imagination. (When the production had trouble finding extras willing to take off their clothes for the robbery scene, they recruited members of a local nudist colony to fill out the background.)

Everyone is soon rescued, relatively free from harm. Finding himself hopelessly smitten with his co-captive, Sean does a creepy thing and shows up on her doorstep the next day to ask her out. (It's very convenient that Daisy broke up with her rich boyfriend during their limo ride home the previous night.) Despite showing up for their date eight hours early, breaking down in tears in her apartment, and then proposing they have sex before they've even left for dinner, Sean is somehow irresistible to Daisy. Cue the cutesy montage of the two of them spending several adorably romantic weeks together.

Daisy Morgan (Sally Field) leaps into the arms of Sean Stein (Michael Caine) on the German VHS cover for *Surrender*. Where are her pants?

It kind of seems like the movie should be ending by this point, what with our two charming balls of quirk happily in love and there being seemingly little standing between them. However, there's still an hour of the movie to go, so it's time to start manufacturing problems to keep our lovebirds on their toes. One of the big issues they face is that Sean is so fearful of becoming romantically entangled with another gold-digger that he pretends to be broke, going so far as to make Daisy—who is actually struggling to pay her bills—pick up the tab whenever they go out on dates. It's also apparent that Daisy isn't completely done with her ex, who returns home after being kidnapped by pygmies (seriously), and appears to be a changed man.

Surrender isn't a romantic comedy classic by any standards, but it's entertaining enough to keep anyone's attention for a breezy ninety minutes. The script has a fair share of laugh-out-loud one-liners and chuckle-worthy sight gags, and probably more than its fair share of unexpected (if inconsequential) plot twists. It's the charming cast who keep the movie afloat when it otherwise would have sagged. *Surrender*'s two main stars had already won three Academy Awards between them when they made this film—Caine for *Hannah and Her Sisters* (1986), and Field for *Norma Rae* (1979) and *Places in the Heart* (1984)—and seem absolutely game to appear in a movie this cheerfully fluffy and dumb.

Caine had been a known commodity in the film industry for more than twenty years by the time he signed on for *Surrender*. He'd long ago received Oscar nominations for his appearances in *Alfie* (1966) and *Sleuth* (1972), made appearances in other noteworthy pictures such as *The Ipcress File* (1965), *The Italian Job* (1969), *Get Carter* (1971), *The Man Who Would Be King* (1975), and *A Bridge Too Far* (1977), and lent his talents to cult films such as Brian De Palma's *Dressed to Kill* (1980) and Neil Jordan's *Mona Lisa* (1986). It was said that every major studio in Hollywood had passed on *Surrender*, but once writer-director Jerry Belson was able to attach Michael Caine, Cannon jumped on the project knowing that his star power would make it easy for them to sell the picture abroad. These days, Caine is widely considered to be one of the most iconic British actors of all time.

Sally Field had risen to fame starring in TV shows such as *Gidget* (1965–1966) and the sublimely nutty *The Flying Nun* (1967–1970) before her critically-acclaimed role in the TV movie *Sybil* (1976) helped launch a more serious career on the silver screen. She soon appeared opposite Burt Reynolds in the blockbuster *Smokey and the Bandit* (1977), which made her a bona fide movie star and a fixture of American movies from that point on. Fortunately for Cannon, Field was married to producer Alan Greisman, who had been helping Belson shop the film to studios. He suggested the project to his wife, who read the script and agreed to sign on so long as Belson took another pass at it to flesh out her character, and turn Daisy into a co-lead rather than a supporting player.

Cannon only needed Michael Caine's headshot to pre-sell the movie to international buyers.

Neither Caine nor Field were at the age when actors typically make romantic comedies, which is something that makes *Surrender* kind of refreshing, even today. Caine was in his mid-fifties, and in five short years would be playing the decrepit Ebenezer Scrooge in *The Muppet Christmas Carol* (1992), which is unquestionably the best-ever cinematic version of Dickens' holiday classic. Field was comparatively young at forty, but was less than a decade away from playing Tom Hanks' dying mom in *Forrest Gump* (1994).

The supporting cast is pretty great, too. Playing the token, incompatible ex-boyfriend meant to stand between our two star-crossed lovers, Eighties mainstay Steve Guttenberg is surprisingly likeable. Perhaps best known for starring in the *Police Academy* franchise, Guttenberg seemed to pop up everywhere during that decade: from *Diner* (1982) to *Cocoon* (1985) to *Short Circuit* (1986). (The biggest hit of his career, 1987's *Three Men and a Baby*, would arrive in theaters just a few weeks after *Surrender*.) Sean's shyster lawyer and lone compadre is played by Peter Boyle, who made his name in the pre-Golan and Globus Cannon hit *Joe* (1970), then went on to appear opposite Robert Mitchum in the excellent *The Friends of Eddie Coyle* (1973), play the monster in *Young Frankenstein* (1974), and have memorable roles in *Taxi Driver* (1976), *Red Heat* (1988), and on *Everybody Loves Raymond* (1996–2005), among others. (Here's a bit of trivia: Boyle, Caine, and Field previously starred together in the abysmal 1979 disaster film, *Beyond the Poseidon Adventure*.)

Daisy's coworker bestie is played by frequent Woody Allen collaborator and former *Rhoda* (1974–1978) sister Julie Kavner, who has one of the most famous voices in the business. Just a few months before the release of *Surrender*, Kavner made her debut playing Marge Simpson in a series of animated shorts that were then part of *The Tracey Ullman Show* (1987–1990), of which she was a cast member. Those were spun off into their own animated sitcom, *The Simpsons*, which would become the longest-running American, primetime scripted television series, and make Kavner one of the highest-paid TV actors of all time. Daisy's dad is played by Jackie Cooper in his final role; the former child star was one of the youngest-ever to be nominated for an Oscar with *Skippy* (1931), and had recently resumed his role as newspaper editor Perry White in Cannon's *Superman IV: The Quest for Peace* (1987). Eagle-eyed Cannon fans should also keep an eye out for Jerry Lazarus, who co-starred in *Treasure of the Four Crowns* (1983), and also had small roles in *Over the Brooklyn Bridge* and *Breakin' 2* (1984), *Hot Chili* (1985), and *The Delta Force* and *Murphy's Law* (1986).

Surrender was the brainchild of writer-director Jerry Belson, who had long been the writing partner of Garry Marshall, and was best-known for scripting episodes of classic TV comedies such as *The Dick Van Dyke Show* (1964–1966) and *The Odd Couple* (1970–1975). He was also a co-creator of *The Tracey Ullman Show*. On the silver screen, he wrote the criminally underseen beauty pageant comedy *Smile* (1975), and did an uncredited rewrite on Steven Spielberg's *Close Encounters of the Third Kind* (1977).

Surrender ultimately came and went from theaters with little more than a whimper.

An ex-rental VHS copy of *Dancers*, formerly of Hollywood Nites in
Denville, New Jersey.

Dancers

Release Date: October 9, 1987
Directed by: Herbert Ross
Written by: Sarah Kernochan
Starring: Mikhail Baryshnikov, Julie Kent
Trailer Voiceover: "At the center of the stage lies a place of dreams, emotions, truth . . . They are dreamers, they are people, they are *Dancers!*"

For the final quarter of the Twentieth Century, Mikhail Baryshnikov enjoyed a level of celebrity to which few professional dancers could ever aspire. The Latvian-born Baryshnikov was practically a household name throughout America, not only for his remarkable talents as a ballet dancer and choreographer, but for being a world-class ladies' man.

Already quite prominent within the world of ballet by the time he defected from the Soviet Union in 1974, the diminutive dancer worked in Canada for several years before settling in New York City, where he'd spend much of his professional career. His fame would grow as a principal dancer for the American Ballet Theatre and New York City Ballet, eventually being named artistic director of the former, and appearing in many nationally televised performances. In the eyes of most critics, he was considered the greatest male dancer in the world.

In the midst of all of this, Baryshnikov would occasionally dedicate himself to a more traditional acting role—albeit, one that heavily featured his abilities as a dancer. The most notable of these roles was in *The Turning Point* (1977), in which he played a famous, Russian ballet dancer—not a big stretch, no—and was nominated for a Best Supporting Actor Oscar. (The film was nominated for eleven Academy Awards in total, but took home none of them.) He'd star again in the film *White Nights* (1985), in which he'd play yet another famous, Russian ballet dancer. Most recently, he took on a recurring role on TV's *Sex and the City* (1998–2004), playing—no, not a famous, Russian ballet dancer, but a famous Russian artist. Big difference.

Despite his protests at being described as such, Baryshnikov was something of a sex symbol. In the '70s and early '80s, he made regular appearances in both the tabloids and at New York City's swanky Studio 54 nightclub. Much of the gossip column fodder dealt with his numerous romantic partners, who were said to include several of his fellow dancers, as well as the actresses Jessica Lange (with whom he had a daughter), Tuesday Weld, Isabella Rossellini, and Liza Minelli. Imagine him as a certified ladies' man in the caliber of George Clooney or James Bond, but perpetually wearing tights.

It's no wonder that Cannon chose to tango with Baryshnikov on *Dancers* (1987), especially considering its pedigree. The movie was to feature the world's premier dancer in one of his signature roles, performing *Giselle* for the cameras. It would also reunite Baryshnikov with Herbert Ross, the director of his most critically-acclaimed film, *The Turning Point*.

Like Baryshnikov, Ross had begun his career as a dancer, making his Broadway debut in the 1940s. By the 1950s he'd become a lauded choreographer, not only for the stage but television and film—he was responsible for the musical sequences in movies such as *Doctor Dolittle* (1967) and *Funny Girl* (1968). He made his directorial debut with the Peter O'Toole musical *Goodbye, Mr. Chips* (1969) and rapidly became very prolific, directing roughly one movie per year for the next twenty-five years. Ross specialized in musicals and stage adaptations, and his films were regularly nominated for awards. Beyond *The Turning Point*, these included *The Sunshine Boys* (1975, with Best Supporting Actor winner George Burns), *The Goodbye Girl* (1977, with Best Actor winner Richard Dreyfuss), *California Suite* (1978, with Best Supporting Actress Maggie Smith), and the incredibly odd, Steve Martin-led remake of *Pennies from Heaven* (1981). He'd also come out with a handful of bona fide hits, such as *Footloose* (1984), *The Secret of My Success* (1987), and *Steel Magnolias* (1989). Needless to say, Ross had earned his respect behind the camera.

Director Herbert Ross and Mikhail Baryshnikov on the set of *Dancers*.

In truth it was Ross's wife, Nora Kaye, who was the person most behind bringing *Dancers* to the screen. A prima-ballerina and one of the founding dancers of the American Ballet Theatre, Kaye brought the project to Cannon, who agreed to produce the film even before her husband was signed on as

887

director. Kaye, who was dying of cancer, mustered the strength to be on set every day of filming in the autumn of 1986. She was credited as an executive producer on the film, but passed away before she could see it released.

In *Dancers*, Mikhail Baryshnikov plays Mikhael Baryshni—*errr*, "Tony Sergeyev," the world's most celebrated ballet dancer. On stage, his transcendent talent can't be denied. Off it, he's an unapologetic cad, sleeping with every pretty ingénue who crosses his stage. (His skirt-chasing is so matter of course that the dancers in his company openly joke about it.) He has a famous girlfriend, yes, but he also has a mistress, and a mistress from his mistress. None of the women in his life seem to mind this a single bit, though, because Tony is "a great artist," and great artists should be allowed to get away with those things, or something like that. He's not kind, nor is he all that charming, but he *can* dance sublimely—something we'll see plenty of in the movie's second half.

When the film begins, Tony is living in Italy and tutu-deep into rehearsals for a filmed version of the classic ballet *Giselle*, which he's directing and starring in. It seems that in spite of Tony's success, his crowds of fawning fans, and nonstop (s)extracurricular activities, he's not happy. Even his agent feels the need to repeatedly inform him that his dancing has begun to lack passion. But what on Earth could possibly fix our horndog hoofer's case of the blues?

Enter teenage, doe-eyed Lisa (ballerina Julie Kent), arriving fresh from America as an emergency replacement for a dancer who broke her toe. Julie is presented as a flagrant symbol of purity and childlike innocence, going so far as to be shown chatting long distance on the telephone with her mother, clutching a teddy bear while a cartoon plays on the TV behind her.

The storyline is meant to reflect the one in the movie's centerpiece ballet, *Giselle*, framing it as a sort of meta-storytelling. Because only a small percentage of Cannon fans are likely to know the plot of a 19th Century French ballet off the top of their heads, it's about a naïve peasant girl named Giselle who's chewed up and spit out by a two-faced, lecherous nobleman. When she learns of his lies, she dies of heartbreak and then spends the second act haunting the slimy bastard who toyed with her affections.

Can you see where this might have a convenient correlation to our characters' plights?

Fortunately, Lisa's story doesn't wind up being nearly as tragic as Giselle's. It doesn't take much effort at all for Tony to seduce her away from a young, Italian stud who's been trying to win her heart with sweet gestures of affection. Tony and Lisa seem to have little in common, but A) he's famous, and B) her boss, so she quickly gives in to his inappropriate advances. Once Tony's fancy fiancée comes to town, though, Lisa's heart is crushed. She abandons the show in tears and, for a moment, appears to have thrown herself over a bridge, but then a few minutes later is revealed to actually be watching Tony's performance of *Giselle* from the wing of the stage, evidently awestruck by his ability to leap and twirl.

You see, most of the second half of *Dancers* is an actual, taped performance of Baryshnikov doing *Giselle*. Or, at least, *Giselle*'s second act, because we already got the gist of the first from Lisa and Tony's melodramatic tale. When the ballet ends, Lisa and Tony have a brief moment of reconciliation, with the young girl walking away from the affair relatively unscathed—that is, save for a tiny tattoo she got to remember their brief time together.

If most of *Dancers* feels like padding, well, that's because that is how it was designed. The film was intended to be a showcase for Baryshnikov's performance of *Giselle*, which would go on tour in the months after the movie's release. A framing story was added to make the film more palatable to mainstream movie audiences, who weren't necessarily the type of people who would normally buy a ticket for the ballet.

The job was doled out to filmmaker Sarah Kernochan, who'd won her first Academy Award in the prior decade for *Marjoe* (1972), a captivating documentary exposing the capitalistic side of evangelism through its magnetic subject, preacher-turned-singer-turned-b-movie actor Marjoe Gortner. (You can read about that film in more detail in this volume's discussion of *American Ninja 3* [1989], which featured Gortner as a villainous businessman who develops a destructive bioweapon with the help of his ninja army.) Kernochan was given a tall order: not only did her script need to mirror the story of *Giselle*, but she was to use as little dialogue as possible, since the cast of real-world dancers couldn't necessarily *act*. The result was a screenplay that was only fifty pages long. This was just enough plot to get the movie to feature-length. Of its 95-minute runtime, approximately forty are from Baryshnikov's performance of *Giselle*, and seven more are dedicated to its slow and drawn-out credits.

Unfortunately, not even the most minimalist approach to dialogue could have compensated for the cast's dearth of dramatic ability. Among the main cast, the best actor in *Dancers* is Baryshnikov—and he's someone for whom English was not his first language, and who was essentially playing yet another variation of himself in a movie. Take after take of dialogue needed to be filmed, as the world's greatest dancer would regularly trip over his lines. (Although this isn't his fault, it certainly doesn't help that with his accent—and his romantic interest being named "Lisa"—he gives off strong vibes of Tommy Wiseau in *The Room* [2003] every time he cries out her name.) Next to his leading lady, though, Baryshnikov looks like Marlon Brando.

Like many of her castmates, Julie Kent was a member of Baryshnikov's American Ballet Theatre. When she auditioned for his dance company at the age of sixteen, Baryshnikov told *People* that he had been "absolutely mesmerized by her looks." When assembling a cast for this film two years later, he immediately thought of Kent—and asked her to take on the role without so much as a screen test. She speaks in a high, nasal voice, and inflects like a stereotypical, '80s valley girl, and that's when she bothers with inflection at all. She went on to have an incredible, acclaimed career in ballet—including twelve years as a principal dancer with the American Ballet Theatre, and serving as a ballet consultant on *Black Swan* (2010)—but her only other notable screen role was as a prima ballerina in *Center Stage* (2000), which speaks volumes about her Hollywood prospects.

Few of her fellow dancers fare much better when asked to speak to one another. It's a shame because there are some witty lines in the script, but this cast delivers them like they're non-actors appearing in a commercial for a local discount furniture warehouse, rather than members of what should have been a prestigious cinematic production.

But, is the ballet itself impressive? What do you think? It's a Mikhail *effing* Baryshnikov production, so of course the dancing is fantastic. The set design by Gianni Quaranta—who won an Oscar for *A Room with a View* (1985) and worked on Cannon's *Otello* (1986)—is also splendid. The musical score fits the movie very well, and was handled by go-to Italian composer Pino Donaggio, who worked on at least ten more of Cannon's films, including *Hercules* (1983) and *The Barbarians* (1987).

In the end, the final nail in *Dancers'* coffin was probably its timing. Coming near the end of a catastrophic 1987 financial year, Cannon was busy bailing buckets of water over the side of their sinking ship when it came time to put out *Dancers*. They barely released the film at all—showing it in a whopping *twelve* theaters in a handful of cities—and when it went to video, didn't seem to understand how to market it. Trailers for the VHS release set it up like a more traditional, romantic dance movie in the vein of *Flashdance* (1983), *Footloose*, or *Dirty Dancing* (1987). They don't even bother to mention that almost half of it is a straight performance of *Giselle*. It's as if Cannon was far more interested in Baryshnikov the heartthrob than Baryshnikov the ballet legend.

Dancers was dragged over the coals by critics—who, judging by box office receipts, were among the only people who saw the movie in theaters. Roger Ebert called it "one of the worst movies of the year." For the *Washington Post*, Rita Kempley wittily referred to it as a "corpse de ballet" and a "disaster." Interestingly, *The New York Times* actually published two reviews—a lukewarm one from film critic Janet Maslin, and a glowing rebuttal by ballet critic Anna Kisselgoff, who seems to be the only person with nice things to say about it. (She predicted that thirteen-year-old girls "who hang Baryshnikov posters on their bedroom walls" would love it, and humorously admits that she's "probably the only reviewer over thirteen who liked the movie.") As someone who's well-versed in *Giselle*, Kisselgoff was able to grasp the deeper symbolism in the film that was clearly lost on anyone who'd never seen the ballet and didn't know all of the story's details.

Perhaps Cannon was feeling gun-shy about doing another straight performance film after the mixed reactions to their *Otello*? If Cannon had simply committed to recording the world's finest dancer in his signature performance—or, if they'd gone in the opposite direction and made the entire thing a modern retelling of *Giselle* instead—you have to wonder if the results would have been more successful. By trying to do both, *Dancers* stumbles and never truly regains its footing.

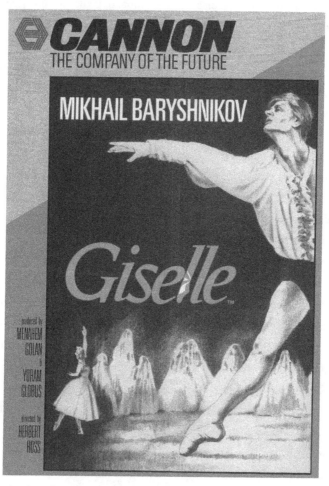

Cannon's 1986 Cannes Film Festival advertisement for the film that would eventually be known as *Dancers*.

Interview: Screenwriter Sarah Kernochan

As the recipient of two Academy Awards—for her Documentary Feature *Marjoe* (1973) and Documentary Short *Thoth* (2002)—Sarah Kernochan is likely the most decorated filmmaker to be interviewed in these books. A true multi-hyphenate who has also worked as an author, journalist, recording artist, and playwright, Kernochan's path crossed with Cannon's when she was hired to write their 1987 ballet film, *Dancers*.

Kernochan's other screenwriting credits include the erotic drama *9 1/2 Weeks* (1986) starring Mickey Rourke and Kim Basinger, *Impromptu* (1991), *Sommersby* (1993), and *Learning to Drive* (2014), and a story credit on *What Lies Beneath* (2000). She wrote and directed *All I Wanna Do* (1998), a.k.a. *Strike!*, a.k.a. *The Hairy Bird*, a comedy set in an all-girl's academy in the 1960s, which starred Kirsten Dunst.

I imagine most career bios will begin with *Marjoe*, but you also wrote for the stage and published a novel in the years between that film and your screenwriting work in the '80s. Had you already met Herbert Ross or Mikhail Baryshnikov while you were part of the New York arts scene?

Sarah Kernochan: Neither. Herbert was curious to meet me for the script job because I had just married James Lapine, who collaborated with Stephen Sondheim on several musicals. Herbert had worked in the theater prior to movies and was friends with Sondheim and his coterie.

At that point in your career, you were fresh off a writing credit on the erotic drama *9 1/2 Weeks*. I know it's easy for screenwriters to get pigeonholed off their first script—was that a danger you faced?

It's very definitely a danger because it happens every time. If you have a successful script in one genre, you get work offered in the same genre. I made sure to bounce around genres, which wasn't a wise career move but kept me from getting bored. As for *9 1/2 Weeks*, I did not get any work based on that because no one was making any erotic movies. That was one of a kind (and bombed theatrically in the U.S.).

All of Cannon's earliest marketing for *Dancers* (pre-shooting) had it titled *Giselle*, which makes me think the decision to add the framing story came later on. Do you know where that idea came from?

Herbert always had in mind a mirror story, and wanted to call it *Giselle/Giselle*. Plain old *Giselle* was a temp title. Cannon thought the generic title of *Dancers*, together with Baryshnikov's billing, would get a more general audience interested and not just balletomanes. Obviously this didn't work.

Can you tell me about your research process, and what you used from it?

I spent a little time interviewing Misha. I needed to know how he prepped for a role and how he saw the character of Albrecht [from *Giselle*], his favorite signature role in all the ballet repertoire. I was to write a contemporary character based on Albrecht, so I wanted that to match Baryshnikov's own interpretation. I also observed American Ballet Theatre rehearsals at the Met.

One of the best reviews for the movie came from the *New York Times'* ballet critic, rather than a film critic, who was familiar with *Giselle* and understood the parallels. Cannon often ran into trouble figuring out how to market their more artistic endeavors—do you feel some of the negative reactions could be due to how the film was sold to viewers?

No. I think it simply wasn't a general audience movie, no matter what Cannon could have tried. Frankly I think the critics treated it fairly, since they were reviewing it as a dramatic film, and it was really more of a hybrid: a skimpy story tacked onto a recording of a brilliant artist in performance for the historical record.

What did you think of the film when you saw the finished product?

I thought, and still think, it didn't work as drama, but is important and should be savored for the ballet itself and the stellar performers.

When it comes to polymaths, I'm always interested in how you tame your muse. Are you able to focus on one creative outlet at a time, or do you find yourself working on several types of projects all at once?

I try to tackle each thing sequentially, one at a time with no overlap. I'm not good at multitasking. And muses should never be tamed, but run wild.

Tony (Mikhail Baryshnikov) takes a personal interest in a young, American ballerina named Lisa (Julie Kent) in *Dancers*.

The unassuming VHS cover of *Barfly*.

Barfly

Release Date: October 16, 1987
Directed by: Barbet Schroeder
Written by: Charles Bukowski
Starring: Mickey Rourke, Faye Dunaway
Trailer Voiceover: "Life on the edge, as seen by Charles Bukowski."

In 1979, filmmaker Barbet Schroeder went to great lengths to hunt down hard-drinking poet Charles Bukowski and ask him to write the screen-play for his next film. When Schroeder first reached him by telephone, Bukowski reportedly told him to "fuck off" and hung up the phone. The filmmaker called back immediately, and sweetened the offer with a $20,000 commission. This began an eight-year saga that resulted in Schroeder standing in the Cannon offices and threatening to cut off his own finger with an electric saw. It also resulted in one of Cannon's most acclaimed films, *Barfly* (1987).

Let's start with Bukowski. The poet laureate of drunkards, brawlers, and gutter-dwellers, Bukowski had been writing for more than forty years by the time *Barfly* was brought to the screen. Born in Germany in 1920 to a U.S.

Army sergeant, Bukowski spent much of his youth in Los Angeles. As a young man he published a few short stories, but failed to make any real headway into the literary scene, then gave it up for most of a decade. It was during this time—after which he'd failed a psychological examination to enter World War II—that Bukowski became something of a professional drunk, bouncing between cities and small jobs, living in dive bars and dirty, rented rooms. These were the years that would serve as his inspiration for *Barfly*'s semiautobiographical screenplay.

By the mid-1950s, Bukowski had shifted gears to focus on poetry. He found some success in magazines and with small-press publishers, but it wasn't until 1969—shortly before his fiftieth birthday—that Bukowski quit his job at the post office and became a full-time writer. Even as he branched out into novels to supplement his prolific output of poetry and short stories—he published more than sixty books in his lifetime—he was never quite as famous in the United States as he was in Europe, where translated copies of his work sold many, many times more than the English-language editions. This led to an infamous 1978 appearance on the French talk show *Apostrophes*, said to have been watched by roughly half of the nation's television viewers every Friday night. Bukowski showed up to the interview already three sheets to the wind, and continued to drink—to the point where he needed to be helped off the set by the crew.

The next morning, Bukowski's books were sold out at every book store in the country.

Barbet Schroeder had binge-read every Bukowski book he could get his hands on while making his 1978 documentary, *Koko: A Talking Gorilla*. Schroeder was a filmmaker whose background stretched across Europe and the Middle East, having been born in Iran to a German mother and Swiss father. His film career began in Paris as a producer on several classics from the French New Wave. Under the umbrella of his production company, Les Films du Losange, Schroeder produced features by Éric Rohmer and Jacques Rivette, and eventually his own directorial work. His first two fiction films,

More (1969) and *La Vallée* (1972), featured original scores by Pink Floyd; his next, the X-rated *Maîtresse* (1975), ignited controversy for its un-simulated depiction of sadomasochistic acts.

His most famous work, however, was a feature-length documentary called *General Idi Amin Dada: A Self Portrait* (1974). Schroeder had struck a deal with the ruthless Ugandan dictator, Idi Amin, who gave Schroeder and his cameraman unprecedented access to film him going about his daily activities in exchange for their help producing a government-approved propaganda documentary. In the film, the bloodthirsty Amin—who was estimated to have murdered more than 100,000 of his people during his regime—is charismatic in a way that catches viewers off-guard; at the same time, it's clear that everything we see was staged at the despot's behest. The results are a film that's surreal, charming, and horrifying all at once. When the paranoid Amin later discovered the version he'd approved was not the same one being shown outside Uganda, he rounded up hundreds of French citizens in a hotel and surrounded them with his army, holding them hostage until the film was re-cut to his liking. Schroeder ultimately agreed, but restored the original footage after Amin was deposed in the late '70s.

After working so closely with a tyrant like Idi Amin, Bukowski must have seemed as friendly as a puppy dog to Schroeder. In Bukowski's works Schroeder saw a kindred spirit, which is why he didn't give up when the poet slammed the phone down on him. Bukowski, who'd grown up on the outskirts of Hollywood during the Great Depression, had a low opinion of filmmakers as being phonies. He did not particularly like movies, and doubted his own ability to write one. Schroeder eventually convinced him, and the two became friends over many long conversations and many more bottles of wine. (Many of their boozy chats were recorded on video, and excerpts were released by Schroeder as 1985's *The Charles Bukowski Tapes*.) It helped that Bukowski was still at this point living check-to-check, and was willing to accept money for an assignment he didn't necessarily want to do.

The German VHS artwork for *Barfly*, by Renato Casaro.

It took Bukowski time to write the screenplay, and Schroeder even longer to find financial backing for the film. Most producers, it turned out, looked at a film about hopeless drunks as something sad—in other words, something no one would want to see. Schroeder spent years trying to convince producers and studio heads that the story should be viewed as life-affirming, and was full of humor.

Nobody bit. This went on for years.

As the 1980s rolled on, Bukowski's legend grew, and a few of his famous admirers caught wind of the *Barfly* project being pitched around Hollywood. One of the most significant of these fans was Sean Penn, hot off critically-revered performances in *Bad Boys* (1983) and *The Falcon and the Snowman* (1985) and his recent marriage to pop superstar Madonna. Penn was said to have been a huge fan of Bukowski's work, and loved the script—so much so that he was willing to waive his growing fee and star in the film for a single dollar. The issue, though, was that he wanted his friend and idol, Dennis Hopper, to direct the film. Hopper had yet to make his post-rehab resurgence with *Blue Velvet* and *Hoosiers* (both 1986) and was still searching for a project to get his career back on track. (He hadn't yet co-starred in *Texas Chainsaw Massacre 2* [1986], either, for what that's worth.) It turns out that Schroeder bore a grudge against Hopper for an argument they'd had many years before, and despised him. Hopper also rubbed Bukowski the wrong way during a long meeting in which the *Easy Rider* (1969) star was, for obvious reasons, the only one in the group who wasn't drinking.

In the end, Bukowski sided with Schroeder and turned down Penn's offer. Bukowski later recounted that after their meeting, Schroeder phoned his lawyer in France and had him rewrite his last will and testament so that if he were to die before the film was made, he gave his consent for another filmmaker to direct *Barfly*—specifically, anyone *except* for Dennis Hopper.

When actor Mickey Rourke heard that Sean Penn offered to do a script for one dollar and was rejected, his ears perked up. Rourke read the script and told Schroeder he wanted to do it. Like Penn, Rourke was a young actor on the rise, with acclaimed turns in Barry Levinson's *Diner* (1982), Francis Ford Coppola's *Rumble Fish* (1983), *The Pope of Greenwich Village* (1984), and the erotic drama *9 1/2 Weeks* (1986) already under his belt. It was Rourke who suggested Faye Dunaway co-star in the film, in case you wondered how Dunaway found herself in yet another Golan-Globus film after she walked out on her pet project, *Duet for One* (1986), when it was already deep into pre-production at Cannon. Suddenly, after seven years of failed starts, the project's fortunes had begun to turn around.

The day after Mickey Rourke had formally committed to the project, Schroeder had a breakfast meeting scheduled with Cannon's own Menahem Golan. In less than half an hour a deal was in place for Cannon to produce *Barfly*. All it took was Golan hearing that Rourke and Dunaway were already attached, and that the movie would have a low budget. The film was co-produced by Francis Ford Coppola's Zoetrope Studios via producer Tom Luddy, who also had a hand in Cannon's *Tough Guys Don't Dance* (1987).

Everything seemed to be progressing smoothly, but that couldn't last. Just before shooting was set to begin, Cannon found themselves nearly broke. Their purchase of Thorn EMI and all of its assets just half a year earlier had left them spread very thin. They had yet to see any returns on their 1987 slate, which included a handful of their most expensive features to date, such as *Over the Top*, *Masters of the Universe*, and *Superman IV*. (Spoiler alert: those movies weren't about to fix their money woes.) Considering they were quite literally forced to turn out the lights on the set of their He-Man movie just a few weeks earlier, they were no longer in a place where they could back an unorthodox comedy about a drunkard poet which no other studio in Hollywood thought would be profitable. And so, Cannon pulled the plug.

This is what led to the most memorable—and most misreported—tale about the making of *Barfly*.

Desperate after spending seven years trying to get the movie made only to see it fall apart at the eleventh hour, Barbet Schroeder staged a short hunger strike in front of the Cannon offices. When this didn't work, he marched into their headquarters with a towel wrapped under his arm. He entered the office of Cannon's main lawyer, laid the towel on his desk, and unwrapped an electric saw. He announced that he'd found new representation from the Black & Decker Law Firm, and produced a syringe full of Novocain. As he readied himself to inject the anesthetic into the pinky of his left hand, he calmly explained to their lawyer that he would cut off his finger, then another, and then another, until Cannon essentially returned the rights to *Barfly* so that they could find a new backer. He plugged in the saw . . .

. . . and within an hour, the film was returned to Schroeder and his co-producers under reasonable terms. The director even got to keep all of his fingers.

It's an amusing story, for sure, but like a lot of tales tied to Cannon, most versions have been exaggerated over the years. Bukowski himself told a version of it to critic Roger Ebert during an on-set visit, but in that one it took place in Golan's office, and it was the Cannon chairman himself watching, horrified, as Schroeder plugged in his saw. Ebert recounted this inaccurate version in both his article about the film and later his book, *Two Weeks in the Midday Sun* (1987). Golan himself often repeated the story in a similar fashion, except that in his memory of the event Schroeder brought a big knife into his office, rather than a saw. (The funniest thing about Golan's "memory"? He wasn't even in Los Angeles when this happened—at this time, he was out of town directing *Over the Top*.) By the time the *Los Angeles Times* covered the story, Schroeder's tiny electric saw had grown into a full-blown chainsaw.

Strangely enough, the most true-to-life version of the Black & Decker tale is probably the one in Bukowski's novel, *Hollywood* (1989), except that the author also placed himself in the room when it happened. Speaking to Schroeder for one of his later films, *Amnesia* (2017), on a magazine assignment, I couldn't help but inquire as to how much truth there was to Bukowski's tale:

"Like all the books of Bukowski, eighty-five to ninety percent of it corresponds to the truth. Sometimes, there is a little bit of improved truth," Schroeder explained. "I was so determined, and at the time I didn't think it would be a problem. I didn't use computers, and I didn't play piano. I didn't think missing part of my little finger would be a big drama. Also, I hoped I could go to the next hospital and have it put back on. In the end that would have cost more than a lawyer, I'm sure, but I didn't have time to get a lawyer, so I chose Black & Decker as my firm."

"The thing that happened that was not in the [book], was that when I walked into the office, they knew exactly what I was going to do, and had made their decision already," Schroeder continued. "They knew it was not worth the trouble if I cut off my finger in their office, or anywhere else. They did not need that publicity. And so, I didn't have to start the saw working. And it was not a big saw! It was very small, for cutting fine wood."

"I was ready to cut my finger, but I didn't need to go any further—he said, 'Okay, okay, I've got the papers, and here, we can promise you this,'" Schroeder said. "Basically, it was not the promise to do the movie that I wanted. I wanted proof that they were going to respect their word. Their word was that I could do the movie with someone outside their company, and they would not ask for one more cent than what they'd spent so far on the movie."

All that said and done, Schroeder and his co-producers still were not able to find anyone else interested in the movie. They returned to Cannon, tails between their legs, and agreed to cut their fees on the already low-budget feature so that the nearly-broke studio could afford it. Even then, Cannon wrote bad checks to the crew, and many of them had to work for several weeks before they were paid.

Dunaway fell ill shortly before filming began, and her recovery meant she didn't arrive on set until two weeks into the thirty-two day shoot. Meanwhile, Rourke himself reportedly didn't make it to set on the first day, as the Rolls Royce that arrived to pick him up and bring him to the location—which was part of his contract—was the wrong color. He also picked a fight over his wardrobe, which he wanted to include bright, Hawaiian-style shirts

904

and custom-made sunglasses with palm tree-shaped frames. (It was a fight Schroeder obviously won, although he compromised by allowing Rourke to briefly try on his custom shades when his character visits the home of the wealthy publisher played by Alice Krige.) For her diva reputation, Dunaway actually made fewer demands than her male co-star.

A Spanish magazine advertisement for *Barfly*.

Schroeder's written agreement with Bukowski included the rare stipulation that no line could be added or altered without the writer's input. The poet was available by phone to make edits whenever a written line came out flat when spoken by an actor. He was also amenable to make rewrites when one of the two leads dug in their heels with a demand. Dunaway requested a scene that showcased her legs, and Bukowski came back with the memorable moment in which Rourke's character admires her legs in Wanda's apartment. Rourke demanded a piece of poetry to recite, and Bukowski inserted the bit where the blood-soaked Henry waxes lyrically into a mirror. There were more, smaller changes and additions, but there was no improvisation on the actors' parts; every bit of dialogue came straight from Bukowski's typewriter. This led to a script that's genuinely the author's work, with as high a number of quotable lines as any film in the Cannon catalog.

Barfly's plot is uncomplicated, about a pair of misanthropic alcoholics nearing the end of their ropes, who find in each other a kindred spirit. They move in together and try to make it work, fully aware that the odds are against them. This gives their messy, wrecked lives a little bit of purpose, and a little bit of hope. Hijinks ensue. *Barfly* alternates between being hilarious and heartbreaking, thanks to its incredibly witty script and a pair of leads who throw themselves fully into the filthy lowlifes they're playing.

Henry Chinaski (Rourke) is a fully-committed drunkard, living in a squalid hotel room above the shitty bar he inhabits from morning to close. It's been this way for a long, long time. During the afternoons he chums around with the other barflies, who appear to get up from their stools even less often than he does. In the evenings, he usually fights the nightshift bartender in the alley behind the establishment, largely for the entertainment of his fellow patrons. On the rare night he doesn't spend lying unconscious next to the back alley's dumpster, Henry retreats to his room to continue drinking, listen to classical music, and scribble down the occasional line of poetry.

Rourke is wonderful in this role, both gross and undeniably charming. In a stained undershirt and equally dirty pants or boxers, Henry struts about like some kind of king ape, his pelvis thrust ahead of him, and his scab-covered knuckles dragging behind. He looks like someone whose features have been ruined by too little food, too much drinking, and too many fists to the face. His expression is usually a sour squint, except when it gives way to a mischievous smile. Most of his lines are delivered in an off-key, sing-song manner, and said in a way that feels like the thoughts were only half-formed by the time the words emerged from his lips. It's hard to discern how much of Henry's behavior is an act, and how much is an illness.

Henry's favorite watering hole, The Golden Horn, was an actual dive bar in Culver City named Big Ed's, selected for its unusual, round-ended bar which gave the camera more options than the standard long, straight bar found in most dives. (Sadly, Big Ed's was torn down a few months after filming to make way for a shopping district.) The crew didn't need to change much about the interior decoration, as it was already as authentic as they come. Even the real-life barflies were allowed to stay and continue drinking there as they filmed, and became extras in the movie. The location certainly lent itself to the screenplay, with a seedy, foul-smelling hotel overhead, and a dirty alley out back making it so that the production didn't need to move far when they went to shoot scenes in Henry's room, or his brawls with the bartender.

The movie's second lead, Wanda (Dunaway), doesn't make her entrance until more than twenty minutes into the film. Like Henry, she's a full-blown addict. She appears even more bitter and world-weary than he is, having lived a longer and sadder life. There is still some dignity beneath her worn, resigned surface, hinting that perhaps she'd seen better times once, but those days are long behind her. Still attractive in spite of the hard-drinking lifestyle and her unkempt appearance, she bounces from man to man—whoever can supply her next liquor bottle, or help pay her rent. And then, Henry comes along . . .

"Just one thing," she explains, some real concern in her voice. "I don't ever want to fall in love. I don't want to go through that again."

"Hey, don't worry," he calms her, a slight smile on his lips. "No one's ever loved me yet."

Izaro films

MICKEY ROURKE
FAYE DUNAWAY
Director:
BARBET SCHROEDER

CANNON

FRANCIS FORD COPPOLA presenta

EL BORRACHO
(BARFLY)

Henry (Mickey Rourke) and Wanda (Faye Dunaway) in *Barfly*.

Barfly only covers a couple days after their first meeting, as the duo try their best not to screw things up, even while screwing things up seems to be the only thing they're any good at. But together, there's a glimmer of hope in their tragic existence.

The film doesn't have a very large cast, but it's a strong one. The bartender who beats Henry to a pulp night after night is played by Frank Stallone, who would return to Cannon for their adaptation of *Ten Little Indians* (1989), and supplied the song "Bad Nite" for his brother's Cannon starrer, *Over the Top*. Stallone's fight scenes with Rourke were among the movie's most-rehearsed. Since Rourke and Stallone were both trained boxers in real life, it took some extra work to make them look like sloppy drunks when they were exchanging blows.

The dayshift bartender who behaves much friendlier to our sorry-ass hero was played by J.C. Quinn, a character actor remembered for roles in video rental favorites such as *C.H.U.D.* (1984), *Maximum Overdrive* (1986), and *The Abyss* (1989).

A larger role goes to Alice Krige, playing the wealthy publisher of a literary magazine who's fallen in love with her romanticized image of Henry Chinaski, the writer. A last-minute replacement for Helen Hunt, Krige is best known for playing the villainous Borg queen in *Star Trek VIII: First Contact* (1996). To track down the writer, she hires a private detective played by the idiosyncratic Jack Nance, remembered for his many collaborations with director David Lynch, including *Dune* (1984), *Blue Velvet* (1986), and *Twin Peaks* (1989–1991), but most of all for his starring role in the quintessential midnight movie, *Eraserhead* (1977).

The author himself, Bukowski, makes a quick cameo drinking a beer a few stools down from where Henry meets Wanda. Although he lived local to the production and was making script edits on a regular basis, he only made a few visits to the set, not wanting to accidentally influence Rourke's performance.

The cinematographer charged with capturing *Barfly*'s scuzzy locales was the great Dutch cameraman Robby Müller, who'd won numerous awards for his team-ups with Wim Wenders (including 1984's *Paris, Texas*) and would later become the go-to lens man for both Jim Jarmusch and Lars Von Trier.

Editing began as soon as shooting wrapped. This being a Cannon project, of course, Schroeder and his team had only four weeks to cut together the film so that it would be ready in time for submission to Cannes. They packed the soundtrack with funky tunes which sound like they're crackling straight from the tube amp speakers of the Golden Horn's smoke-stained jukebox. These included several tracks by Booker T. Jones, with his song "Hip Hug-Her"—performed with the M.G.s—serving as *Barfly*'s theme music.

Although it was nominated for the Palme d'Or at Cannes in 1987, it did not win. This seemed to set a precedence for how the movie would be received, landing a number of impressive (if scattershot) nominations, from a Best Actress nod at the Golden Globes for Dunaway, to Best Male Lead for Rourke and Best Cinematography at the Independent Spirit Awards, none of which it brought home. Audiences, it seems, were torn on whether the film was supposed to be a comedy or a tragedy, and unwilling to embrace something that was both. The movie made back its $3 million budget in theaters, but proved too odd to find the larger audience it really deserved.

In one of the rarer instances you'll find in any volume of *The Cannon Film Guide*, the critics were largely on Cannon's side when it came to *Barfly*. Roger Ebert, who had visited the set to interview Bukowski and Dunaway, gave the film an incredible four out of four stars in his *Chicago Tribune* review, and named it one of his top movies of 1987 in that year's final episode of *At the Movies*. (His partner in criticism, Gene Siskel, on the other hand, disliked the movie and felt Rourke's performance was over-the-top.) In their own glowing review, *Variety* described Rourke's performance as his best since *Diner*. The *New York Times* was similarly impressed.

"To all my friends!" Mickey Rourke in *Barfly*.

For his part, Bukowski maintained a level of cynicism about the filmmaking process—at least for the cameras—by repeatedly telling interviewers who called him up about *Barfly* that he hated movies, and that even if the one he wrote failed, he had at least gotten a book idea out of the experience. That book wound up taking the form of *Hollywood*, a novel first published in 1989 that loosely fictionalized his experience making *Barfly*—which has amusingly been renamed "The Dance of Jim Beam" for the book.

Hollywood is a hoot, and definitely worth a read for any Bukowski, *Barfly*, or Cannon fan. Bukowski does an intentionally half-assed job of disguising the characters' identities, and anyone with a passing familiarity with the Hollywood players of the era should easily be able to figure out who each is meant to be. Cannon, the film company, becomes "Firepower." Menahem Golan becomes "Harry Friedman," while Yoram Globus is now "Nate Fischman." There's a fun passage about Bukowski ("Chinaski") meeting fellow literary icon Norman Mailer ("Victor Norman") at the Chateau Marmont during pre-production on *Tough Guys Don't Dance* (1987), and the two of them carpooling together to Menahem Golan's birthday party. Ultimately, though, it's a story about Bukowski, an old man, watching people make a movie about his younger years—and what a strange experience that was.

After spending much of a decade dedicating himself to bringing *Barfly* to life, at least Schroeder's next few Hollywood films seem like they were a less strenuous process to make. He earned a Best Director nomination for *Reversal of Fortune* (1990)—and helped Jeremy Irons take home a statuette for his lead role in the film. His ensuing thriller *Single White Female* (1992) was a box office hit. When he's not directing or producing movies, Schroeder can sometimes be seen making small cameos in an eclectic mix of films, including a bit role in *Beverly Hills Cop III* (1994), playing the French president in Tim Burton's *Mars Attacks!* (1996), and taking on a part in Wes Anderson's *The Darjeeling Limited* (2007).

A VHS copy of *Under Cover*, formerly rented out by The Movie Barn of Kirtland, New Mexico.

Under Cover

Release Date: December 4, 1987
Directed by: John Stockwell
Written by: John Stockwell & Scott Fields
Starring: David Neidorf, Jennifer Jason Leigh, Barry Corbin
Trailer Voiceover: "They promised him protection—but promises get broken!"

Take the premise of *21 Jump Street* (1987–1991), center it around an undercover "teen" cop with a receding hairline, mix in crack cocaine, a thirst for revenge, and some Southern-fried racism and you've basically got *Under Cover*, Cannon's take on the oft-repeated "going under cover as a high school student" genre.

Under Cover (1987) was the directorial debut of twenty-six-year-old John Stockwell, who you might remember as the star of Albert Pyun's first Cannon feature, *Dangerously Close* (1986). Stockwell had also co-written that film with Scott Fields, his writing partner here. The young, multi-talented Stockwell clearly impressed Golan and Globus, who awarded him with a contract to direct his first feature. This time, the former *Christine* (1983) and

Top Gun (1986) actor wouldn't be appearing on-screen himself, only working behind the camera—except, that is, in a clever cameo where *Under Cover*'s main character can be spotted watching *Dangerously Close* on TV.

Before it really even gets going, *Under Cover* makes a huge ask of its audience. If you're going to buy into the movie's undercover cop plot, you have to be willing to accept that its twenty-five-year-old lead actor, David Neidorf, would believably pass as an undercover high school student. While it's certainly common for older actors to play teenagers in movies, most of those actors don't have Neidorf's high widow's peak. At least the movie acknowledges how preposterous he looks trying to blend in, making several cracks about his hairline and having the character be self-conscious about keeping his head covered with a ball cap. (How's that for lampshading?)Even when disguised in his "teenage" clothing, Neidorf looks closer to thirty years old than the eighteen-year-old senior he's pretending to be. Just roll with it.

The lead actor, David Neidorf, had a relatively short career on screen, but it was packed with critically acclaimed movies. Neidorf had made his big screen debut just one year prior to this in the quintessential basketball flick, *Hoosiers* (1986), playing Everett Flatch, the son of Dennis Hopper's alcoholic assistant coach. The same year he appeared as Tex in Oliver Stone's *Platoon* (1986). Cannon gave him his first starring role in *Under Cover*, but in the month it was released Neidorf could also be seen in Steven Spielberg's *Empire of the Sun* (1987). He followed that up with a role in another classic sports film, *Bull Durham* (1988). Neidorf made a few TV appearances through the early 1990s, then retired from acting in 1995.

The better-known of *Under Cover*'s two leads is Jennifer Jason Leigh, playing another cop who goes undercover as Neidorf's partner. By this point in her career Leigh had already made her breakthrough in the classic coming of age comedy *Fast Times at Ridgemont High* (1982), and had been featured in cult films such as Paul Verhoeven's *Flesh + Blood* (1985) and *The Hitcher* (1986). The 1990s saw her cast in a wide variety of notable movies, including *Single White Female* (1992), Robert Altman's *Short Cuts* (1993), the Coen Brothers' *The Hudsucker Proxy* (1994), and the Stephen King adaptation

Delores Claiborne (1995). Prolific through the 2000s, she'd eventually receive a Best Supporting Actress Oscar nomination for her delightfully foul-mouthed role in Quentin Tarantino's *The Hateful Eight* (2015).

Undercover high-schoolers Jennifer Jason Leigh and David Neidorf in a publicity still for *Under Cover*.

The movie opens with a drug bust gone wrong. Undercover officer Vic Fieldson (John Philbin of *Point Break*, 1991) accidentally makes a pair of dealers aware that he's snooping on them, and is gunned down in the ensuing chase. His former partner and childhood best friend, officer Sheffield "Sheff" Hauser (Neidorf) takes his death extra hard, especially since he feels it's partially his fault. Sheff convinces his lieutenant to send him undercover as a high school student so that he can avenge his partner's death, even after his superior points out that he's too long in the tooth to pass for a teen.

Sheff arrives in South Carolina and is immediately assigned to the undercover drug unit. The cop in charge of cracking down on the shockingly robust, teenage drug trade is Sergeant Irwin Lee, a man seemingly less interested in enacting justice than obstructing it. He's gruffly played by actor Barry Corbin, who played the general in *WarGames* (1983) and would soon be co-starring on *Northern Exposure* (1990–1995). Because these teen drug rings are apparently as big and complex as anything you'd have seen on *The Wire* (2002–2008), there are at least a dozen other rookies being trained for the undercover unit.

Oh—and if you're wondering what these wholesome-looking teens' drug of choice is, it's cocaine, because this was the 1980s. If you're worried, don't be: we only ever see these kids buying and selling coke, never actually using it.

Sheff is assigned a partner in Tanille Laroux (Leigh), a quick-thinking criminal-turned-cop who can actually blend in among the teenagers without looking out-of-place. Sheff objects to having a new partner at first, but he's thankfully overruled. He soon learns that he's really, really not good at this undercover stuff on his own.

Besides looking as old (or older) than most of the teachers, Sheff doesn't follow the teen trends. He can't walk the walk, or talk their talk. At one point he accidentally orders a beer while hanging out with classmates at the local hot dog stand. In one particularly dumb gaffe, he drops his keys on the table while picking up the tab for a friend's Coca Cola, and one of the more rough-and-tumble kids recognizes that he has a handcuff key on the ring. When some of the local hoods confront him about it in the parking lot, Laroux has to jump in and save him—because big, dumb Sheff left his dead partner's badge in the glove compartment, and his police parking tag *tucked in the visor* of his station wagon!

On the plus side of things, Sheff is a talented pitcher and earns himself a place on the school's godawful baseball team, which buys him some cred with the jocks. His best friend on the team is Lucas, a Black classmate from the wrong side of the tracks who is often the target of his hillbilly teammates' racist threats. Lucas is played by David Harris, best remembered as Cochise, a young member of the titular gang in the cult classic *The Warriors* (1979).

Not helping matters any is that Sheff would rather solve his buddy's murder than narc on high schoolers for small drug buys, much to his boss's chagrin. As he follows clues about Vic's fateful evening, he prods at a specific student that he was warned to leave alone, discovers a disturbing truth about his best pal, and uncovers a conspiracy that reaches well beyond the walls of the high school. With his life suddenly on the line, he realizes Tanille—the lady partner he never wanted—is the only person he can trust.

Under Cover is very formulaic, but comfortably so—its twists and turns still manage to thrill, even when you see them coming from half a mile away. Like its predecessor, *Dangerously Close*, the movie was released with a contemporary, MTV-ready soundtrack. (You can hear one of *Dangerously Close*'s featured tracks, the Smithereens' "Blood and Roses," playing during the diner scene in *Under Cover*.) The song "Missionary" by Wednesday Week received a music video made up of clips from the movie, making its premiere on MTV a full eight months before *Under Cover* hit movie theaters. The score itself was composed by the eccentric rocker Todd Rundgren, who had formed the bands Nazz and Utopia before having a productive solo career, and producing classic rock albums such as Meat Loaf's *Bat Out of Hell* and XTC's *Skylarking*.

There are a few more notable faces in the film. Sheff's main ally in the local police department is played by actor-singer Kathleen Wilhoite. She had previously played a much bigger role in Cannon's *Murphy's Law* (1986), as the vulgar car thief, Arabella McGee, who was handcuffed to Charles Bronson. Another one of the cops working with the undercover unit is played by character actor Mark Holton, probably best known as spoiled brat Francis Buxton in *Pee-wee's Big Adventure* (1985).

Under Cover wound up being an effective springboard for John Stockwell's career as a director. The model-turned-actor-turned-director went on to make *Crazy/Beautiful* (2001), *Blue Crush* (2002) and *Into the Blue* (2005), and was the man who finally brought Jean-Claude Van Damme back to the *Kickboxer* franchise with *Kickboxer: Vengeance* in 2016.

David Neidorf with director John Stockwell on the set of *Under Cover*.

Interview: Actor David Neidorf

Although his filmography is relatively sparse compared to many actors, David Neidorf's resume is packed with an impressively high percentage of legitimate classics. Neidorf made his debut playing Dennis Hopper's son, Everett, in *Hoosiers* (1986). He followed that with a role in another classic sports movie: the Kevin Costner-led baseball film *Bull Durham* (1988). His other credits include Oliver Stone's *Platoon* (1986) and Steven Spielberg's *Empire of the Sun* (1987)—for someone who only appeared in ten movies, he's certainly worked with an impressive roster of directors and co-stars.

Usually cast in ensembles, Cannon's *Under Cover* (1987) was the first time Neidorf was given the lead role in a feature, playing undercover cop Sheffield "Sheff" Hauser. Neidorf retired from acting in the mid-1990s, and now owns and operates a successful property management company.

Most of your bios begin with *Hoosiers*, but I'm curious how you got there. Can you tell me about the journey that led you into the film business?

David Neidorf: I was studying acting at The Loft with Peggy Feury and Bill Traylor. Sean Penn, Chris Penn, Michelle Pfeiffer, Nicolas Cage, Laura Dern, and Eric Stoltz also studied there. I probably would never have had the courage to go out and find an agent. Peggy recommended me to her agent at the time, Nicole David at Triad, and she decided to take a shot on me.

My first audition was for *Top Gun* (1986) and I made it through a few rounds. Ironically, that is a movie [*Under Cover* director] John Stockwell acted in. Six months later I booked the part in *Ferris Bueller's Day Off* (1986) that Charlie Sheen ended up playing. I couldn't do it because I booked a much bigger part in *Hoosiers* a few weeks later.

I was not interested in acting when I was younger, but dropping out of college a few times and not having much of a direction in life led me to acting. I seemed to be good at it, and got positive feedback right away.

You played Dennis Hopper's son in *Hoosiers*. This was at a point in his career where he was making a comeback, sobering up after drugs and his erratic behavior nearly killed him. What was your experience like working with him?

Dennis was like a breath of fresh air on the set. He was down to earth, friendly to all of the boys, and even hung out with us on occasion. He was generous and easy to work with. He was fully committed to his part and was great to work with, particularly in the hospital scene.

You mostly worked in ensemble casts before *Under Cover*, which put you in the lead role. What do you remember of the audition process for this one?

I auditioned once, I think. I was just coming off *Platoon*, which was an intense experience and I was a little tired. John Stockwell and I shared the same agency so I think they did a good job of promoting me for that role.

You were roughly the same age as writer-director John Stockwell, who was making his feature debut. How was he to work with?

John was a good guy. I was a little bit insecure being the lead, and was not always easy to deal with. I would say I was stubborn and difficult due to my insecurities. John kept an even keel, and as I look back I wish I had been more supportive of John during filming.

The movie mines a lot of humor from your character looking much older than the teens he had to blend in with. Was that already part of the script when you came on board?

I put that into the script because I didn't feel it was particularly believable that I could be a high school student.

Cannon was having severe financial issues at this time, and many of their other shoots were having their budgets slashed midway through. What was the feel of this production?

It was a low budget movie, so there were the normal stresses of trying to get everything on film at a certain cost. Other than that, we were left alone.

Can you tell me about your castmates? There are some great people in this—Barry Corbin, Jennifer Jason Leigh, David Harris, Kathleen Wilhoite, Mark Holton . . .

There were certainly some very talented actors on the film. Everybody was professional and focused on their work. Jennifer taught me a lot about film acting. She was always very natural when the cameras were rolling, and taught me about the value of relaxation in front of a camera.

Do you have any other, fun memories you can share from the making of this movie?

The fried food from the catering in the Deep South was a revelation. Literally every single item ends up in the deep fryer.

You retired from acting in the 1990s, and you now run a property management company. These two fields seem very different from a spectator's view, but I'm curious if there are lessons you learned from your acting days that have been valuable in your current line of business?

Acting taught me the power of being quiet and observing everything around you. Being sensitive and analyzing how a character's internal life influences their actions. In business, understanding your counterpart's character, position, and motivations better help you craft strategies to create desirable outcomes.

The British VHS release of *Under Cover.*

The VHS cover of *Three Kinds of Heat*, with artwork by Jacques Devaud.

Three Kinds of Heat

Release Date: December 4, 1987
Directed by: Leslie Stevens
Written by: Leslie Stevens
Starring: Robert Ginty, Victoria Barrett, Shakti
Trailer Voiceover: "Three tough agents make three kinds of heat for international crime!"

In May of 1986, Cannon spent an incredible $270 million to buy out the British entertainment company Thorn EMI. This baffling purchase was made largely with money the company had raised from public investors the prior spring, as well as a $100 million revolving line of credit secured from various banks.

This was money that was expected to be spent on, you know, making *movies*. Instead, it went to purchasing cinemas and studio lots, forcing Cannon to tighten their belts when it came to the budgets of the many, many films they had in production at the time. This led Cannon to accrue a massive amount of debt in a matter of months. By that August, the *Los Angeles Times* reported that Cannon was already more than $100 million in the red. Rather than invest in their strengths and continue to churn out low-budget movies for sure profits, or put that money into making sure their larger-budget films like *Superman IV* or *Masters of the Universe* (both 1987) looked as good as they possibly could, Cannon rolled the dice and risked it big on a chance to become a major studio by padding their holdings.

While the gambit failed, you can sort of see why they did it.

In addition to a large chain of English movie theaters and a sizable back catalog of films, the Thorn EMI purchase gave Cannon ownership of the production facilities at Elstree Studios, a famed British lot where hundreds of movies had been shot dating back to the 1920s. These were the massive studios that had housed all three of the original *Star Wars* productions, *Raiders of the Lost Ark* (1981) and *The Shining* (1980), as well as Cannon's own *Lifeforce* (1985). Why a company that excelled in low- to modest-budgeted features felt they needed a facility for making gigantic, big-budget blockbusters is unclear, but we can guess there was some hubris involved. Cannon was forced to sell Elstree Studios just two years later for a scant $36 million, but were able to crank out a few movies in the buildings before doing so. The first of those was the mega-cheap *Three Kinds of Heat* (1987).

Three Kinds of Heat was Cannon's method of breaking in their new digs. As the film's writer-director, Leslie Stevens, candidly described the movie's production to *Variety* in 1986, "It's like sending a dog ahead over the bridge first." Essentially, *Three Kinds of Heat* was a trial run for the higher-profile *Superman IV* (1987) which would start shooting at Elstree a few weeks afterward. If Cannon was going to run into problems at their new facility, it was better they happen on a bottom shelf cheapie like *Three Kinds of Heat* instead of their far more expensive superhero sequel.

The film was director Leslie Stevens' first theatrical feature in twenty-one years. A Broadway playwright whose controversial exploitation feature *Private Property* (1960) made him a surprise darling of the European arthouse scene, Stevens would become a prolific writer, director, and producer of television. In 1963, ABC bought his pitch for a show that at the time was called "Please Stand By"—nowadays, Stevens is most recognized as the man who created *The Outer Limits* (1963–1965).

Essential '80s b-movie jobber Robert Ginty stars in *Three Kinds of Heat*.

Three Kinds of Heat's only well-known star was Robert Ginty, who had previously appeared in Cannon's *Exterminator 2* (1984). The Yale-educated, Shakespearean stage actor had a surprise hit with his leading role in the violent, vigilante flick *The Exterminator* (1980), which had brought in $35 million on a small, independent budget. Although he did not relish taking violent roles, he recognized that cashing in on his unexpected action star image could be lucrative. "I've played a very violent repertory of movies," Ginty told the *New York Times*. "What they've done for me is given me an economically viable career." He spent much of the mid-1980s cashing checks in straight-to-video actioners with titles like *Mission Kill* (1986), *Programmed to Kill* (1987), and *Maniac Killer* (1987). *Three Kinds of Heat* may not have contained the word "kill" in its title like those movies do, but it was similarly cheap.

The movie's other "stars" include Victoria Barrett, an actress whose only prior credits were other Cannon movies, including *Over the Brooklyn Bridge* (1984), *Hot Chili* (1985), *Hot Resort* (1985), and *America 3000* (1986). The actress was a personal favorite of Menahem Golan's—and allegedly his girlfriend, which would explain a lot. Playing the film's third kind of heat was Shakti, a Chinese actress who happened to be director Leslie Stevens' fifth wife, to whom he was newly married and was thirty-four years his junior. As *Variety* learned in 1986, the hope was that *Three Kinds of Heat* might serve as a breakthrough for its relatively unknown female leads.

Let's review, shall we? *Three Kinds of Heat* was Cannon's no-budget trial run for a new studio space, starring a straight-to-video action star, the executive producer's girlfriend, and the sixty-two-year-old director's brand new, twenty-eight-year-old wife. It has to be good, right? Right?

Three Kinds of Heat is a movie. That's about as much as I can say for it.

The film follows three law enforcement agents from three different agencies—the NYPD, Interpol, and the Hong Kong police—as they chase the bagman for a mysterious crime syndicate from New York to London and back to New York again.

The movie's cheapness is apparent from the get-go, when a group of thugs open fire with machine guns at what's supposed to be New York's JFK airport. Civilians are caught in the crossfire between criminals, and only stopped by the intervention of Officer Terry O'Shea (Barrett), a cop working the airport beat. Obviously it would have been too expensive to stage this opening scene in a terminal of one of the world's busiest airports, but Cannon didn't even spring the cash to shoot at *any* actual airport. Instead, they built an airport terminal set on a racetrack near London. The whole thing looks flimsy and barren. There's a lot of smoke and gunfire, but the way the aftermath is so casually handled—a couple paramedics show up to carry out the injured—makes it look like the crew couldn't even be bothered to hire extras. Where are the other cops? Where's the press? Where are the stunned onlookers? Flashing lights? A violent, international gang war just erupted at New York's biggest airport, and the place looks emptier than a shopping mall on a Tuesday morning.

Victoria Barrett and Shakti in *Three Kinds of Heat*.

O'Shea meets two other law enforcement-types who were on the scene. There's Elliot Cromwell (Ginty), an American agent from the State Department who works as a liaison for Interpol, who was staking out the target of the gang's botched hit attempt. We also have Major Shan (Shakti), a Hong Kong police detective trailing the same man. Their shared target is one Harry Pimm, a messenger for Black Lion, one of the world's most powerful crime organizations. It's rumored that Pimm is the only person who knows the identity of the organization's mysterious leader, which is why Interpol is doing everything they can to keep him alive.

Even in their worst movies, Cannon typically maintained a base level of acting talent which separated them from the zero-budget exploitation movies you'd find alongside theirs on video shelves. *Three Kinds of Heat* is one of the few examples—at least, until the company's waning years in the early 1990s—where they failed to hit that lowest of benchmarks. Ginty was a talented stage actor, and was usually reliable to turn in a passing performance even in movies he clearly had no personal investment in. Maybe he commanded separate rates for "showing up" and "giving it a little effort," and the producers opted for the former here—he appears tired and disinterested, even in the movie's limited action scenes. Unlike *America 3000* (1986), the filmmakers opted not to overdub Victoria Barrett's performance this time around, and her lines barely register a blip of excitement or emotion.

It's Shakti, however, whose efforts are most likely to make viewers wince while gritting their teeth. It's hard to pick on her because English obviously isn't her first language, but her husband's low-grade script hardly puts her in a position to succeed. Every attempt is made to mine humor from her mis-pronunciations of words; however, each time she's asked to repeat a phrase like "black lion" ("brack ryan") it feels mean-spirited, rather than laughable. The only time one of these jokes ever lands is when she threatens a low-life by calling him a "mama fucker," though it's impossible to tell whether that particular line was written that way or an accident.

Apparently every other Interpol special agent is too busy to help take down this notorious, international crime league, and so Cromwell's bosses force him to deputize the two women to assist him in chasing down Pimm. In what boils down into a classic case of Two Girls One Cop, neither woman is eager to obey his orders. Each has their own ideas of how the investigation should be handled. What entails is one of the most boring, continents-spanning political "thrillers" imaginable.

Having lost track of Pimm, the trio instead trail his associate, Angelica. This involves taking a trans-Atlantic commercial flight, then following her on a stakeout while she spends a full day dress shopping, which is even more tedious than it sounds. This eventually leads them to a high-end fashion show where, naturally, our leading ladies have no choice but to change into more revealing outfits so they can better blend into the crowd. (The only available outfit that fits Major Shan is a two-piece bikini, because of course.)

At one point, Cromwell is mysteriously removed from the case by his higher-ups, because we needed a bit of drama to break up all the excitement of our heroes sitting on airplanes and watching a woman purchase dresses. It turns out there's a mole working in Interpol, and Cromwell's British handler, Norris, looks awfully suspicious. He's played by prolific journeyman actor Barry Foster, best known as the titular detective on the ITV series *Van der Valk* (1972–1977, 1992–1993) and for a role in Alfred Hitchcock's *Frenzy* (1972). This being a movie full of clichés, Cromwell hands in his badge and goes rogue, allowing him to finish out the case—and begin a romance with his foxy, NYPD counterpart.

They track down Pimm, who hightails it back to New York on a private jet. With seemingly no sense of urgency, our heroes book the next available commercial flight out of London and follow him.

The movie's finale is set in the criminals' warehouse, supposedly on New York's Lower East Side but clearly a dimly-lit soundstage full of cardboard boxes and shipping crates. (We wouldn't be surprised if they actually shot in one of Elstree's storage rooms.) Our heroes crack the case in the stupidest way: by figuring out that the real name of the mysterious crime boss is simply his organization's name—"black lion"—read backwards. This isn't revealed with any particular cleverness, and is especially frustrating as most viewers will have already figured out his true identity within the first ten minutes of the movie. Smarter conspiracy films would have provided at least a few potential suspects to throw the audience off the trail; in *Three Kinds of Heat*, there is no other logical solution even worth considering.

The German VHS cover for *Three Kinds of Heat*, roughly translated as "Three Hardened Supercops," with artwork by Enzo Sciotti.

I hate to tear movies down, even ones that don't aspire to much more than being cheap time-fillers, but it's hard to find much entertainment value at all in *Three Kinds of Heat*. It's a thriller that dares to be excruciatingly boring, despite clocking in under ninety minutes. It has a plot that spans two of the world's most visually recognizable cities, yet takes place almost entirely in darkly-lit storage rooms and the nondescript cabins of commercial airliners. Its script boasts all the humor of a tax form, and a shoehorned romance with all the sexual chemistry of a trip to the DMV. Well aware they had a clunker on their hands, Cannon sat on the film for over a year before they dumped it into a small handful of Los Angeles-area theaters. The few critics who saw the movie justifiably ripped it to shreds.

The bright side of things, though? Elstree Studios didn't collapse around them while they were filming, so Cannon was able to go on and shoot *Superman IV* there before being forced to sell the studio for a loss in 1988.

Whovians, take note: the villainous Harry Pimm is played by Sylvester McCoy, best known for playing the seventh incarnation of the Doctor on *Doctor Who* from 1987 to 1989. He was the last to play the character before the long-running British sci-fi series was put on a two-decade hiatus; his casting in the role was announced shortly after he wrapped *Three Kinds of Heat*. Constantly sneering behind a long, skinny cigarette holder that he chews on like the bastard child of Johnny Depp's Hunter S. Thompson and Burgess Meredith's Penguin, McCoy's *Three Kinds of Heat* baddie is sadly given little to say or do throughout the movie.

Bonus Interview: Actress Lucinda Dickey

During the years covered in the first volume of *The Cannon Film Guide*, there are few actors whose names are as closely associated with Cannon as Lucinda Dickey's. In just one year, 1984, Dickey starred in three of Cannon's highest-profile releases: *Breakin'*, *Breakin' 2: Electric Boogaloo*, and *Ninja III: The Domination*. At a company whose output was typically built around their male stars, Dickey was able to make her mark in three undisputed classics.

Lucinda Dickey with Boogaloo Shrimp and Shabba-Doo in *Breakin'*.

While she had little acting experience prior to her tenure as Cannon's top starlet, Dickey had been dancing her entire life. She began training in her mother's dance studio as a child, and continued her studies as a student at Kansas State University. After touring with a dance group for a period, she moved to Hollywood on a scholarship to an esteemed dance school, Dupree Academy. She was a featured dancer in *Grease 2* (1982) and appeared for a time on *Solid Gold* before she landed the starring role of a utilities worker/dance instructor who becomes possessed by an evil ninja in the wild Cannon classic *Ninja III: The Domination*. From there, she won the role of Kelly, a.k.a. Special K, in the smash hit *Breakin'* and its sequel. All three of her Cannon features debuted in theaters over the space of just eight months.

Dickey has written a memoir that will detail her life and career before, during, and after Cannon.

Unlike many actors, you didn't go to LA to get into movies, but because of a dance scholarship. Did the acting bug really not bite you until you were already in town?

Lucinda Dickey: I moved out to LA to pursue dance. Within a few months I auditioned for the Dupree Dance Academy scholarship and was accepted. One of my very first auditions after the scholarship ended was for *Grease 2* and I was selected as one of sixteen principal dancers. It was during filming that the acting bug bit me. I watched Michelle Pfeiffer and thought, "I could do that." I knew then I wanted to be an actor, not just a dancer. I wanted to be the star. I wanted the red carpet rolled out for me.

For your *Ninja III* audition, you were asked to cold read the movie's wild exorcism scene. How did you manage to impress the casting group with such a difficult scene, and without time to prepare?

Oh Lord, if only I had video of that audition! I guess I somehow tapped into my dark side. I don't know. I remember walking out of there and thinking I'll never hear from them again!

I left the next day for a job in Des Moines, Iowa. I had been hired to entertain as Jennifer Beals' character in *Flashdance* (1983) at a birthday party along with the Venice Chainsaw juggler and a couple of break dancers. It was a wild weekend, to say the least! I stopped in Kansas to see my family before returning to LA, and I found out I had a callback for *Ninja III* the next morning. I think they liked the idea that I was a dancer and a gymnast. I'd be able to handle the martial arts. I don't know that my acting talent was on the top of their list when they chose me.

After you were offered the part, you were needed on location almost immediately. Do you recall your thoughts when you were finally handed a full *Ninja III* script? Was it at least half as wild on the page as it was on the screen?

My callback was on a Thursday morning. My agents called that afternoon to tell me I got the job and needed to leave by Sunday for Phoenix. I didn't have a signed contract or a script. I didn't care. I was starring in a movie!

This was my first acting role—my big break. I had no idea who these Cannon guys were, and no idea whether it was a good or bad script. I loved that my character was tough. I loved that she got possessed by that evil ninja and that I would get to fight all these guys and kick ass. I always knew that my physical ability was my strong suit.

You had one of the world's most generous directors in Sam Firstenberg, and a co-star in Jordan Bennett who seems like a very considerate actor. Was it helpful working with people like these on your first starring feature?

I was very lucky. I hold both of them in very high regard. I was so green. They helped me step-by-step. Jordan and I became good friends. We were stuck together for three months on location. He made me jog with him every morning at 5 AM. I had never run before. It was brutal, but I learned to love running. All-in-all it was a great experience. We worked hard, but had a lot of fun along the way.

I know that Sho Kosugi was displeased with the direction the movie had been taken. Did that make him difficult to work with?

Sho avoided me as much as possible. I had no idea of his history with Cannon or other films he had made. The scenes we had together were shot separately. It made it very difficult for me to do my scenes with the script girl.

I felt it was pretty unfair. I didn't write the script, I was just doing my job. There were a few fight scenes that we had to do together, for obvious reasons. To me, they were very real—he might have chopped me to pieces if I forgot the choreography.

Menahem Golan loved signing deals with big names, but also adored the homegrown stars who entered the spotlight as part of the Cannon family. You were definitely Cannon's in-house star for 1984. Do you recall any of your personal interactions with Golan?

Oh yes! He was quite a character. He loved you to death when things were going well. But there was a lot of bickering, too. It was mostly amongst the crew. I did have a few run-ins with him that I'll never forget!

There was no favoritism when the folks at Cannon started casting *Breakin'*—you had to win the role as part of a general cattle call audition. Do you remember how, or when, you heard they were cooking up a dance movie?

I'd heard about the dance movie while still filming *Ninja III*. At the time, I didn't put too much thought into it. I was battling an evil ninja. I figured I'd be a shoe-in. They seemed very pleased with me in *Ninja III*. When I returned to LA and found out they were interested in another girl I went crazy!

The dance styles you were trained in were very different from what was being spotlighted in *Breakin'*. Did you study up on street dance styles before your audition?

I met with a friend from acting class and we cleared all the furniture out of his living room. He knew a little about break dancing. I knew *very* little. I choreographed a routine for the audition, throwing in as many gymnastic moves as possible. I did butt spins and the worm. It was pretty pathetic! My friend did not get cast in the film.

Were your co-stars helpful in teaching you street dance moves?

LA DOMINACION

Lucinda Dickey in *Ninja III: The Domination*.

Yes, they were. Especially Shrimp. Shabba Doo was more reluctant in the beginning. But, they didn't have a choice! We had many rehearsals with Jaime Rogers, the choreographer for *Breakin'*, and they all helped me learn. I was bruised from head to toe trying to master windmills and head spins and knee spins. I was hell-bent on getting it all down.

A big part of the *Breakin'* movies' charm is that they're wholesome, like '80s versions of the musicals that Judy Garland and Mickey Rooney starred in forty years earlier. What do you think made *Breakin'* such a breakaway hit?

It was fun and refreshing. But mostly, I think people were obsessed with Ozone and Turbo. Everyone had their cardboard boxes out in their driveways trying to imitate those guys.

***Breakin'* was a legitimate phenomenon when it was released. Can you describe your experience being at the epicenter of *Breakin*-mania?**

It was pretty awesome! It all happened so fast. It seemed we'd barely finished filming when *Breakin'* was released. Menahem wanted to beat *Beat Street* (1984) to the box office.

I'll never forget the feeling when we pulled up to Grauman's Chinese Theater for the premier of *Breakin'*. The fans, the flashing cameras, this was my red carpet moment! Afterwards, the three of us were split up and sent on publicity tours to different locations. I toured Japan, Hong Kong, Australia, and Mexico with two other break dancers from the film. Shabba Doo and Shrimp went to the Cannes Film Festival. It didn't seem fair that I wasn't invited to Cannes, but I had the time of my life on tour. I was recognized everywhere I went and I finally mastered the windmill!

You came into these films with so much dance experience, and you had previously worked with both Sam Firstenberg and Bill Goodson, the choreographer on *Electric Boogaloo*. Did you have any room on that second film to suggest your own ideas or moves?

I had been on scholarship with Billy for a year and a half. He knew what my strengths were. I was very happy to be working with him. He hired gymnastic coaches to train us before filming began. Even though I could throw aerials

937

and handsprings, I hadn't trained with a coach since I was fifteen. I felt this was the only thing I could do to keep up with the guys. We had become very competitive. I trusted Billy to help me be at my best when we filmed *Electric Boogaloo*. There was a *lot* more dancing, and it was definitely more my style.

One of the things that delights me most about *Electric Boogaloo* is that it had no reservations about tossing realism out the window, and going full-blown fantasy with its over-the-top dance sequences. Similar to what I asked about *Ninja III*: do your recall your first thoughts once you were handed the *Breakin' 2* script?

I was a little shocked to find out that Kelly had wealthy parents! Nothing let on to that in the first film. The scenes were changed daily so the script was a rainbow of colors. We were handed new pages right up to rolling camera. I can't say I was crazy about the concept, but the large production numbers were incredibly fun.

***Ninja III* was released in between the *Breakin'* movies. What did you think when you saw it all finished and put together?**

I loved filming *Ninja III*. For a first-time film (for me), it was an incredible experience. I truly felt that if I put everything I had into it, which I did, it would be a great film. I was so naive! After *Electric Boogaloo* fell flat in comparison to *Breakin'*, *Ninja III* was not promoted at all and completely bombed. I remember sitting at the back of the theater with some of the cast and crew and I just died a little inside. It was quite anti-climactic, to say the least.

You were briefly in line for Sharon Stone's role in the Quatermain movies. How long were you attached? Were there any other Cannon parts you tried out for, or had discussed?

This is a loaded question! In a nutshell, I had a four-picture deal with Cannon after *Breakin' 2*. I was to star in *King Solomon's Mines* (1985) and its sequel, *Allan Quatermain and the Lost City of Gold* (1986), all to be filmed over five months in Africa with Richard Chamberlain, *Breakin' 3*, and a fourth film to be determined later. After *Breakin' 2*, while on the publicity tour with Shabba Doo and Shrimp, let's just say things went downhill. Very fast. You'll have to read my memoir to get the full story.

Your time in Hollywood was only a handful of years, but these three movies really mean a lot to the people who found and fell in love with them. Are you proud when fans associate you with them?

Absolutely! It was a wonderful, whirlwind experience that not every girl gets to experience. I moved from Kansas to LA dreaming of becoming a professional dancer. To have the opportunity to star in a dance movie was the icing on the cake. I am very proud and very grateful for all the fans that have kept those memories alive.

I can't not mention the untimely passing of Shabba Doo. We were a family during that crazy year, with all that comes with it—the good and the bad. We had reconnected in 2020 for a Zoom interview and it was fun to see and talk to the guys again. How very sad it is to have lost him so soon. He truly was an icon.

Epilogue

By the end of 1987, it was obvious not only to those working directly with Cannon, but to anyone paying attention from the outside, that the company was under serious financial strain. With their purchase of Thorn EMI, Elstree Studios, and yet more theater screens, they had overextended their lines of credit. Worse still, a string of expensive gambles on larger budget movies—*Lifeforce*, *Over the Top*, *Superman IV*, and *Masters of the Universe*—had failed to produce a single hit. Just as their stock prices were hitting an all-time low, they found themselves under investigation by the SEC for allegedly misreporting their earnings. Facing mounting debts, Cannon was forced to start liquidating their holdings just to survive.

With 1988, we head into what one might call Cannon's "dark" period, when budgets shrank and their output increasingly went direct to video. It's a period that involved countless canceled projects, shady new ownership, and a bitter breakup between Golan and Globus, the cousins who—for the last few years—had taken Hollywood by storm. But this period wasn't all doom and gloom, bringing with it an all-new action star named Jean-Claude Van Damme, a shelf full of VHS rental classics, and further features from Cannon's most trusted stars.

Next up ... *The Cannon Film Guide, Vol. III,* with return appearances from Chuck Norris, Charles Bronson, and Michael Dudikoff, and featuring films such as *Bloodsport, Cyborg, Alien from L.A., King Lear, Going Bananas, Hero and the Terror, Platoon Leader, Kinjite: Forbidden Subjects, Rockula, Lambada,* and oh so many more. Stay tuned!

Acknowledgments

Undertaking a project this large would not be possible without the help of a great many people to whom I can't possibly say thank you enough. First, to Ben Ohmart and the BearManor Media team, for being the best possible partners to bring this project to life. To Oisin McGillion Hughes, for applying his vast artistic talents to produce this book's kickass cover art. To Wendy Comeau and Stone Wallace, whose editorial eyes helped whip this book into fighting shape. To my sister Annah Trunick, for sharing her photographic talent. To Cannon ambassadors Sam Firstenberg and James Bruner, for being so supportive throughout the entire process of writing these books, and to all of the interview subjects who shared with me their time and memories.

Special shout-outs go out to my Cannon comrades, Geoff Garlock and Frank Garcia-Hejl of *The Cannon Canon*, with whom I'll be able to commiserate when our missions are one day completed. To david j. moore and Mike McPadden (rest in peace), for inspiring me to try my hand at a cult film guide in the first place. To Paul Talbot and Marco Siedelmann, for writing the definitive tomes on the works of Bronson and Firstenberg. To Mark Hartley, whose incredible documentary *Electric Boogaloo: The Wild,*

Untold Story of Cannon Films (2014) should be the first stop for anyone even remotely interested in the Golan-Globus saga. To Kristian Smock and Dustin Niño, for their ongoing work documenting the careers of b-movies' unsung heroes. And of course, to Eric Reifschneider and the rest of the Cannon Films Appreciation Page folks for years of lively movie discussion.

I would also like to thank the League—Zach, Shawn, Jon, Jen, and Anne—for listening to me talk about these movies constantly, year after year. My mother and mother-in-law, for always taking the kids when I was up against crunch time. Alex Segura, for being my Yoda of hustle. Fellow author Jérémie Damoiseau, for opening up his vast *Masters of the Universe* archives to me, and for providing the ultimate Cannon hook-up in the early days of this project. Andreas Raßbach, for sharing photos from his collection of German VHS tapes. Frank Knösel, for sharing his phenomenal ninja collection. Film art dealers John Di Nardo and Louie Torres, for their extra efforts in helping me track down many of the pieces of ephemera you see in these pages. To Judy Fox, Patrick O'Riley, and Doug Dietz for helping me connect with interview subjects.

A very, very special thanks goes out to the fellow film fans who helped get the word out about the book, including Heath Holland, Joseph Kay, Sam Panico, Andy Gray, Chris Kacvinsky, Tommy Kovac, Mark Krawczyk, Ian Simmons, Scott Weatherly, Brock Smith, Daniel Tribble, Sean Tuohy, Nick Hoffmann, Phil Hall, Bryan Renfro, Michael Hojjatie, Will Padilla, Steven Cristina, Jr., the crew at *The Real Butter Buttercast* (even Poppy), *Cinematic Void*, and so many more.

Most of all I want to thank my wife, Sara, whose endless support (and patience) are the main reasons *The Cannon Film Guide* exists. Thank you for believing in this project, for staying up late with me to discuss the nuances of *Tough Guys Don't Dance*, and for being just as excited as I was once I finally had the chance to speak to Michael Dudikoff.

The author on the *Death Wish* (1974) steps in New York City during the COVID-19 pandemic.

About the Author

Austin Trunick is a Connecticut-based author and film historian. He serves as an editor for the nationally-distributed music and entertainment magazine *Under the Radar*. He has written about movies and pop culture for *Mental Floss* and *Consequence of Sound*. He blames the unrivaled awesomeness of *Revenge of the Ninja* for sending him on this Cannon journey.

Index

Botes, Michelle 138

Bottle Rocket 500

Bottoms, Timothy 421, 424, 438

Bowhay, Morikiyo 723, 726

Boyd, Jan Gan 603, 606, 608, **610**, 611-619

Boyer, Erica 564

Boyle, Peter 33, 368, 877, 882

Brach, Gerard 9

Braddock: Missing in Action III 207, 216, 217, 229, 312, 319, 336, 394, 684

Bradford, Andy 251

Bradley, David 121, 141, 142, 145, 146, 148, 149, 150, 151, **196**, 198

Bradley, Michael 450

Bralver, Bob 121, 153

Brando, Marlon 148, 327, 328, 430, 431, 735, 738, 890

Branigan, Laura 292

Breakfast at Tiffany's 406

Breakfast Club, The 22, 486

Breakin' xx. 25, 31, 41, 42, 43, 44, 289, 314, 568, 732, 932, **932**, 933, 935, 937, 938

Breakin' 2: Electric Boogaloo 29, 41, 42, 44, 50, 114, 122, 131, 132, 163, 258, 289, 777, 883, 932, 933, 937, 938

Brewer, Geoff 319

Briggs, Joe Bob 497

Brimhall, Cynthia 352

Brock, Phil 118, 127, 181, 393

Broeske, Pat H. 629

Bronson, Charles xii, xix, xx, 133, 155, 159, 171, 208, 222, 226, 253, 276, 303, 316, 337, 345, 369, 370, **396**, 397, 399-400, **399**, 401, **401**, 402, 403, 494, 558, 563, 567, 594, **602**, 603, 604, **605**, 608, 609-610, **609**, **610**, 611, 613, **614**, 615-617, **619**, 648, 917, 942, 943

Bronson, Tom 642

Brooks, Randy 606

Garrett, Leif 113, 114, 117

Gatti, Andrew 368

Gayton, Joe 862

Geary, Anthony 817, 820-821, 835

Geeves, David *see* Booth, James

Gelmis, Joseph 855

Gendece, Brian 274, **282**, 283-293

General Hospital 384, 626, 636, 637, 638, 642, 820-821

Genesis Climber MOSPEADA 446

"Genie, The" 695

Geo *see* Clinton, George S.

Gere, Richard 487, 623

Gereighty, Allison 536-537

Gerrish, Flo 31

Get Shorty 569

Gielgud, John 254

Gillis, Jamie 564

Ginty, Robert 128, 361, 923, **925**, 925-926, 928

Giosa, Sue 364, 385

Giraud, Jean "Moebius" 759, 773, 786, 792-793

Glitz 559

Globus, Yoram xiii, xvi, xvii, , **xviii**, xix, 3, 6, 22, 33, 59, 89, 139, 152, 159, 163, 175, 241, 244, 271, 284, 286, 293, 302, 304, 311-312, 319, 320, 323, 357, 358, 362, 364, 368, 387, 390, 402, 410, 445, 470, **478**, 480, 483, 487, 498, 500, 516, 523, 532, 557, 558, 560, 567, 572, 584, 612, 613, 621, 622, 623, 626, 733, 736, 789, 828, 832, 837, 873, 882, 902, 911, 913, 941, 944

Glover, John 557, 564, 566, 648

Godard, Jean-Luc 261, 487, 524, 842

Goddard, Gary 751, 753-754, 758, 763-764, 766, **767**, 767-783, **771**, **776**, **780**, 790, 795, **800**, 803

Goga, Jack Alan 450

Going Bananas 246, 461, 626, 637, 641, 942

Mahon, Richard **270**

Maidstone 841-842

Mailer, John Buffalo 872

Mailer, Norman 261, 839, 840-842, **843**, 844, 847, 848-849, 850, 852, 853, 854, **854**, 855-856, 858, 863, 864-865, 865-866, 867, 869, 871, 872, 911

Making the Grade 24, 114, 244

Mako 389, 392

Maley, Nick 91, **101**, 101-111, **106**

Malovic, Steve 361

Mancini, Henry 92

Mancini, Ric 820

Maniac 215, 496

Maniac Cop 207, 361

Mannequin 479, 481, 635

Manning, Pat 564

Manning, Russ 784

Mansano, Moni 170

Manson, Charles 96, 860

Mantle, Clive 743-744, **749**

Marcos, Ferdinand 135, 180-181, 316

Marcus, Greil 784

Margolis, Mark 314

Maria's Lovers 8, 9-19, **10**, **12**, **14**, **17**, 216, 261, 272, 284, 390, 545, 608, 650

Marjoe (1972) 143, 889, 893

Marrow, Tracy *see* Ice-T

Marshall, Don 319

Marshall, Garry 293-294, 698, 883

Marshall, John 25

Marson, Aileen 255

Martin, Dean 173

Marvin, Lee 222, **225**, 226, 299, 303, 305, 327, 500

Mascii, Jean **395**

Maslin, Janet 100, 891

Mason, James 37, 39

Master Gee 43

Masters of the Universe 413, 423, 504, 748, **750**, 751-815, **755**, **758**, **761**, **765**, **767**, **771**, **776**, **780**, **784**, **794**, **797**, **800**, **802**, **808**, **810**, **813**, **815**, 902, 924, 941, 944

Mata Hari 76, **230**, 231-237, **234**, **237**, 545

Mathews, Thom 413, 663, **664**, 664-669

Matthau, Walter 481

Maxwell, Max 207

May, Elaine 853

May, Mathilda 89, 92, **93**, 94-95, 98, 100, 109, 111

Mayne, Ferdy 30

Mazzoli, Claudio 768, 773

Mazzoni, Roberta 545

McCain, John 687

McCallum, Paul 400

McCallum, Valentine 399, 404, 609

McClure, Marc 736

McCoy, Sylvester 931

McDonald, Priscilla 174

McGill, Everett 597, 600

McGinnis, Scott 113, 114

McKinney, Kurt 141

McLaglen, Josh 640

McMillan, Kenneth 279, **293**, 295

McNally, Kevin 545, 546, 548

McNeil, Randy 348

McNeill, Robert Duncan 761-762, **797**, 797-802, **800**, 806, **810**, 810

McQueen, Chad 123, 178, 185

McQueen, Steve 58, 123, 185

McShane, Ian 73, 76

Rocky IV 626, 633, 754, 756, 770, 774

Rogers Mimi 671, 675

Rogers, Jaime 937

Rogers, Sandy 268

Rollins, Howard 832

Romancing the Stone 184, 241, 243, 572, 588, 660, 662

Romanus, Richard 400

Romeo and Juliet 477, 525, 526, 528

Romero, George A. 215, 496

Roos, Fred 437, 864

Rosenbaum, Jeffery 587

Rosenthal, Mark 731, 735

Ross, Herbert 885, 886, **887**, 893, 894

Ross, Marty 409

Rossellini, Isabella **838**, 839, 842, 845, 853, 886

Rourke, Mickey 278, 331, 893, **896**, 897, 901-902, 904-905, 906-907, **908**,
     908, 909, **910**, 910

Rowlands, Gena 320

Rubbo, Joe 21, 27, 29

Runaway Train 10, 170, 261, **270**, 271-297, **273**, **275**, **277**, **280**, **282**, **285**, **288**,
     291, **293**, **296**, 314, 319, 529, 533, 534, 594, 823

Rundgren, Todd 917

Ryan, John P. 170, 276, 295, 299, 314, 315, 317, 319, 321, 325, **328**, 330-331,
     531, 533, 534, 541

Ryan, John Saint 321

Sabela, Simon 196

Sachs, William 21, 27, 31, 33-36, 648, **654**

Sagall, Jonathan **23**

Saget, Bob 613

Sahara 244, 247, 525, 576, 699

Saito, Takao 410

CPSIA information can be obtained
at www.ICGtesting.com
Printed in the USA
LVHW010718120723
752107LV00005B/96